Contents

Illustrations

FIGURES

Tables

Preface

Michael Graff

George Kenwood and Alan Lougheed published the first edition of *The Growth of the International Economy, 1820–1960* in 1971 and subsequently updated and revised the text repeatedly. The fourth and last revision by these authors, *The Growth of the International Economy, 1820–2000*, came out in 1999. For this, they could refer to data and events up to 1998–9. Their last edition thus covered the collapse of the GDR (East Germany) in 1989, the collapse of the Soviet Union in 1991 and the first years of transition of what had been the centrally planned economies of Eastern and Central Europe into capitalist market economies. The establishment of the World Trade Organization (WTO) and the North American Free Trade Agreement (NAFTA), both in 1994, were included, and the 1997 Asian financial crisis was briefly mentioned as well, although not in much detail, as its outcome had not been obvious when the manuscript was finished.

Although increasing inequality and unemployment and the risk of instability in the international economy of the closing millennium were reflected in the final chapters, as were the sufferings brought about by the dismantling of the social security provisions in the former Soviet bloc countries, this book by and large maintained a thoroughly optimistic attitude towards the advance of the market economy and its effects on living conditions around the globe.

Since then, the Russian financial crisis of 1998–9, the information technology bubble of 1997–2000 and, most importantly, the 2007 burst of the US subprime mortgage bubble that dragged the world economy into recession have occurred. The recent experience has thus generally led to a more sceptical view of globalisation, in particular regarding the financial sector. In international trade, persistent deficits and, correspondingly, surpluses are recorded, and neither economists nor politicians are sure whether the inevitable reversal will proceed smoothly or not. High rates of GDP growth have lifted millions of people above the poverty line, but far too many are still left behind. Migrants from the poorer parts of the world are drowning by the thousands every year in desperate attempts to reach the shores of wealthier economies and seek a better life. Global warming is clearly evident, but no decisive steps to bring it to a halt have been agreed upon so far, nor are any in sight.

We do not know how far George Kenwood and Alan Lougheed would have revised their views, given the experience of the last two and a half decades, had they not both passed away before they could prepare further revisions of their book. The task of preparing a fifth edition in 2013 was hence a delicate one, since they were not there to discuss and could not object.

This applies even more to this sixth edition, given that in the meantime, the international economy has changed profoundly. Given this, I have once more left their structure and text as intact as possible for the sixth edition. In Chapters 1–21, which tell the story from 1820 to 2000, the 'inherited' text basically remains as it was, with minimal revisions – cautious updates and assessments of facts in the light of new evidence and some abbreviations, where the text dealt with events and disputes that appear less important now than 25 years ago. Other changes to these chapters come chiefly in the form of additional sections recommending further readings. The additions to the fifth edition remain, in particular the economic histories of the two World Wars, a 'Prologue' dealing with the international economy before 1820 and several appendices elaborating on economic theories that had previously been only dealt with implicitly in the main body of the text.

Finally, the previous edition's Chapter 22 ('The New Millennium, 2001–2012') is carried forward to 2024, and the final Chapter 23 ('The International Economy until 2015 and Beyond') summarises and offers a tentative outlook into the future. Finally, I have added two appendices to the final Chapter 23: the first looks at global warming from a macroeconomic perspective and the second at the increasing geopolitical tensions.

I am most grateful to the publisher, whose flexibility allowed me to come forward with a coherent account of the most recent events, and to my wife Cintia, who generously gave me the required time to finish this work.

Zurich, September 2025

Abbreviations

ACP	African, Caribbean and Pacific (countries)
AFTA	ASEAN Free Trade Area
APEC	Asian Pacific Economic Community
ASEAN	Association of Southeast Asian Nations
BENELUX	Belgium, the Netherlands and Luxembourg
BIS	Bank for International Settlements
BIT	Bilateral Investment Treaty
BRI	Belt and Road Initiative (New Silk Road)
BSFF	Buffer Stock Financing Facility
CACM	Central American Common Market
CAP	Common Agricultural Policy
CCFF	Compensatory and Contingency Financing Facility
CEEC	Central and Eastern European Countries
CER	Closer Economic Relations
CET	Common External Tariff
CIS	Commonwealth of Independent States
CIT	Country in Transition
CMEA	Council for Mutual Economic Assistance
COMECON	Council for Mutual Economic Assistance
CPE	Centrally Planned Economy
DAC	Development Assistance Committee
EAGGF	European Agricultural Guidance and Guarantee Fund
EBRD	European Bank for Reconstruction and Development
EC	European Community
ECA	Economic Co-operation Administration
ECB	European Central Bank
ECOSOC	Economic and Social Council of the United Nations
ECSC	European Coal and Steel Community
ECU	European Currency Unit
EDF	European Development Fund
EEA	European Economic Area
EEC	European Economic Community

EFF	Extended Fund Facility
EFSF	European Financial Stability Facility
EFTA	European Free Trade Association
EIB	European Investment Bank
EIC	East India Company
EIF	European Investment Fund
EMEA	European-Mediterranean Economic Area
EMP	European Marriage Pattern
EMS	European Monetary System
EMU	European Monetary Union
EPU	European Payments Union
ERM	Exchange Rate Mechanism
ERP	European Recovery Programme
ESAF	Enhanced Structural Adjustment Facility
ESM	European Stability Mechanism
EU	European Union
FDI	Foreign Direct Investment
FPEI	Foreign Portfolio Equity Investment
FPI	Foreign Portfolio Investment
FRG	Federal Republic of Germany
GAB	General Arrangements to Borrow
GATT	General Agreement on Tariffs and Trade
GDP	Gross Domestic Product
GDR	German Democratic Republic
GNI	Gross National Income
GNP	Gross National Product
GSP	Generalised System of Preferences
HIPC	Heavily Indebted Poor Country
IBEC	International Bank for Economic Co-operation
IBRD	International Bank for Reconstruction and Development (World Bank)
IDA	International Development Association
IDB	Inter-American Development Bank
IFC	International Finance Corporation
IIB	International Investment Bank
IMF	International Monetary Fund
IPC	Integrated Programme of Commodities
ITA	Information Technology Agreement
ITO	International Trade Organization
LAFTA	Latin American Free Trade Area
LDC	Less Developed Country
MFN	Most Favoured Nation
MTN	Multilateral Trade Negotiations
NAB	New Arrangements to Borrow
NAFTA	North American Free Trade Agreement

NDB	New Development Bank
NIC	Newly Industrialised (Industrialising) Country
NIE	Newly Industrialised Economy
OAPEC	Organization of Arab Petroleum Exporting Countries
ODA	Official Development Assistance
OECD	Organization for Economic Co-operation and Development
OEEC	Organization for European Economic Co-operation
OMA	Orderly Marketing Arrangement
OPEC	Organization of Petroleum Exporting Countries
R&D	Research and Development
RTA	Regional Trade Agreement
SAF	Structural Assistance Facility
SDR	Special Drawing Right
SEA	Single European Act
SEM	Single European Market
SRF	Supplementary Reserve Facility
STF	Systemic Transformation Facility
TNC	Transnational Corporation
UK	United Kingdom
UN	United Nations
UNCTAD	United Nations Conference on Trade and Development
US	United States
USSR	Union of Soviet Socialist Republics (Soviet Union)
VER	Voluntary Export Restraint
VOC	Vereenigde Oostindische Compagnie
WTO	World Trade Organization

Introduction

A. G. Kenwood, A. L. Lougheed and Michael Graff

The exchange of gifts, goods and services is the means through which independent economic units enter into economic relations with one another and become part of a local or national economic community. As exchange passes beyond a country's boundaries, national economic systems become parts of a broader regional, continental or world economy. Flows of commodity trade are not the only economic links forged between nations, however. People are also highly mobile, and the long evolution of trade from prehistoric exchange to our modern worldwide network of commodity and services exchange has made necessary an intricate system of international credits, loans and investments. These flows of trade, labour, capital and ideas constitute the vital processes of the international economy. The increasing integration of the world economy and the consequences are summarised under the term 'globalization', which goes beyond economic integration, encompassing the wider socio-political and cultural processes and concerns that go along with it, which will be part of the story of this book.[1]

Obviously, our account of the growth of the international economy must be concerned with the measurement and comparison of the rate at which these processes go on over time, but it must also be concerned with examining the ways in which the international economic system is organised to carry out these vital processes, and how the structure, organisation and functioning of these processes change as the international economy expands.

The international economy is studied not as an end, but rather as a means to an end, for in studying its expansion in recent times, we are analysing one of the most potent causes of modern economic growth, which ultimately has a powerful potential to improve human welfare. Yet, in the last decades it also became obvious that unbound economic growth will pose a threat to the survival of humanity, unless it is quickly decoupled from the depletion of non-renewable resources and its negative externalities, in particular the emission of greenhouse gases and the poisoning of the natural environment.

The international economy encourages national economic growth in three ways: (1) by providing opportunities for international specialisation, (2) by allowing increased production and thus benefiting from economies of scale and (3) by acting as a mechanism for

DOI: 10.4324/9781003382171-1

diffusing between nations the apparatus and/or benefits of modern industrial technology. Since specialisation is promoted by trade, and since specialisation and division of labour are major causes of increased productivity and rising per capita real incomes, some comment is called for on the nature of the basis of trade between countries before we say something briefly about the international economy as a means of spreading industrialisation.

International trade may arise simply because countries differ in their demand for goods and services and in their ability to supply them. As far as supply is concerned, the basis for trade can be found in the uneven distribution of economic resources among the nations of the world, coupled with the fact that commodities and services require different proportions of these economic resources in their production. This uneven distribution of resources is partly a matter of climate and geography, and partly a result of each nation's historical development, which has left it with a certain infrastructure, capital goods and a population trained and educated in numerous techniques and skills. Whatever their origin, however, each country's endowment of land, minerals, skills and machinery equips it to produce certain goods and services more efficiently (cheaply) than others. As David Ricardo (1817) famously demonstrated two centuries ago, differences in the *relative* supplies of different productive resources within a country will mean differences in their relative prices and therefore differences in the costs of producing various goods and services. What is important is the relative, not absolute, supply of the factors of production. Thus, China is a country large in area, but, relative to its population's demand for food, land is scarce. On the other hand, Belgium may have a small population in absolute size, but its labour supply, relative to the country's land and capital, may be the most abundant factor. Considering these elements alone, each country would tend to specialise upon those products best suited to its factor endowment, which means those using few of its scarce factors but drawing heavily upon the cheap and abundant ones. Thus, differences in relative factor prices based on the relative abundance or scarcity of economic resources within countries will mean differences in international costs of production and therefore differences in commodity prices. These differences in commodity prices are a basic cause of trade between nations.

However, the international structure of commodity prices and the pattern of foreign trade based on it are not fixed for all time. Over time, changes occur in the distribution of economic resources between countries that alter the comparative cost structure and modify the pattern of world trade. Any country's factor endowment can change radically from internal causes, as technological progress occurs, as population changes, as domestic capital is accumulated and as the economic extent of the land is modified. It can also change from external causes by virtue of international movements of labour and capital and the spread of technical knowledge. The effect of such changes on a nation's relative factor endowment should be obvious. The principal basis for its specialisation and the character of its trade are altered. In analysing the growth of the international economy, therefore, we must consider how changes in factor supplies, technical progress, increasing productivity and changes in demand can transform the structure of comparative costs. Changes in comparative costs affect the pattern of international trade, while developments in international trade, in turn, influence the economic growth processes in the world economy that bring about changes in the international distribution of economic resources.

Whatever the structure of comparative costs at any particular point in time, the size of the trade flows between nations will also depend upon transport costs. Since trade is based mainly on international price differences, it may be severely limited in situations where transport costs largely offset the price advantage of low-cost producers. In other words, the basis for trade, whether international or interregional, lies in comparative cost differences, which are not neutralised by transport costs. It follows, therefore, that any reduction of transport costs due to technical improvements in the carriage of goods enhances the opportunities for trade by allowing international cost and price differences to become more apparent in world markets.

One apparent failure of the factor proportions theorem just outlined is that it does not provide an adequate explanation for the comparative advantage that industrialised nations appear to possess in different industries. This is brought out clearly by the fact that, in this century, trade has tended to expand fastest between the advanced industrial nations, many of which have roughly similar factor endowments. The need to explain the trade advantage of industrial countries has led consequently to an emphasis placed on factors other than simple resource scarcity. One approach to the problem stresses the importance of economies of scale. The technical superiority of certain large indivisible units of capital or the use of specialised labour, both of which depend on the existence of large markets, suggests that a large country, especially one with a big population and high per capita incomes, will be more fruitful for the development of large-scale industry than a smaller country with a similar level of income. Hence, the scale-economy explanation essentially asserts that the country with the largest domestic market tends to specialise in those commodities, which exhibit the greatest scale economies.[2]

The growth of trade between industrial nations has also been explained in terms of the technological gap between nations created by the discovery of new products and new processes of production.[3] According to this theory, trade consists of impermanent commerce, which originates solely in the temporary technological superiority gained by the nation making the industrial breakthrough. In other words, the innovating country's export trade in the new product will last until other countries adopt the new techniques or produce the new product on a scale sufficient to supply their domestic markets and make them independent of imported supplies. The period it will take for the manufacture of a new product to spread from one country to another will obviously depend on a variety of factors, including the threat the new products pose to existing goods and the lure of the high profits earned in the new line of production. At the same time, technological-gap trade may be prolonged by the fact that the innovating country enjoys a peculiar advantage in harvesting scale economies. This advantage arises because the markets for new products expand rapidly at first. The innovator can thus more confidently erect a large plant and secure an entrenched position in domestic and export markets than can successor firms abroad. In this respect, the technological-gap theory is an improvement on the scale-economy theory, since according to the former, a small country that innovates may yet build a large plant, whereas the latter theory simply asserts that the country with the largest home market builds the biggest plant, regardless of when it begins production. Finally, it should be noted that while the technological-gap theory implies that trade between industrial nations is only temporary, the fact that innovation and technical progress are continuous processes means that trade between advanced industrial nations may well persist and even grow over time.

Another explanation of the rapidly expanding trade between industrial nations stresses the importance of domestic demand as a determinant of the products a country will export. Only after the new product is firmly established in the domestic market, it is argued, will the entrepreneur be ready to respond to profit opportunities in foreign markets. Moreover, since income, more than any other variable, appears to determine the consumption and purchasing habits of broad sectors of the population, countries having similar income levels are likely to trade with each other more intensively than countries having different income levels. This explanation of the basis of trade between nations is, of course, dramatically opposed to the factor-endowment theory, which implicitly argues that trade between capital-rich (high-income) and capital-poor (low-income) countries tends to be more promising for the trading partners than exchange of goods between countries whose average income levels are similar, where labour and capital may be expected to be distributed in similar proportions. However, having made this point, it should also be noted that none of the alternative theories just discussed completely dispenses with the factor proportions approach. Indeed, over time, a country's comparative advantage in certain industrial activities may be largely a matter of historical accident, in the sense that past international specialisation based on relative factor endowment may lead to a strengthening and development of natural skills, innovative capacity and investment activity along lines different to those of other countries. Consequently, opportunities for technological-gap trade may emerge and economies of scale assert themselves in the production of commodities and services which will have a ready market in other countries with similar income levels.

Whatever forms the basis of trade between nations, however, there is no doubting the gains from specialisation, which come about because trade between countries provides the opportunity for an international division of labour that leads to a better allocation of economic resources and greater productive efficiency in every country. Indeed, it was these gains from trade, in the form of the extra output made possible by international specialisation, and their distribution among trading nations that formed the basis for the advocacy of a policy of free trade between countries during the nineteenth century. But past experience indicates that the emergence of a truly international economy did much more than just provide a large market suitable for increased specialisation, for it also provided, through international flows of capital and labour as well as of goods, a mechanism for the diffusion of modern industrial technology and a means of transmitting economic growth from industrialising countries to the less developed areas of the world. In short, the expansion of the international economy after 1820 – which is when Britain had transformed from a largely agrarian and stationary economy into the first industrialised and dynamic economy in history – was a major cause of modern economic growth. But in emphasising its function as an 'engine of growth', we should not forget the fact that an expanding international economy is both a cause and an effect of national economic growth. For while the technological diffusion and increased specialisation facilitated by an expanding international economy may provide considerable stimulus to the economic growth of a country, that country's growth, in turn, may, through its increased demand for foreign goods, capital and labour, promote closer economic relations at the international level.

Given the main purpose of this book, which is to describe the growth and assess the economic significance of the modern international economy in the period between 1820 and 2025, its contents fall easily into three parts. After a short prologue that outlines the evolution of the international economy from the beginnings until about 1820, the first part contains a discussion of the forces responsible for the expanding international flows of trade, labour and capital in the years up to 1913 and an examination of the functioning of the international economy as an 'engine of growth' during these years. The impact of the World Wars of the twentieth century on the workings of the international economy is analysed in the second part, and in the light of this analysis, an attempt is made to account for the partial collapse of the international economy during the 1930s. Finally, in the last part, we describe the latest phase in the development of the world economy, 1950–2025, a period which first witnessed unparalleled economic growth, and then — from when the US 2007 financial crisis drove the world economy into a severe recession — persistent economic problems.

The Great Recession of 2008–9, the shocks to the world economy from the COVID-19 pandemic in 2020–1, the geopolitical tensions and hostilities in the Pacific, the Middle East and Eastern Europe, and as this book goes to the printing press, the protectionist trade policies imposed by the US in the first year of the second term of President Donald Trump have started to change the modus operandi of the world economy, so that a simple extrapolation of the previous trends will not do. The future is open. In the concluding Chapter 23 of this book, we will discuss whether the latest period of rapid globalisation that started in the 1970s may now already have passed its zenith.

NOTES

1 For a comprehensive description of 'globalization', see IMF (1997, Chapters 3–4 and the Annex). Stiglitz (2002) provides a critical view.
2 See Krugman et al. (2011, Chapter 6).
3 See Schumpeter (1912).

Prologue

The International Economy from the Beginnings to 1820

Michael Graff

THE PALAEOLITHIC PERIOD

Human-like beings have walked the Earth for maybe as long as two million years, and palaeo-anthropology is rapidly expanding our knowledge about early humans. While the timing and genealogy continue to be controversial, for our purpose it will suffice noticing that humans physically very similar to us existed for hundreds of thousands of years. Most of this time is 'prehistoric' without written evidence from the past, which only began to emerge some 5,000 years ago, and the prehistory of mankind is chronologically almost identical with the Palaeolithic age, which in some places ended about 10,000 years ago, and in others continued until very recently, when unanticipated confrontations with European 'explorers', and later invaders and settlers, regularly brought this way of living to an abrupt end.

During the Palaeolithic age, the essentials of economic activity, governing human life – and survival – from the beginnings to the present, the provision of food and shelter, were achieved by nomadic tribes of gatherers and scavengers, comprising a handful of families that spread slowly from their African origins into Eurasia, and eventually into Australia and the Americas. There is an abundance of Palaeolithic stone axes and similar artefacts, giving evidence for the use of stone tools in the remote past. Tools were certainly also made from other materials, such as wood or bone, but no evidence from the remotest times survived. But the remainders from this era also show that technical change was practically absent, at least until about 50,000 years ago, when some refinement becomes evident. This mode of production implied an eternal rhythm of feast and famine, with limited time devoted to subsistence, and if the surroundings were favourable, the local tribes may have lived in affluence.[1] Life expectancy at birth is estimated to have been 20 years, and even if this number is significantly affected by about 50 per cent of children born alive dying before they were ten years old, very few people would have lived into their fifties.

DOI: 10.4324/9781003382171-2

Thomas Hobbes (1651) famously pictured early prehistory as a state of

> Warre, where every man is Enemy to every man; the same is consequent to the time, wherein men live without other security, than what their own strength, and their own invention shall furnish them withall. In such condition, there is no place for Industry; because the fruit thereof is uncertain; and consequently no Culture of the Earth; no Navigation, nor use of the commodities that may be imported by Sea; no commodious Building; no Instruments of moving, and removing such things as require much force; no Knowledge of the face of the Earth; no account of Time; no Arts; no Letters; no Society; and which is worst of all, continuall feare, and danger of violent death; And the life of man, solitary, poore, nasty, brutish, and short.
>
> (p. 78)

Especially the final words are regularly quoted in texts on economic history and development up to this date. Impressive as they are, we must add that while there is evidence of brutishness and shortness of life of early humans, it is now disputed that this held for all Palaeolithic people, and the alleged lack of culture as well as the solitariness and fragmentation of humans into mutual enemies in their struggle for survival is certainly wrong. Our present understanding of the early humans sees them not only as toolmakers, but also as social and spiritual beeings. Animistic beliefs and incest taboo must have prevailed. Expressions of ceremonial and artistic performance survive to this day as figurines and cave paintings. Also, even with the limited division of labour in Palaeolithic times, survival and eventually progress of the species is unthinkable without cooperation and solidarity at the tribal level. And progress occurred, even if it was painfully slow. First, humans were gradually spreading across the globe; and by the end of this period, the world population may have reached about 10–20 million. For a given inhabited territory, however, technology and population were essentially stationary; growth was 'extensive'[2], resulting from advancing into areas formerly not touched by humans. At the same time, over unnumbered generations, tools gradually improved and archaeological evidence shows that already 500,000 years ago humans had gained some control over fire.

About 10,000 years ago, the Palaeolithic mode of production had been stretched to its limits. The resource for extensive growth – new territory – was depleted and, because of a combination of overhunting and climate change, a considerable number of large mammals that had been favourite prey of the hunting bands became extinct, such as mammoths, mastodons, sabre-toothed tigers and cave bears, as well as the North American wild horses and camels.

During the Palaeolithic era, humans engaged in – mostly cooperative – economic activity to provide the means of subsistence for the tribe, and the latter were common property. The allocation across individuals was governed by ceremonial or, as Karl Polanyi (1944) put it, 'reciprocal' rules deeply rooted in tradition. As there was no private property and no market, exchange was different from trade in the modern sense, where individuals voluntarily agree in a singular interaction that is perceived as beneficial by both parties. Hence, while goods were certainly exchanged in this era, no trade in the modern sense took place.

THE NEOLITHIC PERIOD

During what is now called the 'Neolithic Revolution', subsistence activity shifted from hunting wild animals and gathering wild plants to nomadic pastoralism and eventually food production at permanent settlements, typically comprising from 50 up to 300 villagers. At the dawn of this stage, humans had populated all continents except Antarctica, and the transition occurred independently in different parts of the world, such as the Middle East, Central America, East Asia and the Indian subcontinent. Although the spread of agriculture was a slow process, involving many generations, compared to the inertia of the Palaeolithic period, it is rightly seen as a revolution.

Why did it come so late in the history of our species, and why so suddenly and in areas that could not have had any contact with each other? Most likely, the depletion of resources, as the population frontier was pushed further and hunting parties wiped out more and more of their prey (some to extinction), led to a significant decrease in the marginal productivity of Palaeolithic subsistence activity until it fell below that of initial agriculture, which then in turn experienced increasing productivity through learning by doing (e.g. in irrigation, weeding and eventually breeding).[3]

Its effects on human subsistence were profound. First is the increase in the level and reliability of food production which could sustain a larger population. The domestication of animals not only added dairy products to the human diet; it also added new sources of energy and overland transportation of humans and goods. The new food surplus facilitated the emergence of specialisation in activities unrelated to subsistence, such as handicraft and metallurgy, as well as the rise of complex religions under guidance of a clergy. The latter would usually be related to astronomy and the calendar, as it was now crucial for survival of the villagers to determine the right date for sowing in spring. This required careful observation of natural phenomena, which in turn promoted a scientific approach to knowledge.

The new mode of production gradually spread into most arable areas, almost entirely replacing Palaeolithic reproduction in the course of a few thousand years, with the exception of a few isolated pockets (Australia and parts of Africa and the Americas), where it persisted until recently. But again, this growth of the world economy was extensive, and once the new mode of production had become universal, economy and population were stationary, with 'Malthus' law' limiting population to what the economy could sustain and fixing the level of living close to subsistence for the majority of people.

Moreover, the Neolithic Revolution also changed the nature of property. The once common resources of the Palaeolithic era, fauna to hunt and carrion as well as wild plants and fruits to gather, were now deliberately produced, and the villagers would have defended their now communal property against unfriendly neighbours or nomads. Moreover, livestock was the first truly valuable and (to some extent) durable possession; and the small but steady surplus that this economy provided above subsistence level allowed certain individuals (chiefs, priests, craftsmen) to claim, and in fact acquire, some fraction of what previously was common. Property rights and inequality had become an issue.

There is evidence that particular goods – e.g. obsidian, shells and spices – were travelling long distances even in the remotest past, but 'globalization' as a regular exchange of goods, services, knowledge and – involuntarily – germs between organised communities did not emerge before Antiquity.

The downside of the Neolithic Revolution is that compared to the relatively short time devoted to subsistence in Palaeolithic times, the overwhelming majority of the Neolithic people had to perform monotonous and often back-breaking work from dawn to dusk. Also, the diet typically became less varied and balanced, and living close together along with domesticated animal bred new infectious diseases. The result was deteriorating health status. Last but not least, servitude, inequality and oppression began to rule human life. Arguably, the Christian myth of the expulsion from paradise and similar beliefs in other religions with origins in the Neolithic period reflect the collective memories of better times,[4] and anthropologists have lately gathered evidence that people reverted to hunting and gathering whenever the opportunity arose.[5]

ANTIQUITY

From about 3000 BCE, based on agrarian surpluses of the Neolithic mode of production under particularly favourable conditions – mostly on marshes along rivers subject to annual floods – ancient civilisations emerged in different parts of the world. Their base was the city, and the division of labour as well as the reliable provision of food to its inhabitants required organisation on a scale previously unknown, extending to the surrounding countryside. In fact, agriculture depended on organised flood control and irrigation and required large numbers of labourers engaged in back-breaking work. As cities evolved into regional empires, new classes, ranks and occupations emerged, such as the ruling nobility and clergy, civil servants, artisans, builders, warriors and merchants. Handling the increasing complexity was facilitated by the invention of script, as well as calculating and accounting. Property became increasingly private (individual). Work and life were governed by a strict hierarchy, and throughout Antiquity the vast majority of the population was enslaved or else in servitude.[6]

Antique philosophy and architecture are admired up to this date, but economically, dynamism was very limited. Growth was mostly extensive, a result of conquest; the Antique mode of production, with its reliance on forced labour, provided very limited incentives for innovative activity, for either the rulers or the oppressed. Technology thus largely relied on innovations that pre-date the ancient city states. The difference to the Neolithic mode of production is mainly one of scale and complexity. At the height of this development stands the development of democratic government in Greece and of positive law in Rome.

Continuous rivalry with neighbouring empires fostered an increasingly belligerent and expansionist attitude of the ruling elites; consequently, Antique history is largely about the rise and fall of empires. At the same time, navigation as well as institutionalised money and banking helped establish regular long-distance trade.

The first evidence of 'international' trade points to Mesopotamia about 3000 BCE, where Sumer, lacking raw materials for metallurgy, which it had to import, exported textiles, and along with this adopted standardised weights, prices and bookkeeping. Other evidence for early organised international trade are the permanent Bronze Age 'expatriate' merchant colonies of

Assyrian traders in Anatolia about 2000 BCE. Later, trade spread across the Mediterranean as a profitable enterprise to Greece and Rome.

In the beginning, the cost of transportation over long distances must have been prohibitive for all except a few highly cherished or indispensable goods. Thus, the domestication of the camel by Arabic nomads, dated about 1500 BCE, was a decisive step in the evolution of the international economy. These robust beasts of burden can carry up to 250 kg and walk 30 km each day, requiring water only once every few days, which makes them perfectly suited for overland transport including dry inland regions. Fluvial and maritime transport increased the number of potential tradables even more significantly. The Red Sea and the Persian Gulf, although treacherous to navigate, were (and are) the most important sea routes of the Middle East, connecting Egypt with the Arabic peninsula and Persia. Arabian sailors from early times also crossed the Western Indian Ocean, thereby integrating India into the trade of this era.

In the classic era of Greece and Rome, Mediterranean and Black Sea trade established an extensive intercontinental division of labour. The range of goods traded now extended to staple goods, most notably grain from surplus areas (e.g. Sicily, North Africa and what is now Ukraine) to the Greek cities and the metropolis of Rome.

Possibly the most amazing fact about trade in ancient times is that it was already global. Throughout Antiquity – and up to the end of the Middle Ages – globalisation comprised all inhabited land masses but two: the Americas and Australia. Apart from maritime transport across the Mediterranean and the Indian Ocean, land transport covered vast distances. Most notably, the Silk Road connected East Asia with the Mediterranean. It consisted of a series of previously unconnected stretches of local trade routes that started to be used for trade from China to Rome once both empires had spread and consolidated themselves enough to ensure reasonably safe passage. While 'Pax Romana' covered the Mediterranean and its shores, the Han dynasty negotiated passage for Chinese goods to the Indian subcontinent and Persia, where it would connect with the Roman Empire. The inland route went along the Gobi desert, the Tarim base, the Taklamakan desert, across the Pamir, further to Bukhara, Samarkand and Baghdad to the Levant coast. Apart from this, maritime transport followed the shores of the Chinese Sea, the Indian Ocean and the Persian Gulf to the Middle East.

Neither the sea nor the land route would usually be covered by one and the same travelling party. Rather, locally experienced navigators or traders relying on camels, donkeys or porters to carry the loads would perform transport from one port or trading post to the next, on their own account, adding their costs as well as profits to the final price of the shipped goods at their final destination, where knowledge of the first origin of this trade had been lost.

Given the transport cost, it is obvious that only precious goods could be subject to international trade along the Silk Road: silk, spices, sandalwood and ceramics ('china') from China; and furs and skins, drugs and dyes, jewels, incense, metals and 'exotic' African animals from the West. However, the taste for goods from the West in China did not usually match demand for silk and other Eastern luxuries in the West, so the balance of trade was characterised by a structural and chronic Western deficit that had to be settled in silver or gold.

For the maritime route, the monsoon dictated the direction and rhythm of transport, eastward in spring and summer, westward in autumn and winter. The Indian subcontinent was the hub for the maritime route, which, other than the northern Silk Road, also integrated Africa into the world economy, adding ivory and slaves to the traded goods of this era.

Asian-African contact was intense right from the beginning of this era and led to increased varieties of food crops, e.g. the introduction of the banana from Southeast Asia to Africa. European-African contact was as close as possible during the Roman era, when North Africa served as a main grain supplier for the metropolis.

Globalisation is thus not a new phenomenon. Cultural and economic links between humans living far apart from each other go back to Neolithic times. So does what Bernstein (2008, p. 67) calls the 'trilemma of trade: whether to trade, protect or raid. In the absence of any authority beyond the tribe, entrepreneurs will invariably choose to raid'. Antiquity established some authority beyond the tribe and unified the Mediterranean coasts of Europe, Asia and Africa into a market for staple and luxury goods alike; and the West actively traded with the East, exchanging silks, spices and ceramics for gold and silver via the Silk Road. The medieval period from about 500 to 1500, however, saw the establishment of long-distance trade routes and patterns, which in part prevail up to our era.

MIDDLE AGES

The Middle Ages are conventionally dated from about 500 to 1500. As an epoch, they are mainly a European phenomenon. It started when new socio-economic organisations took shape where formerly there had been the West Roman empire, with the Roman Church as the only unifying force left; and it ended when parts of Europe abandoned Roman Catholicism for local varieties of Protestantism, and Portugal and Spain embarked on their maritime 'discoveries', or commercial and colonial expansion.

Contrary to the widespread picture of the 'Dark Ages', the medieval period was technologically quite dynamic. True, after the collapse of the Roman order, the cities declined and the economy regressed to being practically completely agrarian, but in this they proved inventive. From the sixth to ninth century, among other innovations, the yoke and wheeled cast-iron plough, the overshot water wheel, the spinning wheel, the loom, the horseshoe and the stirrup were invented or adopted from outside. The results were marked increases in agricultural and textile productivity, increasing use of non-human sources of energy, improvements of transport facilities, and last but not least, unprecedented military power in the form of horse-mounted fighting units, the cavalry. The rotation of crops in the three-field system, which also goes back to these times, is estimated to have increased agricultural output by 50 per cent. As a by-product, it led to an increase in fodder crops suitable for horses, and the latter in turn tended to be substitutes for oxen in transport and ploughing. The hub-and-spokes wheel made transport more comfortable and reliable, and four-wheeled wagons replaced the two-wheeled carts of former times, significantly increasing transportation capacity for overland trade. From the tenth to fourteenth centuries, the mechanical clock was invented and spread quickly, and firearms as well as the compass were introduced, the latter based on inventions originating in China. As a result, by the end of the Middle Ages, Europe was – for the first time – technologically and militarily more advanced than any other civilisation and possessed the prerequisites to establish global maritime dominance, along with a Europe-centred trade network.

Initially, the fall of West Rome in the fifth century and, consequently, the end of 'Pax Romana' had disrupted, for a few centuries, the traditional European trade routes across the

Mediterranean and to the Far East. Moreover, the rise and advance of Islam from the seventh century, with the Arabian conquests in North Africa and the Iberian Peninsula, effectively shut the Europeans off from trade with the Levant and North Africa; the latter directed their attention to the South and, in particular, to the East.

On the other hand, the spread of Islam significantly intensified trade within this region; Mohammed himself had been a merchant, so trade was a respected activity, and common beliefs, customs and script facilitated transactions between strangers. Caravan routes connected the Mediterranean with the Red Sea and the Persian Gulf, and at times caravans comprising thousands of camels started crossing the Sahara. Bantu-speaking traders from East Africa conducted trade along the coast up to Persia. 'Pax Islamica' lasted until the eleventh century.

The advance of Islam had cut the remainder of Europe off from its Mediterranean trade routes to Africa and the Levant, but the Christian Reconquista of the Iberian Peninsula from the 'Moors', and from the tenth century the rise of Italian city republics, put an end to the period of Islamic reign over the Mediterranean sea routes. Around the year 1000, Venetian, in alliance with Byzantine, fleets re-opened the eastern Mediterranean waters for intercontinental trade. The strength of the Venetian fleet re-established the former maritime links for centuries to come. For the next 500 years, Venice was the chief European hub. Trade stretched to Europe north of the Alps, to Byzantium, the Black Sea and via the caravan tracks of the Middle East to India. Along with Genoa and other Italian city republics, the northern shores of the Mediterranean thus also became the hub for medieval trade from the Far East via the Levant to the economically rising territories north of the Alps.

From 1095, the crusade motive pushed European expansion into the Muslim world. As a result, European outposts were maintained for two centuries in the 'Holy Land', which, apart from the religious meaning it may have had for devoted Christians at that time, happens to be located at the Levant, the focal point for European–Asian trade since ancient times. Thus, securing safe passage through the east Mediterranean for pilgrims and cross-bearing knights implied safe passage for traded goods as well, which certainly added to the effort.

While the north of present-day Italy held the centre position for European trade, the needs of these merchants in the long-distance trade triggered significant innovations, which economic historians subsume as the medieval Commercial Revolution. It represents the origin of modern banking, comprising the cash account with cheque facility, the letter of exchange, clearing, insurance, double-entry bookkeeping (the importance of which was highlighted by Max Weber) and the notary system ('third party certification of property rights' in modern jargon; its importance highlighted by new institutional economics).

The Commercial Revolution coincided, but was not identical to, the first surge of growth of the European economy as a whole, which took off in the eleventh century and was brought to a brutal end by the Great Plague epidemic of 1348, which itself was a result of long-distance trade that carried infected rats, climbing upon ships on moorings, and their fleas.

The key element of the first surge of growth is most likely found in improved agricultural productivity due to the three-course rotation, as well as large-scale clearance of forested lands for cultivation, which allowed sustaining a growing population.

By the fourteenth century, annual trade fairs emerged in the Champagne, which served as hubs for overland trade, connecting the Mediterranean with the markets north of the Alps.

About a century later, the settlement of trade would mostly be performed by merchants in cities, and on a permanent basis. As a consequence, the financial instruments that had earlier emerged in the trading communities of northern Italy now spread to the new commercial centres in the north and west of Europe.[7]

The successful siege of Constantinople and the fall of Byzantium in 1453 and the subsequent rise of the Ottoman empire once again disrupted west European trade with the east, blocking Venetian access to the Black Sea and the Levant.

Further north, the Vikings by the eighth century had penetrated into the eastern Baltic and from there far into the rivers of Eastern Europe (nowadays Russia and Ukraine), thus establishing a continental trade route to the Black Sea (and along with it, the first statehood on Slavonic territory, the 'Kiev Rus'). Later, in the twelfth century, the 'Hanse', a league of about 200 cities and trading posts across the Baltic under the lead of Lübeck, established a powerful trade monopoly in the region, with outposts (Kontors) in London, Bergen and Novgorod.

For a short period, the Silk Road experienced a revival, during the 'Pax Mongolica' of the High Middle Ages around the thirteenth century. During this time, Mongolian Khans ruled over the land masses of Asia from the Yellow Sea to Europe and re-opened the ancient land route to traders from the east and the west alike.[8]

In the Far East, at the dawn of the Modern Era, China briefly turned into a naval power in search of profitable trade. The peak of this new orientation towards the outer world were the expeditions of Admiral Zheng He, commanding fleets of up to 62 vessels of formerly unknown dimensions, carrying up to 40,000 troops. Zheng He reached Indonesia, India, Ceylon, the Strait of Hormuz and the east coast of Africa. While this advance could have laid the foundation for globalisation taking shape, with China as one of the major hubs, after Zheng He's last voyage in 1433, the empire abruptly and deliberately turned inward again, not only abandoning all coordinated efforts to conduct maritime trade (or expansion), but effectively banning it by outlawing construction of seaworthy ships. China thereafter concentrated on securing its vast land borders against the repeated onslaughts of the belligerent nomadic peoples of Central Asia.

The global economy in the Middle Ages thus had its centre in the Islamic world of the Middle East. Continuous trade connected the hub with Europe, Africa, India, Central Asia and – via Indian traders – China. A lasting result was the diffusion of Islam to the east as far as Indonesia, and of tropical food crops like mangoes, aubergines, melons and lemons to the West. Moreover, slave trade boomed, integrating also the remoter parts of the known world, like Eastern Europe and Central Africa into the international economy. The ties, however, were only loosely knit, and direct contact between the three continents was sparse, as long-distance trade usually involved a long chain of middlemen.

Only decades after Zheng He, Portuguese carracks penetrated into the Western Indian Ocean. Starting in 1415, Portuguese sailors established trading posts along the East African coast; and in 1498, Vasco da Gama sailed into Calicut on the Malabar coast of southwest India.

The monopoly of Islamic trade with the East had been broken, and within a few years, Portugal had established a series of trading posts along the way, which were to become its eastern colonies. Though the Portuguese did not succeed in eliminating Muslim trade between the Middle East and India, they soon took Malacca and established trading posts as far as China and Japan, and for some decades the lion's share of the European silk and spice trade went on Portuguese ships via the Cape of Good Hope and Lisbon. During the sixteenth century, Portugal effective monopolised the European trade with the Moluccan 'Spice Islands', which it had bought from Spain as a bargain in 1529 – then the only source for the highly valued nutmeg, mace and cloves – and Indonesia.

MODERNITY

Modernity is conventionally dated from about 1500, when European invadors reached and violently took possession of the Americas, integrating this formerly largely isolated hemisphere into the global economy. Its dawn coincides with the second European surge of growth. Within Europe, the economic centre now moved towards the Atlantic ports in the west – Lisbon and Seville, later Antwerp, Amsterdam, London and Hamburg. Gutenberg's printing press with movable type drastically reduced the cost of books and thus promoted literacy. Socio-economically, the continuing retreat of feudalism cut the local bonds of servitude and protection between lords and serfs. Feudal lords became landlords, and wage labour relations replaced drudgery. Money and markets were no longer restricted to the cities and the merchant communities, capitalism advanced into the rural economy. Protestantism broke the ideological monopoly of the Catholic Church. In England, towards the end of the sixteenth century, enclosures of formerly common land increased agricultural productivity and created a new class of rural poor. Individual property rights were further strengthened by the 'Glorious Revolution' (1688), which installed a parliament and restricted the power of the crown to levy taxes at its discretion. Technologically, incremental but steady improvements of technical precision laid the foundation for industrialisation, and the upheavals of the mode of production known as the Industrial Revolution (1760–1830) turned Britain into the first industrialised country and the hegemonic power of the nineteenth century.

At the beginning of global trade in the Modern Era stood the rivalry of Portugal and Spain about maritime access to the origins of the treasured spices of the Indian Ocean. In an attempt – futile, as we know now – to reach the treasures of the east by sailing westward, Christopher Columbus in 1492 hit the West Indies (their name up to this date preserves Columbus' failure to realise that he had in fact hit a continent separating the Atlantic from the Pacific). On later voyages, he made landfall on the American mainland, and he, as well as his successors, did not hesitate to claim the land for the Spanish crown, 'saving the souls' of the natives by forcefully converting them to Catholicism, as well as expropriating them of whatever seemed valuable enough to justify the effort.

The European expansion into the Americas was partly driven by the hunger for bullion to settle the chronic deficit in the European–Asian balance of trade. The infamous acts of robbery of the first conquistadores, however, were singular events that offered no relief to the structural imbalance. What was required was a continuous and sizeable flow of bullion from the New World to the Old. In fact, scarcity of bullion in the European economy was followed by abundance, and hence, towards the end of the sixteenth century, people could witness the beginning of a new kind of inflation, subsequently called the 'Price Revolution'. Europe's stock of bullion increased modestly between 1500 and 1580, then rapidly between 1580 and 1620. Before silver mining collapsed and shipments from America fell strongly during the first 20 years of the seventeenth century, the influx of precious metal from the New World elevated the price level in Europe by some 300 to 400 per cent. In 1571, silver was discovered in Potosí (now: Bolivia), in 1546 in San Luis Potosí (Mexico) and in Guanajuato (Mexico). Moreover, in 1571 mercury was discovered in Huencavelica (Peru), which dramatically reduced the cost of silver production. The official records – which do not account for smuggling and privateering – show that as a result, from 1500 to 1650, at least 17,000 tons of silver arrived in Spain. After the 1693 gold discovery in Minas Gerais (Brazil), gold started flowing from Brazil to Portugal. Although there was still a negative balance of trade with the Levant and the East, due to which up to 80 tons of silver per year had to be exported, the overall balance of bullion flows was clearly positive.

The rivalry between the two initial expansionist powers, Portugal and Spain, implied a serious potential for raiding or outright war. The Pope intervened, graciously allocating all 'undiscovered' territories in the west to Spain, and the east to Portugal. The Treaty of Tordesillas between Spain and Portugal (1494) fixed the dividing line at running north-south 370 leagues (1,700 km) west of the Cape Verde islands, which was with hindsight a lucky outcome for the Portuguese, as South America bulges far out to the East, so that Portugal – contrary to the Papal intentions – received a sizeable part of it, too: Brazil.

In the end, Spain gained control over most of the Americas in the west; in the east its only colony was the Philippines. The latter, however, proved to be a highly advantageous possession when the 'Manila galleons' in 1581 started to make their yearly passages across the Pacific from Acapulco to Manila. Bullion from the American mines flew eastward in exchange for silk and other Eastern luxuries for the upper classes in New Spain.

As long as the Portuguese dominated the imports of fine spices into Europe via the Cape of Good Hope, they left the distribution of the precious cargo to European markets to others, in particular the Dutch. Previously engaged in the inter-European trade of salt and herring, their new involvement in the spice business gradually paved the way to eventually joining the Asian trade via the Cape towards the end of the sixteenth century. In a quick and successful series of maritime advances, establishments of trading posts as well as raids on reluctant natives and European competitors, the Dutch would later manage to get a permanent foothold in Indonesia, as well as the monopoly for trade with the Spice Islands.

During the first centuries of the Modern Era, trade between the West and the East or the Americas lay mainly in the hands of a small number of West European national monopoly companies, most importantly the Portuguese 'Casa da India' (chartered 1434), the Spanish 'Casa de Contratación' (1503), the English 'East India Company' (1599) and 'Hudson Bay Company' (1670), the Dutch 'Vereenigde Oostindische Compagnie' (1602) and the French 'Compagnie Française des Indes Orientales' (1646).

Initially, the Portuguese controlled the West European–Asian maritime trade, but towards the end of the sixteenth century, the English and Dutch companies became effective competitors, which in turn led to abandonment of the ancient land route.

After independence from Spain in 1579, from about 1600 to 1820, Holland had the highest per capita income in the world. It was more urbanised than any other part of the world, and less than 50 per cent of the labour force was engaged in agriculture. It reaped the benefits of Ricardian comparative advantage by importing most of its food in exchange for manufactures, which, apart from textiles, mostly related to maritime transport. Free from the burdens of monarchy, with a long tradition of shipbuilding, and with the most sophisticated financial and payment system of its time, the Dutch with unprecedented success turned to international trade and conquest, mostly in Asia, where the Vereenigde Oostindische Compagnie (VOC) acted like a sovereign, and at the cost of the Portuguese. In the end, however, as Portugal before, it overstretched its resources, men and material, to man its ships and defend the outposts.

As early English aspirations in the Far East were effectively rebuffed by the Dutch, they first resorted to India, which was to become the 'brightest jewel in the crown' of the British Empire. Later, when spices had become so commonplace that they were no longer the primary source of profits in the trade with Asia, this accident of history gave England access to Indian cotton, which turned out to be the crucial raw material input in the early stages of the Industrial Revolution.

In the eighteenth century, Dutch supremacy in the world economy was gradually taken over by Britain, a process in which the East India Company (EIC) grew at the expense of the VOC. In a series of wars, apart from Indonesia, the Dutch lost all of their Asian colonies; Britain, on the other hand, succeeded in establishing an overseas empire that by 1820 comprised 100 million subjects on the British Isles proper, in North America, Africa, the Middle East and Australia.

The trading partners in the East never showed much interest in European goods, but rather in silver and gold – the eastward passage was largely in ballast. Westward, spices and silk dominated, later accompanied by ceramics, cotton and tea. It is estimated that maritime trade between Europe and Asia in the early Modern Era until the end of the eighteenth century increased at a rate of 1.1 per cent annually, thus multiplying 25-fold in 300 years. Eventually, annual imports from Asia may have reached 50,000 tons, which is about the load of a modern container ship, but at that time would amount to an average of 0.5 kg per inhabitant of Central and West Europe. Although these imports were luxuries and certainly not distributed evenly, eventually they to some degree found also their ways to people of modest means, thereby enriching the variety of consumer goods, which is not a trivial aspect of globalisation.

When the EIC was expanding in the eighteenth century, the composition of imports into Europe had changed markedly. Apart from cotton, tea, sugar and, later, coffee were the sought-after colonial goods; the trading corporations actively engaged in stimulating demand. Luxury imports for the conspicuous consumption of the wealthy upper classes gradually gave way to imports serving the consumer mass demand in the more prosperous parts of the world, particularly in Europe.

The modern revival of the European–Asian trade, however, was overshadowed by the emerging Atlantic trade. Estimates of imports from the Americas and the Caribbean until the close of the eighteenth century are about twice as high in terms of the average growth rate and three-fold in terms of value (de Vries, 2010).

THE ATLANTIC ECONOMY

European expansion and trade in the sixteenth century were driven by Portugal and Spain, both in the East and the West. As for the East, England and the Netherlands emerge as the first serious competitors in the Atlantic hemisphere. In the seventeenth century, the global wind system had been understood, and circumnavigating the globe was no longer a hazardous adventure, as in the times of Magellan. Europeans reached out for the remaining booty or raided each other's outposts. Dutch, English and French traders and privateers repeatedly tried to establish themselves in Spanish America and Brazil, but were ultimately unsuccessful, so they turned their attention elsewhere. In particular, they turned to North America, where they founded colonies that would eventually become the US and Canada. By this time, the Atlantic economy had taken the shape that it would maintain up to the nineteenth century.

The 'Atlantic triangle' or 'Atlantic system' connected Europe, Africa and the Americas in a particular – hideous and highly profitable – way. The slave labour-based plantation system in the Americas and the Caribbean produced 'colonial goods' for Europe. Sugar cane was the first dominant cash-crop. Formerly a formidable luxury, sugar yielded prices that made other food crops clearly uncompetitive. Food thus had to be imported from Europe or from North America outside the sugar belt; but the main imports were slaves from Africa. Under the atrocious conditions of the sugar plantation system, the slave population did not reproduce itself, thus, it required a constant supply, so that the infamous slave ships kept plying the Atlantic for centuries. It is estimated that from the sixteenth to the nineteenth century close to 13 million Africans were sold to the slave ships anchored at the coast of Africa and waiting until their hulls were filled with human cargo. Apart from sugar, slave labour was later also exploited in cacao, tobacco, coffee and cotton plantations, as well as in other labour-intensive industries, but sugar remained important until the end of the scheme. Europe produced the export goods to be traded for slaves from local merchants at the 'slave coast' of West Africa. Most of the latter trade goods were cloth produced in Britain, and so were the transport services, which meant that Britain profited twice.

The slave trade from Africa was abolished by Parliament in Britain in 1807 and outlawed in the US in the same year; in Brazil transport continued to arrive legally until 1850. But slavery and the plantation system persisted until 1888, when finally, Brazil, as the last major economy, abolished slavery. It had involved cruelties that were revolting, even given the standards of the time.[9] Those Africans that participated in the scheme, hunting and selling people to European traders, profited, but the economic consequences of this particular trade for Africa were clearly a burden, involving the continuous threat to personal liberty, and the mass deportations of healthy and able people significantly reduced the expected returns to investment and education.

By the eighteenth century, the heydays of the national European trade monopolies had passed. Shielded from (national) competition, they had focused more on political influence than cost efficiency in administration and transport. American independence (1776) and the upheavals following the French Revolution (1789) quickly ended their dominance. The new European paradigm would be direct exertion of colonial power to extract resources from overseas, wherever and as long as this was possible.

By the mid-eighteenth century, gradually in the beginning, but steadily and picking up pace during the later decades, the British economy industrialised and eventually became the first technical civilisation. This Industrial Revolution is now conventionally dated 1760–1830, but the dating is disputed, as is the term 'revolution'. Its initial phases see the mechanisation of textile production. The 'spinning jenny', still a remarkably simple device, increased the productivity in yarn; mechanical looms to weave the increased yarn supply followed.

The putting-out system gave way to labour concentrated in the factory. The early factories were powered by water mills. Watt's steam engine took over, developed from the Newcomen engine, a steam pump used to keep water out of mines. The increased manufacturing output pushed into remoter markets, stressing the precarious pre-industrial transport infrastructure to its limits. A boom of canal construction set in, and later the railway took over. As these projects required unprecedented amounts of capital, joint stock companies took care of financing the large-scale investments. While mechanisation of textile production initiated the transformation, the almost complete substitution of mineral fuel (coal, later oil) for timber (including charcoal), animal and human muscle power, wind and running water, completed it.

At that time, Britain also reached out for the last continent which had been left largely unaffected by Europeans: Australia. Portuguese, Dutch and French traders had repeatedly hit the West Australian coast in the seventeenth century when they missed the turn north on their way to Indonesia; but it was not before James Cook charted Australia and New Zealand in the 1770s that firm knowledge of the whereabouts and characteristics of the southern continent was established. Following American independence, the British sought a new place to dispose of their increasing number of convicts, and in 1788 the 'First Fleet' sailed into Sydney Harbour. The convict transport system persisted until the 1860s, but along with the convicts came settlers, and gradually, the British colonies in Australia took shape.

Historians describe the period from the 1780s to the 1820s as an epochal time of change. The invasion into revolutionary France by the First Coalition of the old powers was quickly defeated and in turn triggered the Revolutionary and Napoleonic Wars. The revolutionary order thus first spread over large parts of Europe (with the notable exception of Britain), until Napoleon's armies were finally defeated in 1814.

The introduction of the Code Napoleon in 1804 and its spread through Europe by the French Revolutionary Army constitutes an important legacy for the economic perspectives of those countries, where the Code remained the basis for a corpus of positive law, as in Switzerland, and what are now Belgium, the Netherlands and parts of Germany. In particular, the abolition – or limitation – of the privileges of the church, the nobility and the guilds facilitated the rise of capitalism, as it reduced entry barriers and internal and external trade restrictions.

The 'French Wars' between Britain and France – first royal, then revolutionary – cut many of the links between the advanced European economies and the periphery alike. Apart from the usual disruptions of trade in states of war, during the Napoleonic Wars (1803–15) policies of both Britain (blockade of French ports) and France ('continental system') deliberately aimed at cutting the opponent off from vital resources.

Moreover, at that stage Britain turned into a net importer of grain, and landed interests successfully lobbied for import tariffs on imported corn, as world market prices fell after Napoleon's defeat. The poor were hit by the increasing cost of subsistence, and manufacturers feared upward pressure on the price of their crucial input, paid labour, and tended to favour free trade. David Ricardo took their side and in 1817 provided the theoretical foundation, which is taught to students of international economics to this day: comparative advantage. It took another three decades until the Corn Laws were repealed, but the old debate on the merits and drawbacks of international trade had taken a decisive new turn – from now on, economists would generally see free trade as the preferred regime.

After Napoleon's defeat, the old order of monarchy and clergy was restored in most parts of Europe by the Congress of Vienna (1815), to last for another century; but the American colonies of Spain and Portugal, who had seized the opportunity of the turmoil in Europe, were gone. Also, Britain had emerged from the conflict as the dominant power; it was not only the industrially most advanced economy, but its maritime supremacy was to remain undisputed for the next eight decades. Last but not least, Europeans in the nineteenth century, as no people ever before them, were now aware that technical change and political overthrow could be brought about swiftly; and the church had lost its monopoly on the guidance of reasoning, moral and practical issues for good.

Appendix 1: Economic Output and Macroeconomic Accounting

Michael Graff

Macroeconomic accounting of aggregate economic output of goods and services resorts to the so-called aggregate production function:

$$Y = f\left(X_1, X_2, \ldots X_n\right) \tag{P.1}$$

where Y denotes total output, measured against a standard unit of value, net of intermediate products, and X stands for the factors of production. In the simplest case, output is related to one factor of production only – labour (L). Introductory neoclassical economics nowadays usually refers to labour and physical capital (K), but for agricultural economies the two-factor function would refer to labour and land (T). Of course, the number of factors of production can in principle be extended to many more than two; common are aggregate production functions with three factors L, K and T or L, K and H, where H denotes human capital (or some type of knowledge useful in production). Technology, or 'total factor productivity', is represented by f. Based on theoretical considerations as well as ample empirical evidence, it is assumed that the 'law of diminishing returns' holds, i.e.:

$$\delta Y / \delta X_i > 0, \delta^2 Y / \delta X_i^2 < 0 \tag{P.2}$$

Moreover, as a rule, constant returns to scale as a rule are imposed, so that $\alpha = 1$ in:

$$\lambda^{\alpha} Y = f\left(\lambda X_1, \lambda X_2, \ldots\right) \tag{P.3}$$

When $\alpha > 1$, there are increasing returns to scale ('economies of scale'), which is usually ruled out by discretion; but modern trade theory identifies economies of scale as one of the major potential benefits from trade. Along with comparative advantage (which is the economist's standard pro-trade argument), economies of scale predict that specialising and trading accordingly will increase world output and thus imply that Pareto superior outcomes are achievable due to trade.

To track economic development through history, per capita income (*Y/P*) is the most important variable, reflecting both labour productivity and the achievable standard of living. As a process, expressed in growth rates, the growth rate of per capita income equals the difference between the growth rate $g(\bullet)$ of output and the growth rate of the population:

$$g(Y/P) = g(Y) - g(P) \qquad \text{(P.4)}$$

Relating to the stylised representations of the Palaeolithic and Neolithic economies in this chapter, we find Malthusian equilibria with $g(Y/P) \cong 0$, as any growth of income is subsequently followed by a corresponding growth of the population. In particular, while the transition from the Palaeolithic to the Neolithic mode of production is a period of growing labour productivity, before and after, all growth is 'extensive', i.e. based on increasing factor inputs in a constant returns-to-scale environment, without changes in the production technology. Given the simplicity of tools, the Palaeolithic production function can be expressed as an argument of labour inputs, approximated by the size of the population, and nature, from which they extract their subsistence, given by the territory they can resort to:

$$Y = f(P,T) \qquad \text{(P.5)}$$

With humans spreading across the globe, both factor inputs *P* and *T* increase at the same rate, so does *Y*, and consequently *Y/P* remains constant. This equilibrium can temporarily be disturbed by population pressure, implying a reduction in *Y/P* due to the law of diminishing returns, with consequently increased mortality until equilibrium is restored at subsistence level. Likewise, a decrease in the population-to-land ratio will temporarily increase per capita income, but the resulting population growth will restore the Malthusian equilibrium.

Extensive growth can thus increase, decrease or leave per capita income unaffected, but under Stone Age conditions, a permanent increase cannot be achieved. The Neolithic Revolution changes the production technology, i.e. the way nature is resorted to for subsistence. But as the resulting improvement in labour productivity is not a continuous process, but rather a singular event (or a series of such), the following population growth again fixes per capita income at the subsistence level. Now, extensive growth is possible until the Neolithic mode of production has completely replaced its Palaeolithic predecessor. At this stage, world population and output become stationary.

Intensive growth implies getting more output from the same amount of inputs due to improvements to the production technology in the widest sense, including organisational and motivational elements, as well as economies of scale. This can in principle continue without limit, even with fixed amounts of indispensable factors of production. It will usually imply rising per capita output, unless labour inputs increase at a faster rate than the complementary factors of production so that the law of diminishing returns overcompensates increases in total factor productivity.

Apart from short and isolated periods, intensive growth as a paradigm is basically a result of the Industrial Revolution; and the prospect of ensuring rising levels of living for all inhabitants of the globe in the future crucially depends on the ability to generate sustained intensive growth henceforth.

Appendix 2: Early Financial Manias and Crashes

Michael Graff

A feature of early capitalist economies that may appear recent to contemporary observers is the rhythm of financial euphoria and the following hangover. Quite to the contrary, extraordinary financial follies can be traced back to the Dutch 'tulip mania' of the 1630s, where the price of some tulip bulbs peaked at 3,000 florins (at 0.77 g gold content, this amounts to more than 2.3 kg of gold). The crash left numerous individuals and families impoverished and led, as ever after, to a furious search for scapegoats who could be blamed for the collective madness. Next came two rather similar manias in London and Paris.

The London 'South Sea Bubble' refers to the South Sea Company, chartered in 1711 to take over the crown's debt in exchange for a monopoly on trade with the Americas. Without any serious effort to extract profit from the trade monopoly, the company embarked on emitting shares amidst rumours of fantastic profit opportunities. Share prices peaked and subsequently crashed in 1720.

The French 'Mississippi Bubble' started when John Law (a Scot exiled in Paris) had a bank chartered to fund the royal debt that emitted paper money and likewise ran the Compagnie D'Occident (Mississippi Company), allegedly pertaining to extract gold from the French colony of Louisiana. The result was inflation in paper money as well as in the Mississippi Company's share prices, with the two crashing simultaneously, and as across the channel, in 1720. Interestingly and strikingly familiar to observers of the 2000 IT bubble, dubious free riders had been attracted: 'start-ups' going public with new shares, offering nothing but the vaguest indications of how they would turn the funds thus raised into profitable projects.[10]

For all except the most convinced believers in rational expectations and financial market efficiency, these episodes already highlight four characteristics of the financial boom–bust cycle operational up to this date:

1. the brevity of memory regarding financial events ('this time is different' syndrome);
2. the impressive aura of innovation and sophistication as well as the distinctive financial market jargon, which persuades outsiders (and many insiders) into believing that the latest scheme is extraordinarily clever and absolutely fail-safe;

3 the observation that all bubbles are inflated by credit taken in expectance of certain capital gains;
4 the fact that there are always sceptics, foreseeing the inevitable crash; but that as long as the bubble inflates, standing aside means to forego easy capital gains. Of course, only a very limited number of speculators can pull out at the right moment, so that the sceptics usually suffer the same losses as the believers (this is today called 'rational herding').

Unfortunately, despite all assurances that the lessons of the 2007 crash have been learned and financial sector regulation improved accordingly, it is hard to see how this should affect the mass psychology of financial mania.

Appendix 3: Why Europe? Why Britain?

Michael Graff

Economic historians have long debated, and continue to debate, why the first industrial take-off took place in Western Europe and not in other places of the world, e.g. China, India or the Middle East, which were in many respects at some points in time as advanced – if not more so. There is most likely no single true answer. Nevertheless, a few attempts to explain the fact stand out.

The 'European Marriage Pattern' (EMP) hypothesis relates to the observation that while throughout history marriages were commonly arranged and practically all girls were married as children or at the arrival of puberty, this almost universal pattern was significantly loosened in the European High Middle Ages west of an imaginary line ('Hajnal's line') from Trieste to St. Petersburg, where the average marriage age for girls increased to up to their mid-twenties, and a significant share remained unmarried.[11] There is some dispute regarding the causes of the EMP, among them the principle of consensual marriage advanced by the church, or the scarcity of labour after the Black Death had killed some one-third of the European population in 1348–51, which made labour income available (and attractive) also for girls, thus providing an alternative to staying with their parents or a husband. This, in turn, may also have made human capital investment more attractive. Be this as it may, without effective contraception, postponement of marriage (and 'legitimate' births) is the only effective way to reduce fertility rates, so the EMP contributed to reducing population growth; as such, the Malthusian population trap, which has increases in total subsistence income followed by corresponding increases in population, thus fixing per capita income for all except a few privileged to the subsistence level, was broken. Consequently, the EMP may have helped to generate an agricultural surplus, which is one of the preconditions for industrialisation.

Other arguments relate to a distinctive European praise of hard (manual) labour; or to a relative weakness of religion and tradition after the collapse of the Roman Empire, which facilitated an investigative approach and in turn innovation.

Turning to natural endowments, it is argued that the industrialisation of Britain and other parts of Europe may have benefitted from the fact that hard coal deposits were located close to settlements. Initially used for heating houses, they facilitated the adoption of fossil energy in the industrial revolution. Other parts of the world were disadvantaged in this respect. Particularly in China, coal deposits were mostly brown coal, which is less energy-rich, and they were further away from the population centres. Moreover, the massive shift of labour from agriculture to industry was feasible, because Britain could rely on the foodstuffs from its colonial empire.

More grimly, the profits from the 'Atlantic Triangle' trade that were pocketed by British merchants may have contributed to the initial accumulation of capital, which later helped finance the initial stages of industrialisation.[12] Although this view is at odds with the conclusion that British industrialisation in its initial phases was not as capital intensive as to make the availability of external finance a precondition, this liquidity will have been helpful anyhow. Also, as Rediker (2007) argues, the slave trade and in particular the organisation on board of the slave ships, including the terror, established some of the prototypes of the capitalist production mode. Furthermore, when the mechanisation of textile production in Britain multiplied the demand for fibres, the supply was ensured by North American slave labour. The industrialisation on the Western shores of Europe thus proceeded hand in hand with the expulsion of Native Americans from their lands and expansion and intensification of slave labour.[13]

When the Industrial Revolution was on its way, access to raw materials (cotton) and victuals from the colonies to feed mills and workers was an advantage, as was the British merchant fleet along with the Royal Navy, which ruled the oceans.

Yet other explanations refer to social and cultural obstacles in those other parts of the world that might otherwise have pioneered industrialisation.[14] According to this theory, progress in the Middle East, which until about the twelfth century had been a leader in science, was choked by Islamic zealots gaining influence and claiming that the truthful way of life was established by the Quran, which turned this culture inward-looking, losing interest in innovation. Somewhat different stories are told about China. Self-sufficiency in a great empire that sat behind the legendary wall is brought forward, along with excessive state control of all matters, including economic, as are gender relations keeping women in the home. Abundance of labour may have contributed, reducing the incentive for (labour-saving) innovations. The latter also pertains to India, where the caste system also set insurmountable barriers to economic mobility.

Economic historians have focused on the perspective of the nineteenth-century 'latecomers' of industrialisation. In particular, while the pioneer initially advanced very much in a piecemeal fashion, the latecomers (e.g. France, Belgium, Germany, the US and Japan) usually pushed industrialisation based on large-scale enterprises. Related to this, in contrast to Britain, a banking system able to provide long-term finance and a state that would not only provide a stable and secure environment for economic activity, but actively promote infrastructure investment, education and at the same time offer protection to nascent ('infant') industries from more advanced competitors abroad, was essential. Thus, the 'correct' economic policy may have mattered. One argument is that countries that developed successfully in earlier centuries usually resorted to mercantilist development policies involving economies of scale by investment in transport infrastructure (initially roads, canals and ports). Emphasis was on manufacturing rather than agriculture and mining, infant industry protection and promotion of manufactured exports.[15] Orthodox economists would reply that in the twentieth century import substitution policies were a failure. On the other hand, it is debated to what degree the recent success stories of South Korea, Singapore, Taiwan, Vietnam and, last but not least, China, involve mercantilist features.

Admittedly, some of these theories are highly speculative; and given the complexity of the matter and the indisputable role of randomness, luck and path dependency, it is unlikely that a conclusive explanation will ever be agreed upon. Given this, we have to accept as a fact that by the end of the eighteenth century – when this prologue ends – Britain had emerged as the first and only industrialising country; and that those that would follow soon were its closest neighbours on the European continent.

RECOMMENDATIONS FOR FURTHER READING

For a detailed account of economic history that goes back to the very beginnings, see Cameron (1993, *A Concise Economic History of the World*). Graeber and Wengrow (2021, *The Dawn of Everything*) are also focussing on the beginnings, but from an anthropological perspective. Based on evidence from the past and latest anthropological research, they try to reconstruct the variety of modes of production and societal organisations in Palaeolithic and Neolithic times as well as evidence of resistance to the hardship and restrictions imposed by Neolithic life. The latter aspect is also highlighted by Scott (2016, *Against the Grain. A Deep History of the Early States*). Van Schaik and Michel (2016, *The Good Book of Human Nature: An Evolutionary Reading of the Bible*) turn to the Bible and other religious texts, looking for evidence of Neolithic peoples' memories of better times. Bernstein (2008, *A Splendid Exchange: How Trade Shaped the World*) delivers a highly readable history of international trade from prehistoric times to the present.

The literature on the emergence of money, credit and banking is vast. A mostly ethnological approach is taken by Einzig (1949, *Primitive Money in Its Ethnological, Historical and Economic Aspects*), while Davies (1994, *A History of Money: From Ancient Times to the Present Day*) highlights the economic perspective. Graeber (2011, *Debt: The First 5,000 Years*) and McNally (2020, *Blood and Money*) refute the common assumption amongst economists that money emerged to facilitate trade and instead point to slavery and warfare. Related to this is the history of financial manias and crashes. Prominent references are Galbraith (1990, *A Short History of Financial Euphoria*) and Kindleberger (1978, *Manias, Panics, and Crashes. A History of Financial Crises*). For a more recent text, see Reinhart and Rogoff (2009, *This Time Is Different. Eight Centuries of Financial Folly*).

The question why industrialisation started in Western Europe and not in other places, which may have had equally favourable conditions is the matter of much debate. Pomeranz (2000, *The Great Divergence: China, Europe, and the Making of the Modern World Economy*) gives a comprehensive overview of the many hypotheses put forward so far and argues that Britain's natural endowments (coal) and access to foodstuffs from overseas (colonies) were decisive. Cipolla (1993, *Before the Industrial Revolution: European Society and Economy, 1000–1700*) describes the European Medieval era as a gestation period during which the foundations for industrialisation were laid.

A less benign picture of the roots of industrial capitalism is drawn by Rediker (2007, *The Slave Ship. A Human History*) and Beckert (2014, *Empire of Cotton. A Global History*), which they see in the trans-Atlantic slave trade and the American plantation economies, where expropriation of land and forced labour under a regime of terror formed the bases of a global trade network for the raw materials as well as the manufactured goods of the Industrial Revolution.

NOTES

1 Graeber and Wengrow (2021) argue that the common perception of poor standards of living characteristic for hunters and gatherers results from the fact that most anthropological evidence is from recent field research amongst groups that have survived in unfavourable surroundings without appeal to farmers.
2 For an elaboration of extensive versus intensive growth, see the Appendix 1 to this chapter.
3 Following North and Thomas (1977), the Neolithic Revolution may also have implied the transition from common property to communal property in the early settler communities, which would have prevented outsiders appropriating their production. As a result, the settlers had more incentives to improve their production technology.
4 See van Schaik and Michel (2016).
5 See Graeber and Wengrow (2021).
6 Recent research has asked how humanity could accept to give up liberty. The answer is that in many instances it did not; the oppressed majority revolted or just left (Graber and Wengrow, 2021; Scott, 2016).
7 There, they would soon trigger the inevitable companion of financial development: financial crisis. For details, see Appendix 2 to this chapter.
8 Thus, Marco Polo's legendary voyage to China and back to Venice was indeed accomplishable.
9 It is difficult to treat this topic without moral implication. Foreman-Peck (1995, p. 12) concludes: 'The slave trade was probably the most harmful manner in which the international economy impinged upon lower-income countries. … As a result of the slavery to which the expansion of trade had given such a boost, the ultimate consumers of goods embodying slave-produced materials paid less than would have been required in a world in which all exchanges were voluntary. These consumers throughout the world exploited the slaves, whereas those actually involved in the slave trade and slave plantations are properly described as thieves. Even after the slaves had been freed, the tropical products they supplied were still artificially cheap, because the ex-slaves usually had few alternative sources of employment'.
10 Frequently cited is the company 'for carrying on an undertaking of great advantage, but nobody to know what it is' (e.g. Galbraith 1990, p. 49).
11 See de Moor and van Zanden (2010).
12 This is what Karl Marx (*Das Kapital*, Vol. 1, Chapter 31) sarcastically refers to as the 'rosy dawn of the era of capitalist production'.
13 Beckert (2014, p. 37) stresses that the common perception of the rise capitalism being based on the employment of free labour does not apply before end of the nineteenth century. Violent exploitation of labour under a regime of terror – 'war capitalism' – was supplying the raw materials for 'industrial capitalism'. 'Not secure property rights but a wave of expropriation of labor and land characterised this moment, testifying to capitalism's illiberal origins'.
14 See Landes (1999, p. 52ff.).
15 As Erik S. Reinert (2007) convincingly argues, specialising according to (static) comparative advantage in primary sector activity may amount to specialising in poverty, as increasing returns to scale and experience (learning curves) are usually less pronounced in agriculture and the production of raw materials than in manufacturing and industry.

PART I

The International Economy, 1820–1913

CHAPTER 1

The Causes of the Growth of the International Economy in the Nineteenth Century

A. G. Kenwood, A. L. Lougheed and Michael Graff

To understand why a truly international economy first evolved during the nineteenth century, it is necessary to examine the economic, technical and other changes which were responsible for the massive expansion of capital movements, voluntary as well as forced migration, slave labour in the plantation economy and international trade that occurred during these years. For it was through these flows of money, people and goods that countries hitherto economically independent were fused into the international economy.

TECHNOLOGICAL PROGRESS: INDUSTRY AND AGRICULTURE

The Industrial Revolution, which began in Britain in the late eighteenth century and spread first to the European continent and then to the US during the nineteenth century, and later to Japan, enormously increased the opportunities for trade between countries, for the new technology presupposed a wide variety of resources and an expanding market. Industrialising economies during the nineteenth century had to look outside their own borders for markets in which to sell the surplus output yielded by modern industry, and for the additional supplies of raw materials that were needed when domestic production of these inputs failed to keep pace with rising industrial demand. A similar situation arose in the new centres of primary production overseas, where the use of modern farming techniques produced agricultural surpluses for which markets had to be found abroad. At the same time, the apparatus of improved farming often had to be imported, along with the transport equipment necessary to the opening up of new areas of primary production.

Success in the search for foreign markets for manufactured goods depended very much on whether the new techniques resulted in a new product or in the cheapening of an existing one. Obviously, trade in a new product will grow fastest when many countries are unable to produce it for themselves but want to consume it. For this reason, the rather limited spread of industrialisation before 1913 must have given a powerful impetus to the growth of trade in

DOI: 10.4324/9781003382171-4

industrial goods during the nineteenth century. On the other hand, where innovation involves the cheapening of old goods the effects on trade are often less clear. Thus, foreign trade in cheap machine-made articles often increased at the expense of trade in hand-made substitutes. This happened with British cotton textiles and Indian calicoes during the late eighteenth and early nineteenth centuries, though on balance the revolution in textile manufacturing that occurred in Britain at this time led to a net increase in the volume of cotton goods traded internationally. In other instances, however, where, for example, synthetic substitutes for natural products were discovered, a decline in trade could result from the introduction of the technical improvement.[1]

Taken generally, however, technical progress in the nineteenth century tended to be pro-trade biased. Innovation was widespread, and the opportunities for trade multiplied accordingly. Before 1870, the important innovating industries were textiles (especially cotton) and iron, with steam the new source of power. After 1870, the focus of technical change began to shift, as increasing emphasis came to be placed on the production of steel, machine tools, electrical engineering products and chemicals. Electricity emerged as a new form of energy, and the internal combustion engine as the basis of a new means of transport. The outcome of all these developments was a flood of new goods, including railway equipment, steamships, steel and electrical products, plant and machinery of all kinds, and a growing variety of other manufactured products. In addition, many of the articles already traded internationally became cheaper, especially cotton cloth. The result was a rapid expansion in foreign trade in manufactures.

Part of this trade in manufactures was of a temporary nature, since it was linked with the spread of industrialisation. For, while technical progress in the form of new or cheaper goods undoubtedly favours trade, the diffusion of technology, by encouraging imitation in production and the substitution of domestically produced goods for goods previously imported, tends to be biased against trade. Within a limited area, the diffusion of the Industrial Revolution that began in Britain was fairly rapid. By 1850 it had penetrated into France and Belgium; Switzerland and Germany would follow soon. By 1900, it had reached the US, Scandinavia, Russia and Japan. In certain lines of foreign trade – for example, textiles and clothing – the trade-reducing effect of technical diffusion soon became apparent. On the other hand, the spread of industrialisation may have increased the world innovatory capacity, and there is some evidence of shifts in innovatory capacity occurring after 1870 from Britain to Germany and the US. If increased innovation meant fresh opportunities for trade, shifts in the centre of innovatory activity were obviously important in influencing the geographical pattern of world trade.

In short, despite the spread of industrialisation, nineteenth-century technical progress tended, on balance, to favour the expansion of world trade while bringing about changes in the direction and composition of trade between countries.

Besides providing expanding opportunities for the international exchange of manufactured goods, modern industrial technology created increased opportunities for trade in raw materials. In the early stages of the Industrial Revolution, when textile production expanded rapidly, and machinery continued to be constructed largely of wood, agricultural raw materials dominated these exchanges, especially raw cotton and timber. Later on, however, as industrial technology continued to evolve, manufacturing industry came to rely more on minerals and relatively less on agricultural raw materials. This growing industrial dependence on mineral resources was reflected both in a widening of the range of minerals for which an industrial use was found and in the development of mass consumption of a few of them. While the output of coal and iron ore increased substantially throughout the nineteenth century, after 1850 the output of other metals, such as copper and zinc, grew even faster, and other previously little-used minerals such as petroleum and aluminium had achieved a considerable economic importance by the beginning of the twentieth century.

As industrial growth accelerated in the last quarter of the nineteenth century, the consumption of raw materials increased phenomenally. Between 1880 and 1913, petroleum production doubled every 8.6 years, copper every 13 years, pig iron, phosphates, coal and zinc every 15–17 years, and lead and tin every 20 years. In the circumstances, the tendency to exhaustion of the more readily available supplies of less common metals and fuels was to be expected, and their costs of production rose accordingly. In the search for new and cheaper supplies of minerals that followed, the US emerged as a major producer, capable of not only supplying most of its own needs but also providing a surplus for export to other industrial nations. Russia, too, possessed great, though widely dispersed, mineral resources, and Canada, South Africa, Australia, Chile, Malaya and a number of other countries emerged as other important mineral producers. Indeed, a feature of the growth of world mineral production during these years was the constant shifting of the centre of world supply of these materials from one region to another. Such shifts were recorded for various minerals, including copper and iron ore, and for precious metals, such as gold. Quite obviously, these production shifts had important repercussions on the pattern of world trade, and they also exerted a significant influence on the international flows of labour and capital before 1914.

A similar situation to that found in mineral production developed in agriculture when the spread of industrialisation and the rapid growth of population brought about a phenomenal increase in the demand for foodstuffs and agricultural raw materials, a series of shifts in the geographical sources of supply and, consequently, great changes in the volume and commodity structure of foreign trade. Simultaneously, technological progress and the opening up of new regions cheapened many agricultural products and provided conditions under which mass markets could be supplied with many items formerly classified as luxuries. More and better farm implements and machinery, the use of chemical fertilisers, improved stock-breeding and new methods of checking plant and animal diseases all made significant contributions to the growth of agricultural output. Many of these innovations originated in Europe and eventually diffused to countries overseas. Others were developed in the new farming regions themselves, where labour shortage, drought, short growing seasons and other problems called forth inventions and innovations to deal with them.

The growing demand for tropical products, and in particular for cotton, which fuelled and accompanied industrialisation and the rise of real incomes in Europe and North America, led to a rapid expansion of plantation agriculture in the period after 1850. In the old established areas of European enterprise, the growth of output was achieved primarily by the more efficient use of an abundant labour force. This is what Beckert (2014) calls 'industrial capitalism', to be distinguished from 'war capitalism': Elsewhere, i.e. at the periphery of the world economy, it was to some degree obtained through improvements in peasant farming, but in particular through the spread of the plantation system, which brought with it improved farming methods, higher-yielding plant strains and more use of machinery. The plantation system also introduced new crops. Rubber trees, for example, were introduced into Malaya from Brazil in 1877. Rubber cultivation spread rapidly from there to the Netherlands, East Indies and French Indo-China, and by the end of the century, Southeast Asia had become the chief source of the world supply of natural rubber. In contrast to rubber, the centre of world coffee production shifted in the opposite direction, from Asia to Latin America, following the emergence of Brazil as the world's greatest coffee-producing country. Rice, sugar, tea and tobacco productions were similarly affected by these production shifts as their output grew in response to the expanding demand for primary products in industrial Europe and North America. Last but not least, the world economy experienced a massive surge in cotton production to feed the rapidly increasing number of spindles and looms in the centres of industrial capitalism. The acreage devoted to cotton fields increased in the suitable regions all over the world, but particularly in the southern states of the US, where the number of slaves and the labour intensity imposed onto them by means of terror was pushed to limits right up to the American Civil War (1861–5), after which slavery finally came to an end in North America. It would take another 23 years before the last country which resorted to slavery to mobilise labour for production, Brazil, abolished it in 1888.[2]

TECHNICAL PROGRESS: TRANSPORT AND COMMUNICATIONS

Through cheapening and speeding up the movement of goods and people, improved transport and communications played a vital role in the growth of the world economy in the nineteenth century. By promoting the exchange of a growing volume of goods; by expanding markets, as well as opening up new sources of supply of many products; by permitting the concentration of certain types of production in fewer centres, thereby encouraging specialisation and assisting the realisation of economies of scale; and by allowing a greater interregional flow of people and capital, the new forms of transport and communications made possible the growing economic interdependence of the whole world which is so remarkable a feature of nineteenth-century economic development. Moreover, by making possible a significant relocation of economic activity throughout the world, transport improvements contributed substantially to the rising productivity that lay behind the growth of real incomes in the world economy during these years.[3]

Of these improvements, the application of steam to land and sea transport was of critical importance. On land, steam was rapidly adapted to the railway, which quickly supplanted the existing means of transport. The earliest railways were built in Britain and the eastern US, but they quickly spread, first to Europe and then to the other continents of the world. The extent of this dispersion in the nineteenth century is shown in Table 1.1.

In Europe, the spread of the railway was a contributing factor to the formation of new states, such as Germany and Italy, and the creation of the large markets necessary for industrialisation. In North America and Russia, similar developments occurred, but on a grander scale. Here, the railway permitted the political domination of whole continents by a single government. Outside North America and Europe, railways were essentially instruments of the expansion of the world economy. Financed largely by European capital, the railways of

TABLE 1.1 Railway routes (in 1,000 kilometres), 1840–1910

	1840	1870	1910
Europe	4.2	105	341
North America	4.5	89	428
Latin America	0.2	4	98
Asia		8	96
Africa		2	37
Oceania		2	31
World	8.9	210	1,031

Source: Woytinsky and Woytinsky (1953, p. 341); Woodruff (1966, p. 253).

Latin America, Asia, Africa and Australasia were built primarily to assist in the export of the continents' agricultural and mineral products and, since the abilities of the different countries in these continents to supply the required primary products varied, it is not surprising to find that railway developments were not uniform either within the continents or between them. In Latin America, only Mexico, Brazil and Argentina had networks of any importance, whereas in Africa half the continent's railways at the end of the century were to be found in the Union of South Africa. In Asia, two-thirds of the railway kilometrage in operation at the end of our period were in India, where railways had been built chiefly to ensure political control of the subcontinent. Elsewhere in Asia, railway development had barely begun outside Japan, where over 11,000 km of railway track had been built by 1914.

Compared to the railway, the steamship was slow to establish its supremacy at sea, where the relatively high standard of perfection achieved by the sailing ship during the nineteenth century made it a formidable competitor. By 1869, however, the iron steamship had made serious inroads on the traffic of the sailing ship. The coastal trade had earlier been taken over, while the ocean passenger service and the carriage of mail overseas also passed quickly to steam. With freight, progress was much slower. The steamship cut sharply into the North Atlantic carrying trade, but the Far Eastern trade remained exclusively the preserve of the sailing ship. Here the opening of the Suez Canal in 1869, by providing a shorter route to the East, well served by conveniently located and efficient coaling stations, hastened the replacement of sail by steam. Later, the introduction of the compound engine, which significantly reduced coal consumption, and the conversion from iron to steel in ship-building that took place in the 1880s, made possible a continuous increase in the carrying capacity of the steamship and so increased its competitive power further. From 27 million tons in 1873, the amount of total world freight carried in steamships rose to 63 million tons in 1898, while the steamship proportion of the total world shipping tonnage grew from just over 12 per cent in 1870 to almost two-thirds of the total in 1900.

Despite the rapidly increasing demand for shipping in the nineteenth century, capacity grew sufficiently quickly to bring about a secular decline in ocean freight rates. This decline took place in two phases: between 1815 and 1851, and between 1870–3 and 1908–9. In the first period of decline, freight rates were particularly affected on outward cargoes (from Europe and the UK), on the Baltic and Mediterranean routes and on the North Atlantic run. The causes of the decline in freight rates at this time included technological improvements in sailing ship design and construction, the increased utilisation of ships that resulted from improvements in cargo handling and dock facilities, the reduction of time in ballast and increased knowledge, particularly of winds and currents. In the second period, the greatest decline occurred in the freight rates on long hauls. In bringing about this fall in rates, the steamship exercised a decisive influence, although the performance of sailing ships continued to improve well into the last quarter of the nineteenth century. This lowering of transport costs was of vital significance for the growth of world trade, especially after 1870. Since only those goods that can bear transport costs and still be cheaper than some part of domestic production in the importing country will be traded, a reduction in transport costs will obviously widen the range of internationally traded goods by allowing foreign goods to become even lower in price relative to domestic production. By widening the range of international commodity exchange, and by permitting heavy or bulky products to enter into foreign trade, transport improvements provided a great stimulus to the growth of world trade in the nineteenth century.

In the task of cheapening and speeding up the movement of people and goods, the railway and steamship were supported by a series of developments in related activities. The growth of merchant fleets was accompanied by harbour improvements, the building of docks and warehouses and the introduction of new machines and methods for the rapid handling of cargoes. Sea transport was also speeded up by the cutting of ship canals. Here the two outstanding feats were the opening of the Suez Canal in 1869 and of the Panama Canal in 1915. Other important developments during these years included the completion in 1872 of a new waterway connecting Rotterdam to the North Sea, the opening of the Manchester Ship Canal in 1894 and the Kiel Canal in 1895. The telegraph system was another development of immense significance for the growth of world trade. By the turn of the century new developments in the field of transport and communications, of considerable significance for the future, were already apparent. The internal combustion engine offered an alternative form of land transport, although its ability to compete for traffic with the railways still seemed doubtful. The same could be said of aviation and the passenger traffic on the high seas. Meanwhile, oil began to be used to drive ships, although only some 2 per cent of world shipping was oil-fired in 1914. The telephone had emerged as an improvement on the telegraph, and the invention of the wireless set in 1896 was another step in the direction of bringing the people of the world closer together.

THE ACCUMULATION OF CAPITAL

The importance of capital accumulation for increasing production has long been recognised by economists. Capital accumulation facilitates the introduction of new techniques and provides tools and equipment for a growing population. It also brings about, through increases in the supply of tools and machinery per worker, the use of more efficient methods of production. In particular, the process of industrialisation, with its emphasis on more mechanised methods of production, a rapidly growing consumption of raw materials and the need to supply wider markets, results in substantial additions being made to a country's stock of capital equipment. At the same time, technical progress and continued population growth make necessary a continuous increase in this capital stock if living standards are to be maintained or raised.

The long-term analysis of the process of capital accumulation is made extremely difficult by the formidable conceptual problems involved in appropriately defining and measuring capital. Yet, it is possible to use the available evidence to make a few generalisations about capital accumulation during the nineteenth century.[4] In Britain, for example, the transition from a pre-industrial to an industrial society was neither sudden nor did it involve any dramatic rise in the rate of capital accumulation. Most of the upward shift in the level of national investment associated with the Industrial Revolution in Britain seems to have occurred in the four decades between the mid-1830s and the mid-1870s, when capital formation rose from some 7–8 per cent of national product in the early 1830s to perhaps 14 per cent in the 1870s. This upsurge in the rate of capital accumulation was the result of heavy investment in domestic railways, the coal, iron and textile industries, shipping and its ancillaries, such as docks and harbours, plus substantial investment overseas. After 1875, capital accumulation continued at a high level, with the decline in the relative importance of railway investment being offset by much higher levels of investment in residential building activity and in industry, commerce and finance. Meanwhile, land as a percentage of total national capital declined continuously throughout the nineteenth century from being over one-half of the total capital stock in 1798 to just 7 per cent of the total in 1912.

In other industrialising countries the process of capital formation and the consequent changes in the structure of the capital stock were similar to those experienced by Britain, although the latecomers achieved a high level of capital accumulation much more quickly. But the demand for capital goods was not restricted to the industrial or industrialising countries. The spread of the railway to all corners of the globe set up a growing demand for railway equipment of all kinds, and efforts to exploit the natural resources of the newly settled continents created a heavy demand for agricultural machinery, mining equipment and related types of capital goods. The consequent growth in the world stock of capital provided many fresh opportunities for international trade. The need of developing countries to import machinery and equipment during the early stages of industrialisation created a growing demand for the manufacturing output of those countries already industrialised, as did the demand for capital goods by the primary producing regions of the world. Moreover, differences in the rates of saving relative to investment possibilities in different countries provided profitable opportunities for lending capital on a large scale, which provided a means of financing the purchase of capital equipment needed by the various borrowing countries. In other words, the volume of world trade in the nineteenth century was kept at a high level by two closely connected facts: first, that the new countries, whether industrialising or primary producing, keenly desired a good that the older industrialised countries were well fitted to supply; and second, that the old countries did not demand immediate payment for these goods, but were willing in effect to supply them on credit, so that the volume of trade was continuously larger than it would have been had it depended solely on the opportunities for simultaneous barter.

THE GROWTH OF WORLD POPULATION

Economic growth in the nineteenth century was also accompanied by a rapid increase of population. World population grew from just over 900 million in 1800 to approximately 1,600 million in 1900. At the same time, the distribution of world population changed in a number of significant ways as Table 1.2 shows.

Population grew fastest in the regions dominated by Europeans. In 1900, Asia still remained, as she does today, the most densely populated continent in the world. But in the nineteenth century, her relative position had declined, as had that of Africa, because the populations in the other continents, especially North America and Europe (including Russia) were growing faster. The cause of the rapid increase of population in Europe was that death rates were falling while birth rates continued at a high level, which is known as the 'demographic transition'. In North America, Latin America and Oceania, apart from high rates of natural increase, heavy inflows of migrants, particularly from Europe, contributed to bringing about even faster rates of population growth in these regions.

The rapidly growing world population had important consequences for world trade. In itself a growing population would have meant some increased demand for those commodities already traded internationally. Taken in conjunction with changes in the other factors of production, however, it greatly enhanced the possibilities of trade. For example, in Europe, with the possible exception of Russia, the land–labour ratio became less favourable as population grew, despite improved farming techniques and the reclamation of wastelands. Land became scarce and rose in price, so that agricultural products became more expensive relative to those obtained from other countries overseas. As agricultural price differences widened, therefore, the opportunities for trade increased correspondingly, while in those countries where the growth of domestic production of foodstuffs failed to keep pace with the population increase, imports had to be relied on increasingly to fill the gap. Moreover, the unfavourable land–labour ratio in Europe had another consequence for the international economy. It forced people from the land into the towns and, when domestic urban employment was unavailable,

TABLE 1.2 Growth and percentage distribution of world population, 1800–1900

	Numbers (millions)		Percentage distribution	
	1800	1900	1800	1900
Africa	90	120	9.9	7.5
North America[a]	6	81	0.7	5.0
Latin America	19	63	2.1	3.9
Asia[b]	597	915	65.9	56.9
Europe (including Russia)	192	423	21.2	26.3
Oceania	2	6	0.2	0.4
Total	906	1,608	100.0	100.0

Source: Carr-Saunders (1936, pp. 30–45).

Notes: [a] North America = north of the Rio Grande; [b] excluding Asiatic Russia.

overseas to the new regions of primary production. In these areas, where labour was short, the rapid growth of the incumbent population, aided by immigration, served only to create more favourable conditions for the exploitation of economic resources, particularly natural resources, which had hitherto remained uncultivated partly because of the lack of labour.

THE SUPPLY OF NATURAL RESOURCES

Even if precise measurement of natural resources in economic terms is difficult, if not impossible, the available evidence suggests that a substantial increase in the world supply of natural resources occurred during the nineteenth century.[5] Within Europe, the supply was added to by the cultivation of previously uncultivated land and the discovery and exploitation of new sources of mineral supply. But by far the largest addition to the world supply of natural resources came from the opening up of the vast, fertile and mineral-rich continents of the Americas and Oceania. Sparsely inhabited in many parts, these regions also afforded an enormous increase in living-space for the growing flood of migrants from Europe, who did not consider the indigenous inhabitants of where they settled as owners of the land. If the latter dared to make such claims, the land grab would turn violent.

By 1800 the European-occupied areas in these continents were already more extensive than the whole of Western Europe, whose settled area at this date has been put at between 1.7 million and 2.0 million km^2. In the course of the next 100 years, a further 21–23 million km^2 was added to these European territories overseas, approximately an eight- to nine-fold increase in the occupied area, while the degree of land use became, in every way, a great deal more intense.

Apart from people's willingness and ability to move to these new lands, the key factors in opening them up included an increased knowledge of their natural resources – land, minerals, climate and so on – and their economic accessibility, which largely depended on the availability of cheap and adequate transport. Also important was a sufficiency of capital to clear and work the land and exploit its mineral wealth. In all these respects, the Americas and Oceania stood out, for they possessed a variety of natural resources which, for the most part, were easily accessible and capable of development by known techniques requiring moderate amounts of capital.

In Asia and tropical Africa, on the other hand, the opening up of new lands and the development of new sources of raw materials was a much slower process. Climatic and topographical difficulties, endemic diseases, inadequate knowledge and institutional resistance to change provided the main obstacles to development in these regions. Where development in these continents did occur, however, the availability of natural resources appears to have been a chief factor influencing the location of what have been described as 'export economies'. Situated for the most part in the tropics, the location of these largely plantation and mining activities was determined not by the relative supply of the various factors of production, which existed within a country's borders, but by the location of the least mobile factors of production, such as climate, soil conditions or mineral deposits and by accessibility to markets which, if overseas, meant access to ocean-going transport. Labour, capital and entrepreneurship were internationally mobile and could be applied almost anywhere in the world, so that choice of these industry locations was based on other cost considerations. The most fertile lands and the most promising mineral deposits could be chosen and those requiring the lowest transport costs worked first.[6]

THE GROWTH OF REAL INCOMES

Despite the high rates of population growth, there was a marked rise in real incomes in a number of countries as a result of the increase in productivity brought about by new production methods, better organisation and improved transport. While there are obvious difficulties in measuring this improvement in statistical terms that emphasise the approximate nature of the available national estimates, they suggest a three-fold classification of countries based on the annual rates of growth of real incomes which they experienced in the course of the nineteenth century. Heading the list are those primary producing countries which experienced rates of growth in real income per head in the region of 1.5 per cent per annum. These included the US and Canada after 1850. Per capita real income in Argentina may also have risen this fast in the period after 1880. In Australia, on the other hand, the rate of growth of per capita real income was somewhat slower than 1.5 per cent per annum, and that of New Zealand substantially so. In New Zealand, real income grew at 4.6 per cent per annum, but with population also growing rapidly (4.1 per cent per annum), there was only a 0.5 per cent rise in real income per head. The explanation of this slow growth of per capita income in New Zealand seems to be the high level already attained by the mid-1860s, when average living standards appear to have been significantly higher than those in Australia, which, in turn, were significantly higher than those in either the US or Britain. A further substantial rise in real income from such a high base, with immigration running at a record level, was clearly difficult. Australia's performance was similarly affected by a high initial per capita real income, but in addition she experienced a severe and prolonged depression in the 1890s which depressed average real income to such an extent that it did not regain its 1891 peak until 1909.

Maddison's (1991) estimates of average growth rates of real gross domestic product (GDP) and GDP per capita for selected countries for the period 1870–1913 are shown in Table 1.3. In this group of countries, the performances of Canada and the US are striking, as are, to a lesser extent, those of Germany, Austria and Sweden. Only for Australia, Belgium, the Netherlands and the UK are the average growth rates of per capita income 1 per cent or lower during these years. As was the case for New Zealand, Australia's low per capita growth rate was the result of heavy immigration and a high rate of growth of population between 1870 and 1913.

Another group of countries, making up the greater part of Asia, Africa and Latin America, had annual rates of growth of per capita real income of 0.5 per cent or less. Few statistics are available for these countries. In India, where conditions were more favourable to growth than anywhere else in Asia outside Japan, average per capita income rose at about 0.4 per cent over the period from 1857–63 to 1896–1904. Elsewhere the world, output appears to have grown fast enough to maintain a slowly growing population. Even if per capita real incomes grew in these countries during the nineteenth century, a rate of 0.5 per cent per annum would seem to be the upper limit to what was attainable, given their prevailing economic circumstances.

TABLE 1.3 Growth of real GDP and GDP per capita, 1870–1913 (selected countries)

Country	Annual average compound rates of growth	
	GDP	GDP per capita
Australia	3.5	0.9
Austria	2.4	1.5
Belgium	2.0	1.0
Canada	4.1	2.3
Denmark	2.7	1.6
Finland	2.7	1.4
France	1.5	1.3
Germany	2.8	1.6
Italy	1.9	1.3
Japan	2.3	1.4
Netherlands	2.3	1.0
Norway	2.1	1.3
Sweden	2.2	1.5
Switzerland	2.1	1.2
UK	1.9	1.0
US	3.9	1.8
Arithmetic average	2.5	1.4

Source: Maddison (1991, pp. 49–50, Tables 3.1 and 3.2).

The one exception to this generalisation was Japan, whose total product grew at 3.2 per cent per annum over the period 1870–1913. After allowing for population growth, Japanese real income per capita grew at the relatively high rate of 1.9 per cent per annum.

Changes in income levels have much to do with changes in demand and consequently with changes in the structure of output and the composition of foreign trade. As incomes rise, there is an increased demand for capital goods, manufactured consumer goods and services, and a relatively slow expansion in demand for food, textiles and clothing. Moreover, rising living standards, involving as they do changes in tastes, incomes and, consequently, consumption patterns, not only influence the structure of domestic output but also affect the volume and composition of foreign trade. Thus, the shift in the diet of the US and other Western nations from cereals towards meat and dairy products as the standard of living rose was important both for the domestic producers of these commodities and for the trade flows that existed between these countries. Another example associated with the rise in real incomes is the increased demand for 'colonial' products. Items of trade, such as sugar, tobacco, tea, coffee and cocoa, unaffordable luxuries to all except the richest classes before the seventeenth century, gradually spread across the less well-off during the eighteenth century and came to be regarded as necessities of subsistence during the nineteenth century. Towards the end of this period, the consumption of tropical fruits also became important for the first time.

THE SPREAD OF ECONOMIC LIBERALISM

The period between 1820 and 1913 was characterised by the gradual liberalisation of controls over flows of capital, labour and trade that were to link the countries of the world more closely together as the nineteenth century progressed. International migration as a movement of individuals, almost entirely without control from either the receiving or sending countries and undertaken by single individual or family units took place along with organised migration, where sending countries encouraged the poor to emigrate and labour scarce receiving countries encouraged people to immigrate. Controls over financial transactions were also minimal. Short- and long-term capital could move unsupervised in any direction, and these movements could take any form. Direct foreign investment was undertaken and often encouraged by the governments of the receiving countries. Foreign securities were freely traded on most stock exchanges. Repatriation of profits was unhampered, and the fear of confiscation of foreign investment almost completely absent. In the form of gold coins, foreign currencies mixed freely with the domestic currencies of many countries. Moreover, like in the case of migration, moneyed individuals and enterprises dominated international financial and commercial transactions before 1914, and only rarely were dealings conducted among countries acting as a whole. Finally, whereas international trade had to overcome tariffs during the latter part of the nineteenth century, these were exceedingly low by comparison with those introduced during the interwar years. Furthermore, quotas, import prohibitions and other quantitative restrictions on trade hardly existed before 1913, nor did ideas of economic self-sufficiency, towards the furtherance of which these restrictions on trade were often introduced.

This increase in the degree and extent of economic liberalism contributed to bringing about the formation of an international economy during the nineteenth century, although the true extent of that contribution is difficult to measure, because the spread of economic liberalism was only one factor operating simultaneously with many others, and because in many instances its influence was dependent on the existence of these other factors for its full realisation. For example, freedom to move was not in itself sufficient to generate mass migration, for, among other things, migration also depended on the existence of cheap and speedy transport facilities. This general conclusion is equally true of all the other influences at work taken individually. What is also apparent, however, is that, taken together, these influences brought about the powerful expansion of foreign trade, capital flows and population movements by means of which the integration of the international economy was achieved during the nineteenth century.

THE GROWTH OF INTERNATIONAL TRADE

Before turning to a consideration of the forging of the international links of capital, people and trade that constituted the growth of the international economy in the period since 1820, let us have a look at the growth of foreign trade itself. Table 1.4 describes the long-run growth of the greater part of the world export trade over the period 1820–1913.

In the years up to 1913, the growth of world trade, as measured by the increase in the volume of exports of the world's leading industrial nations, averaged around 4 per cent per annum.

TABLE 1.4 Growth of world exports and world production, 1820–1913

Country	1820–70	1870–1913
Australia		4.8
Austria	4.7	3.5
Belgium	5.4[a]	4.2
Canada		4.1
Denmark	1.9[b]	3.3
Finland		3.9
France	4.0	2.8
Germany	4.8[c]	4.1
Italy	3.4	2.2
Japan		8.5
Netherlands		2.3[d]
Norway		3.2
Sweden		3.1
Switzerland	4.1	3.9
UK	4.9	2.8
US	4.7	4.9
Arithmetic average, exports	4.2	3.9
Arithmetic growth of GDP	2.4	2.5

Source: Maddison (1991, p. 75, Table 3.2, p. 50, Table 3.15).

Notes: [a] 1831–70; [b] 1844–70; [c] 1840–70; [d] 1872–1913.

The final two rows of Table 1.4 show the arithmetic average of the growth rates of the export trade of the 16 countries included in the table and the arithmetic average of the growth rates of real GDP of the same 16 countries. Comparing the two, it can be seen that export growth rates were always higher than output growth rates, which implies growing interconnectedness of the global economy: each unit of output of goods and services goes along with more trade.[7] This reflects an integration of the world economy, i.e. economic globalisation.

In the following chapters, we will see that this also holds for most periods thereafter, with a few notable exceptions and a big question mark for the years since 2008.

RECOMMENDATIONS FOR FURTHER READING

For a detailed history of the world from the French Revolution up to the First World War, covering economics, ideology, politics and imperialism, see Bayly (2004, *The Birth of the Modern World, 1780–1914*). Another useful book dealing with the most important aspects of globalisation in the nineteenth century is O'Rourke and Williamson (1990, *Globalization and History: The Evolution of the Nineteenth-Century Atlantic Economy*). Headrick (1988, *The*

Tentacles of Progress. Technology Transfer in the Age of Imperialism, 1850–1940) gives a useful account of the creation and transfer of technology in the heydays of imperialism.

Marx and Engels (1848, *Manifesto of the Communist Party*) predicted an armed revolution to overcome capitalism, yet they were full of praise for the technical and economic progress of capitalism and the globalisation achieved in the first part of the nineteenth century. These sections in the Manifesto are a masterful summary of the rise of industrial capitalism.

A lot of effort has been devoted to the estimation or creation of economic time series that cover millennia and centuries for which 'official' data are sparse or non-existing. Simon Kuznets and Angus Maddison were outstanding scholars in the field quantitative economic history, or 'cliometrics'. For the period covered in this book, see, e.g., Kuznets (1966, *Modern Economic Growth*) and Maddison (1964, *Economic Growth in the West*; 1991, *Dynamic Forces in Capitalist Development*; and 1994, *Monitoring the World Economy, 1820–1992*).

NOTES

1 Even so, certain other influences could offset the trade-reducing impact of the innovation. Thus, the Germans were responsible for a long series of major discoveries which led to synthetic dyes replacing those made from vegetable products. But the fact that by 1900 German producers controlled some 90 per cent of the world market in dyestuffs indicated a substantial increase of trade in the synthetic product, since consumers of dyestuffs in other countries were mainly dependent on German sources of supply.
2 From today's perspective, the triangular trade and the chattel slavery in the New World can only be regarded as one of the worst crimes against humanity ever. The dehumanisation and commodification of millions of people abducted from Africa, with no hope whatsoever for a return to their origins or freedom for them or their offspring and the violence practiced to keep the system going left their marks well beyond 1888. Previous slave states like the US and Brazil are up to this date characterised by extraordinary inequalities along racial phenotypes and contempt of the poor.
3 As early as 1848, Marx and Engels, in the Communist Manifesto, were full of praise for this epochal achievement of capitalism.
4 For estimates of capital formation, see Kuznets (1966, pp. 75–81). The countries covered include Britain, Belgium, Norway, West Germany, the US, Australia and Japan.
5 Difficulties of measurement arise for many reasons. For example, acreage will not do for land, since different areas of land vary significantly in their climatic features, location and natural fertility. Moreover, once land is worked, it becomes impossible to separate it from other factors, and especially from capital. Measurement over time is complicated by the fact that technical change may alter the economic value, if not the physical characteristics, of a given resource. Thus, petroleum deposits became much more valuable following the invention of the motor car. Finally, the fact that resource discovery and depletion may take place simultaneously makes it hard to decide whether the supply of natural resources available to a particular country has increased over time or not.
6 See Levin (1960, Chapter 4).
7 When export growth rates exceed output growth rates, the ratio of exports to output (X/Y) increases. As on the world scale, exports equal imports (M), the world's 'foreign trade proportion', i.e. the ratio of world trade to world output ((X + M)/Y) is exactly twice the ratio of world exports to output.

CHAPTER 2

International Long-Term Capital Movements

A. G. Kenwood, A. L. Lougheed and Michael Graff

Specialisation in production along the lines of comparative advantage was a major feature of the nineteenth-century international economy, and it was brought about partly by the mobility of capital (and labour) from country to country. In particular, the outflows of people and money from Europe to the vast, fertile and mineral-rich continents overseas helped provide the increased supplies of foodstuffs and raw materials needed to feed Europe's growing population and industry. Consequently, the growth of trade and real income in the world economy that occurred at this time was determined in part by an international redistribution of capital and labour on a scale unique in history. Thus, during the century ending in 1913, some £9,000–10,000 million were invested abroad and some 45–46 million people moved overseas. This movement of capital and population from regions where they were relatively abundant to regions where they were relatively scarce was a necessary condition for the expansion of the international economy.

International movements of capital occur when the residents of one country acquire assets in another (or reduce their liabilities there). Transactions of this sort can occur in a number of ways. For example, a resident in Britain may purchase securities in an American business or the bonds of an American government; or he or she may export goods to the US and leave the proceeds on deposit in that country; or, if he or she owns a business in the US, he or she may 'plough back' the profits of the enterprise instead of withdrawing them as dividends. What all these transactions have in common is the fact that some person (an individual or a firm) resident in Britain acquires either the paper assets of, or property ownership rights in, the US.

One basic distinction between different types of international capital movements is that between long- and short-term transactions. This distinction gives rise to problems of definition, but these can be ignored here by assuming that the foreign long-term capital investment discussed in this chapter consists of capital invested in the expectation that the investment will not be liquidated soon and that it will earn income over an appreciable period.[1]

DOI: 10.4324/9781003382171-5

THE GROWTH OF FOREIGN INVESTMENT

At the beginning of the nineteenth century, the total value of foreign investment was small, and its economic impact on both the borrowing and lending countries was insignificant. It was a business activity undertaken almost exclusively by a few privileged European trading and financial organisations with foreign interests. From the end of the Napoleonic Wars (1803–15), however, foreign investment assumed a new character and an increasing significance. This change came about for several reasons. The establishment and growth of specialised financial institutions in both borrowing and lending countries, such as commercial banks (operating in foreign exchange) and investment houses, made foreign investment easier and less risky, while the accumulation of savings by a middle class willing to invest them abroad supplied the funds needed for an expansion of foreign lending. The flow of funds from savers in one country to borrowers in another was also facilitated by the increasing availability of financial instruments, such as credit money and bills of exchange. In addition, capital markets, such as 'the City' in London, became much more diversified in their business dealings, thereby aiding the expansion of international trade and the growth of foreign investment.

From the end of the Napoleonic Wars until the mid-1850s, about £420 million ($2,050 million) was invested abroad. By 1870, the total value of these investments had more than trebled. But the great era of international lending occurred after 1870, with the capital outflow becoming a flood during the decade before the First World War. By 1900, foreign investments totalled £4,750 million ($23,000 million), and they rose rapidly during the next few years to reach £9,500 million ($43,000 million) in 1914.[2]

DIRECTION OF FOREIGN INVESTMENT

Capital-Exporting Countries

Britain was the major source of supply of foreign capital during the nineteenth century, and France another foreign lender of substance during these years. After 1870, however, when the outflow of loanable funds from the capital-rich countries accelerated tremendously, Germany and the US became major investing countries, and by 1914, they together accounted for one-fifth of the total value of the assets owned abroad by all the capital-exporting nations. Belgium, the Netherlands and Switzerland were other important countries willing to place large surplus savings at the disposal of investors in other countries. But as Figure 2.1a demonstrates, Britain remained by far the most important single source of foreign funds after 1870, with a record as a foreign lender unsurpassed in the whole history of international investment. Thus, between 1870 and 1914, the annual outflow of capital from Britain for investment overseas averaged approximately 4 per cent of national income. Even more striking is the fact that the annual outflow of capital from Britain averaged close to 7 per cent of her national income over the years 1905–13 and reached 9 per cent in the latter year.

Capital-Importing Countries

Figure 2.1b shows the distribution of foreign investments in 1914 by recipient regions. Europe received the largest slice of this investment. Most European countries received some capital

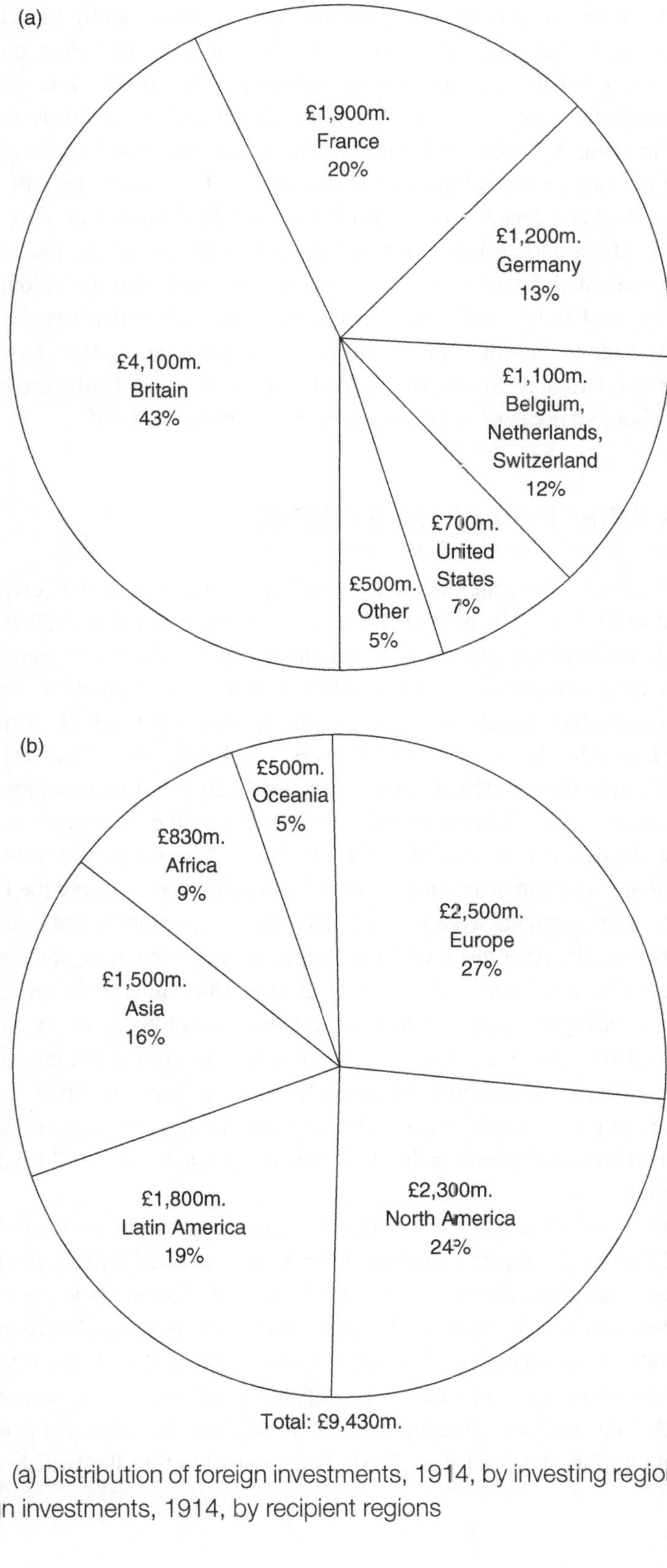

FIGURE 2.1 (a) Distribution of foreign investments, 1914, by investing regions (b) Distribution of foreign investments, 1914, by recipient regions

from abroad at one time or another during the nineteenth century, but by 1914 Russia and the Balkans (including Turkey) were the major borrowers, mainly from France and Germany. Next in order of size of capital inflow was North America. Two-thirds of its share went to the US, and the remainder went to Canada. Argentina, Brazil and Mexico were the most attractive countries in Latin America for foreign investors, and together they accounted for over 80 per cent of the foreign capital directed to that region. In Asia, the bulk of funds went to India, Ceylon, China and Japan, each of which received £200 million or more. By 1914, the Union of South Africa had absorbed approximately 60 per cent of the total funds entering Africa. Egypt accounted for another one-quarter to one-third, and the colonies of Britain, France, Germany and Belgium for most of the remainder. Australia was the major recipient of funds exported to Oceania. If the countries comprising the 'settler colonies' – the US, Canada, Argentina, Uruguay, South Africa, Australia and New Zealand – are taken together, they absorbed about 40 per cent of the capital invested abroad by 1914.

CHANGING DIRECTION OF INVESTMENT

Table 2.1 and Figure 2.2 show the changing geographical pattern of British foreign investment over the period 1830–1914. The bulk of Britain's foreign investment in 1830 was to be found in Europe and Latin America, where British lending during the 1820s had been used primarily to stabilise currencies and to maintain the political status quo. In addition, the boom of the mid-1820s in Britain had stimulated substantial direct investment in Latin American mining activity. In the late 1820s, however, financial reversals in Europe and Latin America left much of the newly incurred debt in default, and consequently British investors turned their attention to the US, where canal and railway building financed by the issue of state and municipal securities created a demand for foreign funds. Yet, North America proved little more reliable than South America as a borrower, and in the difficult years that followed the financial panic of 1837, the state governments were forced to stop interest payments, and two states repudiated their debts outright. As a result of these further financial setbacks, and because domestic economic activity was running at a high level after 1845, interest in foreign investment waned in Britain during the 1840s, although the domestic railway boom of the mid-decade did give rise to railway construction by British contractors in Europe and the colonies. By the mid-1850s, therefore, the distribution of Britain's overseas investment had changed significantly. The share of the total to be found in Europe and in Latin America had declined, while that of the US had increased substantially. The flow of funds to the rest of the world continued to be insignificant.

Between the mid-1850s and 1870, another major change in the regional distribution of British capital occurred. Empire countries increasingly attracted British funds away from Europe and Latin America, whereas the US were barely able to maintain their relative share of the total capital outflow from Britain. These changing preferences of British investors were mainly the result of the changing circumstances confronting British railway builders and investors on the Continent, who found their profits being squeezed by increasing competition from French, Belgian and German entrepreneurs. In addition, the unsettled conditions in the US prior to, and during, the Civil War (1961–5) combined to turn the British investor away

TABLE 2.1 British foreign investment, 1830–1914 (regional distribution)

	1830	1854	1870	1914
	%	%	%	%
Europe	66	55	25	5
US	9	25	27	21
Latin America	23	15	11	18
British Empire: India			22	9
Dominions	2	5	12	37
Other regions			3	9
Total	100	100	100	100
Total investment (£m.)	100	260	770	4,107
($m.)	536	1,266	2,750	20,000

Source: Jenks (1963, pp. 64, 413); Imlah (1952, pp. 208–239); Feinstein (1960); Woodruff (1966, pp. 154ff.).

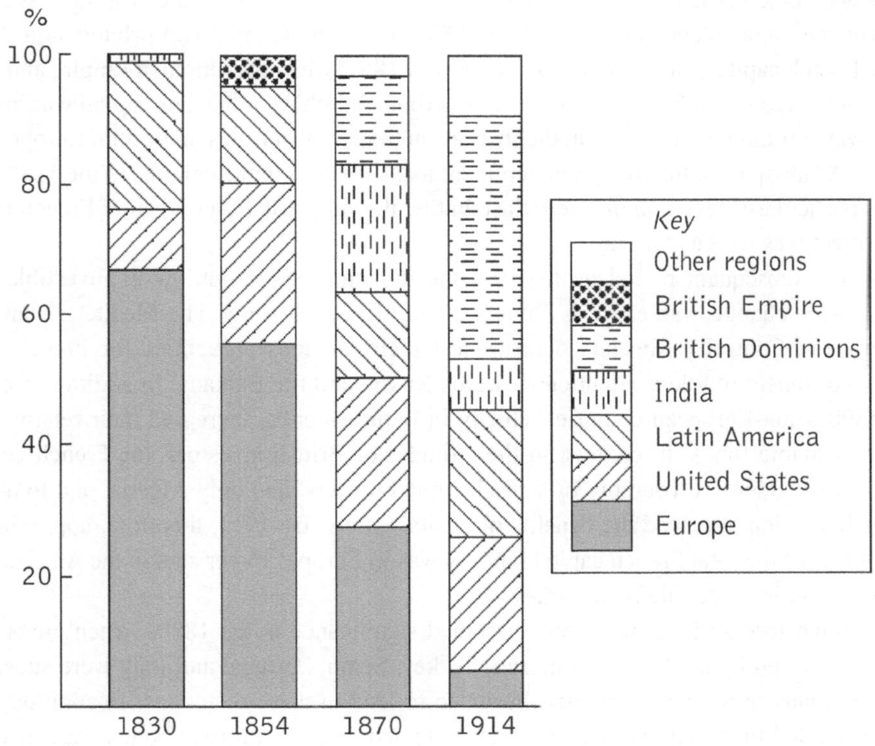

FIGURE 2.2 British foreign investment, 1830–1914 (regional distribution)

Source: Jenks (1963, pp. 64, 413); Imlah (1952, pp. 208–239); Feinstein (1960); Woodruff (1966, pp. 154ff.).

from that country. By 1870, Empire countries accounted for one-third of all British foreign investments. Investment had been heaviest in India, where some £95 million was invested in railways alone between 1845 and 1875, but the volume of investment in Canada, Australia and New Zealand was also growing during these years.

The trend towards investment in Empire countries intensified to such an extent after 1870 that close to one-half of the total British capital abroad in 1914 was in these countries, with the bulk of it invested in the Dominion countries. Australasia during the 1880s and Canada after 1904 were the most attractive Empire regions for British investors during this period, while India's relative share declined considerably. The US continued to receive a high proportion of British capital outflow, chiefly in the form of portfolio investment in railroad companies, and Latin American countries, especially Argentina and, to a lesser extent, Brazil, once again gained favour in the London capital market. On the other hand, Britain's European investments had become relatively unimportant by 1914, chiefly because the Continent had become better able to supply its own capital needs, and while the percentage share going to the rest of the world had trebled between 1870 and 1914, in absolute terms its amount remained small.[3]

French foreign investment during the period 1816–51 amounted to 2,500 million francs (£98 million), the bulk of which was to be found in Spain, the Italian states and Belgium. There was some French investment in the US in the late 1830s, but French capital played only a minor role in development there before 1880. Europe continued to absorb the largest share of the French capital outflow in the 30 years after 1851, while the Ottoman Empire and Egypt also emerged as major borrowers at this time. About one-third of the new capital was invested in railway building, particularly in the Iberian and Italian peninsulas, in Central Europe and in Russia. A large part of the foreign government loans was lost in the defaults of the 1870s, with losses particularly severe in the Near East, but by the early 1880s, a revival of French foreign investment was well under way.

In the subsequent period up to 1914, the direction of the outflow of investible funds from France changed radically, as Table 2.2 and Figure 2.3 show. The Mediterranean, Near Eastern and Central European countries lost their previous attractions for French investors, who transferred their attentions towards Russia and the Balkans. In addition, from the late 1890s, non-European countries, chiefly in Latin America, increased their relative share of the available funds. In contrast to the attitudes of British investors, the French colonies were not considered favourably by French capital owners, and only Algeria, and to a lesser extent Indochina, received the benefits of capital inflow. By 1914, therefore, approximately three-fifths of the total French capital outflow was in Europe, 16 per cent in the Americas and slightly more in Asia, chiefly in Turkey.

German foreign investment only assumed significance in the 1880s, when government securities issued by the Balkan countries, Turkey, Spain, Portugal and Italy were subscribed to in Germany at a time when Paris hesitated to lend in these directions. In addition, loans were extended to Argentina, Venezuela and Mexico, and US railroad bonds were also popular. Following the defaults associated with the financial crises of the 1890s, German foreign lending declined until the early years of this century, when German investors turned away from Europe and towards the US and the German colonies. By 1914 about half of the German foreign investments had been absorbed by European countries, with Austria-Hungary accounting for a substantial part of this capital, and the rest being fairly evenly spread over

TABLE 2.2 French foreign investment, 1851–1914 (regional distribution)

Region	Total investment as in:					
	1851		1881		1914	
	F.000m.	%	F.000m.	%	F.000m.	%
Mediterranean[a]	1.5	60	6.9	39	7.3	14
Central Europe[b]	0.3	12	3.1	18	4.1	9
Eastern Europe[c]	–	–	1.3	7	14.7	28
Northwest Europe[d]	0.6	24	1.2	7	4.1	8
Near Easts[e]	–	–	3.5	20	5.9	11
Colonies	–	–	0.7	4	4.5	9
Western Hemisphere	0.1	4	0.9	5	8.3	16
Other regions	–	–	–	–	3.8	6
Totals (F.000m.)	2.5	100	17.6	100	52.7	100
(£m.)	98		688		2,073	

Source: Cameron (1961, pp. 79, 85 and 486).

Notes: [a] Italy, Spain, Portugal; [b] Austro-Hungary, Germany, Switzerland; [c] Russia, Romania, Greece, Serbia; [d] Belgium, Luxembourg, Netherlands, United Kingdom, Scandinavia; [e] Ottoman Empire and Egypt.

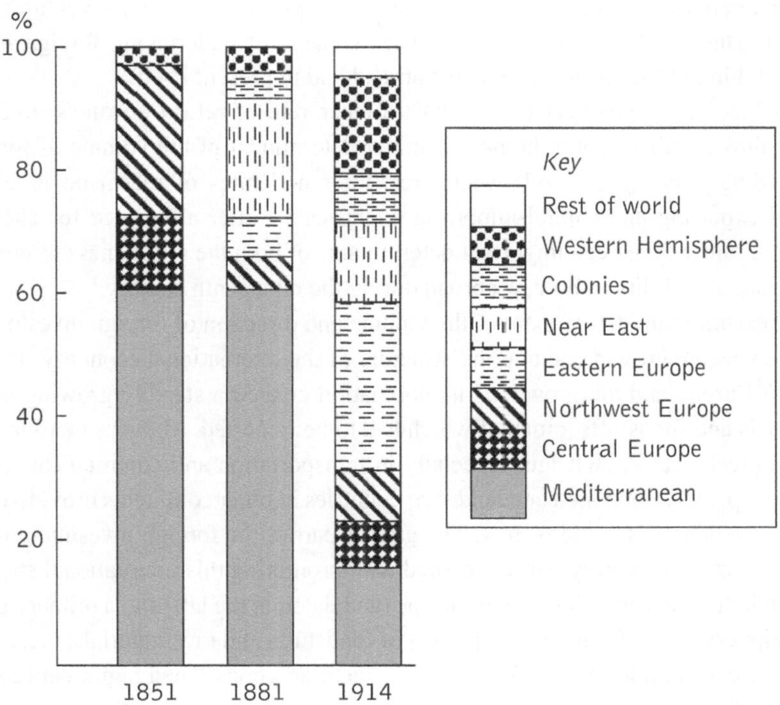

FIGURE 2.3 French foreign investment, 1851–1914 (regional distribution)

Source: As for Table 2.2; Cameron (1961, pp. 79, 85 and 486).

Russia, Turkey, the Balkans, Spain, Portugal, France and Britain. Of the 11,000 million marks (£540 million) invested outside Europe, about 70 per cent went to the Americas and Africa, and Asia (especially the German colonies there) obtained most of the remainder.

Before 1870, US foreign investment was little more than $75 million (£15 million) and was mostly confined to direct investment in mining and manufacturing ventures in Canada, Mexico and South America. By 1899, however, investment in Europe had considerable attractions for American businesses and 80 per cent of the $685 million (£140 million) held abroad, mainly in the form of direct investment, was in Canada, Mexico and Europe. This proportion of total foreign placements of funds declined progressively after 1899 to 66 per cent in 1914, when the total US foreign investment reached $3,514 million (£717 million). During this period of greatly accelerating foreign investment, South America and Asia became important recipients of US direct investment. Manufacturing, the mining of industrial metals and agricultural enterprises, consumed the bulk of the capital outflow.

DETERMINANTS OF CAPITAL OUTFLOW

Before a country could undertake a massive foreign investment programme, a number of conditions had to be fulfilled. First, a considerable degree of economic growth had to be achieved to ensure that domestic savings were accumulated fast enough to provide the surplus of funds. Second, there had to exist abroad government or business enterprises willing and anxious to borrow, or alternatively, numerous opportunities for profitable business ventures for direct investment. Third, a diversified capital market, capable of undertaking foreign investment, was needed. Finally, an incentive to invest abroad had to present itself.

Undoubtedly, the prospect of earning a higher rate of return on one's investment by placing it abroad rather than at home is a major determinant of the volume of foreign lending. Accordingly, changes in relative interest rates and rates of return on investments in the capital-exporting and capital-importing countries — after allowance for changing risk premiums — must have been important determinants of both the willingness to invest abroad and the desire and ability to borrow abroad during the nineteenth century.[4]

Another important determinant of the volume and direction of foreign investment during these years was the growth and altering structure of the international economy. The industrialisation of Europe and the growth of its population created a steadily growing demand for raw materials and foodstuffs, much of which had to be imported. At the same time, important advances in technical knowledge, especially in transportation and communications, and the existence of sparsely populated and land-rich countries in other continents provided the means whereby these demands could be met. The greater part of the foreign investment undertaken during the nineteenth century was concerned with promoting this international specialisation between an industrial centre located in Europe (and, later, in the US) and a primary goods-producing periphery. Apart from being suppliers of foodstuffs and raw materials, these peripheral countries were also important markets for manufactured goods. Their significance as markets provided another incentive for investment in them, especially after 1880, when, because of the industrialisation of Germany and the US and the spread of protection, Britain lost many of her traditional export markets in Europe and North America. Increasingly during these years,

British foreign investment was directed to the Empire, which also now became one of its most important export markets.

According to the neoclassical textbook model, without restrictions, capital would move from where it is relatively abundant to where it is relatively scarce, i.e. from the richer to the poorer countries, with the result of an eventual equalisation of factor prices. But this is not what was (and is) usually observed. By and large, the international capital flows of the nineteenth century rather increased divergence. As O'Rourke and Williamson (1990, p. 245) put it, 'European capital tended to chase after European labor as both migrated to the land-abundant and labor-scarce New World'. The puzzle can at least in part be explained by referring to 'absorptive capacity', which relates to the amount of capital that can be used effectively by a country.[5] Obviously, while it is not possible to measure exactly what the absorptive capacity of an individual country is at a particular time, it is possible to list certain conditions that are necessary for the productive utilisation of capital, whether of domestic or foreign origin. Absorption capacity will be low, for example, when there are inadequate transport facilities, administrative and organisational bottlenecks, deficient qualities of entrepreneurship, a lack of complementary natural resources, scarcities of trained manpower, narrow localised markets and so on. In respect of these conditions, during the nineteenth century some countries, notably the US, Canada, Australia, Argentina, Brazil and a number of European countries, were better placed than others, such as China, India, Egypt and most of Africa. It is not surprising, therefore, to find that by 1913 almost two-thirds of the total foreign investment undertaken during the nineteenth century was to be found in the first-mentioned group of countries, whose capacity to absorb this capital was helped by the international flows of labour that accompanied these movements of foreign capital.

Institutional developments and the spread of protectionism were other important influences at work determining the volume and direction of foreign investment, especially after 1870. The growth and development of financial institutions in both lending and borrowing countries, the movement towards free trade by the 1870s (although reversed in later decades) and the emergence of the gold standard, all contributed in varying degrees to the marshalling of domestic savings in lending countries, the rapid transfer of these funds to borrowing countries and the relatively efficient distribution of the acquired loans to the investors in the latter countries. Especially after the 1870s, foreign direct investment expanded for yet another reason, namely to avoid high tariffs on imports by setting up factories in the tariff-raising countries. This was largely the reason for German direct investments in the US, Russia and a number of other European countries, for British direct investments in Europe and the US and for American investments in Canada and Europe.[6]

Finally, political factors influenced foreign investment. Before 1850, British loans to Greece, Belgium and several Latin American republics were made partly because of the sympathy existing in Britain for the newly independent states. However, this attitude did not prevent British investors from advancing loans to other European governments for other uses aimed at preserving the status quo in European politics. The pattern of French investment before 1850 was also largely determined by political considerations, as well as geographical proximity and cultural and religious affinities to the borrowing countries. In these years 95 per cent of French holdings of foreign government securities were those of Spain, Portugal, the Italian states, Belgium and Austria. After 1850, political considerations continued to exert some influence on the direction of foreign investment, but they became an important determinant only after 1890, when the desire to build up military alliances in anticipation of a future power struggle led to numerous foreign loans being negotiated. The French invested heavily in Russian government securities, and by 1914, 10,000 million francs (£390 million) was owed to French investors. For similar reasons, Russia also received substantial British loans in the years leading up to 1914. Much German investment at this time went to Austria-Hungary and some Balkan countries. Moreover, the political rivalry, which arose in Europe late in the nineteenth century, manifested itself in a burst of imperialism and rapid colonisation in much of Africa and Asia. This development was accompanied by a flow of funds into these regions either to exploit their natural resources or to establish European control over them.

THE USE OF FOREIGN FUNDS IN BORROWING COUNTRIES

During the nineteenth century, foreign investment went into three major fields: government loans; transport and communications; and manufacturing and extractive industries. Compared with most other capital-importing regions, European borrowing tended to be dominated by government loans. Frequently, in the first half of the century, these loans were used to support the extravagance or inefficiency of courts and governments, or for war, defence, insurrection or counter-revolutionary purposes. Towards the end of the century, as the European power struggle gathered force, loans from the west European capital exporters to the governments of Russia, central Europe and the Balkans tended once again to be utilised mainly for military purposes. Of greater economic significance, however, was the heavy investment in railway construction. From the 1840s, the desire of railway builders, at first in Britain, and later in France and Germany, to cover the European continent with a railway network provided most European countries with the economic (and military) benefits to be derived from improved transportation.

Foreign investment in railways was also important for the opening up of other continents. By 1914, $4,000 million (57 per cent) of the total US foreign debt of $7,000 million was in the form of railway securities held abroad, more than half of them in Britain. The British also invested heavily in Indian, Canadian and Australian railways; in Latin America, Asia and Africa railway building absorbed a large share of the investment funds flowing from Britain and Europe to these regions in the period after 1870. While this was providing many countries with more unified domestic markets, the railway investment mainly accelerated their integration into the international economy by allowing cheap and rapid transport of commodities produced in the interior of the countries (raw materials and foodstuffs) to the seaboard for shipment abroad. In this way, international capital movements provided the basis for the international division of labour in the nineteenth century and the resulting expansion of foreign trade.

If other forms of investment in public works were of minor significance when compared with the railways, they were nevertheless important to many countries. The provision of port facilities was a valuable supplement to the railway construction in the Great Plains regions. Canals were built in the US in the 1820s and 1830s, largely with the aid of British capital, and the provision of water and sewerage, roads, bridges, public buildings, telegraph and telephone facilities, gas and electricity financed with foreign funds formed important services for the inhabitants of countries which were experiencing the general benefits of expanding international investment.

For the most part the flow of funds into the manufacturing and extractive industries took the form of direct investment, the extent of which was small in the years before 1870. British capital and enterprise were involved in textile and iron manufacturing on the Continent at this time, and there was also some British capital invested in mining activities in Sweden, Italy and, later, Spain. French industrial investments were concentrated largely in Belgium and Germany, where they were to be found in mining, the metallurgical industries and glass manufacture. After 1870, however, the level of foreign investment in manufacturing and mining increased substantially. In Europe, Germany and France invested heavily in a wide range of manufacturing and mining enterprises in Austria, Italy, Spain and Sweden, but the most striking benefits to be derived from direct investment in Europe accrued to Russia, where a number of industries, including chemicals, metal fabricating, textiles and metal refining were financed by foreign capital after 1880. Foreign investment in oil production, and copper, gold and lead mining also contributed significantly to Russian development. As a result, Russia recorded one of the highest annual average rates of growth of gross national product in Europe between 1870 and 1914.

In the US there was some private portfolio investment in manufacturing after 1870, where foreign investors, mainly British, contributed funds to such firms as US Steel, Eastman Kodak, the United Fruit Company and General Electric. Direct investment by British, Belgian and Dutch firms also went into American oil production, especially after 1901. In Canada, American direct investment expanded production in several spheres of manufacturing, chiefly steel, sugar refining, paper and pulp and mineral refining.

Direct investment in mining and manufacturing also occurred in Latin America and, to a lesser extent, in Australasia and parts of Asia. But these investments remained of minor significance when compared with the much heavier foreign industrial investment in Europe and North America. Even in the latter continents, however, the importance of this type of investment should not be exaggerated. As we have already seen, the bulk of foreign lending went into railways and other forms of infrastructure. Consequently, if foreign lending was of any great significance to the industrial development of the borrowing countries, it made its main contribution indirectly, when better transport facilities widened domestic markets and thereby encouraged the growth of manufacturing industry, and because the availability of foreign capital for investment in overhead capital meant that domestic capital resources were released for use in other forms of domestic economic activity, including manufacturing and mining.

In concluding this section, a brief comment on foreign investment in primary production is relevant. British foreign investment in agricultural and pastoral industries tended to occur in an indirect manner, especially in Australasia and South America, where financial institutions, both British and domestic, accumulated savings through deposits in Britain and lent them to primary producers in the countries concerned. American direct investment was responsible for the establishment or expansion of agricultural industries in Canada, Mexico, Cuba and South America. Direct investment of the colonial type was instrumental in expanding plantation crops such as sugar, rubber, coffee, tea and cocoa, and in developing various mining ventures in Latin America, Africa, Asia and Oceania. British, French and German investors were particularly active in these areas.

ECONOMIC CONSEQUENCES OF FOREIGN INVESTMENT

For capital exporters, there were risks involved in all types of investment, particularly those involving the postponement of interest payments and repudiation of debts. During several periods of the nineteenth century, foreign investors either lost their capital through default or were compelled to wait many years before even interest payments were resumed. This happened to British investments in Europe and Latin America in the 1820s, in the US in the 1830s and in several areas of the world in the 1890s. French investors also burned their fingers in the US in the late 1830s and in Europe in the 1870s, while German investors were estimated to have lost through repudiation or default in the early 1890s as much as 10 per cent of their total capital abroad at the time.

The profitability of investing abroad to a large extent depended on the uses to which the funds were put in the recipient countries. If invested in economically useful and desirable fields, such as in overhead capital or in industrial enterprises located in the growth sectors of the borrowing economy, the likelihood of default was diminished (but not eliminated), for such investments favourably affected growth rates, and at the same time tended to expand exports (or more occasionally reduce imports), so that the means for paying income to foreign investors was provided by the use of the funds. Countries which 'wasted' their loans from abroad in uneconomic pursuits, such as wars, speculation or to support the extravagance or inefficiency and corruption of courts and governments, tended on the whole not to provide such a mechanism for servicing the foreign debt. Thus, default or repudiation was often a virtual certainty. But while much foreign investment was lost in this way, the bulk of it was used productively, and the investment income from abroad, especially after 1870, was of such a size that it tended almost to equal or to exceed the total annual outflow of foreign capital. In other words, for most capital-exporting countries during these years, and especially for Britain, the income receipts on past foreign investment provided the funds out of which new loans for foreign borrowers were provided.

The lending countries also received substantial indirect benefits from their foreign investments. For numerous non-European countries, foreign capital inflow led to an acceleration of international specialisation of production, chiefly in the development of the Great Plains region. By lending surplus savings to these regions to set up railway systems and thereby directly affecting a rapid extension of the land frontier, European countries provided for themselves additional sources of supply of cheap foodstuffs and raw materials, which ensured that the industrialisation of their economies would take place with a minimum of friction and bottlenecks. Such benefits substantially outweighed the occasional losses through default and repudiation, for which irrational actions of the lenders themselves were partly to blame. Indeed, the speedy return of investors to foreign lending after each international financial crisis had passed is indicative of the benefits to be derived from such activity.

The economic impact of foreign lending on the capital-importing country depended on the uses to which the funds were put. In a number of countries capital inflows (accompanied by immigration) acted as a major force, producing rapid and sustained economic growth so that by 1914 these countries were among the most economically highly developed in the world. When countries used their foreign loans efficiently, the problem of servicing the debt incurred was unlikely to produce any significant difficulties. Thus, over time, the only determinant of the borrowing country's capacity to repay was the loan's contribution to the productivity of the economy as a whole and the capacity of the system to skim away part of the increased productivity in taxes or pricing for transfer abroad. In so far as the loans to borrowing countries (largely primary producers) were used to increase the output of primary products and lower their costs of production, an expansion of exports could be expected which, as long as it grew faster than the long-run rate of growth of imports, would produce a balance of trade surplus out of which interest payments and debt redemptions could be met. Where foreign loans were wasted in uneconomic uses, difficulties were predictable, often resulting in non-payment of interest on the debt and sometimes even default.

Foreign investment could also bestow other benefits upon many borrowing countries. It facilitated the diffusion of technological knowledge from the lending to the borrowing countries, thus increasing the likelihood of an increase in productivity. At the same time, the capital flows produced real flows of resources from lenders to borrowers by ensuring that the latter's imports of goods and services could continuously exceed exports for a considerable period of years.[7] To the extent that capital goods increased relative to consumer goods in imports, the growth of productivity in the borrowing country was further enhanced. Thus, for many countries, the diversion of funds received into economically desirable avenues of investment assumed a major role in the development of their economies, even if, at times, the inflow exceeded the absorptive capacity of the industries concerned.

As a country's total production rose, so did savings out of incomes. As time passed, the rate of savings in many capital-importing countries accelerated. Although for most countries the growth of domestic savings did not lead to a reduction of capital inflow, foreign capital tended to be used in different ways, especially in the provision of public works, so that the extra savings could be used to increase production in other sectors of the economy, for example, manufacturing and commerce. Even if there was often much overlapping of the two types of investment in certain industries, the ability of domestic income earners to accumulate savings stemmed in part from the use of foreign funds in the economy.

Direct investment from abroad made contributions to the growth of production in a number of countries because it provided a combination of capital with technological know-how and entrepreneurial ability. In the early stages of industrialisation in both Europe and North America, this type of investment played an important and valuable part. In primary producing countries, however, particularly those in Asia, Latin America and Africa, the concentration of direct investment in export industries, such as plantation crops and mining, in general did little to improve local living standards, and most of the benefits derived from such ventures tended to accrue to the foreign investors in the capital-exporting countries.

To sum up, except for government loans used for military purposes and those frittered away on the upkeep of courts and other royal extravagances, the international capital flows in the nineteenth century aided the economic growth of both borrowing and lending countries. The recipient countries used them to construct infrastructure, creating social overhead capital and to increase their output of export products. The lending countries were at the same time able to intensify their movement towards industrialisation by ensuring rapidly growing supplies of cheap raw materials to feed their factories, and of cheap foodstuffs for their increasing urban populations. The receipts of interest and dividend payments by the capital-exporting countries rapidly grew to such levels as to provide a revolving fund out of which further capital was quickly made available for re-investment abroad. Although the mechanism of international investment occasionally broke down, when the whole period before 1914 is considered, the international flows of capital, and the benefits this investment produced in the form of high rates of economic growth in many countries and a rapidly rising volume of international trade, constituted one of the most significant forces at work in welding together the international economy during these years.

RECOMMENDATIONS FOR FURTHER READING

For discussions of the economic and political circumstances under which international capital flows took place in the colonial world of the nineteenth century, see O'Rourke and Williamson (1990, *Globalization and History. The Evolution of the Nineteenth-Century Atlantic Economy*).

Particular attention to Britain is devoted by Davis and Huttenback (1986, *Mammon and the Pursuit of Empire, the Political Economy of British Imperialism*), Edelstein (1982, *Overseas Investment in the Age of High Imperialism: The United Kingdom 1850–1914*) and Imlah (1958, *Economic Elements in the Pax Britannica*).

Lewis and Schlotterbeck (1938, *America's Stake in International Investments*) and Wilkins (1970, *The Emergence of Multinational Enterprise: American Business Abroad from the Colonial Era to 1914*) direct their focus on the US. Cameron (1961, *France and the Economic Development of Europe 1800–1914*) deals with France, and Körner (2011, *Deutsche Direktinvestitionen 1880–1914: Eine Analyse anhand konkreter Unternehmensbeispiele*) with Germany.

NOTES

1 Conventionally, capital lent for less than one year is said to be short-term; that lent for longer is long-term. The chief difficulty found in implementing this seemingly simple and clear-cut distinction is that the form of the commercial instrument used is not an entirely reliable guide for allocative purposes. Thus, nominally long-term investments, such as government bonds, may in fact be held for short periods if they are readily marketable. This has led to focus on the distinction in terms of the investor's motives. The definition used above is conceived largely in these terms. Long-term investment may also be classified into 'direct' and 'portfolio'. Direct investment occurs when a company in one country sets up a subsidiary, or acquires a controlling interest in a domestic business, in another country. Portfolio investment consists of capital flows from one country to another over the use of which the investors do not have any control — for instance, investment in foreign government loans, in the purchase of a small proportion of share capital in a foreign company, or deposits in foreign financial institutions. Nowadays, for statistical purposes, foreign investments representing 10 per cent or more of a company's capital is classified as foreign direct investment, and as portfolio investments if they fail to meet this threshold. For a critique, see Chapter 17 of this book. In the analysis that follows, we examine foreign long-term capital movements in the nineteenth century. Given the data available, the figures may occasionally include some capital flows with maturity of less than one year.

2 The total value of foreign investments is the gross amount owed by other countries to lending countries. Some lenders, for instance the US, were net borrowers during the period, since they borrowed much larger amounts of foreign capital than they lent abroad themselves.

3 It should be noted, however, that in the late nineteenth century an increasing volume of continental European funds found their way to the London capital market for investment chiefly in foreign issues

and in shares quoted on the London Stock Exchange. See, for example, Michie (1988) and Davis and Huttenback (1986).

4 The relationship between capital movements and the terms of trade, which forms one aspect of this problem of relative rates of return in capital-exporting and capital-importing countries, is discussed in Chapter 10 of this book.

5 Domestic absorption is the sum of private consumption (C), government expenditure (G) and gross domestic investment (I). It exceeds GDP (Y), when net imports ($M–X$) are positive. GDP is the sum of consumption, investment, government expenditure and net exports ($X–M$). On the income side, GDP is spent on consumption, saving (S) and taxes (T). Accordingly: $Y = C + I + G + (X–M) = C + S + T$. Rearranging this identity yields: $M–X = I–S + G–T$. Hence, absorption in excess of GDP can fund private investment in excess of saving, or government expenditure in excess of revenue, or combinations of these.

6 This rationale appears to be part of the motivation for the new import tariffs that US President Trump has been introducing in the beginning of his second term in 2025. For details, see Chapter 23 of this book.

7 This reflects the identity of the balances of the current account and the capital account in the balance of payments. A country with positive net imports (goods and services exports < goods and services imports) must have positive net capital imports (capital exports < capital imports) of the same magnitude, as it must receive loans from the rest of the world to finance its excess imports. Likewise, a country with positive net exports (goods and services exports > goods and services imports) must have positive net capital exports (capital exports > capital imports) of the same magnitude, as it must give loans to the rest of the world to finance the excess imports.

CHAPTER 3

International Migration

A. G. Kenwood, A. L. Lougheed and Michael Graff

If the flow of capital from Europe constitutes a remarkable chapter in the history of the world economy, so does the emigration of labour that accompanied the outflow of capital. As we have just seen, the bulk of Europe's foreign investment in the nineteenth century went to relatively sparsely populated areas where labour was scarce. To these regions also went millions of emigrants from Europe. As farmers, workers and entrepreneurs they complemented and helped to make productive the capital that was flowing after them to these new countries overseas.

EUROPEAN MIGRATION

The emigration statistics suggest a total population outflow overseas of some 46 million during the period 1821–1915. The mass of the migrants, some 44 million, originated in Europe; the remainder came chiefly from Asia. The bulk of the European movement took place after 1880, although with every decade the tide of population movement increased in volume, rising from an average of over 110,000 per year in the period 1821–50 to 270,000 in 1851–80, and to over 900,000 in 1881–1915 (see Table 3.1 and Figure 3.1).

In total, some 11–12 million Europeans emigrated before 1880, compared with 32 million after that date. This acceleration in the rate of emigration from Europe after 1880 was coupled with a significant shift of the source of the population outflow. Before 1880 most of the emigrants came from Northern and Western Europe; after that date the majority were from Southern and Eastern Europe.

Over the whole period, the British Isles were the principal source of supply of people, accounting for approximately 37 per cent of the total outflow from Europe. The other major sources, in order of their importance, were Italy, Germany, Austria-Hungary, Spain, Russia (including what is now Poland) and Portugal. Emigration from Britain was heavy throughout the nineteenth century, whereas the outflow from Italy became substantial only after 1880.

DOI: 10.4324/9781003382171-6

TABLE 3.1 Emigration from Europe, 1821–1915 (millions)

	1821–50		1851–80		1881–1915	
	No.	**%**	**No.**	**%**	**No.**	**%**
NW Europe	3.4	100.0	7.4	91.3	13.7	42.7
Britain	2.6	76.5	4.6	56.8	8.9	27.7
Germany	0.6	17.6	2.1	25.9	2.2	6.9
SE Europe	neg.	–	0.7	8.7	18.4	57.3
Italy	neg.	–	0.2	2.5	7.8	24.3
Spain and Portugal	neg.	–	0.3	3.7	4.3	13.4
Austria-Hungary	neg.	–	0.2	2.5	4.2	13.1
Total	3.4	100.0	8.1	100.0	32.1	100.0
Annual averages	113,000		270,000		917,000	

Source: Ferenczi and Willcox (1929, Vol. I).

Note: Northwest Europe comprises the British Isles, France, Germany, Holland, Belgium, Switzerland, Denmark, Norway, Sweden and Finland; southeast Europe comprises Italy, Spain, Portugal, Austria, Hungary and Russia (including what is now Poland).

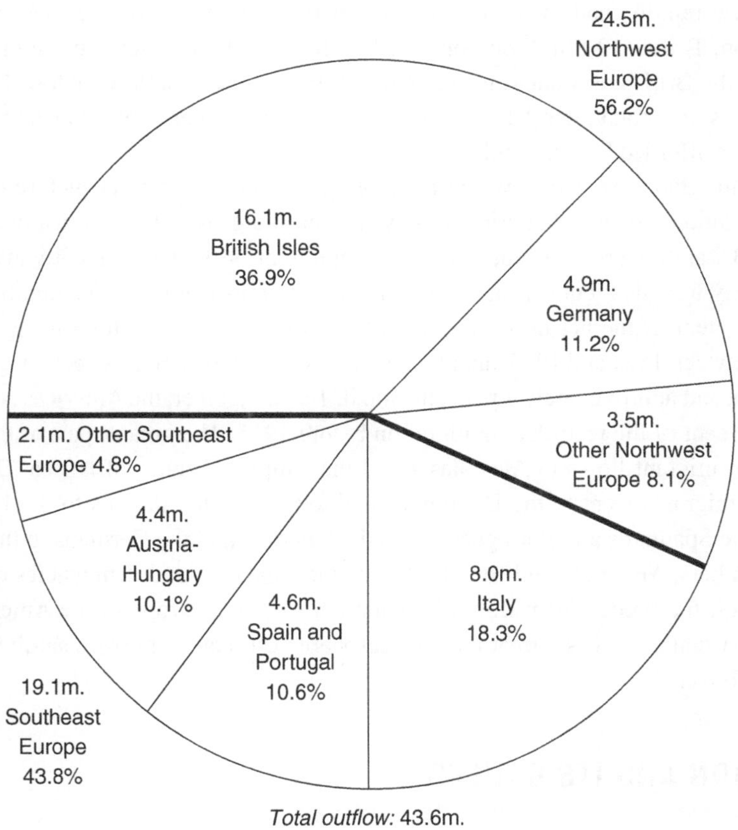

FIGURE 3.1 Emigration from Europe, 1821–1915

Source: Ferenczi and Willcox (1929, Vol. I).

TABLE 3.2 International immigration, 1821–1915 (millions)

Country of immigration	1821–50		1851–80		1881–1915	
	No.	%	No.	%	No.	%
US	2.38	67.0	7.73	68.1	21.76	59.4
Canada	0.74	20.8	0.82	7.2	2.59	7.1
British W. Indies	0.08	2.3	0.27	2.4	0.53	1.4
Brazil	0.02	0.6	0.45	4.0	2.97	8.1
Argentina	–	–	0.44	3.9	4.26	11.6
Australia	0.19	5.4	0.79	7.0	2.77	7.6
New Zealand			0.25	2.2	0.26	0.7
All others	0.14	3.9	0.60	5.3	1.50	4.1
Total	3.55	100.0	11.35	100.0	36.64	100.0
Annual averages	0.12		0.38		1.05	

Sources: Ferenczi and Willcox (1929, pp. 236–288, Table 6); Roberts and Byrne (1966, pp. 125–134); United States Bureau of Census, Statistical Abstract of the United States (https://www.census.gov/about/history/galleries-archives/articles-publications/statistical-abstracts.html).

Then it grew rapidly, and in the first decade of this century it was heavier even than the outflow from Britain (3.6 million compared with 2.8 million). German emigration, which along with the British accounted for the bulk of the European outflow before 1880, became relatively less important after that date, owing chiefly to the alternative domestic employment opportunities afforded by rapid industrialisation.

The immigration statistics, which probably give a fuller and truer picture of intercontinental population movements during these years, show a gross inflow of just over 51 million (see Table 3.2 and Figure 3.2). Not all of these immigrants settled permanently in the countries to which they travelled, but owing to lack of adequate information on the numbers returning home, the extent of the net movement is difficult to gauge. Of the total gross immigration recorded between 1821 and 1915, about 62 per cent entered the US, 9 per cent Argentina, 8 per cent Canada and approximately 7 per cent Brazil. Taken together, the Americas received more than 85 per cent of the recorded immigration before 1915. The greater part of the remainder consisted of migrant flows to Australasia and the temperate zones of Africa. By and large, the British migrants went to the Dominions and to the US, the Italians to the US and Latin America, the Spaniards and Portuguese to Latin America, and the Germans to the US and, in smaller numbers, Argentina and Brazil. Despite the weakness and deficiencies of the migration statistics, the predominant flow of population — from Europe to the Americas, and to the US in particular — is so great that no reasonable estimates of error can alter the picture presented above.

MIGRATION AND ITS CAUSES

In discussions of population movements, a distinction is often made between 'push' and 'pull' migration. During the first 60 years of the nineteenth century, there is no doubt that the forces

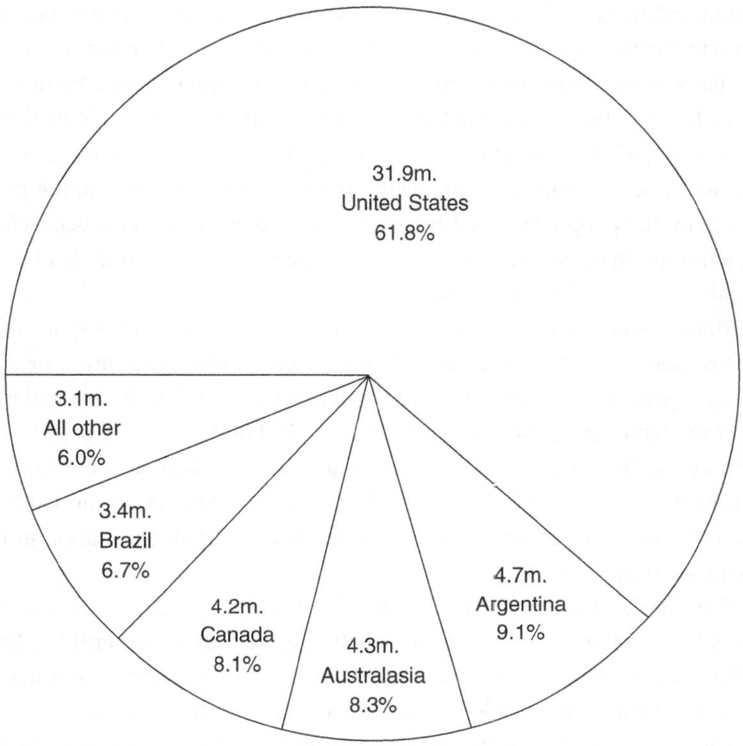

FIGURE 3.2 International immigration, 1821–1915

Source: Ferenczi and Willcox (1929, pp. 236–288, Table 6); Roberts and Byrne (1966, pp. 125–134); United States Bureau of Census, Statistical Abstract of the United States (https://www.census.gov/about/history/galleries-archives/articles-publications/statistical-abstracts.html).

operating to generate intercontinental movements of labour were mainly of the 'push' type, in the sense that the migrant was driven from the homeland by adverse economic conditions or other circumstances, rather than attracted to the country of destination by the more or less vague expectations of a future improvement in his lot. At the same time, the motives for moving were as various as the types of individuals involved. But where a few sought freedom from political or religious oppression, judging by the figures alone, most migrants left for reasons which, although social in their implications, were basically economic in origin.[1]

The root causes of the rise of mass emigration from Europe in the years between 1815 and 1870 were the demographic and technical revolutions that were then transforming the economic and social life of Western Europe. Basically, it was an outflow of rural population brought about by a Malthusian situation of a rapidly growing population — mostly due to marked declines in mortality based on improved hygiene — pressing on limited means of subsistence. Under the pressure of population increase, the land was subdivided until holdings became too small even in good years to support those who cultivated them. Even when improvements in agricultural methods increased productivity, this tended simply to strengthen the trend towards what Friedrich List (1842) described as a 'dwarf economy' (*Zwergwirtschaft*) of tiny marginal holdings. In Ireland and in other countries of the Continent, notably Germany and Scandinavia, the introduction of the potato facilitated the problematic subdivision of land. Where sustenance could be obtained from the potato crop supplemented by the milk of cows or goats, and when no obstacle existed to the minute subdivision of holdings, there was virtually no check to population growth except famine. But if in the western parts of Germany, the 'push' factor took the form of a truly Malthusian 'over-population', in the regions east of the Elbe Germany the people suffered from a social system which produced yields on large estates with a minimum of labour, denying to the peasant farmer not only land ownership and tenancy, but also even regular employment.

Famine finally overwhelmed Ireland in the years 1845–7, and in the space of a few years the country lost about one-fifth of its population by emigration, starvation or disease. Even prior to 1847, emigration had drawn off considerable numbers of the Irish population, but now the losses were much higher, reaching an average of 200,000 per year from 1847 to 1854. If, in subsequent years, the outflow was never again as great as it had been during the 1840s and 1850s, it was heavy nevertheless: 540,000 in the 1870s and 700,000 in the 1880s, and, in the period up to 1890, the Irish continued to contribute to the British emigration to the extent of one-third to one-half of the total annual outflow.

Alternative employment opportunities for displaced rural labour were to be found in urban manufacturing industry or in the construction of railways, but until the last quarter of the nineteenth century, the pace of industrialisation in most of Europe was decidedly slow. Even when it accelerated, the tendency was for emigration to increase in volume, at least in the short run, as countries experienced the disrupting effects of industrialisation and the introduction of capitalistic forms of agricultural production. Ultimately, however, industrialisation in North and West Europe, by increasing employment opportunities and raising relative wages, reduced the 'push' pressures by more than the increase in the American 'pull', which became more pronounced after 1880. Adding to the difficulties of industrial adjustment in Europe in the 1870s and early 1880s was the inflow of cheap American grain, which depressed prices and made much of European agriculture unprofitable. Where, as in Britain, the farmer remained unprotected against this competition, the result was a partial collapse of agriculture and a massive outflow of rural population overseas. Even here, however, the attraction of Empire countries, which often offered subsidised fares, reduced the numbers of migrants going to the US.

These developments resulted in a significant change in the pattern of European emigration after 1880. It was now the turn of the countries of Eastern and Southern Europe to experience on a widespread scale the socially disruptive effects of population growth and economic and technical change. Italy emerged as second only to Britain in importance as a source of emigrants at this time, and after 1900 sent more people overseas than any other European country. There was also heavy emigration from Spain, Portugal, Austria-Hungary and Russia, and while political oppression provided led to some emigration, the bulk of the population movement that occurred during these years took place because of the pressures of rural overcrowding. In short, whatever the diversity of their places of origin, most European migrants during the nineteenth century were either peasants displaced from the soil by the great transformation of European agriculture of these years, or they were artisans similarly displaced by the conversion of handicraft work to factory production.

AIDS TO MASS EMIGRATION

Financial Assistance

The willingness to emigrate under pressure of adverse economic circumstances was not in itself sufficient to bring about a mass outflow of population from Europe. Willingness to move had to be backed by ability to do so. This latter problem, which involved basically the cost of movement, became apparent quite early in the nineteenth century, when the poor and destitute came to constitute a growing proportion of the total emigration from Europe. The peak in this outflow of pauper labour came with the Irish famine of the late 1840s, which had the effect of removing from the land the poorest inhabitants or those who had been living on the margin of subsistence.

During these early years, the growing outflow of people from Europe was made possible partly because the climate of public and official opinion became more favourable to the emigration of the poor. This was shown not only by the removal of restrictions on emigration in countries such as Britain, Germany and Sweden, but also by the fact that the state and other interested bodies — such as philanthropic organisations, emigration and colonisation societies, trade unions and even individuals — appropriated money to pay the costs of emigration of poor people. In Britain, particular importance attaches to the Colonial Land and Emigration Department, which was established in 1840 for the purpose of organising the sale of land in Australia and New Zealand as a means of raising money to assist emigration to these colonies. As a result of its efforts, some 339,339 emigrants went to Australasia between 1847 and 1869 at a cost of £4.9 million, of which £532,000 was raised by the emigrants or their friends, and the rest came from colonial funds. More limited financial aid was provided by the parishes, which were empowered by the British Parliament in the 1830s to raise money on the security of the local rates to assist the emigration of the locally unemployed. Additional help came from philanthropic individuals and societies, as well as from landlords seeking to escape the excessive burden of the poor rate caused by unemployment, while in the towns the trade unions were also active in supporting the emigration of out-of-work members. On the continent, a somewhat similar system of private and state assistance for emigrants developed in Germany, especially after the uprisings of 1848, when state governments came to look on emigration as a means of getting rid of a potentially dangerous proletariat. Only in Baden, however, was there a serious programme of state subsidisation of emigration during these years.

As publicly subsidised emigration declined in importance after the 1850s, financial aid to migrants came increasingly from governments and private persons or groups in the receiving countries. Assisted immigration remained important throughout the rest of the nineteenth century for Britain's Australasian colonies and for some Latin American countries, all of which suffered under the twin handicaps of distance from Europe and North American competition in their quest for migrants. Thus, between 1861 and 1900, the total number of assisted immigrants entering Australia was more than 388,000, compared with a net gain through immigration of some 767,000. In the next decade only 17,700 assisted immigrants reached Australia, but in the following four years (1911–14), they amounted to almost 145,000 out of a total net gain from the UK of 198,500.

In Brazil, free passage, free land and sometimes free machinery, seed and livestock, as well as monthly cash allowances to tide immigrants over the initial period of settlement, were powerful incentives, which eventually attracted a steady stream of migrants to the country. In São Paulo, for example, where the treasury began defraying transportation costs from Southern Europe to the Brazilian coffee plantations in 1887, the number of immigrants reached large proportions. Out of almost 1.5 million entering the state between 1890 and 1913, 65 per cent were subsidised. Liberal financial assistance to cover the costs of travel and settlement was also provided by the Argentinean government, which further encouraged immigration into that country by offers of exemption from military service and immunity from discriminatory taxes.[2]

Another form of financial help to migrants which originated abroad was the remittances sent home by prosperous and successful settlers, which could be used towards paying the fares of relatives and friends who wished to emigrate. The full extent of these remittances is not known, but a few examples of these financial flows between countries are sufficient in themselves to make us aware of the contribution they must have made towards bringing about the large-scale movement of people that took place after 1860. For the UK, the annual inflow of remittance money from the US varied considerably, but between 1848 and 1879 the total amounted to over £21 million, enough to emigrate comfortably no less than 2 million people. Towards the end of the nineteenth century, it was estimated that 79 per cent of the British migrants going to the US had their fares paid by friends and relatives already settled there. Equally striking is the estimated $2 billion remitted to Italy between 1901 and 1923, 80 per cent of which derived from America. Much of this money represented savings repatriated by Italians returning to their homeland, but some of it was undoubtedly used to finance part of the massive emigration from Italy that took place during the early years of this century.

While government assistance to migrants was important for some countries, for example Australia and Brazil, its overall impact on the volume and direction of international migration before 1913 should not be exaggerated. The great bulk of the migrants had to depend on their own resources or those of their families and friends, including people already settled overseas, to finance their movement abroad. At the same time, the fact that so many people were able to emigrate was in no small way due to the availability of cheaper and more accessible transport.

Cheap Transport

In the development of cheaper, faster and more accessible transport the operative factors were the unprecedented expansion of commerce that took place in the nineteenth century and, after 1850, the spread of steamship travel. In the early years of the century, it was the growth of the Canadian timber trade and the expansion of the trade of the US with Europe, particularly in cotton, which gave rise to a considerable increase of unused space on return journeys, so that ship owners increasingly looked to emigrants to provide part of the return freight. As this passenger trade grew, intensive competition between the shipping companies brought fares tumbling down. At Liverpool, the cost of steerage passage to New York fell from £12 in 1816 to just over £3 30 years later, and comparable reductions occurred at the other ports of Northwestern Europe with connections in the New World. But cheaper fares were small compensation for the terrors associated with travel in overcrowded, badly provisioned and often unseaworthy boats, and it was not until the 1840s that interested governments were able to secure better treatment and more comfortable travelling for the migrants. However, the final solution to this problem came only with the growth of the steamship trade, which reduced travelling time substantially and placed the passenger trade in the hands of the more reputable steamship companies.

The spread of steamship travel was rapid after 1850, and although sailing ships still handled about one-half of the emigrant trade in the 1860s, by 1873 the proportion had been reduced to less than 4 per cent. Apart from encouraging emigration by speeding up travel, the steamship companies played a direct role in inducing migration, for in their bid to ensure full passenger lists, their ticket agents combed Europe for migrants, conducting extensive propaganda campaigns in favour of settlement overseas.[3] Even more important as a source of information available to potential migrants was the knowledge of conditions provided by friends and relatives who had already migrated or who had returned home after a period spent abroad. Moreover, as the stock of migrants grew, the volume of information about the opportunities for improvement overseas increased and became more widespread throughout Europe. At the same time, government regulations and competition between steamship companies resulted in continuous improvements in passenger facilities. Despite the better facilities and the long-run decline in the purchasing power of money, the cost of steerage passage varied very little after 1850. Thus, in 1913, steerage rates were £5 10s and £6 15s, compared with an average cost of emigrating Irishmen in 1855 of £5 10s per head.

ECONOMIC CONSEQUENCES OF MIGRATION

Immigrant Countries

The essential economic function of international migration in the nineteenth century was to redistribute some of Europe's rural population surplus to new primary producing regions overseas, where physical and social conditions enabled it to produce more per hand than it would have done had it remained at home. Sometimes, this result was achieved directly, but not always. Many immigrants, although drawn from largely agricultural economies, contributed to the development of new countries by taking non-agricultural jobs, thus releasing more of the incumbent population to expand agriculture. A minority of migrants possessed industrial skills and were responsible for the introduction of new manufacturing techniques. But the chief contribution of immigrants to industrial development in these countries was to be found in the numerical addition to a country's population they made, first as newcomers, and later through high birth rates as parents. These growing numbers provided both the labour force and the large and expanding market so essential to industrialisation and large-scale production.

Whatever the occupational destinations of the migrants, there was a direct connection between immigration and economic growth in the receiving countries. Each inflow of population acted as a powerful force in pushing up the rate of growth of investment, income and employment. Whether these upsurges in economic growth caused the inflow of foreign population or whether immigration stimulated economic expansion — both causal sequences may have operated during the nineteenth century — the contribution of the immigrants to economic growth was obvious. As entrepreneurs, they brought to the recipient countries the capital and knowledge that formed the basis of a wide variety of new manufacturing industries, including, among others, textiles, furniture, chemicals, glassmaking and brewing; and as artisans, they supplied the technical skills necessary to make these new industries an initial success. However, the bulk of the immigrants supplied the construction industries with the working power needed to build railways and other transport facilities, and to erect cities and equip them with public utilities, sanitation and other urban requirements. In addition, where, as in the US, mechanised production was introduced on a large scale, immigrants provided the factory workforce necessary for rapid and sustained industrial growth.

European agricultural skills could not always be used overseas. Only rarely, therefore, did immigrants become frontiersmen or pioneer farmers. In more settled areas, however, many European agricultural techniques proved immensely valuable. The introduction of sugar beet and 'everlasting' clover, the growth of wine production and the diffusion of novel methods of wheat growing are only a few instances of the contributions made by immigrants to the growth of overseas agriculture during the nineteenth century. Moreover, in the neighbourhood of the growing cities, the immigrants often became involved in various types of market-gardening and small-scale intensive agriculture to which local farmers were not accustomed, thus developing a pattern of agriculture that was responsible for bringing about subsequent changes in local consumption habits.

However, immigration involves costs as well as benefits to the receiving country, and the heavy pressures exerted on a country's existing supplies of housing, educational and transport facilities during periods of heavy immigration are characteristic of these. Furthermore, since most immigrants are wage earners, the impact of immigration on the wages of the receiving country is important in the discussion of the economic consequences of migration. Indeed, the threat, real or otherwise, to the living standards of the incumbent population posed by immigrant labour was the occasion for violent anti-immigration demonstrations in many countries during the nineteenth century. Examination of the available evidence suggests that there was no marked tendency for wages in general to fall in the pre-1913 period. But since it is practically impossible to eliminate the effect on the wage level of all the other interacting and continually changing forces, such as technological progress and rising productivity, the spread of industry and the growth of new employment opportunities, it remains a matter of conjecture whether in particular countries immigration did in the long run have an unfavourable effect on the general wage level in receiving countries. On the other hand, if we concentrate on the wages earned in specific occupations, there is some evidence to suggest that heavy immigration did adversely affect wage levels in certain occupations. Thus, in America, the real wages of unskilled workers remained relatively constant in the periods of heavy immigration after 1880, whereas other incomes increased steadily in real terms. Indeed, the 'pick and shovel' man received only slightly more in the US than in Europe, compared with the wide differentials between American and European earnings in other occupations and skills, a fact which was put down by contemporary American observers to the enormous influx of immigrants. On the other hand, as Eichengreen and Gemery (1986, p. 42) have shown,

> over time, initially unskilled immigrants managed to close much of the earnings gap between themselves and their skilled counterparts. Thus, while immigrants who had

> acquired training prior to arrival in the United States initially had the advantage of access to a range of relatively high-paid positions, immigrants who acquired their training after arrival had the advantage of superior opportunities for advancement and earnings growth.

It must be noted, however, that the above conclusion applies to the 'old' immigrant groups, that is, foreign workers born in England, Wales, Scotland, Germany and Scandinavia.

We also find evidence in Argentina and Brazil of heavy immigration retarding the growth of real incomes in certain occupations. But this tendency was not due solely to the increased supply of labour in the market because of immigration. Difficulties are also apparent on the demand side, where the latifundia system, inherited from colonial times, placed the ownership of the land in a few hands; and the slow growth of industry limited the expansion of employment opportunities in both agriculture and manufacturing.

Emigrant Countries

Economic benefits and losses were also experienced by the countries losing population. They suffered a loss in the capital or property which emigrants took with them, as well as the loss of human capital represented by the means expended in rearing, educating and training the emigrants. But the extent of the losses should not be exaggerated. Many of the emigrants were desperately poor. On the other hand, the losing country also benefited from its emigrants in a number of ways. There was the gain in remittances and in the savings brought back to the country by repatriates, and they sometimes returned with new knowledge and new ideas, which could be put to profitable use in the home country. Furthermore, where, as in Ireland, the loss of population was heavy and sustained, there is evidence that emigration did contribute in part to raising real wages and, perhaps more importantly, to increasing the degree of regularity in employment of those who remained. For the most part, however, emigration operated largely as a safety valve for people stranded in declining occupations and places. It did little to raise the real incomes or to expand employment opportunities in losing countries, for these improvements depended more on the spread of industrialisation, technical progress and the growth of productivity than on a simple loss of population. In other words, emigration remained throughout the nineteenth century a palliative rather than a solution for the problems of social and economic change.

INTRACONTINENTAL MIGRATION

The large-scale movement of population was not confined to exchanges between continents. Whereas at the beginning of the nineteenth century the European outposts overseas consisted largely of islands and tide-water settlements, in the following century whole continents were occupied in the Americas and Australasia, as the descendants of earlier stages of immigration, supported by a growing influx of new migrants, turned inland and started cultivating these formerly only sparsely populated lands.[4] The existence of uncultivated lands in parts of Eastern Europe also brought substantial internal migration within Europe. Much of this movement of population was directed towards Russia, where 4.2 million foreigners settled between 1828 and 1915. Two-thirds of these came from Europe, mainly from Germany and Austria. The remainder came from Asian countries bordering on Russia, especially China, Japan, Persia and Turkey. There was also a significant eastward movement of Russians into Asia. Of the 7 million involved in this long-distance internal migration, roughly three-quarters were peasant settlers; the rest, numbering 1.3 million, were prisoners and exiles. These migrants settled mainly in Siberia; others went southwards into the steppe country; still others to eastern Asia and Turkestan. The bulk of the movement took place after 1890. This movement of population into Asiatic Russia forms part of the general redistribution of the Asian population that took place during these years, the nature and direction of which is the subject of the following section.

ASIATIC MIGRATION AND TROPICAL DEVELOPMENT

The Demand for Asian Labour

As the movement of free European people across the Atlantic grew in volume, the centuries-old forcible transfer of Africans to the tropical regions of the New World finally came to an end. Despite its legal abolition in a number of countries, the African slave trade was growing rapidly in the early decades of the nineteenth century and, by 1840, it was estimated to have been almost double what it had been in 1807, when slave trade — but not slavery itself — was outlawed by Britain and the US.[5] During the next decade, however, Britain's efforts to suppress the trade achieved considerable success, and by 1850 the traffic to Brazil was virtually finished, and nearly half of the West African coastline was closed to the slave trade. There was a massive revival of slaving in the 1850s, due mainly to the expansion of cotton production in the US during these years, but the outbreak of the American Civil War quickly put an end to the illegal trade there, as well as in numerous other countries, such as Cuba, where it had been carried on under the protection of the American flag.

The abolition of slavery in the period before 1870 resulted in a serious shortage of labour in the tropical plantation economies, and this was partly responsible for the growing volume of Asian migration during the nineteenth century. But while some of these migrants (which included mainly people from India, China and, after 1870, Japan) went to other continents, the bulk of the population movement was confined to Asia and its adjacent islands. Indian migrants, largely indentured labourers, went to the West Indies, Mauritius, South Africa and South America, and still larger numbers were imported into the plantation and mining economies of Ceylon, Malaya and the East Indies. Chinese intercontinental migration, which was on a considerable scale between 1848 and 1873, was broadly similar in direction and character to that of Indian emigration during these years, but with a somewhat larger number of Chinese emigrating to countries such as the US and Australia. Nearer home, the Chinese went chiefly to Southeast Asia, including Burma, Siam, Indochina and Malaya, and to the East Indies, the Philippine Islands and Formosa (now: Taiwan). The bulk of the Japanese indentured labour went to Hawaii. Large numbers of Japanese also emigrated to Asiatic Russia, America and Korea.

Under the system of indenture, the labourer undertook to work for a fixed period of anything up to five years in return for the cost of his passage, a fixed wage and certain other amenities such as free housing and medical care. On expiration of his contract, the labourer could renew it or settle permanently in the receiving country by taking up alternative employment. After 1857, Indian indentured labourers, who were employed largely in other colonies of the British Empire, could also return home at the expense of the colony which had imported them. From the start the system of indentured labour was subject to grave abuse, and in extreme cases work on the plantations was little better than slavery. The governments of the countries involved in this exchange of labour endeavoured to control the worst of the abuses, and from time to time the emigration of indentured labour was suspended. Even so, the problem of ensuring fair treatment for indentured labour continued to exercise the minds of government officials well into the twentieth century.

The Volume and Direction of Asian Migration

Adequate statistical records exist for only some of the intercontinental flows of Asian migrants. One well-documented movement was that directed to the West Indies, where the freeing of the slaves in 1833 left the sugar plantations with a severe labour shortage. Of the 536,000 mainly indentured labourers introduced into the colony in the period 1834–1918, some 80 per cent (430,000) came from India. Other British colonies outside Asia to which Indians migrated in any numbers during these years were South Africa and Mauritius. Although the full extent of the population inflow into the colonies is not known, a total of 161,000 Indians was recorded in the South African census of 1921. Within Asia, Indian migrants went chiefly to Ceylon (now: Sri Lanka) and Malaya. In Ceylon, the immigrant labour worked mainly in the coffee and tea plantations, and, although for the majority of them their stay was only temporary, the net inflow of Indians into Ceylon between 1839 and 1913 amounted to over 1.8 million people. In total, some 15.8 million people left India between 1871 and 1915, and 11.7 million returned, leaving 4.1 million as net migrants. The heavy return flow is explained largely by the indenture system which, as we have seen, bound a migrant to work for a plantation employer for a fixed number of years.

Like the Indian emigration, the bulk of the Chinese migrants went to other parts of Asia. The Straits Settlements received 5.7 million Chinese between 1881 and 1915, and large numbers of Chinese also went to Siam (now: Thailand) after 1885 so that by 1922 their numbers in that country totalled 1.5 million. A further quarter of a million Chinese migrated to the Philippine Islands, before the American take-over of the islands from Spain in 1898 resulted in the application to the Philippines of the Chinese Exclusion Act already in force in the US. Next to Asia, the Americas attracted the most Chinese. Thus, some 18,000 Chinese entered the West Indies under contract between 1852 and 1884, and by 1862 there were over 60,000 Chinese in Cuba. In Peru, where, as a result of an immigration law passed in 1849, large numbers of Chinese were brought into the country to work on plantations and on the guano beds, the numbers of Chinese entering the country between 1849 and 1874 are estimated at between 80,000 and 100,000. Gold discoveries in California were responsible for the early flows of Chinese into the US, and by the end of the century over 300,000 had entered the country, mainly in the years before 1882, when a reaction against the use of Chinese labour in railway construction and other forms of employment led to the passage of an Act of exclusion. Gold also brought an influx of Chinese into Australia in the 1850s, and by 1861 they numbered 38,000. But with the decline in alluvial gold mining, and following the restrictions placed on Chinese immigration by the various Australian colonies, which culminated in the Commonwealth Immigration Restriction Act of 1901, the number had declined to 22,000 by 1911. Overall, the number of Chinese living abroad increased by perhaps 5 million, but since large numbers of Chinese were recruited for work abroad under the indenture system, the gross outflow was likely to have been substantially greater than this figure suggests.

Japanese emigration was not legalised until 1885, when an agreement was signed by the Japanese government and Hawaiian sugar plantation owners, under which Japanese contract labourers were permitted to migrate to Hawaii. An Imperial edict legalising emigration of Japanese labourers in general soon followed. Consequently, between 1885 and 1907 approximately 540,000 Japanese emigrated, of whom one-third went to Hawaii and a further 14 per cent each to the US and Korea. Other countries receiving more than 10 per cent of the outflow included Asiatic Russia and China. In the following period, 1908–24, a further 643,000 emigrants left Japan. Of these, 38 per cent went to Asiatic Russia and about one-fifth to the US. Smaller numbers went to Hawaii, China, Brazil and Peru. After 1907, Japanese immigration into the US slowed down, following the conclusion of the so-called 'Gentlemen's Agreement', under which the Japanese government undertook to limit the issue of passports valid for continental America to certain selected groups of Japanese migrants. Complete exclusion followed in 1924.

SUMMARY AND OUTLOOK

Before the First World War, migration played a significant role in shaping the global economy. From the earliest waves of human migration in Palaeolithic times to the slave trade of the Modern Era, migration has spread not only labour as a factor of production, but also customs, beliefs, knowledge and ideas. Effective hurdles to migration were the costs and vagaries of transport, rather than legal restrictions. With improvements in transport technology, migration picked up. Economically, the unprecedented international migration in the period 1820–1913 must have significantly contributed to improving the allocation of factors of production of the global economy, raising world output to levels that could not have been achieved under a more repressive regime that was established after the First World War and — with some notable exceptions at a regional scale — remains in force up to this date. This is most unfortunate, because it adds economic loss to the human deprivation, denying people the chance to escape from misery, repression and violence. We shall return to this point in the final chapter of this book.

RECOMMENDATIONS FOR FURTHER READING

The drivers and results of migration from prehistoric times to the present are presented by Goldin at al. (2010, *Exceptional People: How Migration Shaped Our World and Will Define*

Our Future) and Fisher (2014, *Migration, A World History*). Hatton and Williamson (2008, *Global Migration and the World Economy*) are focussing on the economic aspects of migration.

The history of slavery and slave trade is covered by *The Routledge History of Slavery* (2011), and by the four volumes of the *Cambridge World History of Slavery*; for the Modern Era, see Volumes 3 and 4. The history and the role of indentured labour — the other main type of unfree labour in the Modern Era — in shaping the world economy are discussed by Engerman (1986, *Servants to Slaves to Servants: Contract Labour and European Expansion*).

NOTES

1 A chief example of migration because of religious persecution is the flight of 1.5 million Jews from Russia to the US in the 15 years preceding the First World War.
2 Free land or land obtained against a nominal fee was also made available in the US following the passage of the Homestead Act of 1862, and in Canada after the Dominions Act of 1872.
3 Steamship companies and railway construction companies in the US attracted thousands of emigrants by paying much of the prospective emigrant's fares. At one time a single transatlantic steamship company had no fewer than 3,400 agents arranging passages and advancing money from America to emigrants from the British Isles.
4 In those parts of the Americas, Africa and Australasia where the indigenous population before the European invasion had gained their subsistence from Palaeolithic modes of production, the advance of agriculture by European immigrants accomplished what the Neolithic Revolution had achieved elsewhere — albeit considerably more quickly. Where the indigenous population was settled and engaged in agriculture, as in New Zealand and parts of the Americas, the white settlers effectively stole the land from the former occupants.
5 The increase was from 100,000 to 200,000 per year, of whom 150,000 were carried across the Atlantic and 50,000 went to the Arab world.

CHAPTER 4

Commercial Policy in the Nineteenth Century

A. G. Kenwood, A. L. Lougheed and Michael Graff

A country's commercial policy determines the nature of its trading relations with the rest of the world. Although protectionism was widespread before 1850, and was revived again after 1880, during the intervening period there was a general reduction of restrictions on trade. This movement towards freer trade took place at two levels. At the national level, it involved the economic unification of some nation states which later came to play a prominent part in international economic affairs. At the international level, it involved the widespread adoption of free-trade policies, which reached a peak in the third quarter of the nineteenth century, and which marked the end of the system of privileged trading blocs and restricted commerce characteristic of the growth of the colonial empires of Britain, France, Holland and Spain in the period before 1800. At both levels, the perceived advantages of free trade provided the rationale for the movement towards closer economic and political relations.

In Britain, France and the US economic unification had been completed by the beginning of the nineteenth century. In many other regions, however, economic fragmentation was the rule. This was particularly so in Europe, where, as a result of the Congress of Vienna (1815), Germany was organised as a loose federation of 39 states, each economically independent of the others, and Italy was similarly fragmented into politically and economically independent states. Since economic unification was an indispensable prerequisite for the economic development of these countries, as well as for the establishment of a world economy, the economic integration of Germany through the German Zollverein (1834) and the emergence of a unified Italian state in 1861 were important landmarks in the growth of the international economy.

They were not the only examples of national economic integration in the nineteenth century, however, for they were preceded and followed by similar movements in many other European and overseas countries.

Equally striking was the movement towards free trade that reached its peak in the 1870s. Adopted initially by Britain, the policy of free trade between nations gained wide acceptance on the Continent in the years after 1860. Even so, universal free trade was not attained at this time despite the favourable circumstances, and only Britain and Holland adopted policies of

DOI: 10.4324/9781003382171-7

complete free trade. Nevertheless, for a comparatively brief period in the 1860s and the 1870s the world came close to attaining the ideal trading conditions postulated by classical — and later neoclassical — economic theory.

BRITAIN ADOPTS FREE TRADE

In Britain, the intellectual foundations of the case for free trade were laid down by Adam Smith's *The Wealth of Nations* (1776). The main contribution to international trade theory was the dismissal of the mercantilist doctrine according to which countries should strive to achieve a positive balance of trade. The resulting inflow of gold would fill the coffers of the rulers, enabling them to wage wars or build cathedrals, or both. Apart from the fact that it is impossible for *all* countries to have a positive balance of trade — at least one country must absorb the export surpluses — Smith pointed out that in terms of overall material wellbeing, the only reason to export parts of a country's production is to acquire the means to import goods which are not produced locally. His analysis, however, was not without a weakness. Smith saw trade as beneficial if and only if goods could not be produced or did not grow locally so that they had to be imported, or when there was absolute advantage in producing of some good in a country, which then would export some of its production. It was left to other economists, notably David Ricardo (*Principles of Political Economy and Taxation*, 1817) and John Stuart Mill (*Principles of Political Economy*, 1848) to complete the theoretical system justifying free trade begun by Smith. The theory of international trade developed by the classical economists consists of an explanation of the bases of the gains from trade and of the way in which these gains would be distributed among the trading nations. According to the theory, nations, like individuals, should specialise in the production of those goods which they can make with relatively greatest efficiency, where 'relatively' refers to opportunity cost within a given economy compared to opportunity cost in a potential trading partner's economy. Specialisation according to 'comparative advantage' will then result in increasing total output of the trading countries taken together through a more efficient allocation of resources. In short, the gains from trade consist of the extra output generated by international specialisation. Although classical theory is silent about the distributions of the gains from trade between nations, it is the existence of this extra output which in principle makes it possible for each trading country to benefit from the international exchange of commodities. This conclusion of classical trade theory explains why the doctrine of free trade exerted such a powerful hold over economic thought in the nineteenth century and why it is still widely taught and advocated today.[1]

It should be added that economies of scale resulting from trade are another likely outcome of international division of labour. This would be emphasised 200 years after Adam Smith by New Trade Theory with a seminal paper by Paul Krugman (1979). Here, winners and losers can be identified, as with economies of scale, the first-comers can achieve monopolistic power.

The apostles of free trade in Britain had an early success when the Eden Treaty of 1786 relaxed some of the tariffs on trade between Britain and France. But this trend towards trade liberalisation was reversed during the wars with France (1779–83 and 1793–1802), when the need for war finance led to a substantial rise in the British tariff. These trade barriers were only slowly dismantled, despite demands for greater trade liberalisation by the supporters of free trade. Two problems made the adoption of complete free trade impracticable at this stage in Britain's political and economic development. First, the government lacked an alternative source of revenue to protective duties. More importantly, the full realisation of free trade depended upon the repeal of the Corn Laws which, by placing a duty on imports of wheat, protected British farmers from foreign competition. Such legislation, however, was hardly expected from a government which drew its support largely from the agricultural interest of the landed gentry. Even so, a start was made in the years of expanding trade after 1823, when budget surpluses temporarily overcame the revenue difficulty. However, the crucial moves towards free trade were made in the 1840s. In his budget of 1842, Robert Peel abolished the outstanding export duties on British manufactured goods and reduced the import duties on no fewer than 750 articles in the customs list. To make up the expected loss of revenue, the income tax, which had been levied during the Napoleonic Wars (1803–15) and then abandoned, was reintroduced for three years. The next step was taken in 1845 when, with the renewal of the income tax for another three years, Peel swept away 520 customs duties and abolished the remaining export duties on raw materials.

With the income tax likely to replace customs duties as a source of government revenue, free trade for Britain now depended on the abolition of the Corn Laws. But the agricultural interest in Britain remained staunchly protectionist, and despite various attempts at reform, the Corn Laws remained largely unimpaired at the beginning of the 1840s. Britain's economic circumstances were changing, however. Since the end of the eighteenth century, Britain's growing population had made her increasingly dependent on imported wheat and, by the 1840s, she was feeding 10–15 per cent of her population on foreign wheat. Britain was also changing politically, for the growth of manufacturing industry was shifting the balance of political power from a rural to an urban elite, which demanded 'cheap bread' for their workers, as wages were largely determined by the price of grain. In support of these demands, the Anti-Corn Law League, first set up in 1838, maintained an unrelenting attack on agricultural protection. However, it was not the League but the catastrophic Irish famines of 1845–7 that made the repeal of the Corn Laws inevitable. In the face of mass starvation, restrictions on the free import of food could not be tolerated and the Corn Laws were finally abolished in 1846, although a brief respite from foreign competition was afforded to British farmers by not making the Act fully effective until 1849, when, except for a registration fee of one shilling, corn came into Britain free. In that year another pillar of protectionism was removed with the repeal of the Navigation Act, which threw the carrying trade as well as the import of corn open to all nations.

In the course of the next 25 years Gladstone completed the movement towards free trade in Britain. He carried through further tariff reductions in 1853 and equalised the duties on sugar in 1854. For the next few years, the necessity of financing the Crimean War (1854–6) delayed further liberalisation.

Finally, in 1860, Gladstone introduced the first of the series of budgets which completely freed Britain's foreign trade. In that year, the number of dutiable items was reduced to 48, and most of the remaining food duties were abolished. Only those on sugar and confectionery remained an important source of revenue. All preferential duties admitting imports from British possessions at a favourable rate were also abolished at this time. Subsequent budgets put timber on the free list in 1866, removed the registration fee on corn in 1869 and freed sugar of duties in 1875, but for all practical purposes, it was the budget of 1860 that marked Britain's emergence as a free-trade nation within the international economy.

THE SPREAD OF FREE TRADE

Inspired by Britain's example, the classical economists believed that the rest of the world would subsequently move towards complete free trade to the mutual benefit of all concerned. For a brief period after 1860, this anticipation of universal free trade appeared to be approaching reality, as the policy of trade liberalisation spread to other countries through the negotiation of commercial treaties and tariff agreements. How this trend towards free trade was brought about, and the extent to which foreign trade was liberalised during these years, will be examined shortly. First, however, a brief comment on the economic unification of Germany is called for as an example of the operation of the free-trade principle at the national level.

The Zollverein

Prussia played the major role in the economic and political unification of Germany. Beginning in 1819, a series of treaties was signed with other German states, which culminated in 1831 in the formation of the Prussian Customs Union, the first common market of any significance. Meantime, a similar union between Bavaria and Württemberg in 1827 led eventually to the establishment of the Bavarian Customs Union. Finally, in 1833, the Prussian and Bavarian Customs Unions decided to unite to form the Zollverein.

The Zollverein, which came into existence in 1834, included 18 states with a total population of 23.5 million people. The fundamental principle of the union, as with the previous customs unions, was a common tariff (based in the main on the rates in force in Prussia) against all states outside the Union, and the abolition of all duties on goods passing between the various member states. Complete economic integration was not attempted, and each state kept its own commercial code, patent laws and government monopolies. As for the proceeds of the customs duties, these were divided among the states in proportion to population. After its formation, new states were admitted to membership of the Zollverein so that by 1852 it included all the states that were eventually to constitute the German Reich of 1871.

The Cobden-Chevalier Treaty and Its Consequences

The Cobden-Chevalier Treaty of 1860, which represented the culmination of the trends towards trade liberalisation in both France and Britain during the 1850s, was the first of a series of commercial treaties, which in effect converted the greater part of Europe into low-tariff blocs in the 1860s. In Britain, the only duties on manufactures with any perceptible protective quality in the 1850s were on luxuries like lace, cambric handkerchiefs, carpets, shawls and silk. These protective duties interfered almost exclusively with trade between Britain and France, hence the importance of the Anglo-French treaty. Great Britain agreed to abolish all duties on manufactured goods, to lower the duty on brandy to the colonial level and to reduce the import duties on wines. These concessions were offered to all countries alike but would in fact be most beneficial to France. On the other hand, France made concessions only to Great Britain. These included reductions of the duties on British coal and coke, bar and pig iron, steel, tools and machinery, yarns and manufactured goods of hemp and flax.

A number of important results followed from the treaty of 1860. First, it inaugurated a chain of other tariff treaties negotiated in a free-trade spirit, for France now began to conclude similar commercial treaties with other countries for the reciprocal relaxation of tariffs. These included agreements with Belgium and the Zollverein in 1862; with Italy in 1863; with Switzerland in 1864; with Sweden, Norway, the former Hanse towns in Central and Northern Europe, Spain and Holland in 1865; with Austria in 1866; and with Portugal in 1867. Even Britain, despite her inability to offer tariff concessions once she had completed her free-trade programme, secured treaties with Belgium (1862), Italy (1863) and the Zollverein and Austria (1865).

Second, the countries whose economies were linked by low-tariff treaties in the 1860s soon began to cooperate in other matters necessary for the further expansion of international trade. Many conventions were signed during these years to facilitate international communications — railways, canals, telegraphs, postal arrangements and so on. In 1868 the Rhine — a vitally important commercial link in Europe's West — was declared a freeway for ships of all nations. Other agreements liberalised navigation on the rivers Scheldt, Elbe, Po and Danube. In 1857, Denmark and the principal maritime powers agreed to the abolition of the Sound dues. By establishing the Latin Monetary Union in 1865, France, Italy, Switzerland and Belgium agreed to standardise the value of their coinage, which besides temporarily stabilising the international bimetallic standard, naturally facilitated commerce between these countries.

Last but not least, the Anglo-French treaty of 1860 included a most-favoured-nation clause, which also became a feature of most of the following series of commercial treaties. Under this clause, the reductions granted by Britain in its tariff against specific goods imported from France were extended to the same types of goods imported into Britain from all other countries. The importance of the most-favoured-nation clause lies in the encouragement it gave to trade to expand on a multilateral basis. It prevented discrimination because the reduction of duties to one country meant that they were automatically reduced to all other countries enjoying most-favoured-nation treatment with the country reducing them. By including the clause, the treaty of 1860 left a permanent mark on commercial policy, and the existence of the treaty clause became a potent means of restraining tariff increases during the latter part of the nineteenth century. Its use demonstrated that in this era bilateral trade negotiations were the most effective method of tariff reduction, provided they aimed at multilateral trade.

If the movement towards free trade was, in part, the outcome of the general removal of mercantilist restrictions on economic activity, which became widespread in Europe after 1850, the reasons why individual European countries adopted free trade were varied. In the Netherlands, it was largely the result of the pressure exerted by the major export interests, merchants, ship owners and bankers. In France, on the other hand, it were the industrialists interested in cheap raw material and machinery imports rather than exporters, who were the prime movers, although the French government, which appreciated the political gain arising out of the commercial policy, also provided strong support for it. In Germany, the Prussian landed aristocracy's domination of the agricultural export trade accounts for the adoption of a liberal trading policy by an ultra-conservative ruling class. The Italian case seems to be one in which the free-trade doctrine was imported from abroad by a strong political leadership and imposed on relatively disorganised local political and economic interests.

Outside Europe, the independent states were less affected by free trade. In the US, for example, the trend towards freer trade begun in the 1830s was reversed in 1861.

On the other hand, perhaps the most questionable use to which the most-favoured-nation-clause was put was in opening up trade with the East. Here, trade concessions granted initially to Britain and the US by China and Japan, respectively, were later extended to all other Western countries through the principle of most-favoured-nation treatment. As a consequence of these trade treaties with the Western powers, which among other things stipulated the rates of duties to be levied on their imports and exports, both countries were temporarily deprived of their right to determine tariff policy, a loss of sovereignty that for China continued until 1930.

A particularly revolting episode in this context were the so-called Opium Wars (1839–42 and 1856–60), in the course of which the British East India Company (EIC), facing the old trade deficit of the West with the East, had the way for British opium exports into China forcefully opened. The US and France free rode and joined the British in the profitable business in 1844. In China, this is remembered as the beginning of the 'century of humiliation'.

British Colonial Commercial Policy

The adoption of free trade also brought about a change in British colonial commercial policy. In the 1820s, the British colonial system had been transformed from a monopolist into a preferential system, with British goods receiving preferential treatment in the colonies, and colonial produce gaining tariff preference in the British market. In the next 30 years, however, the preferential system was gradually dismantled, and the colonies were free to follow their own commercial policies. The reactions of the colonial governments to this new situation were varied. The removal of preferential duties on wheat in 1849 and the complete abolition of those on timber in 1860 placed Canada in a difficult position. Unable to withstand European competition in the British market, Canada in 1855 signed a reciprocal trade treaty with the US. Despite its abrogation in 1866, trade between the two countries grew rapidly. In Australia, the British preferences were swept away in 1851, and the colonies were free to pursue their own commercial policies, with New South Wales favouring free trade, Victoria protectionism and the others emphasising the levying of duties purely for revenue purposes. New Zealand's early tariffs were also designed to raise revenue and had little protectionist bias. In South Africa, the abandonment of preferential wine duties in 1860 left the country free to fix its own tariff. In 1866–7, a protective tariff was introduced without any opposition from Britain. In India, throughout the 1860s, there was a general tendency to reduce tariffs, especially on cotton manufactures. Apart from revenue requirements, Indian commercial policy reflected the political pressures on the British government to maintain India as a market for British cotton textiles and to prevent its emergence as an export competitor.

Overall, however, the commercial policies adopted by the colonies were of little immediate economic significance for Britain. As the dominant industrial power in a world moving towards free trade, her colonial monopoly was no longer valuable when a world market lay within her grasp. Only after 1880, when the competition of the newly industrialising nations became acute, was there a revival in the importance of the imperial market.

THE ECONOMIC CONSEQUENCES OF FREE TRADE

Stimulated by its release from restrictions, international trade grew apace. The available, admittedly rough, estimates suggest that the value of international trade doubled between 1830 and 1850, corresponding to an annual growth rate of 3.5 per cent, and at least trebled and may have nearly quadrupled, in the next 30 years, which implies annual growth rates in the range of 3.7–4.5 per cent. In per capita terms, world trade grew at a decennial rate of 2.9 per cent between 1800 and 1913 and reached a peak rate of growth of 4.3 per cent annually in the period 1840–70. The rapid expansion of foreign trade that occurred in the third quarter of the nineteenth century was, of course, not solely due to the advent of free trade, and it is difficult to disentangle its effects on trade from those of the other important influences at work during these years. Even so, free trade played its part, and in two respects at least the commercial policies adopted during these years continued to influence economic events in the protectionist period that followed.

The first of these long-run effects of free trade relates to the use of the most-favoured-nation clause in the commercial treaties and agreements during these years. The unconditional form of the clause, by which each country received without any question of reciprocal concessions whatever tariff reductions were granted by every country with which it had a treaty, was a potent means of restraining tariff increases during the latter part of the nineteenth century. In addition, many important treaties, which ran for long periods, contained provisions binding rated items against an increase. These provisions had the effect of preventing any increase of duties on a large list of imports. Moreover, since every country had many treaties containing such provisions and expiring at different dates, it became difficult for any of them to embark upon wholesale tariff increases. In short, the most-favoured-nation clause placed certain limits on the spread of protectionist policies in the period after 1880. The second long-run effect was more general in its influence, and concerns the part played by free-trade policies in generating the atmosphere of liberalism in which economic affairs were conducted in the nineteenth century. Despite the restrictions increasingly placed on trade in the period after 1880, this atmosphere of liberalism persisted up to 1913.[2] In particular, the setting out of the legal rights of aliens in many of the commercial treaties negotiated during these years enabled trade to expand in a world where the rights of the private traders and of private property were guaranteed by an extensive network of treaties. In short, these treaties created a stable world, in which traders were free to come and go, to organise and invest abroad, almost as freely and safely as in their own countries.

THE RETURN TO PROTECTION

For the classical economist, as for many economists today, universal free trade took on the form of an eternal truth, independent of time or place. Yet, the doctrine was a product of its time, for it became the creed of a nation confident in its own power to defeat all rivals in the drive for markets and forced by natural circumstances to depend on the rest of the world for a large part of its supply of food and raw materials. As we saw earlier, Britain had emerged from the Napoleonic Wars (1803–15) as the dominant power. By 1815, it was the industrially most advanced economy, and its maritime supremacy was to remain undisputed until the end of the century, when Germany challenged Britain in a naval dreadnought arms race. Thus, the rise and eventual acceptance of Ricardian free-trade theory in Britain in the first part of the nineteenth century was a reflection of the unique and highly profitable position of the world's supplier with manufactured goods in exchange for food and raw material that Britain had occupied in the global economy.

But if free trade had an obvious appeal for the industrially successful nation, it was the failure of the doctrine to deal with the problem of economic development and the complicated relations between advanced and backward economies that formed the basis of the criticisms levied against it by classical protectionists such as Hamilton and List. The controversy is by no means settled today.

The Case for Protection

The basis of the protectionist argument is to be found in Hamilton's famous *Report on Manufactures* (1791), which remains one of the most elaborate general arguments for protection ever written. In his report to the American Congress, Hamilton stressed both the desirability of national self-sufficiency in manufacturing, and the importance of a sizeable non-agricultural consuming class for a stable and prosperous agriculture. Manufacturing industry, he argued, should be encouraged to grow by a system of bounties and subsidies, and behind a protective tariff, which would free domestic manufacturers from foreign competition, and thus enable them to expand the scale of their operations, thereby achieving economies of scale comparable to those enjoyed by foreign competitors. In this way the 'infant industries' would quickly attain maturity and would then be able to produce at least as cheaply as foreign manufacturers.

Strongly influenced by Hamilton, German economist Friedrich List (1841) in *Das nationale System der politischen Oekonomie* (*The National System of Political Economy*) was highly critical of the classical theory of free trade. In particular, he reproached the British economists with having purposely ignored the differences in economic strength between the nations which they had invited to trade freely with one another on an equal footing. A country's commercial policy, List argued, was related to its level of economic development and it was therefore wrong to advocate one policy as being universally applicable. He concluded that while free trade is beneficial during the early and later (commercial-industrial) stages of development, the transition from an agricultural to an industrial society could be achieved only through a policy of protection. List therefore demanded an 'educational' tariff on the products of infant industries designed to protect them for a limited period from the competition of foreign industries not naturally more efficient but simply more advanced on the learning curve.

Protection in the US

While the debate on protection was going on in the US in the 1790s, the wars between France and England, by blocking the accustomed channels of trade and production, provided a practical illustration of the 'benefits of protection'. The wartime shortages gave an enormous stimulus to those branches of American industry, such as cotton, wool and iron manufactures, whose products had previously been imported. But with the end of the war in Europe came the threat of renewed British competition and a demand for protection from the newly expanded industries. The Tariff Act of 1816 provided the required protection, and for the next 20 years the US followed a continuous policy of protection, moderate at first, but becoming strongly protective after 1824. Protectionist pressures moderated in the 1830s, after the passing of the Compromise Tariff Act of 1833, which provided for a gradual and steady reduction of duties in the years up to 1842, and although tariffs were raised for a while after 1842, liberalisation was resumed in the Tariff Act of 1846 and reinforced by that of 1857. Consequently, for a few years, the US came as near to free trade as it had been since 1816.

Although the trend towards freer trade was reversed in 1861, when the Morrill Act restored the moderately protective tariff levels of 1846, it was the substantial rise in duties needed to pay for the Civil War (1861–5), which laid the foundation of the future American system of protection. During these years the average rate on dutiable commodities rose to 37 per cent in 1862 and to 47 per cent in 1864. After the war, there was a call for tariff reform, but the war tariff remained the basis of the American protective system until the passage of the Act of 1883, when the general tariff level was lowered some 5 per cent. Thereafter the tariff level was pushed up twice in rapid succession. In 1890 the McKinley Act raised the average level of tariffs to 50 per cent. High duties were placed on textiles, iron, steel, glass and tin plate, and to appease the farmers, who were facing increased competition from Canadian imports, tariffs were imposed on a number of agricultural products. The Democrats brought about a downward revision of the tariff in 1894, lowering the average level to 40 per cent, but the Republicans speedily reversed the trend with the Dingley Tariff (1897), which not only restored the McKinley rates, but also raised the average level even higher, to 57 per cent. No further change of any significance took place in the American tariff until 1913, when a Democratic administration passed the Underwood-Simmons Tariff Act, which eliminated specific duties, added over 100 items, including sugar and wool, to the free list, reduced tariffs on nearly 1,000 classifications and increased them on a few others, mostly chemicals. The result of these changes was to reduce the rates of duties on dutiable imports to a remarkably low average of 16 per cent. However, this trend towards free trade in the US had little opportunity to be tested, for within a year war had broken out in Europe. The experiment was not to be repeated until after the Second World War.

Protection in Europe

In Europe, economic and political developments combined to bring about a return to protection after 1880. Economically, it was the desire for industrial development and the competition engendered by successful industrialisation that was responsible for the growing demand for protection. Backing up the economic case for protection was the revival of nationalism in the late nineteenth century, associated with the emergence of new nation states such as Germany and Italy. In addition to embarrassing foreign industrial competition, increasing tariffs provided the larger revenues needed to meet the rising expenditures on armaments caused by the growing military rivalry between the states of Europe, as well as expenditures on education, public health and social services, which were in part manifestations of the nationalist feeling. While nationalism and protectionism are not inevitably associated with one another, in nationalism we do have a force providing at least a predisposition towards protection.[3] Taken together, nationalism and the lag in industrialisation strongly pushed toward protection.

What actually started the swing to protectionism in Europe, however, was neither of these broad economic and political factors, but two specific economic developments of the 1870s. One was the large inflow of cheap grain into Europe from the US and Russia; the other was the depression of 1873–9, the longest and deepest period of stagnant trade the modern world had yet experienced. Farmers and industrialists alike clamoured for relief, and the demands of this coalition of young industry and injured agriculture gave the initial stimulus to protection. Once started, this swing to protectionism was supported and maintained by the deeper and darker forces of nationalism. Over time, pressure groups and vested interests grew in political power and were often able to influence parliaments into granting greater protection to further their own self-interests. Protection also tended to spread across the board, as concessions to one group of industries made it difficult for governments to refuse similar privileges to others. Furthermore, from the 1890s, rate setting tended to become competitive. This tendency arose out of the two-tiered framework yielded by the commercial treaty system developed during these years. Under this treaty system, high general duties were levied on imports from non-treaty countries, and lower rates were applied to dutiable commodities from countries with which treaties had been concluded. As these treaties were renegotiated periodically, immediately before renegotiation an extensive upward revision of the general (or maximum) tariff of each treaty country was legislated to ensure that negotiations would not result in a 'treaty' (or minimum) tariff detrimental to the country's industries. Such a procedure tended to produce higher all-round protection and, in some cases, tariff warfare, detrimental to all concerned. Taken together these developments produced a swing to protection within Europe that became more pronounced as 1913 approached. Over the whole period 1880–1913, only Britain, Holland and Denmark steadfastly adhered to free trade.

Stimulated by the depressed conditions in industry, the increased competition from imported grain and the financial needs of the imperial government, protectionist sentiments gained ground in Germany in the late 1870s. In 1879, moderate tariff protection was extended to both agriculture and manufactures. Raw material imports, however, remained duty-free. Two major upward revisions of duties on grain followed in 1885 and 1888, but the next general revision of the tariff did not come until 1902. By then, the rate increases in the US, France and Russia, together with the lapse of various treaties in which German duties were fixed by agreement, furnished an additional motive and a suitable opportunity for more protection. The new general tariff introduced much higher rates, particularly on finished manufactures, and was more detailed and specialised than the 1879 tariff. The duties on semi-manufactures were kept low, and raw materials continued to be admitted duty-free. A higher level of protection for agriculture was also provided, with increased duties on grain and livestock. The new system remained in being until it was swept away by the outbreak of war in 1914.

Many other countries followed Germany's example. Italy commenced the 1870s with a moderate tariff, but new legislation in 1878 substantially increased protection for manufacturing industry. A year later protection was extended to agriculture. In 1887, rates were raised to a high level and these remained in effect until after the war. The Swiss did not adopt a general tariff until 1884, when duties were imposed which remained only moderately high despite an upward revision in 1891. In 1906, however, new legislation provided high duties on foodstuffs and considerable increases in rates on manufactures. On the other hand, Russia reverted to protection as early as 1868, when manufactured imports were subjected to heavy duties in an effort to promote domestic industrialisation. This Act was not superseded until 1891, but in the interim several all-round increases in duties occurred. The 1891 tariff legislation introduced a maximum-minimum rate structure for purposes of tariff bargaining and placed duties on raw materials and semi-manufactures. The duties on coal, steel, machinery and chemicals were raised so high that import of these goods practically ceased. Further increases of duties in 1893 and in the early 1900s maintained Russia's position as the most highly protected country in the world.

The demands made by French industrialists for protection were hampered by the persistence of a strong free-trade sentiment and by the existence of long-term commercial treaties which effectively pegged the French tariff at a low level. But in the 1880s, growing dissatisfaction in agriculture brought the farmers into line with the industrial advocates of higher tariffs, and in 1890 the combined protectionist forces gained political power. The Meline Tariff of 1892 meant higher duties all round, including an average increase of 25 per cent on duties on agricultural products, and some substantial increases of rates on manufactures. A two-tier system of maximum and minimum rates was introduced for treaty purposes, with the minimum rates themselves amply protective. A general revision of the new tariff structure did not occur until 1910, and then it was aimed primarily at extending the coverage to the many new products, such as chemicals and electrical and rubber goods, that had been developed in the intervening years. The Tariff Act of 1910 predominantly favoured manufacturing industry, and only a few increases were granted on agricultural products. There were few reductions, and raw materials generally were exempted from duties.[4]

THE ECONOMIC CONSEQUENCES OF PROTECTION

Given the multitude of influences at work in the international economy during these years, the effect of the return to protection on the character and the volume of foreign trade after 1880 is not easily determined. However, taking into account the many strong 'trade-creating' forces at work in these years, the moderate level of the protective tariff in some countries, and the existence of commercial treaties that lowered them in many others, the conclusion that tariffs probably did not seriously hinder the growth of international trade in the period before 1914 seems a reasonable one. Indeed, world trade grew steadily between 1870 and 1914, averaging some 3.4 per cent annually over the entire period, and was growing faster than total world production, which averaged 2.1 per cent per annum. Hence, the international division of labour intensified.

If world trade did not suffer unduly from the return to protection, the trade of individual countries may well have done so. Britain's export trade, in particular, could be expected to suffer from the protective tariffs imposed by the newly industrialising nations. Here, woollen exports were the biggest losers, since their best markets were situated in the US and Europe, where competition and protection were most severe, and alternative markets were mostly lacking. In contrast, the cotton textile industry overcame its difficulties by exporting finer-quality cottons to protected markets and by expanding the sales of cheaper cottons to the newly developing countries, where the protected cotton industries of Europe and America were rarely able to compete. Apart from the possibility of switching exports to unprotected markets, there are other reasons for not exaggerating the impact protection had on the overall level of British exports. Tariffs remained for the most part moderate, and Britain could always depend on the most-favoured-nation clause embodied in the commercial treaties of the day to shield her from the worst excesses of her competitors. Moreover, where a long-run decline in British exports did occur, it was more often because of a loss of competitiveness than because of protection. Thus, tariffs may have initially lost Britain markets for iron and steel manufactures in the US and Germany, but later, when German and American producers surpassed the British in efficiency and competitiveness, they became unnecessary to keep British exporters out of these markets. Yet the changes in the composition of British exports due to the tariff were not without their problems for the future, for the shift was towards products which were less profitable and prospectively less capable of expansion. Exports of semi-manufactures grew in importance relative to exports of finished goods, and coal exports expanded rapidly after 1880. The forced specialisation on quality products and semi-manufactured goods, like yarn and pig iron, meant production to satisfy a more volatile demand, thus introducing a greater degree of instability in the British export sector than may formerly have existed. Moreover, the profits of further fabrication, which had previously accrued to Britain, were now passing to those countries which used British semi-manufactures to turn them into finished products. However, the shift into new export lines was made without any great difficulty, and British exports continued to grow.

Although agricultural products became more highly protected as time passed, for much of the period between 1880 and 1914, raw materials and foodstuffs, with the exception of grain into continental Europe, were comparatively free from restrictions, and consequently the 'regions of recent settlement' were not impeded in their growth by prohibitive tariffs. In any case, there was always the British market — the largest in Europe into which primary producing countries enjoyed freedom of entry for their exports, for Britain's response to the decline in the world price of wheat after 1880 was to complete the liquidation of agriculture as an economic sector of any importance. France, Germany and Italy, as we have seen, responded to the new situation by imposing tariffs in an attempt to maintain the relative price of wheat and to protect grain producers. Denmark, however, did not impose a tariff on wheat. Instead, it converted from the growing of grain to animal husbandry and specialisation in dairy production. In carrying out this economic transformation, proximity to expanding industrial markets for dairy products in Britain and Germany was particularly helpful.

As for manufacturing industry, there is no doubt that the raising of tariff barriers in the US, Germany and elsewhere initially contributed to its growth in these countries. But by the 1890s the 'infant industry' argument in favour of manufacturing protection was becoming somewhat threadbare, and the case for protection was being based on a variety of other arguments, such as self-sufficiency, maintaining employment levels, industrial diversification, protection of living standards and wage levels and so on.

Protection does appear to have had some influence on the structure of industry, however. In both the US and Germany, big industrial concerns came to dominate manufacturing, and the resulting concentration of economic power contrasted sharply with the diffusion of economic power characteristic of the early stages of the British industrial revolution. As the amount of capital tied up in a particular venture increased, management became less willing to allow the success of the business to be decided by the uncontrolled operation of market forces. Through trusts, holding companies and business combinations of various kinds, new large business enterprises endeavoured to control the competitive process in an attempt to fix prices and maintain or increase the return on their investment. Protected by tariffs, producers in Germany and the US were able to eliminate domestic competition and create monopolistic or oligopolistic markets. In free-trade Britain, on the other hand, the threat of foreign competition was ever present and attempts at the monopolistic concentration of production were therefore less likely to succeed.

Monopolistic activities also spilled over to the world economy in the form of international cartels. At the beginning of the twentieth century, it was estimated that at least 40 of these cartels were in existence, and in 1912 the figure was put at 100. They covered industries such as shipping, armaments, steel rails, electric bulbs, aluminium, calcium carbide, plate glass, tobacco, enamelware and bottles. The fact that they appeared in industries dominated by a few large firms suggests that protection, since it played some part in creating national monopolies, also contributed indirectly to creating conditions favourable to the international restriction of competition. Moreover, irrespective of the causes of the growth of these international cartels, their fundamental objectives — the control over prices, markets, supply and technological change — are deterrents to specialisation and trade, not only in products directly under their control, but also in other products manufactured in part from cartelised material. To what extent these cartels did restrict world trade in the period before 1914 is difficult to assess. Moreover, the fact that Britain was not a member of most international cartels greatly limited their economic power, because the exercise of their monopoly powers was always subject to the threat of competition from Britain.

An economic 'by-product' of protection is that tariff barriers may stimulate direct foreign investment in protectionist countries. Since the aim of protection is to exclude foreign products from the domestic market of the country imposing the tariff, foreign firms can overcome these trade barriers by setting up branch factories in the markets concerned.[5] Although not widespread before 1914, there were occasions when this kind of direct investment was undertaken. For example, the American tariff of 1883 hit certain cheaper cotton exports from Britain severely. As a result, several Lancashire cotton firms set up branches in the US. Part of the American direct investment in Canada during the pre-1913 period was also due to the existence of the Canadian tariff. While these examples could be multiplied, this type of investment remained comparatively rare before 1913, and direct investment, motivated partly by protection, was not undertaken on a large scale until after the First World War.

RECOMMENDATIONS FOR FURTHER READING

The two contributions from the eighteenth and nineteenth centuries discussed in the text represent important milestones in the history of economic thought and are still worth consulting for sceptical attitudes regarding free trade, in particular for backward economies: Hamilton (1791, *Report on Manufactures*) and List (1841, *Das nationale System der politischen Oekonomie*; 1909, *The National System of Political Economy*).

Economic historian Alexander Gerschenkron (1962, *Economic Backwardness in Historical Perspective*) confirmed that the successful 'latecomers' of the Industrial Revolution in the nineteenth century in fact resorted to 'infant industry' or 'educational' tariffs and pursued an activist development policy, as suggested by Hamilton and List.

Kindleberger (1975, *The Rise of Free Trade in Western Europe, 1820 to 1875*) gives a concise account of the rise of free trade before the Industrial Revolution took hold in continental Europe.

Keynes (1920, *The Economic Consequences of the Peace*) is still impressive today as an essay contrasting the era of liberal movement of goods and people and the world-open mindset of the elites in the late nineteenth century with the horrors brought about by nationalism in the First World War (1914–18) and the resulting hostile and protectionist attitudes and politics of the post-war years.

NOTES

1 In modern economist parlance: if there are overall gains from trade, the set of Pareto-superior distributions of output between countries compared to autarky is not empty. This, of course, is no guarantee that the after-trade allocation will be an element of this set, unless one claims that no country would engage in trade in the first place if this led to a Pareto-inferior outcome.
2 This atmosphere's impression on the European elites is masterfully — and melancholically — described by Keynes (1920, Chapter 1).
3 In 2025, the world just witnessed the spectacular increases of tariffs imposed by US President Trump, which are hard to understand on a purely economic basis — to some degree, they appear to be an act of patriotic grandstanding, attempting to force other countries into political obedience. For more on this, see Chapter 23 of this book.
4 Inter-country comparisons of tariff severity are difficult to make, but one estimate for the early years of this century (Bastable, 1923, p. 106) puts the average tariff in Russia at 28 per cent, in the US at 18.5 per cent, in France and Germany at 9.8 per cent and in Austria at 7.5 per cent.
5 This is likely to be one of the motivations of the enormous tariffs announced by US President Trump in April 2025 to be justifiable with conventional economic reasoning; see Chapter 23 of this book.

CHAPTER 5

Foreign Trade in the Nineteenth Century

A. G. Kenwood, A. L. Lougheed and Michael Graff

The discussion of foreign trade in this chapter will be limited to commodity trade, since long-term data on the international flows of services (freight earnings, insurance and banking, tourism, etc.) are scarce. An analysis of the available services data suggests, however, that earnings on services tended to rise proportionately to commodity trade. Moreover, before 1914, the average proportion of services to commodity tended was, for all except the smallest of countries, limited to between one-tenth and one-sixth. Even so, it should be kept in mind that, for some countries, for example, Britain, services income played an important role in covering deficits on commodity trade, and that for others an export surplus on commodity trade could quickly disappear once payments for services are taken into account.

THE GROWTH OF WORLD TRADE UP TO 1913

Two broad conclusions are suggested by the trends in the foreign trade statistics available for the period 1800–1913. First, that the period was characterised by high rates of growth in foreign trade, and second, that world trade grew at much higher rates than world output during these years. For long sub-periods, of 30 years or more, total foreign trade grew at rates ranging from 29 to 64 per cent per decade (equivalent to annual average compound growth rates from 2.5 to 5 per cent), and, on a per capita basis, from 23 to 53 per cent per decade (from 2.1 to 4.3 per cent annually). The highest decadal growth rates, whether measured in total or per capita terms, were registered in the sub-period 1840–70, with growth rates tending to rise throughout earlier decades and to decline thereafter. At the same time, world output per head appears to have grown at an average rate of 7.3 per cent per decade (0.7 per cent annually) from 1800 to 1913, whereas per capita world trade growth averaged 33 per cent per decade (2.9 per cent annually) over the same period.

The net result of these changes was a marked rise in the proportion of world trade to world output. By 1913, the volume of foreign trade per capita had grown to over 25 times

DOI: 10.4324/9781003382171-8

what it had been in 1800, whereas world output per head had grown only 2.2 times over the same period. This means that during the period 1800–1913, the world's 'foreign trade proportion', i.e. the ratio of world trade to world output, rose to over 11 times (25/2.2) its initial level. Accordingly, as the available statistics suggest, world's foreign trade proportion rose from only 3 per cent in 1800 to about 33 per cent in 1913.

What brought about this marked rise in the world foreign trade proportion? Partly responsible for the faster rate of growth of trade between countries than growth of output within them, was the introduction of more countries into the network of world trade during the nineteenth century. More important was the growing propensity to trade displayed by countries during these years, particularly the more 'developed' (richer) economies of the world, due to the technical and institutional innovations, which made the transport of goods across long distances cheaper, faster and easier.

This marked rise in foreign trade proportions was characteristic of groups of countries and of countries taken individually. These proportions rose markedly in both the developed (richer) and 'underdeveloped' (poorer)[1] parts of the world, with the relative rise in the foreign trade proportion greater for the latter than for the former group of countries, which is not surprising seeing that many of these countries were integrated into the world trading network for the first time during the nineteenth century.[2] Looking at individual countries, the foreign trade proportions of the industrial European countries and Japan rose substantially between 1800 and 1913, while they declined slightly for the younger overseas countries, such as the US and Australia, which already had high foreign trade proportions at the beginning of our period. These 'new' regions could hardly be expected to become even more dependent on foreign trade, once their domestic economies became more broadly based. This was particularly so for the US, with its abundant natural resources while in both Australia and America transport developments seem to have encouraged higher rates of growth of domestic output than of foreign trade. In Europe, on the other hand, limited raw material supplies and a rapidly growing population appear to have increased the continent's dependence on foreign trade throughout the century, so that the foreign trade proportions of European countries grew.

TABLE 5.1 Regional distribution of total world trade, 1876–1913 (per cent)

Region	1876–80			1913		
	Exports	Imports	Total trade	Exports	Imports	Total trade
Europe[a]	64.2	69.6	66.9	58.9	65.1	62.0
North America	11.7	7.4	9.5	14.8	11.5	13.2
Latin America[b]	6.2	4.6	5.4	8.3	7.0	7.6
Asia	12.4	13.4	12.9	11.8	10.4	11.1
Africa	2.2	1.5	1.9	3.7	3.6	3.7
Oceania	3.3	3.5	3.4	2.5	2.4	2.4
World	100.0	100.0	100.0	100.0	100.0	100.0

Source: Lamartine Yates (1959, p. 32f., Tables 6 and 7).

Notes: [a] Including Russia; [b] Central and South America, including all colonial territories in the Western hemisphere.

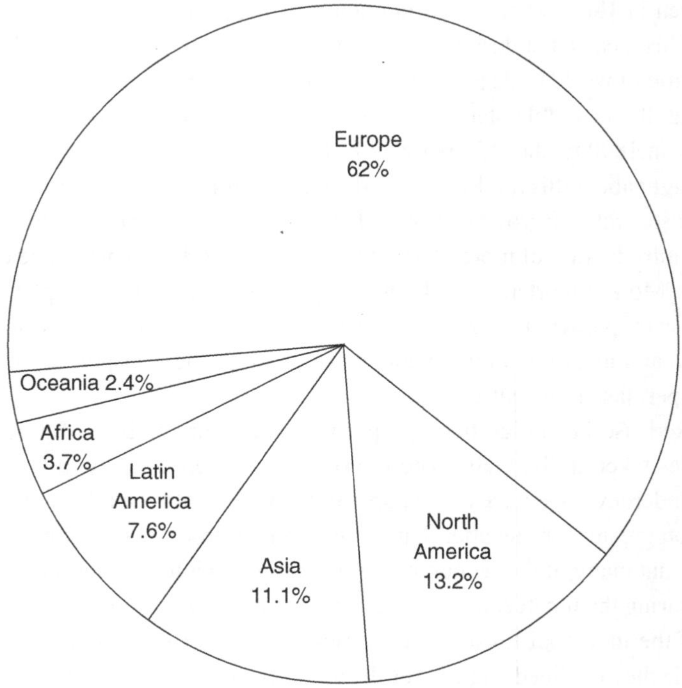

FIGURE 5.1 Regional distribution of total world trade, 1913

Source: As for Table 5.1; Source: Lamartine Yates (1959, p. 32f., Tables 6 and 7).

The distribution of world trade by geographic region over the period 1876–1913 is shown in Table 5.1, while Figure 5.1 illustrates the shares in 1913. Europe dominated world trade in the nineteenth century, when it consisted largely of intra-European trade and Europe's trade with overseas areas, especially those settled by Europeans. This predominance was maintained throughout the period up to 1913, despite the continuous growth of the North American share of world trade, and the tendency for the European and particularly for the UK's shares to fall. In 1913, Europe (including Russia) took some 65 per cent of the world's imports and accounted for 59 per cent of its exports, whereas the North American shares were 12 and 15 per cent, respectively.

THE DIRECTION OF WORLD TRADE UP TO 1913

Because of the spread of industrialisation and the emergence of new centres of primary production overseas, significant changes in the pattern of trade between countries and between regions occurred. For European countries other than Britain, dependence on Europe for imports and for export markets was initially very marked, with the degree of dependence tending to grow as the size of the country concerned diminished. After 1870, however, as the demand for foodstuffs and raw materials drawn from overseas suppliers rose in response to industrial development and population growth, there was some decline in the degree of dependence of European countries on the continental market. At the same time, there were associated changes in the demand for primary products which had important consequences for the different trading countries. Thus, from the 1820s to the mid-1890s, purchases of tropical products grew more slowly than imports of foodstuffs and raw materials coming from temperate regions. Thereafter, however, imports of tropical products from Latin America, Asia and Africa rose significantly.

The tendency for European countries, including Britain, to draw their imports increasingly from continents other than Europe as the nineteenth century proceeded, reflected the heavy dependence of overseas countries on Europe as a market for their exports. The US were no exception. By the 1880s, over four-fifths of its exports were going to Europe; and despite a rapid expansion of American exports to Canada, Latin America and Asia after 1895, the European share was still 60 per cent in 1913. Moreover, two-thirds of US imports came from Europe in the 1850s, and although Europe's share declined thereafter, it remained around 50 per cent of the total after the 1870s. At the same time, significant changes in the relative importance of the different European countries supplying the American market took place. Britain's share of total imports fell from a peak of 46 per cent in the early 1850s to 17 per cent in the years 1911–13. On the other hand, the share of imports coming from continental European countries, and especially Germany, continued to grow throughout the period and accounted for one-third of the total by 1913.

Two-thirds of Latin America's trade was with Europe, with Britain, Germany, France and Spain by far the most important of the countries concerned. If the US is included, the share rises to 90 per cent in the years 1901–5. The trade of Africa and Oceania was even more dependent on the European market than that of Latin America, with Britain in particular a major source of exports to and by far the biggest importer of merchandise from these two continents. Canadian trade, on the other hand, was dominated by Britain and the US. Whereas Britain remained the more important market for Canadian exports throughout the century up to 1913, over the years Canadian imports from the US grew at the expense of those from Britain until, late in the nineteenth century, she lost first place in the Canadian market to the US.

India, China and Britain constituted a tightly knit trading bloc in Asia in the period before 1880. After the 1870s, however, the picture begins to change. The closing down of the opium trade in the 1880s, the rise of Japan as the first Asian industrial power and the economic penetration of China by European powers other than Britain were developments that significantly altered the pattern of international trade in the Far East. As Japan industrialised, the structure of its foreign trade was completely reversed, from one in which raw materials were exported and finished manufactures imported to one in which manufactures were exported and raw materials imported. The direction of Japan's foreign trade changed in line with these developments. Asia replaced Europe and the US as the main source of Japanese imports, supplying almost one-half of these needs by 1913. By that date, Asia had also become Japan's leading regional export market.

Despite the growing industrial importance of the US and Japan in the late nineteenth century, the direction of world trade in the period before 1913 was dominated by Europe's ever-growing demand for foodstuffs and raw materials. Before the First World War, Europe absorbed more than 80 per cent of the exports of Belgium, Holland, Argentina, South Africa and New Zealand; 75–80 per cent of those of Germany and Australia; over 60 per cent of those of France, Italy and the US; and more than half of Canada's and India's. The foreign trade of Britain was distributed almost equally among the Empire, continental Europe and the rest of the world. Europe's share in the imports of these and other countries was somewhat less than its share in their exports. Considering both imports and exports, Britain carried on an extensive trade with all parts of the world; Canada belonged to the American economic community; China and Japan had the strongest commercial ties with Asia; and almost all other nations gravitated towards European markets.

The extent to which Europe dominated world trade before the First World War is seen even more clearly if we consider the percentage distribution of the flow of merchandise trade in 1913. Two-fifths of this trade represented intra-European exchange, slightly more than one-fifth of Europe's imports from non-European countries, and 15 per cent exports from Europe to non-European countries. Thus, trade among non-European countries accounted for less than one-quarter of the world trade in merchandise in 1913.[3]

THE COMPOSITION OF WORLD TRADE UP TO 1913

Data on the composition of world commodity trade distinguishing primary products from manufactured articles go back to the late 1870s. Interestingly, the proportion of primary products to total trade remained remarkably constant until the First World War.[4] This stability was maintained despite the spread of industrialisation and the consequent decline in the relative share of primary production in total output, and despite significant changes in the composition of the export trade in primary products. Since primary products are a large part of the exports of poor countries, and since many such economies were newly integrated into the pattern of world trade with the passing of the nineteenth century, the stability in the share of primary products in world trade can to some degree be explained by these developments, counteracting the growth of trade in manufactures between industrialising countries. Further explanation must be sought in the details of the foreign trade of the regions and countries concerned.

Table 5.2 and Figure 5.2 show the nature of the changes in the regional distribution of trade in primary products and manufactures during the period 1876–1913. In these years, the volume of the export trade in primary products more than trebled. With the exception of 'Other Europe', all regions shared in the expansion, with the growth outside Europe and North America being especially strong between 1895 and 1913. The North American share in this trade grew only slightly, whereas Europe, often overlooked as an exporter of primary products, saw its share rise to almost one-half of the world total around 1900, and then drop back to the level of the late 1870s by 1913. Complementing the export of primary products was the import trade in manufactures. The volume of this trade almost trebled between 1876–80 and 1913, with imports into North America more than quadrupling in volume during these years, and those of continental Europe more than doubling between 1896–1900 and 1913. With the import trade in manufactures growing so strongly in Europe and North America, the share of the poorer countries in this trade fell in the years up to 1913.

Looking at the situation in reverse and concentrating on those regions which predominantly exported manufactures and imported primary products, we find that the most striking features of the world export trade in manufactures were the growth of the North American share and the decline in the UK's share over the whole of the period 1876–80 to 1913. Continental Europe's share remained stable, and Japan accounts for the high Asian proportion. The rest of the world, consisting mainly of the poor countries, was a virtual non-starter in manufacturing production and export by 1913. Turning to the import trade in primary products, the UK's share fell heavily after 1876–80, whereas because of rapid industrialisation and rising real incomes, the shares of North America and continental Europe rose. The growing imports of primary products into the rest of the world after 1896 consisted primarily of food and raw materials for Japan.

Table 5.3 and Figure 5.3, which give the respective shares of primary products and manufactures in total trade, reveal certain other important features in the composition of world trade before 1913.

First, and most obviously, the richer countries chiefly exported manufactures and imported primary products, whereas the trade pattern was reversed for the poor countries, which mainly exported primary products and imported manufactured goods. Moreover, among the rich countries we find that primary products are a much larger element in the

TABLE 5.2A Trade in primary products: regional shares, 1876–1913 (per cent)

Region	1876–80		1896–1900		1913	
	Imports	Exports	Imports	Exports	Imports	Exports
UK and Ireland	29.7	3.1	25.8	3.9	19.0	6.2
Northwest Europe[a]	39.3	22.6	45.0	27.6	43.1	25.2
Other Europe	11.2	20.2	10.4	18.1	12.3	14.7
US and Canada	7.2	16.1	8.5	18.7	11.3	17.3
Rest of world	12.6	38.0	10.3	31.7	14.3	36.6
World	100.0	100.0	100.0	100.0	100.0	100.0

TABLE 5.2B Trade in manufactures: regional shares, 1876–1913 (per cent)

Region	1876–80		1896–1900		1913	
	Imports	Exports	Imports	Exports	Imports	Exports
UK and Ireland	9.1	37.8	10.4	31.5	8.2	25.3
Northwest Europe[a]	18.1	47.1	20.3	45.8	24.4	47.9
Other Europe	13.3	9.2	12.2	10.3	15.4	8.3
US and Canada	7.7	4.4	9.6	7.4	12.1	10.6
Rest of world	51.8	1.5	47.5	5.0	39.9	7.9
World	100.0	100.0	100.0	100.0	100.0	100.0

Source: Lamartine Yates (1959, pp. 47–51, Tables 19, 21, 23 and 25).

Notes: [a] Includes Finland, Sweden, Norway, Denmark, Germany, Belgium, the Netherlands, Switzerland and Austria.

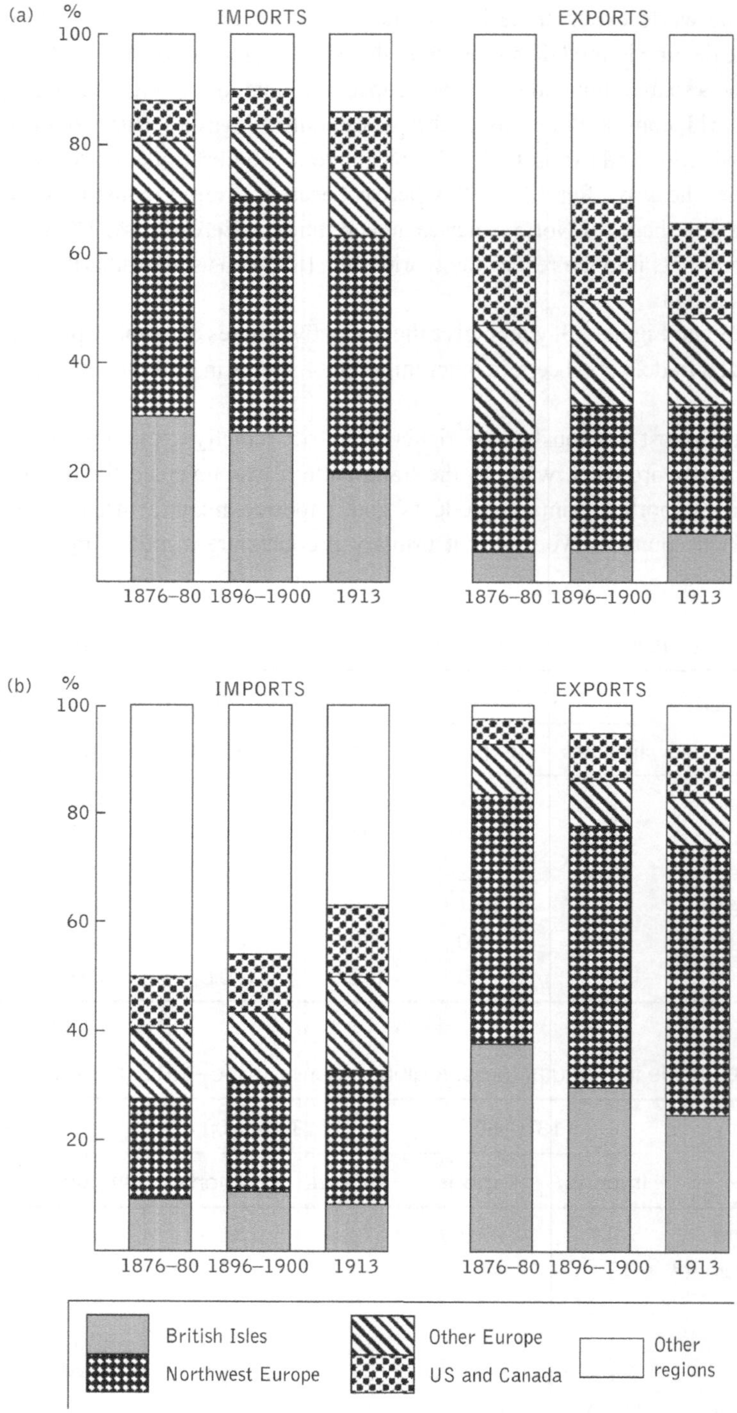

FIGURE 5.2 (a) Regional shares of world trade, 1876–1913, trade in primary products. (b) Regional shares of world trade, 1876–1913, trade in manufactures

Source: As for Table 5.2; Source: Lamartine Yates (1959, pp. 47–51, Tables 19, 21, 23 and 25).

TABLE 5.3 Shares of primary products and manufactures in total trade of each region, 1876–1913 (per cent)

Region	1876–80		1896–1900		1913	
	Primary products	Manufactures	Primary products	Manufactures	Primary products	Manufactures
Exports						
UK and Ireland	11.9	88.1	17.2	82.8	30.3	69.7
Northwest Europe	43.8	56.2	50.5	49.5	48.0	52.0
Other Europe	78.1	21.9	74.9	25.1	75.6	24.4
US and Canada	85.7	14.3	81.0	19.0	74.1	25.9
Poor countries and rest of world	97.6	2.4	91.6	8.4	89.1	10.9
World	61.9	38.1	62.8	37.2	61.8	38.2
Imports						
UK and Ireland	85.8	14.2	82.6	17.4	81.2	18.8
Northwest Europe	60.9	39.1	62.0	38.0	59.9	40.1
US and Canada	63.5	36.5	63.0	37.0	63.4	36.6
Poor countries and rest of world	30.9	69.1	29.2	70.8	40.2	59.8
World	64.9	35.1	65.6	34.3	65.0	35.0

Source: Kuznets (1967, p. 38, Table 8A); see also Lamartine Yates (1959, p. 55, Table 28).

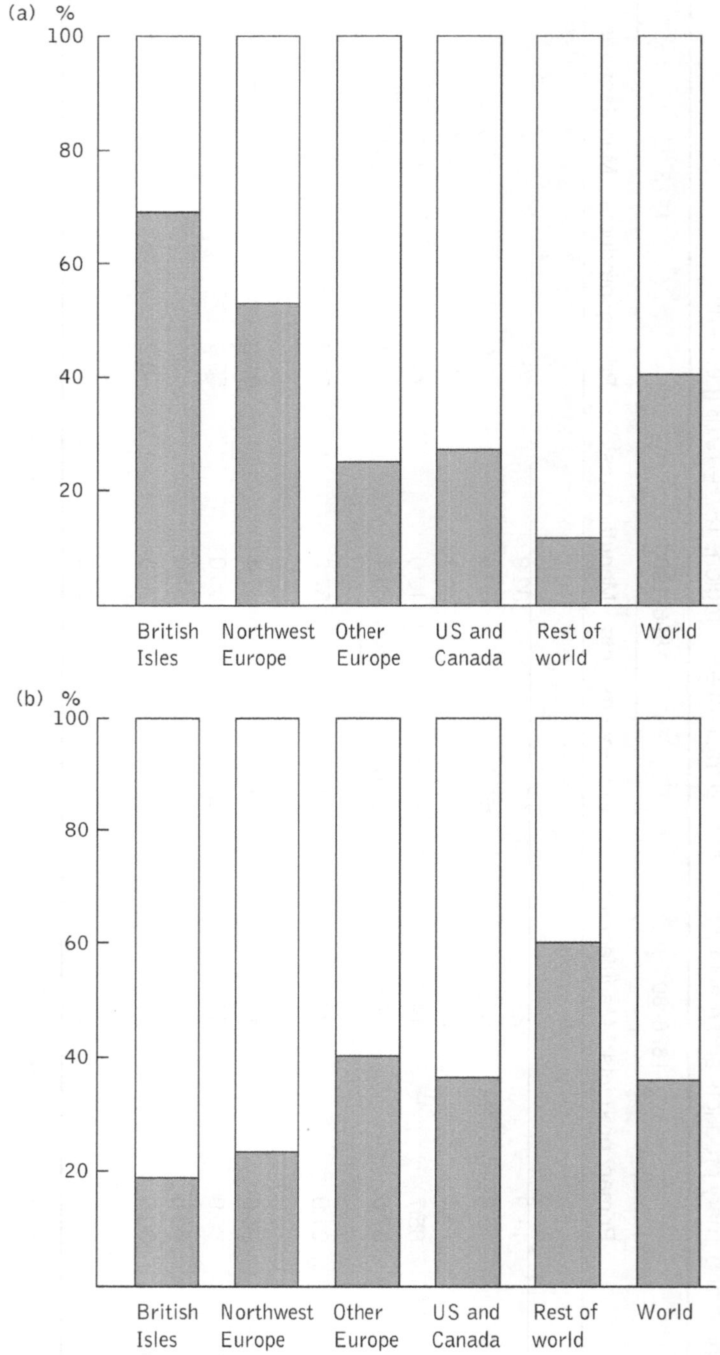

FIGURE 5.3 (a) Shares of primary products and manufactures in total trade of each region, 1913, exports. (b) Shares of primary products and manufactures in total trade of each region, 1913, imports

Source: As for Table 5.3; Source: Kuznets (1967, p. 38, Table 8A); see also Lamartine Yates (1959, p. 55, Table 28).

Note: The shaded area represents manufactures.

exports of the US and Canada, on the one hand, than of the UK and Northwest Europe, on the other. Similar differences are evident in the structure of imports, with primary products a smaller and manufactures a larger element in the import trade of the former than of the latter. Perhaps the most interesting findings of Table 5.3, however, are the trends in the structure of the trade in primary products.

Taking the export trade first, we notice that the shares of primary products rose for the UK and Northwest Europe, and declined for all other regions, both rich and poor. The trends in the structure of the import trade in primary products show declining shares for the UK and Northwest Europe, a stable share for the US and Canada and a fluctuating, if declining, share for Other Europe. It is, however, the trend in the structure of imports of the poor countries that differs significantly from those of rich countries. In the poor regions, imports shifted towards, not away from, primary products; the share of the latter rising from 31 per cent in 1876–80 to 40 per cent in 1913.

Within the manufactures component for the rich countries, a decline in the share of textile manufactures occurred along with a rise in the share of metal manufactures, and a fairly general rise in the share of other manufactures (chemicals, paper and wood products, clay and glass products). These changes in the composition of the exports of the rich countries were partly due to industrialisation and the consequent changes in the structure of domestic output that accompanied it — involving a move away from primary production towards manufacturing, and within the latter a move away from textiles to metal manufactures, chemicals and engineering products. They were also partly caused by the extension of the international economy and the consequently greater international division of labour, which applied within manufacturing activity as well as between manufacturing and primary production. In the changed situation the rich countries found themselves at a growing comparative disadvantage in the production of foodstuffs and raw materials at the same time as their efficiency in manufacturing production was increasing.

One other aspect of these general trends in the structure of world trade that calls for comment is the relative decline of Britain in world trade after 1870. Despite the sharp fall in Britain's relative share of world trade in primary products, from about 30 per cent in 1876–80 to 19 per cent in 1913 (Table 5.2a and Figure 5.2a), there was a marked increase in Britain's dependence on overseas sources of supply. This was to be expected, given Britain's limited supplies of natural raw materials and her free-trade policy. By 1913, seven-eighths of Britain's raw materials (excluding coal) and over half of her food came from overseas. As for manufactured exports, almost all of the decline in Britain's share of this world market appears to have taken place after 1890. Whereas Britain seems to have held her own in textiles, chemicals and non-metalliferous materials, and raised her share of the world export trade in miscellaneous finished goods (furniture, leather, rubber manufactures and so forth) and drink and tobacco products, the losses arose in iron and steel, in metal manufactures and in transport equipment. When Britain's export performance is examined in terms of the distribution of her exports between expanding, stable and contracting commodity groups, a further trend is revealed. Britain was losing ground in commodity groups such as machinery (including motor vehicles) and iron and steel, for which world demand was expanding most rapidly. On the other hand, her export expansion was occurring in those commodity groups (miscellaneous finished goods and drink and tobacco) for which world demand was declining. Her most important single export item, cotton goods, was also a commodity with a declining world market share. Some changes in Britain's overall shares of world trade in manufactures were to be expected, given the structural shifts in the commodity and area composition of trade noted earlier. Even so, the evidence suggests that Britain's export losses were overwhelmingly due to the rise of rivals and, correspondingly, a decline in her competitiveness in foreign markets.

CONCLUSIONS

Between 1800 and 1913, world trade grew rapidly, far outpacing the growth of world output. This trade was dominated by Europe (including Britain), whose trade with the rest of the world consisted largely of an exchange of manufactured goods for primary products. Despite the spread of industrialisation after 1850, the share of primary products in world trade remained remarkably stable, a development which is explained by a slight relative decline in demand for primary products by rich countries being offset by a moderate increase in the exchange of primary products between the poor countries. Throughout the period after the late 1870s, the share of foodstuffs and agricultural raw materials in world trade in primary products tended to decline, whereas that of non-agricultural raw materials rose. A change in the composition of world trade in manufactures is also apparent, with the textiles share declining and that of metal products and other manufactures rising.

This rapid growth of trade during the second half of the nineteenth century and the associated changes in its commodity composition and direction created a new and increasingly more complex network of economic activity and trade embracing whole continents or sub-continents.

The earlier pattern of largely disconnected trading arrangements mainly centred on Britain gave way after 1860 to a new multilateral trading system based on a worldwide pattern of economic specialisation. It involved an exchange of manufactured goods for raw materials and foodstuffs between the rapidly industrialising countries of Europe and North America and primary producing countries situated for the most part in the rest of the world. With the exception of Britain, the newly industrialising countries usually experienced balance of trade deficits with the primary producers. Britain, on the other hand, largely because of her free-trade policy, became a heavy importer of both manufactures and primary produce. She was also the most important exporter of manufactured goods to non-European primary producers, as well as the world's largest foreign lender. Consequently, Britain had a trade surplus with the primary producing countries. This surplus, plus Britain's invisible earnings (payments for services such as banking, insurance and shipping, rendered to foreigners and earnings on foreign investments), provided the foreign exchange she needed to cover her excess of imports from industrialising countries, thus providing these countries in turn with the means with which to finance their deficits with primary producers overseas. This, broadly, was the character of the multilateral system of trade settlement that had emerged by 1913. In the next chapter, the growth and development of this system during the nineteenth century is examined in greater detail.

RECOMMENDATIONS FOR FURTHER READING

For a detailed study of European trade in the nineteenth century, see Bairoch (1974, *Geographical Structure and Trade Balance of European Foreign Trade from 1800 to 1970*). Hanson (1980, *Trade in Transition: Exports from the Third World, 1840–1900*) focussing on the poorer parts of the world, complements Bairoch's account.

A broad and knowledgeable picture of the evolution of the patterns and customs of trade throughout the last few millennia, the winners and the losers, is drawn by Berstein (2008, *A Splendid Exchange: How Trade Shaped the World*). The period 1820–1913 gets its fair share of attention.

NOTES

1 Here and in other parts that follow, the previous editions of this book resort to the terminological opposites of 'developed' versus 'underdeveloped' countries, which was common when the earlier editions came out. Since then, 'underdeveloped countries' has mostly been displaced by 'developing countries', which may appear less offensive, although for many of the poorest regions of the world, it is a euphemism. The most appropriate terminology is perhaps to distinguish between 'rich' and 'poor' countries, which has neither negative nor positive connotation. For this sixth edition, the older terminology has been modernised accordingly, but left unchanged when the context mandates it, i.e. when other texts using this terminology are cited or referred to.

2 See Kuznets (1967, p. 15). Kuznets includes in the developed countries: Canada, the US, Europe, Australia, New Zealand and, after 1880, Japan and the Union of South Africa. The underdeveloped countries cover Africa (excluding South Africa after 1880), Asia (excluding Japan after 1880) and Latin America.

3 See Woytinsky and Woytinsky (1955, p. 71).

4 See Kuznets (1967, p. 33, Table 6).

CHAPTER **6**

The Evolution of a Multilateral Payments Network

A. G. Kenwood, A. L. Lougheed and Michael Graff

INTRODUCTION

An important development associated with the growth of the international economy between 1870 and 1913 was the emergence of a complex multilateral payments network, which facilitated the movements of goods, services, capital and income payments to such a degree that the braking forces of certain impediments to the growth of international commercial relations after 1870 were minimised. Before embarking upon a description of the growth and development of this network of trade and payments, however, it is necessary to define certain concepts of vital significance to the subsequent discussion.

The balance of payments of a country is a systematic record of all economic transactions between the residents of that country and the rest of the world over a given period, usually one year. To simplify the following analysis, we shall assume that only commodities are traded between countries and that only bullion (gold or silver) is used to settle any outstanding trade balances.[1]

Trade and payments patterns between countries may develop along several lines. A bilateral trade and payments system arises when the payments for commodity imports received by country A from country B are offset by payments for exports from A to B. If, under gold standard conditions, these two flows of payments do not entirely offset one another, then a balancing movement of gold will occur from the debtor to the creditor country.

A triangular payments system introduces a third country, C, into the international trading network. Such a system is illustrated in Figure 6.1, where each country in which an arrow originates has a payments surplus with the country at which the arrow is pointed. Consequently, for each country in the system, a deficit in one direction may be partly, wholly or more than offset by its surplus in another direction. Thus, A's deficit with C is just offset by its surplus with B; B's deficit with A is more than offset by its surplus with C; and C's deficit with B is partly offset by its surplus with A. It is essential to note that in the triangular payments

DOI: 10.4324/9781003382171-9

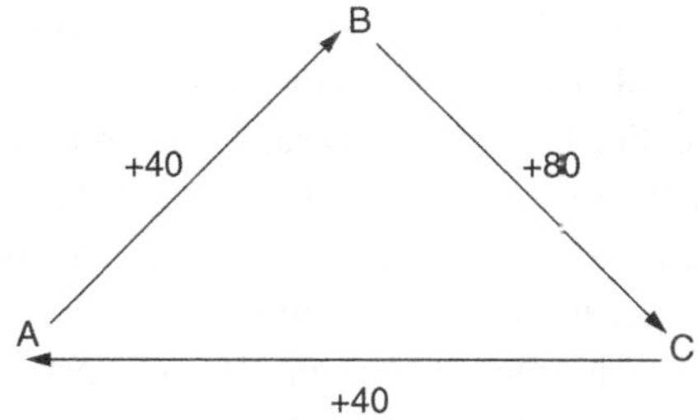

FIGURE 6.1 A triangular payments system

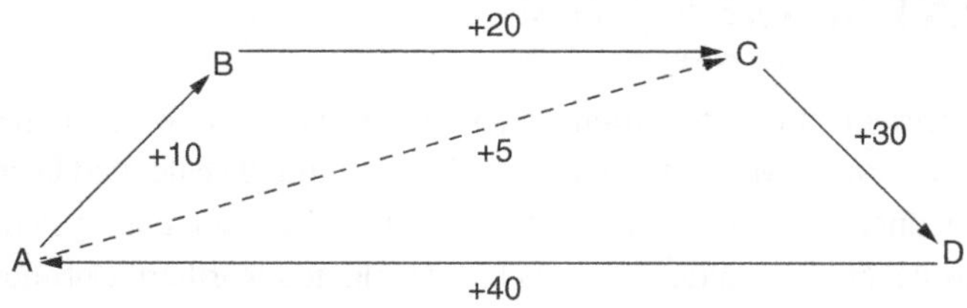

FIGURE 6.2 A multilateral payments system

system a large proportion of the international payments between countries will still be settled bilaterally and that it is only each country's remaining payments surpluses and deficits with other countries that will enter the triangular system. The significance of such a triangular system is that it overcomes the need for balancing each bilateral surplus or deficit and thus reduces the extent of international gold flows. For example, in Figure 6.1, whereas bilateral balancing would produce gold flows of 160, because of triangular settlement, a gold flow of only 40 (from C to B) would occur.

Finally, a multilateral payments system is defined as one including more than three countries or regions (A, B, C, D, etc.). In this situation, which is illustrated in a highly simplified form in Figure 6.2, an extension of the 'roundaboutness' of trade settlements occurs. Once again, the fact that a country's payments surpluses in one direction can offset its deficits in another reduces the need for gold movements as a final balancing item in international transactions. Thus, moving around the rim of the diagram (where the largest positive balances are conventionally recorded), we find that the offsetting of debits and credits leads to a gold flow of only 30 compared with 100 when the outstanding balances are settled bilaterally. But multilateralism involves more than this, for each country will trade with all the other countries included in the system, that is, A will trade with C (the dotted arrow in the diagram) as well as with B and D. It is probable, therefore, that a multilateral payments system will include a number of triangular payments networks like ABC and ACD which will also work to reduce gold flows between countries. Thus, if country A has a surplus of five with country C in addition to its surplus of ten with B, a gold flow of only 25 will now be needed to achieve 'worldwide' balance. It follows, therefore, that the larger the number of countries trading multilaterally, the greater the opportunities for offsetting deficits and surpluses and, consequently, the smaller the flow of gold needed to achieve overall balance between the countries concerned. It also follows that the smaller the demands placed on the available stock of gold in the trading countries, the less is the likelihood of a country restricting its trade with other countries to protect its gold holdings. In other words, in a monetary system that relies on an intrinsically scarce medium of exchange, like the gold standard, the emergence of a multilateral payments system may be a powerful support to the growth of trade between countries. It is estimated that about 70 per cent of all trade was bilateral during the late nineteenth century, and that probably a rather small proportion of the remainder was offset by foreign investment and other non-trade money flows. This means that from 20 to 25 per cent of total world trade was multilateral in nature by the time of the First World War.[2]

DEVELOPMENT OF THE SYSTEM

The multilateral settlement of international transactions was no new phenomenon restricted to the late nineteenth century. Multilateralism, albeit on a limited scale, had been a major feature of international economic relations for centuries. Thus, the triangular system comprising the UK, Western Europe and the Baltic countries had dominated Northern Europe's trade for many years, and the Atlantic (slave) triangle, linking Britain, Africa and the West Indies, provided another example of this type of trading pattern. Other triangular trading systems developed during the first half of the nineteenth century. By the 1860s, for example, Britain's trade deficits with the US were largely covered by her surpluses with Latin America, and a British deficit with China was offset by a surplus with India. But the new payments network that began to emerge after 1870 was essentially different from these earlier trading systems. Whereas the latter consisted of disconnected triangular networks centred on Britain, with each triangle arising out of an entirely different set of trading circumstances, the post-1870 variety was more complicated in nature and wider in scope. It arose partly out of the merging of some of the previously disconnected triangular systems, and partly out of the growing importance in world trade of countries and regions other than Britain. Thus, by 1914, in contrast to the disconnected pattern of trading activities centred on Britain characteristic of the period before 1870, there existed a complicated system of international exchange based on a network of economic activities embracing most parts of the world. Britain still played a central role in the new system, but her trading relations with the rest of the world had undergone a profound change.

Within the new system, which is described in a simplified form in Figure 6.3,[3] the US emerged as a separate link in the chain of international trade and payments in the years after the 1880s. At the beginning of that decade the bulk of American exports, which consisted predominantly of primary products, was shipped to Europe, from which region the US also received more than half of its imports. In this way, the country experienced export surpluses with Europe (including Britain) and trade deficits with the rest of the world. As substantial domestic capital accumulation occurred, however, rapid industrialisation got under way, and by the mid-1890s the US had become a net exporter of manufactures. In consequence, by 1910–14, the early pattern of American trade had altered dramatically. Even when capital flows, interest and dividend payments and other 'invisibles' are taken into account, the US still had a large surplus with the UK, but compared with the 1880s its deficit with continental Europe was smaller. On the other hand, America's import surplus with the Tropics, chiefly India and Brazil, had enlarged considerably, mainly because of its increased demand for raw

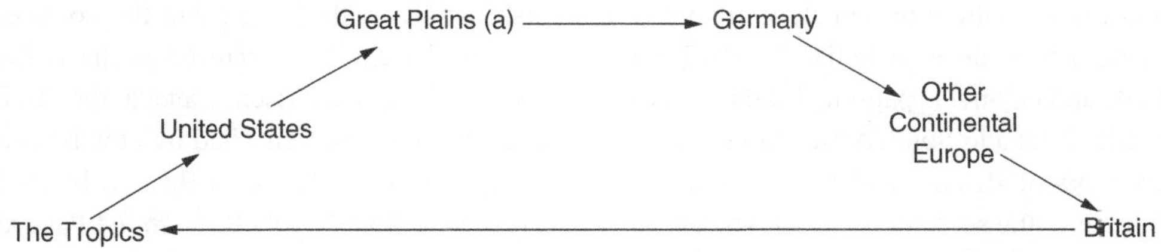

FIGURE 6.3 The multilateral payments system after 1900

Note: (a) Canada, Australia, Argentina, etc.

materials and foodstuffs. Most important of all, however, was the emergence of an American export surplus with the Great Plains countries, especially Canada, which came about largely because of their increased demand for American manufactures. It was this large and growing export surplus with the Great Plains region, rather than the credit balance with Britain or the large reductions in deficit balances with continental Europe, which financed the US's growing deficit with the Tropics.

As the US became less dependent on the European market for its trade, the Great Plains economies were drawn close to Europe by improvements in land and sea transport and by the growth of the European market for agricultural and other land-intensive commodities. On the other hand, despite an expansion of exports to Britain, these land-intensive countries became large debtors of Britain and tended to rely more and more on their positive trade balances with continental Europe to finance their growing imports of British goods and the servicing of their accumulated capital debts and other 'invisibles' payments due to Britain. As time progressed, however, it was with America that these countries came to record their largest import deficits.

After the early 1880s, Germany also emerged as another link in the network of trade. Because of the rapid growth of its manufacturing industries and a relative decline in its agriculture, Germany's demand for raw materials and foodstuffs grew rapidly, and import surpluses with the Great Plains countries developed when they began to replace the US as the German source of supply of these commodities. During the 1890s, moreover, German trade deficits with other major continental countries turned into surpluses when Germany found in these countries a ready market for its increasing exports of manufactures. These other European countries, in turn, increased their export surpluses with the UK, at least until 1900. Although these surpluses declined thereafter, because of heavy imports of British coal and colonial goods, they nevertheless remained fairly substantial and produced a partial offset to the deficits which these countries had developed with Germany and the Great Plains economies.

At the centre of the new multilateral trading network stood Britain, whose major contributions to its development during the period from 1880 to 1914 included her import surplus; her free-trade policy, which greatly facilitated the growth of the exports of other countries by providing a readily accessible market (partly at the expense of British agriculture); and the expansion of her international lending, which produced a positive effect on Britain's current account, as income receipts from these foreign investments continuously increased.

In 1880, when foreign lending was relatively small, Britain's large deficits with continental Europe and the US, and her smaller deficits with Australia, Canada, Egypt and several other countries, were largely offset by positive trade balances with India, South America, Turkey and Japan, with approximately one-third of British deficits with the US and the continent being settled through India. By 1910, however, major changes had occurred in the British trade and payments pattern. Total negative balances with the US had risen, Canada, the Straits Settlements and South Africa (all recipients of large British investment) had by now become creditors of Britain, and South America was no longer a major debtor to Britain. In 1910, therefore, the settlement of British debit balances tended to flow largely through the Far East and Australia. India, which offset approximately 40 per cent of Britain's total deficits, continued to provide the key to the UK's payments system by maintaining heavy export surpluses with continental Europe, the rest of the Empire, China and Hong Kong, and to a lesser extent Japan and the US — in other words, with many of Britain's creditors at the time. The importance of India to Britain became even more marked in the period from 1910 to 1914. The trade balances of Australia, Brazil, Argentina and Canada with Britain turned increasingly positive, but Britain's surplus with India expanded still further. While the Indian market continued to absorb large quantities of British manufactures, the entry of which into many other countries was impeded by tariff protection, Indian products exported to the continent, the US and elsewhere attracted little tariff attention. As a result, Britain was able to absorb large quantities of foodstuffs, raw materials and manufactures from highly protected countries without having to increase her exports to these countries. Had the UK also moved towards protection during the period, international trade would undoubtedly have expanded at a slower rate, for industrial

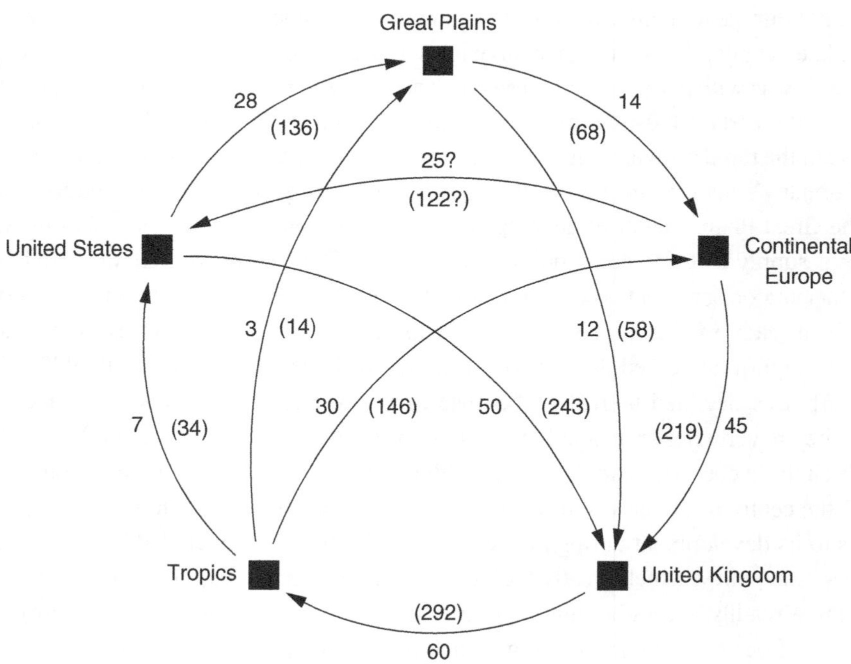

FIGURE 6.4 The system of multilateral trade in 1910

Source: Saul (1960, p. 58, figure 2).

Note: The size of the export surplus between continental Europe and the US is subject to reservation.

Europe and the US would have been compelled to find other markets for their exports or to adjust their industrial production.

An attempt to estimate the pattern of settlement for the year 1910 has been made by Saul (1960). Figure 6.4 is adapted from his 'highly approximate' estimates of the overall trade balances between various pairs of countries or regions for that year, to make the resulting system of multilateral trade comparable to that shown later for the year 1928.[4] The arrows in the figure indicate the balances of merchandise trade, in millions of pounds sterling or dollars (in brackets), pointing from net exporting to net importing countries or regions. For example, in 1910, the UK had an export surplus with the Tropics (India), but import surpluses with the US, continental Europe and the Great Plains of £50 million, $45 million and £12 million, respectively. On the other hand, the US had export surpluses with the UK and the Great Plains but imported more from the Tropics and from continental Europe than it exported to these regions.[5]

When all these trends are considered, the complexity of the multilateral payments network can be appreciated. Not only did it provide a substantial supplement to the bilateral balancing of payments, it also tended to reduce to a minimum the movement of bullion for balancing purposes. It therefore facilitated the smooth working of the international monetary system and promoted a much larger expansion of world trade than would have been possible had this trade been more dependent on the use of gold or silver as the sole means of settling international debts. As a result, numerous countries in the network were able to attain relatively high rates of growth in production and incomes through the consequent increased opportunities for trade.

FOREIGN INVESTMENT AND THE MULTILATERAL SETTLEMENTS NETWORK

The growth of the multilateral payments network also facilitated the massive flows of capital and investment income, which passed between countries after 1870. Although at first sight these flows appear to add strictly monetary factors to a system alleged to concentrate on 'real' flows of goods and services, it is important to note that the settlements network was to a very large extent concerned with 'real' transfers of such capital and investment income from one country to another.

When foreign capital flows from one country to another, its transfer may be effected in several ways, for example, through a shift of bullion from the lending to the borrowing country, through an increase in the capital-receiving country's imports from the lending country (or from other countries), or through a decline in the borrower's exports such that the trade balance diminishes. Gold flows and reduced exports rarely affected the transfer during the late nineteenth century, and for the most part, the transfer of capital from lending to borrowing countries took the form of increased commodity imports by capital-receiving countries. As far as British foreign investment was concerned, there were no 'tied' arrangements under which the borrowing country was committed to use the funds acquired for purchasing only British-made commodities. Nevertheless, for some borrowing countries, such as Australia before 1890, the British market was the major source of manufactured goods. But progressively after 1880, the US and Germany made inroads into British export markets, and a continuously higher proportion of British foreign investment tended to be used by borrowing countries in the purchase of goods from these countries. Other lending countries probably experienced the same sort of trend as Britain, to a lesser or greater degree, depending on the circumstances.

Thus, increasingly towards the end of the period, the international transfer of foreign investments tended to be brought about in an indirect manner and formed an integral part of the entire multilateral payments network. The importance of the network in providing a mechanism supporting the smooth flow of capital during the period is exemplified by the fact that had India not been able to absorb large amounts of British manufactures, the UK could not have invested in Canada to the extent possible after 1904, since much of the large British investment in that country was used to purchase commodities in the US. It was only because America was experiencing a payments deficit with India, and India one with the UK, that the indirect transfer of capital to Canada operated with a minimum of friction. As for the 'real' transfer of the interest and dividends payable on British (and other) foreign investments, whenever this investment income increased and began to exceed new British capital outflows, payments, especially from the Tropics and the Great Plains countries, began to be transferred to Britain partly by way of the trade surpluses these regions had with the US and continental Europe, respectively.

CONCLUDING REMARKS

What was the significance of the multilateral settlements system for the international economy as a whole? First, it allowed countries to obtain international means of payment, which could be used to acquire additional goods and services not available on a strictly bilateral basis; second, it permitted debt servicing to be transferred in a circuitous route from borrower to lender, not possible under a bilateral system without impediments to the free flow of goods; third, it promoted the real transfer of foreign investment on a multilateral basis; and finally, it minimised gold flows for settlement purposes. One result was an enlarged volume of foreign trade. Moreover, because a country was able to finance deficits in one direction through surpluses in another, it was possible for those countries which were neither large debtors nor large creditors to aid debtor countries to pay and creditor countries to receive financial payments due. Under gold standard conditions, the world economy could thus realise benefits from trade and investment without running into difficulty due to lacking means of payments.[6]

During this period, the convertibility of currencies was generally maintained, but from the early 1880s, protective tariffs became widespread in the world economy and tended to slow down the rate of growth of world trade somewhat and altered its direction considerably. In a multilateral trading network, the introduction of restrictive measures on the trade between any two links in the network was likely to affect the trade of all other regions in the system, as well as the financial relations between debtor and creditor countries at opposite ends of the network. In addition, artificial trade barriers could affect the functioning of world commodity markets and thus the prices of staple products sold in those markets. But the fact that Britain adhered to free trade, while possessing a 'safety valve' in India when it came to a settlement of her own foreign payments, helped to minimise the restrictive effects of greater protection in the world economy after 1870. Britain's policy, even if followed unconsciously, allowed the multilateral system to grow rapidly with minimum disruption from tariffs.

Thus, while bilateral settlements between countries continued to predominate in international transactions, the growth of multilateralism, especially after 1870, provided the world economy with an additional mechanism for facilitating trade and payments between countries, and partly for this reason, international monetary crises were comparatively rare during these years, despite tremendous changes in the size and structure of both world production and trade. Yet the most successful years in the functioning of the multilateral trade and payments network also mark the period during which the first seeds of its future destruction were planted; for it was then that there appeared signs of a narrowing of the British payments surplus, upon the size of which the efficient functioning of the system so heavily depended. Although multilateralism was to survive after the First World War, its destruction followed quickly in the early 1930s in the face of a worldwide depression and the continued decline in Britain's international economic position.

One other feature of the functioning of multilateralism in the period up to 1913 is worthy of comment. This is the extent to which foreign capital relied on the multilateral payments network for its effective transfer between countries. In the absence of such a network, capital exports would almost certainly have been lower than they were, and interest and capital repayments more difficult to effect. As we have already noted, the emergence of a multilateral payments network led to economies in the use of gold in international commercial transactions, and this fact partly explains the successful functioning of the gold standard in the period from 1880 to 1913. Nevertheless, any international payment balances outstanding after bilateral and multilateral settlements had been effected had to be settled with gold. It is in order, therefore, to consider the nature and functioning of the international gold standard in the period up to 1913, to which we turn in the following chapter.

RECOMMENDATIONS FOR FURTHER READING

The analyses of the multilateral trade and payments system in the late nineteenth century up to the First World War, on which this chapter is mainly based, are Hilgerdt (1942, *The Network of World Trade*), Hilgerdt (1943, *The Case for Multilateral Trade*), Hansson (1952, *A General Theory of the System of Multilateral Trade*), Saul (1960, *Studies in British Overseas Trade*) and Wright (1955, *Convertibility and Triangular Trade as Safeguards against Economic Depression*).

NOTES

1 In more detail, a country's balance of payments is a record of its commercial and financial transactions with the rest of the world over a period, usually one year. It contains what are called autonomous items and financing items. Autonomous items are classified into current account (goods and services) and capital account. The current account includes the value of commodity exports and imports, the difference between which represents the balance of trade (positive when exports exceed imports and negative when an import surplus occurs), and receipts and payments for 'invisible' items such as transportation,

investment income, travellers' expenditure and other services. The current account is in surplus when monetary receipts for exports and invisibles exceed monetary payments for imports and invisibles. The capital account includes all autonomous capital flows into and out of the country. The financing items offset the autonomous balance and ensure that the whole statement balances, that is, they indicate what happens to the surplus monetary receipts when the autonomous items are in surplus, and how an autonomous deficit is financed. In other words, when all sub-accounts of the balance of payments are summed up, the result must be zero (notwithstanding statistical discrepancies). If a country has, for example, a negative trade balance, this must be set off by (a combination of) receiving loans from abroad, running down central bank reserves or earnings from foreign investments. Under the pure gold standard, the financing items normally comprised changes in the gold stocks of each country. Notice that in practice, balance of payments terminology and booking rules differ substantially across countries and time, so that care must be taken of the definitions when looking at specific balance of payments statistics.

2 For figures demonstrating the nineteenth-century trade and payments systems in chosen years, see Hilgerdt (1943, p. 395) and Saul (1960, p. 58).

3 The diagram is similar to that in Hilgerdt (1943, p. 395).

4 See Figure 14.3 of this book.

5 It is in order to mention that Figure 6.4 does not cover all triangular and multilateral settlement patterns that arose in the period before 1913. A more detailed breakdown would reveal a much more complicated system.

6 Multilateral trade and currency convertibility are two aspects of the same phenomenon, each a necessary condition for the other; see Wright (1955). This applies to an unprecedented degree to the international economy from about 1870 up to the First World War, when barriers to trade and capital flows were minimal and the gold standard effectively established a system of freely convertible currencies.

CHAPTER 7

The Evolution of an International Monetary System

The Gold Standard Until 1914

A. G. Kenwood, A. L. Lougheed and Michael Graff

Whereas trade within a country is made easy by the existence of a single currency common to all its regions, international transactions require a monetary system capable of handling trade involving the use of a variety of national currencies. Of course, international trade can be conducted on a barter basis, and in ancient and medieval times this type of international transaction often occurred. But bartering obviously places severe limitations on the growth of trade, and so during quite early times foreign exchange markets, in which different currencies could be exchanged for one another, made their appearance, thus placing foreign trade on a monetary basis. Bullion — notably gold and silver or alloys thereof — came to be used frequently for payments in international trade, but this had certain drawbacks, particularly in the high cost of acquisition of the means of payment due to its inherent scarcity, the effort and cost of transporting metals from country to country and the risks involved in such transfers. For this reason, the expansion of foreign trade and commerce came to depend very much on improvements in the operation of foreign exchange markets and on the perfecting of devices to reduce the risks attached to fluctuations in the rate of exchange of one currency in terms of another.

With the growth of foreign commerce, financial innovations were quick to appear. The bill of exchange was introduced early, and by the fourteenth century a simple multilateral clearing system had been established. During the seventeenth and eighteenth centuries, the first 'forward' exchange markets were developed to overcome the uncertainty of future movements in the 'spot' rate of exchange, so reducing the risks inherent in fluctuating exchange rates. By this time, Amsterdam had become the most important foreign exchange market in the world, closely followed by London, which was fast assuming a major role in world finance in the eighteenth century. At the beginning of the nineteenth century, foreign exchange markets were quite sophisticated in their operations, and the financing of foreign trade and other international dealings had become quite complex. Throughout its history, the international

DOI: 10.4324/9781003382171-10

financial system had adapted itself to meet the needs of an expanding foreign commerce and the process of adaptation continued during the nineteenth century, when a new international monetary system — the gold standard — evolved in response to the demands of a growing foreign trade and an expanding international flow of capital.[1]

BIMETALLIC AND MONOMETALLIC STANDARDS

At the beginning of our period, only Britain was on a gold standard for both domestic and international dealings. Most other major trading nations at this time were operating either a bimetallic standard, for example, France and the US, or a silver standard, as were most other European countries.

For a country to be wholly committed to a full gold standard, five basic requirements had to be met. First, the unit of account had to be tied to a certain weight of gold; second, gold coins had to circulate domestically and any banknotes in circulation had to be convertible into gold on demand; third, other coins in use had to be subordinate to gold; fourth, no legal restrictions were to be imposed on the melting down of gold coin into bullion; and finally, there had to be no impediment to the export of gold coin and bullion.

Bimetallism, on the other hand, involved the employment of both silver and gold coins as standard money or legal tender under conditions similar to those just outlined for gold. In principle, it promised some relief to the scarcity of money under a monometallic standard. Compared with the gold standard, however, a bimetallic standard had one major drawback: it worked smoothly only as long as the ratio between the values at which the two metals could be freely minted into coins approximated to their values in international bullion markets. If divergence of these values did occur, then the metal with the higher international market value would tend to be sent abroad and be replaced by the other, leaving the country de facto with a monometallic rather than a bimetallic standard. This type of arbitrage is known as 'Gresham's Law', according to which 'bad money drives out good money', or, more specifically, if the legal mint ratio (exchange rate) undervalues one form of money relative to market prices, the legally undervalued ('good') money will be exported or hoarded or melted down and sold at market price, and only the overvalued ('bad') money will continue to circulate.[2]

Due to the inherent instability of the bimetallic system, there were periodic, but not always successful, efforts to achieve international agreement to fix the ratio of the price of gold and silver, bringing the mint ratio in line with the market ratio for bullion. Despite its drawbacks, however, the fear that one metal alone would fail to satisfy the world demand for money and so produce general deflation led to the widespread adoption of the bimetallic standard in the nineteenth century. In fact, for most of the time Britain alone adhered to the gold standard. It was not until the 1870s that other major trading countries began to move gradually in the same direction as that taken by Britain at the end of the Napoleonic Wars.

BRITAIN ADOPTS THE GOLD STANDARD

By the late eighteenth century, Britain had moved to a de facto gold standard, after a long period during which silver had continuously disappeared from domestic circulation. The predominance of gold over silver had begun as early as 1717, when the gold guinea was given a value of 21s. Silver was so undervalued in terms of gold thereafter that it soon came to perform the function of a subsidiary coinage, the silver coins remaining in circulation having become so worn that it was unprofitable to withdraw them from circulation and melt them down for export. Silver's importance as a monetary unit was reduced still further in 1774 when the legal tender status of silver coins was restricted to payments up to £25. The supremacy of gold as a unit of account in Britain was assured from that year.

The movement towards the adoption of a gold standard in Britain was halted during the war years, when, as a wartime measure, cash payments were suspended in 1797 and the Bank of England freed from its obligation to convert its notes into gold. Immediately after the end of the war, however, the de facto gold standard of the late eighteenth century was made *de jure* by the passing of a number of Acts of Parliament. The Coinage Act of 1816 allowed for the minting of a gold sovereign, a 20s gold piece, the first of which was issued in the following year. The gold content of the sovereign was fixed in accordance with the mint price of gold, which had been maintained throughout the eighteenth century at £3 17s 10½d per ounce. Silver coins were legally subordinated to gold and were further restricted by being made legal tender for payments of up to only £2. In 1819, the convertibility of banknotes was restored, when an Act of Parliament committed the Bank of England to resume cash payments in gold bullion and, after 1823, in gold coin. This Act also repealed the law prohibiting the melting down of coin into bullion, and the trade in bullion was declared free. With the resumption of cash payments in 1821, Britain was legally on the full gold standard.

INTERNATIONAL MONETARY STANDARDS UP TO 1870

The task of maintaining stability within the bimetallic system, through exercising control over the world prices of gold and silver, fell to France. The performance of this function imposed few problems in the years between 1815 and 1850, when demand and supply conditions for both metals were fairly stable. There was some withdrawal of gold from circulation, as gold production steadily declined and its market value appreciated relative to that of silver, but France possessed relatively large reserves of both metals and was easily able to absorb silver at the expense of gold without actually moving to a silver standard. The US was also legally on a bimetallic standard for most of the nineteenth century. Until the 1830s, however, the country really operated on a silver standard, because at 15 to 1 the American mint ratio of silver to gold undervalued gold and led to its disappearance from circulation. But a de facto silver standard was inconvenient for a country which traded primarily with another, Britain, which was on a gold standard. It was probably for this reason that the Coinage Acts of 1834 and 1837 reduced the gold content of the dollar and established a new mint ratio of 16 to 1. Since this ratio was above the free market ratio, which generally settled around the French mint ratio of 15.5 to 1, the previous trend towards a silver standard was replaced by a movement to a de facto gold standard similar to that found in Britain during the eighteenth century.

The pressures on the bimetallic standard mounted after 1850, when the discovery of substantial gold deposits in California and Australia produced dramatic changes in currency dealings and metal markets. The relative price of gold fell, and the French mint ratio of 15.5 to 1 proved to be too high for the New World market situation, for it overvalued gold. As silver appreciated relative to gold, France absorbed large quantities of gold, and the French franc de facto became a gold unit, as Gresham's Law became operable. In an effort to stabilise the situation and promote an international bimetallic system, France called a meeting of the franc-using nations in 1865. As a result of this meeting, France, Belgium, Switzerland and Italy (often referred to as the Latin Monetary Union) agreed to regulate their currencies jointly. The agreement, however, did little to alleviate the monetary pressures exerted on the bimetallic countries.

As for the other European countries, by 1870 they were either on a silver standard — the Germanic States, Holland and Scandinavia — or, like Russia, Austria-Hungary, Italy, Greece and, more recently, France, had been forced by wars and revolutions to issue inconvertible paper money which, with the exception of the French issues, were depreciated paper.[3] Outside Europe, the Orient and Latin America were on silver, and the US had inconvertible and depreciated notes, issued during the Civil War, still in circulation. By 1870, therefore, the gold standard was far from being internationally adopted. Britain alone operated on a legal gold standard. Bimetallism existed legally in the US and the Latin Monetary Union, and Germany, Holland, Scandinavia, Latin America and the Orient adhered to the silver standard.

THE SPREAD OF THE GOLD STANDARD

During the 1870s, the movement towards gold accelerated, and silver declined rapidly in importance as an international standard. This sudden change in the international monetary situation was brought about by two developments, each of which drastically affected the relative prices of the two main monetary metals. First, Germany transferred from silver to a gold standard. It did this for several reasons. To begin with, several East European countries, with which Germany had important trading relations, had abandoned a silver standard for inconvertible paper, so Germany no longer derived any advantage from adherence to the silver standard in its commercial relations with these countries. Moreover, most of Germany's commercial relations with non-European countries tended to be financed through Britain, where a gold standard operated. Finally, delegates from a number of European countries to an international monetary congress held in Paris in 1867 had overwhelmingly favoured the adoption of a universal gold standard. Given these arguments in favour of a changeover to gold, the large war indemnity extracted from France by Germany in 1871–2 provided the means for bringing it about. In 1872 a new currency unit, the mark, was adopted to replace the silver thaler, and silver was relegated to subsidiary coins of limited legal tender. Surplus silver bullion and coins of large denominations were used to buy gold in the bullion markets to overcome the domestic shortage of gold for coinage purposes. In two years, Germany acquired £50 million ($243 million) of gold, and so great were the pressures exerted on the markets that the price of silver in terms of gold commenced to decline dramatically.

The fall in the price of silver, and hence its demise as an international monetary standard, was also brought about by the sharp increase in the world output of silver that followed the discovery of large deposits of the metal in Nevada and elsewhere. In the face of the glut of silver in the world market, which was aggravated by the suspension of the minting of silver coins in the US in 1873, the price of silver in terms of gold dropped below 16 to 1, and countries on a silver or bimetallic standard faced the possibility of substantial monetary inflation.[4] As a result, the demonetisation of silver became general after the mid-1870s. Holland, crushed between a gold-using Britain and a gold-using Germany, was the first to go. In 1874, it ceased coining silver and not long afterwards adopted gold as its unit of account. Norway, Sweden and Denmark quickly followed suit. The Latin Monetary Union, under pressure from its inception, encountered extreme difficulties in the early 1870s and its members were compelled in January 1874 to limit their coinage of five-franc pieces. In 1878, they suspended the minting of silver coins altogether, and from that time onwards, France and her colleagues operated on the so-called 'limping' (or 'lame') gold standard. Silver was still legal tender, but it was neither coined nor used to any significant extent in commercial transactions, though banks continued to hold large quantities of the metal. Effectively, however, these countries adhered in all other ways to the gold standard. By 1878, therefore, Britain, Belgium, Holland, France, Germany, Switzerland and the Scandinavian countries were operating on gold, and, since most other continental countries were using irredeemable depreciated paper money, silver was no longer an international standard of value in Europe.

The movement to gold was completed by the end of the century. In the US, bimetallism was not legally abandoned until 1900, but the country was effectively operating on the gold standard once convertibility of paper notes was restored in 1879. Austria moved to gold in 1892, and Russia and Japan in 1897, the year in which India adopted a gold exchange standard by pegging the rupee to sterling. A year later, the Philippine peso likewise became tied to the American dollar. After 1900, other countries, including Siam (now: Thailand) and Ceylon (now: Sri Lanka) in Asia, and Argentina, Mexico, Peru and Uruguay in Latin America, eventually adopted the gold standard, while others were, by the outbreak of the First World War, proceeding in that direction. By 1914, China was alone among major countries in still clinging to a silver standard.

This brief description of the pre-1914 gold standard brings out one of its most striking features, namely its relatively short duration as an international monetary system. Whereas it is not possible to date precisely its beginnings — it did not exist in 1870, but it did in 1900 — the First World War certainly marks its end, for, as we shall see, the post-war restoration of the system was short-lived. Thus, the international gold standard was in full sway only from perhaps 1897 (some would argue 1880) to 1914, less than 20 (or just over 30) years.

THE ROLE OF STERLING AS AN INTERNATIONAL CURRENCY AND THE IMPORTANCE OF THE LONDON CAPITAL MARKET

In the institutional field, the developments in the London capital market were of paramount importance for the efficient functioning of the international gold standard. With Britain's increasing importance in world trade, organised markets were established in London for many types of commodities, a move which was greatly enhanced in the early years by the continued growth of the British re-export trade and later by the adoption of free trade. These markets in turn acted as a stimulus to British shipping and created a growing need for insurance facilities to cover transport risks. As a result of these developments, London grew in importance as a centre of international commerce and finance; and various institutions, such as discount houses, merchant banks, insurance companies and other specialist financial organisations, which were later to provide the essential services for a rapidly expanding international economy, began to increase in number. From the beginning of the nineteenth century, therefore, London forged ahead of Amsterdam, Hamburg and Paris as the leading financial centre of Europe and thus of the world.

While these developments were taking place, a growing proportion of world trade was being financed by short-term credit in the form of foreign bills of exchange. Under these arrangements, by accepting a bill, an importer guaranteed payment within (say) three months of acceptance. The foreign exporter, on the other hand, if he required ready cash before the bill matured, could discount it with a bank (or other financial institution willing to do so) for something less than the face value of the bill, thus allowing interest to the discounter for holding the bill between the date of discounting and maturity and for accepting the risk against default. It was not until the early nineteenth century that these financial arrangements were perfected in Britain by the merchant banks and bill brokers, each of which came to perform a specialised function. The merchant banks, which were well known and respected for their integrity, then began to accept bills on behalf of reliable businessmen and firms, whose names were less familiar than theirs. In other words, for the payment of a small commission, the merchant banks, by endorsing a bill of exchange, would guarantee that it would not be dishonoured on maturity. In this way the merchant banks ensured that a large number of bills would be available for discounting. The discounting function was performed initially by the bill-broker — a financial go-between who accumulated bills of exchange and sought out banks with surplus funds, with a view to persuading them to invest in the bills in his care. For his trouble and his knowledge, he charged a small commission. Some years later, the bill-broker began to give way to the dealer, who was himself a principal and not merely a commission agent. Supplementing his own sizeable funds with money borrowed on call or short notice from the large London banks, he used the money to discount bills on his own account. Still later came the discount houses, which were little more than large-scale dealers. They had more capital to invest; they took deposits from the public and paid interest on them; and they did a much greater volume of business.

The acceptance houses did not restrict their business activities to the market for short-term credit. With the growth of British investment abroad after 1820, they came to specialise in foreign security issues as well, and before 1850 they were also important dealers in foreign exchange and bullion. Later, however, the various merchant houses came to specialise either in the acceptance business or in the issue of securities, and foreign exchange dealings came to be concentrated in the hands of the branches of foreign banks in London. These branches increased rapidly in number after 1870, when the growth of the London capital market and the extent of Britain's foreign trade made it essential for many foreign banks to establish branches in the centre. Increasingly, in the years up to 1914, the operations of these foreign branch banks presented a growing challenge to the supremacy of the bill on London as an instrument of international payments. For, with the telegraphic process, the accumulated sterling reserves in these foreign branches tended to replace the bill on London as a method of payment across the exchanges.

The growing importance of the London capital market, especially after 1870, was associated with the increasing use of sterling as an international currency. Throughout the nineteenth century, Britain maintained a continuous surplus on current account in its dealings with the rest of the world. But she did not amass large gold reserves, chiefly because of her willingness to invest the surplus abroad. Yet, from experience over a number of decades, foreign institutions and traders confidently accepted the ability of Britain to maintain the convertibility of sterling into gold. The stability of sterling was unrivalled, and the possibility of its devaluation never even considered. Sterling was as good as gold, and in some respects even better, because it was more convenient, in the sense that British exporters and importers, who dominated world trade, preferred to draw and to be drawn on in pounds sterling, and because it brought in an income, for holders of sterling received interest payments, whereas gold holdings earned nothing.

Given the general acceptability of sterling throughout the international economy, it is not surprising to find that gold played only a minor role in settling international debts. The vast majority of payments were made either by the transfer of bills payable in sterling, or by the purchase and sale of bills payable in foreign currencies, or simply by the transfer of credits in the books of banks, although the volume of business conducted under the latter two heads was never large before 1914. Hence sterling bills of exchange were used not only to finance the exports and imports of Britain, but also those of a large part of the rest of the world. The reasons for this worldwide preference for the pound sterling as a medium of international payments were numerous. It came about partly because Britain was the world's largest trader, the dominant carrier in world trade and the largest single source of foreign capital. In part also, it was because the value of the pound sterling was kept stable throughout the period from 1821 to 1914 by rigorous adherence to the gold standard. But equally important was the high standing of the British acceptance houses and the assurance that any bill receiving their endorsement could be readily discounted, at the world's most favourable rates, in the London discount market. Combined, these forces turned London into the financial centre of the world, and the pound sterling into an internationally acceptable currency.

THE WORKING OF THE GOLD STANDARD

Whereas sterling was used to finance the bulk of international financial transactions in the nineteenth century, gold remained the ultimate means of settling balances which could not be adjusted in any other way. Moreover, the international acceptability of sterling in settlement of debts depended on its ready convertibility into gold. For these reasons, it is necessary to examine in some detail the working of the gold standard in the period until 1914.

Under the gold standard, because the basic monetary unit of each country on the gold standard had a fixed gold content, the value of each country's currency was fixed in terms of all other currencies at the 'mint parity' or 'par' value. But if the par rate of exchange between two currencies, say the pound sterling and the dollar, was fixed by the gold content of each currency, the market rate of exchange was determined by the forces of demand and supply. In the market, if the demand for dollars rose relative to their supply, the market rate of the dollar in terms of sterling would rise; if the demand declined, the market rate would fall. Under the gold standard, however, the fact that residents in member countries could export or import gold freely placed limits on the extent to which the market rate could rise above or fall below the par rate. If the demand for dollars in London increased so much relative to the supply that the market rate of exchange (dollars per pound sterling) rose above the mint parity rate by more than the cost of exporting gold, it would have been profitable for those demanding dollars to buy gold in London, ship it to New York and sell it for dollars in that market. Similarly, if the demand for dollars had fallen relative to the supply forthcoming so that the market rate of the dollar had declined below the mint parity by more than the cost of shipping gold, those willing to supply dollars (and thus demanding sterling) would have profited by shipping gold from the US to London and selling it for sterling.

The cost of shifting gold from one financial centre to another allowed a certain degree of flexibility in foreign exchange rates. Consequently, the market rate could fluctuate according to the forces of supply and demand between two values, termed the 'gold export' and 'gold import' points. These limiting rates of exchange were established at values above and below the par value determined by the cost of transporting gold. The distance between the gold points could change over time if transport and other costs, such as insurance, altered. Similarly, the distance between the two points was relatively large or small depending on the distance between the two countries whose currencies were linked together. In general, the spot rate of the dollar in London would move towards the gold export point when Britain experienced a deficit in its balance of payments with the US (an excess demand for dollars and an excess supply of sterling in the exchange market). Similarly, a British surplus with the US would produce an excess supply of dollars (demand for sterling) and a decline in the market rate of the dollar towards the gold import point.

Normally, most transactions would have been conducted in foreign exchange, and only large and persistent imbalances between the two countries would have produced gold flows. But while gold flows produced short-run balancing of the supply of and demand for foreign exchange, they obviously could not be continued indefinitely, for a country could not sustain gold exports forever without running out of the metal. Gold imports could go on somewhat longer, perhaps, but eventually the importing country's trading partners would exhaust their supplies of gold. What then was the nature of the longer-run mechanism of adjustment under the gold standard which prevented these situations from arising?

One answer to the question was given by the classical economists, such as David Hume, Adam Smith and John Stuart Mill, who worked out the 'price-specie-flow' mechanism. According to this explanation, price changes induced by gold flows were supposed to bring about the adjustment. Suppose a country develops a balance of trade deficit because of excessive imports and proceeds to export gold to cover this excess. This loss of gold will reduce the domestic money supply, since either gold circulates as money in the country, or the banking system keeps the country's internal supply of money adjusted to the quantity of its gold reserves. According to the Quantity Theory of Money (see Appendix 2 to this chapter), a decrease in the domestic money supply will lead to a decline in commodity prices, since less spending with output unchanged means lower prices. Lower prices for goods will, in turn, increase exports, as foreigners find the country a cheaper place in which to buy. Lower domestic prices will also reduce imports, since domestic substitutes for foreign goods become cheaper relative to foreign supplies. In the gold-receiving country, the process is reversed. The inflow of gold increases the domestic money supply and raises commodity prices, which makes exporting more difficult and the importing of cheaper foreign supplies more attractive.

These changes in the export and import capacities of the two countries will alter the supply and demand conditions in the foreign exchange market and bring about adjustments in exchange rates until equilibrium is re-established between the gold points.

Late in the nineteenth century this price-specie-flow mechanism was elaborated in a number of ways, the most important of which concerned the effects of gold movements on the monetary policy of the central banks. In Britain, it was argued that gold flows led to changes in the Bank of England's discount rate. Thus, as gold exporters obtained gold from the Bank of England, the bank's ratio of reserves to liabilities would decline. If this decline persisted, the bank would eventually raise its discount rate automatically to prevent further depletion of its gold reserves. Such action would produce increased interest rates generally and a restriction of credit. This would have an adverse effect on business activity and employment and lead to a fall in prices and wages, which would reinforce the direct effects of the price-specie-flow mechanism. On the other hand, when a gold inflow took place, the increased money supply would mean an abundance of credit and interest rates would fall. Declining interest rates would stimulate domestic activity and generate an upward pressure on wages and prices. If interest rate policy was, in this way, a 'rule of the game' requiring strict observance by monetary authorities, the gold standard mechanism would truly have been an automatic system. The combination of specie flows and interest rate changes would have produced an era of stable exchange rates, and, given a moderately large stock of monetary gold in each country, although its size was subject to fluctuation, it would not be in danger of permanent depletion, since a loss of gold would be automatically corrected by the operation of the adjustment mechanism.

DIVERGENCE BETWEEN CLASSICAL THEORY AND EMPIRICAL EVIDENCE

The weakness of the price-specie-flow theory of adjustment is that it fails to conform to the empirical evidence on the functioning of the pre-1914 gold standard. Thus, contrary to the classical theory's prediction of divergences between the movements of exports and imports both within countries and between countries on the gold standard, we find a high degree of parallelism of movements in these trade flows.[5] Second, export prices in a number of countries moved together over time, although the classical theory would have called for more frequent divergences. Third, there is evidence that prices and especially wages were less flexible in a downward direction than was implied in the classical theory, and thus other forces would have been required to supplement any downward pressures which may have occurred when efforts were being made to restore a country's balance of trade to equilibrium. Fourth, major central banks often ignored the rules of the game and neutralised the foreign payments imbalance by refraining from using discount rate policy when such use would adversely affect the domestic economy. If, for example, it became necessary to increase interest rates to reinforce the deflationary tendencies required to improve the competitiveness of domestic industries and thus ensure that the trade balance became more favourable, central banks often allowed interest rates to decline in an endeavour to avoid the deflationary situation created by the outflow of gold. Fifth, the importance of capital movements was entirely neglected in the price-specie-flow theory, despite the fact that the current account of the lending countries remained for many years in continuous surplus, and the recipient countries continuously experienced a negative balance on current account. In short, classical theory tended to be too preoccupied with the trade account and industrial competitiveness.

Since international capital flows depended to a large degree on economic conditions in the lending countries, it was the recipient countries which suffered most from changes in the level of foreign lending, particularly by way of instability in their exchange rates and their external balances. Finally, the discount rates of the major central banks in surplus and deficit countries tended to move together as the automatic adjustment mechanism came into action, and not, as one would expect from classical theory, in a divergent manner.[6]

OTHER FEATURES OF THE ADJUSTMENT MECHANISM

As noted earlier, the classical theory was over-simplified to the extent that it concentrated on the current account balance and neglected capital movements, the existence of which allowed the current account to remain unbalanced for several years. Later theorists supplemented classical theory by including capital movements, but early in the twentieth century economists were still at a loss to explain the rapidity with which the gold standard adjustment mechanism had in many cases produced external balance. The answer was eventually found in the changes in incomes which accompanied the price movements. Thus, a fall in a country's exports reduces the income of its export industry and through multiplier effects brings about a reduction in spending on wages, salaries, raw materials, consumption goods and savings. There will also be a decline in the country's demand for imports, which, by offsetting the fall in its exports, will tend to bring about balance in the country's external payments position. On the other hand, a rise in exports, by increasing domestic incomes, will tend to work in the opposite direction, reducing the payments surplus generated by expanding exports by encouraging a greater volume of imports.[7] As Scammell (1965, p. 49) points out, 'the potency of income adjustment can be judged from the fact that, on certain occasions, balance of payments adjustment has taken place in spite of simultaneous neutralising action by the central bank to offset the effects of gold flows'. In other words, there is a strong case for arguing that the major burden of adjustment in the gold standard was carried by changes in income.

In one respect at least the classical theory was correct — it predicted few international monetary problems. Once cannot help being impressed by the relatively smooth functioning of the nineteenth-century gold standard. Despite the relatively rudimentary state of economic knowledge concerning internal and external balance and the relative ineffectiveness of government fiscal policy as a weapon for maintaining such a balance, the external adjustment mechanism of the gold standard worked with a higher degree of efficiency than that of any subsequent international monetary system. Trade and capital movements proceeded smoothly over the gold standard period (1880–1914), exchange rates, especially among major trading countries, remained comparatively stable and quantitative restrictions on trade and other payments were remarkably absent. What made this efficient functioning possible? Perhaps the chief reasons accounting for the successful working of the gold standard are to be found in the position of the United Kingdom in the international economy, the growth and strength of sterling as an international currency and the working of the multilateral settlements network. Britain remained the major trading country throughout the century and the most important source of investible funds. Although it acquired and maintained a persistent trade deficit, it experienced a continuous current account surplus through its large 'invisibles' earnings from shipping and foreign investments. Nevertheless, Britain's gold reserves remained relatively low throughout most of the period, for the current account surplus tended to be offset to a large extent by the capital outflow which occurred during the period. To a more limited extent, other West European countries tended to follow this pattern when they, too, became major lenders.

The gold standard period was an era of rapid industrial growth in the world economy, and in the circumstances, it was possible to achieve adjustment without the appearance of deflationary tendencies. Changes in demand could readily be met by alterations in industrial structures, and if the adjustment process demanded price changes, these could be accomplished without widespread unemployment and reduced profits. In other words, the international economy was mostly dynamic and flexible in its operation. Often, too, an adverse payments situation did not lead to large reductions in international reserves because of the cushioning effect provided by the longer-term credit facilities which increasingly became available during these years. Furthermore, there was a greater degree of discretion exercised by central banks in the implementation of their policy than the classical theory admitted. This was true even of the Bank of England. While protection of its gold reserves remained of paramount importance in determining the Bank of England's monetary policy, it nevertheless exercised considerable discretion in the choice and timing of its actions and was always aware of the need to achieve external balance with a minimum of interference with the level of domestic business activity. Finally, the growth of a complex multilateral settlements network by providing a variety of ways of offsetting payments between countries considerably reduced the need for gold flows to balance international accounts. This reduced the need for countries to hold large stocks of gold for balancing purposes and thus helped to prevent a shortage of gold from developing as more and more countries came to adopt the gold standard in the years after 1870.

CONCLUSIONS

During its relatively brief existence, the gold standard was not the standardised or automatic international monetary system it was widely believed to be in the 1930s. There were various versions of the gold standard, including the gold exchange standard; and the discretionary monetary policies of governments exerted some influence on the automatic functioning of the mechanism. Even so, the system worked smoothly, without large and frequent lapses of confidence in the parities of major currencies. This success was due in part to the growth of a multilateral settlements network, and in part to the predominance of Britain in the international economy, which led to the increasing use of sterling as a supplement to gold in the settlement of international commercial transactions. Moreover, due to the increasing use of credit money (paper currency and bank deposits), which perhaps accounted for over 90 per cent of the total expansion of money from the 1870s to 1914, gold was becoming less important as a domestic currency towards the end of the nineteenth century.

Appendix 1: History of Money from Its Origins to 1914

Michael Graff

The Origins

The conventional view, which can be traced back to Adam Smith (and is repeated in textbooks ever since), holds that there is a natural human impulse to trade and barter. Accordingly, trade would have emerged before money, which in turn was invented to facilitate indirect exchange. After money was established, credit came to its aid as a means of acquiring purchasing power by those that are presently short of money. However, whether money and the monetary system resulted from trade, or vice versa, is a disputed question. The problem with the conventional economist's view is that there is no evidence of any society — past or present — that established trade based on *economic* considerations before it had been using money. On the other hand, there is abundant anthropological evidence of *ritualised* barter, without money or profit motive. Also, trade did most likely not emerge between individuals, but between clans or tribes, which puts doubt on Smith's assumption of the inherent human impulse to trade. Moreover, the first 'financial institutions' known of are the antique temple banks of Mesopotamia, which resorted to credit, but not to (coined) money. Thus, money is likely to have preceded organised trade.

Recently, David Graeber (2011) has argued that credit emerged even before money, and financial markets — or any markets — did not emerge spontaneously, but as a result of organised power: the state or the gods and their representatives on Earth, the clergy. Notably, also according to Graeber, the amendment of (coined) money to credit is due to war, specifically to pay soldiers in durable money rather than in terms of credit, a promise that becomes obsolete when a war-waging party is defeated. Also, slavery promoted the use of money. Accordingly, the economy of Antiquity at the same time became dominated by warfare, slavery and coined money. Thereafter, during the early Middle Ages, money was partly abandoned, along with slavery. Both return on the scene in the Modern Era, when the European economy was flooded with silver and gold from the New World, and slave ships kept crossing the Atlantic. The history of coined money as a means of payment may thus have to be considered as a special case within the broader history of money and credit. It is to the former that we turn now in more detail.

Early standardised means of transactions (pre-monetary currency) were *marketable*[8] goods, where the value of money was identical to the commodity value of the circulating means of exchange. Due to practical requirements, such as homogeneity, durability and divisibility, metals and bullion soon formed the basis of early commodity money. Since metal or bullion does not provide any obvious, intrinsic units or cuts, at this stage, the problem of standard weighting arose. The solution was to define standardised units of weight for bullion that would be used as currency, and to cut it to size accordingly. In the second century BCE, bullion with *private* stamps was used for monetary purposes. Around the end of the eighth century BCE, the first *royal* stamps confirming the purity or weight are found in Asia Minor. Although these early forerunners to coinage were rather clumsy lumps, the sovereign's stamps confirming their weight implies that they can indeed be considered as coins in economics terms. Coinage quickly spread through the Eastern Mediterranean as well as through the Middle East. Technical improvements soon followed, such as the disc shape, which continues in use today, embossing instead of casting and, while the first coins carried stamps on one side only, later the entire surface of the coin was richly embossed, making it increasingly difficult to clip or rasp bullion off the coin's edges, or to commit outright forgery. On this basis, the new medium of exchange gained acceptance. While it may have been customary to weigh the coins in the early days, a trusted seal from a chartered mint would contribute to eliminating the need for weighing for many, if not most, transactions. Thus, the prototype of the full-bodied coinage, minted under official charter, came about.[9]

Notably, full-bodied metal currency has remained the basis of the conception of 'money' until very recently. Coins below their intrinsic value were rare, and generally just those of low value. *Money was bullion.* Based on the antique design, this monetary system lasted for some 2,500 years. Apart from a minuscule fraction that the mint would charge for its services — usually far less than 1 per cent — money that consisted of full-bodied coins was a standard that referred to arbitrarily defined quantities of bullion. Underweight coins would either be rejected or circulate at a discount; and undervalued coinage would vanish from circulation as soon as its face value dropped below the commodity value (plus cost of melting and selling the metal). Price stability was guaranteed by the intrinsic scarcity of gold and silver. As the use of bullion for *monetary* in addition to ornamental or technical purposes created additional demand that would raise the price of bullion in terms of other commodities, the scarcity of bullion was further enhanced, which helped to keep the prices of other goods low. This contributed to the trust in the purchasing power of bullion as well as in the monetary system based upon it.

Yet, with money came inflation, a phenomenon that is accordingly known since Antiquity. The earliest systematic debasements of coinage go back to the Greek city-states. Performed as reductions of the share of gold or silver in the alloy to be minted, or by hiding cores of low-value metal within the coin, debasements were initially carried out with caution, and probably only in wartime, so that they would not be permanent threats to acceptance of the money as a means of payments at face value. The noticeable increase in price levels in ancient Greece was not brought about by debasement, but by the influx of large amounts of Persian gold after the conquest of Persia under Alexander the Great. In Rome, when the Punic

Wars were stressing the state finances, debasement was more common, and indeed, the first long-term inflation in history is due to systematic coin debasement in the Roman Empire, when in the course of roughly a century with average inflation rates of up to 4 per cent, the price level increased by a factor of 50.

The Dark Ages and the Commercial Revolution

The fall of the Western Roman Empire in 476 heralded the start of the European 'Dark Ages', stretching on to the eleventh century. During this period of organisational decay and stagnation, the ancient monetary standards largely disappeared and non-Byzantine Europe experienced progressive demonetisation. Coinage crumbled away and money vanished from circulation. Although Roman currency still served as a measure of value, there was no intrinsic difference between coins, jewellery or other valuables. Credit was largely limited to consumption loans in times of hardship and denominated in quantity of goods rather than in monetary units. Accordingly, investment had to rely on internal finance, and an occasional surplus would be hoarded.

Isolated resumptions of European coinage are documented for the eighth century, and by the tenth century, in northern Italy new coinage reappeared in large numbers, resulting in effective re-monetisation. This marks the beginning of the Commercial Revolution, which from the eleventh to the thirteenth centuries shaped the prototype of the modern financial system, including the settlement of payments, banking and insurance. The driving factor for this surge of innovation was the international trade in goods that had recommenced on a large scale, with northern Italy as its hub. Merchants in Genoa, Venice, Florence and the cities of Lombardy and Florence created an unprecedented need for finance and liquidity as well as constant demand for financial services such as currency exchange and naval insurance. With the return to the regular minting of money based on full-bodied coins, the related problems do not fail to re-emerge. In addition to wear and tear, the clipping of coins (by the public) and periodic debasements (by the authority) regularly contributed to reducing the bullion content of the coinage, which sooner or later inevitably would result in devaluation. The history of money, which for the most part is the history of full-bodied money, is hence mostly a chronology of debasements and subsequent monetary reforms to restore the old standard or to establish a new one with modified mint parity. The significance of this chapter of economic history consists in illustrating that the ancient monetary system quite effectively ensured that money as a unit of measurement would correspond to a well-defined quantity of bullion. Significant deviations from the official parity would sooner or later be detected and not tolerated, hence resulting in monetary reform. Inevitably, the authority at some stage would feel that its coffers were unduly depleted and again be tempted to debase the coinage, so that the cycle of debasement and reform would continue.

Though coined money as a rule would conform rather closely to the mint parity, the risk of receiving underweight coins was certainly too high to be neglected. Accordingly, for *large* payments settled in cash, the requirement to verify purity and weight persisted. This inconvenience triggered the path-breaking innovation of credit money. To reduce the number of payments that would finally have to be settled in cash, the merchants of northern Italy developed a number of new financial instruments. The most straightforward was to grant customers trade credit for later settlement. By softening the liquidity constraint of the cash economy, this contributed to making investment and consumption decisions less dependent on current liquidity. Another — arguably more important — innovation was the private cash account ('giro di partita') at the new 'banchi di scritta' or 'banchi del giro'. Apart from the peace of mind from knowing that coins or bullion were stored securely in the coffers of the bank, this innovation soon delivered a new kind of payments service, as payments from one customer of the bank to another — usually members of the local merchant community — could be performed as transfers between accounts. Initially both payer and payee would have to appear at the bank in person, but soon a written order by the payer, stating the payee and the sum to be transferred, was sufficient. Thus, the earliest known cheque was issued in 1368. This innovation made the settlement of payments safer and at the same time markedly reduced transaction costs.

Since the early cheques represented intrapersonal transfers of an existing claim on coins or bullion in the coffers of the bank, they did not increase the quantity of money, at least as long as the banks held 100 per cent reserves, as their statutes required. It would not take long, however, until some banks quietly began to breach the rules and offer standing overdraft facilities to their most trustworthy customers, which marks the beginning of fractional reserve banking. The most important implication for money and banking was that fractional reserve banking in principle allowed expanding the means of payments — the quantity of money — far beyond the rigid limits previously set by the quantity of bullion. Yet during the Commercial Revolution, bank money, important as it was to the merchant community, occupied a relatively small niche. Hence, despite its potential, the effect that this innovation had on the quantity of money initially remained very limited. In fact, it was not before the twentieth century that it became common for payments affecting the wider public.

Another important financial innovation was the medieval letter of exchange, an instruction to a merchant or a banker in another city to pay a specified amount to a third party.[10] Since before this inter-city or international trade had required risky shipments of coins or bullion, the letter of exchange was highly significant in supporting the expansion of trade. Apart from this, the letter of exchange helped to evade the ecclesiastical usury regulations of that time. Instead of charging explicit interest, it could disguise it as a 'discount'. For transactions between areas of different coinage, the exchange rate provided an opportunity to effectively charge interest without arousing the potentially dangerous attention of the church.[11]

Though the Commercial Revolution took place in the centres of trade — the towns — money and credit soon, and increasingly, affected also the rural population of medieval Europe. Initially this was because the growing population in the towns would buy victuals from the surrounding countryside for money, with the result that using money became common among rural people. Moreover, while serfdom prevailed, from the tenth century an increasing part of the rural population was employed as wage-labourers.[12] In addition, lords of feudal properties were increasingly being paid in money instead of feudal service or payment in kind. They, too, hence started to measure profit in money. Thus, throughout the medieval society, economic activity was directed more and more at the realisation of money revenue, and prototypes of the capitalistic enterprise emerged. In addition to this, the way of life of the aristocracy further promoted monetisation and credit. On the one hand, there were the expenses related to taking up public office. Also, gambling was endemic — almost obligatory — in aristocratic circles and resulted in huge gains and losses. As the bourgeoisie copied the habits of the aristocracy, gambling spread beyond the nobility. As a result of these developments, within a few centuries the largely cash-free society of the 'Dark Ages' was transformed into an economy that was monetised 'from head to toe' (Spufford, 1988, p. 378). Yet though the Commercial Revolution successfully developed credit money, and clearing soon became common practice, liquidity was ultimately restricted and depended on access to gold and silver: unbalanced accounts — at the bank or with a trading partner — would finally require settlement in full-bodied coins or bullion.

Modern Times

In late medieval Europe, the demand for money started to outstrip supply, so that in relative terms, currency became scarcer than in the preceding centuries. The mining and refining of bullion failed to keep pace with the increase in economic activity that was settled in cash. In addition, money in circulation was depleted through normal wear and tear as well as through hoarding, which, in times of unrest, often meant that coins were buried in depots and abandoned when their possessors lost their lives.

Furthermore, the world economy at that stage required a constant flow of gold and silver to the East. While Oriental goods were sought-after in Europe, in the East there was little interest in European commodities. Hence, the European balance of trade with the East was constantly negative and bullion had to be shipped to the East for settlement. The 'Great Bullion Famine' that resulted from these developments formed the empirical basis for European mercantilism, and particularly the doctrine of 'bullionism'. Indeed, for an economy in which the means of payment was predominantly restricted to full-bodied coins, bullionism was a well-founded strategy to counter a downward pressure on prices and hence to avert deflation and depression. However, with a production of bullion that was minor relative to the stock inherited from the past, so that the supply of money was practically exogenous, bullionism, once adopted by all relevant European economies, turned effectively into a zero-sum game. Consequently, the economic policy of mercantilism could offer no remedy to the scarcity of money and the 'hunger' for bullion in Europe as a whole. The only promising strategy for Europe was to find substitutes for bullion that were not subjected to the same inherent scarcity and yet were suitable to serve as money.[13]

Hence, at the dusk of the Middle Ages, the European monetary system was lacking innovation that would deliver substitutes for its bullion currency, which by now had become both common in usage and scarce in supply. Yet it took centuries for the sustainable solution to this problem to gain widespread acceptance — currency that circulated below a parity corresponding to its commodity price. In fact, the final dissociation of money from bullion did not take place before the 1970s, when the convertibility of the US dollar into gold was suspended.[14] Apart from institutional inertia, the most important retarding factor in the spread of credit money was a result of what has been called the 'Age of Discovery', the European expansion. It was driven by the hunger for bullion as much as — if not more than — by the desire to spread Christianity and succeeded in establishing a continuous and sizeable flow of bullion from the New World to the Old, thus increasing the supply of bullion-based money and alleviating the scarcity of currency. 'The famine of precious metal that had strangled the European Economy during the Middle Ages was over' (Cipolla, 1993, p. 214), implying that monetary innovation became far less urgent. In fact, scarcity of money was followed by abundance, and hence, towards the end of the sixteenth century inflation began that was to last for 150 years. This historical account of an obvious correlation between the stock of money and the price level for centuries constituted the empirical basis for the Quantity Theory of Money (see Appendix 2 to this chapter). Yet, the relief to the European bullion famine though influx from the New World was temporary and hence not a way to put an end to the scarcity of money for good. When the shipments started to decline, innovation was back on the agenda. By that time, it was not only triggered by the scarcity of money but also by the inconvenience of full-bodied coins for the settlement of large payments, as the early prototypes of credit money that were developed in Italy during the Commercial Revolution had not yet diffused from their niches. This now started to change. When the medieval trade with the East, taking the Silk Road to the Levantine Coast, then by ship across the Mediterranean to the trade centres of northern Italy, was replaced by the Africa route, new centres of trade and commerce emerged in the European ports of the Atlantic. By the seventeenth century, the financial instruments developed during the Commercial Revolution had been adopted in the Northwest. From that time, until 1914, the world's centres of money, banking and finance were found in Northwestern Europe; first in Antwerp, then in Amsterdam and Hamburg, and, after the Napoleonic wars, in London. Now financial development gained momentum and various local variants of secured and unsecured credit were added to the Italian prototypes, including different types of negotiable debt instruments. In particular, the medieval letter of exchange underwent important modifications, and its successor, the bill of exchange, became a negotiable instrument for credit and payment. An essential prerequisite for negotiability was that personal trust in the ability and willingness of the issuer to meet his obligations had to be substituted for by some more formal — institutional — guarantee. The solution found was bill discounting. For this purpose, in the larger centres of trade and commerce municipal discount houses were chartered. The first of these was in 1609 the Amsterdamsche Wisselbank, and here as elsewhere, credit and payment for regional as well as international trade were considerably facilitated.

Yet the bill of exchange never became a local means of payments. In Amsterdam this function was eventually taken by the Wisselbank's guilder (florin), which was credited to personal accounts for discounted bills as well as against deposits of full-bodied coins or bullion. The Wisselbank's guilder soon became the dominant currency for trade and commerce in Amsterdam and far beyond; in 1720, when the peak was reached, almost 300 local and foreign merchants held bank guilder accounts with the Wisselbank. The opportunity to settle payments by transfers denominated in a widely accepted bank deposit currency was much safer and more convenient than shipments of coinage or bullion, particularly in the face of the dreadful coinage mayhem of the sixteenth and seventeenth centuries.

As others, Adam Smith was impressed by the convenience that the Wisselbank meant to trade and commerce.[15] Yet he also realised that the Wisselbank did not restrict its activity to bill discounting and the issue of bank guilder against deposits of full-bodied coinage or bullion. In fact, although the statutes of the Wisselbank required the bank's guilder to be backed by 100 per cent reserves, in practice, credit-worthy customers could transfer guilder in excess of their deposits. In other words, the Wisselbank engaged in fractional reserve banking and made personal loans. As the beginnings of fractional reserve banking can be traced back to the Commercial Revolution and to the early goldsmith bankers of London, the Wisselbank's practice was not strictly an innovation. But now fractional reserve banking was performed by a public bank that was supervised by the authorities, and at a much larger scale than ever before. Hence, economic historians tend to identify the Wisselbank as the starting point of credit money.[16] In the seventeenth century, more than 20 public banks were chartered, modelled on the Amsterdam example, e.g. in Barcelona (1609), Hamburg (1619), Delft (1621), Nuremberg (1621), Rotterdam (1635), Stockholm (1656) and London (1694). Although the creation of money through fractional reserve banking was not covered by any of these banks' charters, it soon became accepted practice.[17] Bank money had thus become a reality.

Another type of credit money that emerged in the Modern Era is the banknote, or paper money, an impersonal means of payment which is characterised by the fact that, whatever its face value, its commodity price is practically zero. In Europe,[18] paper money was first issued in 1661 by the Swedish Riksbank, followed by the Bank of England in 1694 and the Bank of Scotland in 1695. From 1690, paper money was issued in New England and in the early eighteenth century in France as well as in various Italian and German states.

From a theoretical perspective, the numerous innovations in money, finance and the payments system during this period can be summarised as a gradual substitution of credit for commodity as a means of payments. This process had started during the Commercial Revolution, but it gained momentum in modern times. Still, until recently, credit money was confined to a relatively narrow range of economic activities, and bank money was not common in everyday life until well into the twentieth century. The move towards credit money freed the monetary system from the material restrictions of the past. However, the downside of removing the natural and technical constraints that the use in Antiquity of full-bodied money minted from bullion had laid on the quantity of money is that without these restraints, the potential for inflation is infinite. And indeed, while moderate inflations and tinkering with coinage have been recorded since the first coins were minted, hyperinflation has exclusively affected credit money.[19] Due to this imminent danger, opposition to uncovered paper money ('fiat money') has been fierce well into the twentieth century, both among the public and among those responsible for the stability of the monetary system.

For the nineteenth century, Peel's Bank Act of 1844 is revealing in illustrating the dilemma.[20] It declared the notes of England as legal tender, which could be perceived as a decreed 'fiat money'. However, at the same time the Act included the obligation that two-thirds of the notes in circulation had to be covered by gold in the bank's coffers. This effectively allowed supplying liquidity to the economy in excess of the stock of bullion. But with mandatory reserves of two-thirds, the public could trust that the notes were indeed convertible into gold, at least in the absence of circumstances that might trigger a run on the coffers of the bank. Other European countries soon followed this example, which indeed proved reasonably flexible in supplying money and liquidity for the fast-growing economies of that time.

With the onset of hostilities in 1914, the situation to cause a flight from paper into gold had arrived and consequently, convertibility into gold was suspended in all belligerent nations. This marks the beginning of a process at the end of which, in the 1970s, the link between money and bullion, which had been established thousands of years ago, would be cut for good and the world's currencies eventually all turned into uncovered paper money. But this is a later story.

Appendix 2: The Quantity Theory of Money

Michael Graff

The Equation of Exchange

Before we turn to the epistemology of the quantity theory, it will be helpful to lay out its twentieth-century formalisation, the equation of exchange. Let M denote the amount of money in the hands of the public, T the economic transactions paid for with M within a given period, P the price level of T and V the velocity of the circulation of M. With these definitions, we can write down the following identity:

$$MV = PT \tag{7.1}$$

which is the version of the equation of exchange associated with Irving Fisher (1911). The right-hand side of the equation denotes the volume of transactions paid for, quantified in terms of their prices. With M defined as the stock of means of payments at hand to settle the volume of payments given by PT, V is the number of times per period that the stock of money must pass from payer to payee to satisfy the equality condition, which is another way to look at the concept of the velocity of money.

M, V, P and T have empirical correlates that in principle can be quantified. In practice, however, measurement of any of the four variables is fraught with formidable difficulties. Regarding M, for periods before the advent of bank money, the stock of bullion and full-bodied coins may serve as a useful approximation. Since liquid bank liabilities have become the major means of payments, measurement is not as straightforward, which is illustrated by the fact that applied economics nowadays refers to various definitions such as M1, M2 and M3 (occasionally M4), where a higher ordinal number indicates a wider aggregate. The textbook definition for M1 is legal tender (notes and coins) plus demand deposits with banks in the hands of the public. Aggregates with higher ordinal numbers consecutively add bank liabilities of lesser liquidity, implying that money's core function as a means of payments, which is the focus of M1, is amended by its quality to serve as a means for storage of wealth and financial investment. Hence, M1 is most in line with M in the equation of exchange. Yet, not even the narrow aggregate M1 consists of homogenous elements, and in fact, Irving Fisher's original equation of exchange

$$MV + M'V' = PT \tag{7.2}$$

takes account of this, where 'M signifies the quantity of money in circulation; V, its velocity of circulation, or rate of turnover per annum; M', the volume of deposits subject to check; and V', its velocity of circulation, or rate of turnover per annum'.[21] The distinction between two categories of means of payments, with the possibility of different velocities, adds realism to the equation, and monetary statistics nowadays allow distinguishing between cash and demand deposits. For the time being, let us consider the measurement issues regarding M as manageable. However, the same does not hold for T, which includes intermediary products and services. Since the commonly available measures of aggregate economic activity like gross domestic product (GDP, or Y) exclude intermediary products and services, $Y < T$. Referring to Y, for which useful approximations are usually available, rather than to T, hence requires us to define a modified identity given by

$$MV^Y = PY^r \tag{7.3}$$

which is the GDP version of the equation of exchange (7.2). Equation (7.3) is the norm today. Y^r denotes real GDP and V^Y the velocity of money related to GDP. Since $Y < T$ by definition, from (7.1) and (7.3), we can derive $V^Y = V(Y^r/T) < V$.

At first glance, the difference between the transaction and GDP versions seems minor, but it should be noted that in (7.1) and (7.2), money is strictly referred to as a means of transactions, whereas in the GDP version, V^Y cannot readily be interpreted as the velocity of money. Yet, as long as the fraction Y^r/T is constant, the growth rate of V^Y will be the same as that of V, and with estimates of Y^r/T, we can compute V^Y from V. In other words, V^Y is essentially representing the same concept as V, implying that it is characterised by the same benefits or drawbacks.

The Epistemology: Important Steps in the Evolution of the Quantity Theory

Medieval Thought Foreshadowing the Theory of Money

Scholasticism (the most prominent proponent, Thomas Aquinas, died in 1274) tried to reconcile secular aspects with normative theological considerations. Important in our context is the 'just price doctrine', which on the one hand postulates the exchange of equivalents, but on the other insists that individual incomes should secure the means of living corresponding to social status (including the means to be able to give to charity). Prices were hence seen as phenomena that should reflect market forces as well as normative aspects.[22]

Empirically, in medieval Europe, apart from all innovations brought about by the Commercial Revolution, the stock of money usually grew rather smoothly, without sudden increases or decreases that would have led anyone to contemplate possible links between the quantity of money and the level of prices. Yet, when the bubonic plague swept over Europe from 1347 and within a few years reduced the population by an estimated one-third or more, this had an impact on prices that did not escape the attention of a thoughtful observer, Nicolai de Oresmius (1325–82). He was the bishop of Lisieux, an astronomer, mathematician and, last but not least, advisor to Charles V on financial matters. In his tracts on economics, he mainly argued against coinage debasement (even if ordered by Charles V). In today's terminology, Oresmius' opinion was that reducing the bullion content of coins that maintained the same face value had led to a corresponding increase in prices, so that in the end, the king had not gained anything by the debasement.[23] However, Oresmius tract 'De Origine, Natura, Jure, et Mutationibus Monetarum' of 1355 is probably also the first statement of the quantity theory. Now it is important to note that this publication came three years after Europe's above-mentioned first medieval plague epidemic (1347–52). The resulting decline of aggregate economic activity economic was — in today's terminology — a dramatic negative supply shock. Accordingly, the price increases that attracted Oresmius' attention were only partly due to coinage debasement; the supply shock was probably the major factor. Though it may seem an anachronism to discuss earlier contributions in terms of the equation of exchange, the effect of the plague on the price level can easily be captured by the GDP version of the equation of exchange (3) with time subscripts:

$$M_t V_t = P_t Y_t^r \tag{7.3a}$$

Let $t-1$ denote the time before the outbreak of the plague, so that $Y_t^r < Y_{t-1}^r$. Now, in a currency system where money is bullion, the stock of money M is practically constant in the short term. Hence, without a dramatic decline in V, it follows that $P_t > P_{t-1}$. While we can speculate that some hidden money was permanently lost when people fell victim to the plague, and that the survivors tended to hoard money more than previously (leading to a decline in V), the decline of Y to appears to have outweighed the declines of M and V. The price increases that Oresmius observed were, then, caused by a sharp decline in transactions that had to be settled in money in an economy that had inherited a stock of money from a far more numerous population. Of course, this does not contradict the debasement story. As can be seen from the equation of exchange, without a decline of V, both an increase in the *nominal* supply of money M and a decrease of Y will result in a higher price level P.

Classical Quantity Theory

The classical quantity theory is referred back to Jean Bodin's (1530–96) 'Réponse aux paradoxes de Monsieur de Malestroict touchant l'enchérissement de toutes choses' (1566). Malestroict had blamed the widespread practice of coin clipping, i.e. debasing of coins by the public, for the general acceleration in prices 'de toutes choses', which had become noticeable by the middle of the sixteenth century. Bodin took a different stance. He argued that the price level had risen together with the stock of money, or more precisely, with the amount of bullion available for monetary purposes. Bodin witnessed the results of fifteenth- and sixteenth-century shipments of bullion from the Americas to Europe and the resulting 'price revolution', and was able to draw the right conclusion about the link between the two. The classical Quantity Theory of Money is thus a reflection of the history of money in the early Modern Era. It preceded the advent of classical economics by two centuries.

The classic's final version of the Quantity Theory is the proportionality theorem, which postulates that the price level reacts proportional to changes to the stock of money. For the classics, the Quantity Theory was a major device to overcome the doctrine of mercantilism, according to which the money supply — in these times given by the stock of bullion within state borders — is the deciding determinant of economic prosperity. This was contested by the proportionality theorem, which can be documented by numerous citations from the classical literature. For our purpose, it will be sufficient to refer to a few examples. David Hume explains (1752, p. 127): 'If we consider any one kingdom by itself, 'tis evident, that the greater or less the plenty of money is of no consequence; since the prices of commodities are always proportion'd to the plenty of money'. After thus having presented the proportionality theorem as self-evident, Hume explains that the acquisition of bullion would be to the detriment of foreign trade, as the domestic export goods would become more expensive. He concludes (p. 133): 'In my opinion,' tis only in this interval or intermediary situation, betwixt the acquisition of money and rise of prices, that the increasing quantity of gold and silver is favourable to industry'. With these reflections, known today as the 'price-specie-flow' mechanism, Hume formulated the theory of the balance of trade in an international bullion (or gold) standard, where the flow of 'specie' would tend to equilibrate the balance of trade.

Some 50 years later, in the 'bullionist controversy', David Ricardo (1772–1823), perhaps the most influential classical theoretician, was a devoted proponent of the Quantity Theory with a strictly bullionist concept of money. Consequently, Ricardo (1809) advocated a strict correspondence between the issue of banknotes and the bullion in the issuing banks' vaults.

Finally, let us cite the last great advocate of classical economics, John Stuart Mill (1848, p. 15f.):

> If the whole money in circulation was doubled, prices would be doubled. If it was only increased one-fourth, prices would rise one-fourth.... So that the value of money, other things being the same, varies inversely as its quantity: every increase of quantity lowering the value, and every diminution raising it, in a ratio exactly equivalent.

More formally, the classical Qantity Theory's proportionality theorem can be derived from the equation of exchange (7.3) as follows:

$$MV^Y = PY^r \Leftrightarrow P = \left(\frac{V^Y}{Y^r}\right)M \qquad (7.4)$$

$$\Rightarrow$$

$$P = f(M) \qquad (7.4a)$$

In the history of economic thought, the classical quantity theory is a theory of the general price level, as formalised in equation (7.4a). Assuming an exogenously given level of potential output and full employment, in the short term, Y^r can be treated as a constant. Assuming further that the income velocity of money V^Y is exogenous and constant, equation (7.4a) can be specified as $P = aM$, where a is the proportionality constant. Notice that under these assumptions, money is 'neutral' in the sense that real output is completely independent of the stock or changes to the stock of money. Money affects the price level, and nothing else.

Finally, to derive a theory of the price level (7.4a) with empirical content from the identity stated by the equation of exchange (7.3), the following conditions must be met:

1 M is an exogenous variable and independent of P, Y^r and V^Y. (Otherwise, there is no conclusive causality.)
2 V is an exogenous variable; in particular, it is independent of P, M and Y^r. (Otherwise, the link between money and prices is indeterminate.)
3 Y^r is independent of M, i.e. neutrality of money holds. (To the degree to which real output is a positive function of the money supply, extra money would raise output but not prices.)

Quantity Theoretical Inflation Theory

Yet another approach to derive a positive theory from the equation of exchange is to transform it into growth rates and to solve for the growth rate of the price level, i.e. inflation. Taking logarithms and time derivatives of the equation (7.3) following t result in

$$d(InM)/dt + d\left(InV^Y\right)/dt = d(InP)/dt + d\left(InY^r\right)/dt \tag{7.5}$$

$$g(M) + g\left(V^Y\right) = g(P) + g\left(Y^r\right) \tag{7.5a}$$

$$\pi = g(M) + g\left(V^Y\right) - g\left(Y^r\right) \tag{7.5b}$$

where $g(X)$ represents the growth rate of a variable X and $\pi \equiv g(P)$. As can be inferred from equation (7.5b), if the velocity of money is a constant, hence $g(V^Y) = 0$, any growth rate of the money supply exceeding that of real output, leads to inflation. This is the basis of perhaps the most famous, and most often quoted of Milton Friedman's statements that 'inflation is always and everywhere a monetary phenomenon in the sense that it is and can be produced only by a more rapid increase in the quantity of money than in output' (Friedman, 1994, p. 49).

It is in order to note that the observed correlation between π and $g(M)$ does not prove that causality runs from $g(M)$ to π; inflation could also be the cause and $g(M)$ the consequence, especially in hyper-inflationary situations. Moreover, this inflation theory must assume super-neutrality of money, i.e. independence of the growth rate $g(Y^r)$ from $g(M)$. The question of super-neutrality of money in the inflation process has not been empirically clarified so far.[24] But if $g(Y^r)$ reacts positively to a change in $g(M)$, the correlation between $g(M)$ and π is not as narrow as the equation of exchange suggests.

RECOMMENDATIONS FOR FURTHER READING

For a detailed studies of the international monetary system and its history, see Hawtrey (1927, *The Gold Standard in Theory and Practice*, London), Bloomfield (1959, *Monetary Policy under the International Gold Standard 1880–1914*), Triffin (1968, *Our International Monetary System: Yesterday, Today and Tomorrow*) and the book edited by Eichengreen (1985, *The Gold Standard in Theory and History*).

For the history of money and credit — discussed in Appendix 1 to this chapter — see Menger (1892, *On the Origin of Money*), Einzig (1949, *Primitive Money in Its Ethnological, Historical and Economic Aspects*), Davies (1994, *A History of Money. From Ancient Times to the Present Day*), Galbraith (1995, *Money. Whence It Came, Where It Went*) and for an anthropological perspective Graeber (2011, *Debt: The First 5,000 Years*).

For the Quantity Theory of Money — discussed in Appendix 2 to this chapter — see Fisher (1911, *Recent Changes in Price Levels and Their Causes*) and Blaug (1995, *Why Is the Quantity Theory of Money the Oldest Surviving Theory in Economics?*).

NOTES

1 For a detailed exposition of the history of money and its driving forces, see Appendix 1 to this chapter.

2 Once the mint ratio and the world market ratio diverged, it paid those who could do so to engage in arbitrage at the various exchanges. Suppose, for example, that the Paris exchange is offering 15.5 ounces of silver for one ounce of gold and that an American merchant holds 1,000 ounces of gold. If the US mint ratio is 15 to 1, he can obtain 15,000 ounces of silver for his 1,000 ounces of gold at an American mint. But if the gold is sent to Paris, he can get an extra 500 ounces of silver for it. It will pay him, therefore, to convert his gold into silver in Paris and to reconvert all his Parisian silver into gold in Washington. The result of this process is, of course, that all gold leaves the US and silver becomes the circulating medium. Gold was 'undervalued' in the US and, according to Gresham's Law, that 'bad' money drives out 'good', the gold coinage does not circulate there.

3 'Irredeemable' or 'inconvertible' legal tender notes could not be converted into gold on demand, but only when the government is willing to allow it. Normally, of course, in a gold standard country, banknotes were convertible into gold on demand. An inconvertible currency may depreciate relative to gold, if the quantity issued is excessive, and lead to inflation.

4 Following Gresham's Law, maintaining bimetallism in this situation would have meant a de facto move to a silver currency with a rapidly expanding monetary base, which, according to the Quantity Theory of Money, would lead to inflation. For an elaboration, see Appendix 2 to this chapter.

5 The price-specie-flow theory predicts that a deficit country's exports would rise, and its imports fall during the adjustment period. Conversely, a surplus country would experience opposite changes in the volume of its import and export trade.

6 See Triffin (1968) and Scammell (1965).

7 This point corresponds to the Keynesian view that quantities react quicker than prices. The resulting 'export multiplier' can be formalised as follows: Aggregate output Y equals consumption C, investment I plus net exports X–M. Assuming that aggregate consumption and imports are constant fractions of income ($C = cY$ and $M = mY$), whereas aggregate investment and exports are autonomous (with respect to Y), implies that $(1-c+m)\ Y = X+I$. The export multiplier is given by the partial derivative of Y with respect to X, $\partial Y/\partial X = 1/(1-c+m)$. The export multiplier thus increases in c and decreases in m. If $c > m$, it exceeds unity, so that an increase (decrease) in exports increases (decreases) aggregate by more than the original volume change.

8 See Menger's (1892) seminal contribution.

9 The next notable improvement in the production of coinage, the screw press, followed in the early Modern Era.

10 In the judgement of Max Weber (1924, p. 229), the medieval letter of exchange had the same irreplaceable function as a means of making payments over distances that the cheque had in Weber's time. Yet, the letter of exchange was not accessible to everybody, since it depended on close relations with trustworthy and liquid business partners. Merchants would most likely refer to networks consisting of relatives, which were common among Sephardic Jews or Calvinist families.

11 Canonical prohibition against interest for clerics was enacted in 325; from 806, it was extended to lay people. A breach could lead to condemnation by the church. A gradual relaxation took place from 1516, when money lending was tolerated on charitable grounds if the interest rate was modest. The Protestant rejection of interest prohibition can be traced back to Calvin in 1574. In the Napoleonic *code civil*, interest payments were explicitly allowed, which at the time could have had a catalyst effect, at least in Catholic Southern Europe. Although, as indicated above, ecclesiastical prohibition of usury could be circumvented, the normative power of medieval religious authority should not be underestimated. The fact that credit at interest spread throughout business circles despite the 'usury' ban owes much to the fact that agents and traders had to have an adventurous spirit and be willing to take risks in view of the precarious nature of land and sea travel. Moreover, due to their nomadic way of life outside of the ordered medieval world, it was probably easier for merchants than most other people to distance themselves from the prevailing values and mores. However, a deliberate, rational, anticlerical rejection of interest prohibition was not able to evolve until well into the time of the Enlightenment.

12 Yet, this transformation proceeded slowly and initially only in a limited number of places; in Italy and Russia, its completion took until the nineteenth century.

13 We note in passing that, given the knowledge of the nature of chemical elements at that time, *alchemy* was a rational attempt to fight the bullion famine, although — as we know now — it was doomed to fail.

14 Yet, let us recall that economic history provides a host of examples of monetary decay and disintegration, illustrating that organisational and institutional progress is reversible, as during regressions to a barter economy or a commodity money standard. Frequently cited in the economic literature are the 'cigarette standards' in Sicily, Germany and in the Pacific after 1944, see, e.g., Radford (1945).

15 Smith 1776 (Book 4, Chapter 3). See also Sombart (1916, Vol. I, p. 424ff.), who cites a considerable number of observers, reflecting how contemporary merchants greeted the improvement that the new money meant to trade and commerce.

16 See, e.g., Galbraith (1995, p. 8), according to whom the founding of the Wisselbank was nothing short of 'a step that joins the history of money to the history of banking'.

17 Some economists maintain that the Wisselbank strictly upheld its statutes, i.e. ensured that its bank money was backed 100 per cent. However, there is no dispute that the public banks that followed the Wisselbank's example soon established the practice of fractional reserve banking.

18 See, e.g., Born (1972) and Rittmann (1975, p. 483ff.). The oldest known paper money circulated in China from the seventh century. However, at the end of the Ming Dynasty in the seventeenth century, it perished.

19 Initially, governments issued uncovered paper money in times of crisis, war or revolution. The first European issue of government paper money occurred in pre-revolutionary France where, after the revolution, the notorious 'assignats' were emitted. Other early examples are the paper monies in North America during the War of Independence, in England during the Napoleonic Wars and the greenbacks from the US Civil War. As Friedman (1994, p. 45) remarks, these emergency measures without exception quickly resulted in inflation and ultimately disruption of the paper currency, after which stability had to be restored under a bullion standard.

20 See Born (1976, p. 20ff.). Robert Peel was Prime Minister of Great Britain in 1834–5 and 1841–6.

21 Fisher (1911, p. 38). Note that Fisher did not consider demand deposits (which are not directly convertible into bullion) as proper money. Yet, inclusion of M' into the equation of exchange proves that he considered it a fully functional means of payment. In 1911, the ancient identity 'money = bullion' still reigned in economics.

22 Setting prices clearly different from the 'just' price was a case for the secular jurisdiction, so that the just price doctrine certainly had normative power.

23 For this, see Gordon (1987) and others. According to Mundell's (1998, p. 3) judgement, Oresmius's 'De Moneta' (written during the reign of Charles V, when no less than 86 coin devaluations took place) is the first traditional version of Gresham's Law, and the most important work on the theory of money in the period prior to the sixteenth century.

24 Traditionally, economics would not usually assume super-neutrality of money, as individuals easily err about the rate of inflation. Contrary to this view, 'neoclassical macroeconomics' today frequently refers to rational expectations of the expected rate of inflation, and money is therefore not only neutral, but also super-neutral; see McCallum (1990).

CHAPTER **8**

International Aspects of Economic Growth in the Nineteenth Century

The Spread of Industrialisation

A. G. Kenwood, A. L. Lougheed and Michael Graff

INTRODUCTION

The international economy played a major role in promoting the spread of economic growth in the nineteenth century. The flows of trade, capital and labour, which linked countries together economically, not only provided the means whereby the benefits of economic growth, in the form of higher real incomes, could be transmitted from country to country, but they were also the mechanism through which the technological and social innovations that are the essence of modern economic growth could be diffused. As a result, the economic growth of most countries came to depend as much on their ability to take advantage of the opportunities for trade and for the acquisition of new knowledge and additional factors of production presented by the international economy as on the quantity and quality of the economic resources domestically available to them.

Obviously, the international diffusion of modern technology and the stimulation of economic growth through an expansion of foreign trade are economic processes that are not independent of each other, if only because export-led growth implies some measure of technological and social change.

The nineteenth-century world economy is best viewed as being composed of a centre and a periphery, with growth at the centre building up economic pressures tending to diffuse the development process to the periphery. Initially, Britain stood at the centre of this growth process, but as the century progressed, continental Europe and, in particular Northwest Europe, came to play a larger part in fostering the spread of economic development overseas. Britain's central role in the world economy during these years rested on a technological revolution that had begun in the second half of the eighteenth century with the Industrial Revolution, and continued from 1820 to 1880 to transform a predominantly agrarian economy into the world's first industrial nation. But imitators were not lacking and, partly through a flow of capital and skilled labour from Britain, the new industrial technology spread first to continental Europe

DOI: 10.4324/9781003382171-11

and then to the US, so that by the 1870s, when Britain's rate of industrial growth began to slow down, these other countries began to play their part in the process of transmitting growth to the less developed regions of the world.[1]

The peripheral regions were incorporated in this international growth process through a steady and persistent increase in the demand for primary products, which many of these areas were able to produce. Industrialisation in Britain soon exposed her limited range of natural resources and her growing inability to feed a rapidly growing population. Increasingly, Britain was forced to rely on other countries to supply her mounting needs for foodstuffs and industrial raw materials. To a lesser extent the other industrialising countries of Europe also came to depend on overseas sources of supply of primary products. The growing pressure of industrial demand on the centre's natural resources and supplies of foodstuffs and raw materials, and the resulting tendency towards rising prices, prompted a search for cheaper supplies in the periphery and an outflow of capital and skilled labour to develop peripheral sources of supply. In this way, a cumulative process of growth was initiated in a number of countries overseas by the relation between the export demand for primary products and the inflow of foreign capital and labour that was associated with the expansion of the export sector. Particularly favoured by these developments were the US and, later, the 'regions of recent settlement', including Canada, Argentina, Uruguay, South Africa, Australia and New Zealand, each of which, at different times and to varying degrees, came to depend on growth through primary product exports and the inflows of foreign capital and labour associated with it. At the other end of the spectrum were those peripheral countries which remained largely unaffected by these revolutionary changes, or those which became 'enclave economies', that is, countries in which foreign demand and the new technology served to modernise the export sector while leaving the rest of the economy virtually unchanged.

The failure of the expansion and modernisation of the export sector of the enclave economy to spark off growth in the rest of the economy is only one of the problems arising out of the international record of economic growth in the nineteenth century. There are many others. Why, for example, did economic growth spread to only a limited proportion of the total world population? What accounts for the slow spread of industrialisation? For even in Europe and the US, rapid industrialisation occurred only after 1870, more than a century after the new technology had emerged in Britain. More pertinent to the present discussion is the question of whether these 'failures' in the diffusion of economic growth reflected weaknesses in the functioning of the international economy or whether they were the result of the existence of other obstacles to the spread of economic development. These questions, and many others like them, are the subject of a continuing and lively debate.

THE SPREAD OF INDUSTRIALISATION

The diffusion of technology is closely related to the problem of mobility — of goods, people, ideas and behaviour. Clearly, mobility in this sense was greatly enhanced during the nineteenth century by innovations in transportation and communications and in the field of international finance, which greatly facilitated the large-scale movement of goods, people and capital between countries. These flows of economic resources were, in turn, important channels for the diffusion of the new industrial technology, since physical capital embodied it, immigrant artisans and entrepreneurs possessed the required technical skills[2] and imported goods provided opportunities for adaptive imitation.

Given the opportunity for adopting new methods of production presented by the international economy, the spread of technical innovation also required an economic incentive. Probably the most effective stimulus to innovation is the market to be supplied: both its size and the rate at which it is growing. A large and rapidly expanding market creates an environment that is highly conducive to technological advance and to all forms of innovation, including the adoption and adaptation of foreign techniques.

THE CONTRIBUTION OF THE INTERNATIONAL ECONOMY

The emerging international economy was itself an important form of market expansion in the nineteenth century. Without legal barriers and problems created by exchange rate uncertainty — which, as we have seen, were minimal in the late nineteenth century — foreign trade is in principle simply an extension of domestic trade; and expanding opportunities for the international exchange of commodities did encourage the spread of industrialisation. In Britain, industrialisation was initially based on a rapidly expanding export of cotton textiles, and later it came to depend increasingly on exports of iron manufactures and coal. In the US before the Civil War (1861–5), raw cotton production — mostly based on the expansion and intensification of slave labour — played a part in supporting early industrial development in the country; and industrialisation in Germany late in the nineteenth century was also closely tied to an expansion of manufactured exports. Even in Russia and Japan, where governments created domestic markets for industrial goods through their own demands for military and railway equipment, the ability to develop an export trade, in wheat for Russia and in cotton textiles for Japan, was necessary to provide the foreign exchange needed to service the inflow of foreign capital or to purchase the foreign machinery essential to industrialisation. Whether the demand for industrial goods was satisfied directly through an expansion of manufactured exports, or whether it was created indirectly through the growth of primary products exports leading to a rise in domestic real incomes, expanding foreign markets created an environment highly favourable to technological diffusion.

The growth of markets, both at home and abroad, is closely related to improvements in transportation, since poor transport facilities automatically restrict the size of the market, thus limiting the scope for the use of modern technology. For this reason, good transport was perhaps the most powerful single means for accelerating the importation of modern industrial techniques in the nineteenth century. In this respect, foreign investment was often of vital significance, since much of it went into railway building on the Continent and in North and South America and Australasia. Some of this capital also went into the development of shipping lines, the construction of docks and harbours, improvements in communications and the provision of other ancillary services necessary for an expanding foreign trade.

The size of the domestic markets of some countries was also increased by immigration, which allowed populations to grow faster than they would have done if dependent only on natural increase. Moreover, where the immigrant population could be used in combination with unexploited or unused economic resources, per capita real incomes often rose (thus further increasing market size) because a larger workforce permitted greater specialisation and the use of more productive techniques. Furthermore, part of the immigrant workforce could be utilised in constructing the transport network.

Finally, for a number of countries within Europe, the movement towards larger domestic markets was aided by the gradual reduction of internal barriers to trade by such trade-liberalising measures as the freeing of the Rhine to all shipping, and by the setting up of customs unions such as the German Zollverein. At the same time the spread of free-trade policies after 1850 provided most countries with expanding opportunities for the international exchange of goods and services. Later in the nineteenth century, however, the widespread adoption of protectionist policies, while reducing the size of foreign markets, encouraged industrialisation in some countries by preserving the domestic market for local producers.

On the supply side, a country's rate of physical and human capital accumulation is obviously a major determinant of its capacity to absorb new ideas and new methods of production. Where, for example, technical change is embodied in capital equipment, a country's rate of capital investment is all-important, since, in general, the more investment the greater the degree of technological progress. Capital shortage may therefore hinder technological diffusion in several ways. For example, it will place limits on a country's stock of social overhead capital, especially transport facilities. The need for relatively abundant supplies of capital is also stressed, where innovations in techniques cannot be made singly but require simultaneous development in various industries. Moreover, the fact that techniques can rarely be borrowed without adaptation further adds to challenges. Finally, the fact that industrialisation in the nineteenth century was accompanied by population growth and urban development meant that there were heavy demands on capital in the form of housing, public utilities and the additional tools and machines needed to equip an expanding workforce. While, in most countries, the bulk of their capital needs were satisfied out of domestic savings, the availability of foreign funds could be crucial to finance infrastructures and other social overhead capital — especially transport facilities, communications and public utilities.

For some countries foreign trade and immigration flows also partly overcame the obstacles to industrialisation caused by lack of natural resources, skilled labour and enterprise. In so far as the adoption of modern industrial techniques in the nineteenth century was dependent on natural resources, geographical location or some other unequally distributed endowment, growth opportunities were not equally available to all countries. Limited natural resources were restricting industrialisation in some countries of Europe. French economic development, it has been argued, suffered from a shortage of coal. But whatever the relevance of scarcity of natural resources as an obstacle to technological diffusion, it must have become less important with time, as progress during the nineteenth century began to make alternative processes possible, or to make imported resources effective substitutes for scarce and therefore expensive domestic supplies. Moreover, if the raw materials necessary for industrial development could be imported from abroad, so too could the necessary skills and organisational ability. Historically, the trader from abroad and the immigrant artisan have long been the main channel for the importation of foreign techniques; where the nineteenth century differed from earlier times was in the scale on which these movements of labour occurred and in the wider range of skills people carried with them — their 'human capital' — when they moved from country to country.

International Transfer Mechanisms

What prompted the greater part of the flow of labour, capital and trade between countries were differences in the relative prices of these resources in different countries. In the case of both labour and capital, non-economic considerations exerted some influence on their movement internationally, but for the most part it was differences in wage rates and the rates of return on investment that prompted the flow of factors of production from regions where earnings were low to those where they were higher. With commodity trade, too, the exchange was prompted by differences in the relative prices of the goods traded, which reflected in turn differences in the costs of production in the various countries engaged in foreign trade. In so far as the flows of goods, capital and labour took place in response to differential economic advantages of this kind, they acted as spontaneous or 'natural' carriers of modern technology and ideas. On the other hand, specific and direct attempts were often made by governments and other interested bodies to transfer technologies internationally. In addition to sending students abroad to study the new techniques, governments also encouraged the inflow of foreign skills and capital through subsidies to immigrant entrepreneurs and guarantees of dividends on foreign loans. Implicit in such policies was the assumption that the diffusion of the new knowledge, either nationally or internationally, was likely to be slower than desired in the absence of conscious efforts to encourage technological change.[3]

CAUSES OF THE LIMITED SPREAD OF INDUSTRIALISATION

International

Despite the existence of these natural carriers of technology on a scale previously unmatched in history, and despite the efforts made by some governments to reinforce the market influences determining the volume of direction of these trade and factor flows, the rate at which the new technology diffused was slow, and the spread of modern industry limited. Thus, by 1913, the spread of industrialisation had affected Western Europe, North America and Japan, but the rest of the world remained largely untouched. An important question is thus whether the slow rare of diffusion of modern industrial growth across borders reflected weaknesses in the functioning of the international economy as a mechanism for transmitting growth between countries, or whether it was largely the result of local obstacles to the absorption of modern technology. We can offer a few general observations.

To begin with, if the diffusion of modern industrial technology was limited before 1914, it was partly because the supply of capital and labour available for international transfer was limited, and because not all countries desiring to import these productive resources were equally well placed to attract them. North America, and especially the US, were particularly attractive for foreign investors and migrant labour; and Western Europe, because of its compactness and its proximity to Britain, the seat of the Industrial Revolution, was also conveniently placed to take advantage of the new technology. The fact that these two regions received the lion's share of the economic resources that did shift internationally during these years meant simply that there were fewer of these resources available for other capital- and labour-importing countries, and their prospects for industrial development suffered correspondingly.

Moreover, in some countries primary production continued to be more profitable than manufacturing, so that real income could be increased more rapidly by specialising in agricultural and mining production and exchanging the surpluses of primary products for manufactures produced elsewhere. As long as the real incomes of primary producers were sustained by the mounting demand for foodstuffs and raw materials of the industrialising regions at the centre of the international economy, the spread of industrialisation to peripheral countries was limited by the economic advantages accruing to them from the growing territorial division of labour which formed the basis of the expanding international economy of the nineteenth century.[4]

National

While the international economy may have functioned in such a way as to limit the spread of industrialisation in the nineteenth century, for the most part the major obstacles to the diffusion of modern technology were to be found within countries rather than between them. The available evidence for this period suggests that the diffusion of modern industrial technology between countries was much faster than its diffusion within countries. Thus, Watt's steam engine, first brought out in England in 1776, was introduced into France in 1779, into Germany in 1788 and into Italy in 1816. On the other hand, within Britain the steam engine did not come into general use until after 1850. In the other European countries, however, the lag was even greater, and in Italy the steam engine was still far from widely used even in 1913. A similar situation developed in the US, where the steam engine was introduced towards the end of the eighteenth century and quickly adopted for use in river boats. But it was not widely used in American industry until after the Civil War (1861–5). Another example is the spread of the idea of interchangeable parts and standardised production. Developed in the US well before 1850 and introduced into the British government's arms factory at Enfield in the 1850s, these innovations were adopted only very slowly by British manufacturers. While further evidence of disparate rates of technological diffusion between and within countries exists — for example, in the spread of new textile machinery and modern metallurgical processes during the nineteenth century — what obviously needs explanation is the cause of this disparity. Why, with easy international movement of inventions, a country's capacity to absorb and adopt new techniques on a wide scale should be so difficult to foster or impart.

As we have already indicated, the adoption of modern technology in the nineteenth century was partly dependent on the availability of capital, natural resources and the necessary labour skills (initially, above all else, literacy) and organisational ability. But while limited markets and shortages of productive resources could be partially overcome with the help of foreign trade, the available domestic supplies of capital and organisational skills were often crucial in bringing about successful industrialisation. Moreover, non-economic influences, particularly social attitudes, customs, beliefs and motivation to succeed economically,[5] are important determinants of the rate at which new techniques are diffused throughout an economy. The incompatibility of the new industrial technology with existing institutional arrangements, the reactions of merchants and businessmen to the uncertainty and risks attached to new ways of doing things, and the concern for social and political stability are only a few examples of the forces generating the social rigidities and resistance to change likely to be encountered in an industrialising society. The existence of such forces serves to remind us that technological change is a cultural, social, psychological and political process. Yet on the question of whether major structural shifts in the socio-political fabric must precede or accompany the adoption of industrial technology, the facts are not unambiguous. In France, for example, a very strong concern for continuity in the social and cultural sphere meant that technical change was relatively slow, and that the government did not play a major role in promoting economic development. Germany, on the other hand, achieved rapid industrialisation despite the fact that the old order retained much of its force. Denmark and Sweden also appear to have created expansionary economies as much by changing the direction of their economic efforts as by altering the structure of their institutions or the habits of their peoples. In South and East Europe, however, the existence of an essentially feudal system, and the rigid social stratification which accompanied it, as well as the low social value attached to industry and profit in the culture of some of these countries, constituted insurmountable barriers to the adoption of the new industrial technology, backed up as they were by deficiencies of resources, scale of markets and education. Only Russia, in this part of the continent, succeeded in industrialising to any significant extent, and then only after the resistance of the government and other conservative forces had been overcome, largely by outside events, notably the lost Russo-Japanese War of 1904–5.

Outside Europe, the spread of industrialisation to the US, Canada and, to a lesser extent, the other regions of European settlement overseas was helped by a level of receptivity to the new technology that was at least as high as that in Britain and the more industrially advanced countries in Europe, with which countries they shared a common social, economic, cultural and linguistic background. These ties were also useful in fostering periodic inflows of European capital and labour, which considerably assisted the diffusion of industrial techniques within the countries concerned.

High receptivity to the new technology was not confined to European countries or their off-shoots overseas, however. In Asia, Japan began industrialising rapidly towards the end of the nineteenth century, and in this respect, it is interesting to contrast the experiences of Japan and China before 1914 when confronted by Western technology and economic intervention. Displaying a common policy of exclusiveness and virtual absence of contracts with foreign countries, as well as a social structure and system of land ownership that acted as a barrier to industrialisation, their responses to Western intervention in their affairs were totally different. Whereas Japan adopted Western industrial techniques rapidly and succeeded in achieving economic 'take-off' seemingly without any major social or cultural changes, the Chinese government remained contemptuous of Western civilisation and opposed to all forms of social and economic change.

Some idea of the extent of the spread of modern industrialisation by 1913 is given in Table 8.1, which contains indices of output of manufactures per head of the population for a wide range of countries. These output indices are based on the average share of manufacturing output for the period 1925–9 allocated to each country and taken back to 1913 by the use of industrial production indices. The measure of industrial output for each country was then divided by its population and the result expressed as a proportion of US output per head. Given the manner of their construction, the indices contained in Table 8.1 obviously should be treated as orders of magnitude, with wide margins of error.

TABLE 8.1 Index of output of manufactures per head of population, 1913

US	100	Poland	13
		Russia	9
Europe		Yugoslavia	6
UK	90	Romania	6
Belgium	73	Greece	4
Germany	64		
Switzerland	64	**Other**	
Sweden	50	Canada	84
France	46	Australia	75
Denmark	46	New Zealand	66
Netherlands	44	Argentina	23
Norway	39	Chile	17
Austria	31	Japan	6
Czechoslovakia	28	Mexico	5
Finland	27	South Africa	5
Italy	20	Brazil	2
Hungary	19	India	1
Spain	15		

Source: Lewis (1978, p. 163, table 7.1). For a more detailed explanation of the construction of the table, see Lewis (1978, p. 313, footnote 9).

What the table reveals is the relatively limited spread of the new industrial technology by 1913. The US, Britain and most of Western Europe were relatively well industrialised by this time, as were Canada, Australia and New Zealand, whose highly productive agriculture provided, as in the other industrially advanced countries, a strong domestic demand for manufactured goods. Elsewhere, however, in East and South Europe, in much of Latin America and in most of Asia and Africa, the process of modern industrial developments had barely begun by the outbreak of the First World War.

CONCLUSIONS

The spread of industrialisation from Britain to continental Europe and North America was assisted by the functioning of the international economy. The flows of capital, labour, goods and services and ideas, which linked together the countries of the world, provided the channels through which modern industrial technology diffused between nations. If the extent of this technological diffusion was limited in the nineteenth century, it was partly because the stock of capital and labour available for international transfer was limited, and partly because not all countries desiring to import these extra productive resources were equally well placed to attract them. But what was an even greater obstacle to the spread of industrialisation was the fact that many countries, even when they received inflows of foreign labour and capital, lacked absorptive capacity — the knowledge base, institutions and flexibility necessary to take advantage of the changing technological opportunities that presented themselves. It was this weakness that accounts for the limited industrialisation up to 1914. To industrialise successfully, there had to be capital formation, technical change and reallocation of resources, as well as changes in social, political and cultural attitudes to economic activity. Since in most countries, 'traditionalism' and along with it the forces of inertia were strong and deeply entrenched, the spread of industrialisation was inevitably a slow process.

RECOMMENDATIONS FOR FURTHER READING

For a detailed introduction into the field of development economics, the textbook by Todaro and Smith (2020, *Economic Development*) is a highly recommendable reference.

For texts which focus on the process and spread of industrialisation until 1914, see Milward and Saul (1973, *The Economic Development of Continental Europe, 1780–1870*) and (1977, *The Development of the Economies of Continental Europe, 1850–1914*), Pollard (1981, *Peaceful Conquest: the Industrialization of Europe 1760–1970*) and Cameron (1985, *A New View of European Industrialization*).

The contribution to the book edited by Spencer and Woroniak (1967, *The Transfer of Technology to Developing Countries*) discusses the chances and challenges for poor countries in the absorption of advanced technology from abroad.

NOTES

1 But, as Rondo Cameron has stressed, 'It is necessary … to distinguish between the mere diffusion of technology and the distinctive pattern of industrialisation that occurred on the continent as a result of this diffusion' (Cameron 1985, p. 10). Cameron goes on to argue (Cameron 1985, p. 22f.) that, besides the British model of industrialisation, there were several others in which such factors as the availability of coal and the needed human resources formed two basic ingredients, with international investment and financial institutions performing subordinate roles.

2 For an account of the paramount importance of migration of skilled artisans at the dawn of the Industrial Revolution in Europe, see Cipolla (1972).

3 These two methods of transmitting technical knowledge enable us to draw a distinction between technological diffusion, on the one hand, and technological transfer, on the other. Whereas the former term can be used to describe a natural spontaneous process of knowledge transmission, technological transfer is based on deliberate effort, see Spencer and Woroniak (1967). Both mechanisms played their part in the process of economic development in the nineteenth century.

4 In this context, Argentina may be cited as the prime example.

5 For an elaboration of this point, see Inkeles (1983).

CHAPTER 9

International Aspects of Economic Growth in the Nineteenth Century

A. G. Kenwood, A. L. Lougheed and Michael Graff

INTRODUCTION

Outside the industrialising countries, economic growth was primarily a reflex action to the steady and persistent rise in the world demand for primary products. In these peripheral countries, economic growth took place for two reasons. First, trade was one of the means whereby the benefits of technological progress in Europe diffused to the rest of the world, mainly through the exchange of manufactured goods for foodstuffs and raw materials. At the same time, specialisation in the production of those primary products most suited to the economic resources of these countries tended to raise the general level of their skills and productivity. Moreover, this increased productivity, along with the continued growth of exports and the accompanying rise in real incomes, provided an incentive to the establishment and expansion of other forms of economic activity and paved the way for further economic development. In this way, an expansion of primary product exports could induce growth in the rest of the economy.

Faith in the transmission of development through trade was not too difficult to justify in the light of what was happening during the nineteenth century. Great Britain, for example, was developing successfully, first on the basis of textile exports, and later by expanding her exports of coal and iron. More relevant for primary producing countries, however, was the experience of the US, which before the Civil War (1861–5) experienced rapid economic development, albeit largely because of a rapid expansion in their raw cotton exports, based on an increasing amount of slave labour under a regime of terror. Less violent nineteenth-century examples of successful development based on primary product exports include Denmark, Sweden, Australia, Canada, New Zealand, South Africa and, to a lesser extent, Argentina and Brazil. In certain other countries, the export trade, if not a leading sector, was still a most valuable support to economic development. In Russia, for example, wheat exports provided the foreign exchange needed to import the foreign capital goods essential to industrialisation, whereas

DOI: 10.4324/9781003382171-12

in Japan, where the creation of a domestic mass market was precluded by the low-income condition of the peasants and workers, the expansion of foreign markets was imperative as an outlet for the products of the country's new manufacturing industries.

Yet, if, during the nineteenth century, there were many countries in which exports played an important part in inducing growth in the rest of the domestic economy, there were many others, accounting between them for the bulk of the world's population, in which foreign trade failed to generate conditions conducive to self-sustaining growth. Broadly speaking, two explanations have been advanced to account for this breakdown in the transmission of growth through trade. The first explanation emphasises the drawbacks and disadvantages of dependence on exports of primary products for promoting economic growth, while the second attempts to explain why growth in the export sector fails to carry over to the other sectors of the economy and cause a general expansion of the economy.

The first approach concentrates on the drawbacks to a country specialising in primary production. In particular, the disadvantages arising out of a country's dependence on a single export product are stressed, with all that this means for the country's future development should the world demand for the product fall, or should superior sources of supply be discovered elsewhere. Other disadvantages to primary production include the excessive price fluctuations displayed in the markets for primary products and their influence, through a country's foreign exchange earnings, on its financing of economic development. In particular, low elasticity of demand in the rich countries, along with a high incidence of supply-side shocks, may result in extremely volatile export revenue. Moreover, there is the declining terms-of-trade argument ('terms-of-trade pessimism', also 'Prebisch–Singer thesis'[1]), which runs to the effect that specialisation in primary production is an undesirable policy in the long run, since it condemns primary producers to ever-declining terms of trade (export prices relative to import prices). According to this argument, while the gains of technological progress in industrial countries are distributed to producers in the form of higher incomes — because of the existence of industrial monopolies and upward pressures exerted on wages by well-organised trade unions — in the primary producing countries competitive pressures ensure that the gains from technical improvements in agriculture and mining are passed on in the form of lower prices. Consequently, it has been claimed that in the long run, the prices of manufactured goods (the imports of primary producers) have tended to rise relative to the prices of primary products (the exports of these countries). This, in turn, has meant that primary producing countries were able to purchase fewer and fewer manufactured goods with a given quantity of primary product exports. The Prebisch–Singer version relates an empirically observed long-term decline in the poorer countries' terms of trade to the income elasticity of demand for primary and manufactured goods, which is higher for the latter than for the former. Thus, with rising incomes, the increase in demand for manufactures exceeds the demand for primary sector output. Prebisch's and Singers' observations have been challenged in recent decades to the degree that their thesis was largely viewed as discredited by the evidence, but as more data are becoming available, it now appears that their terms-of-trade pessimism is, in the long run, warranted.[2] Finally, as has been stressed by Erik S. Reinert, specialising in primary production, i.e. according to the comparative advantage of the poorer countries, in dynamic perspective implies choosing those activities in which innovation and change occur at significantly lower rates than in manufacturing and industrial production.[3]

The second explanation of the sluggish growth in the periphery concentrates on the factors limiting the carry-over of growth from the export sector to the rest of the economy. It is this carry-over problem which lies at the centre of the successful or unsuccessful transmission of growth through trade.[4]

REGIONS OF RECENT SETTLEMENT

In discussing the carry-over problem, it is useful to draw the distinction between those countries in which, despite immigration, labour was scarce but land abundant, and the densely populated countries of Asia. The former group of countries, often described collectively as the 'regions of recent settlement' — or 'settler colonies'[5] — include Canada, the US, Australia, New Zealand, South Africa and Argentina, and they constitute for the nineteenth century the outstanding example of growth through trade in primary products. In them, a large inflow of European labour and capital supplied the factors needed for export industry production, with the immigrant workers and entrepreneurs making up a rapidly integrated and largely homogeneous society, conversant with European needs and markets and receptive to the forces of innovation and change. In some of these countries, such as the US and, to a lesser extent, Canada and Australia, the large size of the country could give rise to internal economic development independent of any significant impetus from the export sector, while in all of them abundant and readily accessible natural resources attracted foreign capital with the profits to be made from their exploitation.

Moreover, with the exception of Argentina, these were high-wage economies. Generally speaking, we should expect to find higher wage levels in sparsely populated countries than in densely populated ones, as well as a tendency for wage levels to show a rising trend over periods of rapid expansion of output requiring more (scarce) labour. These expectations are broadly borne out by experience in the newly settled regions of North America and Australasia. What is even more important, however, is that high wages assisted economic development in two ways. First, they provided buoyant markets, even in countries with relatively small populations. Second, through the efforts of entrepreneurs to counteract high wage costs and overcome labour scarcity, they generated technical progress in the form of labour-saving innovation, which in turn supported and enhanced the high productivity that came in time to provide the basis upon which these high wages were paid. This interaction between rising productivity, high wage levels and expanding domestic markets was not experienced by all labour-scarce countries. In Argentina, for reasons shortly to be discussed, the high-wage/low-rent economy never materialised in the nineteenth century, and the opportunities for the further development of the economy were correspondingly reduced, despite very high rates of growth in the country's export sector. It is for this reason that we include Argentina in the following discussion of those countries in which export expansion was unsuccessful or only partially successful in generating self-sustaining growth.

THE EXPORT ECONOMIES

Owing to the steady growth in the world demand for primary products characteristic of the period, the demand side does not need detailed elaboration in attempting to explain the failure to establish a transmission of growth through trade that occurred in many countries during the nineteenth century. To explain the phenomenon, we concentrate on the supply side, where two major problems presented themselves to peripheral countries desiring to benefit from the growth forces generated by European industrialisation. First, these countries had to integrate themselves into the expanding lines of trade created by the rising European demand for foodstuffs and raw materials. When this was achieved, the expansionary forces generated within the export sector of these integrating economies had then to be diffused throughout the rest of the economy. In other words, the lack of successful economic growth in underdeveloped countries during the nineteenth century can be explained either by inadequate or late integration into the world economy or by the obstacles which prevented the growth forces originating in the export sector from transmitting themselves to the rest of the economy.

Late integration into the world economy partly explains the relative backwardness of many African economies. Although there was a rapid expansion of African exports in the late nineteenth century, the extent of the continent's integration into the international economy was seriously limited by transport difficulties. In a continent with few navigable rivers, where the ravages of the tsetse fly restricted the use of animal power and where, as a result, porterage was the chief means of transport, the transition from an economic system based on slave labour to one based on wage labour tended to have a paralysing effect on transport and, through it, on internal trade. Apart from gold and ivory — and, until slavery was finally abolished in the Western hemisphere in the late nineteenth century, abducted and commodified human beings —, there were few commodities that could bear the high cost of porterage from the interior.

When it arrived, even the railway could provide only a limited system of communications in the absence of animal-drawn wheeled transport and feeder roads. As far as low-value bulky commodities were concerned, a radius of 50–65 km from a railway, or a navigable river for that matter, was the extreme limit of profitable production for export under conditions of porterage. This transport deficiency blunted the impact of world demand on the African economy and accounts for the persistence of a substantial African subsistence economy which, through its low productivity and lack of monetisation, slowed down the overall economic growth of the continent.

In those regions and countries which did achieve relatively early and successful integration into the world economy, the problem is one of explaining the lack of successful export-led growth. Here, two broad categories of explanations have been put forward, one economic, the other political and socio-cultural. The economic explanations tend to concentrate on the differential effects on economic growth of the various export commodities according to their production characteristics. In particular, this approach singles out for attention the export sector's demand for inputs, its effects on income distribution and the creation of markets and the opportunities it provides for the diffusion of technical, organisational and administrative skills. The second approach stresses such factors as land tenure systems, the basic values and attitudes of the population, political conditions including the effects of colonialism, and other largely non-economic considerations. In fact, neither set of explanations is completely independent of the other. In discussing the failure of export-led growth to materialise in any given country, both must be taken into account, although the weights to be allocated to each will obviously vary from one country to another.

The economic explanations centre on the different types of productive activity to be found in the primary producing countries and their differential effects on income distribution and the opportunities for long-term development. In particular, the distinction is drawn between peasant farmer export economies, on the one hand, and those economies primarily dependent on exporting the products of mines and plantations on the other. These basically different patterns of productive activity are important because they generate different export-income distributions between foreign and domestic producers, and because they provide differing opportunities for improving the skills and productivity of the indigenous population.

Peasant farmer exports, which include such commodities as rice, palm oil, cocoa, cotton, rubber and copra and other coconut products, are important in Africa and a number of Asian countries. Apart from land, peasant production typically requires very little durable capital equipment, since it amounts to little more than an extension of the traditional economic organisation and technology of the subsistence sector. It is also a form of production which has little need of outside capital and labour. In fact, where the peasant combines the growing of cash crops with other crops intended for his own personal consumption, export production is largely self-financing. Typically, too, peasant production draws little or no labour from outside the household. Two links, outside the peasants' control, are needed, however, to connect them to the world markets for which they produce. Improvements in transport and communications can help open up new areas of production, and a middleman is often necessary to collect, process and convey the peasant's produce to foreign buyers as well as supply the imported goods that act as an inducement to increased export production, since by stimulating new wants among the peasants, the expansion of imports can act as a major dynamic force encouraging the expansion of exports.

In the last quarter of the nineteenth century the output of many peasant economies increased substantially in response to a growing world demand for their products. Between 1870 and 1913, peasant rice exports from Burma (now: Myanmar) and Thailand grew some 10–13 times. Egyptian cotton production rose from 22,500 tons in 1860 to 140,000 million in 1879 and 350,000 tons in 1913. On the west coast of Africa, palm oil and oil-seed accounted for over three-quarters of the total value of Nigerian exports in 1913, and cocoa contributed 80 per cent to the value of the Gold Coast's total exports in the same year.

Despite these impressive export performances, in most countries their impact on the rest of the economy was limited or insignificant. There were several reasons why this should be so. The partial commitment to export production implicit in an economic set-up where the peasant household continued to provide for its own subsistence requirements in addition to growing cash crops limited the spread of a money economy. If, in addition, market transactions were restricted largely to an exchange of exports for imports, then the monetised sector obviously had little impact on the rest of the economy. On the other hand, complete export specialisation, while more conducive to the development of the domestic market — since peasant families producing for export would set up a cash demand for locally produced foodstuffs and other locally produced goods and services — was not without its drawbacks.[6] The peasants were now completely at the mercy of an often unstable export market. More important, their activities ceased to be self-financing, so that in the event of drought, plant disease or a fall in world prices, they might be forced to fall back on outside sources of credit, including money-lenders who charged high rates of interest. In these circumstances, partial specialisation often represented a rational response to the prevailing set of economic conditions under which the peasants operated.

The spread of a money economy was also restricted by lack of transport which, as we have already seen, accounted for the persistence of a subsistence sector in large areas of Africa. Limited technical knowledge, simple methods of production and poor-quality produce also reduced the level of peasant income, either by keeping productivity low or by influencing the prices received for peasant produce on world markets. In some countries the increase in production and exports achieved during these years was absorbed partly by an increase in population and partly by a rise in the level of living of the upper and middle classes and by a much smaller rise in that of the bulk of the population.[7] There was also the possibility of a part, and often a substantial part, of the peasant's income passing into the hands of some person or group in the export sector, especially when the middleman handling the peasant's crops could exercise monopoly power. Thus, a few foreign import-export firms could combine to purchase the peasants' output at low prices, while selling them imports at highly inflated prices. Alternatively, this monopoly power could be exercised by a government agency, such as the 'Nederlandsche Handel-Maatschappij', which was set up in the Dutch East Indies in the 1820s to purchase peasant produce at low, fixed prices or to acquire it as taxes in kind. Exploitation of the peasant could also occur when the peasant's crops had to be processed at a company factory possessing a local monopoly. This appears to have happened in Cuba, where improvements in sugar technology and an influx of foreign capital led to a reduction in the number of sugar mills and an increase in the manufacturing capacity of those that survived. At first, competition between the mills worked in favour of the sugar farmers. But later, when, in order to ensure adequate supplies of sugar cane, the mill companies created territorial monopolies by purchasing plantations and by building private railways to transport the cane to the mill, the surviving farmers found themselves completely at the mercy of one or other of the large companies.[8]

While peasant farmer export economies have certain features that are potentially favourable to the spread of economic growth, from its very beginnings, plantation-type production displayed characteristics highly inimical to successful economic development. This type of agriculture predominated in the former 'extractive colonies' of Latin America and the Central American and Caribbean regions where sugar, bananas, coffee and cotton were the major plantation crops grown. It was also to be found in Ceylon (now: Sri Lanka), parts of India and in Southeast Asia, where the emphasis was on tea, coffee and rubber. In Africa, plantations developed relatively late. By the 1890s cocoa, coffee and tobacco plantations had been established in the German Cameroons, and sisal was first introduced into Tanganyika in 1892. Banana plantations in the Cameroons, tea plantations in Nyasaland and East Africa and oil-palm plantations in the Belgian Congo were not established until the start of this century.

Originally based on the use of slave labour, in the nineteenth century plantation production was characterised by: a high degree of foreign ownership and control; the provision of finance by foreign banks and agency houses; large-scale, factory-style operation of the plantations using large amounts of labour specially imported from abroad for these purposes; control of the import-export trade by foreigners; and virtually complete reliance on imported supplies of capital equipment, estate supplies and, often, even food for the workforce. These key characteristics of plantation production had important consequences for the working of the export sector and its capacity to transmit growth to the rest of the economy.

Where the export sector consisted almost wholly of foreign-owned plantations employing foreign capital and imported labour, it constituted an enclave economy which, because the income it generated was largely remitted abroad, contributed little to the formation of the domestic market and the promotion of local economic growth. Low wages with no rising trend (despite rapid growth of output) were also characteristic of those export economies where use was made of indigenous labour. In some countries, such as the Central American republics, where the coffee and banana plantations depended on the local population for their workforce, money wages, plus a variety of devices designed to cut off the peasant from free access to land, were used to force the local population into employment at low wages. When these methods proved insufficient, the governments often resorted to more direct, coercive measures to meet the labour requirements of the rapidly growing export sector. Similar policies, including the imposition of money taxes on the indigenous population, were used in Africa to drive the natives into paid employment in the mines and plantations. In other plantation economies, the relatively abundant supply of cheap labour imported from India and China tended to depress wages in the export sector as well as in the economy generally. In so far as the local population was deterred from entering employment in the export sector by the prevailing low level of wages, they tended to crowd into alternative paid occupations, thus depressing wages in those industries as well. Alternatively, the local population was forced to fall back on the subsistence sector, with its associated low productivity and lack of market contact.

The outcome of this situation was a high concentration of a country's income and wealth in the hands of a small group of people, whether of local or foreign origin, and, as a consequence, an underdeveloped domestic market. Foreign ownership also meant leakage of export income overseas; but even when the plantation owners were local entrepreneurs employing local capital, their contribution to local economic growth, either through their consumption or their investment expenditures, was often minimal. In some economies the local entrepreneurs formed too small a group to permit economic production for their domestic demand; in others, contact with Western culture and consumption patterns turned them into large-scale importers of foreign goods and services. In both situations the result was the same, the creation of a group of 'luxury importers' who contributed little to the promotion of a domestic market, either by way of consumption or of investment.

If the market contribution of the export sector to domestic economic growth was small, so too was the technological contribution in the sense of improvement in the quality of the workforce. Since there was little pressure from labour for higher wages, the entrepreneur had no interest in replacing his labour by capital or in improving the skills of his workforce. The same arguments apply to land where it was in abundant supply. Lacking any incentive for improvements in methods of cultivation or of labour skills, the tendency for the entrepreneur to invest new capital in the simple extension of his plantation was reinforced. Given the prevailing pattern of resource availability, with capital scarce and land and labour abundant, the method of production used and the form of investment taken were rational ones, although their capacity for promoting growth in the rest of the economy was limited. Potentially, mining was the most effective form of production for diffusing technical skills and raising the level of labour productivity. In fact, its potential was rarely ever realised. Initially the use of modern mining techniques inevitably meant that foreign skills had to be imported as well, and the indigenous workers could find employment only as unskilled labourers. Over time, the structure of the mining labour force changed very little, either because of discrimination against local workers, which prevented them from gaining promotion and the opportunity to acquire new skills, or because the nature of the local workforce gave the employer no incentive to impart new skills to it.[9] The outcome of all this was a tendency for the low wages paid to the local workforce to persist, along with no or little improvement in its average level of skill.

Whether in plantation or mining economies, these low wages eventually became institutionalised in a cheap-labour policy which was justified on a number of grounds, including the low productivity of the workforce, its customarily low material standard of living, its lack of response to the incentive of high wages, and the prejudice that, in general, indigenous labour not only had low productivity but that it also had limited capacity for improvement. Since low wages meant low productivity, the cheap-labour policy became self-justifying, and through the vicious circle of low wages and low productivity the productivity of the indigenous workforce even in thinly populated countries was fossilised at its very low initial level. It was the pattern of low wages and productivity perpetuated by the cheap-labour policy of the mines and plantations, rather than primary production as such, that accounted for the failure of exports in underdeveloped countries to be a leading sector initiating growth in the rest of the economy.

The other set of factors relevant to this discussion comprises the social, political, cultural and legal constraints on the propagation of export-led growth. These constraints largely reflected the psychological and ideological attitudes generated by the export economy's one-sided orientation, wherein agricultural production for export was what really counted. Change in the existing socio-political system, in so far as it occurred, was effected only to the extent required for the realisation of this objective. This is seen all too clearly in the land tenure system that developed in the plantation economies. Where property in land became economically meaningful only when coupled with technical and commercial know-how and easy access to finance, the resulting system of land ownership was rapidly structured around the plantation as the central type of organisation in agricultural export sectors. This structuring of the export sector was often brought about by deliberate government policy. In the Central American republics, for example, the inability of the respective governments to raise capital on international markets made them dependent upon foreign firms, particularly banana producers, for the building of railways and the improvement of port facilities. In return, these plantation companies received generous land grants and other government incentives, including exemption from taxes. In other countries, what government policy failed to do in the way of discriminating between those who could and those who could not own land, the market did through unequal access to financial and commercial processes and institutions and through differences in technical knowledge. Whatever the forces at work, be they government or free-market inspired, the outcome was almost always the same — a bimodal property distribution with a few enormous plantations at one end of the scale and many very small farms at the other.

Although it was not a plantation export economy, a similar situation developed in Argentina. Here, the early growth of an export economy based on cattle-raising led to the fertile areas of the Pampas passing into the hands of a few large cattle ranchers. Later, when new export lines were developed, particularly wheat, the lack of readily accessible land for occupation by immigrant farmers seriously impeded the growth of output and employment in the rural sector.

The tendency towards concentration of land ownership affected the development of agriculture and of the economy as a whole in a several ways. First, it restricted the growth of rural output and employment as well as the growth of domestic markets. The lack of available agricultural land held back rural output by discouraging immigration, since the immigrant was obliged to work as a tenant farmer or as a low-paid field hand. Alternatively, immigrants were forced into the towns, thus swelling the supply of manpower for urban employment and forcing down wages in these labour markets. Second, the concentration of land ownership led to a stratified society in which the bulk of the country's income and wealth went to a few people, while the mass of the population lived on incomes barely above the subsistence level. With income concentrated in a few hands, there was a disproportionate demand for luxury consumption and investment, usually met out of imports, whereas the low income level of the bulk of the population restricted the latter's demand for manufactured goods and was therefore an obstacle to industrial development. Industrial growth was also limited by the free-trade policy adopted by nearly all these countries. The landowning class constituted the ruling political group and, mindful of its own interests and those of foreign circles to which it was linked in a variety of ways, it advocated a free-trade policy which, by allowing the unrestricted entry of foreign manufactures, limited the development of the basic industries needed to integrate the whole economy.

ECONOMIC IMPERIALISM AND COLONIALISM

Economic development was also hindered for various reasons in those territories that became colonised following the burst of imperialist expansion that occurred in the late nineteenth century. Beginning in the 1880s, a wave of 'colony grabbing' began that continued until the outbreak of war in 1914. Africa was divided among the European powers; British control was extended over Burma (now: Myanmar) and Malaya; France consolidated its Indo-Chinese empire; and the US was not free from the desire for political and economic expansion — the Philippine Islands were seized during a war with Spain, and political intervention occurred in Hawaii, Mexico, Costa Rica, Dominica, Colombia and Nicaragua.

The root causes of this burst of imperialism in the late nineteenth century are complex, as the numerous theories put forward to explain the phenomenon indicate. Some explain the acquisition of colonies in these years in purely political terms, seeing the colonies either in strategic terms or as political bargaining counters for use in the game of international diplomacy. Others see the new imperialism as a manifestation of a popular and emotional concern for national prestige and power. Economic explanations of the phenomenon abound. The commercial needs of Europe are stressed, including the growing need for new markets fostered by the spread of protection and the growth of industry; the desire to gain control over supplies of raw material, particularly tropical products; and the need to find alternative outlets for surplus capital for which domestic investment opportunities did not exist. Providing an additional pretext for intervention in the affairs of other countries and possibly leading to their eventual acquisition as colonies, were the missionaries, planters, labour recruiters and traders of the colonising countries. These people, who through their activities (maybe unwittingly) undermined the established order in the foreign territory, often forced their country's government to step in to protect their lives and property and to restore political stability.

The aspiration for colonies has often been rationalised in purely economic terms, yet the available evidence suggests that the colonial annexations of the late nineteenth century were of limited economic benefit to the colonising powers. Most of these tropical colonies were too poor to provide valuable markets for manufactured exports, and while some of them were suppliers of important industrial raw materials, for example metals and crude rubber, the combined share of the colonies in the raw material markets of the world was relatively small. Consequently, except for Britain, whose empire was by far the largest and provided uniquely favourable markets and a wide variety of raw materials, trade with the tropical dependencies was only a small fraction of the total trade of their owners. Moreover, even when the trend towards protectionism became intense, the fact that up to the First World War and beyond, Britain, Holland, Belgium and Germany retained liberal commercial policies in their dealings with their colonies meant that non-colonial nations generally had easy access to the colonial markets of these states.

If tropical colonies were not acquired to provide exclusive markets and sources of raw materials and foodstuffs for the metropolitan country, neither were they an important outlet for the surplus capital of that country. Indeed, there is very little geographical correlation between capital exports and the acquisition of new colonies after 1880, and compared with foreign investment in Europe and the 'regions of recent settlement', the funds invested in Africa and Southeast Asia were relatively insignificant. Thus, whereas by 1914 almost $11,000 million of British investments were to be found in the US and the British Dominions, only some $600 million was invested in West Africa, the Straits Settlements and the rest of Britain's recent overseas acquisitions. Furthermore, many imperialist powers — notably Russia, Italy, Portugal and Spain — far from having an embarrassing surplus of capital, were net importers of capital and must therefore have had other motives for making annexations. Nor, when it was undertaken, was investment in the tropics always highly profitable. Studies of the type of loans issued in the heyday of colonial expansion reveal that the greater part was in fixed-interest government securities; that the profitability of this investment was only marginally higher than that of domestic investment; and that in the end some European investors lost their money through defaults. On the other hand, the return on some risk capital (equities) was often high, and probably higher than could be obtained at most times on industrial investments in Europe or America. Yet the high profits earned on colonial equity investments were more the result of the heavy industrial demand for particular products, for example metals and rubber, the scarcity of local capital and the superior bargaining position of Western countries in their dealings with politically and economically weaker societies, than the outcome of the exercise of formal imperial power as such.

Whatever the nature and extent of the benefits accruing to the metropolitan powers from the possession of colonies, however, there can be little doubt that colonisation placed severe limits on the economic development of the annexed territories. In these countries, the indigenous population could not resist penetration by Westerners into the heart of their economy, or the reorganisation of their laws and institutions according to the interests of Western entrepreneurs and governments. Changes in the system of land tenure, the conditions of labour supply and the nature of the economic activities of large populations were imposed by colonising governments. At the same time, the setting up of an orderly framework of government administration and the introduction of sanitation and other public health measures caused a rapid growth of population in many colonies. The result was a disruption of the traditional balance between population, natural resources and technology.

The case of India may be cited by way of illustration. Here, the British need of an efficient and simple method of raising land revenues resulted in two systems of land tenure being introduced. In the Presidency of Bengal, the land was concentrated in the hands of a group of great landlords who were expected to remain strongly pro-British, since their income and security depended, in the last analysis, upon the strength of the British regime. Elsewhere in India, the British made land settlements on a field-by-field basis with the individual cultivating peasants, as in southern Madras, or on an estate basis with groups of leading families in the villages, as in the central parts of India. Where peasant farming predominated, the nature of the revenue and land tenure systems — annual payment of taxes in money and in full, plus the private property structure of landholding which permitted mortgaging, transference, alienation — meant that in time of drought or other financial difficulty, the peasant was forced to turn to the moneylender and merchant for credit. Whichever land tenure system operated, however, it afforded to the landlord and moneylender a means for drawing away from the peasant everything but the mere minimum required to keep cultivation going.

Another result of British rule which served to undermine the position of the peasantry was the increase in population. Political stability and improvements in sanitation and other public health measures served to reduce the death rate, while leaving the birth rate unchanged. The population rose, exerting pressure on the available supply of land. Industrialisation could have provided the answer to the population pressure in rural areas by taking up the surplus labour, but so long as India remained a major market for British manufactures, a full-blooded industrial policy was out of the question. When industrialisation did get under way in India towards the end of the nineteenth century, its scale was inadequate to deal with the emerging population problem. The rural overcrowding which, in the absence of attempts to improve agricultural techniques, placed severe limits upon the ability of the agricultural sector to generate surpluses of crops for sale and for export. In short, the overall nature of the economic situation in India was much the same as that described earlier for the plantation economy: a concentration of income and wealth in a few hands; the vast mass of the indigenous population subsisting at a low level; and a commercial policy which hindered the spread of industrialisation within the economy.

In many poor countries the choice was not between foreign-inspired development and indigenously stimulated growth, but rather between what happened and nothing. European economic expansion in the nineteenth century, despite its destructive elements, was a powerful agent of modernisation.[10]

RECOMMENDATIONS FOR FURTHER READING

Marx and Engels (1848, *Manifesto of the Communist Party*, translated by Samuel Moore in cooperation with Friedrich Engels, London, 1888) stress the progressive characteristics of globalisation.

For the detailed discussions of the impact of colonialism and its heritage on the economic performance of the periphery, see Latham (1978, *The International Economy and the Underdeveloped World 1865–1914*), Reinert (2007, *How the Rich Countries Grew Rich ... and why Poor Countries Stay Poor*) and Acemoglu, Johnson and Robinson (2001, *The Colonial Origins of Comparative Development: An Empirical Investigation*).

Lenin (1917, *Imperialism, the Highest Stage of Capitalism*) highlights the antagonisms within the imperialist centre of the late nineteenth century that led to the disaster of the First World War.

The unequal trade debate was triggered by Prebisch (1950, *The Economic Development of Latin America and Its Principal Problems*) and Singer (1950, *The Distribution of Gains between Investing and Borrowing Countries*). Harvey et al. (2010, *The Prebisch–Singer Hypothesis: Four Centuries of Evidence*), 60 years later, summarise the evidence from quantitative economic history and largely confirm the Prebisch–Singer hypothesis.

NOTES

1 See Prebisch (1950) and Singer (1950).
2 See Harvey et al. (2010).
3 Reinert (2007). A thought experiment suggested by Reinert pushing this argument to its limits goes as follows: Imagine a tribe that was previously living isolated with a Palaeolithic mode of production is discovered and integrated into the world economy. Advisers trained in contemporary mainstream economics should recommend specialisation according to comparative advantage, which is production of hand axes in exchange for modern goods like computers. Obviously, this strategy amounts to 'specialising in poverty'. Also, Ricardo's famous example of England and Portugal from the beginning of the nineteenth century is hardly less instructive. England specialised in cloth, as advised and Portugal in wine. England soon after industrialised, triggered by innovations in cloth production, while Portugal stuck to primary production and up to this date remains one of the poorest countries in Europe.
4 A country's ability to overcome the difficulties inherent in monoculture and unstable primary product prices depends very much on the flexibility of its economic structure. This question of flexibility is closely connected with the problem of the carry-over in export-led growth.
5 Acemoglu et al. (2001, see also Acemoglu and Robinson, 2012) must be credited for bringing the present generation of economists' attention back to history, in particular colonial history. They emphasise that where European colonisers experienced high mortality and hence were reluctant to settle permanently, economic activity and the ruling institutions would be 'extractive', i.e. exploiting natural resources and (slave) labour for quick take-home profits. On the other hand, in more temperate climates, colonisers would settle and engage in activity and institution building that was more favourable to the development of the colonies proper. The colonial rule ended at some stage, but the legacy of the institutions prevails to this day.
6 The extreme situation was reached in Malaya during the rubber boom at the start of the twentieth century, when so much rubber was planted by Malayans and to a lesser extent by Chinese and Indian smallholders that the country came to depend upon imports for much of its staple food supply.
7 This appears to have been the case in Egypt in the half century before 1913; see Issawi (1961, p. 11).
8 See Guerra y Sánchez (1964).

9 For example, the unskilled workforce in African mining consisted largely of migrant African workers who spent only a limited time in paid employment before returning to their tribal areas.

10 Contrary to many present sceptics of globalisation, Marx and Engels were full of praise of what they witnessed in the nineteenth century and prominently stressed the progressive characteristics of globalisation in the Communist Manifesto, in a way worth citing at length (1848): 'The need of a constantly expanding market for its products chases the bourgeoisie over the entire surface of the globe. It must nestle everywhere, settle everywhere, establish connexions everywhere. The bourgeoisie has through its exploitation of the world market given a cosmopolitan character to production and consumption in every country. To the great chagrin of Reactionists, it has drawn from under the feet of industry the national ground on which it stood. All old-established national industries have been destroyed or are daily being destroyed. They are dislodged by new industries, whose introduction becomes a life and death question for all civilised nations, by industries that no longer work up indigenous raw material, but raw material drawn from the remotest zones; industries whose products are consumed, not only at home, but in every quarter of the globe. In place of the old wants, satisfied by the production of the country, we find new wants, requiring for their satisfaction the products of distant lands and climes. In place of the old local and national seclusion and self-sufficiency, we have intercourse in every direction, universal inter-dependence of nations. And as in material, so also in intellectual production. The intellectual creations of individual nations become common property. National one-sidedness and narrow-mindedness become more and more impossible, and from the numerous national and local literatures, there arises a world literature. The bourgeoisie, by the rapid improvement of all instruments of production, by the immensely facilitated means of communication, draws all, even the most barbarian, nations into civilisation. The cheap prices of commodities are the heavy artillery with which it batters down all Chinese walls, with which it forces the barbarians' intensely obstinate hatred of foreigners to capitulate. It compels all nations, on pain of extinction, to adopt the bourgeois mode of production; it compels them to introduce what it calls civilisation into their midst, i.e., to become bourgeois themselves. In one word, it creates a world after its own image. The bourgeoisie has subjected the country to the rule of the towns. It has created enormous cities, has greatly increased the urban population as compared with the rural, and has thus rescued a considerable part of the population from the idiocy of rural life. Just as it has made the country dependent on the towns, so it has made barbarian and semi-barbarian countries dependent on the civilised ones, nations of peasants on nations of bourgeois, the East on the West. The bourgeoisie keeps more and more doing away with the scattered state of the population, of the means of production, and of property. It has agglomerated population, centralised the means of production, and has concentrated property in a few hands. The necessary consequence of this was political centralisation. Independent, or but loosely connected provinces, with separate interests, laws, governments and systems of taxation, became lumped together into one nation, with one government, one code of laws, one national class-interest, one frontier, and one customs-tariff. The bourgeoisie, during its rule of scarce one hundred years, has created more massive and more colossal productive forces than have all preceding generations together. Subjection of Nature's forces to man, machinery, application of chemistry to industry and agriculture, steam navigation, railways, electric telegraphs, clearing of whole continents for cultivation, canalisation or rivers, whole populations conjured out of the ground — what earlier century had even a presentiment that such productive forces slumbered in the lap of social labour?' What is missing here, of course, is the question 'cui bono?'. Marx and Engels assumed that the distribution of the benefits of globalisation would be taken care of by those left behind in due time.

CHAPTER **10**

Trends and Fluctuations in the International Economy up to 1914

A. G. Kenwood, A. L. Lougheed and Michael Graff

Along with economic growth, fluctuations in economic activity may be transmitted from country to country through the operation of the international economy. Since economic fluctuations appear to be a characteristic feature of industrial economies,[1] and since the nineteenth century saw the emergence of a number of these economies closely linked with each other through trade, labour and capital flows, it is not surprising to find evidence of a tendency for economic expansion and contraction in one industrial country to spill over into other industrial countries. But the spill-over effects of these fluctuations did not stop there. They also spread to primary producing countries, producing excessive fluctuations in the prices and volume of their exports which, through their influence on these countries' foreign exchange earnings, placed severe constraints on their capacity to generate sustained economic growth. Potentially more damaging to the long-term prospects of growth in these countries, however, is the claim that the spread of modern technology has been associated with a secular tendency for primary product prices to decline relative to the prices of manufactured goods. If true, this movement of the terms of trade against primary producers meant that they were, and are, faced with the possibility of a long-run decline in their real export incomes.[2]

THE INTERNATIONAL TRANSMISSION OF BUSINESS CYCLES

The historical evidence suggests that in the past there has been a substantial degree of business cycle conformity between countries, especially when the fluctuations have been violent ones. The international impact of the great financial crises of the nineteenth century has long been recognised and is amply borne out by an examination of the business annals of numerous countries for the period,[3] but the annals tell us little about the mechanism by which it was affected or the predominant direction of these effects.[4]

Before 1890, the international economy consisted of a number of self-contained trading networks, with little economic contact between the countries in each network, except through

DOI: 10.4324/9781003382171-13

Britain, which stood at the centre linking them together. Thus, a slump in the US would affect, say, Australia, only indirectly through its impact on the British economy, where the consequent fall in the American demand for British exports, by reducing the level of economic activity in Britain, would lead eventually to a decline in the British demand for Australian exports. But after 1890, because of the spread of industry and the accompanying growth in the world demand for industrial raw materials and foodstuffs, direct trading relations between continental Europe and the US and the primary producing countries overseas, especially those in the British Empire, became more common. The system of separate trading blocs gradually coalesced into a single network of world trade and the possibility of fluctuations being transmitted directly from one part of the international economy to another became more and more real.[5]

LONG SWINGS AND THE INTERNATIONAL ECONOMY

The existence of long swings in economic activity, averaging between 15 and 25 years in duration, is now an undisputed fact. Investigations have revealed such fluctuations in building activity, where the phenomenon has long been recognised, railway construction, public utilities and migration. They are also evident in the merchandise imports and exports of several countries, as well as in the flows of capital between countries. Of particular importance in this context is the evidence of long-term inverse movements in British home and foreign investment and the related tendency, at least in the period after 1870, for general long swing movements in economic activity in the US and Canada to vary inversely with swings in British building and domestic investment generally.

Table 10.1 illustrates the nature of this inversion. The figures in columns 1 and 2 describe the opposing movements in Britain's home and foreign investment. Domestic investment rose in the 1870s and 1890s and early years of the present century and declined in the 1880s and in the years after 1906. Foreign investment, on the other hand, moved in the opposite direction, falling in the 1870s and 1890s and rising in the 1880s and 1900s. Outflows of population from Britain[6] move parallel to the outflow of capital. Since a large part of both flows of men and money went to the US and Canada after 1870, these countries received substantial injections of population and capital from Britain, as well as from other European countries, in the 1880s and 1900s. These were periods when domestic investment and economic activity were running at high levels in the North American economy. In other words, in those periods when domestic investment and business activity were depressed in Britain, the US and Canadian economies were growing rapidly, and this economic growth was sustained partly by the outflow of population and capital from Britain to these countries. On the other hand, in those periods when the British economy was growing rapidly, the outflow of capital and population slowed up, and the growth of the North American economy was correspondingly reduced.

The long-cycle mechanism offers an attractive framework within which to study the growth process associated with the functioning of the international economy in the years before 1914. That these long fluctuations are to be observed in the international flows of capital, population and trade emphasises this fact, for these flows represented some of the real forces at work influencing changes in the level of economic activity in different parts of the

TABLE 10.1 Great Britain, the US and Canada: inverse long swings in economic activity, 1871–1913

Period	Britain			US		Canada		
	Net domestic fixed capital formation £m.	Capital outflow £m.	British immigration ('000s)	Net capital inflow $m.	Net capital expenditures railways $m.	Immigrant arrivals ('000s)	Net capital inflow[a] $m.	Total fixed capital formation $m.
	(1)	(2)	(3)	(4)	(5)	(6)	(7)	(8)
1871–5	358	373	370	896	940	181	166	n.a.
1876–80	381	124	178	–348	383	162	93	n.a.
1881–5	297	309	385	258	996	477	167	n.a.
1886–90	174	438	423	1.045	642	409	242	n.a.
1891–5	289	260	195	392	726	182	202	n.a.
1896–1900	540	202	76	–807	–130	157	124	n.a.
1901–5	686	245	201	–730	328	556	317	1.061
1906–10	446	729	325	238	1,808	1,088	830	2,025
1911–13	267	618	191	–66	1,216	1,108	1,156	2,919[b]

Source: column 1: Mitchell and Deane (1962, p. 373f.); column 2: Imlah (1958, pp. 72–5); column 3: US Bureau of Census and Statistics (1960, p. 56f.); column 4: Williamson (1964, p. 280f., table B19); column 5: Ulmer (1960, p. 256f., table C1); columns 6 and 8: Urquhart and Buckley (1965, p. 23, 138); column 7: Bloomfield (1968, Appendix I, pp. 42–4).

Notes: [a] excluding net short-term capital flows; [b] for the years 1911–15; n.a.: not available.

world at this time. Whatever the true nature of the mechanism generating these inverse long swings in economic activity, its functioning obviously depended on the complicated interplay of many variables, including immigration, the terms of trade, and lenders' preferences.[7]

LONG-RUN TRENDS IN THE TERMS OF TRADE

Before commencing a description of trends in the terms of trade for during the nineteenth century, it is necessary to consider briefly the nature and significance of the terms of trade concept. The commodity (or net barter) terms of trade compare the changing relationship between export and import prices for a particular country over a number of years. A weighted index is usually constructed for both export and import prices in terms of base year prices, and from these two indexes the terms of trade index is derived by calculating the export price index as a percentage of the import price index. The main use of the terms of trade index is to determine (purely on the basis of relative price changes), whether over a number of years a country gains additional real income or loses it. If, for instance, a particular country's export volume remains unchanged in two successive years, but export prices increase by 10 per cent on average, the money incomes of exporters will increase by 10 per cent despite the fact that total production remains unchanged. If, at the same time import prices are constant, the country is able to obtain a greater volume of imports for the same volume of exports. In other words, the country experiences a gain in terms of real income. On the other hand, if export prices declined by 10 per cent, other things remaining the same, a reduction in real income would eventuate. To summarise: a net gain will always accrue to a country so long as its import prices increase at a slower rate, or decline faster, than its export prices. On the other hand, if import prices increase faster or decline more slowly than export prices, the country will tend to lose real income purely from changes in international prices.[8] On the production side, increased export prices, especially if the trend is sustained for a period of several years, would tend to produce a transfer of factors from other sectors into export industries, thus altering the country's distribution of productive factors. In this way, long-run trends in the terms of trade can have an important effect on the economic growth path of a country whose development is highly dependent on its export income.

When we come to examine the long-run trends in the terms of trade during the nineteenth century, we find that reasonably accurate information exists for only a handful of countries, and that for most of them the data relate only to the period after 1870. The longest terms of trade series available are those for the UK and US, both of which cover the period 1800–1913. Taking the British estimates first, these reveal a general long-run decline in the commodity terms of trade during the period from 1802 to the mid-1850s, followed by a sustained upward trend over the rest of the period. The tendency for the UK terms of trade to deteriorate over the first half of the nineteenth century arose because British cotton export prices fell faster than raw cotton import prices. Between 1814 and 1843, the prices of raw cotton imports fell by almost 80 per cent, while cotton textile prices declined even more sharply, partly because of the fall in raw cotton prices, and partly because of the technological advances occurring in the production of cotton textiles. The heavy weighting of cotton textiles in British exports and the precipitate fall in cotton textile prices led to a decline in the weighted average of British export prices that was greater than that of import prices, with a consequent deterioration in the British commodity terms of trade. Indeed, if textile manufactures in general are removed from the terms of trade series, the residual series exhibits a fluctuating pattern with no long-run tendency to deteriorate.

Between 1857 and 1873, there was a decided improvement in Britain's commodity terms of trade as export prices rose, while import prices fell. Thereafter, up to 1881, deterioration set in, caused by a heavy fall in export prices. From 1882 to 1913, both export and import prices moved together, declining in the years up to the mid-1890s and rising in the remainder of the period up to 1913. As a result of the relative movements of the two series, the British terms of trade tended to become progressively more favourable, initially because import prices were falling generally faster than export prices, and later because export prices tended on the whole to rise faster than import prices. Thus, except for the trough in the series between 1873 and 1884, the terms of trade index moved in such a way as to allow Britain to experience considerable gains from trade as the result of price changes for more than half a century.

The American terms of trade improved substantially during the second half of the 1790s and then deteriorated sharply in the years up to the end of the Napoleonic Wars, when wartime shortages brought about a sharp rise in import prices. This was followed by a period of generally improving terms of trade between 1815 and 1860, the most favourable periods being 1816–19, the mid-1830s and 1849–60. Import prices followed a general downward trend until the late 1840s, after which they tended to rise. On the other hand, export prices fluctuated more widely, with the most favourable improvements occurring during the 1830s. Over the 20 years after 1860, the American commodity terms of trade appear to have continued an upward trend, although there was some deterioration in the early 1870s. In the remaining years up to 1913 there is little apparent upward or downward trend in the US terms of trade. Thus, from the end of the Napoleonic Wars until the First World War, movements in international prices tended on the whole to benefit the US economy, with perhaps the most unfavourable effects of price movements occurring during the late 1880s and the 1890s.

Terms of trade estimates are available for a few European countries after 1870. What is most striking about the German series, especially after 1880, is its exceptional stability, for even during the one period of marked change — the years of deteriorating terms of trade between 1901 and 1913 — the index fell only 12 per cent. It is therefore highly unlikely that Germany either lost or gained real income during these years as a result of changes in international trade prices. The French experience was very similar to that of Germany. Like Germany, with the possible exception of the last decade before the First World War, when a deterioration of approximately 20 per cent is apparent in the French terms of trade, the French economy tended not to be too greatly disturbed by movements in the relative prices of its imports or exports.

The only other countries for which reasonably acceptable statistical series have been constructed for periods of 30 or more years before 1914 are India, Japan, New Zealand and Australia. Despite the violent fluctuations exhibited by the Indian series, it has a definite upward trend over the period from 1861 to the mid-1890s, followed by a general levelling out during the remainder of the period. On the other hand, the Japanese terms of trade rose in the years up to 1900 and then displayed a tendency to fall thereafter. Despite the deterioration in the Japanese terms of trade in the 1900s, however, the available evidence suggests that neither Japan nor India experienced any significant loss of real income because of relative movements in international trade prices. The New Zealand data suggest that the terms of trade deteriorated throughout the 1860s, recovered in the early 1870s, and followed a sustained upward movement over the remainder of the period. Contrary to expectations, the Australian data exhibit different characteristics from those of New Zealand. There appear to have been favourable terms of trade for Australia during the 1870s, an adverse movement during the 1880s and the first half of the 1890s, and then a sustained improvement over the remainder of the period. Although it can be reasonably concluded that New Zealand received fairly substantial increases in real income from international price movements, such a conclusion is harder to sustain in the case of Australia, given the economic difficulties experienced by that country during the 1880s and the early 1890s.

Thus, an analysis of the available data on the terms of trade suggests that only in relatively few periods did any of the countries considered experience a long-run loss of real income because of sustained adverse movements in world prices — for example, Britain between 1800 and 1850, the US in the 1820s and 1890s, and Australia between 1880 and 1895. Generally speaking, however, these losses in real income resulting from deteriorating commodity terms of trade were offset by other changes, such as increased productivity reducing costs of production in export industries, so that any net loss of real income, if it occurred, was unlikely to have been very large. Even more interesting is the conclusion that primary producing countries such as Australia, New Zealand and India, all of which traded extensively with the UK, could experience improving terms of trade at the same time as Britain did. This could happen because of the effect of falling freight rates on the prices of internationally traded goods. Thus, the price of a primary product could fall in the country importing it despite increased production costs in the exporting country, if a reduction in transport costs more than offset the rise in production costs. It could also come about because of the different production mixes of the exports and imports of the different countries involved in trade with each other. It is noticeable, for instance, that because of the similar commodity composition of the two indexes, the Australian import price index follows fairly closely the trend in the British export price index from 1870 to 1913. On the other hand, great divergences exist between the Australian export price index, which was heavily influenced by the prices of a few products of major importance, such as wool, and the British import price index which incorporated a much wider range of commodities. Given the different commodity composition of imports and exports and variations in the movement of the prices of individual commodities, the possibility of the import and export price indexes of different countries, and consequently their commodity terms of trade, moving together are greatly enhanced. It therefore does not follow that an improvement in the terms of trade of an industrial country must lead inevitably to deterioration in the terms of trade of the primary producing country.

Long-run fluctuations in the prices of agricultural products play a significant role in the explanation of world economic growth during the Modern Era, as put forward by Walt W. Rostow (1978) and Arthur Lewis (1978). According to Rostow, for example, the process of world economic growth involves basically the interaction of three forces: the adjustment of food and raw material production to the growth of population and industrial production; the impact on total production and prices of the classic sequence of leading sector 'complexes' (cotton textiles; railways and iron, steel, chemicals and electricity; and the motor-car); and a housing cycle responding to population growth and migration. Technological change clusters around the opening up of new areas of primary production and the leading sector complexes with their associated backward and forward linkages. Although Rostow argues that the existence of such 'Kondratieff' long waves (cycles)[9] is not an essential element in his dynamic theory of world growth, he claims nevertheless that the international economy has experienced four marked, if irregular, Kondratieff cycles between 1790 and 1972 in the relative scarcity and abundance of foodstuffs and raw materials. Kondratieff expansions are marked by high or rising prices of primary products and interest rates; and an income shift towards a rapidly expanding agriculture, towards 'profits' and away from the urban wage share. Kondratieff contractions exhibit opposite changes in these variables.[10] Lewis also gives a central role to long waves in prices and the terms of trade, which, he argues, are related to changes in the rate of growth of supplies of agricultural products.

PHASES OF GROWTH

The long-run growth of the international economy has figured importantly in the work of two economists, Angus Maddison and Solomos Solomou.

Maddison (1982) concedes that major changes in the growth momentum during the capitalist epoch have occurred, in his view their explanation can be sought not in systematic long waves, as postulated by the Kondratieff thesis, but in specific disturbances of an *ad hoc* character. Major system shocks, such as the depression of the 1930s, change the momentum of capitalist development at certain points. Thus, Maddison holds that for a better understanding of the evolution of the international economic system, it is worthwhile to divide the period since 1820 into separate phases of growth, which have a meaningful internal coherence in spite of wide variations in individual country performance within each of them. His analysis is based on the aggregate economic performance of 16 major economies over the period from 1871 to 1981, and his phases of growth refer essentially to the functioning of the international economic system. Moreover, while Maddison's statistical analyses cover only the period from 1871 to 1981, he suggests, on the basis of the more limited statistical data available for the period between 1820 and 1870, that in most respects experience during these years was similar to that in 1871–1913. Maddison states that since 1820, there have been four distinct phases of development. These were a liberal, market-oriented order, which ended with the First World War; a period of conflict and autarky from 1914 to 1950; a 'golden age' of fast growth to 1973; and a phase of slower growth and accelerated inflation thereafter. These successive phases of growth were not initiated by collective planning decisions, innovative ideas or changes in the ideology of domestic and international policy. Rather, the transition from one phase to another has in practice been determined by some kind of exogenous system shock, such as war, deep depression or the collapse of a long-standing international payments mechanism. The phases do not represent 'stages of growth' in the international capitalist system, nor, because the lengths of the phases vary, are they cyclical in the Kondratieff long wave sense.

In the account of the long-run growth of the international economy by Solomou (1988), the relative backwardness of countries and the differential growth rates across nations that this gives rise to play a central role. Like Maddison, Solomou rejects a Kondratieff wave phasing of post-1850 economic growth, preferring to view the era between 1856 and 1937 as one complete 'catching-up wave', with the accelerating trajectory of 1856–1913 — or 1856–1929 if the break in the war years is allowed for — ended by the world depression of the 1930s. Accordingly, the world economy has not grown along a steady and balanced path, but has experienced a series of transitions from one steady-state growth path to another due to the effects of world wars and changes in the international economic structure. Solomou's 'catching-up' waves are waves of irregular length and amplitude, and do not fall in the Kondratieff periodicity. Finally, Solomou emphasises the fact that since backwardness and therefore a desire to catch up still exists in the world economy, this is a sufficient condition for a catching-up wave growth path continuing into the future, once rapid economic growth is resumed.[11]

Appendix: International Business Cycles — Concepts and Definitions

Michael Graff

The concepts of 'international business cycles' or a 'world business cycle' have long captured the imagination of economists. In either case, a cycle must affect more than a single country. In a fully integrated world economy, we might find a dominant world business cycle with no pronounced regional variation, whereas in a less than fully integrated world, some of the transnational cyclical co-movement will be confined to geographical regions or economic blocs. Accordingly, a reason- able assumption is that, presently as well as in the past, different layers of business cycles proceed at the same time. Formally, this structure can be represented as a layer of cycles, where the cyclical position $P_{i,t}$ of country i at time t is determined by country-specific ('idiosyncratic') factors $I_{i,t}$, supra-national developments $S_{j,t}$ business conditions within structurally defined groups of countries $G_{k,t}$, and a world business cycle W_t, so that

$$P_{i,t} = f\left(I_{i,t}, S_{j,t}, G_{k,t}, W_t\right) \tag{10.1}$$

Theoretical Considerations on International Business Cycles

The earliest theory of cyclical patterns in economic activity attributed them to nature: climate and weather, relating to predominantly agricultural economies. With the share of agriculture in output declining, the cyclicality of economic conditions in the secondary and tertiary sector is traditionally referred to as an investment cycle, where at some stage over-investment leads to more or less severe corrections until a new boom sets in. The underlying assumption is that a considerable number of market participants are reacting to the same signals. These may be the employment outlook, profits, order books, raw material and intermediate goods prices, inventories, exchange rates, demand for exports or news about international crises and war or peace.

Apart from this view, a school dominated by theoretical economists that until Great Recession 2008–9 put a bold question mark over its conjectures — was highly influential in academics, suggests a 'real business cycle'. Based on the assumption of rational and informed agents, this theory sees the origin of cycles exclusively in exogenous shocks (technical innovations or political interventions) to an otherwise smooth evolution of the market economy.

Moreover, though they do not represent the mainstream, some economists continue to refer to the theory of the business cycle by Joseph Schumpeter (1939). This theory ascribes the business cycle to clusters of innovations which lead to a general phase of prosperity. New products and procedures deliver monopoly rents to the pioneers; on the other hand they make some of the inherited capital stock obsolete in economic terms. This 'creative destruction' triggers vigorous price adjustments and, consequently, entrepreneurs and bankers face difficulty in assessing the profitability of further innovation and investment. Moreover, at that stage, a considerable part of investment is getting speculative rather than innovative. Once the initial cluster of innovations has diffused through the economy, profits converge towards zero. The boom is over and the economy returns to a stationary state. This may even manifest itself as a depression. Typically, however, the price adjustment that happened through the recession forms the basis for new innovative activity which again culminates in a cluster of innovations. Evidence for this business cycle theory is sparse so far. Yet it cannot be ruled out that the 'Second Industrial Revolution' (within the IT sector) has brought about a convergence of technological trajectories, which would result in a clustering of innovations and hence constitute the basis for a new 'Schumpeter cycle'.

These theories comprise a number of arguments that can likewise serve as theoretical explanations for a *supra-nationality* of business cycles. Generally, a systematic commonality of economic activity across different territorial units has to be attributed to cyclical forces operating across regions.[12] These could affect either prices or quantities or both, and relate to goods and services, factors of production, financial securities or to psychological factors such as consumer confidence or the 'animal spirits' of entrepreneurs. Hence, as far as economic agents react to signals from abroad, we would expect to find transnationality in business cycles. Real business cycle theory directly implies that the business cycle will be supra-national if this is true for the driving forces, i.e. the technology and policy shocks that are hitting the international economy.[13] From a Schumpeterian perspective, a common technological trajectory would constitute the basis for supra-nationality of the business cycle.[14]

Economic theory hence states a number of plausible arguments for the emergence of international business cycles and identifies potentially triggering factors as well as likely channels for international transmission and diffusion. Some of the factors that drive the business cycle operate predominantly domestically, while others have more international significance. In this context, we would expect that countries are not necessarily affected to the same degree by the factors that drive international cycles. Geographic, cultural and technological proximity would imply more similar reactions to impulses from the international economy. Moreover, 'cyclical proximity' is affected by economic and political integration (or disintegration) and thus is not time invariant.

The post-Second World War economic integration of Europe is an important illustration of these considerations, as it has shaped or at least deepened a distinctive European business cycle.[15] The cyclical integration is nevertheless far from complete. In particular, private consumption is still heavily affected by country-specific idiosyncrasies.[16] Furthermore, according to some findings, it appears that the overall deepening of cyclical integration in the EEC/EU has flattened out in the new millennium, and the ongoing economic and financial crises that goes along with severe problems in some countries of the Eurozone puts a bold question mark over the assertion that European economic integration is continuously deepening. Intra-European frontiers hence continue — to some extent at least — to be boundaries for the business cycle.

RECOMMENDATIONS FOR FURTHER READING

For a detailed research on cycles or phases of economic development in the nineteenth century, on which this chapter is partly based, see Rostow (1978, *The World Economy: History and Prospect*), Lewis (1978, *Growth and Fluctuations, 1870–1913*), Maddison (1982, *Phases of Capitalist Development*), van Duijn (1983, *The Long Wave in Economic Life*) and Solomou (1988, *Phases of Economic Growth, 1850–1913: Kondratieff Waves and Kuznets Swings*).

Kindleberger (1956, *The Terms of Trade: A European Case Study*) and Morgan (1959, *The Long-Run Terms of Trade between Agriculture and Manufacturing*) are useful contributions relating to the discussion of the terms of trade in this chapter.

The 'Kondratieff cycle' is presented by Kondratieff (1935, *The Long Waves in Economic Life*) and discussed in Garvy (1943, *Kondratieff's Theory of Long Cycles*).

Empirical and theoretical evidence for international business cycles from the last few decades can be found in Norrbin and Schlagenhauf (1996, *The Role of International Factors in the Business Cycle: A Multi-country Study*), Fatás (1997, *EMU: Countries or Regions? Lessons from the EMS Experience*), Clark et al. (2001, *Borders and Business Cycles*) and Ambler et al. (2004, *International Business Cycles: What Are the Facts?*).

NOTES

1 In the first few years of the new millennium, a considerable number of economists where convinced that business cycles and crises had been overcome once and for all (they called this the 'Great Moderation'; for more detailed discussion see Chapter 22). The events of 2007 and the subsequent difficult recovery taught them better. Indeed, the comparably smooth growth after the 2001 recession brought about by easy monetary conditions may be a crucial driving factor of the asset price bubble as well as its inevitable burst in the US that triggered the 2008–9 recession and the associated global financial turmoil. For a detailed discussion, see Quiggin (2010).
2 See the discussion of the Prebisch–Singer thesis in Chapter 9 of this book.
3 See Thorp (1926); especially useful is Section VI of the Introduction, which deals with international relationships between business cycles.
4 See the Appendix to this chapter for a general discussion of the potential drivers and transmission channels of international business cycles up to the present.
5 See Saul (1960, pp. 111–116).
6 The immigration figures in column 3 of Table 10.1 refer only to British immigration into the US, but total British migration to all countries during these years followed a similar pattern — falling in the 1870s and 1890s and rising in the 1880s and 1900s.
7 For a fuller discussion of some of the problems raised in this section, see Hall (1968).
8 The terms of trade argument should not be restricted to changes in prices alone, since other factors are also important in determining the gains from trade over time. For example, improvements in productivity in export industries may reduce the costs of producing exports faster than the fall in their prices, thus nullifying the loss of real income implied in a deterioration of a country's commodity terms of trade. To take these factors into account, a number of other terms of trade concepts have been developed, some

of which can, and some of which cannot, be measured statistically. For practical purposes, however, the commodity terms of trade provide the easiest way in which to use the available data, despite the difficulties that inevitably arise in constructing such an index.

9 Acceptance of the existence of long waves in economic activity of 40–60 years' length is largely the result of the work of Russian economist Nikolai D. Kondratieff during the 1920s (see Kondratieff 1935). For a critique of the Kondratieff hypothesis, see Garvy (1943).

10 According to Rostow (1978, pp. 299–304), the four long waves in price movements cover the periods 1790–1848, 1848–96, 1896–1936 and 1936–72.

11 Since the 1990s, renewed interest in the ultimate causes of economic growth, along with the availability of comprehensive international data sets, has led to a huge amount of empirical work assessing the evidence for catching up and convergence across the countries of the world from about 1960–70 (which is the usual coverage of the available cross-country data). Unsurprisingly, the findings differ, but it is fair to say that catching-up and convergence are missing on the global scale but can be found within groups of countries ('convergence clubs', usually medium or high income; see, e.g., Ben-David, 1998) with similar characteristics. Accordingly, even if it is obvious that Solomou's 'desire to catch up' still exists in the world economy, it definitely is not a sufficient condition for its accomplishment. For preliminary accounts of the results of this research programme, see Levine and Zervos (1993) and Sala-i-Martin (1997).

12 See, among others, Clark and van Wincoop (2001) and Artis (2003).

13 Norrbin and Schlagenhauf (1996) find 'limited support' for real business cycles in the form of industry-specific cycles with international business cycles. Imbs (2000) shows that OECD countries with similar industrial specialisations are characterised by distinctive co-movement of economic activity.

14 This might especially affect groups of countries with a similar human capital endowment, allowing for a quick diffusion of clusters of innovations; see Comin and Hobijn (2004).

15 See Fatás (1997).

16 See Ambler et al. (2004).

PART II
The First World War and the Interwar Years

CHAPTER **11**

The International Economy from 1914 to 1939

A. G. Kenwood, A. L. Lougheed and Michael Graff

The international division of labour that had emerged in the nineteenth century was severely disrupted with the outbreak of war in 1914. Four years of fighting left a legacy of problems to the international economy that were never completely solved in the economic reconstruction that followed. Consequently, the post-war international economic system was ill-prepared to withstand the shock of a worldwide 'Great Depression' in the early 1930s, and a rapid breakup of the world economy followed. Six more years of even more disastrous war (1939–45) were to elapse before another attempt at restoring the international economy could be undertaken.

THE FIRST WORLD WAR

The First World War — known as the 'Great War' until 1939 — was an imperialist war. It was motivated by claims for land, in particular a redesign of European borders and, to a lesser extent, for colonies. It was launched as a result of disastrous diplomacy failure in the summer of 1914, when on 28 July Austria-Hungary declared war on Serbia, which resulted in declarations of war based on mutual defence alliances, so that by 4 August the European Great Powers — Britain, France, Russia, Germany and Austria-Hungary — were all at war.[1] Enthusiastically greeted in all belligerent nations in a wave of nationalist frenzy, it turned into unprecedented disaster and tragedy for all parties involved; and while the armistice of 11 November 1918 manifested military victory and defeat, it is hard to see any benefit of the war to anyone that was worth the price,[2] with the possible exception of the US.[3] It was launched by a military and political elite that lacked both intelligence and moral virtues;[4] and the organised working class, which in the pre-war years had solemnly sworn to prevent the predictable slaughter by general strike and refusal to point guns at one another, had one of its darkest moments in the summer of 1914, when — with minor exceptions — rank and file of left-wing parties and workers' unions abandoned their international anti-war coalition in favour of primitive and aggressive patriotism. The war cost the lives of nearly 10 million soldiers and about

DOI: 10.4324/9781003382171-15

7 million civilians who died as a result of military action or from disease and famine brought about by the war; it brought an end to the pre-war period of optimism, internationalism and economic liberalism; and it marked the beginnings of the 'Age of Extremes', as the dreadful twentieth century has been termed by historian Eric Hobsbawm (1994).

The opponents comprised as major participants the Austro-Hungarian, German and Ottoman Empires, and from 1915 Bulgaria (the 'Central Powers') on the one hand, and Serbia, the British, French, Russian and Japanese Empires as well as, from 1915, Italy, from 1916, Portugal and Romania, and from 1917, Greece, and — last but not least — the US (the 'Allies' or 'Entente Powers'). As the European colonies, dominions and overseas possessions in Africa, Asia, Oceania and the Americas participated on the side of their colonial rulers, or home countries, providing both troops and supplies, the Great War was truly global, although the actual fighting took place mainly on the battlefields of Europe, and to some extent also in North Africa and the Far East, where Japan conquered and occupied the German colony of Tsingtao on the Chinese mainland, and all German colonies in the Pacific were occupied by the Entente. Sub-Saharan Africa was a minor war theatre where colonial armies had their skirmishes without sizeable impact on the war as a whole.

All parties initially believed in quick victory as a matter of weeks, or perhaps months. Yet, after the initial advance of German troops into French territory (via Belgium and Luxembourg, violating their neutrality) in the West and defeat of Russian advances in the East in 1914, most front lines settled down for the long remainder of the war, forcing the Central Powers to fight on two fronts. The resulting trench warfare implied heavy losses for the attacker, which — if 'successful' — would bring minimal gains of some 100 m, usually with no strategic value whatsoever. Thus, the war effort turned from quick strategic advances of troops to mobilising as many men, guns and artillery shells as possible for the trenches in order to outweigh the opponent in numbers and tons. The resulting cynical strategy of 'bleeding out' the enemy, however, turned against friend and foe alike, and in essence the murderous stalemate would persist until 1918, when the Central Powers had eventually depleted their resources and asked for an armistice. As Broadberry and Harrison (2005, p. 2) put it:

> In battles that were intended to be won by the last man left standing, resources counted for almost everything. Once the German military advantage had failed to win an immediate victory in the west, it seems inevitable that the greater Allied capacity for taking risks, absorbing the costs of mistakes, replacing losses, and accumulating overwhelming quantitative superiority should eventually have turned the balance against Germany.

More specifically, the Entente's superiority was based on about five times as many people and three times the output compared to the Central Powers. Without the element of surprise and quick success, which did not materialise, the Central Powers thus did not stand a realistic chance of winning.

In the course of the war, as it became obvious that resources mattered most in what turned out to be a prolonged warfare of attrition, both Central Powers and the Entente bargained for allies, often with the promise of compensation with land and colonies after victory was won. Victory seemed to be in reach for the last time for the Central Powers when Russia withdrew from the war after the Russian Revolution in November 1917, accepting harsh peace conditions, thus freeing German troops in the East for a final assault in the West in March 1918. However, with 10,000 US troops arriving at the western front per day, the Allies resisted, and when Bulgaria, and eventually Austria-Hungary, too, stopped fighting, the German army, finally facing defeat, asked for an armistice, which became effective on 11 November 1918.

Economically, mobilising resources for the war meant combinations of making men disposable for combat and supplying them with provisions and war materials without starving the civilian population. The latter required increasing total output or at least maintaining it at pre-war levels; making a significant share of it disposable to the government; and directing it from peacetime to war uses. As no belligerent party had anticipated a long war and no plan existed for this possibility, mobilisation efforts were initially *ad hoc* but gradually turned the major warring countries into pronounced wartime economies. The war effort of all belligerent nations mobilised some 65 million men into the armed forces, for which substitutes had to be found. Thus, working hours increased and women entered factories and offices on a large scale.

From the very beginning, Britain imposed a naval blockade on Germany, which was later retaliated against by German submarine warfare to cut Allied supply routes across the Atlantic. Unrestricted U-boat warfare was opened in 1917. Initially, it threatened to have a critical impact on Britain, but it brought the US into the war on 6 April 1917. Also, the Allies adopted a convoy system, which greatly reduced vulnerability to submarines. At that stage total output was increasing and above 1913 levels in Britain and the US, while Russia and France, as well as the Central Powers of Germany and Austria-Hungary, were facing output levels lingering significantly below pre-war magnitudes.

The share of GDP at the disposal of government increased in all belligerent nations, and in the richest economies it reached unprecedented levels of as high as 50 per cent.[5] War finance operated through three channels: taxation, debt and central bank credit to the government and the resulting inflation, i.e. 'inflation tax'.[6] Furthermore, as Galbraith (1994) notes, a widely neglected aspect of war finance in 1914–18 is that those who suffered most and faced the highest personal risk of injury and death also paid most in economic terms, since common soldiers — volunteers or conscripts — were paid only insignificantly. In other words, while governments had to acquire the purchasing power to buy the material resources to wage the war, the manpower in the battlefield and on the battleships consisted largely of grossly underpaid and forced labour services.

The Russian Empire had collapsed in October 1917, when the Bolsheviks seized power (and maintained it in a bloody civil war), but the revolutions in Germany and Hungary were defeated by internal opponents. The Austro-Hungarian and the Ottoman Empires were broken up after the armistice by the Allies along ethno-linguistic lines, and the German Empire was considerably reduced.

The Treaty of Versailles (1919), which in fact was not so much a result of peace negotiations and compromise as an arrangement imposed on the defeated at the threat of renouncing the armistice and reopening hostilities, ceded parts of German territory to France, Belgium, Denmark and the newly created state of Poland, thus demonstrating what the Great War really had been fought for. More importantly, perhaps, it demanded from Germany payment for all Allied damage and losses caused by the war and four years of occupation of extended territories in the West. While today the ill design is obvious, apart from the Germans, who considered it as unjust from the start, few contemporary observers in responsible positions remarked on its insanity.[7] Not only did the imposed reparations grossly exceed Germany's ability to pay (indeed, only a fraction was ever paid; most was simply written off by the 1930s), the objective of real transfer of resources from Germany to the Allies would have required a positive balance of trade for generations to come, with the resulting loss of output and employment in the recipient economies ('transfer problem'). None of this happened to any sizeable degree, as the reparation demands were repeatedly reduced and the lion's share of more than 85 per cent finally de facto written off under the Hoover moratorium in 1931.[8]

Planning for the post-war period thus appears as dilettantish, as had been, four years before, the planning for the war. It aimed at preventing another war by dividing the multi-ethnic Austro-Hungarian and Ottoman Empires into 'national states' and by restricting Germany's industrial base and military power. German revanchists thus had an easy play in winning public opinion, which culminated in the Nazi Party's rise to power in 1933. The lesson that in order to ensure peaceful relations it may be better to rely on trade and integration than containment had yet to be learned.

THE INTERNATIONAL ECONOMY AFTER THE FIRST WORLD WAR

The First World War affected the whole structure of the international economy. Trade patterns altered significantly, as the diversion of productive resources in Europe from manufacturing for export to turning out war materials led to the emergence of alternative sources of supply overseas. With the coming of peace, most of this trade returned to its normal channels, but some of the changes persisted, creating difficult problems of economic adjustment for a number of countries, including Britain. The gold standard was another casualty of the war years, when most countries went off gold. Although restored in a modified form by the late 1920s, it never again functioned as effectively as it had done before 1914, and by the early 1930s it had been reduced to a state of near collapse by a series of financial crises. In only one important respect did pre-war trends continue into the inter-war period: in the field of commercial policy, the movement towards protectionism became more marked, as international considerations were increasingly subordinated to national monetary and employment policies made necessary by post-war reconstruction and, later, by the onset of an unprecedented world depression.

Associated with these monetary and trade problems was a tendency for the rate of growth of the world supply of primary products and manufactures to outstrip the rate of growth of demand for these commodities. This came about largely because of technological progress and the continued spread of industrialisation, which, along with population changes and rising real incomes, led to significant adjustments in the structure of world output and demand. How these real changes affected the orderly functioning of the international economy is the subject of the remainder of this chapter, while the international monetary problems created by the First World War are discussed in the chapter that follows.

PRIMARY PRODUCTION

Technological progress was particularly rapid in agriculture during the inter-war years. In temperate latitudes, improvements continued to be made in the breeding of plants and animals, and the use of artificial fertilisers became widespread. Mechanised agriculture was also spreading, with improvements in the efficiency of tractors and the introduction of a growing range of ancillary equipment. Many new developments were also evident in tropical and sub-tropical agriculture. Particularly important were the selective breeding of plants, the increased use of fertilisers, the greater attention paid to the control of plant diseases and pests, and the growing use of selective weed killers. There was also considerable progress in mining operations and in the initial processing of minerals during these years. The mechanisation of mining proceeded rapidly in many countries. There was even more rapid progress in the processing of metallic ores, where flotation techniques developed in the early years of the twentieth century made possible the exploitation of low-grade ores and complex ores containing several metals. Their use in working the low-grade ores of Chile, for example, made that country one of the world's largest producers of copper. Even more striking was the rapid development of the world's petroleum resources during this century. Along with the opening up of the oilfields and the advances made in drilling and refining techniques went the growth and spread of the world's oil-refining industry. Activity was particularly marked in the Middle East, where oil refineries were established in Bahrain and Saudi Arabia by US engineers, and in Iraq and Lebanon by British and joint European enterprises.[9]

The widespread adoption of new techniques in agriculture and mining during the 1920s led to a substantial rise in the output of primary products that was added to by the appearance of new sources of supply, many of which had been brought into being by wartime demand and post-war shortages. Consequently, there appeared in the late 1920s a rather general tendency for supply to outrun demand, and there was an appreciable fall in prices as a result. While there were considerable differences in commodity price movements, some rising and others falling or remaining stationary, when it occurred, the fall in prices was mainly in raw materials, though the prices of certain foodstuffs, particularly sugar and wheat, also declined heavily. Even when substantial price falls occurred, however, they did not always reflect the true extent of the changes in market forces, since the sale of some primary products was subject to monopolistic influences with the result that their prices were often higher than they would have been had competitive conditions prevailed. Thus, commodity control schemes existed for varying periods in the 1920s for products such as rubber, coffee, sugar, wheat and copper, and during 1927 and 1928, attempts were made to establish partial restriction of output schemes for petroleum, lead and zinc, although without any really significant effect on prices.

The downward pressure on primary product prices was not due solely to increased productivity and the opening up of new areas of production. Other forces were also at work. The speedy revival of Europe's sugar-beet industry was certainly a more important cause of excessive world sugar supplies than the rapid technical progress achieved in Cuba and Java during these years. Weaknesses in the management of the industry's commodity control scheme, which by holding prices at too attractive levels tended to induce further plantings, were as much a cause of the overproduction of coffee in Brazil as the opening up within the country of new, rich coffee lands. In explaining the overproduction of wheat during these years, the decline in per capita consumption, due to a shift to more expensive foods as living standards rose, needs to be taken into account, along with the increased acreage under cultivation, greater mechanisation and the increased yields due to the application of scientific methods in the selection of seeds and plants. Indeed, as real incomes grew, changes in demand pervaded the world economy. Thus, there was a relative decline in the world consumption of cereals and a substantial growth in that of fruit, dairy products and certain tropical foodstuffs. Canned products, ready-cooked meats and vegetables were eaten far more than in the pre-war period. The consumption of cigarettes increased enormously all over the world, while the demand for cigars and pipe tobacco in general declined. Cotton and wool gave way to silk and artificial silk, as lighter and finer clothing increased in demand. Overall, however, rising incomes were associated with a declining percentage spent on food and an increasing proportion spent on other commodities, especially manufactures.[10] Of course, these shifts in demand were not universal, but where they did occur they were strong enough to call for marginal adjustments in production which became more difficult to bring about as economic conditions deteriorated.

Despite the growing difficulties faced by the primary producing countries, the evidence suggests that the incomes and foreign exchange earnings of these countries as a whole were reasonably well maintained until the late 1920s. The economic benefits that flowed from the expansion of trade and output in primary products during these years were not evenly shared, however. The recovery of primary production in Europe in particular was slow, whereas it was in Oceania, South America and Africa, with their specialisation in meat, dairy products, wheat, sugar, coffee and vegetable oils, where the really substantial gains were achieved. The same was true of mineral production, where oil and rubber producers were the main beneficiaries.

POPULATION GROWTH AND MIGRATION

The difficulties facing primary producers may also have been due partly to the slowing up of the rate of growth of Europe's population, which reached its peak during the 1920s. Thereafter it declined, largely because of a fall in the birth rate that had begun in Northwest Europe and then spread gradually to the east and south.[11] Even more striking was the decline in North America where, under the influence of the depression, the annual rate of growth of the population fell from 1.4 per cent in the 1920s to 0.8 per cent in the 1930s. In Asia and Africa, on the other hand, population began to increase more rapidly than in Europe. In India, for example, the first clear signs of a rise in life expectancy appeared in 1921–31, when a significant fall in the death rate took place. The result of all these demographic changes was a slight decline in the relative importance of the European population. If the combined populations of Africa and Asia are taken as a rough measure of the world population of non-European stock, it accounted for 75 per cent of the world total in 1800, had fallen to 61 per cent in the 1920s, but then recovered slightly to 62 per cent of the total by 1940.

Despite the slowing up in the rate of growth of Europe's population, the pressure to migrate continued to be high. But with few great fertile and readily accessible areas of the world remaining unoccupied, and with the US in particular showing less willingness to absorb immigrants than it had done in the past, the outflow of population from Europe fell heavily. It declined even further with the onset of the depression, and for a short time in the 1930s Europe became an area of immigration rather than of emigration. Thus, compared with an annual outflow of 1.5 million between 1909 and 1914, European emigration declined to around 700,000 annually in the 1920s and to 130,000 in the 1930s. Britain remained the most important single source of migrants, and South and East Europe continued to provide well over half of the total outflow of population from Europe (Tables 11.1a and 11.1b and Figure 11.1).

TABLE 11.1A Growth and percentage distribution of world population, 1920–40

Region	Number (m)		Distribution (%)	
	1920	1940	1920	1940
Europe (including USSR)	487	573	26.9	25.5
North America	117	146	6.5	6.5
Latin America	91	131	5.0	5.8
Asia	966	1,213	53.4	54.0
Africa	140	172	7.7	7.7
Oceania	9	11	0.5	0.5
Total	1,810	2,246	100.0	100.0

Source: US Demographic Yearbook (various); Woytinsky and Woytinsky (1953); Woodruff (1966, tables 111/4 and 5).

TABLE 11.1B European emigration, 1921–40

Country/region	Number ('000s)		Distribution (%)	
	1921–30	1931–40	1921–30	1931–40
Northwest Europe	3.11	0.53	45.4	43.1
Britain	2.15	0.26	31.3	21.1
Germany	0.56	0.12	8.2	9.8
Southeast Europe	3.76	0.70	54.6	56.9
Spain and Portugal	1.56	0.24	22.7	19.5
Italy	1.37	0.24	19.9	19.5
Poland	0.63	0.16	9.2	13.0
Total	6.87	1.23	100.0	100.0

Sources: As for Table 11.1a; Sources: US Demographic Yearbook (various); Woytinsky and Woytinsky (1953); Woodruff (1966, tables 111/4 and 5).

Even though direct restriction of immigration into the US was inaugurated by the Quota Act of 1921, which set an upper limit on the number allowed into the country during one year, the US still took the largest share of gross immigration during the inter-war years. Compared with the pre-war period, however, there was a substantial drop in US immigration in the 1920s and 1930s, when the annual average intake fell to less than quarter of a million, compared with an annual average of nearly 1 million in the nine years before 1914 (see Table 11.1c and Figure 11.2).

Of the other countries of immigration, Canada and Australia continued to absorb large numbers of British migrants as well as a smaller number of migrants from other European countries. Much of Canada's ability to attract and absorb immigrants came from the rapid expansion of its manufacturing and construction industries, and from the 1920s onwards the country showed a preference for the skilled industrial workers essential to its industrial progress. In Australia, where rapid industrialisation also set up a growing demand for labour, the Empire Settlement Act of 1922 and the '£34 million agreement' reached between Great

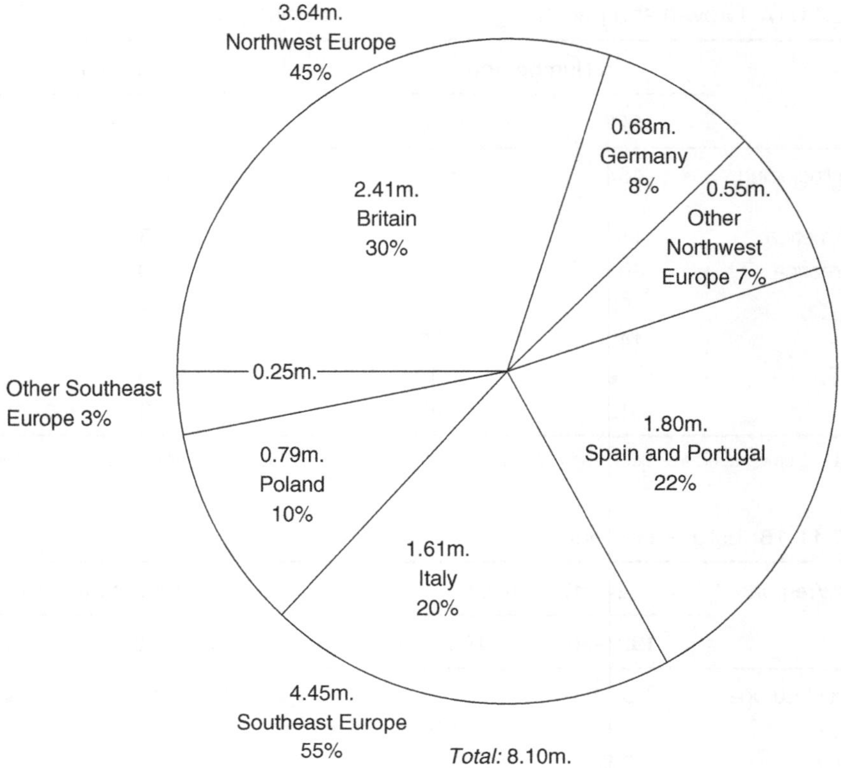

FIGURE 11.1 Emigration from Europe, 1921–40

Source: As for Table 11.1; Sources: US Demographic Yearbook (various); Woytinsky and Woytinsky (1953); Woodruff (1966, tables 111/4 and 5).

TABLE 11.1C Gross immigration into selected countries, 1921–40

Country	Number ('000s)		Distribution (%)	
	1921–30	1931–40	1921–30	1931–40
US	2.72	0.44	37.5	31.9
Canada	0.99	0.08	13.7	5.8
Argentina	1.40	0.31	19.3	22.5
Brazil	0.84	0.24	11.6	17.4
Australia	0.95	0.14	13.1	10.1
Others	0.35	0.17	4.8	12.3
Total	7.25	1.38	100.0	100.0

Sources: As for Table 11.1a; Sources: US Demographic Yearbook (various); Woytinsky and Woytinsky (1953); Woodruff (1966, tables 111/4 and 5).

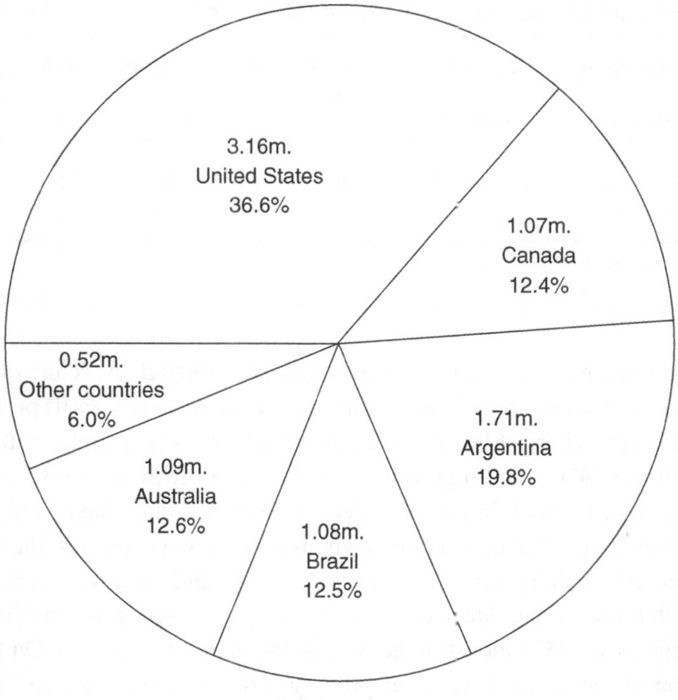

FIGURE 11.2 International immigration, 1921–40

Source: As for Table 11.1; Sources: US Demographic Yearbook (various); Woytinsky and Woytinsky (1953); Woodruff (1966, tables 111/4 and 5).

Britain and the Australian government in 1925 provided for government loans to assist migration to Australia. Planning for some 500,000 migrants in ten years, the project proved to be overambitious. All the same, there was a net inflow of over 300,000 migrants in the 1920s of whom two-thirds were assisted.

Large numbers of European migrants also went to Brazil and Argentina during these years. In Brazil, where the First World War had provided the initial stimulus for industrialisation, the immigrants came mainly from Italy and Germany in the 1920s, and there was also a record inflow of Japanese in the 1930s. In Argentina, the immigrants came overwhelmingly from Latin Europe, mainly Spain and Italy. As with all other countries of immigration, the Argentinean population inflow, which was substantial in the 1920s, fell heavily in the 1930s, when a catastrophic fall in agricultural prices and land values reduced the flow of immigration and encouraged the Argentinean government to introduce restrictive legislation.

MANUFACTURING PRODUCTION

The continued spread of industrialisation was stimulated by both the war and the depression. Cut off from European sources of supply during the war years, manufacturing industry

TABLE 11.2 Percentage distribution of the world's manufacturing production, 1913–38

Period	US	Germany	UK	France	Soviet Union	Sweden	Japan	India	Rest of world	World
1913	35.8	14.3	14.1	7.0	4.4	1.0	1.2	1.1	21.1	100.0
1926–29	42.2	11.6	9.4	6.6	4.3	1.0	2.5	1.2	21.2	100.0
1936–38	32.3	10.7	9.2	4.5	18.5	1.3	3.5	1.4	18.7	100.0

Source: League of Nations (1945, p. 13, table 1).

Note: The 1913 percentages represent the distribution according to the frontiers established after the First World War.

developed rapidly in a number of countries overseas, and although the return of normal peacetime production saw the collapse of some of these nascent industries, tariff protection ensured the survival of many others. After the war, industrialisation was rapid in the US, Canada and Australia in the 1920s, and high rates of industrial growth were also achieved during these years in Brazil, Finland, India, New Zealand, South Africa, Japan and — last but not least — the Soviet Union. Relative to the newly industrialising countries, the older industrial nations experienced declining rates of industrial growth, and even the US failed to achieve industrial growth rates comparable to those of the newly developing nations during the 1920s, while in the depressed 1930s industrial activity in the country stagnated. On the other hand, the deterioration in the terms of trade of primary producing countries and the network of restrictions on trade in primary products, which grew up in the 1930s, forced the governments in a large number of non-industrial countries to foster secondary industry behind tariff protection to safeguard living standards and to keep down unemployment. As a result, industrialisation in these countries proceeded with undiminished vigour despite the depression.

Taking 1913 as 100, the world index of manufacturing activity averaged 185 in the years 1936–8, whereas the index for the US stood at 167, Germany 138, Britain 122 and France 118, all well below the world average. In contrast, many newly industrialising countries had grown at an enormous pace: the Soviet Union's index rose to a stunning 774, Japan reached 529, Finland 289, India 230 and Sweden 223. Over the whole period, therefore, the slower growth of the old countries was largely offset by the rapid progress of the new industrial nations and, as Table 11.2 clearly shows, significant changes in the distribution of the world's manufacturing production occurred as a result. The notable features of this table include the dominant position of the US in world manufacturing during the late 1920s and its subsequent decline during the depression years; the increased shares in world manufacturing activity of the Soviet Union and Japan; and the decline in the relative shares of the old-established European industrial powers, Britain, France and Germany.

Too much should not be read into these production figures, however. They tell us nothing about the significant differences in the nature of the industrial growth experienced by the various countries concerned. In the newly industrialising countries, growth took the form of the expansion of textile manufactures and other types of fabrication typical of a country in the early stages of industrialisation. On the other hand, in the US, and to a lesser extent in some of the old industrial countries, industrialisation during these years involved the rapid growth of new industries, such as motor cars, household appliances and chemicals, as well as the increasing use of new methods of production, such as the assembly line. These new industrial techniques involved a considerable increase in the use of capital and of power. They also brought about significant changes in the composition of world manufacturing output.

As the US experience suggests, the inter-war period was marked not so much by startling new inventions as by remarkable advances in the efficiency of already familiar techniques. Fuel economies were achieved in iron and steel production and in the generation of electricity, with the best power stations halving fuel consumption between 1918 and 1939. The variety of materials available for engineering was greatly extended with the introduction after the war of new alloys, especially the light alloys based on aluminium. There was also an increasing use of plastics. Few radical improvements were made in machine tools, although the use of tungsten carbide as a tool material after 1926 was a significant advance. Refrigeration techniques improved greatly, and substantial increases in the efficiency of gas engines, petrol and oil engines, including diesel and steam turbines were also achieved during these years. But with the exception of the gas turbine, which passed through the critical stages of development shortly before the outbreak of the Second World War, the 20 years between the two wars were not remarkable for the invention of prime movers.

By far the most important development in production methods during these years was the widespread adoption of the assembly line. Initially developed by Henry Ford as the key to the efficient, large-scale — and therefore cheap — production of motor cars, the assembly line system was widely used in the US after the First World War to mass-produce such items as washing machines, radios and refrigerators. In addition, many other products, including shoes, stockings, glassware and chinaware, were passed through factories in a continuous process from raw material to finished product. By enormously increasing the volume of output, and thereby reducing costs, the assembly line led to a marked rise in productivity and a consequent increase in real incomes, which was partly used to purchase the growing output of consumer goods made possible by the new industrial techniques.

Indeed, this emphasis on durable consumption goods is only one of a number of ways in which the new industrial technology was marked off from that of the nineteenth century, for the new industries were as much concerned with mechanising the home as they were with mechanising production. This trend, which began around 1900 with the introduction of the telephone, the gramophone, the bicycle and the motor car, was continued after the First World War when, with the development of the vacuum cleaner, the washing machine, the refrigerator and the radio, machines became familiar in the home. Moreover, the growing range of household electrical appliances and the increasing use of electricity for domestic lighting and cooking, along with the rising industrial consumption of electrical power, enormously increased investment in electricity-generating capacity during these years and created a growing demand for electrical plant and equipment of all kinds.

Apart from the rapid development of the aeroplane, the inter-war years did not witness many revolutionary changes in the means of transportation. Railway networks continued to grow, particularly in the poorer continents, where railway kilometres increased from about 250,000 in 1920 to 300,000 in 1940. Railway construction was especially heavy in the Soviet Union, where the railway network increased by half again between the wars. On the railways, locomotive performance continued to improve, and the diesel-electric locomotive appeared in the US in 1924. Other railway improvements introduced during these years related to traffic control systems, the air-conditioning of trains and better communication systems for trains.

Many of these innovations were the result of efforts to increase railway efficiency in the face of the growing competition of motor transport. This competition was most apparent in the US where, despite the efforts of the railway companies to counter road competition, the railway network in operation in the country declined by about 30,000 km between 1920 and 1940. At sea, oil-burning ships were gradually replacing the coal-burner, while improvements in the design of ships led to substantial reductions in fuel consumption. Here, too, competition was beginning to make itself felt, at least for the ocean passenger trade, as air travel became faster, safer and more regular.

Rapid technological change and the spread of industrialisation to new regions brought with them the problem of economic adjustment in established industrial economies. In no country was this more important during these years than in Britain, where the coal and cotton industries declined absolutely in the face of competition from new producers and the development of substitutes for their products. Other British industries in trouble during these years included shipbuilding, which lost ground because of the worldwide excess capacity created by the war, the failure of foreign trade to grow as rapidly as industrial production and the continuous growth of overseas shipbuilding. While the great staple industries of Britain stagnated and their trade declined, her iron and steel and engineering industries continued to expand, and new industries, notably motor cars, electrical goods, chemicals and rayon, underwent a vigorous expansion. Even so, the growth of these industries and the support they gave to British exports failed to offset the decline in Britain's traditional industries. Accordingly, a major change in the international division of labour was the stagnation of the British economy and the associated decline in her international commercial and financial position. This also — at least partly — helps explain why the international economy failed to function as smoothly during the 1920s as it had until 1914.

GROWTH OF WORLD INCOMES

Between the wars, the rate of growth of world incomes slowed down appreciably as a result of the economic problems thrown up by the war and the onset of the depression in the early 1930s. Table 11.3 compares the annual rates of growth of national income, income per capita and population for selected regions during the two periods 1860–1913 and 1913–29.

Whereas growth was by no means negligible after 1913, growth of total income and income per head slowed down considerably between 1913 and 1929. The rate of growth of world income declined by just under one-quarter in the period 1913–29, but with world population continuing to grow at about the same rate as that of the pre-war period, income per head fell by about one-third. The per capita income growth rate in Northwest Europe was almost halved, while that of the even more economically and politically troubled areas of Southern and Eastern Europe fell even more heavily. More striking still is the stagnation of per capita income growth in Oceania, where it was Australia that was responsible for the poor result. Australian per capita income experienced some growth in the 1920s, but it failed to offset the contraction of real incomes during the war years, so that by the end of the 1920s Australia's income per head was some 10 per cent down on that of 1913–4.

The main beneficiary of the war years was Japan, whose economy grew even more strongly — almost twice as fast — after 1913 than before. Somewhat surprisingly, growth in

TABLE 11.3 Annual compound growth rates of national income, income per head and population for selected regions, 1860–1929

Region	1860–1913			1913–29		
	Income	Population	Income per capita	Income	Population	Income per capita
North America	3.8	2.1	1.7	2.8	1.6	1.2
Oceania	4.0	3.1	0.9	1.7	1.7	0.0
Northwest Europe	2.1	0.8	1.3	0.9	0.2	0.7
Soviet Union	2.2	1.2	1.0	1.1	0.5	0.6
Southeast Europe	1.9	0.8	1.1	1.6	1.3	0.3
Latin America	2.3	1.4	0.9	2.8	1.9	0.9
Japan	2.4	0.9	1.5	4.0	1.2	2.8
Far East	2.8	1.6	1.2	2.4	1.6	0.8
Southeast Asia	1.1	0.5	0.6	0.9	0.6	0.3
China	0.4	0.3	0.1	0.5	0.3	0.2

Source: Aldcroft (1987, p. 288, table 11).

North America also slowed down after 1913, despite the fact that this area, like Japan, stood to benefit from the war.

Estimates of income growth rates comparable to those in Table 11.3 are not available for the period 1929–39, but Maddison (1962) has calculated annual compounded rates of growth of GNP for the worlds more important trading nations covering the period 1890–1938. These estimates are given in Table 11.4. Although the sub-periods chosen by Maddison differ from those of Table 11.3, the general picture that emerges is the same. With few exceptions, the countries listed in the table all experienced declining income growth rates during the inter-war years.

Although Germany, Norway and the UK recorded income growth rates in the period 1925–38 that compared more than favourably with their growth rates in the pre-1913 period, most of Europe was merely making up ground lost during the war and immediate post-war years, in the period after 1925. Both the US and Canada suffered an appreciable decline in the rates of growth of their real incomes after 1913, with the decline being most marked for the US in the years after 1925. Of the major trading nations, only Japan appears to have experienced sustained and substantial economic growth throughout the inter-war years.

THE INTENSIFICATION OF PROTECTIONISM

Within the world markets for primary products and manufactures, adjustments in supply and demand to take into account the changed economic conditions of the inter-war years were made difficult by the spread of restrictions on foreign trade. The war itself was responsible

TABLE 11.4 Annual compounded rates of growth for select countries, 1890–1938 (per cent)

	1890–1913	1913–25	1925–38
Belgium	3.1[a]	−0.9[b]	2.3[c]
Denmark	3.5	1.8	2.4
France	1.4	1.4	−0.2
Germany	2.9	−1.7	4.1
Italy	2.1	2.0	1.8
Netherlands	2.2[d]	3.1	1.3
Norway	2.6[e]	2.3	3.4
Sweden	3.6	1.6	3.1
Switzerland	2.4	2.1	1.9
UK	1.7	0.2	2.5
Europe	2.1	−0.3	2.2
Canada	4.3	1.0	1.8
US	3.9	3.0	1.0
Japan	2.3	3.5	3.8

Source: Maddison (1962, p. 141, Table 5).

Notes: [a] 1895–1913; [b] 1913–24; [c] 1924–38; [d] 1900–13; [e] 1887–1913.

in a number of ways for the intensification of protectionism. In Japan, India, Australia and some Latin American countries, the disappearance of European competition in many lines of manufacturing for four years called forth considerable local production. Some of these 'war babies' died a natural death with the return of peacetime trading conditions, but many others, inspired by motives of self-interest and national security, clamoured for and obtained the support of tariffs. In Australia, for example, iron and steel, machinery, railway materials and chemicals were given protection; in India, iron and steel, cotton textiles, paper and chemicals; in Argentina, pharmaceutical manufactures.

Protectionism also flourished in Europe, where the post-war creation of entirely new nations in Central and Eastern Europe lengthened Europe's tariff frontiers by close to 20,000 km. Behind these barriers, new governments, faced with economic dislocation and production shortages of all kinds, endeavoured to achieve some measure of economic stability. Currency disorders were an added problem in many countries, encouraging the use of tariffs and the introduction of many direct restrictions on trade, such as import and export licensing, quotas, prohibitions and exchange controls. France, Germany (after 1925), Italy, Spain, Belgium and the Netherlands were among the many European countries that introduced tariffs for the first time or revised existing tariffs upwards during the 1920s. These tariffs were not restricted to manufacturing industry or to the control of balance of payments problems created by currency disorders and production difficulties. Agricultural protection also became more widespread and severe in Europe. It played its greatest role in Italy, where, behind high protection, the fascist government in 1925 launched a 'Battle for Wheat' to reduce the country's heavy dependence on outside sources of supply of grain. But the movement towards agricultural self-sufficiency was general throughout Europe at this time, and its consequences for the growth of world trade in primary products were grave.

In Britain, the McKenna Act of 1915 imposed duties of 33.33 per cent on cars, motorcycles and certain other manufactures. This effort to save wartime shipping space and foreign exchange laid the foundations for a return to protection after the war, when the Act remained in force and was extended to commercial vehicles and tyres. Further protection to British industry was afforded by the Safe-guarding of Industries Act and the Dyestuffs Importation Act, both passed in 1921, which placed duties on the products of a number of key industries, including optical glass and instruments, considered to be vital for national security, and prohibited the importation of all synthetic dyestuffs and intermediate products. Even more crucial for the international economy was the introduction by the US of the Fordney-McCumber Tariff of 1922. This Act, which raised US tariffs to the highest level in the country's history up to that time, was utterly inconsistent with the newfound role of the US as the world's most important creditor nation. Since high tariffs made it difficult for the debtor nations to earn dollars with which to make interest payments on US loans and to repay war debts, and since gold was in short supply, the difficulties of the US's debtors were prevented from becoming glaringly obvious only by the willingness of US investors to lend capital abroad.

Protection also became a feature of many primary goods-producing countries, where the desire to support war-induced manufacturing industries was supplemented by the need to reduce dependence on foreign manufactures in the face of deteriorating terms of trade. Whatever the reason for introducing protection in these countries, however, one feature of the international economic situation in the 1920s is perfectly clear: the growing range of restrictions placed on trade between nations reflected an enlargement of the objectives of protectionist policy. In particular, the use of commercial policy during these years came to be extended from the protection of certain industries to the protection of a country's balance of trade and its gold reserves against declining export prices and the effects of the prevailing currency disorders of the 1920s. Later, during the depression years, commercial policy developed another function, that of creating employment through the setting up of domestic manufacturing industries to cater for demands formerly satisfied by imports, which were denied access to the domestic market by the use of tariffs or other restrictive measures.[12]

The spread of protection, the frequent adoption of deliberately high duties for bargaining purposes[13] and the introduction of quantitative restrictions on trade imposed a severe handicap on the recovery of world commerce in the 1920s, and in an attempt to remedy the situation, the League of Nations called a World Economic Conference in 1927 which had an immediate, though short-lived, effect on trade relations. Through autonomous measures and bilateral agreements, such as the Franco-German Commercial Treaty of August 1927, which laid the basis for an integrated European treaty system, the rising trend in tariffs was temporarily checked. Another conference held in the same year tried to deal with the problem of quantitative restrictions on trade, but it dragged on until 1930 without achieving anything of real value. What finally defeated the efforts of both conferences, however, was the onset of depression and the threat of even higher tariffs in the US.

This failure of international policy-making highlights a fundamental weakness in the international economy during the inter-war years. Whereas the major economic problems of the day demanded solution at the international level, the authorities through which existing regulation was exercised were, with few and partial exceptions, national. International attempts to produce solutions to the world's economic problems were made, but they were rare and largely unsuccessful. The League of Nations, which played a constructive role in the early 1920s, particularly in negotiating international loans for countries wishing to stabilise their currencies, had a less active role in the 1930s. It produced a large number of reports and inquiries on both international and national affairs, but their effect on policy appears to have been minimal.

This lack of determined international policy-making is due to a number of reasons. The post-war difficulties would soon be overcome, it was felt, once the pre-war international monetary mechanism had been restored to full working order. Even more of an obstacle to international cooperation was the decline of faith in economic liberalism, which became a marked feature of the inter-war years. If the exigencies of war forced most governments to become more involved in economic affairs, the political changes and economic difficulties of the inter-war period ensured that this involvement would continue and even intensify. The powerful stimulus given to economic nationalism by the war, the economic and financial difficulties of the 1920s and the depression of the 1930s made it inevitable that the government would play a larger role in the economic life of the nation than formerly. Indeed, fascism and related ideologies, which emerged and came to power in an increasing number of countries in the 1920s and 1930s, elevated one's own nation above others and often pursued a pronouncedly aggressive approach vis-à-vis the rest of the world. The increasing dependence on purely national solutions to economic problems thus made international cooperation difficult, if not impossible.

Economic nationalism also affected monetary policy, where, despite the professed reverence for the gold standard mechanism, the independent national control of the domestic supply of money came to supplant the pre-war principle of the international gold standard, according to which any nation's stock of money was dependent upon the ebb and flow of gold. By giving to the central bank the power to influence strongly the supply of money inside the country, the government tended to insulate the national monetary system from international forces, and in doing so it impaired the very mechanism upon which so much faith in future economic progress had rested.

RECOMMENDATIONS FOR FURTHER READING

Highly influential contributions to the question of how Europe in 1914 tumbled into the abyss of war are found in the books of Fischer (1961, *Griff nach der Weltmacht: Die Kriegszielpolitik des kaiserlichen Deutschland 1914/18*; 1967, *Germany's Aims in the First World War*) and Clark (2012, *The Sleepwalkers. How Europe Went to War in 1914*). While Fischer highlights the German government's responsibility for the rising tensions in the summer of 1914, Clark attributes the outbreak of war to the activities of war mongers on all sides along with the inability of the responsible people to anticipate the upcoming catastrophe. Hobsbawm (1994, *The Age of Extremes. A History of the World, 1914–1991*) shows how the violent the history of the twentieth century up to the end of the Cold War in 1991 goes back to 1914.

Broadberry and Harrison (2005, *The Economics of World War I: A Comparative Analysis*) deliver a detailed account of the economic aspects of the four years of the First World War.

Keynes (1920, *The Economic Consequences of the Peace*), a member of the British delegation to Versailles in 1919, delivered an economic critique of reparations imposed on

Germany after the war and correctly predicted the resulting disintegration of the German currency.

The economic history of inter-war years up to the Great Depression is discussed by Aldcroft (1987, *From Versailles to Wall Street, 1919–1929*).

Recommendable contributions of the economic origins of the Great Depression and its consequences are Kindleberger (1986, *The World in Depression, 1929–1939*) and Bernanke (2000, *Essays on the Great Depression*).

NOTES

1 Although imperialistic ambitions were shared by all European belligerent nations, who regarded the possibility of war as an opportunity rather than a risk, the subsequent interpretation of the role of German diplomacy in the summer of 1914 became particularly important, as the Peace Treaty of Versailles in 1919 assigned full responsibility for the war to Germany. This 'guilt thesis' formed the basis for the enormous war reparations imposed on her. Not surprisingly, it found little support in Germany in the post-war years, which in turn facilitated the rise of German Fascism ('National Socialism'), with its core objective being the revision of the outcome of the First World War (along with the destruction of the left-wing labour movement and the extinction of the Jews). In the 1960s, German historian Fritz Fischer (1961) made a strong point that Germany, rather than de-escalating the rising tensions, deliberately fuelled them and pushed Austria-Hungary to declare war on Serbia, which, given the web of treaties in 1914, inevitable would trigger a major European war. Having said that, a tragic aspect of the Great War is that — contrary to claims and beliefs on all sides — it was not fought for any high-standing humanitarian ideas, but for land and economic dominance, which makes its devastating blood toll particularly depressing.

2 In fact, losses of life in absolute numbers were higher on the victorious Entente side than in the defeated Central Powers; in relative terms, however, the Central Powers lost about 5 per cent of their population, while total deaths in the Entente amounted to 1.2 per cent.

3 Compared to other Great Powers, the war effort of the US was rather marginal. While the US death toll was not negligible (it is estimated at about 100,000), US industrial output was not mobilised for warfare before 1917. On the other hand, US exports increased, both to belligerent nations and to substitute former European exports, in particular to Latin America. As a result, at the end of the war, the world saw massive levels of indebtedness to the US, which was a crucial factor in the relocation of the financial centre of the world economy from London to New York.

4 This point is highlighted by Galbraith (1994), who argues that despite the economic dominance of the bourgeoisie in the capitalist countries at the onset of the war, the political and military power was still largely in the hands of the land owners and the nobility: 'The aristocratic and landed tradition was, indeed, a nearly perfect design for ensuring that both government and armed forces would be in the hands of leaders of minimal competence. Selection was by inheritance, not by intelligence'. Worse, with industrial capitalism firmly established by 1914, aristocracy had essentially become obsolete and had no function apart from war, which thus became a matter of self-interest of the political elites (see De Long, 2022).

5 Estimates of peak government spending shares of GDP reported by Broadberry and Harrison (2005, p. 27) are 53.5 per cent for France, 59.0 per cent for Germany, 37.1 per cent for the United Kingdom and 16.6 per cent for the US.

6 As an increase in the supply of money beyond corresponding increases of economic output decreases the purchasing power of all monetary balances, government-induced inflation can be regarded as a tax on money.

7 An exception to the rule is John Maynard Keynes. Apart from a detailed account of the lack of realism regarding the German ability to pay the imposed reparations, his 'The economic consequences of the peace', written in 1919, correctly predicted the disintegration of the German currency.

8 The reparations were initially not fixed. Germany had to hand over 7,000 tons of gold and its merchant fleet. After first having claimed 269 billion gold marks, the sum was fixed in 1921 at 132 billion gold marks; in real times equal to about 3.5 times Germany's GDP of 1913. For details on the subsequent remissions, see Chapter 12 of this book.

9 The rise of the petroleum industry in the early twentieth century is responsible for the dramatic challenges of global warming that humanity is presently facing. With the benefit of hindsight, it should never have happened.
10 The widely observed regularity that the share of income spent on food declines as household incomes rise is referred to as 'Engel's Law', named after the statistician Ernst Engel (1821–96), who made this observation in 1857.
11 This process is referred to as the 'demographic transition'. It first started in Britain and other parts of Northwest Europe around the middle of the nineteenth century, triggered by a marked decline in death rates, mainly due to improvements in sanitation and hygiene. With birth rates remaining at high levels for a few generations, population growth accelerated until the subsequent decline in birth rates would drive it down to lower — in some societies eventually even negative — levels. For an elaboration of the concept, see Kirk (1996).
12 In today's economists' jargon, this is called 'beggar-thy-neighbour' policy.
13 A century later, the world would witness the same policy intention, when on 9 April 2025, US President Donald Trump declared 90 days 'pause' on the spectacularly high tariffs imposed a week before on imports from almost all countries, in order to give time for negotiating 'deals'.

CHAPTER 12

The Restoration of the Gold Standard and the Economic Recovery of the 1920s

A. G. Kenwood, A. L. Lougheed and Michael Graff

The war years saw the end of the gold standard when its two basic requirements, interconvertibility between paper money and gold and the free export of gold, were suspended. Initially, most of the belligerent countries were able to maintain adequate gold reserves and familiar exchange rates, chiefly by taking gold coins out of domestic circulation and concentrating them in official hands. As the years passed, however, it became increasingly difficult for the warring countries to support the pre-war pattern of exchange rates. For Britain and France, the difficulty was overcome finally by the receipt of US loans, following that country's entry into the war early in 1917. Lacking such support, the German and Austro-Hungarian currencies were in a state of collapse by 1918. But for most countries, including the US, Britain and the Empire, France, Italy, the Netherlands, Spain, Sweden, Japan, Argentina and Brazil, exchange rates at the end of the war diverged remarkably little from the pre-war pattern despite the upheaval of the previous four years.

POST-WAR INFLATION AND THE RESTORATION OF THE GOLD STANDARD

This apparent normalcy in the pattern of exchange rates cloaked the profound changes war had brought. In particular, the war economies had all experienced varying degrees of price inflation, the true extent of which had been disguised by price controls and rationing. In the immediate post-war years, a reconstruction boom plus the widespread dislocation of trade and production in Central Europe caused a further inflationary rise in prices, which reached a peak in most countries in 1920, and then gave way to a couple of years of business depression and heavy price declines. In Germany, France and Central and Eastern Europe, however, inflation continued for several more years, and in the process the old money units of Austria, Hungary, Poland, Germany and Russia were practically destroyed.[1]

DOI: 10.4324/9781003382171-16

To achieve monetary stability, international financial conferences were held in Brussels (1920) and Genoa (1922). Shortly afterwards, with the help of large international loans from the US and Britain, financial reorganisations were carried out in Austria (1922) and Hungary (1924). In 1925, further loans for stabilisation purposes were made to Poland and Czechoslovakia, followed by similar arrangements with Bulgaria, Italy and Romania. The outstanding event in post-war financial progress, however, was the stabilisation of the German mark in 1923, which was accompanied by the drawing up of the Dawes Plan for the settlement of the German war debt.

The post-war hyperinflation in Germany was due mainly to the government's inability to balance its budget. The resulting government deficits were financed initially by borrowing, but when the deficits persisted and even increased in size because of rising prices, the German public refused to take up more government securities, and the government was forced to issue treasury bills to cover its excess expenditure. These only added to the quantity of money in circulation and led to a further rise in prices. Eventually, the expanding money supply and rising prices by depreciating the value of the mark caused it to be spent more rapidly. From the combined force of large quantities of money being spent faster and faster, runaway inflation inevitably developed. In the final stages of hyperinflation, the rise in domestic prices left the increase in the quantity of money far behind, and it was the consequent acute shortage of money which eventually provided the government with the opportunity to bring the inflation under control. The 'Rentenmark' — allegedly secured in value by land holdings — introduced late in 1923 was quickly taken up by a public long inconvenienced by the lack of a stable currency. This enabled the government to cover its expenditures with new issues of money while taking steps to balance its budget through spending cuts and tax increases. A decline in the velocity of circulation of money as inflationary pressures abated sufficed to offset any further monetary expansion. Stabilisation of the mark was completed with the receipt of an international loan of 800 million marks (£40 million) under the Dawes Plan of 1924.

The Dawes Plan was the outcome of a reconsideration of the whole German reparations problems that had followed the financial collapse of the mark. The Treaty of Versailles (1919) had established the principle that Germany should indemnify the Allies for their war losses and had created a Reparations Commission to assess the amount. In 1921 the Commission assessed the war damage at 132 billion gold marks (equal to £6,600 million) and laid down a time schedule of payments. It soon became obvious, however, that Germany was in no position to meet these obligations. Under the Dawes arrangements, Germany was required to make reparations payments, rising in five years from £50 million to £125 million per annum, the number of years of payments being left undetermined. The first payment was made possible by the floating of an international loan (the Dawes loan), which also enabled Germany to return to the gold standard in 1924 with the introduction of a new currency, the Reichsmark, at the old pre-war gold parity of 23.8 cents. Foreign countries now became interested in investing in Germany, and for the rest of the 1920s, both the government and private firms were able to borrow large sums abroad. The German economic situation was stabilised.

This massive foreign borrowing, however, led to the emergence of a precarious financial situation in Germany in the late 1920s, when one last attempt was made to solve the reparations problem. Under the Young Plan of 1929 the reparations figure and period of payment were revised, the annual payments being scaled down to £100 million and the payments terminating in 1988 (sic!). The new agreement took effect in April 1930, supported by a $300 million loan. But with the onset of the worldwide Great Depression, Germany was quickly engulfed in a financial crisis which led to a moratorium on reparations payments in June 1931 and, in the following year, their complete abandonment.

Linked with the problem of German reparations was the question of the repayment of inter-Allied war debts. Italy, France and Belgium had emerged from the war in debt to one another and to Britain, while all of them, together with several other countries, had received loans totalling $7,700 million from the US by the end of 1918. Post-war lending for relief and reconstruction added to these debts, until by the end of 1922, the debt owing to the US stood at $9,400 million, of which the share of Britain was $4,100 million, France $2,900 million, Italy $1,600 million, with the remainder divided among Belgium, Cuba, Czechoslovakia, Greece, Romania, Russia and Yugoslavia (Lewis and Schlotterbeck, 1938, p. 362).

Since many of the Allied countries came to regard German reparations payments as a means of liquidating their US debts, there developed a chain of debt payments commencing in Germany and ending in the US. For these debt repayments to proceed smoothly, two requirements had to be met: large sums of marks had to be extracted annually from the German people, and these sums had to be transferred regularly into other currencies — ultimately, a large proportion into dollars. These requirements could be met by increasing German taxes sufficiently to release a flow of goods and services for export large enough to earn the foreign exchange needed for reparations payments. But because the German government lacked the gold and foreign exchange necessary to make the initial reparations payment and was also never able to achieve a budget surplus, and because the creditor countries were opposed to accepting the large inflow of German goods needed if the country was to earn the foreign exchange with which to make reparations payments, the transfer process was never able to function effectively.[2]

In the event, the problem of reparations and inter-Allied war debts was not settled until the mid-1920s, when Germany began receiving large loans of foreign capital, mainly from the US. Then the chain of debt repayments began to function smoothly, but when this foreign lending to Germany ceased in the late 1920s, the transfer of reparations also stopped, and with it the repayment of the related war debts.

The repayment of the Allies' war debts also created difficulties, but the several attempts to solve these all foundered on the US's insistence that they be paid in full. When, however, the Allies were forced to give up their claims on German reparations in 1931, war debts, too, were soon abandoned. Between 1918 and 1931, the US received $2.6 billion of the original $12 billion in repayments from the Allies.

Germany's return to the gold standard, following the floating of the Dawes loan in 1924, was the start of a general return to the gold standard in the next few years. In Britain, the wartime peg of the pound/dollar rate had been abandoned in March 1919 so that a temporarily fluctuating rate could be used to measure progress in deflating British prices enough relative to US prices to make pre-war parity workable again. It was not until April 1925, however, that the pound rose near enough to parity with the dollar for a return to gold to be announced. This decision was made legal shortly afterwards by the Gold Standard Act passed on 13 May 1925. The French inflation, on the other hand, continued until mid-1926 and went far enough to prevent a return to pre-war parity. When, at the end of 1926, the franc was eventually stabilised de facto by official dealings on the foreign exchange market, it stood at about one-fifth of its pre-war parity. *De jure* ratification of this 80 per cent depreciation followed in June 1928, when a law was passed redefining the gold content of the franc in line with the prevailing exchange rate.

Between 1925 and 1928, the reconstruction of the international monetary mechanism was substantially completed. By early 1926 some 39 countries had returned to gold, either at their pre-war parity or at a devalued level or had displayed exchange rate stability for a full year. This list included Great Britain, the Netherlands, Sweden, Denmark, Switzerland, Germany, Austria, Hungary, Finland, Czechoslovakia, Yugoslavia, Bulgaria, Russia, the British Dominions, most Latin American countries and the US, which had returned with ease to the full gold standard in 1919 and thereafter had been the guidepost for the realignment of other currencies. By 1931, most of the countries which had not already done so returned to gold, the most notable being France, Italy and Argentina.

WEAKNESSES IN THE POST-WAR GOLD STANDARD: INTERNATIONAL INVESTMENT

With the restoration of the gold standard, it was widely assumed that the most essential aspect of post-war economic reconstruction had been achieved. As it turned out, these hopes were largely illusory. The belief that a familiar and highly efficient international monetary mechanism had been restored to full working order overlooked the fact that, to function successfully, the pre-war gold standard had required a special kind of environment which no longer existed, and that the pre-war machinery was in many essential respects quite different from that which had now replaced it.

Nowhere were the changes so marked, compared with the pre-war period, than in the field of international investment, for the war had brought about shifts of unprecedented magnitude in the structure of international debt. As we have already seen, the war created a whole series of new international debts in the form of reparations and Allied war loans. Moreover, the US had emerged from the war as the principal creditor on private account, whereas Germany had been transformed from a major creditor country to a debtor. The war had also weakened Britain's international lending position by forcing her to liquidate part of her long-term assets, while further losses arose because of the confiscation of British assets in enemy countries and in Russia. French and German losses on these accounts were relatively greater even than those of Britain. On the other hand, the US had not only repatriated US securities held by British and French investors during the war years, but had also invested heavily in foreign securities, while granting considerable war credits to the Allies.

Britain's efforts to re-establish her international financial position in the post-war years were complicated by her poor export performance. Her problem of expanding exports in the 1920s on the basis of a stagnant economy and in the face of growing foreign competition meant that with imports growing faster than exports, the resulting trade gap absorbed a steadily increasing proportion of Britain's invisible earnings. The result was small current account surpluses, seldom reaching one-third or one-half of the pre-war real size (allowing for price rises), which failed to cover the long-term foreign security issues floated in the London capital market.

In these changed circumstances, the US became the chief source of international loans, followed by Britain and France. US foreign investments grew from $7,000 million in 1919 to $17,000 million in 1930 (including $2,000 million invested in the short term). Just over one-half were direct investments, almost one-half of which went to poor countries, mostly in Latin America. In the London capital market new overseas issues averaged £125 million per annum from 1921 to 1930, or about £80 million to £90 million ($390–$440 million) after allowing for loan repayments and foreign participation in the new issues.

Apart from the emergence of the US as the world's principal creditor, the other striking feature of international investment activity during the interwar years was the large-scale borrowing of foreign capital by continental European countries in the years after 1924. Germany was the chief capital-importer, absorbing close to $4,000 million from 1924 to 1929, inclusive. Other European borrowers during these years included Austria, Bulgaria, Czechoslovakia, Greece, Hungary, Poland and Romania. Elsewhere, Argentina and Australia, after having exported capital during certain of the early post-war years, returned to their traditional roles of heavy borrowers in the 1920s. The Union of South Africa also raised loans during the middle and late 1920s. Canada, on the other hand, only began to borrow from 1929 onward, when the capital exports from the chief creditor countries were declining. Broadly speaking, London contributed relatively little to the European investments but supplied a very large share of the money invested in the Empire, including a number of Asian and African countries. On the other hand, investments in Europe and Canada, and those in Latin American countries, were raised chiefly in the US.

The pattern of foreign investment activity that emerged in the 1920s had a number of weaknesses that acted as powerful destabilisers during the early stages of the Great Depression that developed after 1929. To begin with, in contrast to pre-1914, when European capital had gone to countries that supplied the foodstuffs and raw materials demanded by Europe's expanding markets, much of the US'S investment in the 1920s went to countries, particularly those in Europe, whose exports were competitive with, rather than complementary to, those of the US. Moreover, trading relations between the US and Europe had changed significantly. Largely as a result of industrialisation in the US, Europe never regained its pre-war position as a supplier of US imports, averaging only about 30 per cent of the total in the 1920s compared with over 30 per cent before 1914. The US, however, had become an important market for raw materials and foodstuffs, and since several of these commodities were supplied by countries with whom Europe had export surpluses, the US's growing export surplus with Europe depended in considerable measure upon the volume of US imports from these third-party countries. Thus, the world pattern of settlements in the 1920s and particularly the growing US trade surplus with Europe depended upon US capital exports in Europe and elsewhere, a high and stable US demand for the products of third countries, and the existence of a European surplus on current account with these latter areas which was settled in gold and dollars. When, therefore, along with a drastic decline in its imports of raw materials and foodstuffs, US capital exports practically dried up in the early 1930s, a world payments crisis was inevitable.

Another source of weakness was to be found in the debtor countries, especially those primary producers faced with declining world prices for their exports. Apart from the possibility that some of the foreign lending of the period, by financing a further expansion of primary production, may have contributed indirectly to bringing about these price falls, the heavy demand for foreign capital in the 1920s was accompanied by a rise in the percentage return on the outstanding investments. Thus, the annual net outward payments of interest and dividends by debtor countries (excluding regular amortisation payments and reparations payments) rose from $1,400 million annually around 1920 to about $2,500 million in 1928. This increase in net payments of interest and dividends was not evenly distributed among debtor countries, however. Whereas Canada's net outward payments during these years remained stable, others, such as Australia and Argentina, rose by between 50 and 100 per cent. But the heaviest increases occurred in Central and Eastern Europe. These rising debt charges came at a time when falling export prices made it increasingly difficult for some of these debtor countries to earn the foreign exchange necessary to finance needed imports and to meet the debt payments on heavy borrowings at high rates of interest. The effect on a country's balance of payments of these developments could be concealed only as long as creditor countries were prepared to fill the gap with new loans and thus give at least an appearance of equilibrium to a situation fraught with instability and danger.

One further threat to international economic stability came from the heavy and frequently unpredictable movements of short-term capital, which became a feature of the interwar period. French foreign investment in the 1920s, particularly after 1924, was largely of the short-term kind, involving temporary investment on short-term account or in securities bought on foreign stock exchanges. Some of it also took the form of a flight of French capital for investment in stable foreign currencies, more especially the dollar and sterling, brought about by the instability of the French franc in the mid-1920s. However beneficial these capital inflows were to the receiving countries, they represented de-stabilising capital flows, since a rapid withdrawal could easily bring about a major financial crisis in the centre experiencing the loss of funds. A difficult situation was made even worse by the practice that grew up of British and US financial institutions using these funds to lend, in their turn, on long- and short-term bases. This meant that a cessation of French lending, involving possibly the repatriation of French capital, could bring about a chain reaction in the sphere of international finance involving the whole community of international borrowers and lenders.

INSTITUTIONAL WEAKNESSES OF THE RESTORED GOLD STANDARD

The emergence of New York as a major international financial centre had important consequences for the functioning of the restored gold standard. In particular, it involved the decentralisation of the international clearing function. Whereas pre-war international transactions had been centralised in London, with payments typically being made in a relatively simple way by transfer of bank balances held in London, the post-war system became decentralised, with New York and Paris taking over a large part of the function hitherto performed by London. The existence of more than one major financial centre made international clearing more complex and less efficient, for the various centres now had to arrange for offsetting claims among themselves and to hold balances with one another for this purpose. Moreover, the existence of a number of financial centres created exactly the conditions under which foreign-owned funds were liable to move erratically from one financial centre to another in response to changing interest rates, changes in confidence or distrust in currencies. This 'hot-money' danger — well-known up to the present — had been far less serious before 1914, when no centre rivalled London as a place where short-term funds might move and be profitably held.

These difficulties were added to by the institutional shortcomings of the new financial centres. New York lacked the experience of London in the role of distributing international securities to investors. The overwhelming importance of the financial requirements of the domestic market in economic life of the US, the small fraction that foreign trade constituted in total value added, together with the minor role of international investment banking in the US at that time, prevented the establishment of a close connection between a surplus in the US's current account and its level of long-term international lending. Moreover, even when capital was lent abroad, US commercial policy placed major obstacles in the way of debt repayment, since the high tariff policy adopted by the US during these years made it difficult for foreigners to earn dollars in the US market. Borrowers were thus able to make these payments mostly by further borrowing rather than by export expansion.

The functioning of the international monetary system was also hindered by a shortage of gold, and the rather uneven distribution of the existing gold stocks brought about by the war. US holdings, as a proportion of the world's gold stock, had grown from 24 per cent in 1913 to 44 per cent at the end of 1923, while those of Britain had risen from 3 to 9 per cent. On the other hand, certain other countries, including Germany, Italy, Russia, India and Brazil, had suffered not only a relative but also an absolute loss of gold during these years. Given this shortage of world gold reserves, some other acceptable means of international payment had to be found to supplement gold. This was the significance of the widespread adoption of the gold exchange standard during the 1920s, which was officially recommended by the 1922 Geneva Conference as a means of alleviating the world shortage of gold. Under this system, assets in the form of foreign currencies could be counted as part of a country's international monetary reserves. In other words, a country was allowed to stabilise its currency in terms of a foreign currency that was convertible into gold and to hold its reserves in the form of that currency.

This system was not new. Before 1914 it had been adopted by Russia and Austria-Hungary, among others, in Europe, and elsewhere by India, Japan and Argentina, which tied their currencies to sterling, and by the Philippine Islands, which linked its currency to the dollar. During the 1920s, however, the spread of the gold exchange standard was largely a European phenomenon. As it operated in the 1920s, the gold exchange standard had several glaring weaknesses. The first concerned how some countries built up their reserves of convertible currencies. In the absence of a current account surplus or of access to long-term borrowing, many countries acquired reserves by borrowing on short-term bases. Such reserves, however, were highly mobile and particularly vulnerable to changes in confidence. Faced with a foreign exchange crisis, a country was thus likely to find that its foreign reserves tended to disappear at the very moment they were most needed. The weakness of London as an international financial centre was another flaw in the system. Since gold exchange standard countries kept claims on sterling and dollars as reserves, both London and New York had to hold larger stocks of gold than were necessary simply to back their own trading transactions. New York had adequate gold reserves for this purpose, but London had not, and adequate stocks were never acquired. Indeed, London had difficulty preventing a loss of gold in the 1920s, largely because it was lending abroad more than its current account balance permitted. One answer to the difficulty would have been to place temporary restrictions on capital exports, but such a policy would have been inconsistent with London's claim to be a centre of international finance.

One further drawback to the gold exchange standard — and the one which eventually brought the system to an end — was that the most important countries regarded their use of the system as a temporary expedient. Since the holding of foreign exchange instead of gold was considered by some policy makers as damaging to national prestige, transfer to the gold standard was for them only a matter of time. Of the countries on the gold exchange standard, France alone accounted for more than one-half of the total central bank foreign exchange holdings at the end of 1928.[3] When, in that year, France decided to take nothing but gold in settlement of the large surpluses accruing to her from the repatriation of French capital that followed the advent of financial stability at home and from the favourable trade balance generated by an undervalued franc, the end of the gold exchange standard was in sight.

Finally, because many central banks adopted policies of offsetting or neutralising the domestic monetary effects of gold inflows and outflows, the traditional corrective to current account disequilibria — the 'price-specie-flow' mechanism — did not occur promptly and actively under the restored gold standard of the 1920s. While offsetting was not entirely absent from the pre-1914 system, it may often have been automatic rather than the result of deliberate official policy, as was frequently the case in the 1920s. Thus, the US pursued a policy of 'gold sterilization' during these years — the Federal Reserve Banks deliberately offsetting some of the country's gold receipts by reducing their holdings of government securities. A similar policy was followed by the Bank of England in the six years after the country's return to gold in 1925. In France, where post-war inflationary experiences may have influenced government policy, gold movements were also not allowed to have their traditional influence on domestic money supplies.

In summary, the gold standard of the late 1920s was little more than a façade. Gold disappeared from active domestic circulation, and the adoption of the gold or gold exchange standards, with all their drawbacks, represented further attempts to economise on gold. Neutralisation or offsetting of international influences on domestic money, incomes and prices was widespread so that gold standard 'price-specie-flow' mechanism of balance of current account equilibration was largely destroyed, but without being replaced by any alternative mechanism. Exchange rate adjustments had been carried out by many countries to take account of changed economic conditions, but some rates were clearly pegged at the wrong levels. With both the prices and incomes and the exchange rate mechanisms of current account adjustment inoperative, it was only the large injections of US capital into the world economy that prevented the system from collapsing.

THE ECONOMIC BOOM OF THE LATE 1920s

Despite its weaknesses, the restoration of the gold standard marked the beginning of a major industrial boom centred on Europe. After the economic collapse of 1920–1 and up to 1925, Europe suffered a relative decline in its economic standing in the world. Whereas European production did not regain pre-war levels until 1925, it increased by 20 per cent between 1913 and 1925 in Asia and Oceania, by 25 per cent in North America, and by even more in Latin America place temporary restrictions on capital exports, but such a policy would have been inconsistent with London's claim to be a centre of international finance.

One further drawback to the gold exchange standard — and the one which eventually brought the system to an end — was that the most important countries regarded their use of the system as a temporary expedient. Since the holding of foreign exchange instead of gold was considered by some policy makers as damaging to national prestige, transfer to the gold standard was for them only a matter of time. Of the countries on the gold exchange standard, France alone accounted for more than one-half of the total central bank foreign exchange holdings at the end of 1928.[3] When, in that year, France decided to take nothing but gold in settlement of the large surpluses accruing to her from the repatriation of French capital that followed the advent of financial stability at home and from the favourable trade balance generated by an undervalued franc, the end of the gold exchange standard was in sight.

Finally, because many central banks adopted policies of offsetting or neutralising the domestic monetary effects of gold inflows and outflows, the traditional corrective to current account disequilibria — the 'price-specie-flow' mechanism — did not occur promptly and actively under the restored gold standard of the 1920s. While offsetting was not entirely absent from the pre-1914 system, it may often have been automatic rather than the result of deliberate official policy, as was frequently the case in the 1920s. Thus, the US pursued a policy of 'gold sterilization' during these years — the Federal Reserve Banks deliberately offsetting some of the country's gold receipts by reducing their holdings of government securities. A similar policy was followed by the Bank of England in the six years after the country's return to gold in 1925. In France, where post-war inflationary experiences may have influenced government policy, gold movements were also not allowed to have their traditional influence on domestic money supplies.

In summary, the gold standard of the late 1920s was little more than a façade. Gold disappeared from active domestic circulation, and the adoption of the gold or gold exchange standards, with all their drawbacks, represented further attempts to economise on gold. Neutralisation or offsetting of international influences on domestic money, incomes and prices was widespread so that gold standard 'price-specie-flow' mechanism of balance of current account equilibration was largely destroyed, but without being replaced by any alternative mechanism. Exchange rate adjustments had been carried out by many countries to take account of changed economic conditions, but some rates were clearly pegged at the wrong levels. With both the prices and incomes and the exchange rate mechanisms of current account adjustment inoperative, it was only the large injections of US capital into the world economy that prevented the system from collapsing.

THE ECONOMIC BOOM OF THE LATE 1920s

Despite its weaknesses, the restoration of the gold standard marked the beginning of a major industrial boom centred on Europe. After the economic collapse of 1920–1 and up to 1925, Europe suffered a relative decline in its economic standing in the world. Whereas European production did not regain pre-war levels until 1925, it increased by 20 per cent between 1913 and 1925 in Asia and Oceania, by 25 per cent in North America, and by even more in Latin America

CHAPTER 13

The Collapse of the Gold Standard and the Disintegration of the International Economy

A. G. Kenwood, A. L. Lougheed and Michael Graff

The Great Depression of the 1930s had its origin in the US. It is true that signs of declining production had already appeared at various times between late 1927 and mid-1929 in a number of countries, including Australia, Germany, Canada and Argentina, and that commodity prices in the world as a whole began to fall in the second half of 1928. But the economic crisis did not become widespread and severe until after the industrial downturn in the US in mid-1929 and the collapse of the stock market in October of that year. It is usual, therefore, to date the beginning of the world depression from the US stock market crash, for the subsequent collapse of the US economy not only intensified the economic difficulties of those countries already suffering from depression, but it also brought about a rapid economic decline in most other parts of the world.

CRISIS IN AGRICULTURE

By the middle of 1929, many primary goods-producing countries were experiencing financial stringency as falling export prices and declining capital inflows gave rise to acute balance of payments problems. Partly responsible for the decline in foreign lending, particularly by the US, was the rise in US interest rates during 1928 and 1929, as the stock market speculation intensified. Both the rise in interest rates and the prospect of earning speculative profits kept US funds at home and attracted substantial funds from abroad. This difficult international lending situation was further aggravated by the repatriation of French capital that followed the stabilisation of the franc in 1928. The British credit market, under pressure from these and other developments, was in no position to fill the gap created by the withdrawal of France and the US from foreign lending. The result was a general tightening of credit everywhere and a

DOI: 10.4324/9781003382171-17

lack of finance at the very time when the pressure of falling primary product prices was worsening the financial position of the agricultural debtor countries.

When the US stock market crash finally came, it was followed by a virtual end to US lending abroad and a repatriation of US funds. As a result, the economic difficulties in the agricultural debtor countries rapidly approached crisis proportions. In a desperate effort to balance their international accounts and obtain the foreign exchange needed to service their external debt, these countries endeavoured to expand exports still further, which only added to the heavy surpluses of primary products thrown on the market. At the same time, the commodity control schemes, which had operated in the 1920s to maintain relatively high prices for some primary products, collapsed because of the lack of foreign capital to finance the withholding of inventories from the market, releasing a flood of accumulated products onto an already depressed market. The dominant feature in the deepening economic depression in 1930–1, therefore, was the collapse of agricultural and raw materials prices, which strengthened the already existing depression in primary producing countries. In this rapidly deteriorating situation, an improvement in the current account of the debtor countries could only be temporary, since successful export expansion only depressed commodity prices further, thus making even greater export volume increases necessary in the future if the improved trade position was to be maintained. Furthermore, the restrictions on imports of manufactures imposed by some primary producers tended to spread the depression to industrial countries, which reduced their ability to import foodstuffs and raw materials. Moreover, the policy of expanding exports and restricting imports created a dangerous tariff situation. Thus, a number of European governments reacted to the flood of cheap primary products from overseas by protecting peasant producers at home. Even more damaging for the debtor countries, however, was the Smoot–Hawley Act of June 1930, which substantially increased the US tariff level. Coming on top of the rapid decline in income and production in the US, the tariff increases only served to reduce further US purchases of foreign goods.

The greatest number of the heavier duties included in the Smoot–Hawley Act was imposed upon manufactured articles, so that exports of European countries, and particularly of Germany, to the US, were most affected. As a result of the First World War, Europe was, on balance, a large debtor to the US. Europe thus required new loans to be available to roll over the existing debt, or ready access to the US market for its exports. Hence, Europe had to seek to mobilise dollar resources by exporting to third countries, which had accumulated dollar surpluses. But in 1929 and 1930 these raw-material-producing countries were in serious trouble, and it was not feasible to increase exports of manufactured goods to them. In any case, the US tariff indirectly made matters even worse for European countries, since many of the third countries retaliated by raising their duties markedly on products of particular importance to the US, chiefly manufactures, which were also their main imports from Europe.

The deepening of the economic crisis throughout the latter months of 1930, therefore, was due largely to the growing difficulties of the debtor countries, especially those among them which relied mainly upon exports of raw materials and foodstuffs. There were many other complications, perhaps the most important being the steady repatriation of French short-term balances and the imposition of the Smoot–Hawley tariff. The former was accompanied by a persistent drain of gold to France, which not only weakened the financial standing of sterling and the dollar, but also hindered the revival of large-scale, long-term capital exports from the

US and Britain. The latter still further hampered the free exchange of commodities which alone could make possible the heavy payments on account of debt services.

FINANCIAL CRISIS IN EUROPE

Until the late spring of 1931, the Great Depression in many respects appeared to be following the course of ordinary business slumps of the past. A number of primary producing countries had gone off gold, but no major international trading country had been involved, and the gold standard was still intact in Western Europe and America. Moreover, there were some signs of a definite easing of the economic situation. Although the debtor countries continued to experience financial difficulties, all the changes in official bank rates were downward, suggesting conditions of monetary ease in the chief creditor countries, and the accumulation of liquid capital funds. Steadiness or slight rises in seasonally adjusted figures of industrial production in Germany and the US during the early months of the year even afforded some hope that the revival was not very far away.

This hesitant optimism was soon shattered by the outbreak of an international financial panic. It began in Austria, where a revaluation of the assets of the Creditanstalt of Vienna revealed the bank as insolvent. Despite quick action by the Austrian government to guarantee all deposits of the bank, this flaw in Austria's financial structure led to a heavy withdrawal of foreign short-term credits. This was stemmed only when loans by the Bank for International Settlements (BIS) and the Bank of England to the Austrian government enabled it to guarantee the Creditanstalt's existing liabilities to foreign creditors, while, for their part, the foreign creditors of the bank undertook not to withdraw their advances for a period of two years.

Meanwhile the panic had spread to Germany, which had come under suspicion mainly because of its close commercial ties with Austria. A run on the Reichsbank developed, and attempts were made to end it by raising an international loan in support of the bank and by the announcement of a year's moratorium on reparations and war-debt payments. Withdrawals continued, however, and were accelerated when the disclosure of enormous losses by Nordwolle (North-German Wool Company), involving the shutdown of the Danat-Bank (Darmstädter und National Bank), converted a run mainly of Germany's foreign creditors into a flight from the mark into foreign exchange by Germans as well. The German government reacted to this new crisis by temporarily closing the banks and stock exchanges and by raising the discount rate from 7 to 10 per cent. Steps were also taken to introduce exchange controls and to place restrictions on bank payments. The international loan granted earlier was renewed, and, with the panic subsiding, the signing of a standstill agreement, immobilising for six months the funds owed by Germans to foreign banks, consolidated the movement towards more normal conditions.

Britain, too, was now suffering a steady loss of gold and, throughout the summer months, the bank rate rose steadily until it reached 4.5 per cent at the end of July. Her difficulties were closely linked with those of Germany and Austria, for British bankers had advanced them a large amount of short-term credit which was rapidly becoming 'frozen' by the inability of the debtors to meet their foreign obligations. In Germany alone, British short-term holdings amounting to $70 million were locked up under the standstill agreement. Unwanted attention was drawn to the volume of short-term claims in London by the publication on 13 July 1931 of the report of the Macmillan Committee, which revealed that London's short-term claims on foreigners, including those 'frozen' on the continent, amounted to only £153 million, whereas deposits and sterling bills held in London by foreigners amounted to £407 million. While there is nothing unusual about a banker having demand liabilities far in excess of immediately liquid assets, knowledge of the fact is inconvenient in time of crisis. Almost as damaging to Britain's international financial standing was the publication on 31 July 1931 of the May Committee report on the country's public finances. This revealed an impending deficit in the government budget and recommended cuts in government expenditure, as well as tax increases. In an age when the first canon of orthodox finance was a balanced budget, this report served only to convince foreigners of the waywardness of Britain.

With the withdrawal of short-term balances and the sale of British securities intensifying the strain on Britain's gold reserves, the Bank of England secured on 1 August 1931 a credit of £50 million from French and US banks. The run continued, however, despite the resignation of a Labour government unwilling to implement the May Committee recommendations on cuts in government expenditure, and the election of a coalition government pledged to put the economies into effect. On 29 August, a further credit of £80 million was arranged, but the drain continued. The introduction by the government of a supplementary budget on 10 September 1931 designed to balance the government's accounts failed to halt the run, which developed panic proportions following reports of an alleged naval mutiny at Invergordon (Scotland) on 15 September caused by proposed naval pay cuts. During the following three days, over £43 million were withdrawn from the London money market, making a total withdrawal of over £200 million in the preceding two months. On 21 September 1931, therefore, legislation was passed suspending the Bank of England's obligation to redeem its notes in gold. The bank rate was raised to 6 per cent, and the Stock Exchange was closed for two days. Temporary restrictions were also imposed on all foreign exchange dealings.

Immediately after Britain suspended gold payments the pound sterling fell heavily in relation to currencies still on the gold standard.[1] In order not to be put at a trading disadvantage, many other countries quickly followed Britain off gold. By the end of 1932, when 32 countries had suspended gold payments, Scandinavia, Portugal, Egypt, Latvia, most of Latin America, Japan and all British territories and dominions except South Africa were also off gold. Only France and the US among the big nations, and Belgium, the Netherlands and Switzerland among the smaller states, remained on gold for the time being.

Britain's abandonment of gold in 1931 marks the beginning of the 'sterling area'. Several factors, both non-economic and economic in character, explain why some countries sought to tie their currencies to the pound sterling. A non-economic consideration was the sentimental ties which existed between Great Britain and the other members of the British Commonwealth of Nations. Sentimentality, although important, was not the major reason for adherence to sterling, however, since a number of countries not members of the British Commonwealth joined the sterling area, and one of the more important British dominion countries, Canada, did not — Canada's economic ties being much stronger with the US than with Britain. Fundamentally, three economic factors accounted for the willingness, and desire, of some countries to enter the sterling area. First, sterling was an important currency in the world, it was widely used, and its prestige was relatively high. As gold ceased to be an international standard of value, certain countries sought to tie their currencies to another standard of value, in this case the pound sterling. Second, Britain constituted the major market for the exports of many countries. These countries sought to promote a close currency link between Britain and themselves to protect this commercial relationship. In tying their currencies to sterling, the exporting countries were able to protect commodity prices and the competitive position of those producers dependent upon the British market. Third, a number of countries were debtors of Britain, and they accordingly fixed exchange rates between their currencies and the pound sterling in order to preserve a constancy of cost in servicing their debt obligations.

THE END OF THE GOLD STANDARD

After Britain left gold in September 1931, the international panic centred on the US, and nearly $2,000 million in gold left the country in the fiscal year ending June 1932. To stop the drain, the US monetary authorities adopted a savage deflationary policy to the accompaniment of rising unemployment and still deeper depression. When, therefore, the US came to leave the gold standard, it was because of a deliberate act of policy, aimed at relieving the desperate financial and economic conditions existing in the country rather than because of any external balance of payments difficulties as such. In its search for a policy to combating the depression, the newly elected Roosevelt administration believed that a revival of the US economy could only follow from a general rise of domestic prices, and for this reason a number of government policies were initiated and aimed at bringing this about. Finally, on 20 April 1933, the US suspended gold payments in the belief that if the price of gold was raised commodity prices would automatically rise in direct proportion, thus encouraging business expansion.

The abandonment of gold by the US marked the virtual end of the gold standard. The next year saw the gradual polarisation of countries around a few major industrial powers and the eventual emergence of a number of regional currency systems. At its peak, this decentralised currency mechanism consisted of the sterling area, centred on Britain, the dollar area, headed by the US and composed chiefly of Latin American countries, the exchange control area of Central and Southeastern Europe, in which Germany played a leading role, the yen area dominated by Japan the Far East and the gold bloc in Western Europe.[2] Although it was not formally constituted until after the collapse of the World Economic Conference in mid-1933, the gold bloc began to take shape when the central banks of Belgium, France and the Netherlands began to experience foreign exchange losses following the depreciation of sterling in 1931. The remnant of the gold standard was not long in existence, however. As the depression continued, doubts were entertained about the ability of the gold countries to resist devaluation. Consequently, a speculative flight of capital began in these countries, reinforced later by growing fears of war. Belgium was the first to go, devaluing its currency by 28 per cent in March 1935. The other members of the gold bloc followed at the end of September 1936. France devalued by 30 per cent, and Switzerland by approximately the same amount. No definite margin of devaluation was set by the Dutch, but a newly established equalisation fund kept the exchange rate against the dollar in the vicinity of 20 per cent below the old parity.

GROWTH OF RESTRICTIONS ON FINANCE AND TRADE

The widespread exchange and trade regulations, which accompanied the collapse of the gold standard, while offering greater resistance to uncontrolled capital movements, prevented a return to a steady capital outflow from creditor to debtor countries during the 1930s. Exchange control hindered the repatriation of capital, while trade regulations eliminated a large portion of the multilateral trade, through which returns on foreign direct investments as well as the service of foreign loans had been transferred. Moreover, the volume of lending declined during these years, and the direction of the loans became even more circumscribed than formerly because of the emergence of the regional currency blocs. The loans floated in London were thus, with few exceptions, confined to members of the British Commonwealth and other countries within the sterling area. Countries with overseas territories confined themselves chiefly to supplying these territories with funds, and Japan invested largely in Manchuria. Other loans, based on geographical proximity or close economic relations, included those by the US to Canada, by Sweden to other Scandinavian countries, and by Belgium, the Netherlands and Switzerland to France. France and the other members of the gold bloc also recorded heavy capital exports during the middle and late 1930s. But only a small part of this capital went to debtor countries. The bulk represented capital seeking refuge in other creditor countries, particularly the US, because of the menacing monetary instability in Europe and, after 1936, because of increasing political instability and the growing threat of war.

The depression of the 1930s and the financial difficulties associated with it also had a profound influence on commercial policy during these years. Confronted by a worldwide depression, no country escaped untouched, and there was consequently a reaction against international economic interdependence. Each nation fell back on its own resources and pursued a policy of fostering internal recovery first and foremost. In such an atmosphere, the regulation of foreign trade and financial transactions was a natural and inevitable development. Broadly speaking, these controls took two main forms: those aimed directly at controlling the making of payments between countries, and those affecting in the first instance the movements of individual commodities between countries. The former group included exchange controls and all the various blends of clearing and payments agreements associated with it; the latter, tariffs, import quotas, prohibitions and the like. While the distinction between the two types of trade controls is not completely clear cut, for in operation they overlapped at every stage, it does provide us with convenient headings under which to discuss the developments in commercial policy during the 1930s.

Foreign Exchange Controls

Although any form of government intervention that affects the level of foreign exchange rates is, in a broad sense, exchange control, the narrower and more common interpretation of the term refers to various forms of official restrictions upon private transactions in foreign exchange. Where such restrictions were introduced during our period, governments, often through central banks, assumed control of foreign exchange by requiring exporters to surrender the foreign money received from sales abroad and by requiring importers to purchase foreign exchange from authorised sources, with both the buying and selling of foreign exchange taking place at official rates fixed by the government. Whereas few countries passed through the depression without resort to some exchange restrictions, if only for a short period, severe and thoroughgoing systems of control were implemented in debtor countries faced with difficult payments problems and, sometimes, the danger of a simultaneous flight of both domestic and foreign capital. In these countries, of which Germany is a leading example, the government attempted to control all transactions that affected the demand for and supply of foreign exchange. Inevitably the system of control grew more complex, as it became necessary to implement the overall regulations with a host of detailed provisions designed to eliminate evasion.

The increasing severity and persistence of exchange control policies in the 1930s was partly the result of a broadening in the objectives supporting its introduction and retention in the countries concerned. While the original object of exchange control was to curb the outflow of capital associated with the financial crises of the early 1930s, with the deepening of the depression the objectives of such a policy soon multiplied. Thus, the insulation given to an economy by exchange control afforded an opportunity to introduce domestic expansionary measures to raise incomes and increase employment. Exchange control was also necessary if a country wished to maintain an official price of the domestic currency higher than that resulting from the interplay of forces operating on the foreign exchange market, either because it feared exchange depreciation would lead to inflation, or because depreciation would lead to subsequent increases in the burden of debt service.[3] It could also be used to protect domestic industries, since such a policy enabled a country to allocate foreign exchange for imports on a product-by-product basis, so that the exclusion, or carefully controlled admission, of particular imports brought about by the lack of foreign exchange also served to protect the home market for domestic producers. Finally, exchange control was used to acquire revenue for the government. By setting a higher rate (or rates) for selling than for buying foreign exchange, the difference accrued to the government as profit. A number of countries (e.g. Argentina and Chile) employed exchange control for this purpose, among others.

Bilateral Trading Agreements

As a matter of historical fact, however, the main change of emphasis that occurred in the use of exchange control during these years related to the control of trade. The shortage of foreign currency, which made exchange control necessary, was not merely general, but tended to be relatively greater for some currencies than for others. Moreover, the fact that some currencies were relatively scarcer than others led to bilateralism, that is, to a deliberate balancing of accounts between pairs of trading countries. Bilateral arrangements had advantages other than just that of overcoming the trading difficulties associated with shortages of foreign currencies. They were attractive in situations where the opportunities for trade discrimination afforded by exchange control enabled one country to gain from its monopoly control of the trade of other, often smaller, countries. Germany, in particular, was able to take advantage of this sort of situation in its trade with Eastern and Central European countries in the 1930s. These arrangements could also be used to settle the problem of blocked balances held by exchange control countries. These bilateral arrangements, however, included one significant new element. Whereas the bilateral trading arrangements for dealing with problems other than those of blocked balances almost invariably involved only exchange control countries, the problem of blocked balances often involved free exchange market countries as well.

What all these bilateral arrangements had in common was that they were agreements between pairs of trading countries, designed to keep trade at a relatively high volume, but to do so without the accumulation of 'soft currencies', which could not be used to settle 'hard currency'[4] deficits, and without incurring deficits payable in hard currencies. In other words, these agreements sought to reduce the need for settlement in gold or scarce foreign exchange. Such agreements took three major forms: (1) private compensation agreements, (2) clearing agreements and (3) payments agreements.

Compensation agreements, the simplest of the new trading devices, were merely a modern form of the age-old principle of barter. Obviously, no currency transactions were necessary when two countries could agree to an exchange of goods of equal value. Where governments were involved in such barter deals, the arrangements were described as a compensation agreement. More often, however, the negotiations were conducted by private individuals or firms, in which case the term private compensation was used to describe the transaction. A considerable volume of German trade came under these compensation deals in 1932 and 1933, including the exchange of some 9 million marks worth of German coal for Brazilian coffee, and the exchange of German fertiliser for Egyptian cotton. In some countries, the growth of these trading practices was encouraged by the setting up of organisations to act as middlemen in these barter deals. The Polish Company for Compensation Trade, which began operations in November 1932, was one of the more important of these organisations. In Germany, on the other hand, the Chambers of Commerce established the clearing information bureau for this purpose; and in Copenhagen five importing firms organised, in 1934, the Association for Commodity Exchange to arrange private compensation transactions with foreign firms.

Private compensation agreements, even when assisted by barter agencies, involved enormous difficulties, since they required the offsetting of individual exports and imports in each transaction. Clearing agreements, which were also entered into during these years, avoided these difficulties by providing a broader and more general procedure for offsetting claims. Under such arrangements each country agreed to establish, usually in its central bank, an account through which all payments for imports and exports were to be cleared. For example, under the German clearing arrangement with Yugoslavia, German importers of Yugoslavian goods would pay marks into an account at the Reichsbank, where they were credited to the account of the Yugoslav clearing agency. German exporters to Yugoslavia were then paid marks from this fund, debited to the Yugoslav account. In Belgrade, the opposite process took place. Yugoslav importers made payments into the clearing account in dinars and exporters received dinars from the account.

As with many developments in the exchange control field during these years, the Germans led the way with clearing arrangements. The first was signed in 1932 with Hungary, and by 1937 Germany had negotiated clearing agreements with every European country except Britain and Albania, as well as with Argentina, Chile, Uruguay and Colombia. The principal feature of these clearing procedures was that they covered not only payments arising from merchandise trade, but also various other payments, including the transfer of interest and dividends, travel expenditures, shipping services, remittances and so on. In each case, exchange clearing provided a way of settling individual transactions between two countries in terms of their respective domestic currencies.

Payments agreements differed from clearing agreements chiefly in that they covered a wider range of transactions and used the normal method of payment over the foreign exchanges rather than special clearing accounts. In addition, a payments agreement often linked an exchange control country with a free exchange country, whereas clearing agreements were negotiated only between exchange control countries. Consequently, most of the payments agreements in force in the summer of 1939 were between free exchange countries of Western Europe, on the one hand, and exchange control countries in Central and Southeastern Europe or Latin America, on the other.

The chief reason for free exchange countries becoming involved in bilateral agreements during these years was the difficulty of realising frozen debt and service payments in exchange control countries. A major item of frozen debt arose out of the standstill agreements negotiated during the financial crisis of 1931. Britain had been deeply involved in these developments, and it is not surprising, therefore, to find that the first creditor country to make use of payments agreements in its relations with debtor countries was the United Kingdom. Thus, the Anglo-German Agreement of November 1934 is generally regarded as the model of subsequent payments agreements, although the British government had first employed the payments principle in the Roca-Runciman Agreement of May 1933 with Argentina. The Anglo-German agreement earmarked 55 per cent of the value of German exports to Britain for payment of British exports to Germany, and the surplus 45 per cent was partly used to service the Dawes and Young Plan loans in Britain and to cover other charges, including the payment of freight expenses in sterling, the remainder being placed at the free disposal of the Reichsbank.

Confined to preventing capital movements, exchange control need not result in restrictions in trade, discrimination between countries or protection of particular producers. Indeed, it was currency overvaluation rather than exchange control as such that was ultimately responsible for the contraction of trade that took place during the 1930s. Once exchange control is applied in support of currency overvaluation, payments made in the currencies of control countries lead towards the accumulation of blocked balances. Bilateral trading arrangements, which are themselves only instruments of policy, then become necessary to liquidate these frozen claims. In the process, trade is distorted and discrimination against countries inevitably practised. It is then but a short step from this type of discrimination to discrimination with a view to economic domination. Throughout the process, however, exchange control and bilateral trading arrangements are essentially instruments or tools of policy.

Whatever the reason for adopting a policy of exchange control, however, its use led to a loss of world real income, because by distorting trade from its normal channels into bilateral grooves, the resultant trade represented less specialisation according to comparative advantage than trade carried out under multilateral conditions. Yet given that the setting of equilibrium exchange rates and the liberalising of international payments was impossible in the depressed conditions of the 1930s, bilateral trading arrangements did make possible trade in specialised commodities that would not otherwise have taken place. Both partners to clearing payments agreements gained. Exports to other exchange control countries increased, despite the economic difficulties of the early 1930s, and these additional exports made it possible to acquire useful imports. Moreover, exchange clearing made possible the liquidation of frozen balances, and permitted the maintenance of debt service owed to creditor countries.

Tariffs and Other Restrictions on Trade

Despite the spread of exchange control, tariffs remained the greatest single obstacle to the international movement of goods in the 1930s. The upward movement of tariffs, which characterised the early depression years, continued well into the mid-1930s, when there was some relaxation of restrictions from late 1936 onwards. But in 1938 the decline in world trade and a fall in primary product prices led to a resumption of the upward movement. By the end of the 1930s, therefore, close to half the world's trade was restricted by tariffs alone.

Britain's conversion to whole-hearted protectionism represents the major single development in the tariff history of the period. In practice, Britain was still predominantly free trading at the beginning of the 1930s, for out of £1,030 million of imports, £138 million paid revenue duties, and only £13 million were subject to McKenna or Safeguarding Act duties. But the situation changed radically with the passing of the Import Duties Act of March 1932. This Act imposed a general duty of 10 per cent ad valorem on all imports into the United Kingdom, except Empire goods and those named on a free list, which included most foodstuffs and raw materials. The Act also set up an Import Duties Advisory Committee to recommend additional duties. In April, a 33.33 per cent duty was placed on most kinds of steel; the general level of duties on manufactured goods was raised to 20 per cent, on luxury goods to 24–30 per cent and on a few items (including some chemicals) to 33.33 per cent. With a few exceptions, British Empire products again received exemption from these charges.

The other significant feature of commercial policy in these years was the spread of import quotas and other forms of quantitative controls over trade France was the first country to adopt import quotas on a wide scale as a means of combating the depression, and she was quickly followed by a number of other countries. By the end of 1932, 11 countries had fully fledged quota or licensing systems. Despite their further spread, import quotas remained primarily a European instrument of trade control. At the beginning of 1939, 28 countries, 19 of them European, operated quota or licensing systems applying to a substantial range of commodities.

There were various reasons for adopting quantitative import controls. They could be used to protect domestic manufacturing and, perhaps even more importantly, to protect domestic agriculture from overseas competition that followed the violent fall in primary product prices in the early 1930s. Import quotas were also of vital importance to the gold bloc countries after the abandonment of the gold standard by Britain and the US. With their currencies becoming overvalued in the face of currency depreciation elsewhere, these countries experienced severe balance of payments pressures. Denied the use of exchange control by their adherence to the gold standard, they imposed severe control on imports to bring their foreign trade into balance. Moreover, import quotas often formed part of national recovery programmes. In 1933, for example, the United Kingdom introduced quotas on agricultural products in support of national marketing schemes aimed at reviving British agriculture and in favour of Empire producers. Import quotas were also used for purposes of retaliation and commercial bargaining

Import quotas were even more damaging to international trade than tariffs, since a quota directly limits the level of permissible imports and thus operates independently of the price mechanism. Thus, while it is always possible for the foreign exporter to beat the tariff by lowering his price sufficiently to make him competitive with domestic producers even when the tariff is added to his price, the quota limits the importation of a commodity to a fixed amount irrespective of supply and demand conditions (or prices) in the domestic or foreign markets. But while appreciating the additional restrictions placed on foreign trade by import quotas as compared with tariffs, the extraordinary difficulties of the 1930s should always be kept in mind when considering the welfare implications of these additional controls on international exchange. In the depression years, tariffs proved completely inadequate in protecting domestic industry, whether agriculture or manufacturing, from distress sales of foreign goods induced by serious deflationary pressures abroad. Only import quotas could ensure the strict limitation of these imports, thus reducing the damage they inflicted on domestic production and employment. Moreover, where balance of payments difficulties called for the reduction of a country's imports, import quotas or the licensing of imports provided the only certain way of confining the total value of imports within predetermined limits. It is not surprising, therefore, to find that import licensing and other forms of quantitative restrictions on imports were often used in connection with systems of exchange control.

INTERNATIONAL FINANCIAL COOPERATION

The Bank for International Settlements (BIS) was set up in Basel in Switzerland in 1930 under the Young Plan to facilitate the flows of reparations payments from Germany to the recipient countries. After the reparations moratorium of July 1931, it continued — and continues up to this date — to perform its once only-subsidiary function of promoting central bank cooperation. The monthly meetings of its board members, mostly central bankers, provided a venue for discussion and attempts at cooperation. As noted above, the BIS arranged loans to the Austrian government after the Creditanstalt disaster. Throughout the 1930s, the bank also provided short-term credit facilities to a number of central banks. Nevertheless, its attempts to encourage central bank cooperation at this time were of minor importance.

By the middle of 1932 the opinion was widespread that international action was necessary to combat the breakdown of international trade and finance and to promote economic recovery. Consequently, a World Economic Conference was held in London in June 1933, to discuss, among other things, the question of currency stabilisation. However, shortly before the meeting was convened, the dollar went off gold and was allowed to fluctuate freely without any immediate hope of stabilisation. With the future of the dollar uncertain, international agreement on currency stabilisation was impossible, and the Conference was adjourned without having achieved any worthwhile success.

The need for some measure of international financial cooperation arose again in 1936, when the abandonment of the gold standard by the gold bloc countries created problems for those countries operating exchange stabilisation funds. Meanwhile all major obstacles to an agreement between the major financial powers in the world had been removed by the final collapse of the remnants of the gold standard and by the change in the US government's attitude to international currency stability following the stabilisation of the dollar in 1934. The result was the Tripartite Monetary Agreement between France, Britain and the US, which was concluded just before the French devaluation in September 1936, and which was later joined by Belgium, Holland and Switzerland. While it would be a mistake to exaggerate the concrete accomplishments of this agreement, which were largely in the field of technical cooperation, it was important, nevertheless, because it endorsed the principle of managed exchange rates which had come to replace the free exchange rates associated with the gold standard, and because it involved recognition of the need for effective international cooperation in a managed exchange rate system. In this sense the Tripartite Monetary Agreement of 1936 was a forerunner of the International Monetary Fund.

The interwar period witnessed the beginnings of the gradual transfer of international financial hegemony from Britain to the US, which was completed by the end of the Second World War. In the 1930s, the US's domestic economic difficulties still had tended to take precedence over her involvement in international economic affairs. Also, whilst Britain's abandonment of the gold standard in September 1931 brought about the total collapse of the international monetary standard, which she had pioneered in the early nineteenth century, she nevertheless remained the head of one of the strongest regional economic entities — the sterling area — to emerge from the ruins of that system.[5]

REGIONAL ECONOMIC COOPERATION

The failure to achieve international agreement on matters of trade and finance in the early 1930s led many countries to consider the alternative possibility of trade liberalising agreements on a regional basis. An early example of this type of economic cooperation was that between the Danubian agricultural countries, Hungary, Romania, Yugoslavia and Bulgaria, which in the early 1930s obtained tariff preferences for their chief exports in a number of individually negotiated bilateral agreements with European industrial countries. The regional economic pact between Italy, Austria and Hungary brought about by the Rome Agreements of 1934, and the series of agreements reached in the 1930s between the 'Oslo Group' of nations, comprising Denmark, Sweden, Norway, Finland, the Netherlands, Belgium and Luxembourg, provide further examples of these attempts at regional economic cooperation. In the Americas the Pan American Conference attempted to deal with the problem of trade restrictions in the Western Hemisphere. The US concluded several reciprocal trade agreements with Latin American countries in the years before 1939, and a number of trade liberalising agreements were also concluded between pairs of Latin American countries. Owing to their relative importance in Latin American trade, even more such agreements were negotiated with European countries. Although, on balance, these regional agreements were probably trade diverting rather than trade creating in their effect on the international exchange of goods and services, they did help to revive business confidence and reverse the trend towards economic nationalism.

By far the most important regional economic pact of these years was the establishment of a general preferential system within the British Commonwealth as a result of the Ottawa agreements of 1932. Under these arrangements, Commonwealth countries agreed to extend to each other increased import preference. As for tariff reductions within the Empire, the results were meagre. What was achieved by way of increased trade within the Commonwealth was achieved not by the reduction of tariffs within the Empire, but by raising them to those countries outside it. Moreover, although imperial preference increased Britain's share in the trade of Empire countries, it also deflected foreign competition into other markets where Britain's position was less favourable. The drawbacks to Britain of this changed pattern of trade only became apparent in the period after the end of the Second World War.

In colonial territories, the open-door policy formerly favoured by the chief colonial powers was gradually abandoned with the onset of the depression and the growing impact of Japanese competition in colonial areas in the Far East and elsewhere after 1931. Complete tariff assimilation between the mother country and its colonies constituted the policy pursued by France, the US and Japan in relation to certain of their colonies. On the other hand, within the British, French (non-assimilated colonies), Portuguese, Spanish and Italian Empires, tariff preferences were extensively employed. At the same time, import quotas and foreign exchange regulations provided convenient openings for discrimination in favour of intra-imperial trade.

INTERNATIONAL COMMODITY CONTROL SCHEMES

International commodity schemes constituted practically the only significant multilateral economic agreements concluded in the 1930s. These intergovernmental agreements, between leading producing countries, or between the producing and leading importing countries as well, were concerned with matters relating to the production and marketing of certain primary products. Where only producers were involved, the object of these agreements was to control production and exportation to stabilise prices, or even to raise them. Some of these international agreements evolved from private cartels set up in the 1920s to control the prices of certain products, such as rubber, tea and tin, while others grew out of the attempts of individual governments to deal with the problem of surplus production and unstable prices. Cases in which international commodity agreements evolved through government sponsorship included coffee, sugar and wheat.

The collapse of these earlier control schemes and the depressed prices of primary products during the early 1930s led to the establishment of several international commodity agreements in the years from 1931 onwards. These included agreements covering tin and sugar (1931), tea and wheat (1933), rubber (1934) and copper (1936). Together, these schemes covered 80–90 per cent, or even more, of exportable production, and, with the partial exception of the tin scheme, all relied on quantitative control of production. Pricing policy was largely one of opportunism or expediency. Overall, however, these schemes did not play an important part in the history of primary production during the 1930s. Their influence was decisive only for tea, tin and rubber, and they had some influence on the production and export of sugar and copper. Even if these achievements were confined to a limited field, however, the mere fact that control schemes were set up for so many products, and that their marketing was sufficiently well organised to enable the schemes to operate reasonably efficiently is important as a pointer to what might have been achieved had a more vigorous international economic policy been fostered by the major trading powers.

Private and government-sponsored cartel agreements between normally competitive firms located in two or more countries became more frequent in manufacturing industry, because the interwar period with its falling prices and substantial excess capacity in many lines proved especially favourable for their emergence. Thus, at the outbreak of the Second World War, it is estimated that the number of international cartels amounted to 179, of which 133 involved manufactured and semi-manufactured goods, including steel, chemicals, electrical products, oil and aluminium. These cartels had as their central objective the reduction of competition to stabilise prices and, where possible, enjoy monopoly profits. They were also used occasionally as instruments of government policy. This happened in Germany in the 1930s, when various cartels dominated by German producers were used by the Nazi government to maintain German exports at the expense of other countries, and to assure the German economy of supplies of foreign currency.

Like monopolies, cartels tend to restrict the volume of world trade and divert its channels. In the interwar years, international cartelisation tended to divide the world into spheres of commercial influence by allocating to the nationals of certain countries exclusive selling rights in certain territories. Thus, in the cartel arrangements of the 1930s, US firms were normally assigned the US market, sometimes the whole of North America and, on occasion, part of Latin America. British firms laid special claim to Empire territory, while the growing strength of German firms in several cartels won them increasingly large areas of Europe as their exclusive market. It is perhaps in those situations where markets were allocated among the members of the cartel that the reduction of trade was most apparent — for example, where the US market became the exclusive preserve of US firms, for under these arrangements potential trade is simply stopped at its source.

CONCLUSIONS

The worldwide Great Depression of the 1930s, and the collapse of the gold standard which accompanied its onset in the early years of that decade, were responsible for the spread of financial and trade practices which severely restricted the exchange of goods between countries. Even when devices such as bilateral trading agreements promoted trade flows between countries, which might not otherwise have taken place, the benefits derived from this increase in the volume of international trade were offset by the loss of welfare to its participants consequent upon the trade being conducted through bilateral rather than multilateral channels. Distortions of trading patterns and consequent reduction of specialisation according to comparative advantage were also characteristic of those regional economic blocs operating preferential trading arrangements. The net outcome of all these developments was a substantial slowing up in the growth of international trade during the interwar years, which is examined in detail in the next chapter.

RECOMMENDATIONS FOR FURTHER READING

The disintegration of the international economy during in the 1930s is dealt with in detail by Gordon (1941, *Barriers to World Trade*), Calleo (1976, *The Historiography of the Interwar Period: Reconsiderations*) and Costigliola (1985, *Awkward Dominion. American Political, Economic and Cultural Relations with Europe, 1919–1933*).

NOTES

1 Sterling fluctuated freely on the foreign exchange market until April 1932, when the Exchange Equalisation Account was established. Operated by the Bank of England under Treasury control, the Account's purchases and sales of sterling in the market were supposed to smooth out excessive short-run fluctuations. In particular, the Account operated to protect the domestic credit base from the effects of international short-term capital movements.

2 A number of countries with diverse commercial and financial ties, such as Canada and Argentina, did not fit naturally into any one of these groups, and had to maintain an intermediate and precarious position in this system of group exchanges.
3 Since foreign loans are ordinarily expressed in the currency of the lending country, an appreciation of the lender's currency increases the amount of domestic money that the debtor country must pay out to acquire the lender's currency necessary to service the foreign debt. Later in the twentieth century, economists would refer to this potential danger for a country with borrowing denominated in foreign currency as the 'original sin'.
4 A 'hard currency' is widely accepted for international payments, whereas 'soft currencies' are not. The latter may only be accepted in the issuing countries or blocs, and at the extreme, not even there.
5 For a more detailed discussion of this transfer of leadership, see Calleo (1976).

CHAPTER **14**

International Trade during the Interwar Period

A. G. Kenwood, A. L. Lougheed and Michael Graff

THE GROWTH OF WORLD TRADE IN THE INTERWAR YEARS

Between the two world wars there was a sharp break in the expansion of world trade. Although the volume of foreign trade continued to grow, the average annual rate of growth of total trade declined from an average of almost 3.4 per cent in the period 1881–1913 to 1.3 per cent in the period 1913–37. The decline in per capita trade, from an annual average of 2.9 per cent in the period 1881–1913 to 0.3 per cent in 1913–37, was even more striking.

Given the economic difficulties of the interwar period, this decline in world trade is not surprising. What was disconcerting about foreign trade developments during these years, however, was that the reduction in the rate of growth of world trade was clearly more marked than that in the rate of growth of world product, whether measured on a total or per capita basis. Thus, over the period 1913–37 the total product of 13 developed countries grew at an average annual rate of 2.0 per cent and 1.2 per capita, compared with an increase of about 1.0 per cent in total trade and a decrease of about — 0.3 per cent in per capita trade.[1]

This tendency for output to grow faster than trade was not uniformly maintained throughout the interwar years, however. Largely on account of the expansion in the US, industrial production emerged from the war less battered than trade. In the 1920s, however, trade revived rapidly and was probably growing slightly faster than world output towards the end of the decade. This improvement in trade relative to output was maintained in the early years of the 1930s, when the loss in the volume of international trade because of the depression was less than the decline in world industrial output. But with recovery world production revived more rapidly than world trade, and by 1937 industrial production had grown to 104 per cent of the 1929 figure, whereas world trade registered only 97 per cent.

These trends in world output and world trade suggest that the foreign trade proportion, that is, the ratio of world trade to world product, declined during the interwar period, despite an increase in the number of trading nations, largely brought about by the post-war political

DOI: 10.4324/9781003382171-18

settlement in Europe, which created several new nation states. During the war years the world foreign trade proportion probably fell, but it was the depression of the 1930s and the Second World War that sharply reduced the volume of foreign trade and the world trade proportion, so that by the late 1940s and early 1950s it was probably at its lowest since 1913.

THE DIRECTION OF WORLD TRADE BETWEEN THE WARS

The First World War interrupted the customary flow of trade between continents and nations, bringing about a decrease in Europe's trade and an increase in that of the US. The decline in Europe's share of total world trade continued during the interwar years, despite some recovery in the 1930s when the depression checked the expansion of American trade. Consequently, by 1937 Europe was responsible for just over half of world trade compared with almost two-thirds in 1913, as can be seen in Table 14.1.

This decline in Europe's importance in world trade came about for various reasons. It was due partly to the fall in the trade share of Russia (the Soviet Union, respectively), which accounted for close to 4 per cent of total world trade in 1913, but only some 1.5 per cent in the late 1920s and around 1 per cent in the late 1930s. It also reflected the continued growth in the importance of the North American continent in world trade, whose share in 1937 was larger than it had been in 1913, despite the set-back of the 1930s. An even more important cause of the shift in relative shares over the period was the continuous increase in the proportion of world trade of the then still largely poor regions of Asia, Africa and Oceania. In 1913, they accounted for 17 per cent of world trade; by 1937 their combined share had grown to almost one-quarter of the total trade.

The same trade picture is examined from a somewhat different angle in Table 14.2, which shows the changing shares of the industrialised and the poorer countries in world

TABLE 14.1 Distribution of world trade by geographic regions, 1913–37 (per cent)

Region	1913		Total trade	1928		Total trade	1937		Total trade
	Exports	Imports		Exports	Imports		Exports	Imports	
Europe[a]	58.9	65.1	62.0	48.0	56.2	52.1	47.0	55.8	51.4
North America[b]	14.8	11.5	13.2	19.8	15.2	17.5	17.1	13.9	15.5
Latin America[c]	8.3	7.0	7.6	9.8	7.6	8.7	10.2	7.2	8.7
Asia	11.8	10.4	11.1	15.5	13.8	14.6	16.9	14.1	15.5
Africa	3.7	3.6	3.7	4.0	4.6	4.3	5.3	6.2	5.7
Oceania	2.5	2.4	2.4	2.9	2.6	2.8	3.5	2.8	3.2
Total	100.0	100.0	100.0	100.0	100.0	100.0	100.0	100.0	100.0

Source: Lamartine Yates (1959, p. 32f., Tables 6 and 7).

Notes: [a] including Russia/Soviet Union; [b] Canada and US; [c] Central and South America, including all colonial territories in the Western Hemisphere.

trade during the period 1913–37, measured in constant prices, excluding the Soviet Union. Here it can be seen that the decline in Europe's share in world trade during the interwar years is accounted for solely by the decline in the share of Industrial Europe, since Other Europe's share was slightly larger in 1937 than it had been in 1913. The pattern for North America from Table 14.1 is repeated here, with the region's share in total trade growing in the period up to 1928 and then declining in the 1930s. The trade of Japan and the newly industrialising areas of South Africa and Oceania expanded continuously as a proportion of world trade, as did the share of the rest of the world, although the trade improvement experienced by the latter group of countries was largely concentrated in the period between 1913 and 1928.

Despite the various changes in the direction of world trade that occurred during the interwar years, the trade conducted between non-European nations only rose from just under one-quarter to just over one-quarter of total world trade, and Europe still dominated the trade picture in 1938, as it had done before 1913, as can be seen in Table 14.3. Whereas intra-European trade fell substantially from 40 per cent of the total world trade in imports in 1913 to 29 per cent in 1938, this fall was largely offset by an increase in trade between European and non-European countries. In other words, the economic difficulties of the interwar years, while restricting trade within Europe, tended at the same time to sustain and even encourage trade between Europe and the rest of the world.

TABLE 14.2 Shares of developed and less developed countries in world trade, 1913–37 (per cent)

	Constant prices (excluding the Soviet Union)					
	Industrial Europe	USA and Canada	Oceania, South Africa, Japan	Others	Of which	
					Other Europe	Rest of world
1913	54.4	14.5	5.4	25.7	5.7	20.0
1928	43.1	18.8	6.9	31.2	7.9	23.3
1937	43.8	16.5	9.5	30.2	6.3	23.9

Source: Kuznets (1967, p. 11, Table 2).

TABLE 14.3 Percentage distribution of world trade in imports, 1913–38

	1913	1938
World trade	100	100
Intra-European trade	40	29
Imports to Europe from non-European countries	22	27
Imports to non-European from Europe	15	17
Trade among non-European countries	23	27

Source: Woytinsky and Woytinsky (1955, pp. 71–80).

THE CHANGING COMPOSITION OF WORLD TRADE

The broad nature of the changes in the commodity structure of world trade during the interwar period is illustrated in Tables 14.4a and 14.4b and Figure 14.1, which describe the trends in the regional shares in world trade in primary products and manufactures.

As far as the world trade in primary products is concerned, the most striking development during these years was the rapid growth of the export share of the poorer countries, from just over one-third of the total in 1913 to around half in 1937. Taken together, these countries exported the whole range of tropical and temperate foodstuffs, as well as all the non-ferrous metals and petroleum, the demand for which was growing rapidly at this time. Even more striking, however, was the heavy decline in Europe's share of the world export trade in manufactures, from over four-fifths of the total trade in 1913 to approximately two-thirds in 1937. Within the total European share, the UK's share continued the decline that had begun well before 1913, but the decline in that of continental Europe was a completely new trend which became apparent only after 1913. Offsetting the falling European share were increases in the shares of this trade originating in North America and Asia, chiefly Japan. As for the import

TABLE 14.4A Trade in primary products: regional shares, 1913–37 (per cent)

Region	1913		1928		1937	
	Imports	Exports	Imports	Exports	Imports	Exports
UK and Ireland	19.0	6.2	19.9	4.8	22.9	4.8
Northwest Europe[a]	43.1	25.2	34.2	14.5	33.7	15.6
Other Europe	12.3	14.7	10.5	16.0	8.5	13.7
US and Canada	11.3	17.3	16.7	20.0	15.8	15.5
Underdeveloped and rest of world	14.3	36.6	18.7	44.7	19.1	50.4
World	100.0	100.0	100.0	100.0	100.0	100.0

TABLE 14.4B Trade in manufactures: regional shares, 1913–37 (per cent)

Region	1913		1928		1937	
	Imports	Exports	Imports	Exports	Imports	Exports
UK and Ireland	8.2	25.3	9.1	21.8	8.8	19.5
Northwest Europe[a]	24.4	47.9	17.5	40.9	17.5	41.8
Other Europe	15.4	8.3	15.7	4.6	13.3	5.8
US and Canada	12.1	10.6	12.8	19.2	10.6	19.7
Underdeveloped and rest of world	39.9	7.9	44.9	13.5	49.8	13.2
World	100.0	100.0	100.0	100.0	100.0	100.0

Source: Lamartine Yates (1959, Tables 19, 21, 23 and 25).

Note: [a] Finland, Sweden, Norway, Denmark, Germany, Belgium, Netherlands, France, Switzerland and Australia.

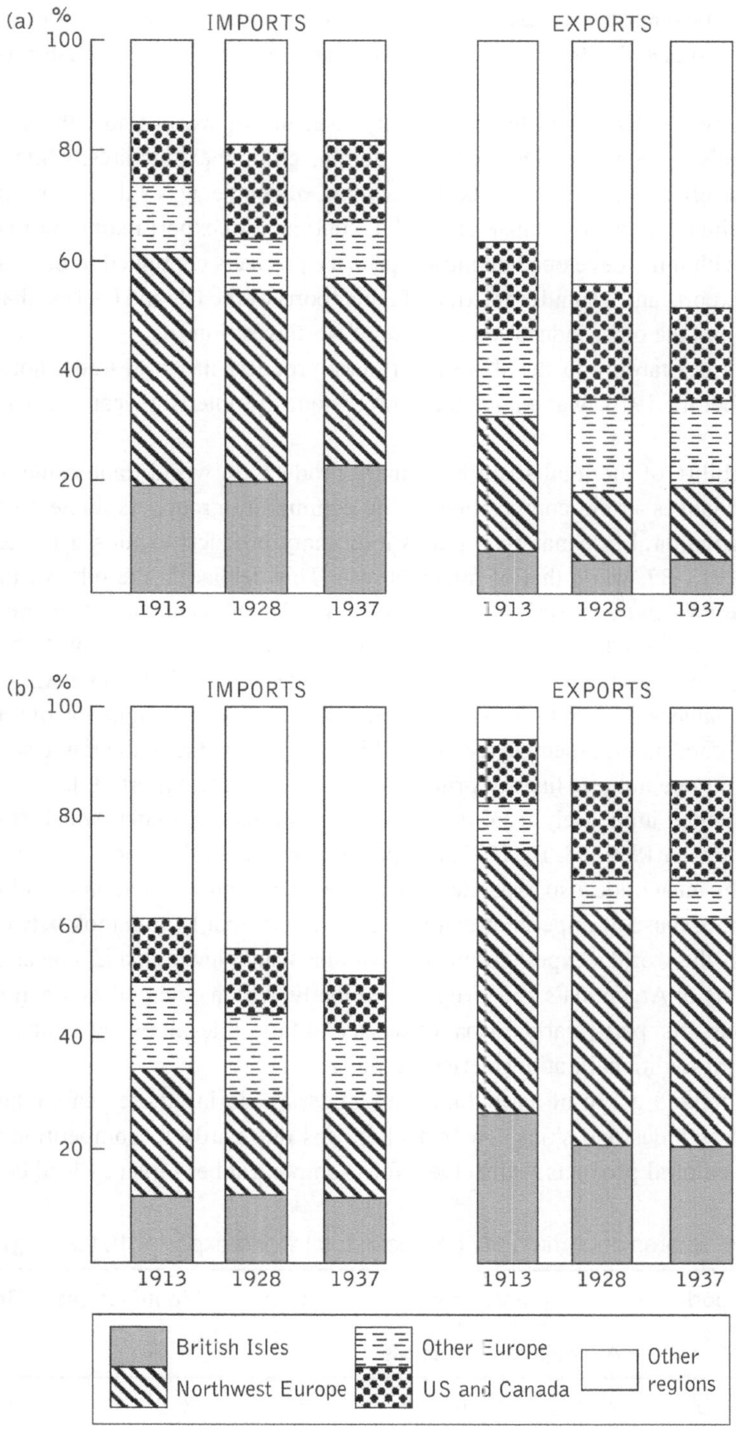

FIGURE 14.1 (a) Regional shares in total world trade, 1913–37, primary products. (b) Regional shares in total world trade, 1913–37, manufactures

Source: As for Tables 14.4; Source: Lamartine Yates (1959, Tables 19, 21, 23 and 25).

trade in manufactures, the tendency for the share of the industrialised countries in this trade to decline was associated with an extension of the share going to the non-industrialised countries of the world.

Despite these changes in the commodity structure of world trade, the export trade of the industrialised countries continued to be dominated by manufactures, while their imports consisted largely of primary products. The reverse, of course, was still the case for the rest of the world which, apart from Japan and India, continued to export mainly primary products. Moreover, within the developed countries, primary products continued to be a larger proportion of the exports and a smaller fraction of the imports of the US and Canada than for the UK and Ireland and the other industrial countries of Northwest Europe.

Finally, the stability in the share of primary products in world trade, noted earlier for the period before 1914, was maintained throughout the interwar years, as can be seen in Table 14.5.

The stability of the total share of primary products in world trade came about despite significant changes in the composition of the commodity group. As Table 14.5 shows, the food and agricultural raw materials shares in primary products exports declined throughout the period 1913–37, while that of minerals rose. This decline in the relative importance of foodstuffs in foreign trade was associated with several significant changes in the composition of world trade in food during these years. The trade in certain tropical foodstuffs, particularly cocoa, coffee, bananas and citrus fruits, increased substantially in the interwar years, both in volume and value terms. On the other hand, there was the relative stagnation of trade in certain non-tropical foodstuffs, especially cereals, which was partly due to the rising self-sufficiency of Western Europe in these lines of primary production. In the export of dairy products, New Zealand benefited immensely from the growing world trade in butter, which reached a peak of 615,000 tons in 1934–38. By 1937, it supplied a quarter of the world's butter exports. The volume of the meat trade also expanded during the 1920s and suffered only a minor fall in the 1930s when, because of imperial preference and the fact that Britain took between three and four-fifths of the world's exports of meat, Australia's and New Zealand's meat exports grew at the expense of Argentina's and Uruguay's. Finally, Africa emerged as a major supplier of tropical foodstuffs, particularly cocoa, oilseeds and fats, a development which took place at the expense of traditional Latin American exports.

The depressed group of agricultural raw materials during these years included cotton, silk as well as hides and skins. Their decline was due partly to competition between the various agricultural products themselves; for example, rubber replaced leather in a number

TABLE 14.5 Shares of commodity groups in total world exports, 1913–37 (per cent)

Year	Food	Primary products		Total	Manufactures	Total trade
		Agriculture	Minerals			
1913	27.0	22.7	14.0	63.7	36.3	100.0
1927	24.3	21.5	15.8	61.6	38.4	100.0
1937	23.0	21.0	19.5	63.5	36.5	100.0

Source: Lamartine Yates (1959, p. 44, Table 16).

of uses, and wood pulp in the form of rayon competed against cotton and silk. Competition also came from the mineral realm, where petroleum-based compounds made synthetic rubber and, later, nylon; and synthesised chemicals provided dyes and drugs previously obtained from the juices of plants. With the growing production of man-made fibres, the European demand for raw cotton declined during the interwar years, being only partly offset by rising Japanese imports. The foreign trade in raw cotton was also reduced by the spread of cotton manufacture to countries that produced their own raw cotton, such as Brazil and India. Among the raw cotton exporters, the salient changes were the rise of Brazil, the continued expansion of Egypt and India and the decline of the US. The growth of rayon production also brought about a heavy fall of raw silk exports from Japan and China. Unlike cotton and silk, the volume of the wool trade continued to grow in the 1920s and held its own in the 1930s, and its greater stability compared to the other textiles may be put down largely to the lack of competition from synthetics. The world consumption of natural rubber also increased throughout the interwar period and was accompanied by a significant shift in the source of supply. Whereas, in 1909–13, 80 per cent of the rubber traded came from the Amazon basin, Central America and Central Africa, by the end of the 1930s it came almost wholly from Southeast Asia.

The rise in mineral exports indicated in Table 14.5 is attributable to petroleum and, to a lesser extent, non-ferrous metals. Other significant changes in world trade in minerals during these years included: the switch of the US from being an exporter to an importer of copper, lead and zinc; Europe's growing deficiency of minerals; and the rising importance of Africa and Latin America as producers of minerals, including copper, lead, zinc, iron ore and petroleum. For the then newest of the non-ferrous metals — bauxite and aluminium — demand grew rapidly during the interwar years. Apart from America, mining was located mainly in Europe — Italy, Hungary, Yugoslavia and France. Some supplies were obtained from the Netherlands East Indies, and in the 1930s a start was made in the Guyanas. Among the fuels the growth of petroleum stood out. From virtually nothing in 1913 the trade grew to $1,170 million in 1929. Europe was the main importer, while the US, the Netherlands Antilles and Venezuela were the main exporters. In international trade, coal continued to be important, and as late as 1938 it was surpassed only by cotton. But whereas the combined exports of coal of continental Europe fell very little between the wars, Britain's exports of this product declined substantially.

The interwar years also witnessed significant changes in the commodity composition of world trade in manufactures, as can be inferred from Table 14.6 and Figure 14.2.

The most striking change was the continued shift away from textiles and towards engineering products. Metals and chemicals showed a slight upward trend, while miscellaneous manufactures, composed largely of consumer goods, showed a downward movement after 1929. Indeed, the trends in the various commodity groups included in Table 14.6 suggest that during the interwar years, international trade in manufactures moved away from consumer goods and towards capital goods, with trade in manufactured materials remaining fairly stable. In support of this conclusion, it has been estimated that the combined shares of textiles and other consumer goods in the world export of manufactures fell from 52 per cent to 38 per cent between 1913 and 1937, while that of manufactured materials, including iron and steel, rose from 29 to 33 per cent, and of capital goods from 19 per cent to 29 per cent.

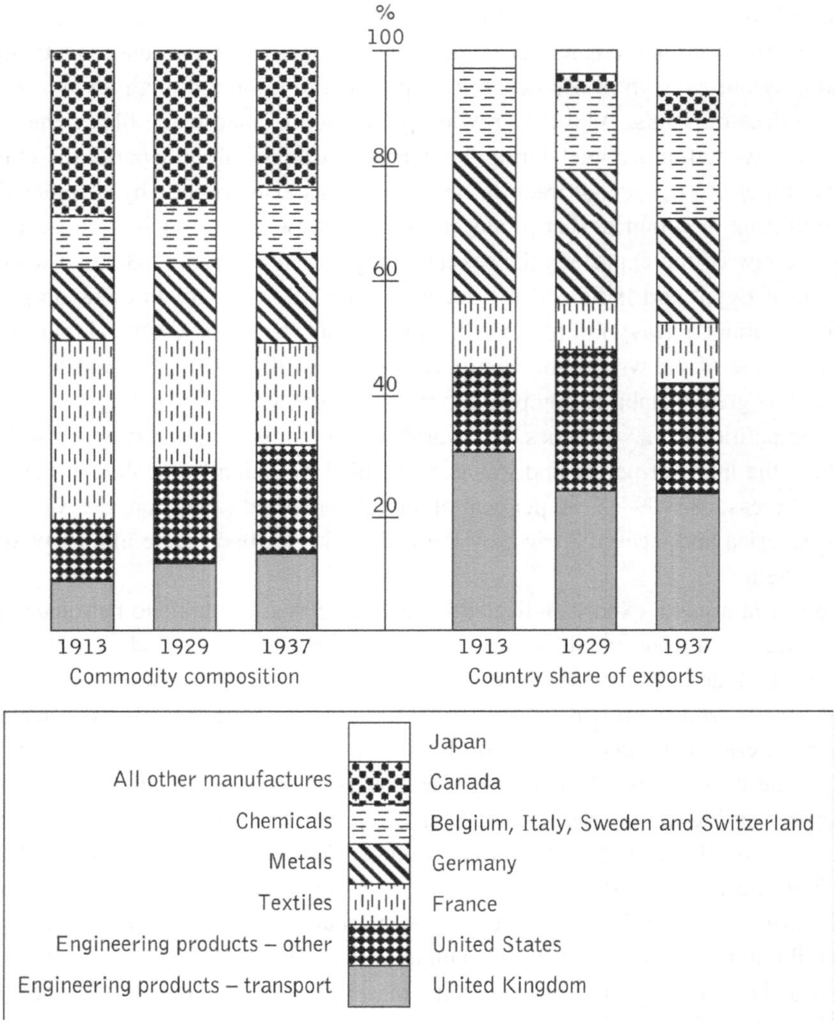

FIGURE 14.2 Shares of commodity groups in total world exports, 1913–37

Source: As for Tables 14.6 and 14.7; Source: Cairncross (1955, p. 235, Table 4, and p. 244).

The changes in the composition of export trade in manufactures were associated with a significant change in the direction of this trade. Up to the early 1930s, the greater part of the expansion in manufactured exports went to the non-industrial parts of the world, trade in manufactures within the industrial group of countries accounting for rather less than half of the total increase. During the remainder of the 1930s, however, this intra-trade declined much more heavily than did manufactures exported to non-industrial countries, chiefly because the trade restrictions of these years affected the intra-trade far more severely than exports to non-industrial nations. As we have already noted, inter-European trade in manufactures fell precipitately during these years, a development which was partly offset by a rapid expansion of trade in manufactures between the US and Canada. The overall effect, however, of a net

TABLE 14.6 Commodity patterns of trade in manufactures (exports), 1913–37 (per cent)

	1913	1929	1937
Engineering products	19.6	27.2	30.2
Non-electrical	9.7	11.4	12.9
Electrical	2.6	4.0	4.9
Transport	7.3	11.8	12.4
Textiles	28.2	23.2	18.2
Metals	13.8	12.7	16.0
Chemicals	8.5	8.1	9.5
All other manufactures	29.9	28.8	26.1
Total	100.0	100.0	100.0

Source: Cairncross (1955, p. 244).

TABLE 14.7 Shares of leading exporters in world trade in manufactures, 1913–37 (per cent)

	1913	1929	1937
UK	30.6	23.8	22.4
US	13.0	21.4	20.3
France	12.7	11.1	6.1
Germany	27.5	21.9	23.4
Belgium, Italy, Sweden and Switzerland	13.1	14.3	15.4
Canada	0.7	3.4	5.0
Japan	2.5	4.1	7.5
Total	100.0	100.0	100.0
£m.	1,292	2,342	1,723

Source: Cairncross (1955, p. 235, Table 4).

decline in trade in manufactures between industrial countries and an expansion of such trade between industrial and non-industrial countries was that the share of manufactures in total world trade changed very little during the interwar period.

Table 14.7, along with Figure 14.2, shows the changing shares of the leading exporters in world trade in manufactures between 1913 and 1937. The shares of the UK, France and Germany declined through the period, their combined share falling from just over 70 per cent of the total world trade in manufactures in 1913 to about 52 per cent in 1937. On the other hand, the US share advanced from 13 per cent to 20 per cent over these years, despite a set-back in the 1930s because of the Great Depression. Even more striking are the rise of Japan and the equally rapid emergence of Canada as large industrial exporters. The American advance was mainly in the expanding export lines, such as engineering products and transport equipment, Canada's in the stable group of miscellaneous manufactures, and Japan's chiefly in the declining textile group.

The evidence suggests that changes in the relative position of countries in world trade in manufactures during the interwar years were not so much due to structural shifts in the world

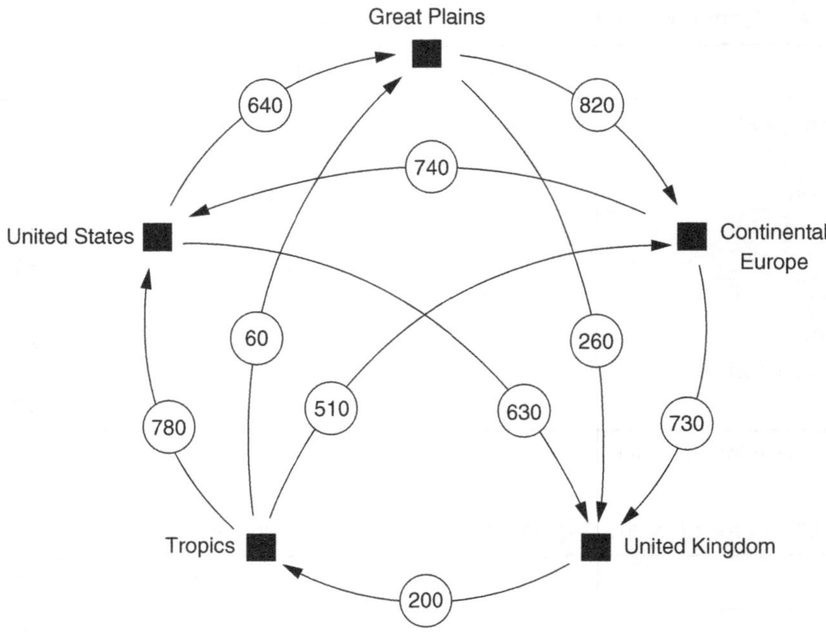

FIGURE 14.3 The system of multilateral trade in 1928

Source: Hilgerdt (1945, p. 77, Table 44); Hansson (1952, pp. 59–68).

demand for these exports as to each country's ability to compete in markets for individual groups of commodities. Accordingly, the main reason for the fall in Britain's share in world trade in manufactures between 1899 and 1937 was her failure to compete in export markets for iron and steel and engineering products.

The network of world merchandise trade calculated for the year 1928 and shown in Figure 14.3 describes the situation as it emerged in the 1920s following the end of the First World War, and before the Great Depression led to the disintegration of the international economy into a series of regional trading blocs. The countries included in the trading system in 1928 accounted for nine-tenths of the world's trade, and the arrows in the figure indicate the direction of balances of merchandise trade, in millions of dollars, between the countries and regions in the system by pointing from net exporting to net importing groups.

The dominance of the US in the post-war international trading system is obvious, with export surpluses with every region except the tropical raw materials and food-producing countries. On the other hand, by 1928, the times when Britain was the world's leading net exporter were definitely gone. She had become a substantial net importer from all regions except the Tropics.

What impressed observers of economic activity during the interwar years, however, was not so much the poor or strong export performances of individual countries as the declining importance of foreign trade in general. The slow growth of trade in manufactures between 1913 and 1929, the extreme declines of this trade in the depression years, and the tendency for the ratio of foreign trade to national income to decline in many countries were unprecedented.

RECOMMENDATIONS FOR FURTHER READING

For a detailed studies for the changing composition and direction of world trade in the inter-war years as dealt with in this chapter, see Tyszynski (1951, *World Trade in Manufactured Commodities, 1899–1950*), Cairncross and Faaland (1952, *Long-term Trends in Europe's Trade*), Cairncross (1955, *World Trade in Manufactures since 1900*) and Baldwin (1958, *The Commodity Composition of Trade: Selected Industrial Countries, 1900–1954*).

Latham (1981, *The Depression and the Developing World, 1914–1939*) looks specifically at the poorer parts of the world.

NOTE

1 See Kuznets (1967, pp. 4–6, Table 14.1). The 13 countries covered by Kuznets' statistics are the United Kingdom, America, France, Germany, Belgium, Denmark, Norway, Sweden, Canada, Japan, Italy, Switzerland and the Netherlands. The computation of annual average growth rates is ours.

CHAPTER 15

The Great Depression

An Overview

A. G. Kenwood, A. L. Lougheed and Michael Graff

THE US AND THE GREAT DEPRESSION

What were the underlying causes of the Great Depression of the 1930s? Where did it originate, and why was it so widespread, so deep and so long? Was it caused by real or monetary factors? There is no general agreement among economists and economic historians as to the answers to these questions. Practically every feature of the international economy in the 1920s can be argued to have contributed to the great slump, and some economists have, in fact, developed explanations of the depression which take account of such features: for example, the instability of the gold exchange standard (Triffin, 1960), the troubles of primary producers (Lewis, 1949) or the dislocations resulting from the First World War, including the trend towards increased protection evident in the post-1918 period (Arndt, 1944).

Notwithstanding these arguments, the origins of the world economic crisis, which began in 1929 are to be found in the US, which, by reducing its capital exports and imports of goods, placed an impossible strain, directly and indirectly, upon the international economy. Given the sheer economic weight of the US economy in 1929, representing as it did more than half the industrial world, and the impact it was bound to have because of this on world prices, and through prices on world investment, it is difficult to argue that the depression was somehow forced on the US by the rest of the world.

If the US was a dominant part of the international economy of the 1920s, what were the underlying causes of its domestic slump? Gordon and Wilcox (1981) argue that the 1929–30 downturn in the US was at least partially monetary in origin. They point to the rapid monetary growth in 1928, which came to a halt in 1929, thus aggravating the boom and collapse in both US output and the stock market, and to the bank failures, which contributed to reducing aggregate demand. Yet, they conclude that most of the decline in nominal spending in 1929–31 was due to non-monetary factors.

Which were the real and monetary factors that drove the US economy into the depression? A major driver was the decline, from 1925 onwards, in both residential and non-residential

DOI: 10.4324/9781003382171-19

construction. The main causes of the decline in housing construction were a catching up with wartime arrears, the falling off in family formations, brought about by a slowing down of population growth in the 1920s, and the shortage of mortgage credit in competition with speculative borrowing in 1928–9. On the other hand, non-residential construction continued at a high rate throughout the decade, but this created actual or latent surplus capacity, which any significant curtailment of demand was sure to reveal as serious.

A second major source of weakness was to be found in the agricultural sector, which was still important enough in the late 1920s to exert a powerful influence on the total economy. Farm incomes ceased to rise after 1925, as increasing world supplies caused downward pressures on the prices of most agricultural products, and in the great agricultural centres of the US few manifestations of boom psychology appeared after 1926.

Another development that played a part in the decline of 1929 was the continuing shift to durable consumer goods, which in the US had begun around the turn of the century. In the 1920s, there was a large expansion of productive capacity in the motor car, radio and electrical appliances industries, which was assisted by the introduction of hire purchase, or 'instalment credit' as it is known in the US, as a means of paying for the more expensive items. By 1925, the volume of instalment credit outstanding in the US was $1,375 million, and by 1929, it had grown to $3,000 million.

But the continued growth of sales of these new products required not only high and expanding consumers' incomes but also solid consumer of confidence about the future. Towards the end of the 1920s there is evidence that consumer confidence was fading and that some durable consumer goods markets were becoming saturated. This slowdown in the growth of consumer demand may have been due in part to a tendency for incomes to become progressively more unevenly distributed, as growing productivity tended to favour profits at the expense of wages and salaries. As Kindleberger (1986, p. 1047) notes:

> Business was in trouble long before the [Wall Street] crash … March [1929] was … the peak of automobile production, which fell from 622,000 in that month to 416,000 in September, at the height of the stock market … The industrial production index fell after June, and the decline in industrial production, prices and personal income from August to October was at annual rates of 20, 7.5 and 5 per cent.

The collapse of the stock market quickly revealed the structural weakness of the US banking system. Since the early nineteenth century, it consisted mostly of small banking units that — given the absence of a determined lender of last resort — were required to provide their own liquidity; as asset prices fell, these banks simply lacked the resilience that a few large banks — their fortunes not tied up with any one locality — would have had.[1] Unsurprisingly, during the depression years, several waves of bank failures shook the economy. The first came at the end of 1930 and the beginning of 1931, just when there were signs of an economic upturn. The second came late in 1931, after the Federal Reserve System had raised the rediscount rate to staunch an outflow of gold. The third, and most disastrous, began in mid-1932 and continued almost to the point of total breakdown of the banking system in the winter of 1932–3. In all, 8,812 banks suspended convertibility of their deposits in the years 1930–3, nearly half the number going under in 1933 alone. The failure of the Federal Reserve

System to act as a lender of last resort, along with its contractive monetary policies markedly worsened the depression in the US during the years 1931–3.

OTHER FACTORS IN THE GREAT DEPRESSION

Apart from the collapse of its economy, there were several other ways in which the US dealt blows to the international economy. First, the drying up of US foreign capital flows placed severe financial strain on debtor countries, with a resultant decline in economic activity. The primary producing countries of the periphery were doubly disadvantaged by this decline in lending, for they not only suffered a direct loss because of the reduced capital inflow from the US, but they also experienced the indirect effects of the decline in US lending, which by ensuring tight monetary policies in the major industrial countries of Europe, probably contributed to a decline in European long-term lending to the periphery, and to a decline in the growth of demand for the exports of the periphery.

Even more damaging for some debtor countries, however, was the Smoot-Hawley Act of June 1930, which substantially increased US tariffs. Coming on top of the rapid decline in incomes and production in the US, the tariff increases only served to reduce further US purchases of foreign goods. Indirectly, the US tariff made matters even worse for some European countries, since in retaliation other countries, particularly those primary producers whose exports of raw materials had been affected by the tariffs, raised their duties markedly on US goods, such as manufactures, which were also their main imports from Europe.

Whatever the relative importance of the effects of the decline in American lending and trade for individual countries, it is likely that their combined effect was more important than any form of 'overproduction' in determining the rapid decline in primary product prices and the export revenues of the periphery during the depression years. The collapse of primary product prices contributed to the extent and depth of the depression because its ramifications were so wide. Faced with growing economic difficulties, primary producing countries were either driven off the gold standard or forced to take other measures to protect their international payments, measures which started a train of restrictions on international trade and payments and harmed industrial producers as well.

Apart from structural dislocations in primary product markets, practically every other feature of the international economy in the 1920s can be argued to have contributed to the Great Depression. The difficulties of post-war adjustment, including the problems of reparations and war debts; the weaknesses of the gold exchange standard, including the possible overvaluation of the pound sterling and the undervaluation of the French franc; the spread of protectionism; and the adoption of more nationalistic economic policies involving a considerable degree of government intervention in the economy, have all been advanced by way of explanation of the origins of the Great Depression, or its length and severity.

Furthermore, some explanations of the depression deal not so much with origins as such, but with changes that might have prevented the depression, reduced its length or moderated its severity. Thus, Friedman and Schwartz (1965) argue that the rigid exchange rates prevailing under the gold standard made the rapid spread of the US depression to other countries inevitable. They argue further that if, in 1931, other countries had followed Britain and depreciated their currencies promptly in terms of gold instead of waiting for years, international liquidity would have increased quickly and the vicious spiral of deflation, import restrictions and more deflation would have been cut short. Lewis (1949) suggests that the maintenance of agricultural prices through the operation of buffer stock schemes would have had a dampening effect on the depression.

Kindleberger (1986) also explains the severity of the 1929 depression in terms of the malfunctioning of the international economy. He starts from the observation that the international economy is basically unstable, and that in the 1920s this instability was aggravated by the financial distortions resulting from the First World War. This instability, he argues, could have been overcome only by effective international leadership which involved: (1) maintaining a relatively open market for distress goods; (2) providing counter-cyclical long-term lending and (3) discounting in crisis.

In the nineteenth century up to 1913, Britain provided the leadership. After 1918, the British could not, and the US would not, play the role of leader. Instead, the US destroyed the trade mechanism through the Smoot-Hawley Tariff; it was unwilling to serve as a lender of last resort in 1931; and it engaged in aggressive currency depreciation by bidding up the price of gold and silver. The need for during the depression years is not in doubt. Indeed, at the onset of the Great Depression, there was no overwhelming reason why the US should adopt some form of effective international leadership. It is certainly true that after the Second World War, because of the US's opposition to the spread of what was perceived as 'communism', along with its deepening involvement in international economic affairs, it was prepared to exercise such economic leadership, but between the wars, US international economic activity was largely peripheral to a continued and overwhelming commitment to domestic economic expansion. In any case, given the fundamental weaknesses in the US banking system, it is doubtful whether it could have effectively exercised the international leadership necessary. In short, if the US could not save itself from so severe a depression, how could it be expected to save the rest of the world?

LONG-RUN FACTORS AND THE GREAT DEPRESSION

As the economic crisis deepened in the US, there were some economists who claimed that the depression of 1929–33 marked not merely a cyclical downturn, but the start of a period of secular stagnation, chiefly caused by a decline in the population growth rate along with a higher propensity to save and the resulting slowdown of aggregate demand growth.[2]

The performance of the US economy after the Second World War puts the stagnation thesis under a cloud. But if the stagnation of the 1930s was due to the special circumstances of the time, the boom from the 1945 into the mid-1970s was likewise no more than an episode, shaped by the special circumstances of the period.

With the onset of a worldwide recession in the 1970s, attention once again focused on the possible existence of long-term periodicities or rhythms in the evolution of the international capitalist system; and the same of course holds for the 'Great Recession' of 2008–9, which, like the Great Depression, originated in the US economy and spread from there across the globe. In this context, it is noteworthy that Ben Bernanke, who was chairman of the Federal

Reserve Board from 2006 to 2014, is a renowned scholar of the Great Depression; and it was clear from the onset of the US financial crises in 2007 that he was determined not to repeat the mistakes made during the Great Depression, foremost the contractionary monetary policy which — as Friedman and Schwartz (1965) claimed — bears a significant responsibility for the length and the severity of the contraction.[3]

Another view sees the causes of the Great Depression of the 1930s in the real forces underlying the long-run growth and development of the world economy. Thus, for Rostow (1978), the inter-war years were characterised by chronic surpluses in primary products, caused in part by the distortions of the war and post-war years, and in part by the chronically depressed state of demand. Primary producers in general suffered a relative decline in income, limiting their capacity to purchase industrial goods and to invest in new methods and techniques. Their catastrophic loss of income between 1929 and 1933 was one major factor accounting for the depth of the depression throughout the world. Most advanced industrial countries, on the other hand, faced a double structural adjustment after 1920: an adjustment to the potentialities of cheapened supplies of foodstuffs and raw materials, and an adjustment to the potentialities of a new leading sector complex in the form of the internal combustion engine, electricity and chemicals. Whereas the US largely benefited from successful adaptation to both kinds of structural change in the 1920s, Britain took advantage of the favourable terms of trade, but because of chronic unemployment and the depressed state of domestic demand, she failed to make the necessary structural adjustments to her manufacturing industry. In general, the adoption of policies of agricultural protection meant that continental European countries sacrificed to some degree the benefits of the lower world prices of primary products and, like Britain, they failed to make the structural shifts to new leading sectors at a pace sufficient to avoid abnormally high levels of unemployment, even during the best years of the 1920s.

Another non-monetarist explanation of the depth and duration of the depression in the US sees it as the outgrowth of secular trends in the world economy. Thus, according to Bernstein (1987), by the 1920s, the American economy had entered an era characterised by the emergence of dramatically new demand patterns and investment opportunities. The failure to respond to these new opportunities derived from the difficulty of altering technology and labour skills to meet these new demands at a time of severe financial instability. Moreover, recovery was lacking in the 1930s because at the time the long-run potential for growth was shifting under the influence of a secular transformation to sectors whose presence in the aggregate economy was still relatively insignificant. The growth of these industries was, in turn, a response to the emergence of new demand patterns of an increasingly affluent population.

To sum up, we have enough reasons to suggest that, along with events and policies that were specific to the inter-war period important, forceful long-run trends in the capitalist world economy were operating to bring about the depression of the 1930s in a complex interaction to produce a worldwide depression.[4]

RECOMMENDATIONS FOR FURTHER READING

The literature on the Great Depression is huge, for a key reference, see Kindleberger (1986, *The World in Depression, 1929–1939*).

The monetarist view of the origins of the Great Depression — the foundation of orthodox explanations — is perhaps best reflected by Friedman and Schwartz (1965, *The Great Contraction, 1929–1933*) and by the contributions to Brunner (1981, *The Great Depression Revisited*).

Heterodox (non-orthodox) approaches to understanding the Great Depression that are explicitly or implicitly dealt with in this chapter can be found in the contributions by, or to, van der Wee (1972, *The Great Depression Revisited. Essays on the Economics of the Thirties*), Temin (1976, *Did Monetary Forces Cause the Great Depression?*), Barber (1978, *On the Origins of the Great Depression*), Rostow (1978, *The World Economy: History and Prospect*), Bernstein (1987, *The Great Depression. Delayed Recovery and Economic Change in America, 1929–1939*) and last but not least by Bernanke (2000, *Essays on the Great Depression*).

The exceptional situation of the Soviet Union in the 1920s and 1930s is discussed by Allen (2003, *Farm to Factory: A Reinterpretation of the Soviet Industrial Revolution*) and by Gregory and Sailors, (2003, *The Soviet Union during the Great Depression: The Autarky Model*).

NOTES

1 The problem of bank failures was apparent well before the onset of the depression in 1929. Over the nine-year period 1921–9, 5,411 banks failed. Most of them were small country banks, but some were national banks and among the largest in the country.

2 See, e.g., Hansen (1938) and Barber (1978).

3 Most economists, and central bankers in particular, have adopted this 'monetarist' perspective. Thus, since 2007, there was no shortage of central bank money; quite to the contrary, most money markets are up to this date virtually flooded with liquidity.

4 It is important to keep in mind that while the capitalist world plunged into its worst economic slump, the Great Depression left the Soviet Union virtually unharmed. At that time, instead of relying on the 'invisible hand' of the market, the Soviet Union was the only country conducting deliberate economic planning, and the first three five-year plans (1928–33, 1933–7 and 1937–41) brought about rapid industrialisation and economic growth in the Soviet Union — in a period that neatly coincides with the Great Depression.

PART III

The Second World War and the Post-1945 International Economy

CHAPTER **16**

The International Economy from 1939 to 1950

A. G. Kenwood, A. L. Lougheed and Michael Graff

The economic slump of the 1930s was barely over, and the armistice of the Great War had come into force little more than 20 years ago, when the dominant powers, and with them the world turned to war again. For six years, from September 1939 to August 1945, changing coalitions of belligerent countries took part in a war that exceeded all other military conflict before or after, in terms of mobilisation of economic and human resources for warfare, as well as level and scale of violence, atrocity, crime and the total number of victims. The Second World War was far more disastrous than the preceding disaster of 1914–18 in any respect, except for the fact that once the outcome had obviously tipped in favour of the anti-Hitler coalition in 1943, coordinated efforts were undertaken to establish the outlines of a post-war economic order that would secure peace and prosperity better than before.

THE SECOND WORLD WAR

The Second World War was, unlike 1914–18, not a traditional imperialist contest for dominance. It was launched through unprovoked aggression by the criminal governments of Germany and — to a lesser extent — her allies Italy and Japan (the 'Axis'). It was triggered as the culmination of a series of expansionist and militarist moves by German chancellor Hitler with the attack on Poland on 1 September 1939, poorly disguised as a response to a staged Polish hostility.[1]

An obvious motif for this aggression was reversal of the outcome of 1918, along with revenge for Versailles. But the reasons lie deeper: a vicious combination of Hitler's ambitions to make Germany the dominant military power in Europe and eventually of the globe, racial hubris and a quest for 'lebensraum' in the east, along with pathological hatred of the Jews, who mostly lived in places determined for conquest and servitude or 'Germanification'. Much of this had by 1939 sadly been embraced by the German leadership and large parts of the German population, who thus were ready to follow Hitler and fight to the end.

DOI: 10.4324/9781003382171-21

Japan's aggressive militarist, expansionist and racist policy predates the Second World War, but German success in the initial years of the war encouraged Japan to embark on the conquest of large parts of Asia, which had already begun previously with the invasion of Manchuria in 1931. Similarly, Mussolini's fascist Italy had begun her aggressive policy already in 1935 and seized Abyssinia (now: Ethiopia) as a first step in the preposterous attempt to turn Italy into a modern-day reincarnation of the Roman Empire.

The Second World War, like the Great War before, was truly global, and this time the actual fighting was not confined to the battlefields of Europe. Except for the Americas and Australia, which were never invaded, all settled continents experienced fierce fighting. With a few exceptions (Ireland, Portugal, Spain, Sweden, Switzerland and Turkey, plus some micro-states), all European countries were involved in the conflicts. Outside Europe, under the rule of empires as the world was, the colonies and dominions fought with little choice, and after Japan attacked the US at Pearl Harbor, Hawaii, in December 1941, the only independent territory outside Europe not engaged in the war up to the end was Afghanistan.

Both 'Axis' and 'Allies' comprised changing coalitions. The former initially was a military pact of Germany, Italy and Japan. It was later joined by Slovakia (a pro-fascist satellite state installed after the demolition of Czechoslovakia in March 1939, which took part in the attack on Poland), Romania (participating in the attack on the Soviet Union in June 1941), Hungary (declared war on the Soviet Union after the German attack in June 1941) and Bulgaria (declared war on the Allies after Pearl Harbor). Along with the Germans also fought divisions of volunteers from occupied territories and politically close and supporting countries such as Franco's Spain.

The 'Allies' initially comprised only Germany's first victim, Poland, and the latter's allies, France (including colonies) and Britain (including colonies/dominions). The Soviet Union found itself in the camp of the Allies when it was attacked in June 1941. The US had been reluctant to join the war on the Allied side — though they effectively supported the Allied case with supplies — until they were attacked by Japan in December 1941. Further support to the Allied side came from exile governments and volunteer troops from Axis-occupied territories who had managed to escape from the occupants.

Until 1942, the Axis held the initiative, advanced from victory to victory in all theatres of war, and thus appeared invincible to many contemporary observers. Many countries hence chose cautiously not to take sides prematurely. When the Allied victory eventually became obvious and could be regarded only as a matter of time, many of the so-far-neutral countries joined in: Romania (formerly a German ally) in August 1944, Persia (now: Iran) in September 1944 and Syria and Saudi Arabia in February 1945. In Latin America, Argentina — not without sympathy for the Axis powers in earlier stages of the war — was the last country to declare war on Germany in March 1945. The worldwide powerful coalition, which eventually defeated the aggressors until unconditional surrender in 1945, thus emerged painfully slowly.

As in 1914, Germany had to rely on quick success in all her campaigns; and the same held for Japan, since the resources available to the Allies — people as well as industrial and agricultural output — vastly outnumbered the reserves of the Axis. Victory depended on quick military advances and defeat of the Allies before they could fully mobilise their superior economic potential for warfare. Indeed, Axis powers initially took the initiative and advanced on all fronts they chose to open. Poland was taken in four weeks, and though it was not a serious opponent for the German army, the pace of the campaign impressed. A 'phoney' war followed between Germany and the UK and France. In April 1940 Germany invaded and occupied the neutral states of Belgium, the Netherlands and Luxembourg, as well as Denmark and Norway. In June 1940, France was driven out of the war in another quick and crushing campaign of six weeks. Hitler was at the height of his triumph, having forced the French army to capitulate in June 1940, and the British Expeditionary Force to withdraw across the Channel — four years of bloodletting (1914–18) had not achieved this. Only Britain was still opposing a German continental power that stretched from the Atlantic to the Soviet Border. A negotiated peace on German terms seemed within reach, but instead Hitler launched an air campaign to neutralise the Royal Air Force, a prerequisite for an invasion of England. The Battle of Britain in June 1940 resulted in a stalemate with high losses of aircraft and men on both sides and was abandoned by Germany in September, and an invasion of Britain was off the agenda.

In the Balkans, Italy took Albania in 1939 and attacked Greece in October 1940, albeit with little success, and consequently, in April 1941, Germany, Hungary and Bulgaria intervened and attacked Yugoslavia and Greece. Yugoslavia fell in two weeks, and pro-Axis satellite regimes were installed in its provinces. Greece fell within three weeks, except for Crete, which was later taken by German paratroopers. By May 1941, the Balkans and most of the Mediterranean — with the notable exceptions of Malta, Gibraltar and Egypt — were thus under Axis control.

In North Africa, Axis and Allies fought for control of the Suez Canal and the oil reserves of the Middle East from June 1940 to May 1943; and it was only in late 1942 that the balance finally and decisively tipped in favour of the Allies. Importantly, American troops had joined in; and the eastern front absorbed the better parts of the Axis fighting power.

Thus, in early 1941, with Britain practically facing the Axis powers alone, a negotiated peace on Axis terms was more likely than ever throughout the war. But then Hitler turned against the Soviet Union to complete his self-assigned mission. Less than two years before — despite the deep ideological antagonism between fascism and Bolshevism, and hence to the surprise of most contemporary observers — a German–Soviet Non-Aggression Treaty had been signed, with a secret protocol dividing the spheres of influence in Eastern Europe. While this was obviously nothing but a tactical move by Hitler, Stalin appears to have taken the pact more seriously. Until June 1941, the Soviet Union was a major source of raw materials supporting the German war machine, and Stalin doubted and thus ignored all incoming intelligence on an imminent attack. On 22 June 1941, Germany and her allies thus took the Red Army by surprise.[2] The Russian front collapsed and was not stabilised until December 1941, when the advance had already reached the outskirts of Leningrad and Moscow. But at that stage, the German surprise strategy had failed. The resilience of the Red Army and the Soviet people, and their willingness to resist the aggressor after the first crushing onslaught, had been grossly underestimated, and no adequate preparations had hence been made by Germany for a prolonged war and for the harsh Russian winter.[3]

A new Axis offensive in 1942 towards the Caucasus and the oil fields of the region advanced as far as Maikop, Grozny and Stalingrad, but there, after months of fierce resistance, the Red Army in January 1943 took the initiative and encircled and annihilated the 6th German army. Arguably, Germany had lost the war in Russia already a year before the capitulation of the 6th Army by overstretching her reserves in the winter of 1940–1, but it was

Stalingrad where defeat became manifest; and to any informed observer it became decisively clear that the tide of war had changed against the Axis.[4] Even if the largest of the battles in the east — the Tank Battle of Kursk in July 1943 — was yet to come, and the eastern front would consume millions of soldiers before the Red Army could take Berlin in the spring of 1945, from January 1943 to May 1945 the German armies in the east were on the retreat.[5]

Meanwhile, after the attack on Hawaii in December 1941 Japan had defeated and occupied Malaya (including the British naval base of Singapore), most of the Philippines and Dutch East India (now: Indonesia), Australian-governed Papua and New Guinea, and Burma (now: Myanmar), and it was reaching out to India and Australia. It took all the force the US could mobilise in 1942 to bring the Japanese campaign to a stop in the battles of the Coral Sea in May and Midway in June and thus to secure ongoing American presence in the Pacific.[6]

The unequal Allied coalition of 1941–5 between the Western Powers and the Soviet Union against the Axis held until its objective — unconditional defeat of the aggressors in Europe and the Pacific — had been reached, but it was plagued by ongoing mistrust. In particular, while the Soviet Union received vast amounts of material supplies, repeated Soviet demands to open a second front in Europe to relieve the Red Army, whose soldiers were practically alone fighting the Axis on the ground in Europe, remained without consequence until July 1943, when Americans, British and Canadians landed in Sicily, and on the Italian mainland in September 1943. Meanwhile, Italy had lost faith in Mussolini and changed sides. Despite fierce fighting, the German armies in Italy, who had turned from ally into occupant, capitulated only in April 1945.

The real onslaught of the Western Allies on Hitler's 'fortress Europe', which delivered the final blow to the German army, started in June 1944 with the Allied landing in Normandy. By this time, the Red Army had reached Belorussia and, in August, Poland. German defeat was now inevitable even without the second front, but it diverted German forces and thus contributed to achieving the Allies' first goal of the war, Germany's unconditional surrender, considerably quicker than otherwise.

In August 1944, the Allies took Paris, and by September they reached the German border, where resistance stiffened. With the Soviet Union advancing towards the eastern border while British and US troops approached from the west, German defeat was sealed, although the fronts did not collapse and the Allies had to fight for another seven months until war came to an end in Europe. In April 1945, the Western Allies had crossed the Rhine and advanced into Germany, and the Red Army launched its successful attacks against Vienna and Berlin in April 1945. German unconditional surrender on all fronts took effect on 8 May.

Could a second front have been opened earlier, maybe as early as 1942? The invasion in 1944 succeeded with an overwhelming superiority of material and practically complete dominance in the air, after the American armaments programme had gained steam and after the Luftwaffe had been pulverised in years of attrition on the eastern front and strategic bombing in the west. Though a certain hesitation to confront the main enemy directly cannot be overlooked — thus the North African and Italian campaigns — the likelihood that a Western invasion in 1943 or even more so in 1942 would have resulted in disaster — then without the prospect of mobilising public support for another try — is not insignificant.

Consequently, while the Red Army did the ground fighting for three appalling years from June 1941 to June 1944, the Western Allies were mainly engaged in naval and air battles.

They were keeping open vital supply routes across the Atlantic against German submarine warfare, which by 1942 threatened to starve Britain. Increasing Allied air superiority eventually contributed in 1943 to the defeat of the German U-boat campaign. Superior air force also played a decisive role in the halting of the Japanese advance in the Pacific in 1942. At the same time, Britain and the US launched their massive programme of 'strategic bombing' against the Axis powers and the territories occupied by them. It had some first disastrous effects in 1943 — notably the destruction of large parts of Hamburg in a fire storm — but until D-day the striking distance of Allied bomber and fighter aircraft did not allow them to penetrate deep into Germany. This changed after the Allied landing in June 1944, and for the remainder of the war Allied planes dominated the skies over the front and the German hinterland, and city after city was reduced to rubble.

Strategic bombing, which in practice could not make a distinction between enemy combatants, industrial workforce and other civilians, is one of the most controversial aspect of the Allied efforts to defeat the aggressors in the Second World War. Ignoring any ethical implications,[7] were the opportunity costs too high? Strategic bombing absorbed vast resources — planes, guns, ammunition, explosives, fuel and trained men — and casualty rates of the bomber crews were among the highest of all Western fighting units. With the benefit of hindsight, it is obvious that the objective to break the will of the enemies' populations to continue the war effort by destroying their dwellings and threatening them with random death was not met. On the other hand, the scale of destruction which was achieved against Germany and Japan in 1944 and 1945 clearly had a significant impact on industrial output and supply lines. Repeated alerts deprived the workforce of sleep, and absentee rates jumped in the wake of major attacks. Production went underground or was spread across smaller units, which were less vulnerable to attacks, but reduced economies of scale. By the end of the war, the cumulative effects of strategic bombing may have deprived German troops of half of the armaments they otherwise would have been able to access.

Finally, to contribute to the defence of the cities against the armadas of bombers, a significant share of the remaining — and declining — Axis fighter aircraft was diverted from the fronts to the hinterland. Strategic bombing thus indirectly supported the ground troops of the Red Army and later of the Western Allies, saving uncounted Allied lives.

The only power to direct considerable resources into the development of nuclear weapons in the Second World War was the US, which employed more than 100,000 people in the 'Manhattan Project' and successfully produced four atomic bombs. The first was ignited in July 1945 in the New Mexican desert, only nine weeks after the surrender of Germany and the end of the war in Europe. Unfortunately for the inhabitants of Hiroshima and Nagasaki, the Japanese leadership was slow to negotiate peace or surrender, and on 6 and 9 August 1945 atomic bombs were dropped on their cities, causing tens of thousands of immediate casualties and uncounted more in the years to come, resulting from radiation. Japanese unconditional surrender was announced on 15 August 1945. Unlike against Germany, bombing rather than invasion concluded hostilities in Asia.

The war effort of the main belligerent nations (Germany, Italy, Japan; France, UK, USSR and US) mobilised unprecedented numbers into their armed forces; about 12 million in 1939, 24 million in 1940, 25 million in 1941, 34 million in 1942, 43 million in 1943–4 and 44 million in the final year of the war.[8] The share of Gross National Product (GNP) devoted to military expenses in many instances increased to levels far beyond those of the First World War (with an overall maximum of about 50 per cent) in practically all belligerent nations. For the US and the USSR, the military share in 1944 is estimated at 53 per cent, for Japan at 76 per cent and for Germany (in 1943) at 70 per cent. Both world wars were wars of mass production and mass mobilisation, which pre-industrial economies could never have fought, since they would not have been able to free as many resources for prolonged periods from agricultural production for the armed forces, supplies and armaments production. While the share of the labour force in the major belligerent economies in military service is estimated to have amounted to about 15 per cent in the First World War, in the Second World War it was close to 20 per cent. As the war proceeded, Germany not only relied on women to keep production going — like anyone else — but increasingly on slave labour by civilians from the occupied territories, prisoners of war and from the victims of the concentration camps.

The number of lives lost due to the Second World War is estimated to have exceeded that of the already disastrous First World War by a factor of three to five, with a share of civilians vastly higher, mainly due to genocide and strategic bombing. Deaths brought about by violence or war-related deprivation amount to about 55 million. The Soviet Union suffered the highest number of casualties (more than 25 million), followed by China (13 million), Germany (7 million), Poland (5.5 million), Japan (2.5 million) and Yugoslavia (1.7 million), France (0.6 million), and Britain and the US (both 0.5 million). The comparatively low number of war-induced casualties in Britain and the US reflect the fact that they were never invaded and preferred strategic bombing to fighting on the ground until they had achieved overwhelming superiority.

Allied victory may have been a moral necessity for humanity, but it was not an inevitable result of moral superiority; it did require an unprecedented mobilisation of resources and had to be fought for in bloody battles to the very end. As a result, the aggressors were defeated,[9] and for the next four decades the world was to be dominated by two antagonistic military 'superpowers', the US and the Soviet Union and their economic spheres of influence. War as a means of politics was not brought to an end in 1945, but military conflict has since moved from the core to the periphery, and any direct confrontation between the great powers has so far been successfully avoided.[10] With increasing geopolitical tensions, the Russia-Ukraine war, and the increasingly belligerent attitudes in Europe as well as in the US, where the rise of the China is leading to increasing fears that the days of US hegemony may be numbered, direct confrontation between today's military superpowers — all of them equipped with atomic weapons — now unfortunately seems less unlikely than some years ago. (We will come back to this in Chapter 23.)

Richard Overy (1995) convincingly argues that it misses too many aspects to reduce the reasons why the Axis powers were defeated to superior strength in output and numbers of people. Also, apparent mistakes by the Axis' political and military leadership do not explain the defeat, as the Axis marched from success to success until 1942. Instead, he stresses different shapes of the learning curves in the Axis and Allied camps: whereas the Axis power initially exploited their superior military skills, based on tradition and training as well as adoption of modern tactics based on different combinations of infantry, tanks and air force, as well as submarines, with crushing success, the initial victories made them slow to adapt their tactics when the fortunes of war changed. On the other hand, the Allies took care to learn all the lessons from their initial series of defeats. Most importantly, as the war turned into one of attrition, they quickly and successfully turned to standardised mass production of armaments, which from 1943 onwards effectively translated their superior access to resources into military supremacy. Had the Axis powers succeeded in Russia and the Pacific in 1941 and 1942, which they failed at only by a close margin, the material superiority of the Allies would not have played a role. Finally, both Allies and Axis exercised considerable efforts — in terms of both material resources and casualties — to deprive their enemies of the resources they already had, or to cut them off from their vital supplies. Submarine warfare against Allied supply routes posed a dangerous threat in 1942, and strategic bombing from 1943 to 1945 perceptibly affected the war efforts of Germany, Japan and Italy.

How decisive, then, was the access to resources to the outcome of the war? Until late 1941 this was clearly less the case than from 1942 to 1945. Initially, the Axis powers were better prepared in terms of armaments, military training and strategy; and ruthlessness, deception and surprise were on their side. But in late 1941, the Axis' advances on all fronts were halted, the war turned into a stalemate and then, gradually, into a war of attrition, where the Allies' material superiority was decisive. Allied material superiority, however, took time to become manifest. After the defeat of France, and before the Soviet Union and the US were attacked and joined the Allies, the Axis powers' balance of resources and men had even tilted the war in their favour. But after the disaster of 1941, from 1942 onwards the Soviet armaments industry clearly outproduced the enemy, particularly in tanks, self-propelled guns and ammunition. Last but not least, once the American industry had its mass production turned from cars towards war material its output of ships, fighter and bomber aircraft and machine guns dwarfed that of all other belligerents. It is illustrative of the situation that as the war entered its final stage in 1944, Allied infantry was practically fully motorised, whereas Germany increasingly had to resort to horses.[11]

Why were Germany and her allies not more successful in mobilising resources for the war once they had achieved victories that turned most of Europe into their economic hinterland? There are many more or less convincing answers, but two stand out.

First, the occupied territories supplied far fewer resources than anticipated due to a combination of mismanagement and silent rebellion in the face of the aggressors' attitude and behaviour towards the conquered populations, which included anything from the extraction of slave labour, random shootings of hostages to open genocide, and thus alienated even people that had initially welcomed the occupants.

Second, Germany produced a wide range of sophisticated weaponry, but production was expensive (labour and resource intensive) and did not try systematically to exploit economies of scale in standardised mass production of armaments until 1944, when it was already too late, since the material superiority of the Allies had become unbeatable and strategic bombing shattered whatever efforts were made despite the unbridgeable backlog.

Unlike its predecessor, the Second World War was nowhere greeted enthusiastically, not even in the aggressor states, where bewilderment reigned. But unlike the armistice achieved in November 1918, the capitulation of Germany on 8 May and of Japan on 15 August 1945 put an end to governments that had deliberately promoted aggression, cruelty and murder, so that the exceptional price paid appears justified — even with the benefit of hindsight of more than 50 years.

As Allied victory came within reach, the leadership of the Soviet Union, the US and Britain decided that Germany should be disarmed and occupied until a final settlement was reached in a peace treaty. After 8 May 1945, the Great German Reich of Germany and Austria was dissolved and both countries divided into occupation zones under Soviet, American, British and French military rule. However, with the common enemy defeated for good, by 1948 the political antagonism between the Western Allies and the Soviet Union became so manifest that constructive cooperation seemed impractical, and both parties proceeded to secure their spheres of domination and influence. Unsurprisingly, Soviet influence, by and large, reached as far as the Red Army had advanced in May 1945, which included Poland, Czechoslovakia, Hungary, Bulgaria and Romania, as well as the Soviet occupation zone in the east of Germany, including Berlin.[12] The latter attained statehood as the German Democratic Republic (GDR) in 1949 and remained a devoted follower of the Soviet Union until 1989. In the West, the Federal Republic of Germany (FRG) was formed out of the American, British and French occupation zones. Both GDR and FRG remained occupied and without full sovereignty for four decades. They were quickly integrated into the West European/Atlantic and Soviet bloc economies, and in the mid-1950s they were rearmed as antagonistic front states in the Cold War. Both remained loyal to the US- and USSR-led alliances until the Soviet bloc began to disintegrate in 1989.

Japan was disarmed and occupied but not divided into zones. It remained occupied by the US until 1952, when a peace treaty came into force. Japan gave up her imperial territorial ambitions in the Pacific and military aggression and became a close ally of the US in the Cold War.

In 1955 Austria committed to neutrality and never again to form a unified state with Germany, as from 1939 to 1945. The Austrian State Treaty was signed, which effectively ended occupation by the end of the same year. A similar suggestion to establish a unified neutral state was rejected by West Germany, which feared that neutrality was the first step towards domination by the Soviet Union. Consequently, two antagonistic German states persisted until 1990. When the Soviet bloc was in full dissolution, the GDR was incorporated into the FRG, and Germany gained full sovereignty.

Apart from the German partition, another unintended outcome of the Second World War, resulting in particular from the genocide committed behind the eastern front, was the foundation of the state of Israel in 1948 in Palestine, a British mandate since 1922. Jewish migration into Palestine had already taken place before the First World War, picking up in the end of the nineteenth century, promoted by Zionist movements in Europe. In the 1930s, the official anti-Semitism in Nazi Germany caused more Jews to seek refuge in Palestine, until they were trapped in Nazi-occupied Europe. After Germany's defeat, numerous Jews that had survived the genocide were held in camps in Germany as 'displaced persons'. They had neither any desire to go back to what had been home, where local anti-Semitism had facilitated mass murder, and no relatives or friends — or any Jews at all — were left, nor the required visas to go elsewhere. Many of these found their way to Palestine. Tensions between Jews and Arabs rose, and with Britain in the process of withdrawal from the mandate, the United Nations General Assembly decided upon the establishment of a Jewish and an Arab State in Palestine in November 1947. Thus, Israel came into being in May 1948, and unfortunately, a peaceful settlement of the resulting Israeli-Arab conflict over land, borders and statehood has never been reached and is not in sight.

PLANNING THE FUTURE INTERNATIONAL ECONOMY AND THE TRANSITIONAL PERIOD, 1944–50

The 1930s witnessed the collapse of the multilateral trade and payments system, which had emerged in the late nineteenth century. In the field of commercial policy, severe restrictions, often of a discriminatory nature, tended to prevail, while the international payments system degenerated into a multitude of exchange controls. In consequence, international flows of capital and labour were severely retarded, and the future of world trade appeared to be particularly gloomy. With the outbreak of war, the financial and commercial restrictions on trade were intensified. Even while the war was still in progress, however, it was realised that strenuous efforts to reduce trade and exchange barriers would be needed to ensure the proper functioning of the international economy in the post-war years. Preliminary discussions along these lines followed the signing of the Mutual Aid Agreement between the US and Britain in 1941, which, although predominantly concerned with lend-lease arrangements, also committed the two countries to cooperate in international economic affairs after the war. Subsequently, numerous discussions were held in Washington and London with a view to producing a set of rules or a code of conduct in international monetary affairs to be implemented after the war.

At the beginning of these discussions, two plans submitted by the British negotiators (the Keynes Plan) and the American negotiators (the White Plan) were considered. The first proposed the establishment of a clearing union and the creation of a large amount of credit (*bancor*) to be allotted among all trading nations. It was envisaged that the $35 billion of bancor to be created would not only be used for financing capital account deficits but also serve to help the financing of post-war reconstruction. This plan was unacceptable to the US negotiators, who claimed it had inflationary tendencies and because its operations would be too automatic and not allow member country governments enough discretion in their balance of payments policies. The White Plan, which concentrated on the setting up of international institutions under the control of member countries, was then debated and out of the many discussions in which compromises were reached, emerged the International Monetary Fund (IMF) and the International Bank for Reconstruction and Development (IBRD).

THE BRETTON WOODS CONFERENCE

In July an international conference that should eventually determine the international economic order of a large part of the world[13] was held at Bretton Woods, New Hampshire. At the Bretton Woods Conference in July 1944, representatives from 45 countries, dominated by the leaders of the anti-Hitler coalition, agreed to a plan to restore currency convertibility. This conference demonstrates that the Second World War, which was launched by Germany merely 21 years after the end of the last world war, had taught the leaders of the winning coalition a lesson: for a durable peace, it was not enough to win the war, and apart from disarming the aggressor, an international economy to the benefit of all would have to be established.

The US dollar was fixed to gold at a parity of 1/35 ounces, and since no other currency was convertible into gold, the dollar became the 'anchor currency' of the Bretton Woods system, with the other participating currencies pegged to the dollar within a relatively narrow band of ±1 per cent. Consequently, as soon as a currency was made convertible into US dollars, it was de facto indirectly pegged to and convertible into gold. Hence, a link from paper to gold, albeit indirectly via the US dollar, was re-established for another three decades. The end of the Bretton Woods system came in 1971, when the US government suspended convertibility of the dollar into gold. Consequently, not only the dollar, but all currencies that were pegged to it, suddenly were stripped of the provision — as hypothetical as it may have been — to redeem paper into gold at a fixed rate.

The link between money and bullion, which had been established thousands of years ago, was suddenly cut and the world's currencies turned into uncovered paper money. Understandably, the public — as far as people were interested in the nature of money — was concerned. At the same time, central banks were urgently looking for an alternative to 'anchor' potentially worthless 'fiat money' to a solid base. The quantity theory of money, at that time widely discussed and forcefully promoted by the influential monetarist school, delivered this device (see the Appendix to Chapter 18 of the book).

THE INTERNATIONAL MONETARY FUND

The goal of the IMF's operation was to create the conditions under which the transfer of goods and services from one country to another could take place unfettered by restrictions on trade or controls over international payments. To achieve this end, the Fund had three main objectives, each of which reflected the lessons learned during the interwar years. First, a multilateral system of payments based on a worldwide convertibility of currencies was to be achieved through the elimination of exchange controls.[14] In addition, reasonable stability of exchange rates was to be maintained, competitive currency devaluations avoided and, where exchange adjustments were necessary, these were to be carried out in an orderly fashion. Finally, to enable member nations to pursue domestic policies of full employment, the Fund undertook the virtually impossible task of combining exchange rate stability with national independence in monetary and fiscal matters.

To eliminate foreign exchange restrictions and thus eventually to restore currency convertibility, members of the Fund were to refrain from imposing new restrictions on current account transactions after the end of the war and to avoid practices that discriminated against any currency. But, realising that exchange controls might be necessary in the difficult early post-war years, the Fund allowed for a transitional period of readjustment and adaptation, ending in 1952, after which members still retaining exchange restrictions were to consult with officers of the IMF about their continuance. Exchange restrictions on capital account transactions were not forbidden but were retained as a guard against the destabilising effects of flights of capital on a country's balance of payments. Indeed, the Fund expected members to introduce controls to prevent such capital movements. Currency discrimination was also sanctioned by the IMF under certain conditions, particularly where a currency was officially designated a scarce currency. As long as it was so designated, member countries were to be permitted to impose discriminatory exchange controls on the use of that currency.

To achieve stability of exchange rates and an acceptable mechanism of international adjustment, the Fund Agreement borrowed some elements from the gold standard and some from the rival system of flexible exchange rates. Thus, under the provisions of the IMF

Agreement, each member country was obliged to establish a par value for its currency fixed either in terms of gold or of the dollar, and to peg the exchange rate of its currency against other currencies within a range of 1 per cent above or below that par value. Within this 2 per cent band, the market rate of exchange could move subject to market forces but, if the market rate approached the lower or higher limits of the band ('support points'), the central bank would be required to prevent the exchange rate from moving outside the band. To deal with pressures on these exchange rates due to short-term disturbances in a country's balance of payments or to the difficulties associated with the early stages of more deep-seated payments problems, the Fund established a pool of currencies upon which members could draw. This was made up of the contributions of members, based on assigned quotas, the individual size of which was determined by the level of the contributing country's gross national product and its importance in world trade. The subscriptions themselves were to consist of two components: 25 per cent of the quota was to be contributed in gold and dollars, and 75 per cent in the member's own currency. Apart from determining a country's drawing rights on the Fund, the size of its quota also determined a country's voting rights in the Fund's deliberations. The largest quotas were initially assigned to the US ($2,750 million), Britain ($1,300 million), China ($550 million), France ($450 million) and India ($400 million).[15] Provision was made for a periodic review of quotas, and changes in quotas could be made if the Fund deemed such a step desirable for the proper functioning of the international monetary system.

To deal with short-run balance of payments difficulties, members were to be allowed to draw on the foreign currencies held in the pool, so that these drawing rights, in effect, provided a form of reserves supplemental to the members' own international reserves. In making such a drawing, a member country would surrender domestic currency to the Fund equal in value to the foreign currencies drawn. A member drawing from the Fund was also expected to make a future repurchase of the domestic currency thus transferred to the Fund with gold and/or convertible currencies. A drawing within the gold tranche (up to the value of the gold subscribed by a member to the Fund) was to be automatic, but to obtain a larger drawing, a member would be required to gain the consent of the Fund. The repurchase provisions were included to preserve the efficacy of the Fund by ensuring that, in the short run, its stocks of currencies in strong demand would not be rapidly depleted. However, where widespread drawings made a currency scarce in the Fund, additional supplies of it could be obtained from the scarce currency country in exchange for gold or by borrowing the currency from the member country. Alternatively, the Fund could declare the currency scarce as noted above, and the Fund could take steps to ration its meagre supply of the currency.

To deal with a fundamental disequilibrium in a country's balance of payments the Fund turned to supervised flexibility of exchange rates. Members were to be allowed to change the initial par value of their currencies (i.e. devalue or revalue) only to correct fundamental disequilibria. Such a change was to be approved by the Fund, unless the change altered the exchange rate by no more than 10 per cent of the currency's initial par value.

The new international monetary system was constructed on the supposition that each member country would experience fluctuations of its current account, with deficits in some years and surpluses in others. Over a period of several years, however, it was expected that surpluses would tend to offset deficits. When a particular deficit was very severe, and a country's international currency reserves fell to a dangerous level, it could approach the Fund for a drawing to carry it over its difficult period. But if the payments deficit persisted over a period of several years and the country thus had to make frequent use of the Fund's resources, a devaluation of its currency would then become acceptable to the Fund, especially if the country's domestic economic policies were not the most immediate cause of the difficulties. A country with persistent current account surpluses, on the other hand, would simply amass reserves and would not be under any monetary pressures to rectify the situation comparable to those faced by the persistent debtor country whose reserves were being depleted. But the Fund's powers under the scarce currency clause were deemed sufficient either to deter the surplus country from continuing to amass reserves or to compel it to eliminate its current account surplus by an upward revaluation of its currency or by some other such measure. When the international monetary system was functioning smoothly, the Fund's operations were expected to be of minor importance. On the other hand, should imbalances and other difficulties arise, the Fund was considered to possess ample reserves and sufficient powers to return the world monetary system quickly to stability.

THE INTERNATIONAL BANK FOR RECONSTRUCTION AND DEVELOPMENT

The other institution set up at Bretton Woods in 1944 was the IBRD, commonly called the World Bank. Originally designed to help finance post-war reconstruction, the Bank was later to help extend aid to the developing nations. At first it was intended that the Bank's loan capital, which was set at $10,000 million, would be subscribed by member countries, each of which was asked to provide 20 per cent of its subscription (2 per cent in gold or dollars and 18 per cent in its own currency) when the Bank began operations. The other 80 per cent remained on call to meet the Bank's future obligations. By 1959, however, the Bank's capital had been increased to $21,000 million, and the bulk of the Bank's lending resources was derived from borrowing in capital markets through the issue of bonds, which were guaranteed by the governments of the countries in whose currencies these issues were denominated. Furthermore, the function of the Bank had been extended to cover development loans to member countries for specified projects. Such loans were normally tied to the direct foreign exchange costs of the imports needed for the completion of these projects, and the IBRD was given powers to stipulate the foreign country from which the required imports were to be purchased. These development loans were to be repaid in the currencies originally made available, and borrowers were to be charged rates of interest determined by the prevailing rates in capital markets where the Bank's bonds were sold. The Bank was also allowed to lend to private enterprise in member countries.[16] Finally, in addition to its lending function, the IBRD was given powers to offer technical assistance in the use of the funds it provided and to conduct general surveys to help member countries assess their economic potential and prepare development programmes.

THE GENERAL AGREEMENT ON TARIFFS AND TRADE

The efforts to re-establish multilateralism through the setting up of the IMF would have been defeated if trade controls, over which the Fund had no authority, replaced arbitrary controls over international payments. But experience in the 1930s had underlined the close connection between exchange controls and trade restrictions and consequently, between 1943 and 1945, when the formation of the IMF was under consideration, American, British and Canadian officials were also discussing the possibility of extending the principle of international organisation into the field of commercial policy. In 1947, a conference called by the Economic and Social Council of the United Nations (ECOSOC) began working towards the establishment of an International Trade Organization (ITO) with a view to extending to trade the same philosophy underpinning the IMF in the monetary field. At the same time, the US, under its Trade Agreements Act, began talks with a view to the reduction of worldwide import duties. At Geneva, in 1947, negotiations organised by ECOSOC produced the General Agreement on Tariffs and Trade (GATT), which was to be applied until the full ITO was concluded. The provisions for the latter organisation were incorporated in the Havana Charter of 1948. However, the US and several other countries refused to ratify the proposed ITO.[17] They objected to the provisions relating to full employment policies, international cartels and the stabilisation of primary product prices. At the same time, the success of the first GATT session in Geneva in 1947 did much to reduce the urgency of the creation of such an organisation.

The GATT incorporated in it the objective enshrined in the US Trade Agreements Act of 1934 (renewed in 1945), which allowed the US administration to negotiate reciprocal tariff reductions with other countries.[18] Thus, the procedure adopted at the negotiations in Geneva in 1947, in which 23 countries participated, involved bilateral bargaining on a product-by-product basis to obtain the maximum reductions possible in existing duties. Concessions agreed on in this manner were generalised by being granted to all other countries represented at the conference by the adoption of the most-favoured nation principle. Altogether, 123 sets of negotiations covering 50,000 items were completed and incorporated in the GATT, which was signed on 30 October 1947.

The code of conduct included in the GATT involved two major principles: first, a multilateral and non-discriminatory approach to international trade and, second, condemnation of quantitative trade restrictions. The first principle was implemented through the inclusion of the most-favoured nation clause, under which preferential trade arrangements designed to favour one nation over others were prohibited. Exceptions to the rule were allowed, however, and included those preferential systems that had existed in mid-1939, the formation of customs unions or free trade areas and the use of discrimination for temporary balance of payments purposes or by developing countries to aid their economic growth. As for quantitative restrictions, the code precluded them in principle but allowed exceptions in certain circumstances, namely for short-term balance of payments purposes and to allow developing countries to protect their infant industries. Finally, an escape clause allowed a contracting party to impose quotas to regulate internal marketing of a product so long as it concurrently restricted domestic production of the commodity to such an extent that imports maintained the same share of total domestic consumption as before the imposition of the restrictions. The first GATT allowed for the setting up of a Secretariat with its headquarters in Geneva, and thus the General Agreement became institutionalised. The basic philosophy underlying the GATT code of conduct was that each contracting party should enjoy reasonable access to the markets of its trading partners in return for offering the same sort of access to its domestic markets to foreign exporters. In this way, world trade would expand rapidly, with all countries experiencing fair trading relations.

As a result of these arrangements in the monetary and commercial policy fields, the countries which joined these post-war international economic organisations could expect at least to avoid the enormous problems they had encountered in their international economic relations in the 1930s. The architects of these institutions, by establishing codes of conduct in international monetary and commercial dealings acceptable to all member countries, expected that a post-war international economy would emerge relatively unimpeded by quantitative restrictions on trade and exchange controls on current account transactions.

POST-WAR RECONSTRUCTION

Many parts of the world experienced difficult times in the early post-war years. A long war had deprived consumers in many countries of basic commodities and semi-luxuries, and personal savings had grown as a consequence of these shortages. When peace returned, therefore, consumers were anxious to use these savings to satisfy their deprived desires for all types of goods and services. On the other hand, especially in Europe and Japan, the war had reduced millions of people to desperate poverty. In addition, much of the productive equipment in the warring nations, with the notable exception of the US, had been destroyed or replacement and new investment had been delayed, so that whole industrial complexes required rebuilding. As a result, the demand for goods and services for consumption and investment purposes outran the available world supplies, while the problem of increasing output was made all the more difficult by the problems of the change-over from wartime to peacetime production. The consequent excess demand that persisted throughout the immediate post-war years produced tremendous inflationary pressures in many countries, which were only partly contained in some by the continuation of wartime rationing and other physical controls. Other countries were not so fortunately placed, and eventually currency reforms were needed to put a stop to runaway inflation. The shortage of fuel and the inability of the agricultural sector to provide the population with adequate supplies of food added to the extreme economic difficulties which existed in Europe.

For several years after the end of the war, then, the international economy experienced abnormal conditions. The only major country to enter world trade and commerce without undue stress was the US, which had emerged from the war in a highly favourable economic position. For a few years, many of its industrial competitors were barely able to meet domestic requirements for manufactures and were thus unable to compete with American exports in foreign markets. Furthermore, European demand for foodstuffs, raw materials and capital goods was such that US firms and farmers were able to benefit considerably from supplying part of the demand and consequently recorded pronounced and persistent surpluses in trade with Europe. Such a situation led directly to a dollar shortage which became almost universal in the late 1940s.

From 1945 to 1948, world production rose and economic recovery continued, but in Europe the rate of growth of industrial output was generally too slow to catch up with demand or to increase exports sufficiently to achieve external equilibrium. In the late 1940s, however, two developments occurred which, perhaps more than any others, were responsible for transforming the economic situation in Europe. These were the European Recovery Programme (ERP), inaugurated in April 1948, and the devaluations of September 1949.

The ERP, largely inspired by a fear that any further economic deterioration in Western Europe would make the countries in the region more sympathetic towards communism, was proposed by the American Secretary of State, George Marshall, in 1947. This programme, aimed at the economic reconstruction of Europe, called Marshall Aid, was to be implemented through the Economic Co-operation Administration (ECA) in the US and the Organization for European Economic Co-operation (OEEC), established in Europe in April 1948. The OEEC comprised 16 European countries. From April 1948 to the end of 1951, over $11,000 million was provided through the ECA to Europe, with France, Britain, West Germany, the Netherlands and Italy receiving 75 per cent of the total. After 1951, Europe received a further $2,600 million, mainly in the period up to mid-1953. The aid offered under the ERP took the form of grants of commodities produced predominantly in the US, foodstuffs, fertilisers, fodder and fuel initially, but, by 1951, raw materials, semi-processed goods and machinery accounted for more than half the commodities supplied under the Plan.[19]

While Marshall Aid represented only about 5 per cent of the recipient countries' gross national incomes, because of its strategic importance for industrial construction, its economic impact was quickly noticeable. Total manufacturing output in the OEEC countries rose by 13 per cent in 1949, and by 1952 it was 39 per cent above the 1948 level. While many other factors undoubtedly contributed to European recovery during these years, the contribution of Marshall Aid remains a very significant one.

The other major event that helped the European recovery, and that led to an improvement in the trade balance of several countries, was the widespread use of currency devaluation in September 1949, when 19 countries, accounting for almost two-thirds of total world trade, devalued their currencies relative to the dollar by approximately 30 per cent. The basic reason for the devaluations were the distortions which had developed in the pattern of international payments. Even before the Second World War, exchange rates had not been adequate to produce high levels of production and employment in all trading countries, while the war and the abnormal conditions after 1945 had created new forces to change the trade and payments patterns in the world economy. For these reasons, the initial par values of many currencies established in 1946–7 did not truly reflect the differences in domestic purchasing power of the currencies of the various trading countries. As a result, the countries with overvalued currencies were not capable of earning the export receipts needed to buy urgently required imports.

The position in Britain is worthy of special mention. During the war she had liquidated a large part of her overseas assets to obtain funds out of which to purchase war materials. War demands also forced her to incur vast debts to other countries in the form of accumulated sterling balances, as well as to borrow heavily from the US. Late in 1945, she was forced to seek further financial assistance from the US. Under the Anglo-American Financial Agreement of July 1946, the US undertook to advance $3,750 million to Britain in the next four years, while lend-lease and other debt obligations were consolidated into a lump sum of $650 million. In return for this aid, Britain undertook to make sterling freely convertible on and after 15 July 1947. The size of the credit proved to be totally inadequate to Britain's needs, however. Within 12 months, over $2,000 million of the loans had been used up and, when the pound was made convertible in mid-1947, the rest disappeared overnight, forcing the suspension of convertibility of the pound by the end of August.

Despite Britain's difficulties, economic recovery was rapid in Europe after 1947 and, confronted by sellers' markets, exporters had few problems with which to contend. By 1949, however, the picture was changing. The increased availability of goods in Europe and North America now favoured the buyer, and price considerations once again became decisive in export markets. Overvalued European currencies, not a serious hindrance to exports as long as shortages persisted, now became a major obstacle. A revision of exchange values was inevitable. Britain went first, devaluing the pound by 30.5 per cent on 18 September 1949. Within a few days many other countries followed her example, including all the sterling area (except Pakistan) and 11 West European economies.

In addition, European production continued to expand, thus reducing the region's dependence on foreign goods, especially those of the US. Intra-European trade was also beginning to revive with the return to more normal trading conditions. By 1952 the international economic situation had improved considerably. Although controls over trade and payments were to last in varying degrees of intensity from country to country for the remainder of the decade, by 1952 the extreme pressures of the immediate post-war years had almost disappeared.[20]

RECOMMENDATIONS FOR FURTHER READING

The economic aspects of the Second World War are discussed by Harrison (1998, *The Economics of World War II*), Overy (1995, *Why the Allies Won*) and Tooze (2006, *The Wages of Destruction: The Making and Breaking of the Nazi Economy*).

Kuznets (1964, *Postwar Economic Growth: Four Lectures*) and Milward (1984, *The Reconstruction of Western Europe 1945–51*) deal with the recovery of the international economy after 1945.

For the Bretton Woods Conference in 1944 and the institutions that emerged from it, recent references are Toussaint (2023, *The World Bank. A Critical History*) and the contributions to Scott-Smith and Rofe (2017, *Global Perspectives on the Bretton Woods Conference and the Post-War World Order*).

The international monetary system after 1945 is discussed in detail by Tew (1960, *International Monetary Co-operation*), Horie (1964, *The International Monetary Fund*) and Scammell (1964, *International Monetary Policy*).

NOTES

1 The open intervention of Germany and Italy in the Spanish Civil War 1936–9 supporting Franco's coup d'état against the Spanish democratic republic, which in turn was aided by the Soviet Union, can be seen as the first incidence of warfare between the future major opponents 1941–5 in Europe. In 1931, Japanese troops invaded and conquered Manchuria, followed by a full-scale invasion into China in 1937, which marks the beginning of the hostilities in Asia.
2 The German leadership thus hoped that as a consequence of the attack, what had previously been imported from the Soviet Union could henceforth be plundered.
3 Following Overy (1995, p. 24), the 'central question of the war' is how the Soviet Union could keep on fighting once the front had reached Leningrad and Moscow, and most of the industrial and agricultural

heartland was occupied by the aggressor. Among the more obvious answers are the depth of Russia that allowed for prolonged retreat and relocation of production to the east, the moral superiority on the side of the attacked, who knew that defeat meant either death or servitude and misery, and who to prevent this outcome produced weaponry in 12–16-hour shifts and fought to the last man standing, and Western supplies that were convoyed to the USSR in large numbers — including everything from spam to lorries and tanks. Apart from that, the Soviet command economy and the accomplished collectivisation of agriculture help to explain why against all expectations the Soviet economy did not collapse in 1941.

4 Not even German propaganda could conceal the defeat at Stalingrad and the fact that victory was thus out of reach. Why, then, did Germany fight on for another two years that should prove terrible beyond imagination? Regarding Hitler, a convincing explanation is that once he realised that the war of conquest against Russia — and 'Bolshevism' — was lost, he directed the German war effort towards his second obsession, the destruction of the European Jews. Indeed, while the eastern front held — offering continuous and fierce resistance in a painfully slow retreat — the extermination camps in Poland continued to operate up to January 1945 and thus almost completely accomplished the genocide (see Haffner, 1978). For those Germans that did not share Hitler's pathological hatred of the Jews and the 'Bolsheviks', fear of Soviet revenge, given widespread knowledge of the atrocities committed in the east by Wehrmacht, police and SS, may have induced many to continue the increasingly unequal fight. But loyalty to the leadership and comradeship with fellow soldiers as long-trained military virtues certainly played a role, too, along with the increasing level of terror against deserters, defectors and saboteurs towards the end of the war.

5 While the Soviet war effort has rather been downplayed in the West during the Cold War years, it is now generally acknowledged that the decisive fighting happened in the east. Along with the biased Western reception of the war effort within the Allied camp, the Soviet government tended to downplay the number of Soviet victims (20 rather than more than 25 million military and civilian), as the true numbers in part also reveal the failure of the government to take adequate defensive measures in 1941.

6 Indeed, in 1942 the American war effort was mainly directed against Japan.

7 It is estimated that Allied strategic bombing killed 800,000 Germans and 500,000 Japanese, along with 50,000 Italians and 70,000 French civilians; about 150,000 Allied crew members died in action.

8 Broadberry and Harrison (2008).

9 Remarkably, this time this had lasting effects. Up to this date, military ambitions of the ex-Axis countries appear comparatively modest.

10 However, on two occasions since 1945, the world was close to war between the US and the Soviet Union (and their allies): the Korean War of 1950–3 and the Cuban missile crisis of 1962. Rational behaviour by both US and Soviet political and military leadership has thereafter safely prevented disaster. Technical flaws (false alarms) have since then been a more dangerous threat.

11 A few numbers from Broadberry and Harrison (2008) reflect the Allies' material superiority: the Allied-to-Axis wartime GDP ratio is estimated at 2.0 in 1941, 2.1 in 1942, 2.3 in 1943, 3.1 in 1944 and staggering 5.0 in 1945. The ratios of Allied and Axis 1942–4 weaponry production are 3.0 for aircraft, 3.1 for rifles, 3.4 for mortars, 3.8 for guns, 4.0 for machine guns and 22.9 for machine pistols. The Allied-to-Axis ratios of population and territory (boundaries of 1938) are 7.5 and 22.7.

12 To symbolise the victors' unity, the German and Austrian capitals, Berlin and Vienna, were also divided into four occupation zones. Unintended in 1945, this established West Berlin (consisting of the three Western zones) in 1949 as a capitalist island in the Soviet-style economy of the GDR. West Berlin was isolated economically, and to prevent movement of people from East Berlin and the rest of the GDR and to this enclave a wall was constructed in 1961.

13 Although the Soviet Union took part in the conference, the antagonism between the major Western countries and the Soviet Union that quickly re-emerged after the end of hostilities in 1945 effectively kept the Soviet camp out of the Bretton Woods institutions (and out of the world economy governed by them) until its dissolution in the 1990s. The People's Republic of China is another part of the world that stayed apart for an extended period (WTO member since 2001, IMF since 2004).

14 Convertibility of a currency is a term that has undergone a definitional change. Whereas under the nineteenth-century gold standard it signified convertibility into gold on demand, since 1940, at least, it has referred to a situation in which there are no restrictions on the conversion of one currency into another for current account purposes.

15 The Soviet Union was given a quota of $1,200 million but eventually declined membership of the Fund.

16 It has always been the Bank's policy not to offer loans where funds are obtainable in private capital markets on reasonable terms. Its underlying pro-markets orientation stresses promoting private investment, not competing against it.
17 Despite the failed attempt to establish the ITO in 1948, efforts were never completely abandoned, and in 1995 the World Trade Organization (WTO) came into being as the successor of the GATT. For details, see Chapter 19 of this book.
18 The Americans had embarked on a programme of trade liberalisation in the 1930s when, under the Reciprocal Trade Agreements Act of 1934, the president was authorised to sign commercial agreements with other countries, reducing existing American duties by as much as 50 per cent in exchange for parallel concessions. This Act was renewed in 1945 for a further three years to allow the administration to negotiate up to 25 per cent from the rates current at the beginning of that year.
19 Arguably, had the Keynes Plan been chosen instead of the White Plan, the scarcity of dollars outside the US and, consequently, the need for Marshall Aid might have been markedly less pronounced.
20 The recovery of the world economy after the Second World War was further strengthened by a new outbreak of violence, the Korean War (1950–3), which raised the level of world demand considerably. In fact, while war is horror for those affected by its atrocities, it is good for business. As Polish-German Rosa Luxemburg, one of the few European left-wing politicians who, as a 'revolutionary defeatist' categorically opposed the First World War sarcastically commented in 1916: 'Die Dividenden steigen, und die Proletarier fallen' [The dividends are rising, and the proletarians are falling].

CHAPTER **17**

The International Economy, 1950–2000

A. G. Kenwood, A. L. Lougheed and Michael Graff

ECONOMIC GROWTH: AN OVERVIEW

The Golden Age, 1950–73

By the early 1950s, the first stage in the post-war recovery of the international economy had largely been completed. The European economies had been reconstructed, and normal peace-time production had been resumed in most of them. Inflation had given way to price stability and currency overvaluation had been corrected by the widespread devaluations in 1949. These signs of economic improvement meant that, in contrast to the depressed conditions of the 1930s and the grim austerity of the war and early post-war years, the 1950s and 1960s were decades of rapidly rising living standards for the greater part of the population in Western Europe, North America and Oceania. From 1950 to 1973, real GDP of the top 16 OECD[1] countries rose at an average annual rate of 4.8 per cent, while labour productivity (GDP per hour or labour) grew at a rate of around 4.5 per cent per year on average. This resulting transformation in living standards was epitomised in the new and ever widening range of consumer durables, which quickly became an accepted part of the consumption patterns in these countries. Where income levels did not allow immediate purchase of these goods, greater security of employment increased the attractiveness of living on credit,[2] which permitted a more rapid accumulation of these material goods than would otherwise have occurred. In this age of affluence, advertising took on a new importance and television provided the advertisers with a new medium with which to practise their highly specialised selling techniques. Notably, the increased importance of advertising not only reflected the growing affluence — which meant that producers could no longer count on unlimited consumer need and had to make sure to stimulate them — it also reflected the industrial evolution of the international economy in this stage of capitalism. The new techniques that brought about the increase in industrial productivity, which largely supported the rise in living standards that was apparent during these years, almost inevitably demanded large-scale operations. In secondary and tertiary industries,

DOI: 10.4324/9781003382171-22

'bigness' became a necessity and oligopoly the predominant form of market structure. Since the size of the competing firms and the large financial resources over which they had command, plus the need to guarantee some minimum level of profitability to satisfy shareholders, ruled out price-cutting, firms resorted increasingly to competitive advertising, the promotion of after-sales service and other forms of non-price competition. Contemporary trade theory refers to the notion of 'monopolistic competition' when supra-national markets are served by a limited number of firms that succeed in convincing consumers that their products (de facto almost perfect substitutes) are unique — hence the recent emphasis on corporate identity branding, logos and the like.[3]

Innovation became a form of dynamic inter-firm competition, since product improvement and the development of completely new products quickly gave a firm an advantage over its rivals. The threatened loss of markets and profits was more than enough to keep most large business enterprises abreast of current technical developments and, in so far as these changes could be affected by what the firm itself did, particularly by its programme of research and development, the level of investment in the enterprise was raised correspondingly. Investment was not only the means of ensuring the short-run efficiency of the firm's plant and equipment, it also became the means of promoting the long-run growth of the firm.

The shift of emphasis from short-run to long-run considerations evident in the investment behaviour of industrial large-scale businesses toward the end of the century was also reflected in macroeconomic policy theorising, where long-run economic growth became more prominent than fighting unemployment or macroeconomic fine tuning. For reasons of political power or prestige and because of the consequent rise in living standards, securing high rates of economic growth became an important object of economic policy.

Beneath the welter of affluence there developed attempts to improve the economic welfare of the poorest countries of the world. This was the outcome of several motives. The threat posed to their affluence by the poverty and misery that abounded in these regions was keenly felt in most Western countries, especially as this fear was reinforced by the appeal of Soviet style socialism as a political programme and a model for the political, social and economic development of the poorer parts of the world. It was also felt that, while a few advanced countries with special positions to protect might be hurt by the changes brought about by successful economic development elsewhere, the economic benefits to be gained from an all-round rise in living standards and the greater opportunities for trade between nations that would arise as countries became richer would more than offset these losses. Furthermore, the achievement of independence of former European colonies in other continents committed the former colonial powers to the granting of favourable treatment to these emerging nations to ease the burdens of adjusting to their newly won independence. Some of the interest of people in developed countries in the fate of their counterparts in the poorer countries stemmed also from genuine altruism, a fact which is most evident in the succession of voluntary appeals for food, medical supplies and clothing for the inhabitants of the stricken areas of the world. Whatever the motives, however, the channelling of aid from the richer to the poorer countries of the world represented a major change in the field of international capital flows as compared with the pre-1939 period, while the concerted efforts to overcome the problem of economic backwardness remains of immense significance for the future of the international economy.

As a result of this support and of their own effort, the developing market economies as a group experienced high rates of economic growth, averaging around 6 per cent annually between 1960 and 1973. Yet, per capita growth rates were well below those of the advanced countries due to higher rates of population growth in the poorer parts of the world. The centrally planned economies also recorded high annual growth rates between 1950 and 1973, averaging close to 5 per cent increases in real GDP.[4]

Limited Growth and Economic Problems, 1973–90

This period of rapid growth came to an end after the boom of 1973. World inflation had risen from 5.9 per cent in 1971 to 9.6 per cent in 1973 and was to exceed 15 per cent in 1974, so that national monetary and fiscal policies were increasingly directed towards controlling price increases. In addition to a commodities boom in 1972–3, an expansionary monetary policy in the US and the convergence of the trade cycles of most industrial countries for the first time in the post-war era, all contributed to the boom. As it subsided, the consequent decline in industrial production in the major advanced countries was worsened by contractionary monetary and fiscal policies increasingly implemented against the inflationary forces stimulated by the boom. Conditions changed in the world economy after 1973, with higher inflation rates and higher unemployment levels. At first, the industrial world moved into recession throughout 1974 and most of 1975 at a time when the trend towards higher prices was exacerbated by the first 'oil crisis' — the substantial increases in oil prices of 1974.[5] Recovery commenced late in 1975 but, despite a 5.2 per cent increase in real GDP for the OECD as a whole in 1976, economic growth was uneven and averaged only 2.8 per cent for the period 1974–80, compared with an average of just under 5 per cent for the years from 1950 to 1973. At the same time, productivity declined considerably. To a large extent, the lower growth rates of the 1970s were the result of the restrictive economic policies pursued by central banks and governments in their attempts to deal with the problem of inflation. Indeed, guided by the monetarist approach to economic policy, the long-run growth policy which had been so successful between 1950 and 1973 succumbed to the short-run policy of containing inflation, despite its impact on economic growth and employment.[6] During the period 1973–80, consumer prices rose at an average 10 per cent compared with 4 per cent from 1950 to 1973, while unemployment grew substantially in all OECD countries to exceed 4 per cent by 1975 and 5 per cent by 1979.

The second 'oil crisis' — the price hike in 1979–80 — largely accounted for a second major recession in the world economy between 1981 and 1982.[7] While recovery commenced in 1984, economic performance was patchy during the remainder of the 1980s. Real GDP for the OECD recorded an average annual growth rate below 3 per cent. Inflation rates were reduced from 7.5 per cent in 1982 to 2.7 per cent in 1986 but then crept up to around 4 per cent on average towards the end of the decade, while unemployment remained persistently around 8 per cent. The poorer countries were also affected in much the same way. The exception was a group of the newly industrialising countries[8] that were able to maintain high growth rates throughout this difficult period.

Changes in the 1990s

Another change in the world economy began in the 1990s as economic globalisation accelerated. International economic relations brought economies even closer together, and a new approach to domestic economic policy became evident, under which many of the elements of a laissez-faire economy became popular, just at a time when central planning became discredited. Worldwide economic policies were concerned with short-run economic objectives, such as the containment of inflation, economic efficiency, increased productivity and greater profitability. These objectives were associated with others, including small government, privatisation of state-owned enterprises, downsizing of the workforce in private industry and public service, and labour market and other microeconomic reforms. In these changed circumstances, it was argued, the market mechanism would lead to economic growth and eventual full employment. By the 1990s, however, the new approach had led to high and intractable unemployment rates in some countries and the disappearance of minimum wage thresholds in others, producing a new class of people, the 'working poor'. In addition, a widening of the gap between the rich and the poor became evident.[9]

Other major changes in the 1990s included the intensification of European economic integration, the breakdown of central planning in the East European countries and the emergence of a group of newly classified 'advanced' countries. Despite the steady increase in the geographic size and economic power of the European Economic Community as its membership grew, it appeared during the early 1980s that it was not performing as well economically as Japan and the US. Steps were therefore taken to stimulate technical improvements in the region and to increase productivity and competitiveness through the removal of various economic restrictions within the Community.[10]

Finally, the creation of an Economic and Monetary Union (EMU) was begun in 1992 by the general member acceptance of the Maastricht Treaty, which aimed to create a single currency (the euro) and a common central bank (the European Central Bank (ECB)). It was intended that all member countries would meet certain conditions, aimed at creating convergence of the various economies, considered essential for the success of the Monetary Union. By 1997, however, when the members were to meet all the conditions for entry, the slow movement of some of them led to a weakening of these conditions to allow several of them access to the Monetary Union. In 1998, the 11 successful members to form the EMU in 1999 were declared, leaving out only the UK, Denmark, Sweden and Greece.[11]

The shift towards a market economy in Central and Eastern Europe and the breakup of the USSR into the Countries in Transition[12] occurred at the beginning of the decade. Later, in, the IMF reclassified some 'Newly Industrialized Countries' (NICs) as 'advanced' economies, namely China-Hong Kong, China-Taipei (Taiwan), Korea, Singapore and Israel. In the same year, however, the Asian members of the group, along with Thailand, Malaysia and Indonesia, went into a financial crisis on a scale rarely experienced anywhere else in the world between the Great Depression 1929–33 and the Great Recession that struck in 2008/9. The 1997 Asian financial crisis wiped out much of the gains from growth that these economies had achieved since the 1970s.

POPULATION GROWTH AND MIGRATION

From 1950 to 2000, the world's population rose from 2.5 billion to 6.1 billion, at an average annual rate of growth of 1.8 per cent. The highest growth rates ever — 2.1 per cent —were recorded in the 1960s. Since the 1970s, the world population has been steadily declining, and in 2000, it had fallen to 1.4 per cent.

During these years, the population of Europe rose at only 0.5 per cent annually — chiefly because of declining birth rates and because emigration was relatively high in the 1950s — while North America recorded 1.2 per cent. All other regions experienced annual increases at or above the world average, the highest being in Africa (2.6 per cent). For Latin America and South Asia, it was 2.3 and 2.2 per cent, for Oceania 1.8 per cent, and East Asia recorded an annual average increase of only 1.7 per cent.

Immigration contributed substantially to population growth in Oceania and South America, and in many countries in these two regions the natural increase in the 1950s rose above its pre-war average and served to augment the growth through immigration. In Asia, medical improvements and public health measures lowered the death rate drastically, and with hardly a fall in the birth rate, the population grew rapidly. Given the rapid growth of the world population during 1960s, concern was soon expressed about the capacity of the world economy to provide adequate supplies of food and raw materials to support the growth in numbers. The subsequently fall in the population growth rate has gradually made this a lesser matter for concern.

From 1945 to 1960 the major source of migrants was Europe, notably, the British Isles (2.2 million), Germany (1.5 million) and Italy (1.3 million). Altogether, just under 5 million people emigrated from Europe during the 1950s, much lower than the totals of each decade from 1880 to 1910. The chief countries of destination were the US, Canada, Australia (each of which absorbed more than 1 million people), Argentina and Brazil. In this period, there were substantial restrictions on the inflow of people into the US and other recipient countries. Unlike the European emigrants of the nineteenth century, whose efforts overseas expanded the supplies of foodstuffs and raw materials for the European market, the bulk of the immigrants of the 1950s entered manufacturing and tertiary industries in the immigrant countries, some of which were competitive with European export industries.

From 1960 to 1990, intercontinental migration slowed down somewhat. While the traditional flows continued — for example, British emigration to Canada and Oceania — high rates of economic growth in Western European countries increased the demand for labour so rapidly that millions of foreign workers from neighbouring countries were absorbed into the national workforce of these boom countries. While some immigrants came from other continents, such as those from Turkey to Germany and from Algeria to France, large intra-continental flows emerged and grew, such as the workers who moved from Portugal, Yugoslavia and Greece into the industrial regions of Western Europe. Moreover, the provision of free movement of labour within the European Community[13] added to the general shift of workers within Europe. Germany recorded a large net population inflow between 1958 and 1973 and, in some years, absorbed over 1 million immigrants. Access to foreign workers prevented shortages of labour from developing within the Community and thus reduced the pressures of wage inflation. Moreover, with the slowdown in economic activity in the late 1970s, there was a net outflow of labour from Western Europe as foreign workers returned to their homelands in large numbers, thus easing the unemployment problems in the host countries. As economic activity in the EC recovered in the 1980s, the inflow of foreign workers was renewed, but not on the same scale as before 1973, in which year there were over 6 million foreign workers in Western Europe. Towards the end of the 1970s another form of intercontinental migration began — that of refugees from Asia, mainly Vietnam. During the 1980s, hundreds of thousands of East Asians were absorbed by several developed countries, including the US, Canada and Australia.

High unemployment in Europe after the 1970s did little to revitalise immigration into that continent, and many of the inter- and intra-continental migration flows during the 1980s and 1990s have been the movement of refugees from poverty, political prosecution, war and civil strife and in many parts of the world. Within Asia there have been substantial international shifts of labour, largely from the Philippines, Bangladesh and Indonesia, into Malaysia, Thailand and the Middle East. From 1975 to 1995, some 12 million Asian workers were employed in other countries, over 60 per cent of them in the Middle East or elsewhere outside the Asia region. Other major migration movements in the early 1990s were from Asia and Central America to the US, and from North Africa and North Asia to Europe.

INTERNATIONAL CAPITAL FLOWS: PRIVATE INVESTMENT

International flows of financial capital have accelerated the globalisation process. Such flows can be classified in terms of foreign direct investment (FDI), involving the acquisition of ownership and/or control of an organisation in the 'host' country by the investing company in the 'home' country, or foreign portfolio investment (FPI), in which the home investor obtains shares in a host country's company, say, on the stock exchange (foreign portfolio equity investment — FPEI) or part control of other forms of investment in the host country without gaining ownership or majority control. It is important to notice that in international statistics FDI is nowadays defined somewhat arbitrarily as when the result is ownership by a foreign investor of 10 per cent or more of the ordinary shares or voting power of an incorporated enterprise or the equivalent. This may, but need not, coincide with the notion of 'greenfield' investment, in which an investing company sets up an entirely new firm in the host country. What is recorded as FDI may thus also consist of cross-border mergers or acquisitions, or plainly financial investment in the secondary market for corporate stock without any interest or involvement in the fates of the firms. FDI can also be 're-invested earnings' — earnings not repatriated to the home country to evade taxation or held in the host country to finance some future capital project. While a high proportion of FDI in the 1950s and 1960s was greenfield, from the early 1970s to the late 1980s, cross-border equities and acquisitions became much more important, rising to a peak of 70 per cent of all FDI inflows. In the 1990s, however, greenfield FDI may have regained some of its previous importance. Financial transactions recorded as FDI, but in fact motivated by tax evasion, have clearly gained importance, although the very nature of offshore finance makes it difficult to arrive at reliable numbers. The accumulated stock of FDI in 2000 was highest in the US, the second most important recipient was Hong Kong. Singapore stood is at rank 15, the British Virgin Islands at rank 29, the Cayman Islands are number 34 of more than 200 countries, ahead of Indonesia, Nigeria, Turkey and India, to name just a few. Clearly, offshore financial services for firms or wealthy individuals reluctant to pay taxes to their domestic authorities must be held responsible for this pattern.

FDI: In Total

The world total FDI, transmitted from home country to host country, rose rapidly to around $20 billion per year in the early 1970s, much of it the result of the US's multinational corporations (now often called transnational corporations — TNCs) investing in Europe to overcome the European Economic Community's (EEC's) common tariff. Thereafter, European transnationals rapidly grew in number, while a feature of the 1980s was the rise of the Japanese TNCs. By 1985, both FDI inflows and outflows recorded around $45 billion annually. But a boom in FDI was to occur after 1985, with annual outflows reaching $280 billion in 1991. After a brief downturn, a further acceleration occurred to a new high of $345–$350 billion in 1996. By the mid-1990s, however, many other countries, including Hong Kong, Korea, Singapore, Taiwan, China, Mexico and Brazil, could boast their own TNCs. Altogether, in 1996, there were some 45,000 parent companies, 7,900 of them based in the NICs and other developing countries, that had set up some 280,000 foreign affiliates, and the total FDI stock of which was $3,200 billion. The worldwide assets of these foreign affiliates were valued at $8,400 billion. This value had been increasing faster than the world gross fixed investment during the decade to 1996.[14]

A major cause of this accelerated growth in the 1990s was the liberalisation of investment criteria in many countries. In addition, a rapid increase in gross saving in several countries provided funds for greater investment. Another reason was the rapid increase in the number of bilateral investment treaties (BITs) aiming to protect and promote investment. In 1996, there were some 1,330 BITs covering 162 countries, a tripling in numbers since 1991. This growth of TNCs led to a rapid increase in international production (the total output of all foreign affiliates), which was valued in 1995 at $7,000 billion in world sales. The growth of these sales from 1987 to 1995 was greater than the growth of exports of goods and services by 20–30 per cent. The gross product of foreign affiliates rose almost threefold between 1982 and 1995.

Yet another reason for the rapid rise in the world sales of TNCs was the opening up of the domestic economies and financial markets of many countries to actors from abroad to improve domestic productive efficiency. Safeguards against the possibility of monopolisation and other devices to restrict trade and competition were sometimes implemented, but action in these areas has been limited.

Transnational companies have tended to concentrate on manufacturing (chemicals, pharmaceuticals, electronics, computers and foodstuffs), petroleum, telecommunications and finance. Their entry into a country may confer benefits on it in terms of increased production, investment and employment, and the introduction of new managerial skills. It can favour export expansion or import replacement and promote the diffusion of new technology. At the same time, the concentration of a number of these international firms in one country may pose serious problems for its government, especially if they control a large part of the country's exports. These problems include the possible relocation of export orders from the local affiliate to another affiliate elsewhere in the world, or the movement of liquid assets out of a country experiencing balance of payments difficulties, thus compounding them.

FDI: National Features

Table 17.1 shows direct investment by home and host country from 1985 to 1996. The US was the major host and home country in 1996, by a substantial margin in both cases. For many years after 1945, the US, almost alone, was in a position to export capital on a large scale. Between 1938 and 1973, its total FDI rose from $11.7 billion to $107 billion, of which re-invested foreign earnings accounted for $8.1 billion of the total. US FDI expanded much

TABLE 17.1 Foreign direct investment, by home and host country, 1985–95 (billion dollars)

Country	Average annual			End stock	
	1985–90	1993	1996	1985	1996
Home country					
World	155.6	239.1	346.8	690	3,178
US	21.6	74.8	84.9	251	794
UK	25.2	25.5	53.5	100	356
Germany	12.9	15.3	28.7	60	288
Hong Kong	2.0	17.7	27.0	37	112
France	14.3	20.6	25.2	2	206
Japan	27.8	13.8	23.4	44	330
Netherlands	8.8	12.3	19.9	48	185
Belgium/ Luxembourg	3.6	4.9	9.0	5	73
Canada	4.8	5.9	7.5	41	111
Singapore	0.6	2.0	4.8	6	37
Other	34.0	46.3	62.9	96	686
EU_{15}	80	97	160	286	1,404
Host country					
WORLD	141.9	218.1	349.2	745	3,233
US	48.6	43.5	84.6	184	645
China	2.7	27.5	42.3	3	169
UK	19.0	15.5	30.1	64	345
France	7.2	20.8	20.8	33	168
Belgium/ Luxembourg	4.1	10.7	13.9	9	101
Singapore	3.0	4.7	9.4	13	66
Indonesia	0.6	2.0	8.0	25	59
Canada	5.3	5.0	6.7	65	129
Netherlands	5.6	8.8	6.3	25	119
Germany	2.3	1.8	3.9	37	171
Other	43.5	77.8	123.2	287	1,261
EU_{15}	53	81	99	226	1,219

Source: UNCTAD (1997, Annex B).

more slowly during the difficult years of the 1970s and the early 1980s but then grew rapidly after 1984.

By 1996, it had risen to an accumulated value of almost $800 billion, and by which year it recorded an outflow of $84.6 billion. Almost half of the FDI outflow in 1996 comprised the re-invested earnings of the foreign affiliates. In the 1990s, the European Union absorbed around 40–45 per cent of the total US FDI outflow, Canada 8–10 per cent and developing countries, mainly in Latin America, around 30 per cent.

In these years, manufacturing accounted for some 35 per cent of the non-bank FDI, mainly transport equipment (8 per cent), chemicals and allied products (6 per cent), food (3 per cent) and industrial machinery and equipment (3 per cent). In addition, finance (excluding deposit institutions) claimed 37 per cent, petroleum 8 per cent and communications 5 per cent.

In these years, the US have become an important host country. Of the total FDI inflow in 1996 of $85 billion, the European Union contributed around $57 billion, Japan $14 billion, Canada $7 billion and other developed countries $6 billion.

By 1996, FDI inflows into the EU had risen to just under $100 billion. The UK claimed the largest share (30 per cent), followed by France (21 per cent) and Belgium (14 per cent). Over half the EU FDI inflow during the years between 1986 and 1997 came from other EU members and the US. In addition, European FDI outflow rose to $160 billion in 1996, with the UK (33 per cent), Germany (18 per cent), France (16 per cent) and the Netherlands (12 per cent) supplying most of it. While much of this outflow from EU countries went into other EU countries, between 1992 and 1996 the EU share of new FDI dropped from 72 to 55 per cent because of the poor economic conditions in many EU countries.

The US and developing countries also received much of the EU capital outflow. In addition, the amounts going to Eastern European countries, hesitant at first, grew rapidly after 1994, when the transformation of these countries from command economies to market economies was well under way. Poland, Hungary, the Czech Republic and Russia received the bulk of these capital flows, mainly from Germany. Much of the EU FDI went into finance, distribution, chemicals and allied products, transport equipment, petroleum, non-ferrous metals and non-electrical machinery. A feature of EU inward FDI has been a decline in mergers and acquisitions, seemingly indicating a growing shortage of EU firms to be taken over by outsiders.

As Table 17.1 shows, the UK in 1996 remained the largest home and host country in the EU. At first, in the 1950s, British FDI went mainly to Commonwealth countries but, in the 1960s, the focus shifted towards the Continent, particularly after 1973. By 1980, when the total value of British FDI reached $80 billion, the EC share was 20 per cent of the total and that of the US 33 per cent. During the 1980s and 1990s British FDI rose rapidly and exceeded $350 billion in 1996. Its geographic spread was much the same in the latter year as before, with the EU, US and Commonwealth countries accounting for the major shares. The annual inflow of FDI into Britain rose to some $30 billion by 1996, most coming from the US, Japan and other EU countries. In that year, the total value of FDI stock in the UK was some $356 billion.

German FDI has concentrated mainly on Europe, East and West, although North America's share had increased to over 20 per cent by 1996. France has continued to invest largely in its former colonies, other EU countries and the US. The Netherlands has been the other major foreign investor within the EU, investing mainly in other EU countries and the US.

Since the 1970s, the importance of Japan as a foreign direct investor increased considerably until the second half of the 1980s, following which its impact deteriorated rapidly. North America was Japan's favourite region for investment. It received just under 50 per cent of the total outflow in 1996. Asia (especially China, Indonesia, Hong Kong and Thailand) accounted for around 25 per cent, and Europe 17 per cent. Of the total Japanese FDI in 1996, 42 per cent went into manufacturing, especially electrical and transport equipment. Banking, insurance and real estate were also highly favoured. In the early 1990s, the newly advanced countries of Asia — especially Hong Kong, Singapore, Taiwan and Korea — began to invest in other Asian countries, especially China and Cambodia. Their total foreign stock in 1996 was valued at $191 billion, of which Hong Kong contributed $112 billion. Their industrial preferences include electronics, trading, transportation, electrical goods, construction and hotels. The financial crises of 1998 placed a temporary hold on such investments.

Portfolio Investment

Portfolio investment (in public sector and other bonds and corporate stock) also tended to grow very rapidly from the 1970s, as the world's capital markets became more integrated. Although it is difficult to obtain completely reliable figures, it appears that FPEI rose from around $10 billion in the early 1970s to exceed $150 billion by 1986. The growth of capital markets in emerging countries, especially in East Asia and East Europe, and the increasing globalisation of such markets, led to a sharp rise in the flows of FPEI to these areas from around $1 billion dollars in 1988 to $45 billion in 1993. However, a financial crisis in Mexico near the end of 1994 led to sharp reductions in the annual flows of this type of capital and, although a recovery occurred in 1996, the crises in Asian share markets towards the end of 1997 and in most world markets in 1998 affected this type of foreign investment dramatically.

Japan emerged as a major portfolio investor in the late 1980s and in some years accounted for well over 50 per cent of the total. Japan, Germany, France and the Netherlands were the principal portfolio investors in 1995, while Germany, Japan, Italy and Canada were the main recipients, but the available information is fraught with great volatility over time. In the emerging markets, Europe and Central Asia, Latin America and, to an important extent, East Asia, appear to have been the major recipient areas. Singapore and Hong Kong also became important portfolio investors.

Another form of portfolio investment, commercial bank lending to foreign national governments and private firms, has also become important since the late 1970s. At first the expansion of international bank lending occurred when the terms of trade of the borrowing countries and their currency reserves were falling while real interest rates were rising, and debt servicing became a major problem. Some large debtor countries — such as Mexico, Brazil and Argentina — experienced severe financial difficulties which persisted during the rest of the 1980s and, for some, into the 1990s, despite rescheduling and other forms of aid introduced after 1982. In the 1990s, bank lending to both national governments and to private firms abroad was facilitated by the greater freedom of capital movements. Despite large annual changes in the banks' long-term lending in the early 1990s, recording –$300 million (net inflow) in 1993, the net aggregate rose rapidly to reach $34 billion in 1996. Sixty per cent of all bank loans to developing countries went to private companies, large amounts went to Chile, China, Indonesia, Malaysia, South Africa, Thailand and Turkey. The financial problems of East Asia in 1997 were partly attributable to some of these loans. Commercial bank loans to the governments of developing countries are used mainly for large-scale infrastructure projects, especially power.

In the 1980s and 1990s, there were other innovations in international capital markets, including derivatives. While the expansion of forward exchange facilities largely fulfilled the desire for risk avoidance in a system of floating exchange rates, other changes emerged which helped to free up the world capital markets. The growth of derivatives (instruments whose values depend on the values of other financial assets) — for example, currency or interest rate futures, call and put options and swaps on stock exchange indexes, interest rates and currencies — was so rapid that they quickly became central to the operation of financial markets, for they acted as instruments for hedging risky investments and for speculative activity. Derivatives fall into one of two classes, 'exchange-traded' (bought and sold on a market, the price determined by market pressures) or 'over-the-counter' contracts between two parties (prices determined by negotiation between the parties involved). The rapid growth of derivatives transmitted disturbances across markets and institutions. By the end of 1996, the notional amounts of exchange-traded instruments (futures and options) outstanding totalled $9,885 billion, of which interest rate futures ($5,900 billion) and interest rate options ($3,300 billion) were the most popular. Over-the-counter instruments amounted to $24,292 billion and interest rate swaps accounted for over half of this amount. International capital markets thus widened considerably during the 1990s, became more complex and less regulated, and until the end of the millennium, the resulting 'financialization' was mostly greeted with enthusiasm by professionals as well as laymen.

INTERNATIONAL CAPITAL FLOWS: FOREIGN AID AND OTHER RESOURCE FLOWS TO DEVELOPING COUNTRIES

While private capital flows to developing countries rose rapidly during the 1990s, official aid flows tended to stagnate. Generally speaking, the net flow of resources to the developing countries includes the net flow of direct and portfolio investment (outlined above), foreign aid and other resource flows which include bank loans to national governments. Strictly speaking, foreign aid refers to grants or gifts of money or goods from one country to another for development purposes or for alleviating economic crises, such as famine, flood or drought relief. However, it is conventional to broaden the definition to include long-term development loans offered to one country by another as well as aid provided for military purposes. Foreign aid, thus defined, is provided by individual countries, by regional organisations consisting of a number of countries such as the EU and by international institutions such as the World Bank and its affiliates. Voluntary private aid, collected by private organisations within a country, is another source of assistance provided for the poorer countries.

From 1945 to 1960, around $26 billion was granted as Official Development Assistance (ODA) to the poor countries by the Development Assistance Committee (DAC) countries, the

US donating $16 billion of this amount. The centrally planned economies (CPEs) advanced over $6.5 billion. Some $14 billion of all this aid went to Asia, mainly India. In the 1960s the net foreign aid contribution in the form of ODA from the DAC countries was $61 billion, and other 'official flows' totalled $5 billion. The CPEs provided over $8 billion, of which the USSR granted $3.8 billion. A feature of foreign aid in this decade was the recognition of the debt-servicing problem encountered by such high-debt countries as India, and the need for more concessional terms in bilateral loans.

The foreign aid (ODA) from DAC countries in the 1970s, amounting to $150 billion, was thus provided on more favourable terms than previously. At the same time, over $40 billion flowed from members of the Organisation of Petroleum Exporting Countries (OPEC) to the non-oil-exporting developing countries, and Eastern Europe offered in excess of $10 billion. It was during the 1970s that private flows to developing countries began to grow rapidly. FDI rose from $3.7 billion a year in 1970 to over $10 billion in 1980, while portfolio flows, including bank loans, rose from below $700 million to over $17 billion between these years. As a result of all these aid flows to the developing countries, their total net external debt reached $650 billion in 1980. In that year, the ODA of DAC countries represented only 36 per cent of the total resource flow, while private investment accounted for 54 per cent. Despite a United Nations target of 0.7 per cent of GNP for each donor country's ODA to be achieved by 1975, few DAC members reached this goal, even by the end of the 1980s, the average for the group remaining persistently below 0.4 per cent. In addition, high inflation rates reduced the real value of the annual fund flows to the recipient countries.

From 1981 to 1990, the ODA from DAC countries amounted to some $434 billion but, in real terms, because of high inflation rates the average annual increase was very small. During the 1980s, much attention was also paid to the high interest rates and, at times, the increasing value of the US dollar, both of which accentuated the debt-servicing problems of the recipient countries. The high and rising external debts of some of these countries reached crisis levels. Mexico, for example, recorded a severe debt crisis in 1982. Even when inflationary pressures abated in the donor countries in the late 1980s and interest rates were somewhat lower, the debt problems remained. At the same time, despite the high cost of borrowing, the total external debt of the developing countries rose from $650 billion in 1980 to $1,500 billion in 1990. Countries such as Mexico, Brazil, Argentina and those in sub-Saharan Africa were the most severely affected by this problem. Several measures, including debt rescheduling and debt cancelling, reduced the heavy debt burden for some recipient countries.

During the 1980s, private financial flows to the developing world, especially commercial bank loans, increased considerably. This type of development financing arose from the decline of exchange controls and the evolution of international banking. Initially, it was based on sound banking practices assisted by the presence of a number of credit-worthy developing countries. The debt of these countries to the banks in the industrial countries rose from around $17 billion in 1973 to $392 billion in 1989. Largely, the growth of this form of debt arose out of the inadequacy of ODA to meet all the investment requirements of the most successful developing countries, but the debt problems noted above applied to these loans also. In addition to FDI and bank loans, portfolio investment in equities was also growing during this decade.

The foreign debt of the CPEs increased from $5.2 billion in 1971 to peak at $72.6 billion in 1982. When, at the end of the decade, central planning in these countries gave way to a transition to market economies, their aggregate cumulative debt was over $260 billion and, by 1996, had expanded even further to $450 billion, as finance was required to fund the transition. Foreign aid from these countries in this decade has been negligible.

During the first half of the 1990s, ODA from DAC countries reached almost $40 billion. Of this amount, just over 70 per cent was provided by EU members. During these years, there were several major changes in the nature of the financial resource flows from the donors to the recipient countries. ODA peaked in aggregate in 1991 and its relative share fell from 55 per cent of the total resource flows in 1990 to 14 per cent by mid-decade — such a decline representing an even greater fall in real terms. In addition, the traditional role of ODA, the financing of long-term development and faster poverty reduction, gave way substantially to the funding of emergency relief and so-called 'peacekeeping' activities, and in supporting the reforms of the transition economies of Eastern Europe and the former USSR. On the other hand, for the heavily indebted poor countries (HIPCs), a debt initiative was introduced to help some of them overcome their debt problems. While sub-Saharan Africa has absorbed up to 40 per cent of this concessional aid, Europe and Central Asia (the transitional economies) increased their share from $166 million in 1989 to around $9 billion in 1996. Nevertheless, donor countries expressed only a modest interest in granting non-concessional aid to these countries in the early years of their transition.

Altogether, total private capital resource flows to the developing countries rose annually from $44 billion in 1990 to $243.8 billion in 1996. The innovations of the 1980s were continued and enlarged in the 1990s and private commercial resources, such as bank loans, replaced much of the ODA of the DAC countries, which had previously been considered crucial to the development of the poor countries. The globalisation movement, however, tended to 'privatize' these official ventures.

Regional arrangements for promoting aid to the developing countries began in 1958, when the EC set up its European Development Fund (EDF) to assist the development of its 'associated territories', mostly the former French, Belgian and Italian colonies in Africa. Under the Lomé Convention in 1975, the EDF covered all former EC members' colonies in Africa, the Caribbean and the Pacific regions (the ACP countries). In 1961, the Organisation of American States created the Inter-American Development Bank (IDB) to help finance development projects, especially of a social overhead nature, within the Americas. The total cumulative lending by the IDB, to 1995, was $40.5 billion, net of cancellations and exchange adjustments. The Asian Development Bank began to operate in 1968 and, to 1995, had advanced $32.3 billion for over 1,000 projects in over 30 countries. The African Development Bank was established in 1963 and the African Development Fund in 1973. The total loans and grants of these two institutions to the end of 1995 was $17.2 billion. These regional development institutions gave priority in their loans to agriculture and agro-industry, public utilities, transportation and energy, in the form mainly of technical assistance.

Multilateral financial assistance was initially channelled through the World Bank, which began operations in 1946. To 1960 it had approved 260 development loans worth a net $5 billion. Its lending rose rapidly after 1960, averaging $1 billion per year by 1970. Further acceleration then occurred as inflation became a major problem in all recipient countries. By 1981, the Bank had lent $68 billion, of which 32 per cent had gone to Latin America, 28 per cent to Europe and the Mediterranean countries and 23 per cent to Asia and the Pacific. Asia's share began to rise in the 1980s at the expense of that of Europe and the Mediterranean countries. By the 1990s, however, the opening up of the world's capital markets gave the recipient countries of World Bank loans another source of funds and, from 1991 to 1995, the Bank recorded a relatively small decrease in its net disbursements due to repayments exceeding loans. From 1988 to 1995 the cumulated assistance provided by the Bank rose from $155 billion to $164 billion, all the increase being non-concessional flows. The main sectors attracting World Bank loans by the 1990s were economic infrastructure (over 60 per cent) and social and administrative infrastructure. Apart from financial aid, the Bank also offers technical assistance on a growing scale to an increasing number of developing countries.

The International Development Association (IDA) was established as an affiliate of the World Bank in 1962 to provide developing countries with access to 'softer' loans than those offered by the World Bank. Such loans carry a long period of grace (ten years) and a long maturity of 50 years. Recipients pay a service charge on loans of 0.75 per cent. In 1995, when the cumulated total of IDA concessional flows had reached $79 billion, $31.3 billion had been granted after 1987. Sub-Saharan Africa absorbed around 40 per cent of IDA loans, while the Middle East, North Africa and Southern Europe took over 20 per cent. It was aimed at improving social, administrative and economic infrastructure, agriculture and programme assistance. Because the IDA concentrated its lending on the poorer developing countries, its existence allowed the World Bank to extend its relatively 'harder' loans mainly to the not-so-poor developing countries. The International Finance Corporation (IFC) is another affiliate of the World Bank that was created to promote and encourage the growth of private enterprise in member countries by making loans to private firms. While its limited financial resources have prevented the IFC from having any significant economic impact on developing countries, it encourages outside private investors to participate in its investments, thereby often stimulating private investment flows into many projects in developing countries. In the 1990s it advanced an average $1 billion per year in non-concessional loans to developing countries.

The United Nations, through its numerous agencies, has initiated considerable flows of concessional funds to the developing world. These flows averaged around $5.6 billion per year between 1990 and 1995. Altogether, between 1991 and 1995, a net disbursement of $70 billion of concessional aid and $36 billion of non-concessional aid flowed from multilateral organisations.

In the changing world of the 1990s, foreign aid, itself, came under scrutiny. Some commentators argued that it was wasteful in the hands of the recipients and that alternative sources existed for countries to borrow to satisfy their development needs. A further argument was that, if aid was still to be disbursed, it should be given only if it is used properly. Even IDA loans, which are offered only to the least developed, poorer countries, should be granted only to those that are already reforming their economies. On the other hand, it is noted that bilateral aid is not always altruistic; much of it is tied to the donor countries and therefore indirectly aids the donor's exporters. Moreover, during the Cold War, aid to countries at the periphery was also provided with the intention to ensure political and geostrategic support, and some of the poorer countries found themselves in a situation where they could sell their support to the highest bidder. The collapse of the USSR and the Soviet bloc along with it put an end to this.

TECHNICAL CHANGE AND WORLD TRADE

Let us now consider in which ways technical change influenced the post-war pattern of world trade. Partly because of the backlog of promising, unused innovations built up during the 1930s, and partly because of the research stimulated during the Second World War, which had considerable peacetime significance, technical progress was very rapid after the war. In later years, innovative capacity was sustained at a high level by a large increase in the funds, both public and private, devoted to research and development (R&D). According to the United Nations Conference on Trade and Development's (UNCTAD) statistics, in the US, the amount spent on R&D rose from 1 per cent of GDP in 1950 to 2.8 per cent in 1960 and, in the USSR, during the same period, it grew from 1.2 to 2.5 per cent. This trend was repeated in most other advanced countries. By 1993, the US still spent 2.8 per cent of GDP on R&D, while Germany (2.5 per cent), France (2.4 per cent), the UK (2.15 per cent) and South Korea (2.1 per cent) were other major investors. Thus, billions of dollars were spent annually, and by the year 2000 at least 5.8 million full-time-equivalent personnel were employed in R&D.

This innovative activity created an ever-growing range of new raw materials, productive processes, energy resources and production and consumption goods. The period witnessed the introduction of the transistor, the micro-chip and the various products in which it was used, such as compact disc players, video recorders and mobile telephones. Other examples include plastics, synthetic resins, man-made fibres, including oil-based synthetics, new metals and metal products of aluminium and alloy steels, and whole ranges of antibiotics and other life-saving drugs. New production processes were installed in most industries and prefabrication became a common method of production. Nuclear energy production was introduced in several countries, while the possibilities of solar and wind power were also explored. Many types of electronic devices, including television and radar equipment, which are the basis of automation and cybernetic methods, were more widely adopted. The list is far from complete, but it is long enough to show the nature of the far-reaching technical changes that occurred after 1945.

While technical progress in the production of goods provided increased opportunities for trade, transport improvements continued to assist the international movement of commodities and people. Railway construction remained an important form of transport investment in many poorer countries after 1945, but in the highly industrialised nations, the relative importance of the railway declined in the face of rising road transport. The growing use of motor transport and of the aeroplane enormously increased the consumption of petroleum and other oil products, and this was reflected at sea by the rapid enlargement of oil-tanker capacity. Importantly, from the late 1950s, containerisation became a major means of speeding up the handling and transportation of goods.

Increasingly, after 1945, air transport of people and goods by domestic and international airlines made substantial inroads on land and sea transport. Air travel made possible the rapid extension of the international company by providing the necessary face-to-face communication needed to administer complex affairs with appropriate speed and reasonable cost. Later, domestic and international communications have been improved by satellite transmission, improved telephony, facsimile (fax) and electronic mail (email), with the internet further encouraging the speed of international exchange and contributing to the vast increase in information that has altered the very nature of many productive and household activities.

In terms of the flow of technology resulting from the build-up of FDI and other means of transfer, technical diffusion occurred at an accelerating rate. The international flows of royalties and other technologically related flows give some idea of the size and direction of technical diffusion and of the success of such ventures. UNCTAD's breakdown of the receipts and payments of the income flows of the five major investing countries shows that the US dominated in the receipts of royalties and licence fees, its share being over 50 per cent, that a major proportion of these income flows occurred within a small group of countries — the US, the UK, Japan, Germany, France and the Netherlands — and that while there were only small technology flows to the developing countries, some of them, including Mexico, Brazil, China and India, were important recipients of industrial know-how.

Trade among the rich countries was stimulated not only because it provided a channel for the diffusion of the fruits of technical progress between the industrial countries, but also because manufactured products became more sophisticated and consumer tastes varied with respect to the different brands of products being produced in different countries. Thus, for instance, Asian cars are sold in Europe, and European cars are sold in Asia. In some respects, developing countries lost out from the advances made in synthetic products and the economies made in the use of natural materials, for instance through electrolytic tin-plating and the systematic recovery and reprocessing of metals. The demand for such staple exports as crude rubber, wool, silk, indigo, nitrates, jute, hemp, vegetable oils and hides and skins declined during the period — in most cases as the outcome of the technical advances made in the chemicals industry — and, as a result, many developing countries lost valuable export markets while, at the same time, rich countries gained new export industries. But this trend was not all in one direction for, through FDI, licensing, joint ventures and other means, a number of developing countries, especially in East Asia, became the major producers of many of the new products because of the cheapness of their factors of production, and thus provided reverse trade flows of these technical products back to the rich countries. Indeed, their development strategy revolved around such production and trade.

CONCLUDING REMARKS

In the second half of the twentieth century, international economic relations became more complex, more extensive and much closer than in any previous period. The world became divided into three general areas, the advanced industrial nations, the developing countries and the centrally planned (later: transitional) economies. International cooperation produced large flows of resources, commodities, ideas and technology from country to country and from continent to continent. During the period up to 1973, many countries experienced a long period of unparalleled economic growth. For various reasons, especially the persistence of severe inflationary pressures, the next decade was fraught with economic difficulties, which did not completely disappear despite all attempts to deal with them. Lower levels of inflation in the industrial countries were achieved in the second half of the 1980s, but low growth and high unemployment remained major economic and social problems, persisting in many countries up to the end of the 1990s. Given the increasing degree of globalisation and along with it the increasing economic interdependence since the 1950s, most countries were adversely affected by the downturn in the industrial world in 1974 and the relatively poor economic performances generally prevailing thereafter. Within the developing countries, however, the NICs, particularly those of East Asia, were able to achieve high rates of economic growth during the last few decades despite the quantitative restrictions placed on many of their manufactured exports by the industrially advanced countries. Much of their production was the result of the adoption of technology from the richer countries.

It was also after 1973 that the debt problems of many developing countries increased in intensity and, although the many efforts to curtail the growth of external debt yielded some success, at the end of the millennium severe debt problems persisted in several countries because of the 'Asian crisis' of 1997–8 and the turmoil in world commodity and financial markets in 1998.

RECOMMENDATIONS FOR FURTHER READING

The backbone of economic and monetary policy in up to the economic crises of the 1970s was the observed trade-off between unemployment and inflation. The seminal paper on what was coming to be known as this 'Phillips curve' is Phillips (1958, *The Relationship between Unemployment and the Rate of Change of Money Wages in the United Kingdom, 1861–1957*).

A seminal paper on the catching up of poorer countries, the underlying reasons and the difficulties is Abramovitz (1986, *Catching Up, Forging Ahead, and Falling Behind*).

For a detailed study of the emergence and the destructive role of 'tax havens' in the world economy, see Shaxson (2011, *Treasure Islands. Tax Havens and the Men Who Stole the World*).

NOTES

1 The OECD is an institution created out of the OEEC in 1960 and initially mainly comprised the major advanced countries of Western Europe, North America, Japan and Oceania. Its self-declared goal is to advance economic cooperation among its members in such a way as to improve the economic performance of the world economy. In 2024 it comprised 38 members, including recent entrants (since 1995) Chile, Columbia, Costa Rica, the Czech Republic, Estonia, Hungary, Israel, South Korea, Latvia, Lithuania, Poland, Slovakia and Slovenia. Lately, it has gained some prominence as a platform to combat international tax havens.

2 However, this process, attractive as it appeared while it lasted, eventually proved unsustainable in the Great Recession, which started with a financial crisis in 2007 and with far-reaching consequences that still linger; for an elaboration see Chapter 22.

3 A telling example is the fierce resistance of the tobacco industry against the plain cigarette packaging standard introduced in Australia in 2012. As cigarettes are an almost perfect example of an identical product whose perceived uniqueness rests on branding, plain packaging most effectively undermines the industry's marketing strategy. Of course, the goal of the legislator is not only to annihilate the nimbus of the cigarette brands but along with it the public's unhealthy desire to consume these products at all.

4 The CPEs, or 'socialist' countries, included the USSR, Poland, Hungary, Bulgaria, Czechoslovakia, the German Democratic Republic, Romania, Yugoslavia, Mongolia, China, North Vietnam, North Korea, Cambodia, Albania and Cuba. Many of these countries were grouped under the Council for Mutual Economic Assistance (CMEA or COMECON).

5 On 6 October 1973, the Arabian camp, headed by Egypt and Syria, attacked Israel in what was later called the 'Yom Kippur' war, referring to this day in the Jewish calendar. When it became clear that the threat to Israel's existence had failed, the Organization of Arab Petroleum Exporting Countries or the OAPEC (consisting of the Arab members of OPEC, plus Egypt, Syria and Tunisia) proclaimed an oil embargo on the US in particular and on Israel's supporters in general. The resulting cartel effectively quadrupled oil prices and sent the oil-addicted economies of the capitalist West into recession.

6 Pre-monetarist economic policy had (explicitly or implicitly) been based on the assumption of a trade-off between inflation and unemployment. Phillips (1958) had pointed to an empirical observation that lower unemployment was related to higher wage increases and vice versa. From this, the so-called Phillips curve was derived, suggesting a policy trade-off to secure low unemployment in return for inflation. This interpretation was challenged in the 1970s based on the argument that higher inflation would only lead to lower real wages if the workers were subject to money illusion. Without this, the 'classical dichotomy' is restored, where money in the long run affects nominal aggregates only, and the Phillips curve is vertical. Interestingly, while this neoclassical view quickly became dominant in academic circles, even the most orthodox central banks up to this date rely on an upward-sloped Phillips curve for inflation targeting: a positive output gap is associated with higher than tolerable inflation *and* higher than desired employment, so that monetary policy needs to slow down GDP growth (and along with it employment) to steer the economy back into the monetary authority's comfort zone (and vice versa). Thus, while a link between monetary policy and unemployment is solemnly denied, it is in fact taken for granted for the time horizon subject to monetary policy.

7 The second oil crisis also originated in the Middle East, but unlike the first, it was not designed to penalise the West for its support to Israel, but resulted from the uncertainty due to internal conflicts in the region: the overthrow of the Shah regime in 1979 and the establishment of an Islamic regime in Iran with a temporary suspension of Iran's oil exports, and the First Persian Gulf War between Iran and Iraq (1980–8) that followed.

8 At that time, the newly industrialising countries (NICs) included: Hong Kong, India, Indonesia, Israel, Korea, Singapore, Taiwan, Argentina, Brazil, Mexico and in Europe Greece, Portugal and Spain.

9 The mainstream economic policy recommendations of that time are now commonly known as the 'Washington Consensus'; for a more detailed discussion see Chapter 22.

10 See Chapter 20 for a fuller discussion of these points.

11 For a more detailed discussion of the EMU, see Chapters 22 and 23.

12 The CITs included the CEECs (Albania, Belarus, Bosnia and Herzegovina, Bulgaria, Croatia, Czech Republic, Estonia, Hungary, Latvia, Lithuania, Macedonia, Moldova, Poland, Romania, Slovakia, Slovenia, Ukraine, Yugoslavia, Transcaucasia) and the Central Asian countries (Armenia, Azerbaijan, Georgia, Kazakhstan, Kyrgyz Republic, Mongolia, Tajikistan, Turkmenistan and Uzbekistan). Russia was also classified as a CIT.

13 The terms EEC (European Economic Community), EC (European Communities) and EU (European Union) tend to be used when each one was current.

14 These figures and some other information in this section come from UNCTAD (1997, p. 3). UNCTAD has calculated that the stock of FDI, which had reached $1,000 billion in 1987, doubled by 1993 and reached $3,200 billion in 1996.

CHAPTER **18**

International Monetary Relations, 1945–2000

A. G. Kenwood, A. L. Lougheed and Michael Graff

At Bretton Woods it had been expected that post-war reconstruction and the restoration of normal trading and commercial relations between countries would be largely attained by 1952. In fact, it was not until the late 1950s that most of the industrial countries were willing to consider the adoption of currency convertibility, a necessary step for the International Monetary Fund (IMF) system to function smoothly.

THE IMF: 1947–61

The IMF began its operations on 1 March 1947, by which date members had submitted the initial par values of their currencies and had paid their subscriptions into the IMF. Thereafter, despite the pervasiveness of inflationary pressures and other problems of post-war reconstruction, including a worldwide shortage of US dollars, the IMF's currency transactions up to 1952 did not exceed $850 million. The IMF's limited role in international economic affairs during these years came about because of the continuing use of exchange controls, the exclusion of Marshall Aid recipient countries from IMF drawings, the 1949 devaluations and the need for countries to implement suitable monetary and fiscal policies to contain inflation before IMF aid became available. Yet the IMF endeavoured with moderate success to recreate a multilateral system of trade and payments by attempting to reduce the use of exchange restrictions, quantitative import controls and multiple exchange rate practices.

Multilateralism, however, could be fully realised only when current account convertibility was widely adopted, and this could not occur until IMF members had amassed adequate reserves of convertible currencies with which to conduct their international monetary transactions and establish realistic exchange rates. Only the US dollar was available as a major convertible currency at the time. The first move to this end, the widespread currency devaluations of September 1949, was aborted in the following year by the resumption of inflationary pressures in most devaluing countries following the outbreak of the Korean War. Moreover,

DOI: 10.4324/9781003382171-23

economic recovery had only just begun to restore industrial production in Europe, and the basis for expanding trade relations had still to be laid. By 1952, therefore, the transition to a stable world economic environment was still not completed, and the IMF's position in international monetary affairs had still to be asserted.

In the 1950s, despite the continued shortage of the dollar, world trade expanded rapidly and the payments situation improved for many of the nondollar countries, especially those in Western Europe and the developed primary producers. The European payments improvement resulted not so much from an increased demand for European products as from the increasing worldwide competitiveness of the European export industries as they regained their pre-war position as major exporters.

The year 1958 marked a turning point in international monetary relations, when the US recorded its first annual payments deficit of the post-war years, and a massive outflow of gold and dollars to the rest of the world occurred. This deficit resulted from a deteriorating trade balance, an expansion of foreign investment and a continuing high level of US government outlays abroad. It was this large outflow which facilitated the concerted move towards greater currency convertibility. In December 1958, 14 European and 15 other countries announced their adoption of non-resident convertibility, which meant that, in future, the exchange regulations of these countries would allow foreigners, but not residents, to shift funds for current account purposes freely from one country to another. Further improvements in international monetary conditions led, on 15 February 1961, to the adoption of the IMF's current account convertibility requirements (currencies to be convertible into others on demand for current account purposes) by ten member countries, namely, Belgium, France, West Germany, Ireland, Italy, Luxembourg, Netherlands, Peru, Sweden and the UK.

The IMF began to assume a more positive role in international monetary affairs in 1956, when it granted the first large drawing of $562 million, to the UK, to ease payments problems stemming from the Suez crisis of that year. In 1958, the first review of quotas occurred, and a 50 per cent increase was agreed on, with larger increases for Canada, West Germany and Japan. The IMF's financial resources rose by $5.1 billion to $14.5 billion. Thus, when the post-war transitional period eventually ended in 1961, the IMF, with larger resources and greater prestige, was in a position to start operating as had been intended at Bretton Woods.

REGIONAL PAYMENTS ARRANGEMENTS

One reason for the failure of the IMF to play a leading role in international monetary affairs before 1956 was that many European countries resorted to regional devices for overcoming their payments problems. One such arrangement was the European Payments Union (EPU), which arose out of the need for greater flexibility in intra-European payments if Marshall Aid was to work effectively. This scheme incorporated automatic clearing of all payments deficits regardless of size, the automatic settlement of reciprocal deficits and machinery for correcting intra-European payments disequilibria. The Bank for International Settlements (BIS) acted as the agent of the member countries. The IMF opposed the formation and existence of the EPU, chiefly because it provided a rival mechanism for settling balance of payments difficulties. The EPU became redundant in 1958 when most of its members accepted non-resident convertibility.

Another regional payments arrangement in existence during these years was the sterling area, which had contracted sharply with the outbreak of the Second World War to include the British Commonwealth (other than Canada), the Colonial Territories, Ireland, Egypt, Sudan, Iceland and Iraq. The need to conserve gold and dollars for war purposes had led, in 1939, to the introduction of exchange controls which remained in force until the late 1950s. The principle underlying the system was simple. All gold and foreign currency earned was directed into a single pool, the Exchange Equalisation Account, and all external payments from the area were made from that pool. Within the area itself, there was free movement of currencies, whereas payments into or out of the bloc were subject to regulation. The relevance of the sterling area disappeared in 1961 when the UK adopted IMF convertibility.

An Overview of the 1950s

The long period of currency inconvertibility to 1961 not only prevented the efficient working of the IMF, which depended on the widespread convertibility of member countries' currencies, but it also produced a situation which ensured the Bretton Woods system would never be implemented in the form originally proposed. To begin with, the economic rivalry between the US and Western Europe, a major factor in the eventual breakdown of the Bretton Woods international monetary design, began to appear early in the 1950s. Since the IMF was regarded as largely US dominated and because the IMF refused to play an active role in solving the immense monetary problems being experienced in Europe at the time, the West European countries created a purely European substitute — the EPU. This shift in the direction of institutionalisation of a supranational European economy was carried further in 1957 with the formation of the European Economic Community. Second, the IMF architects had not foreseen the large increase in world trade and commerce, which began in the mid-1950s, and the inadequacy of existing gold stocks and gold production to cope with the large increase in the demand for foreign currency reserves that accompanied it. As a result, most countries turned to 'key' currencies to perform the major role in the accumulation of reserve assets. The US stipulation that only dollars (or gold) would be accepted in payments settlements and the US payments surpluses in the 1950s produced a large increase in the demand for the dollar as a reserve asset, a development which bypassed the IMF system. In short, in the 1950s, the international monetary system moved towards a gold exchange standard similar to that of the 1920s, which had collapsed at the end of that decade. The emphasis was on virtually rigid exchange rates and on the accumulation and use of key international currencies as reserves. Even before the acceptance of non-resident convertibility in 1958, the dangers inherent in such trends were being stressed by international monetary experts but, as we shall see later, these dangers were largely ignored. The major role of the IMF under the new gold exchange standard was the provision of short-term liquidity through its drawings mechanism to those countries experiencing balance of payments problems and a consequent rundown of their gold and key currency reserves.

THE IMF IN THE 1960s

Innovations in the IMF

IMF quotas were increased further in 1965 and again in 1970, raising the institution's resources to over $29 billion by the end of 1973. Throughout this period a much greater use was made of the IMF than previously, and between 1960 and 1973, total drawings amounted to $23 billion.

Several other changes in the IMF's financing arrangements occurred during this period. The shortage of dollars in its stocks in the 1950s led to the sale of gold by the IMF to relieve this shortage. By 1960, dollars to the value of $606 million had been obtained in this way. During the 1960s, the IMF's holdings of several European currencies was also threatened with depletion and, from 1961 to 1973, further sales of gold to the value of $3.3 billion were to obtain additional stocks of these currencies. At the same time, the IMF's powers to borrow currencies from member countries were formalised in 1962 by the establishment of the General Arrangements to Borrow (GAB) which allowed the IMF access to the currencies of ten of the major trading countries (the 'Group of Ten') up to specified limits. The total borrowing power of the IMF under the GAB was $6 billion and, by 1973, the IMF had borrowed $2.65 billion, almost exclusively in continental European currencies. Borrowing from outside the GAB amounted to $500 million.

The First Amendment to the IMF's Articles of Agreement was adopted in 1969 to address the need to increase the availability of reserve assets for member countries. As the world's gold production could not expand enough to meet the growing need for international liquidity induced by a rapidly expanding world trade, member countries could increase their reserve assets only by accumulating key currencies such as the US dollar and the pound sterling. For such accumulations of a particular currency to occur, however, the issuing country had to be willing to run deficits in its own balance of payments. Should the key currency countries refuse to tolerate such deficits and attempt to reduce or eliminate them, the major source of international liquidity might well dry up and jeopardise the continued growth of world trade. It was with this latter prospect in mind that the First Amendment was adopted to introduce into the system the Special Drawing Right (SDR, or 'paper gold', since the value of one SDR was initially equal to one US dollar, which in turn corresponded to 0.888671 grains of gold) as a new international monetary unit of account, held as book entries in the IMF, but available to supplement the international reserve assets of member countries. The new facility became effective on 1 January 1970, when the first allocation of SDRs to members on the basis of quotas was made. By the end of 1973, almost 6.2 billion SDRs had been allocated in this way.

Finally, two other innovations of this period included, first, the introduction of a compensatory and contingency financing facility (CCFF), beginning in 1963 to aid members experiencing a sudden shortfall in their export receipts below the medium-term trend (compensatory) or an anticipated shortfall (contingency). This facility eventually allowed such members to draw up to 100 per cent of their quotas in the year in which the shortfall occurred. From 1963 to 1973, 29 countries obtained access to the CCFF, drawing a total of $870 million. Second, there was the Buffer Stock Financing Facility (BSFF), set up in 1969 to allow a member to draw as much as 50 per cent of quota to aid the financing of an international buffer stock scheme.

The IMF and the International Monetary System

The gold exchange standard, complete with highly inflexible exchange rates which emerged in a complete form during the 1960s, had several implications for the future of the IMF. First, whereas the Bretton Woods agreement allowed for changes in the external value of a country's currency whenever it was apparent that a 'fundamental disequilibrium' existed in the country's balance of payments, the new arrangements implicitly placed currency devaluation in the 'last resort' category. Countries compelled by the seriousness of their payments situation to devalue their currencies (such as the UK in 1967) were virtually accused of gross financial mismanagement. The prevailing prescription for balance of payments adjustment was internal deflation and, if necessary, substantial borrowing to control the outflow of speculative capital.

Second, as the 1960s progressed and the US continued to run substantial payments deficits in support of the demand for increased international liquidity, another problem emerged — that of confidence in the dollar. This problem was compounded by the growing current account surpluses of the industrial countries of Western Europe, as they improved their international competitiveness relative to the US. Through these surpluses, countries such as Germany, France, the Netherlands and Italy increased their foreign exchange assets considerably — from $5 billion in 1960 to $34 billion at the end of 1973. Despite the growing shortages of the currencies of these countries in the IMF, the use of the scarce currency clause was never considered by the IMF. Rather, it purchased additional quantities of such currencies with gold or borrowed them under the GAB. It was the rivalry between the US and Western Europe which largely created this impasse. The US had assumed the role of provider of reserve assets to the rest of the world and, to do so, ignored its overall payments situation. Western Europe, on the other hand, ignored its own surplus position and was reluctant to consider upward valuation of its currencies. A few upward revaluations (of the deutsche mark and the guilder in 1961 of 5 per cent) did occur, but these were rather isolated events.

Moreover, while the Europeans argued increasingly that adjustment should be made by the US, they were witnessing the growth of the Eurodollar market in the 1960s, which aggravated the instability of the dollar. A Eurodollar is a deposit denominated in US dollars placed in a bank located in another country — for example, in Britain. This market had emerged in the mid-1950s, when some British banks began to accept deposits in foreign currency, mostly American dollars. Importantly, foreign banking supervision and prudency regulations, and the cost associated with them, did not apply in this peculiar market segment. Thus, the rate of interest paid by the bank to depositors of a Eurodollar was higher than that obtainable for such a period in the US, and the rates charged by the bank to borrowers were lower than such borrowers could obtain in their own countries or in the US. The name stuck, but nowadays the Eurodollar market comprises trade in all major currencies. The unifying element is that currencies are traded outside their emitters' jurisdictions ('offshore') and hence not subject to their supervision and regulation. The smaller gap between borrowing and lending rates in offshore banks compared to 'onshore' demonstrates the greater profitability of such operations relative to domestic operations. In addition, the secrecy and complexity involved in such operations make offshore finance attractive for tax evasion and money laundering. Obviously, this is an attractive business model for the parties involved.[1] The drawback is that it increases the riskiness of the global financial system and reduces the tax base. The costs are thus borne by the outsiders, common taxpayers.

The Eurodollar market appeared after the acceptance of non-resident convertibility by the major trading countries in 1958. It was to grow rapidly after the oil price increases in 1973–4, the oil exporters feeding dollars into the market and oil-importing countries becoming major borrowers. In addition, this market became an important source of funds for the major debtor nations of the 1980s. The 'Big Bang' of 1986, the deregulation of financial markets by the Thatcher government, turned the London Eurodollar market into the largest source of funds anywhere. By 1995 it had grown to around $4,000 billion. Other European currencies — such as the deutsche mark, sterling, Swiss franc — and the yen have appeared and have grown in importance since the 1960s and, in 1995, the total was around $2,000 billion.

Another departure from the IMF system was the setting up of the Basle Arrangements and reciprocal swaps. The first was an agreement among European central banks to aid each other when flows of 'hot' (speculative) money produced pressures on their currencies. In several of the British payments crises of the 1960s, the Bank of England was able to maintain the value of sterling by borrowing extensively from continental central banks at the critical moment. Reciprocal swaps involved similar arrangements between Western European central bankers and those of the US and Japan. Tacit cooperation thus prolonged the life of the gold exchange standard. For example, the 'dollar overhang' (an excess of dollars held abroad over the value of the US gold holdings) which developed in the early 1960s, could have forced the US to suspend dollar convertibility if a rush by European central banks to convert their holdings of dollars into gold had developed, thereby ending the IMF system. Agreement among European central bankers not to upset the system in this way ensured its extension during the late 1960s. Second, eight Group of Ten countries formed a 'gold pool' in 1961 with the Bank of England as its agent, to hold the free-market price of gold at around $35 an ounce, the price established in 1934. The Bank would sell gold from the pool when upward market pressures appeared and buy gold if the price tended to fall. The arrangement worked well until the pound was devalued in 1967 when confidence in the key currencies weakened. France's withdrawal from the pool in 1968 led to severe upward pressures on the gold price and, to prevent the gold reserves of the pool from depletion, the Bank of England withdrew from the market, allowing the price of gold to increase. Thereafter, lack of confidence in the international monetary system forced the gold price to rise to a record height of over $900 an ounce in 1978. From 1968, a two-tiered system existed, with the official gold price remaining at $35 an ounce, considerably below the free-market price.

Meanwhile, because of the declining US competitiveness and its continuing heavy private foreign investment, which transferred production abroad and reduced domestic exports, its trade account moved into deficit late in the 1960s. Thus, the US 'deficit' policy in support of international liquidity became untenable. In August 1971, US President Richard Nixon arrived at this conclusion and rendered the dollar inconvertible into gold and, to improve the US balance of trade, placed a 10 per cent surcharge on all imports, a measure justified in the US based on allegedly 'unfair' exchange rates.

Thus ended the gold exchange standard with its problems of liquidity, adjustment (or lack of it) and confidence. For the first time since the invention of coined bullion to serve as money, except for periods of war and revolution, the world's major currencies were off gold. Fiat money had become the rule, and the public, politicians and, last but not least, central bankers were looking for a new anchor to secure price stability. They found it in an updated version of the

Quantity Theory of Money, which served Chicago economist Milton Friedman (1912–2006) to spread his message that economic police should foremost control the quantity of money. To ensure adequate scarcity of money, in the 1970s monetary targets assumed the role that for millennia had been enacted by the intrinsic scarcity of precious metals. Success was quick, but it did not last. Starting in the 1990s, monetary targeting was abandoned by a steadily increasing number of monetary authorities in favour of inflation targeting, and the process was completed in 2003 when it was dismissed by the last important central bank having rhetorically stuck to it, the European Central Bank.[2]

UNCERTAIN YEARS, 1971–6

As noted earlier, this five-year period witnessed an upheaval in the international economy. The commodity boom which ended in 1973, the worldwide high rates of inflation, exacerbated by the huge increase in the price of oil late in 1973, and government endeavours to curb inflationary pressures led to a world recession in 1975. At the same time, the immense flow of financial resources to the oil-exporting countries led to large payments imbalances among the oil-importing countries. By the mid-1970s, a high degree of uncertainty existed in the world economy, and it was against this background that reform of the international monetary system was attempted.

In response to the measures introduced by the US in August 1971, namely, the inconvertibility of the dollar and the 10 per cent import surcharge, the Smithsonian Agreement of December 1971 produced what were to be temporary and marginal changes in the international monetary system. Although it was an agreement concluded within the Group of Ten, the IMF gave its blessing to the changes, which involved a re-alignment of exchange rates, including a 10 per cent devaluation of the dollar against gold and the SDR, and a wider margin for fluctuation of the market value of a currency around the par value (now called the central rate) before the currency had to be supported by the central bank. As for the future, the growing solidarity among the developing country members of the IMF ensured that any substantial reform of the system would be conducted under the control of the IMF, which had much wider representation than the Group of Ten. With the setting up within the IMF of a Committee of Twenty in 1972 to produce proposals for the reform of the system, it would appear at first sight that the IMF had regained a central role in the system, but this was not entirely so. In February 1973, the US dollar was again devalued (by 10 per cent) relative to gold and the SDR in an attempt to improve the US balance of payments which, had again deteriorated badly. In March, the deutsche mark was revalued upward by 3 per cent, but the change was only a prelude to the introduction of the 'European snake', the joint floating of most of the currencies of the European Economic Communinty (EEC) relative to the dollar. This arrangement ensured that fluctuations in the values of these currencies were contained within prescribed limits relative to one another while they floated together relative to the dollar. The snake arrangements formed an integral part of the European Monetary System which came into effect in March 1979 with its European Currency Unit (ECU).

The dismantling of the 'old' system continued in 1973 with the ending of the two-tiered gold policy, when the former gold pool members terminated their agreement not to sell gold in the private markets; with an increase in the size of the reciprocal swaps arrangements within the Group of Ten from $6,250 million to $17,980 million; and with a general movement within the industrial countries towards the 'managed floating' of their currencies — a considerable change from the rigid exchange rates of the immediate past.

In January 1974, the Committee of Twenty abandoned its two-year timetable for international monetary reform, agreeing that the altered conditions in the world economy, such as the oil price crisis and the movement into recession on a wide scale, required priority to be given to monetary arrangements which would solve or at least contain the new problems in the short term. When, in June 1974, the Committee concluded its deliberations, it advocated the setting up of an Interim Committee to continue with 'an evolutionary approach' to international monetary reform, the establishment of guidelines for the management of floating exchange rates, the establishment of a special oil facility within the IMF and the valuation of the SDR on the basis of a standard weight of a basket of 16 currencies. The last was advocated to break the nexus between the SDR and gold (and the dollar). All these recommendations were put into effect in the months that followed. The IMF's oil facility allowed drawings by countries whose balance of payments was severely affected by the need to increase payments for oil imports. Such drawings were financed from funds provided largely by the oil-exporting members.

The creation of the Interim Committee ensured that there was virtually no cessation to the discussion on monetary reform. Early in January 1976, this committee produced the Jamaica Agreement, which was to form the basis of the Second Amendment of the Fund Agreement and was to guide international monetary affairs through the next two decades. While the Jamaica Agreement stressed the need for monetary cooperation, it legalised the floating of the currencies of member countries as well as the right of central banks to interfere in the float. The IMF was to maintain surveillance over the managed floating of currencies and over the international liquidity policies of member countries. A 32.5 per cent general rise in quotas and larger increases in the quotas of oil-exporting countries were to bring the IMF's resources up to SDR39,000 million. The international monetary system was to move in an evolutionary manner towards an SDR system, and gold was to be downgraded as a reserve asset. The IMF was to sell 25 million ounces (one-sixth of its gold holdings) by tender, and profits from these sales were to be used to set up a trust fund to assist poor countries with 1973 per capita incomes of no more than SDR300. The Second Amendment, incorporating these proposals, was effective from April 1978. Even so, another increase in quotas occurred in 1983, raising the total to almost SDR90 billion.

THE POST-JAMAICAN PERIOD, 1976–2000

The high inflation and unemployment of the second half of the 1970s continued into the 1980s, partly because of a second large increase in the price of oil. Serious international debt problems were created for many non-oil-exporting countries, and these were perpetuated throughout the decade.

First, only 51 of the 181 currencies of that time were floating independently, including (in March 1997) those of the US, the UK, Japan, Canada, Australia, Italy, Sweden, Finland, Switzerland, New Zealand, of several poorer countries, and some East European currencies.

The currencies of many other countries were tied to the SDR or leading key currencies, and for them recourse to drawings was still necessary when their capital accounts deteriorated.

Second, increased quotas enlarged the IMF's facilities for granting drawings to countries with payments difficulties.

Third, the total allocation of SDRs rose from 9.315 billion in 1976 to 21.5 billion in 1989 and the use of SDRs increased accordingly. Fourth, since 1976, several other financial facilities have been created in the IMF to enlarge its resources available to developing countries, especially the poorest of them. These included the structural adjustment facility (SAF) with commitments of more than SDR1.7 billion, operational from 1987, and an enhanced structural adjustment facility (ESAF), commenced in 1989 on a renewal basis, which provides resources on concessional terms to support medium-term macroeconomic adjustment and structural reforms in low-income countries with heavy balance of payments problems. These loans drew an interest rate of 0.5 per cent per year only. In addition, a temporary systemic transformation facility (STF) was established in April 1993 to provide financing to members with balance of payments problems associated with their changeover from non-market price setting to market-based pricing. With the collapse of the centrally planned economies (CPEs) at the beginning of the 1990s, the IMF supported the transition of these countries to market-based economies. After their admission to membership, large amounts of funds were made available to them, their use being subject to certain conditions regarding the monetary, fiscal and other policies of the respective governments. The STF was primarily set up for this purpose while general drawings and stand-by credits were also used. Users were expected to switch to a stand-by arrangement of ESAF rapidly. Largely aimed at the countries in transition (CITs), it ceased to operate at the end of 1995. Up to April 1997, these facilities had provided some SDR13 billion (SAF loans, SDR1.8 billion; ESAF SDR7.1 billion; and almost SDR4 billion in STF). The CCFF continues to offer its own special type of aid. 'Conditionality'[3] applies whenever recourse to these facilities is requested. Furthermore, in December 1997, the IMF introduced a supplemental reserve facility (SRF) to provide financial assistance to a member experiencing substantial payments difficulties owing to a large short-run financing need brought about by a sudden and disruptive loss of market confidence displayed by pressure on the capital account and the member's reserves. South Korea was the first country to be offered aid under the SRF, early in 1998.

Fifth, through the profits from its gold sales ($4.6 billion), the IMF was able to set up a Trust IMF of SDR3,000 million, out of which it could make loans to the poorest of the developing countries. Finally, to upgrade the prestige of the SDR to the position of major reserve asset, several abortive attempts were made to establish a substitution account by means of which key currencies held as official reserve assets could be exchanged for SDRs.

In the 1980s, the IMF adopted a positive role in attempts to alleviate the large debt problems of several poorer countries. In the 1990s, its support helped to overcome the enormous economic problems faced by East European countries in their transition to market-based economic systems. Finally, in 1997, the IMF was called upon to assist Thailand, Indonesia, Malaysia, the Philippines and Korea in dealing with the sudden collapse of their economies.

It was against this background that the IMF quotas were raised by 45 per cent in 1998, the total reaching SDR212 billion ($288 billion). Moreover, by the mid-1990s, the IMF's powers to borrow from member countries increased substantially. The GAB amounted to

SDR17 billion from the 11 members (the Group of Ten and Switzerland, which joined the GAB in 1982, after having had a loose arrangement with the IMF since 1962) and SDR1.5 billion under an associated agreement with Saudi Arabia. From the commencement of the GAB in 1962 up to 1997, the IMF took advantage of the arrangements to borrow nine times. Early in 1997, new borrowing arrangements were approved to enhance the IMF's ability to safeguard the international monetary system. These were included in the NAB (New Arrangements to Borrow), under which 25 members and institutions can lend to the IMF additional resources up to SDR34 billion ($47 billion), to supplement its regular quota drawing rights to deal with unusual pressures in the international monetary system.[4] The NAB did not replace the GAB but became the facility of first recourse and remains in force initially for five years. Activation of the NAB is more flexible than that of the GAB. The massive IMF financial relief for countries such as Korea, Malaysia, Thailand, the Philippines and Indonesia was possible later in 1997 only through the existence of the increased quotas and other facilities, including the IMF's borrowing rights.

Meanwhile, in the EU there was a steady move towards full monetary integration. The role of sterling as a key currency had been ended in 1977, when the Bank of England arranged a Basle agreement with the central banks of eight industrial countries to ensure this. Whereas Britain had floated the pound sterling separately after 1973, the ECU also floated against the dollar, but the members of the European Monetary System (EMS) had to adhere to an adjustable peg relative to the ECU. This EMS began in 1979 and covered the currencies of Belgium, Denmark, France, Germany, Ireland, Italy and the Netherlands. It had some success in its aims to achieve the downward convergence of the inflation rates of member countries and to insulate the exchange rates of member currencies against the fluctuations among themselves, though not against the dollar. Nevertheless, from March 1979 to September 1992, there were 11 currency re-alignments within the EMS, with several temporary withdrawals of currencies from the system, followed by a foreign exchange market crisis which lasted from September 1992 to August 1993, when each currency was allowed to fluctuate in the market to a greater extent.

The Maastricht Treaty of December 1991 was a plan for the full monetary integration of the EU, including the introduction of a European currency (later to be named 'euro') to replace the numerous national currencies and central banks of the member countries. The European Monetary Institute (EMI) was set up in 1994 and converted into the European Central Bank (ECB) in mid-1998. At the beginning of 1999, the euro replaced the former national currencies of Austria, Belgium, Finland, France, Germany, Ireland, Italy, Luxembourg, the Netherlands, Portugal and Spain, based on the 31 December notation via the ECU, the currency basket that had been established in 1979 and had since then served as a unit of account only. From then on, the participant's national currencies that continued in circulation were euro in disguise, and on 1 January 2001, the actual cash changeover took place. On this date, Greece, which initially failed to fulfil the strict fiscal convergence criteria, was admitted as the twelfth member state. Denmark, Sweden and the UK would have been allowed to introduce the euro but opted to stay aside.

Because of the floating of several major world currencies, the consequent abundance of international liquidity and the lack of demand for further SDR allocations, the expected SDR standard failed to materialise. In 1996, the IMF accepted that the SDR was unlikely to become the main reserve asset of the international monetary system, nor would it become a fully-fledged world currency. Nevertheless, for several reasons, including a possible need for its use if the world economy got into serious difficulties, it was agreed that it should not be abolished.

Increasingly throughout the 1980s, and widespread during the 1990s, was the adoption of the 'Washington Consensus' economic stabilisation philosophy mentioned earlier in this book. It was adopted by the IMF at the Madrid meeting of the Interim Committee in October 1994 for inclusion in its advice to countries requiring financial aid. Unemployment did not enter the equation because it was argued by orthodox macro-economists and accepted by the IMF that unemployment was largely a structural problem, the solution of which required labour market reforms. A steadfast belief within the IMF in macroeconomic stabilisation (maintaining low levels of inflation) and structural reform influenced the IMF to take a greater interest in the internal affairs of the member countries and to impose its recommendations on those who applied for credits.

In the 1990s some emerging markets experienced major monetary crises, especially Mexico in 1994 and the Association of South Eastern Asian Nations (ASEAN) countries, Hong Kong, Taiwan and Korea in 1997, while Japan's long-term banking problems left much to be desired. With the expansion of the global financial system, weaknesses in it became more apparent. Greater freedom of movement of money from country to country enhanced the activities of speculators willing to shift funds very quickly at the first sign of trouble, thus compounding for the countries concerned whatever economic problems had appeared in them.

The Thai baht had been pegged to the US dollar for about a decade when, in July 1997, it was attacked by speculators, forcing the central bank to abandon fixed exchange rates. The baht soon lost some 60 per cent of its value against the US dollar. The Indonesian rupiah, the Malaysian ringgit, the Philippine peso and the South Korean won also experienced pronounced depreciation versus the US dollar, albeit to a lesser degree than the baht. Notably, the 1997 Asian financial crisis had hit economies that by and large had followed the recommendations of the 'Washington Consensus'. This was 'rewarded' by massive inflows of foreign capital, but when the mood changed, capital flows reversed, and contagion affected the whole region. What made the crises severe was the devaluation of the affected Asian currencies. The affected economies were faced with short-term debt denominated in foreign currency that corresponded to rapidly increasing amounts in domestic currency.[5] Most affected countries plunged into recession in 1998, but recovery followed quickly, and by 1999 the worst was over in this region. Meanwhile, the Russian economy had suffered from lower prices for its raw material exports, and worries increased that the peg of the rouble would not be maintained. In August 1998, panic spread, and resulting capital flight brought about the feared devaluation of the rouble. The wisdom of open capital markets became questionable, and in 1998, Malyasia was the first major economy to re-install strict capital controls.

The opening up of capital markets on an international scale had begun after the adoption of floating exchange rates in the 1970s, thus accelerating the free movement of capital funds into and out of countries. Capital controls were lifted in the US and Germany by 1975, in Britain in 1979, in Japan in 1980 and in the rest of Western Europe by 1990. By 1997 almost all of the advanced countries and 25 per cent of developing countries dispensed with capital controls. Moreover, the booming offshore markets did not know capital controls in the first place; quite to the contrary, one of the reasons for their existence was to circumvent regulation and controls.[6]

These changes brought about capital account convertibility in the balance of payments and thus promoted the further globalisation of financial markets. While such capital movements advanced the process of international economic integration, they also made economies more vulnerable to outside shocks and, along with floating exchange rates, created the need for risk-avoiding instruments.

Floating exchange rates and a globally free capital market undoubtedly intensified international monetary crises by encouraging international currency speculation. The large increase in the volume of portfolio capital in the international monetary system, combined with the rapid growth of derivatives, tended to make the international monetary system more prone to international contagion, and it became increasingly likely that such crises would spread around the globe.

CONCLUDING REMARKS

The first stage in the development of the post-Second World War international monetary system came to an end in the early 1970s. Attempts at reform of the system failed, which is not surprising, given that the shift towards more flexible exchange rates and the continuing use by many countries of the US dollar as an international reserve asset reduced the pressures for far-reaching changes in the international monetary area. Several new problems confronted the system in the final years of the twentieth century. These included the enormous financial problems of the CITs and their need for massive amounts of investment funds and the Asian financial crisis. Both were at least in part products of floating exchange rates and easily obtainable investment funds ('hot money') searching for profitable avenues of investment.

The introduction of the European single currency was an unprecedented and courageous large-scale experiment, and its impact on the participating economies as well as on the international monetary system still remain to be fully evaluated, even if contrary to the beliefs of many sceptics, it has now survived 35 years.

The conditionality approach of the IMF was (and remains) another matter for concern. Based on the 'Washington Consensus', the economic policy measures imposed on borrowers caused major social upheavals in several countries because of the hardship for the poor and the unemployment such a policy engenders. Nevertheless, the IMF was equipped with new and massive sources of funds to maintain its operations for maintaining sound balance of payments positions in its member countries.

Appendix: The Quantity Theory as a Theory of the Demand for Money

Michael Graff

The equation of exchange introduced in Appendix 2 to Chapter 7 can serve to derive a simple money demand function.

$$MV^Y = PY^r \tag{18.1}$$

Let us define $k \equiv 1/V^Y$ and $Y \equiv PY^r$. Equation (18.1) can then be rearranged into the 'Cambridge Equation'

$$M = kY \tag{18.2}$$

$$\Rightarrow$$

$$M^d = f(Y) \tag{18.2a}$$

The Cambridge Equation is seen a money demand function, a behavioural equation where M is interpreted as the demand for money M^d and the 'Cambridge constant' k shows the proportion of real income that individuals want to hold in liquid form. As k is the inverse of V, stability of V^Y in (18.1) implies a stable money demand function (18.2a).[7]

The Monetarist Liquidity Preference Theory

The success of the monetarist liquidity preference theory among economic theorists and practitioners around 1970 reflects the political and economic situation of these days. 'Vulgar Keynesianism', with particular emphasis on deficit spending to combat underemployment, had taken root as orthodoxy, whereas monetary policy, at best, was allowed an auxiliary role. At that time, it became apparent that inflation picked up along with unemployment, which went against the predictions of the theory. Moreover, with the end of the Bretton Woods system, monetary policy suddenly had to take on new functions, so a revised theoretical foundation for monetary policy became the order of the day.

In these circumstances, Friedman's version of Quantity Theory was readily accepted as the appropriate paradigm, leading to new directions in macroeconomics. What made Friedman's version so attractive? It offered clear guidance to monetary policy by directly addressing the main weaknesses of the classical Quantity Theory, namely ignorance of the velocity of money and its determinants. Let us hence look at his seminal work in some detail: Friedman (1956) approached the demand for money like the demand for any good would be analysed in a microeconomics textbook. M^d is hence a function $f(\cdot)$ of

- the price of the relevant good; here the price level P, where a high price level implies a low 'price of money' so that $f'(P) > 0$;
- the prices of substitutive goods; here interpreted as the real return of other financial claims, such as yields from fixed-interest bonds r^b, shares r^e as well as the yield from holding real assets, where $f'(r^b) < 0$ and $f'(r^e) < 0$. The yield from holding real assets rather than financial claims corresponds to the rate of inflation, so that $f'(dP/dt) < 0$;
- the budget constraint; here represented by Friedman's famous *permanent income* Y, where $f'(Y) > 0$;
- the degree of liquidity of an individual's total assets; here Friedman defines w as the ratio of non-human assets to human capital. As human capital is less liquid than non-human assets, it follows that $f'(w) < 0$;
- preferences; here Friedman writes down u, but remains vague, so this should be regarded as a catch-all term to make sure that the money demand function lists all arguments.

Friedman's money demand function hence reads as follows:

$$M^d = f\left(P, r^b, r^e, (dP/dt), Y, w, u\right) \tag{18.3}$$

Now, as monetarism assumes the people are free from money illusion, the nominal demand for money M is linearly homogeneous in nominal variables (here: P and Y), so that

$$M^d / Y = f\left(P/Y, r^b, r^e, (dP/dt), 1, w, u\right) \tag{18.4}$$

$$\Rightarrow$$

$$M^d = f\left(P/Y, r^b, r^e, (dP/dt), 1, w, u\right) Y \tag{18.5}$$

A comparison between equation (18.5) and the Cambridge Equation (18.2) reveals that the function $f(P/Y, r^b, r^e, (dP/dt), 1, w, u)$ is an elaboration of the Cambridge k.

Now, if f can empirically be handled as a stable function of traceable macroeconomic variables, Friedman's *neo-Quantity Theory* can be called upon as the basis for an economic policy that is focused on control of the money supply. Solving (18.4) for Y and referring to the equilibrium condition $M^d = M^s$, we get:

$$Y = M^s / \left[f\left(P/Y, r^b, r^e, (dp/dt), 1, w, u \right) \right] \tag{18.6}$$

With a stable money demand function f and the money supply M^s exogenously set by the monetary authority, nominal output Y can be directly controlled. Hence, from the monetarist point of view, the money supply is, or should be, the central variable of economic policy.

RECOMMENDATIONS FOR FURTHER READING

For studies of the international monetary system and the major events in the period covered in this chapter, refer to MacBean and Snowden (1981, *International Institutions in Trade and Finance*), Williamson (1982, *The Lending Policies of the International Monetary Fund*) and Garritsen de Vries (1986, *Balance of Payments Adjustment, 1945–1986: The IMF Experience*).

The theoretical foundation for the revival of the Quantity Theory in the 1970s is Friedman (1956, *The Quantity Theory of Money: A Restatement*).

IMF conditionality, imposing austerity on loan-seeking countries, is addressed by Gupta et al. (2020, *Revisiting IMF Expenditure Conditionality*), who find its outcomes in general to be beneficial, and Stiglitz (2002, *Globalization and Its Discontents*), Chief Economist of the World Bank from 1997 to 2000, who finds that conditionality often worsened poverty and inequality.

NOTES

1 The City of London's fierce resistance to European tax harmonisation in general, any financial transaction tax in particular and, of course, against an adoption of the euro in the UK in 1999 is very clear from this perspective.
2 For an elaboration of the rationale of monetary targeting, see the Appendix to this chapter.
3 Under the conditionality approach, a country requesting a Fund drawing has to satisfy the Fund that certain policies would be followed in an effort to eliminate the payments problem that caused the need for the required funds. Some countries regard conditionality as undue interference by the Fund in domestic affairs, whereas it is looked upon by the Fund as essential to the maintenance of the revolving nature of the Fund's financial resources. The conditionality rule was tightened during the 1990s. Essentially, conditionality implies interference in national sovereignty, but as access to the IMF's resources is voluntary and on otherwise favourable terms, governments are faced with a trade-off. What remains an open question is whether the typical 'Washington Consensus' conditionality measures reflect more than the prevailing beliefs of a notoriously presumptuous professional elite with close ties to the ruling classes.
4 The countries included in the NAB were Australia, Austria, Belgium, Canada, Denmark, Finland, France, Germany, Hong Kong, Italy, Japan, Korea, Kuwait, Luxembourg, Malaysia, the Netherlands, Norway, Saudi Arabia, Singapore, Spain, Sweden, Switzerland, Thailand, the UK and the US.
5 This potentially dangerous currency mismatch for countries that cannot borrow in their own currencies (practically all countries except those with the major international currencies) is nowadays referred to amongst economists as the 'original sin'.
6 In economic terminology, the extra incomes earned by offshore finance are 'rents'; based on the provision of 'scarce resources' like secrecy, conspiracy and tax rates close to zero. Scarcity is inherent, as the scheme would not work if all countries tried to extract such rents.
7 On the aggregate level, stability of (18.2′) is based on the premise that k reflects the amount of money M that is required to process the volume of monetary transactions associated with Y, when payment habits as well as the technical and institutional features of the payments system are considered as given.

CHAPTER 19

The GATT, the WTO and International Commercial Policy, 1947–2000

A. G. Kenwood, A. L. Lougheed and Michael Graff

THE EARLY YEARS, 1947–60

Despite the diversity of interests among the contracting parties to the GATT and the variety of commercial policies they pursued, the GATT achieved considerable success in a number of areas during the 1950s. While the early success recorded in the 1947 tariff-reducing negotiations was not again repeated in the subsequent meetings at Annecy (1949), Torquay (1950/1) and Geneva (1955/6), some progress continued to be made and, by the mid-1950s, a net reduction in US duties of 50 per cent had been achieved since 1934 by tariff concessions alone, the greater part of which occurred after 1945. Even more striking, GATT membership grew from 23 signatories in 1947 to over 70 in 1960, covering over 80 per cent of total world trade. In addition, by providing a forum for conciliation and discussion, the GATT resolved, often through arbitration or adjudication, commercial disputes which might otherwise have caused continuing bad feeling, reprisals and even diplomatic breakdown.

Progress in dealing with quantitative trade restrictions was much slower than that with tariffs, partly because the economic difficulties of the late 1940s and 1950s led many countries to retain controls over their trade, and partly because the GATT's powers over quantitative restrictions were weak, for it could only consult with members to persuade them to reduce these restrictive measures. But the GATT's constant review of the individual commercial policies and its persistent attempts to reduce trade restrictions must have contributed something to the general, gradual elimination of such restrictions which occurred in the late 1950s. Moreover, the GATT's existence may have prevented the use of new preferential arrangements similar to those adopted in the 1920s, but this did not preclude the growth of regional trading blocs under the exceptions to the no-new-preferences rule which eroded the GATT's powers to some extent.

DOI: 10.4324/9781003382171-24

The Advent of Regional Trading Blocs

A number of small customs unions, France-Monaco, Italy-San Marino, Switzerland-Liechtenstein and Belgium-Luxembourg, emerged unbroken from the Second World War.[1] After the war, the trend towards economic and/or political integration gathered pace. The first step had been taken with the formation of Benelux in 1944, when liberated Belgium, the Netherlands and Luxembourg agreed to establish a tariff community with a common external tariff as a prelude to complete economic integration in later years.

In 1950, the Schuman Plan to set up a European Coal and Steel Community (ECSC) under a waiver of the GATT's no-new-preferences rule was adopted by the Benelux countries, France, West Germany and Italy. The ECSC gradually removed duties on coal and steel, subsidies and other restrictions and discriminatory devices between member countries, under the guidance of a supranational authority. But it was only a forerunner of bigger things to come. In 1955, discussions began on the formation of a customs union by ECSC members, with far-reaching implications for the international economy as a whole. The structure of the European Economic Community (EEC) was agreed upon in March 1957 and incorporated in the Treaty of Rome, the provisions of which came into operation in 1958 after GATT's recognition of the regional trading bloc.

The economic aim of the EEC, by establishing a common market and by progressively harmonising the economic policies of the member states, was to promote the development of economic activities in the region, increase economic stability, and accelerate improvements in the living standards of the population. But it would be misguided to reduce the early stages of the post-war European unification process to its economic aspects. By introducing a supranational High Authority, the ECSC took control of steel and coal production — the indispensable resources to wage the mechanised wars of the twentieth century — out of the hands of national governments. Thus, governments of nations that had gone to war against each other twice in just four decades, with the resulting inevitable sentiments of bitterness, hatred and lust for revenge, had deliberately made a third war between them impossible. This policy found its logical continuation in the establishment of the European Atomic Energy Community in 1957. Political unity thus clearly formed a long-run aim, even if it was only implied in the treaty.[2]

Other features provided for the free movement of people, services and capital within the region, common agricultural and transport policies and the setting up of a Social Fund and an Investment Bank. The treaty also provided for association of the EEC with the dependent overseas territories of the member states.[3]

THE HABERLER REPORT

The general improvement in trading conditions between the Western industrial nations evident in the second half of the 1950s led to increasing dissatisfaction among the primary producing countries. They were inclined to look upon the GATT as an institution designed largely to allow commercial policies which favoured the richest industrial contracting parties. Consequently, a panel of experts was appointed to investigate and report on the working of the General Agreement since 1947. The Haberler Report was presented to GATT in 1958. It emphasised two major points: that agricultural protectionism in the industrial countries had minimised the benefits that the traditional food-exporting countries could have expected to receive from their membership of GATT, and that many of the developing countries had also been disadvantaged by the commercial and other policies of the industrial nations.

THE GATT, THE WTO AND COMMERCIAL POLICY, 1960–2000

After the Haberler Report

Out of the deliberations on the Haberler Report came the setting up of three committees to consider further tariff reductions, agricultural protectionism and the specific trade problems of the developing countries. The first committee produced the Dillon and Kennedy Rounds of tariff negotiations in 1961 and 1964–7. The second committee, after much research, concluded that 'the extensive resort to non-tariff protection of agriculture had impaired or nullified tariff concessions or other benefits which agricultural exporting countries expect to receive from the General Agreement'. The third committee on the trade problems of the developing countries in 1964 achieved the incorporation of a new chapter in the GATT allowing discrimination in favour of developing countries. This paved the way for the establishment of the Generalised System of Preferences (GSP), introduced by most industrialised countries in the 1970s — for example, by the EEC in 1971 and the US in 1976.

The Formation and Development of UNCTAD

As we have already seen, a major source of grievance within the GATT in the 1950s was the relatively poor export performance of many primary producing countries. Whereas some of the reasons for this state of affairs were to be found in the domestic policies of the primary producing countries themselves, many of them found that the industrial nations had used the exceptions in GATT to protect their own relatively inefficient agricultural industries to the detriment of foreign primary producers. Furthermore, until the Kennedy round in the mid-1960s, agricultural products did not enter into discussions on tariff reductions. Rightly or wrongly, the less developed countries (LDCs) came to look upon the GATT as a 'rich man's club' and, early in the 1960s, they turned to the United Nations, the only forum in which they had considerable voting strength, for an answer to their trade problems. The result was the first meeting of the United Nations Conference on Trade and Development (UNCTAD) in Geneva in 1964.

UNCTAD became institutionalised in much the same way as the GATT, and up to now, conferences have been held in New Delhi (1968), Santiago (1972), Nairobi (1976), Manila (1979), Belgrade (1983), Geneva (1987), Cartagena (1992), Midrand (1996), Bangkok (2000), São Paulo (2004), Accra (2008), Nairobi (2016) and Bridgetown (2021). UNCTAD membership includes most developing countries, while developed nations maintain observers at all discussions. UNCTAD cannot force its recommendations on the industrial countries, but even so, by highlighting the inequities of the trade system and other aspects of international economic relations, which favour the economically powerful, it has often influenced the richer nations into offering concessions that otherwise may not have been made. In the 1970s, it highlighted the call for a 'new international economic order' and for a 'North-South' debate on the existing and mounting problems of the Third World. At Manila in 1979 (UNCTAD V), there was widespread support for the introduction of an integrated programme of commodities (IPC) and the establishment of a Common Fund, with a view to stabilising primary product prices, thereby eliminating some of the uncertainties surrounding the export earnings of many of the developing countries.

Discrimination in World Trade

From the early 1960s, the undermining of one of the basic principles upon which the GATT had been founded — non-discrimination in trade and no new preferences — was carried even further than it had been in the 1950s, with the formation of the EEC.

Up to 2000, the original six EEC members were joined by Denmark, Ireland and the UK in 1973, by Greece in 1981, by Portugal and Spain in 1986 and by Austria, Finland and Sweden in 1995, thus covering 15 European nations. By 1997, 14 countries had applied for membership and a number of countries in Central and Eastern Europe were separated out for accelerated movement towards membership. Along the way the Community had acquired the reputation of being a powerful economic and political entity.

In 1960, as a counter to the EEC, the European Free Trade Association (EFTA) was formed by Austria, Denmark, Norway, Portugal, Sweden, Switzerland and the UK. EFTA was a much looser organisation than the EEC for, while each member country was committed to reducing its tariffs on the other member countries' goods, each country could follow an independent policy with regard to its import duties on goods coming from non-member countries. While Finland became an associate member in 1961 and Iceland joined EFTA in 1970, and Liechtenstein in 1991, EFTA was weakened by the entry of Denmark and the UK into the EEC in 1973, followed by Portugal, Austria, Finland and Sweden in later years. In 1994, Norway voted 52.2 per cent against joining the EU. Also, EFTA gained somewhat from the free trade agreement with the EEC on non-agricultural goods in 1972 and by the creation of the European Economic Area (EEA) in 1994, again with the EEC (EU) Single Market for goods, services, capital and, last but not least, labour. Of the EFTA countries, Switzerland, however, voted 50.3 per cent to remain outside the EEA. With only four members (Norway, Switzerland, Iceland and Liechtenstein), all small and one of them a microstate, the reasons for the continued existence of EFTA remain vague.[4]

In addition to the expansion of the EU borders, internally, greater consolidation occurred with the introduction of the Single Market programme of 1986, ensuring the elimination of internal non-tariff barriers to trade in commodities and services, which was completed by the end of 1992.

As a result of the development of the Cold War, the Eastern European centrally planned economies (CPEs) in 1949 set up their own trading bloc, COMECON (Council for Mutual Economic Assistance) also known as CMEA (Council for Mutual Economic Assistance), originally comprising the USSR as the dominant economy, Albania (until 1961), Bulgaria, Czechoslovakia, Hungary, Poland and Romania. The German Democratic Republic (GDR) joined it in 1950, followed by Mongolia (1962), Cuba (1972) and Vietnam (1978). It organised a centrally planned division of labour between its members and operated until the end of the 1980s.[5] In 1991, following the breakdown of the GDR (1989) and the Soviet Union

(1991), it was formally dissolved. The abrupt end of this international division of labour sent most of the new economies in transition into deep and long-lasting recessions. Several of them applied to the EU for membership and in 2000 found themselves in the entrance queue.[6]

As many as 17 trading blocs were established in other parts of the world in the 1960s — regional arrangements of varying degrees of integration covering more than 80 contracting parties. These included the Latin American Free Trade Area (LAFTA) of seven countries, set up in 1961, and the Central American Common Market (CACM), which was to become fully integrated by 1967. In Africa, the seven former French West African colonies formed a new trading bloc, and Chad, Gabon and the Central African Republic formed the Equatorial Customs Union. The successful Association of Southeast Asian Nations (ASEAN), covering Brunei, Indonesia, Malaysia, Philippines, Singapore and Thailand, was set up in 1967. In 1992, ASEAN established the ASEAN Free Trade Area (AFTA), accepting Vietnam as a member in 1995 and Burma (now: Myanmar), Laos and Cambodia in 1997. The Australia–New Zealand Closer Economic Relations (CER) agreement commenced in 1965. Other preferential arrangements were established elsewhere, but they were important only within their own region and many of them did not last for more than a decade.

LAFTA succumbed in 1968 when it was replaced by the Andean Pact, covering Bolivia, Chile, Colombia, Ecuador and Peru. This organisation was in difficulties by 1975 and the CACM disintegrated in the 1970s after Honduras left it. Nevertheless, such regional groupings were revitalised in the 1990s. CARICOM is an association of Caribbean states including Cuba; while, in South America, the Andean Group by the year 2000 comprised Venezuela, Colombia (between which two countries trade has increased rapidly), Ecuador, Peru and Bolivia. This group now favours free trade within its borders. Out of the former LAFTA emerged the most successful Latin American group — Mercosul (in Portuguese, 'Mercosur' in Spanish) — introduced in 1991, comprising Brazil (the economically and politically dominant constituent), Argentina, Paraguay and Uruguay, and which became a full customs union in January 1995 but with, however, a number of national exceptions, especially in sugar and motor vehicles. Early indications suggest that this region has benefited from the closer ties. Before the end of the millennium, Chile and Bolivia had made approaches on membership; Chile became an associated member in 1996, Bolivia in 1997.

At the instigation of France, the first Yaoundé Convention of the EEC in 1963 granted association status to the former French, Belgian and Italian colonies in Africa. Under this convention, these newly emerging African countries received preferential treatment for their exports within the EEC and, also, a European Development Fund (EDF) was set up to offer them financial aid. These arrangements received a hostile reception from other developing countries, which were discriminated against by the preferences granted. Subsequently, however, the adoption of GSP by the EEC in 1971 did much to reduce the degree of preferential treatment accorded to the former colonies. In 1975, the Yaoundé Convention was superseded by the Lomé Convention, which extended the preferential arrangements to include the former colonies of Britain and widened the area covered by including countries and colonies in Africa, the Caribbean and the Pacific (ACP) countries. Given that the degree of trade preferences afforded under this agreement were small, the major benefit to be derived by the countries in the ACP region from association with the EEC arose out of a particular scheme, under which these countries were to be compensated for any shortfall in their export earnings on several commodities sold to the EEC. Such compensation was financed out of the EDF.

In addition to these conventions, the EEC negotiated preferential trade treaties with numerous other countries, especially in the Mediterranean area and in South America. In 1972, the preferential bilateral trade agreements which had been concluded by the EEC with individual Mediterranean countries after 1968 were multilateralised for the region, and a highly preferential system was created. By 1973, fewer than half a dozen countries were confronted by the EEC's most favoured nation (MFN) duties under these arrangements. All of these arrangements (including the free entry into the EEC of non-agricultural goods from EFTA members after 1972) show up the weaknesses of the GATT, more particularly its inability to prevent further erosion of one of the principles on which it was founded, non-discrimination in trade and no new preferences. Meanwhile, the stalwart of non-discriminatory trade dealings, the US, introduced tariff preferences on a list of commodities in favour of certain Caribbean countries and took the first steps towards a free trade area with Israel.

Having witnessed the increasing economic integration of the EU for a number of decades, the US, Canada and Mexico eventually formed the North American Free Trade Area (NAFTA), commencing in January 1994. In the east, attempts have been made since 1989 to form another important free trade area, APEC (Asian Pacific Economic Community), which is a wide grouping of economies, including, amongst others, the US, Canada and Mexico, the People's Republic of China along with Hong Kong and Taiwan, Russia, Japan, Malaysia, Thailand, the Philippines, South Korea, Australia and New Zealand. It is described as embracing 'open regionalism'. Somewhat over-ambitiously, APEC declared in 1994 that it would turn into a free trade area by 2020. This failed to materialise, given the increasing geopolitical tensions in the Eurasian and Pacific world.

Agricultural Protectionism

World trade has been severely distorted by the actions of the developed countries. By far, the most damaging departure from the principles of GATT in the 1960s was the introduction of the Common Agricultural Policy (CAP) by the EEC in 1962. Its origins go back to the memories of supply shortages, rationing and famines during or in the aftermaths of the devastating wars, which let autarky in agriculture (although practically unachievable for most of densely populated Europe) appear as the most desirable condition. This, along with a romantic notion of peasants' lives, an apparently universal conviction that domestic foodstuff is qualitatively superior to imported and, last but not least, effective lobbying by the agricultural sector helps explaining the paradox that the supra-national organisation of one of the most industrialised regions of the world where agriculture contributed only a marginal share of value added, was captured by the interest of its farmers and agro-business. In practice, the CAP aimed at ensuring that farmers in the Community would be able to enjoy incomes comparable with those obtained in other domestic industries. This was achieved through restrictions on the entry of foodstuffs from non-member countries, the use of support prices for agricultural products and the disposal of agricultural surpluses when necessary. To restrict imports, a variable levy system was introduced and used in such a way that imports of foodstuffs were priced higher than the same commodities produced by EEC farmers. The levy could thus be used as effectively as quantitative restrictions on agricultural imports. The pricing policy was subject to annual review and, as applied to some commodities, it led to overproduction and the accumulation of surpluses — for example, in sugar and butter. One way of disposing of such surpluses was to dump them on world markets, financing the required export subsidies out of an agricultural fund (the European Agricultural Guidance and Guarantee Fund (EAGGF)), which was fed by financial contributions from the member governments.

Britain's accession to the EEC in 1973 created almost insuperable difficulties for several countries, among them Australia and New Zealand, that had long-established markets in Britain for a number of primary products. They were compelled to rationalise their efficient agricultural sectors and/or cultivate new markets elsewhere in the world. Ironically, this search for new markets was hampered by the EEC's and, from the mid-1980s, US policy of dumping agricultural surpluses in world markets.

Over the years the enormous costs associated with the CAP attracted substantial criticism. As a result, in the early 1990s, radical reforms to the CAP were suggested. At the same time, the agricultural discussions which took place in the Uruguay Round concluded that quantitative restrictions on imports of agricultural products should be 'tariffied'; that these tariffs should then be reduced by 36 per cent from the 1986/8 base over a period of six years from mid-1995; that some domestic support (which distorted production or trade) should be subject to 20 per cent reduction; and that export subsidies be reduced by 21 per cent from 1995. Implementation of such proposals, which were greeted by most member states, was however hampered by the EEC's/EU's principle of unanimous decisions in essential matters, of which the CAP is one, so that every government effectively has a veto right to which it resorts as soon as it feels that its farmers will be subject to a reduction of subsidies or protection. Needless to say, under such constitutional constraints change can only be painfully slow.[7]

Non-Tariff Trade Restrictions

A second area of concern for promoters of free trade arose in the 1970s when frequent and widespread resort to non-tariff restrictions on imports by the industrial countries occurred. The types of measures used were varied in character, but orderly marketing arrangements (OMAs) and voluntary export restraints (VERs) were the most common. The effectiveness of Japan's penetration of American and European markets was of major concern to those countries and was the initial reason for such restrictions.

Third, under the GSP introduced in the early 1970s, tariff preferences were extended to a wide range of exports from the developing countries but, at the same time, it became common to fix annual maxima to the quantities of the commodities allowed into the countries offering such preferential treatment. Finally, the worsening economic conditions which prevailed in all industrial countries after 1973 led to a general claim by domestic producers for greater protection against imports. As a result, this form of protection became even more widespread.

Multilateral Trade Negotiations, 1960–2000

From 1960 to 2000, four rounds of multilateral trade negotiations (MTNs) have been concluded. The Dillon round of 1961 achieved very little, and it became apparent that the method of product-by-product negotiations had finally reached its practical limits and was no longer useful in bringing about substantial reductions in the levels of protection.

Next, the Kennedy round (1964–7) was notable because linear reductions in tariffs on a wide variety of products were negotiated, which achieved an average reduction in industrial tariffs of between 36 and 39 per cent. At the same time, over 60 per cent of the reductions were in excess of 50 per cent. Thus, some tariff harmonisation also occurred. The Kennedy round favoured the trade of the industrial countries, although it also benefited some developing countries to the extent that the lowering of tariffs on manufactured goods allowed the rapid growth of manufactured exports from the NICs such as Brazil, Taiwan, Korea, Hong Kong and Singapore. Although the terms of negotiation of the round required that some regard be paid to the reduction of agricultural protection, little progress was made. A new International Grains Agreement was the only concession to agriculture made by the EEC and the US, and this Agreement lasted only three years.

The third round of MTNs since 1960 was the Tokyo round (1973–9). For the first time, it appeared that, in addition to the usual reductions in tariffs on manufactures, the negotiators were committed to a consideration of ways of reducing the barriers to trade in agricultural products and non-tariff trade barriers, as well as a general consideration of the trade problems of developing countries. While a number of factors contributed to a delay in the commencement of the negotiations until 1977, the Trade Negotiations Committee had by then established that discussions would proceed along seven lines:

1 tariffs on industrial products,
2 non-tariff barriers to trade,
3 the sectoral approach, that is, the technique of coordinated reduction or elimination of trade barriers within particular product groups,
4 agricultural products,
5 tropical products,
6 the adequacy of the multilateral safeguards system,
7 special differential treatment for developing countries.

In addition to the general hostility in Europe against the reduction of agricultural protectionism, the lower growth performances of industrial countries increased rather than reduced the prevalence of non-tariff trade barriers. Contracting parties outside the US and the EEC took little part in the deliberations. The outcome included around 30 per cent reductions in tariffs on industrial products, including some tariff harmonisation. The reductions were larger on finished goods than on raw materials or intermediate products, and small reductions in tariffs occurred for temperate-zone agricultural commodities on which non-tariff barriers remained unchanged. Agreement on relatively minor aspects of trade, which were of interest primarily to the EEC and the US, was also achieved. Given the extent to which non-tariff barriers, in the form of OMAs and VERs, had been introduced, particularly in Europe, to counter competition from Japan and the NICs, the relatively minor agreements reached highlighted the manner in which many of the fundamental trade restrictions which were supposed to receive the bulk of attention of the round were side-stepped in the negotiations.

Japan, the NICs and some developing countries desired the introduction of a code of conduct to be followed by countries introducing import controls aimed at preserving orderly marketing on certain products in their domestic markets, but the EEC insisted on maintaining the right to implement such controls on a unilateral basis when they became necessary. Given the rhetoric with which the Tokyo round was introduced, it was a failure. Little was achieved of direct benefit to contracting parties outside the industrial world and much that was achieved was peripheral to the major issues upon which the round was justified. Largely, the industrial countries, and especially the EEC, set out to protect their positions, but the round was necessary precisely because the policies then being followed by the EEC and other countries were contrary to the fundamental philosophy underpinning the GATT.

The Uruguay Round, the sixth round of GATT negotiations which commenced in 1986, was the most ambitious of them all, taking seven years of hard bargaining in areas of trade which, for decades, had been considered too difficult, namely, trade in agriculture and trade in services. It also aimed to reduce the prevalence of the new protectionism, popular after the early 1970s. The agriculture problem held back the completion of the round for three years. There were important successes. The major features of the agreements included the replacement of the GATT by the World Trade Organization (WTO). The WTO was given a broader range of activities, including agriculture, the textile and clothing trades and the trade in services. The trade-related aspects of investment and the protection of property rights and some internal policy issues such as trade and the environment, competition policy and labour standards, which may feature as protection issues, were also covered by the new body. For the settlements of disputes, the WTO was offered greater power in that only a 66 or 75 per cent vote of contracting parties was required instead of GATT's 100 per cent.

In addition to the setting up of the WTO, tariffs on industrial products were reduced from an average of 4.7 to 3 per cent, while the percentage of goods with zero tariffs was to increase from between 20 and 22 to between 40 and 45, and no tariffs were to be placed on pharmaceuticals, construction equipment, medical equipment, paper products or steel. Quotas on the imports of agricultural commodities and of textiles and apparel (under the MFA) were to be replaced by less restrictive tariffs over a ten-year period — on agricultural products by 24 per cent in developing countries and by 36 per cent in developed countries. Tariffs on textiles were to be reduced by 25 per cent.

The volume of subsidised agricultural exports was to be reduced by 21 per cent in six years; government subsidies for industrial research were to be limited to 50 per cent of applied research costs. While the use of anti-dumping laws was not banned, faster and harder action was required to end disputes arising out of their use. On safeguards, the temporary use of trade restrictions was allowed if an increase in imports severely damaged a domestic industry, but using health and safety standards simply to restrict trade was not allowed.

Finally, intellectual property such as patents, trademarks and copyrights was to have 20 years' protection, with a ten-year phase-in period for developing countries for patent protection of pharmaceuticals.

The name change from GATT to WTO was effected in Geneva in January 1995. By then, the WTO included 127 members. Its first meeting was held in Singapore in November 1996. It included in its agenda the working towards an agreement on labour standards, investment and competition policy, government procurement and an information technology agreement (ITA), an attempt to liberalise trade in computer-related products worth about $1 billion per year. Yet, as in GATT, the emphasis was on items of special interest to North America and Europe.

Commodity Agreements

Widely fluctuating export prices of primary products have posed a major problem for countries with a narrow primary-product export base or for whom these exports provided a large part of their national incomes. Between the two world wars there were 72 commodity agreements signed, and almost all faded away by 1945. After the Second World War, several attempts were made to ensure orderly world marketing of primary products with international agreements covering such commodities as wheat, sugar, tin, coffee, cocoa and petroleum. These had limited success. Few lasted long and those that survived produced only marginal improvements for the exporters of those commodities. Only OPEC (and illegal drug cartels) have had the right combination of factors allowing long-term survival. The many failures show only too well the tremendous difficulties surrounding any attempt to draw up such agreements, each of which must satisfy the many exporting and importing countries covered, and with each country concerned with the protection of its own interests.

As noted above, increased instability in world commodity markets in the 1970s led UNCTAD to press for an IPC covering some 18 traded commodities to aid the financing of the buffer stocks of commodities to which these international commodity agreements would give rise. In 1979, a Common Fund was established, but its role was less ambitious than that intended by UNCTAD, for its resources, made up of government contributions, were limited to $4.7 billion. In addition, as noted in Chapter 18, a modest compensatory finance scheme had already been set up by the IMF in 1963 in its compensatory and continuing financing facility (CCFF) and, later, a buffer stock financing facility (BSFF) was established for a similar purpose. The CCFF aided those developing countries whose exports in a particular year fell below their average value of the previous five years. In 1975 the EEC adopted a similar scheme to provide a $400 billion fund for the 57 members of the ACP. Nevertheless, both of these compensatory schemes were only modest in their scope.

CONCLUDING REMARKS

Immediately after the Second World War, a concerted effort was made to set up a multilateral trade system through the elimination of controls over trade and commerce and a reduction in the amount of protection afforded to domestic industries by contracting parties to the GATT. The MFN principle and the no-new-preferences rule were intended to prevail in the tariff field. Discriminatory devices were to be rejected by all participants in Western trade, and non-tariff barriers to trade were considered objectionable by the GATT.

By 1960, the situation was, in practice, almost the complete reverse. As a result of the escape clauses in GATT and the inclusion of what was considered at the time to be a relatively minor exception to the general rules governing trade liberalisation, the international economy was heading towards regionalisation to such an extent that, within each regional free trade area, the MFN principle and the no-new-preferences rule were sidestepped as individual member countries within them discriminated in favour of other member countries and against outsiders.

After 1960, the international economic power which has come with the economic union of several of the major trading nations and others has led to many of the original rules of GATT becoming inoperative, and the failure of GATT negotiators to come to grips in the past with the major inequities which govern world trade demonstrates the fact that the record of GATT compared with its original basic objectives is one of failure. Yet the GATT was partially successful in that tariffs on manufactured imports were reduced substantially over the years by the advanced countries.

The successes of the Uruguay Round and the setting up of the WTO did not solve the major trade problems. The topics under discussion were (and still are) predominantly those which best served the interests of the major trading groups' intra-trade. As in the past, the powerful are only interested in what concerns them.

RECOMMENDATIONS FOR FURTHER READING

MacBean and Snowden (1981, *International Institutions in Trade and Finance*) and Hoekman and Kostecki (2009, *The Political Economy of the World Trading System: WTO and Beyond*) deliver useful summaries and analyses of the institutions of international trade in the second half of the twentieth century.

Special emphasis of the position of the poorer countries can be found in Golt (1978, *Developing Countries in the GATT System*), Davenport (1986, *Trade Policy, Protection, and the Third World*), Pomfrey (1988, *Unequal Partners: The Economics of Discriminatory International Trade Policies*) and MacLaren (1995, *The Uruguay Round Agreement on Agriculture: A New Order?*).

NOTES

1 A customs union involves the economic integration of a number of countries in such a way as to produce free trade among members of the union and a common external tariff levied against all non-members; a free trade area differs from a customs union in that member nations follow independent tariff policies with respect to other countries.

2 Consequently, if somewhat belatedly, this coordinated effort of a generation of responsible and visionary politicians that had learned their lessons from the disasters of the world wars was awarded with the Nobel Peace Prize to the European Union in 2012.

3 From an international economics perspective, trading blocs are an ambivalent phenomenon, as they may simultaneously tear down barriers to trade and erect new ones. They may still prove beneficial to countries outside the union by improving the welfare of the participants and creating additional opportunities for trade. But it is necessary to consider not only their trade-creating potentialities, but also the trade diverting effects of such unions, that is, the extent to which the formation of a customs union will lead to a diversion of the trade of one member country from third countries to another member of the union. The rest of the world can benefit economically from the setting up of a customs union if the creation of new trade opportunities exceeds the extent of trade diversion.

4 Interestingly, the two countries for which the doors to the EU are wide open but in which the electorate has effectively blocked entry are Norway and Switzerland. With per capita incomes among the highest in the world, they apparently found that they had more to lose than to win. Also, despite the pronounced protection of agriculture within the EU, these two countries — with even more pronounced comparative disadvantage in agriculture due to adverse climates and terrains — are even more protective, so that the votes against the EU/EEA can also be understood to be an expression of support to the domestic farmers.

5 For example, the public transport in these countries relied on trams from Czechoslovakia, while Hungary supplied the buses.

6 Many of them were admitted in 2004; for details, see Chapter 22.

7 Two points are worth mentioning in this context: first, as a large economy the EEC/EU may be the single largest distorter of trade in agricultural products; yet others, notably the two European bystanders Norway and Switzerland, are even more protective, and the US is resorting to protection of its farmers whenever it appears internally appropriate.

CHAPTER 20

Trade and Growth in the International Economy

The Developed Countries, 1945–2000

A. G. Kenwood, A. L. Lougheed and Michael Graff

WORLD TRADE

Total Trade

Despite the restrictions on foreign trade which existed in one form or another from the end of the Second World War to 1960, the total value of the merchandise exports of the market economies rose from $53,300 million in 1948 to $112,300 million in 1960, or at an average annual growth rate of over 6 per cent. This is a remarkable record, especially when it is realised that the prices of traded commodities were about the same in 1960 as they had been in 1948. From 1960 to 1973, growth rates were even higher, at an average annual rate for the volume of exports of around 8 per cent. But 1973 marked the end of the rapid growth of exports, the annual increase dropping to average around 4.5 per cent from 1973 to 1979, to 1.5 per cent from 1980 to 1989, and then rising to 4.5 per cent in 1990–5. The rates were still high in most years, however, when compared with the rate of growth of world trade from the beginning of the nineteenth century to 1950. From 1950 to 2000, the volume of world trade fell in only three years, in 1958, 1975 and 1982.

Another important feature of world trade during this period was that, in almost every year, the increase in its volume exceeded the increase in the volume of world production. In other words, the international division of labour deepened, as every dollar or world value added corresponded to an increasing value of cross-border transactions — either trade production inputs (raw materials and intermediate products, capital goods) or in final output.[1] This also applied within the broad categories of products in most periods, as Table 20.1 illustrates.

The evidence provided on world trade and world output in Table 20.1 shows that even during the relatively low-growth period after 1973, trade was still expanding faster than production in most years. The different regions of the world, however, did not share equally in this rapidly rising trade. Excluding the centrally planned economies (CPEs), the rates of growth of the industrial countries of Europe, North America and Japan were higher than the

DOI: 10.4324/9781003382171-25

TABLE 20.1 World merchandise exports and production, total and by category, 1953–95

Period	Total increase in volume (per cent)							
	Agriculture		Mining		Manufacturing		Total	
	Trade	Output	Trade	Output	Trade	Output	Trade	Output
1953–63	65	29	[a]	[a]	126	86	94	68
1963–79	96	47	101	99	282	149	200	120
1890–9	16	28	13	21	71	21	48	25
1990–5	25	8	25	10	37	5	34	8

Source: GATT and WTO, *International Trade*, various issues.

Note: [a] Included in agriculture.

TABLE 20.2 World exports by major area, 1953–95 (per cent of total)

Exporting region	Per cent of total						
	1953	1963	1973	1980	1985	1990	1995
Industrial area[a]	58.1	64.3	68.2	60.9	64.4	71.1	69.7
Australasia, South Africa	2.0	2.8	2.7	2.6	1.9	2.1	1.9
Developing countries[b]	39.5	20.7	19.2	28.8	22.9	21.9	22.2
CPEs/CITs[c]	0.3	12.1	9.9	7.7	10.7	4.9	6.1
Total	100.0	100.0	100.0	100.0	100.0	100.0	100.0

Source: As for Table 20.1; Sources: GATT and WTO, *International Trade*, various issues.

Notes: [a] Includes all Western Europe, US, Canada and Japan; [b] of which the oil exporters recorded 5.9, 7.3 and 12.8 per cent in 1963, 1973 and 1980, respectively; while the newly advanced Asian countries (Korea, Hong Kong, Taiwan and Singapore) recorded 4.7, 5.7 and 6.7 per cent from 1985 on (excluding reexports); [c] from 1990, these were the CITs. China is also included here.

world average in the 1950s and, as a result, these countries increased their relative share of total exports from 61 to around 70 per cent. Other developed countries in Europe, Australasia and South Africa experienced a reduction in their share from 9 to 7 per cent and the share of the developing countries fell from 30 to 23 per cent. These changes largely reflected the different rates of growth in the output and exports of manufactures and primary products of the different regions.

Table 20.2 shows that the shares of all groups of countries in total world exports between 1963 and 1995 fluctuated from time to time. The industrial area, however, commanded around 70 per cent of the total towards the end of the period as the share of the countries in transition (CITs) (including China), the former CPEs, fell substantially in their change-over to market economies. The share of developing countries fluctuated between 20 and 25 per cent while, in the latest period, the inclusion in this group of Korea, Hong Kong, Taiwan and Singapore maintained the healthy share of this group of countries, contributing 4.7, 5.7 and 6.7 per cent, respectively, to the totals in the years 1980, 1990 and 1995. The large increase in the share of developing countries in 1980 reflected the increased returns to the oil exporters of the Middle East as a result of the large oil price increases of the mid-1970s. The decline in the share of the CPEs to 1985 shows the lesser importance this group of countries placed on trade, while the drastic fall in the 1990s shows some of the problems of switching from planned to market-based economies.

The Direction of Merchandise Trade

The differences in the trade growth rates by the different groups of countries in Table 20.2 are reflected in the shifts that have occurred in the direction of trade, as can be seen in Table 20.3. Except for the rise of developing countries in the 1970s and early 1980s, as the oil-exporting

TABLE 20.3 Matrices of world exports for selected years 1953–95 (per cent of total)

Exports to from	Industrial countries	Developing countries	CPEs/CITs	Total
1953				
Industrial countries	37.1	19.3	1.5	61.4
Developing countries	17.5	6.7	0.6	25.4
CPEs	1.1	0.4	8.0	9.6
Total	58.6	27.0	10.1	100.0
1963				
Industrial countries	44.6	14.7	2.3	64.1
Developing countries	14.2	4.5	1.7	20.8
CPEs	2.3	1.1	8.3	11.9
Total	63.6	20.8	12.3	100.0
1980				
Industrial countries	42.6	14.3	3.0	61.3
Developing countries	19.5	6.8	1.1	27.8
CPEs	2.9	1.6	4.5	8.9
Total	66.3	23.1	8.6	100.0
1990				
Industrial countries[a]	55.4[a]	12.6	2.2	71.7
Developing countries	13.9	5.7	1.3	21.2
CPEs/CITs	2.6	1.7	2.5	7.1
Total	71.9	20.0	6.0	100.0
1995				
Industrial countries[a]	51.0a	15.0	3.6	71.1
Developing countries	15.4	8.7	1.3	25.6
CPEs/CITs	2.0	0.5	0.7	3.1
Total	68.8	24.1	5.5	100.0

Source: As for Table 20.1; Sources: GATT and WTO, *International Trade*, various issues.

Note: Discrepancies due to rounding; [a] includes Australasia and South Africa. They accounted for 3 per cent of the total and traded was principally with industrial countries.

TABLE 20.4 Distribution of the export trade of major industrial countries, 1937–95 (per cent of total)

Country	1937	1950	1960	1973	1980	1985	1990	1995
UK	20	20	14	9	10	9	9	8
US	23	32	28	20	21	19	20	20
France	7	10	9	11	11	10	10	10
Germany[a]	16	6	15	19	18	20	20	17
Other W. Europe[b]	20	20	21	23	23	23	23	23
Canada	8	9	7	6	6	6	6	7
Japan	6	3	5	12	12	13	14	15
Total	100	100	100	100	100	100	100	100

Source: Maizels (1963, p. 426 f.); GATT/WTO, *International Trade*, various issues.

Notes: Discrepancies due to rounding; [a] after 1945, Germany had to cede extensive territories in the east, and in 1949, it was partitioned into two states, which lasted until 1991, only West Germany is considered during these years; [b] includes Belgium, Luxembourg, the Netherlands, Italy and Sweden. On a similar basis, the EU accounted for 37, 40 and 38 per cent of the total in 1985, 1990 and 1995, respectively. The figures presented are for the 15 members of the EU, although some were not members in 1985 or 1990.

countries gained larger shares, there were no major shifts in any of the series until the 1990s. The fall in the share of the CPEs/CITs in the 1990s occurred because of the major upheaval in production and trade as most of these countries changed to market-related economies. At the same time, the rise in the developing countries' share in the 1990s not only reflected this fall but represented the substantial increases in the export trade of several East Asian countries, including China, as they industrialised.

When we examine the export performances of the chief industrial nations since 1937, as shown in Table 20.4, we find that by 1960 the increase in the share of the US was achieved largely at the expense of the UK, and that Germany and Japan by that year had barely regained their pre-war trading positions. From 1960 to 1973, the trade shifts became even more marked. Most striking was the doubling of the Japanese share and the large decline in the shares of the UK and the US. The continental European countries also increased their shares substantially. After 1973, however, comparatively few major changes occurred, except the ever-increasing rise of the Japanese share. Moreover, since unification, the German share fell somewhat. The estimates for the EU suggest that there was little change in the share of the Union's export trade with the rest of the world between 1985 and 1995.

Composition of World Trade

The trends in the direction of world trade ran parallel with the changes in the composition of total merchandise exports. As Table 20.5 and Figure 20.1 show, the increased importance of manufactures in world exports was matched by a corresponding decline in the importance of trade in food and raw materials, at least up to 1973 and again after 1979. In the late 1970s

TABLE 20.5 Shares of commodity groups in world merchandise exports, 1937–95, by value (per cent of total)

Year	Primary products			Manufactures	Total exports
	Food	Raw materials	Total		
1937	23	40	63	37	100
1950	23	34	57	43	100
1960	20	25	45	55	100
1973	15	23	38	62	100
1980	11	32	43	55	100
1985	11	26	37	63	100
1990	10	18	28	73	100
1995	9	17	26	74	100

Source: Lamartine Yates (1959, p. 44); GATT/WTO, *International Trade,* various issues.

Note: Raw materials include fuels and non-ferrous metals.

and early 1980s, the energy crisis brought about a marked but temporary increase in the share of raw materials in world export trade, but economies in the use of oil and a decline in its price in the 1980s reduced this share by 1990.

Outside these countries, the East Asian 'newly advanced' countries (Korea, Hong Kong, Taiwan and Singapore) and the Asian NICs (including Malaysia, Thailand and Indonesia) improved their combined share of total manufactured exports from 3.9 per cent in 1973 to 6.7 per cent in 1995 if reexports are excluded.

The changing composition of trade in manufactures followed the pattern established in the late nineteenth century and continued during the interwar period (see Table 20.6 and Figure 20.1).

The shift away from textiles towards engineering products intensified, although the use of non-tariff import restrictions on textiles by the industrially advanced countries after 1970 accounts for some of the decline in the relative importance of this group. The decline in metals (iron and steel) after 1963 is particularly evident, while chemicals have continued to become more important. All other manufactures lost ground in the 1960s but recovered somewhat from the late 1970s onwards. On the whole, there was a continuation and intensification of the movement away from consumer goods (and semi-manufactures) towards capital goods which had begun in the interwar years, a trend that is consistent with the greater trade among the industrial nations that occurred after the Second World War.[2]

Table 20.7 illustrates the trade in services from 1980 to 1995. It shows the importance of Western Europe in the trade in commercial services, albeit a slightly declining one, as the current account figures for the region increased more slowly than those of other areas and countries. The share of the EU fell from 46.5 per cent in 1980 to 42.5 per cent in 1990. As the European share declined, that of North America, in particular, rose substantially.

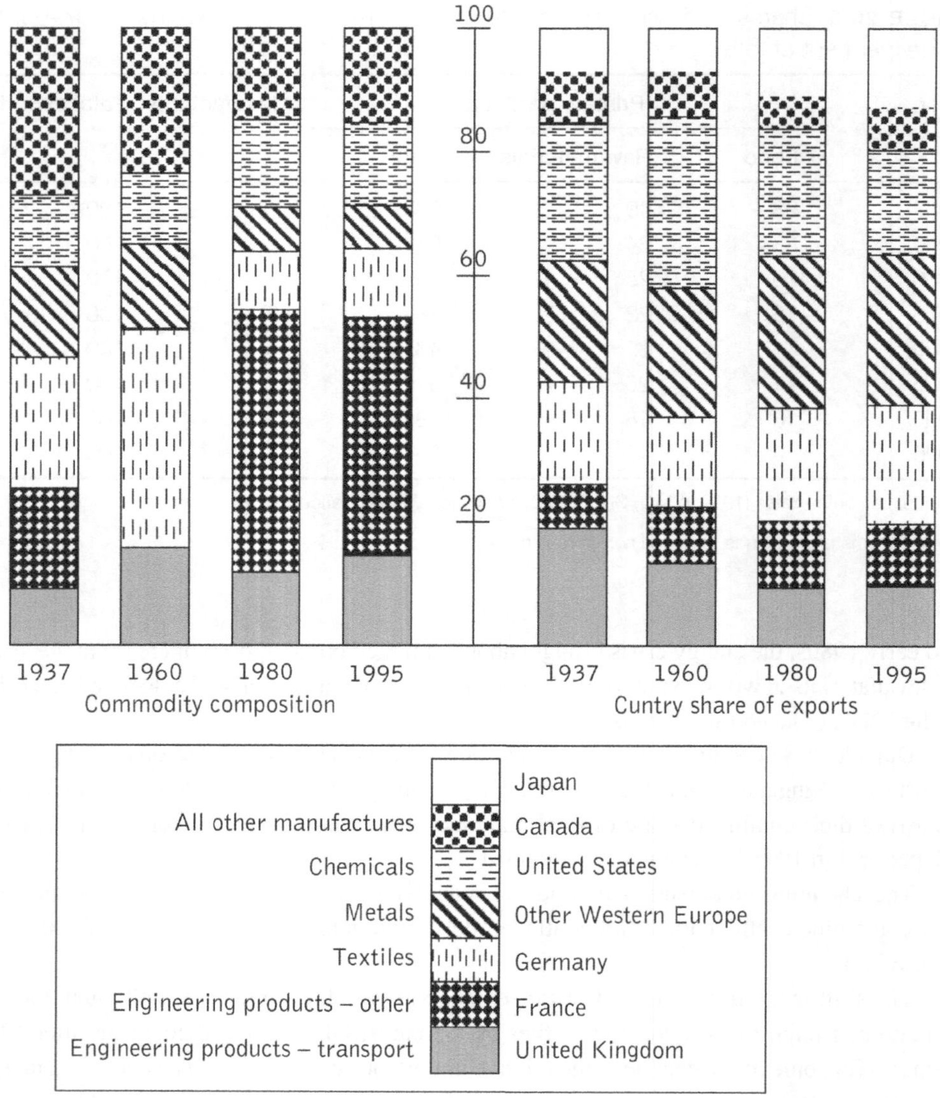

FIGURE 20.1 World trade in manufactures, 1937–95, commodity composition and country share

Source: As for Tables 20.4 and 20.6; Cairncross (1955, p. 244); Maizels (1963, p. 426 f.); and GATT/WTO, *International Trade*, various issues.

CONCLUSIONS

It is apparent from the above account that the rich industrial countries were able to obtain greater shares from the growth of international trade after 1950 than most other countries. The relative shift in the world demand away from foodstuffs and raw materials towards capital goods produced a change in the direction of total trade in favour of trade among the industrial

TABLE 20.6 Commodity pattern of trade in manufactures, 1937–95 (per cent of total)

Group/year	1937	1950	1963	1973	1980	1990	1995
Engineering products	26.5	34.9	51.8	54.2	54.2	50.4	52.2
Machinery	16.0	20.7	43.0	42.8	42.6	n.s.	n.s.
Transport[a]	10.5	14.2	8.8	11.8	11.6	n.s.	n.s.
Textiles, clothing	21.5	19.9	11.4	10.3	8.7	9.2	8.5
Metals[b]	15.3	12.9	9.1	8.2	7.0	4.4	4.1
Chemicals	10.6	10.5	11.9	12.0	13.9	12.2	12.8
All other	26.0	21.9	15.8	15.3	16.4	23.8	22.4
Total	100.0	100.0	100.0	100.0	100.0	100.0	100.0

Source: Cairncross (1955, p. 244); GATT/WTO, *International Trade*, various issues.

Notes: n.s. = not separated out; [a] from 1963, road motor vehicles; [b] iron and steel from 1963.

TABLE 20.7 Trade in commercial services, 1980–95, million dollars (per cent of total)

Country/region	1980	1985	1990	1995
World	402.0 (100)	405.0 (100)	802.2 (100)	1,198.0 (100)
North America	43.7 (11)	64.3 (16)	134.2 (17)	210.6 (18)
Western Europe	230.2 (57)	205.5 (51)	431.2 (53)	588.1 (49)
Japan	18.9 (5)	20.7 (5)	41.1 (5)	64.0 (5)
Singapore	6.0 (1)	6.3 (2)	12.7 (2)	29.3 (2)
Hong Kong	4.3 (1)	7.7 (2)	18.1 (2)	35.9 (3)
Australia	3.7 (1)	4.2 (1)	9.7 (1)	15.5 (1)
All other	95.2 (24)	96.3 (24)	155.2 (19)	254.6 (21)

Source: GATT/WTO, *International Trade*, various issues.

countries and against the exports of the poorer to the richer countries.[3] Even so, several developing countries were able to use the growth of world trade in manufactures to achieve industrial take-off during the 1980s. These (mainly Asian) countries, despite the setbacks of the late 1990s, are continuing on the path to advanced country status. The historical record outlined above shows that trade in the post-Second World War period grew at annual rates never before experienced and, what is more significant, it was the trade among the industrial countries which possessed similar ranges of factor endowments that rose the fastest. Several reasons have been advanced to explain this.

First, it has been argued that much of this increased trade between industrial countries was merely a return to a more normal rate of foreign economic relations following the lowering of restrictions on trade and payments introduced during the 1930s and in the early post-war years.

Second, since patterns of domestic demand are influenced to an important degree by per capita income, countries having similar income levels are likely to trade with each other more intensively than they are with countries having different income levels.

Third, the theory of 'monopolistic competition' argues that economies of scale and path dependency may result in a situation where the world market is served by a limited number of large firms that succeed in convincing consumers that their products (de facto almost perfect substitutes) are unique.[4]

ECONOMIC GROWTH IN THE ADVANCED COUNTRIES, 1950–2000

The Record of Growth

World production was more severely affected by the Second World War than by the First World War, but reconstruction in the years after 1945 was much more rapid and, in most countries, the 1938 levels of GDP had been exceeded by 1950. The major exceptions were West Germany and Japan, where the recovery was not concluded until the mid-1950s.

Beginning in the early 1950s, the industrialised countries[5] experienced over 20 years of sustained economic growth. Real GDP grew at an average of just over 5 per cent from 1950 to 1973, which compares favourably with the averages of 2.6 per cent from 1870 to 1913 and 1.9 per cent from 1913 to 1950. Between 1973 and 1980, however, the average annual growth rate fell to 2.9 per cent, and even lower rates were recorded in 1980–90 and 1990–97, as shown in Table 20.8 and illustrated in Figure 20.2.

Economic growth was not uniform within this group of countries, however. During the 1950s and 1960s, Japan grew much more rapidly than other countries, averaging 9.8 per cent annually, followed by West Germany (6.3 per cent), Italy (5.6 per cent) and Finland and France (5.0 per cent). The lowest growth rates were recorded by the US (3.5 per cent) and the UK (2.8 per cent). From 1973 to 1980, only a few countries recorded 3 per cent or higher growth rates: Norway (4.9 per cent), Canada (4.3 per cent), Japan (3.6 per cent), the Netherlands and Austria (around 3 per cent).

TABLE 20.8 Comparison of economic growth rates in developing and developed countries, 1955–98

	Averages of annual growth rates (per cent)					
	1955–60	1960–5	1965–73	1973–9	1980–8	1989–98
Developing countries						
Real GDP	4.6	5.5	6.6	4.9	4.3	5.8
Real GDP per capita	2.4	3.0	4.1	2.7	2.0	3.6
Advanced countries[a]						
Real GDP	3.2	5.2	4.6	2.9	2.9	2.5
Real GDP per capita	2.0	3.9	3.5	2.2	2.3	1.8

Source: World Bank, *Annual Report* and *World Development Report*, various issues; IMF, *World Economic Outlook*, various issues.

Note: advanced economies from 1980 to 1988, including Hong Kong, Israel, Korea, Singapore and Taiwan. CITs recorded 2.9 per cent and −2.9 per cent in real GDP in the last two periods, and 2.3 per cent and −3.0 per cent in real GDP per capita.

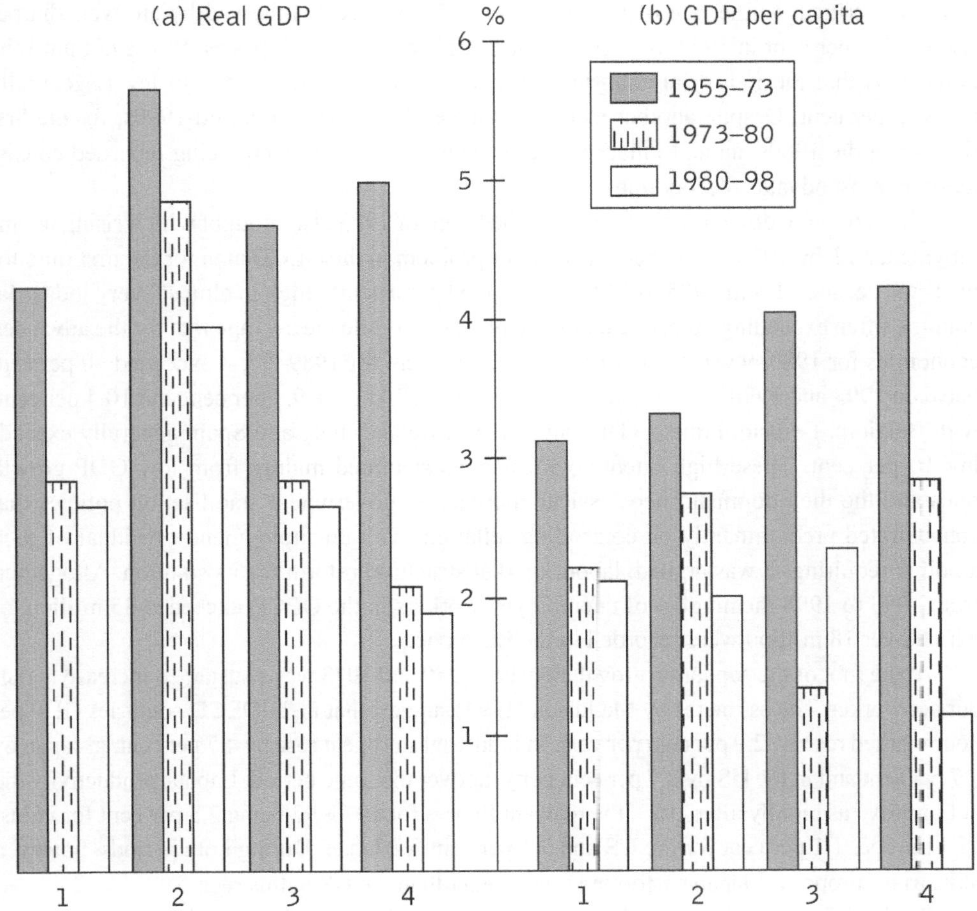

FIGURE 20.2 Average annual rates of growth in GDP and per capita GDP, 1955–98 (selected country groups)

Source: As for Table 20.8; Maddison (1989); IMF (1998, annex tables).

The OECD countries as a whole recorded an average annual increase of 2.8 per cent and 2.7 per cent for the periods 1973–80 and 1980–90, and 2.2 per cent for 1990–7. The leading growth countries of the 1980s were Japan (3.8 per cent), Finland (3.7 per cent), Ireland (3.4 per cent), Australia (3.3 per cent), Iceland (3.2 per cent) and Canada (3.0 per cent), and in subsequent years to 1997, Ireland (6 per cent), Norway (3.7 per cent) and Australia (3.0 per cent) recorded average annual growth rates of 3 per cent or higher. At the same time, the newly advanced countries of Asia experienced much higher rates of economic growth: Singapore (8.2 per cent), Korea (7.1 per cent), Taiwan (6.5 per cent), Hong Kong (5.3 per cent) and Israel (4.6 per cent).

The rate of change in both consumer prices and levels of unemployment in the industrialised countries altered substantially after 1973. The average rate of inflation in the OECD area from 1950 to 1970 was just over 5 per cent (largely influenced by the higher rates recorded towards the end of the 1960s). Between 1973 and 1980, it averaged 9.9 per cent. The year

1973 was critical as the rate of inflation rose to 7.3 per cent, followed by an even sharper rise to 12.5 per cent in 1974 as a result of the huge increase in oil prices. It was not until the mid-1980s that the industrial countries were able to pull inflation back to levels generally below 5 per cent. Despite another increase in the early 1990s, in the mid-1990s, for the first time since the 1960s, annual inflation rates of below 3 per cent were being recorded consistently in most advanced economies.

The economic downturn that followed the boom of 1973 also brought with it rising unemployment and, by 1975, it had become a major problem in the OECD area for the first time for over two decades. From 1975 to 1990, it remained persistently high in almost every industrial country, often exceeding 10 per cent of the workforce. While the average rate for the advanced economies for 1980–9 was 6.9 per cent and 7.1 per cent for 1989–97, it exceeded 10 per cent between 1993 and 1998. The respective figures for the EU were 9.1 per cent and 10.4 per cent, with Belgium, Finland, France, Germany, Greece, Ireland, Italy and Spain generally exceeding 10 per cent. These high unemployment rates stemmed mainly from low GDP growth rates and the then dominant neoclassical approach to government stabilisation policies that concentrated predominantly on controlling inflation, with unemployment a residual of such a policy requiring, it was argued, labour market structural reform for its solution. Altogether, from 1993 to 1998 the number of unemployed workers in the OECD exceeded 35 million, of which over 18 million were recorded in the EU alone.

At the root of the economic growth between 1950 and 1973 was a sustained increase in output per worker. The estimates by Maddison (1994) suggest that in 21 OECD countries GDP per hour worked rose by 2.9 per cent per year. In industrial Europe it rose by 4.7 per cent, in Japan by 7.7 per cent and in the US by 2.7 per cent per year over the same period. Labour productivity did not improve as rapidly after 1973, the relevant figures for 1973–92 being 2.3 per cent for industrial Europe, 1.1 per cent for the US and 3.1 per cent for Japan. During both periods, however, industrial Europe and Japan performed much better than the US in this regard.

Productivity increases were higher in agriculture than in manufacturing in all countries except Japan and France, while they were decidedly lower in services than in the other two sectors. At the same time, employment in agriculture declined at an average rate of 3.3 per cent between 1950 and 1973, whereas employment in manufacturing and services rose at annual rates of 1.0 and 2.3 per cent, respectively — trends which partly explain the relative changes in productivity.

The annual average rate of growth of real GDP for the industrial countries fell from an annual average of 5 per cent between 1963 and 1973 to 2.5 per cent (1973–9), 2.7 per cent (1980–9) and 2.2 per cent (1990–7). Consumption fell from an average growth rate of 5 per cent in the first period to 3.0 per cent in the second and third periods and to 2.8 per cent in 1989–98. In addition, the rate of investment expenditure during the 1980s remained at low levels until the last few years of the decade, when a revival began. An annual average of 2.8 per cent was recorded for gross capital formation from 1979 to 1988. This revival was relatively short lived, fading out by 1990. For 1989–98 an annual average of 2.6 per cent is estimated for the industrial countries, which rose after 1993. It is clear, therefore, given the relatively high rates of investment during the rapid growth period to 1973, that the decline in investment expenditure and a smaller proportionate decrease in real consumption expenditure both made a contribution to the lower growth rates in GDP after 1973.

In Europe, in order to improve the productivity and competitiveness of the European Community and to stimulate the region's technological achievements, the Single European Act was legislated in 1985. The thrust of the Act was to eliminate, by the end of 1992, the non-tariff trade restrictions the Treaty of Rome of 1957 had not addressed but which hampered intraregional trade. The 1992 programme included the elimination of all barriers to trade and the offer of equal access for all member countries to the markets of the others.

It has already been noted that, in 1997, some Asian NICs were reclassified by the IMF as 'advanced economies', namely Hong Kong (returned to China in 1997 but allowed to continue to function as an independent entity), China-Taipei (or Taiwan), Korea, Singapore and Israel. These economies experienced very rapid economic growth and at annual rates much higher than those of most other countries or regions. Much of this growth was concentrated in their export industries. In addition, they were very strongly tied to Japan by trade relations and by investment flows. The first major setback to their growth performance came with their stock exchange and currency crises, which began in September 1997.

Factors Influencing Economic Growth Rates

Economic growth in many parts of the world economy in the 1950s and 1960s was significantly influenced by the rapid expansion of industrial Europe and Japan, if only because the foreign trade of these countries rose faster than that of other countries and regions. At the same time, the foreign demand for the exports of industrial Europe and Japan was a major factor influencing the high growth rates in these countries. Progressive tariff reductions and the continuous elimination of other restrictive trade barriers, especially within Europe itself, also contributed a great deal towards the growth of this trade.

Another feature of the growth of industrial countries from 1950 to 1973 was the high ratio of investment to GDP. Directly and indirectly, investment generated substantial additions to GDP by raising demand in many sectors, increasing the amount of capital per worker, and allowing a high degree of innovation. This was aided by high degree of confidence in the continuation of prosperity and rapid changes in technological knowledge, which produced incentives to introduce new products or to modernise production methods.

Finally, for the period up to 1973, it has been argued that the industrial countries were able to maintain their high growth rates by paying low prices to the developing countries for their raw materials, including oil — a feature of the times that was to change in the early 1970s.

Thus, many factors, reflecting both favourable demand and supply conditions, were responsible for the unprecedented growth rates experienced by most industrial European countries and Japan between 1950 and 1973. While many of these growth forces were domestic in origin, others had their origins in the international economy. In particular, the growth of foreign demand for manufactures was of considerable importance in stimulating an expansion of industrial.

Japan experienced explosive economic growth from the mid-1950s on, largely through unprecedentedly high levels of investment, a rapidly expanding labour supply, a shift out of low-into high-productivity industries, a growing foreign demand for Japanese exports, the ability of export industries to remain highly competitive, collaboration between the private sector and the public sector, an absence of economic waste through low military expenditure, and significant advances in education.

The US and Canada recorded lower growth rates between 1950 and 1973 than most European countries, partly because they had experienced large increases in production from 1945 to 1950, before European recovery was complete. European and Japanese economic growth in the 1950s and later involved an element of catching up.

In Australia, New Zealand and South Africa, growth rates also fell below those of Europe and Japan. These countries had grown rapidly in the years immediately following the Second World War. Moreover, the spread of agricultural protectionism in later years had a depressing effect on the exports of the Australasian countries, which was reflected to some extent in their lower growth rates.

After 1973, economic conditions deteriorated, average growth rates were lower than in the period before 1973 and investment proceeded at much lower.

In the 1990s, the industrial countries were confronted with low and fluctuating rates of economic growth. While inflation was reduced to minimal rates and inflationary expectations tended to weaken, unemployment in most industrial countries remained a major problem.

Finally, the relatively low growth rates in most industrial countries during the 1980s and 1990s may suggest that, once countries achieve high levels of per capita income, the pressure for maintaining high growth rates may diminish as workers and others place a higher value on leisure. However, the doctrines guiding economic policies of these years and the emphasis placed on free movement of capital along with 'slim' states and low taxes widened the gap between the rich and the poor in society. This destroyed the leisure goals of much of the workforce of the industrial world, replacing them with uncertainty concerning the opportunities for future employment, especially in unskilled areas.

The movement towards globalisation following the completion of the Uruguay Round of the GATT/WTO, and the adherence to the new economic philosophy of economic rationalism, emphasising the control of inflation above all other government economic objectives, especially in the US, while the deflationary pressures in Western Europe, as countries attempted to conform with the procedures involved in passing the Maastricht tests, have possibly been the major causes of the aberrations of the late 1980s and the 1990s.

Economic Fluctuations

The high rates of economic growth attained by most advanced countries after 1950 substantially altered the character of the economic fluctuations they experienced. Between 1950 and 1960, the US suffered three recessions, but only in two of them — in 1953 and 1958 — did GDP fall. Each setback, however, was followed in the succeeding year by higher than average increases in GDP. Western Europe, on the other hand, recorded recessions in only two years — 1952 and 1958. Moreover, as Lamfalussy (1963) observed, during the immediate post-war years, it was in those two years alone that world trade declined, if only slightly.[6]

From 1960 to 1973, only three industrial countries recorded a reduction in GDP: Australia (1961), Germany (1967) and the US (1970). In each case, the decline was no greater than 0.3 per cent and, in each case, higher than average rates of growth were recorded in at least two of the next three years. Apart from their short duration and the fact that they were invariably followed by an immediate and substantial recovery, the recessions of this period were generally marked by changes in the rates of economic growth rather than fluctuations in absolute levels of economic activity characteristic of previous recessions and depressions. There was also a weak transmission of cyclical downturns between the US and Europe. Thus, the recessions of this period contrasted markedly with those experienced during the interwar years.

In 1972 and 1973, however, and for the first time since the end of the Second World War, the economic cycles in the US, Western Europe and Japan roughly synchronised and by the end of 1973 all of the industrial countries slid into a recession which was worsened by the emerging oil crisis. In 1974, four countries, Japan, the US, the UK and Denmark, experienced a fall in GDP while in 1975, the worst year in the four decades from 1950 to 1990, ten industrial countries recorded declines in total output. Given the partial economic recovery in the OECD after 1975, few countries in the region experienced declining annual output until 1980, when another widespread recession was triggered by the second oil crisis, the price increases of 1979–80. In 1981, European countries collectively recorded a marginal increase in GDP while in 1982 the OECD as a whole experienced no growth.

Recovering in 1983, most countries experienced varying rates of growth during the remaining years of the 1980s. In 1990, the US experienced a fall in its growth rate below 2 per cent for the first time since 1982 and went on to record a fall of 1 per cent in real GDP in 1992. In Europe, France, Italy, the UK, Austria and Belgium, in addition to Canada and Australia, followed the same path as the US. In 1991, eight OECD countries recorded falls in their GDP. It was the worst year economically since 1982. After 1991, economic growth has been spasmodic, without more than a weak recovery throughout the whole OECD region up to 1998, at least. Of the major industrial countries, Japan has suffered most, in stark contrast to that country's performance in the 1960s.

The instability of the times, the greater uncertainty concerning the future and the continuing presence of inflation along with high and rising unemployment ensured that more attention was paid to cyclical behaviour after 1973 than had been the case in the 1950s and 1960s.

RECOMMENDATIONS FOR FURTHER READING

Denison (1967, *Why Growth Rates Differ: Postwar Experience of Nine Western Countries*) is a seminal paper on the drives of growth in the industrialised world in the first decades after the Second World War.

Lamfalussy (1963, *International Trade and Trade Cycles*) and the contributions to Boltho (1982, *The European Economy: Growth and Crisis*) direct their attention to the cycles and crises of the post-war industrial world.

Maddison (2001, *The World Economy: A Millennial Perspective*) provides detailed data on and discussions of the world economy over the second half of the twentieth century.

NOTES

1 A third category that can safely be assumed to have gained importance since the period under consideration is international trade within multinational corporations, where 'transfer mispricing' of, e.g., intra-firm services is used to record profits in tax havens rather than where the value added is generated.

By the nature of this activity, it is notoriously difficult to find quantitative information on this type of trade. Frequently cited is the Tax Justice Network's claim (www.taxjustice.net/cms/front_content.php?idcat=139): 'It is estimated that about 60 per cent of international trade happens within, rather than between, multinationals: that is, across national boundaries but within the same corporate group. Suggestions have been made that this figure may be closer to 70 per cent'. Academic research has barely touched this subject; a notable exception is Neiman (2008), who estimates that '[b]etween a third and a half of all U.S. trade occurs between related parties, or intrafirm, such as trades between a parent and subsidiary of the same multinational corporation'. Of course, only a fraction of all international trade within multinationals is an accountancy phenomenon to evade taxes, but the very existence of offshore and consultancy related to 'tax optimization' indicates that it must be significant.

2 During the interwar years, when this trend first revealed itself, it was associated with a substantial decline in the volume of trade between roughly the same group of countries. Moreover, at the same time, the trade in capital goods was chiefly with the NICs.

3 Only the growing importance of the trade in fuels in the 1970s and early 1980s tended to go against this trend.

4 For an elaboration, see Krugman et al. (2011, Chapter 8); see also Chapter 17 of this book, in particular endnote 3.

5 Here, they comprise the 16 most industrialised countries at the time: the EU members (excluding Greece, Ireland, Portugal and Spain), Australia, Canada, Japan, Norway, Switzerland and the US.

6 After 1958, the period of uninterrupted positive annual growth of world trade impressively lasted for 50 years; to be interrupted only twice so far: in 2008 by the Great Recession and in 2020 by the worldwide economic slump due to the measures taken during the COVID-19 pandemic.

CHAPTER 21

Trade and Growth in the International Economy

The Periphery, 1945–2000

A. G. Kenwood, A. L. Lougheed and Michael Graff

THE DEVELOPING ECONOMIES

Economic Growth

From 1955 to 1998, in every period chosen, the rate of growth of production in the developing countries was higher on average than in the developed countries, as can be seen in Table 20.8. But so, too, has population increased more rapidly in the former group of countries than in the latter. As a result, the average rate of growth in per capita production or income in developing countries did not exceed that of the developed countries to the same extent as the growth of production. The large increases in the average growth rates of GDP and per capita GDP of the developing countries in the 1990s are in stark contrast to the decline in each of these series for the advanced countries, which include some countries previously in the developing countries group.

These aggregate figures in Table 20.8 hide considerable heterogeneity, however. On a regional basis, 'East Asia' has been by far the most successful in terms of increases in per capita income since 1955. While 'Europe, the Middle East and North Africa' recorded a high average rate of growth to 1973, thereafter the region's performance declined and, in the 1980s, it experienced little growth in per capita terms, largely due to the poor experience of the oil-exporting countries. A slight recovery occurred in the 1990s. 'Latin America and the Caribbean' exhibited a similar pattern of growth to that of Europe and the Middle East, while sub-Saharan Africa consistently recorded the lowest growth rates of all the groups. Within the most successful group, 'East Asia', manufacturing production recorded much higher than average increases than it did for the developing countries as a whole.

It is common to classify developing countries into several groups such as the newly industrialising (or 'industrialized') countries (NIC5), the least developed, and the others. The last of these groups has been further distinguished as to whether its constituent countries are rather more or rather less industrialised. The 'heavily indebted poor countries' (HIPCs)

DOI: 10.4324/9781003382171-26

is another sub-group that has emerged in the literature as a legacy of the large borrowing programmes of the 1980s. The highest rates of economic growth in the 1970s were recorded by the oil-exporting countries, but in the early 1980s, when oil prices began to decline, their growth rates were very low in per capita terms. The NICs, on the other hand, especially those in East Asia, became increasingly more industrialised, experienced rapid economic growth and recorded high export performances despite the quantitative restrictions placed on their manufactured exports by the industrial countries. In essence, the NIC grouping is a half-way classification for emerging countries between 'developing' and 'advanced' status, and in 1997 the IMF 'granted' the latter classification to Hong Kong, Taiwan, Israel, Korea and Singapore. China, Indonesia, Malaysia, Thailand and Vietnam recorded rates of growth of GDP generally in excess of 8 per cent during the 1990s, until the Asian financial crisis of 1997 affected their performances.

During the 1970s, inflation rates increased within the developing countries. If we exclude the six high-inflation countries — Argentina, Chile, Ghana, Israel, Turkey and Zaire, in each of which consumer prices rose at more than double the average for their groups — the oil exporters averaged an annual increase of 18 per cent in consumer prices from 1973 to 1980; the major exporters of manufactures 33 per cent; the low-income countries 17 per cent; and the remainder 24 per cent. Inflation became a greater problem for most countries after 1978 when the second major oil price increase occurred. Averaging 25 per cent per year from 1973 to 1982, the inflation rate of developing countries as a group remained above 30 per cent until 1988, when it rose sharply. It was lowest in Asia, generally below 10 per cent, and highest in Latin America, where in 1990 it peaked at over 440 per cent. By the mid-1990s, the average rate of inflation in developing countries had fallen from 68 per cent in 1990 to 10 per cent (1997), although it was still high at an average of 15 per cent in Africa and 22 per cent in the Middle East in that year.

Foreign Aid and Economic Development

Economic growth in the developing countries was accompanied by a massive inflow of foreign capital. In addition to the influx of long-term private capital, which went principally into mining, oil production and manufacturing, a further $800 billion was provided in the form of official foreign aid to these countries between 1950 and 1995. The aid offered recipient countries some help in their efforts to overcome two obstacles, which might have frustrated their attempts to achieve sustained economic development.

On the one hand, if a country's development programme entails greater investment expenditures than can be sustained by the level of domestic savings, it can undertake the additional expenditure without inflation only if the excess of domestic expenditure over current output is covered by external financing. On the other hand, a trade or foreign exchange gap will appear when a country's shortage of foreign exchange becomes an effective barrier to its economic development by denying it access to imported commodities, especially capital goods, essential for its economic growth. Foreign assistance is then needed to allow the projected investment of the development plan to take the desired form — that is, investment may require necessary imports that cannot be alternatively supplied from substitute domestic sources. If domestic saving does not result in an adequate increase in exports (through reducing the demand for domestically produced goods, thus freeing them for export), or a reduction in imports of consumer goods so as to provide sufficient foreign exchange for the imports needed to support the higher rate of capital formation, foreign assistance will then be required for balance of payments reasons quite distinct from the need for aid as an adjunct to savings. Thus, a country in which savings are relatively abundant may still experience a foreign exchange gap.[1]

It should also be pointed out that, whereas a savings gap requires a transfer of external resources in the form of aid, a trade gap may be filled by foreign exchange obtained in a number of ways, for instance, through aid receipts, improvements in the terms of trade and/or higher export earnings.

Fears have been expressed that developing countries would come to depend upon foreign capital assistance, and that this state of dependence will never end. But assuming that the foreign capital is used successfully to promote economic development, the consequent increase in productivity and income may create a source of potential saving that can at some point take over the burden of supplying the capital needed for continuing development. In order to achieve successful growth, the foreign capital should make a net contribution to a country's development. It must not lead to a diversion of domestic investment funds into inventory accumulation, luxury building, speculation, graft and corruption or military expenditure. At the same time, a country's capacity to make effective use of foreign aid will depend on a wide range of conditions, including the stability and efficiency of government, the availability of complementary inputs, the size of the domestic market, the extent of social overhead capital — especially in transport and communications — so important for the mobility of goods and people, and finally, the prevailing social attitudes towards change and institutions and habits that influence growth. Even if successful economic development is achieved, however, a country's increased savings potential may be absorbed by population growth or by wasteful types of government expenditure.

The foreign aid policies adopted by donor countries can also influence for good or ill the way in which their financial assistance to the developing countries is used. Thus, tied aid — that is, loans and grants that can only be used to purchase goods in the donor country — denies the recipient country the opportunity of buying its imports in the cheapest market or of obtaining the collection of goods most suitable for its development requirements. Untied aid, which has no restrictions on the uses to which it is put, is obviously to be preferred. When, in the 1950s, the Cold War made aid-giving an instrument of foreign policy for most donor countries, its economic effectiveness was reduced. Moreover, a large part of foreign aid advanced since 1945 was in the form of military assistance and this has conferred few economic benefits on the countries receiving it. At times it was used to prop up dictatorships or military rule, with little of the money being used for economic purposes. Political considerations in the past have tended to produce gross distortions in the pattern of foreign aid. Thus, India, which has a high capacity to import capital, was, relatively speaking, starved of foreign funds because of its political policy of non-alignment.[2]

On the other hand, other countries, because of their political stance, obtained funds out of all proportion to their capacity to use them effectively. One way of overcoming this problem is to channel a greater part of the aid flow to developing countries through international agencies such as the International Development Association (IDA) rather than national governments.

Some aid to developing countries was in the form of grants with no repayment, but most aid involved loans with or without interest payments, and with a short or long maturing period. Where interest must be paid and where loans have to be amortised, these payments constitute a direct cost to the recipient country. To meet the service charges on foreign capital, the borrowing country must somehow generate a surplus of foreign exchange. If it achieves a rapid rate of economic development, the growth of new savings may ensure the release of a corresponding value of real resources which can be exported or can be substituted for imports. There will thus appear a similar surplus of foreign exchange receipts over payments for imports which can be used to cover debt service charges. If, however, development lags or if the population grows too rapidly, a borrowing country can only ensure that the debt charges will be covered by directing foreign capital into the production of exports or import substitutes, or by the imposition of restrictions on both imports and domestic consumption. The problem of debt-servicing has received much attention from the mid-1960s onward and a general movement towards debt restructuring and softer loans, incorporating lower interest rates and longer periods of grace and maturity, ensued. In addition, grants became more prevalent in the 1970s and 1980s. At the same time, however, the annual increases in the total amount of foreign aid in real terms tended to decline after the economic crises of the mid-1970s.

Increasingly, during the 1980s, when some relatively successful developing countries found their annual aid flows inadequate to finance their development projects, they turned towards the international loan market, in which many commercial banks in the US and elsewhere were increasingly willing to lend to the governments of such countries. These were not 'soft' loans, however, and interest payments were quoted in US dollars. The increasing international interest rates of the 1980s and the rise in the value of the US dollar soon found several borrowing countries in payments difficulties. Thus, in 1982 and in 1994 Mexico experienced debt crises, which had to be resolved with the aid of the international financial and foreign aid community. In addition, in the 1980s and increasingly in the 1990s, business firms and domestic banks in some of the 'richer' developing countries resorted to loans from financial institutions in the industrial countries.

Indeed, the foreign aid approach to financial assistance to developing countries altered in nature and in effect during the 1990s. From funding long-run economic development and reducing poverty, foreign aid was directed increasingly towards emergency relief and so-called 'peacekeeping' activities. Traditional foreign aid was reserved for the poorest countries and the HIPCs. On the other hand, given the opening-up of world financial markets, foreign aid or official development finance, which fell from $56.3 billion in 1990 to $40.8 billion in 1996, was increasingly replaced by private resource flows, which grew from $44.4 billion in 1990 to $243.8 billion. These private flows included foreign direct investment (FDI) (an increase from $24.5 billion in 1990 to $109.5 billion in 1996), commercial bank debt ($3 billion to $34.2 billion) and bonds ($2.3 billion to $46.1 billion). Portfolio investment rose from $3.2 billion to $45.7 billion at this time. Thus, after the end of the Cold War in 1990, when the need for foreign aid as a political weapon disappeared, official aid gave way to foreign private borrowing on a large-scale and official financial assistance began to wither.

Foreign Trade and Economic Development

The trade performances of primary producers during the 1950s and later were relatively poor. Several reasons were advanced to account for this. They include the change in the composition of industrial production in the industrial countries within their manufacturing sectors, i.e. from industries normally demanding a high raw materials content in the finished product to those whose products have a low raw materials content; the relatively low-income elasticity of consumer demand for many agricultural products; agricultural protectionism in the industrial countries; the substantial economies in the industrial uses of natural materials obtained through improved production methods; and the displacement of natural raw materials by synthetic and other manmade substitutes. Declining prices, due largely to falling demand brought about by these changes, also affected the export earnings of many primary producing countries. The resulting poor export performances of many developing countries placed severe constraints on their growth and, while foreign aid tended to alleviate these difficulties to a certain extent, by allowing the developing nations to import larger quantities of manufactures from industrial countries than their trading positions warranted, this offset to the relatively low growth of exports was far from complete for the group as a whole. As for a solution to their trade problems, although trends in demand and in technical progress cannot easily be reversed, the developing countries felt that the protectionist and fiscal policies of industrial countries could be moderated to allow greater rates of growth in at least some of their trade. At the same time they believed that a greater degree of stability in primary product prices could have been achieved through commodity agreements and other such arrangements.

The protection given by the advanced countries to their relatively inefficient domestic primary producers in the 1950s and 1960s was a major cause of discontent in the developing world. In addition, the levying of fiscal taxes in Europe on such agricultural products as tea, coffee and tobacco also caused concern. Since these taxes were often more severe than the customs duties already imposed on the products, they had a very damaging effect on the exports of certain developing countries. But there was still more in contention.

The developing countries felt that they were at a disadvantage in trying to raise their share of the world trade in manufactures. Particularly significant in this respect in the 1960s was the argument that their manufactured exports should receive preferential treatment by the industrial nations, since the most favoured nation (MFN) clause included in the General Agreement on Tariffs and Trade (GATT) was just only if all trading nations had reached the same level of economic development. More specifically, it was felt that the manner in which tariff reductions were agreed upon in the GATT, namely, reciprocal reductions on the part of the negotiating countries, was inappropriate for the developing countries, since tariff reductions brought about in this way could adversely affect their development programmes. Moreover, the tariff structure of the developed countries was detrimental to the growth of manufactured exports of developing countries by being lowest on raw materials and highest on finished goods, favouring the last stages of manufacturing production to be carried out in the industrial world. In addition, the use of quantitative import restrictions by the richer countries to protect high-cost domestic producers against competition from developing countries tended to cover a number of commodities, such as leather and leather goods, jute and coin manufactures, electric motors, sporting goods and textiles, many of which the developing countries had been able to export in great amounts.

These difficulties led to a growing disenchantment in the developing countries with the GATT. As we have already seen, one outcome of all this activity was the establishment of UNCTAD, which held its first meeting in Geneva in 1964. In addition, the new chapter written into the GATT, allowing preferential treatment by the industrial countries of the imports of products from the developing countries, led to the introduction of the Generalised System of Preferences (GSP) in the 1970s by most industrial countries. However, despite the GSP, the tropical products agreement during the Tokyo Round, and the movement towards the establishment of a Common Fund in relation to commodity agreements, it is highly questionable whether these innovations went far enough. In addition, the non-tariff barriers erected against the entry of manufactures into the industrial countries, especially in Europe, multiplied after 1973 and adversely affected the development of the NICs, some of which were among the most debt-ridden countries in the developing world. The negotiations under the Uruguay Round in the early 1990s have, to some extent, reduced the effectiveness of many of these barriers to entry into the industrial countries.

Throughout much of the period during which the developing countries placed an emphasis on an expansion of trade with the rest of the world they experienced a deterioration in their terms of trade. Towards the end of the 1950s they found that their efforts at development were being undermined in this way. While little deterioration occurred for the non-oil developing countries from the early 1960s to 1972, adverse effects appeared once again during much of the 1970s when, despite an improvement of 7.5 per cent in the 1973 boom, a rapid decline in the next two years and a further fall after 1978 meant that, from 1972 to 1980, a deterioration of 11 per cent on average had occurred. A further 2 per cent decline in the terms of trade of the non-oil-exporting developing countries was recorded between 1980 and 1989, but, thereafter to 1998, despite some annual fluctuations, on the whole little change occurred.

It has been argued that developing countries should trade more with each other — that primary producers should supply the NICs and other exporters of manufactures with raw materials in return for manufactured products. In fact, trade within the developing countries has fluctuated in relative terms over time but increased substantially in the 1990s. Second, it is increasingly recognised that a major drawback to development in many poor countries is the lack of an efficient food-producing sector. Numerous countries quite often find it necessary to use valuable foreign exchange to purchase urgently needed food from the richer countries. An improved agricultural sector can not only provide a growing urban sector with its food requirements but can also act as a growing market for the output of the urban manufacturing sector of an economy.

Long-Run Economic Growth of the Developing Countries

The concern about the slow rate of economic growth in the poor countries is a continuation of a debate which developed at the end of the Second World War concerning the long-run tendency for most developing countries to grow more slowly than the industrial world over the past century and a half. Broadly speaking, explanations of economic underdevelopment have evolved in the form of two largely opposed theories: 'traditional society theories' and 'world economy theories'. The first set of theories sees the problem of slow growth and underdevelopment as originating within the poor countries themselves, whereas the second set places emphasis on the economic domination of poor countries by the industrialised West; that is, underdevelopment is a consequence of the way in which the international economy has evolved in the past.

In 'traditional society theories', the influence of the advanced countries on the underdeveloped economies is seen as basically development-promoting, and underdevelopment is analysed as a function of indigenous social, cultural and psychological factors that block development. Thus, while the advanced countries may supply the economic preconditions for development, in the form of capital, technology and trade, and may also encourage the emergence of modernising elites concerned with promoting development in imitation of Western entrepreneurs and political leaders, underdevelopment persists, despite all this, because poor societies are unable, because of their very nature, to respond adequately to the stimulus of industrialisation. They may fail to encourage change and innovation, hampered as they may be by a rigid social structure or powerful and corrupt official bureaucracies or a dictatorial army-controlled and regimented political system. In short, these societies lack the existence or quick emergence of a political, social and institutional framework which exploits the impulses to expansion and development available to them. In sum, traditional society theories argue that underdeveloped countries are insufficiently open to the development-promoting world economy created by the industrial nations.

'World economy theories' make precisely the opposite argument. They see underdevelopment as a result of the integration of the periphery into the international economy on unfavourable terms. These theories attribute underdevelopment and slow growth to the dependent position of the poor countries in an international economy that is constructed to benefit the Western industrial nations. In short, the influence of developed nations on the underdeveloped countries is seen as basically development-blocking, not development-promoting. Underdeveloped economies are seen as primary producing satellites, providing a flow of cheap agricultural and mineral products to the West. Colonialism tended to reinforce this pattern of economic development, which often led to dependence on a limited range of primary products and the creation of 'enclave economies' brought about by foreign investment in the export sector. It is argued, moreover, that primary product export prices showed a long-run tendency to decline and this limited improvements in domestic living standards and seriously hindered industrial development by limiting the export earnings available to finance it. Industrial development in the poor countries was hampered in other ways. Colonialism involved the loss of autonomy in tariff protection, and the unrestrained competition of foreign manufactured goods often led to the collapse of native handicraft industries. Moreover, when industrial development did occur, it was often dominated by foreign-owned enterprises. In these and other ways the domination of the international economy by the industrially advanced countries was seen as providing the major obstacle to economic development in the poor countries.

Neither set of theories outlined above is likely to provide the complete explanation of the problem of underdevelopment and slow economic growth. Only through detailed study of the experience of *individual* countries will convincing answers to the question of the origins of underdevelopment and slow economic growth in so many parts of the world be found More-over, in the later decades of the twentieth century not all developing countries have remained underdeveloped. Countries as South Korea, Hong Kong, Taiwan, Singapore, Indonesia,

Malaysia and Thailand have all taken great strides towards becoming advanced advances. An investigation of the reasons for the success of these countries may provide additional useful insights.

THE CENTRALLY PLANNED ECONOMIES

Economic Growth

In Europe, the centrally planned economies (CPEs) emulated Western economic progress during the 1950s and 1960s.[3] From 1951 to 1973, the Soviet Union recorded an annual average rate of growth of real GDP of 5 per cent, and the other CPEs (excluding Albania) 4.7 per cent. Bulgaria (6.1 per cent) and Romania (5.9 per cent) were the fastest-growing economies during these years. In per capita terms, the Soviet Union averaged 3.6 per cent per year while the rest averaged 4 per cent. In China, GDP rose at around 6 per cent per year in the 1950s and 4 per cent per head of population.

After 1973, however, economic growth slowed down rapidly in the European CPEs. From 1974 to 1982, the Soviet Union's annual rate of growth of GDP averaged around 2 per cent and just under that figure from 1983 to 1988. The other European CPEs averaged 1.9 per cent between 1974 and 1982, and 2.7 per cent from 1983 to 1988. In per capita terms, the Soviet Union barely exceeded a growth rate of 1 per cent per annum after 1973, while the rest of East Europe was able to increase its per capita performance from 1.3 per cent per year (1974–82) to 2.3 per cent in the late 1980s. After 1982, however, only Poland (4.2 per cent) was able to record a GDP growth rate above 3 per cent. China, on the other hand, achieved an average annual growth rate of 5.2 per cent between 1965 and 1987. As a result of numerous economic reforms in the 1980s, including the encouraging of village-township small-scale manufacturing enterprises, the country was able to achieve an average of 9 per cent for the period 1979 to 1987. In addition, China opened its doors to direct foreign investment, and from 1979 to 1985 over $16 billion entered the country, principally from Hong Kong (61 per cent) and Japan (10 per cent).

A feature of the growth of the CPEs from 1960 to 1975 was the high rate of real investment, with the Soviet Union averaging 7.5 per cent per year and the other East European countries 10 per cent. The situation changed dramatically after 1975, with investment growth slackening to an average of 3.2 per cent to 1980 and 2.2 per cent from 1980 to 1985. Partly for this reason, the economic performance of industry (manufacturing and construction) worsened during the 1980s. While this sector grew at an annual average of 5 per cent from 1961 to 1980, over the next eight years this average fell to 2.5 per cent in the Soviet Union (about the same as in the Western industrial countries) and 1.3 per cent in other East European countries. As for agriculture, while it virtually stagnated in the Soviet Union in the 1980s, its growth in other CPEs rose from 1.0 per cent annually between 1961 and 1980 to 2.3 per cent per year from 1981 to 1988.

Various reasons have been advanced for the relatively poor performances of the European CPEs from 1973 to 1988. While they were affected by the same growth-inhibiting factors which also reduced growth rates in the Western industrial countries, the Cold War's Western embargoes, boycotts and technology transfer restrictions, and finally, the nuclear armaments' race that the NATO initiated in the 1980s, created additional challenges. Apart from this, it is argued that the lack of competitive pressures prevented the growth of productivity and the drive towards greater efficiency within the industrial sector of the CPEs. In addition, the difficulty in obtaining the information required to ensure that central planning could be effective in all sectors of the economy also played an important role. During the 1980s, recognition of the defects in central planning led to moves towards the introduction of market-oriented structural reforms in an endeavour to correct the deficiencies of the planning system.

Foreign Trade

In conjunction with the goal of development through industrialisation, trading with the rest of the world was considered necessary only to obtain raw materials and other commodities which could not be produced domestically, and exports were considered essential only to the extent necessary to pay for the required imports and to dispose of surplus production. Even so, trade with the West was higher in the late 1940s than in the 1950s when, for several reasons, including the commencement of the Cold War in 1948 and the formation of COMECON (or the Council for Mutual Economic Assistance (CMEA)) in 1949, intra-bloc trade expanded at the expense of trade with the West. By 1960, intra-bloc trade was around four times the size of that undertaken with the Western industrial countries, the latter consisting largely of exchanges of food, fuel and raw materials for steel products and machinery and equipment.

The CMEA was set up to achieve broader economic cooperation within Eastern Europe, but it was not until 1955 that an elaborate scheme for the coordination of production and the development of a pattern of national export specialisation was completed, which was designed to eliminate duplication of output and to achieve the benefits of large-scale production. But political difficulties in Hungary and Poland in 1956 and Romania's objection to being a supplier solely of primary products meant that, although intra-bloc trade and commercial exchanges grew rapidly from 1957 to 1962, little progress was made toward the multilateralising of planning and development.

At first the character of the foreign trade of the CPEs was bilateral, with each country attempting to balance its trade each year with each of its CPE trading partners. This practice, however, tended to ensure that trade within the region would not be maximised. To initiate a movement away from such bilateralism, the International Bank for Economic Co-operation (IBEC) was established in 1964, and a new trade currency, the 'transferable rouble', created. Each CMEA member country could then record deficits with some of its neighbours and surpluses with others, with the IBEC using transferable roubles to settle deficits and surpluses within limits. Trade with the West still tended not to be balanced bilaterally, but an overall external balance was always a goal of the East European bloc.

In 1963, intra-bloc trade accounted for 66 per cent of the total exports of CMEA members, trade with the Western industrial countries for 19 per cent and with developing countries for 12 per cent. From 1963 on, however, trade with the non-CPE world became much more important than it had been in the 1950s. This growing importance came about largely because the East European countries increasingly recognised that greater trade with the West could play an important part in their development programmes by providing additional supplies of scarce currencies and thus greater access to the benefits of modern industrial technology. By the 1980s, intra-area trade accounted for between 48 and 52 per cent of total exports, trade with the Western industrial countries for 27–33 per cent and with developing countries for 14–17 per cent. But the expansion of trade with the West was fraught with problems, both political and economic.

In the 1970s, a widening trade deficit with Western countries emerged as the East European countries found it increasingly difficult to expand their exports in line with their demand for technologically advanced machinery and equipment from the West. There were several reasons for this, including: the Common Agricultural Policy (CAP) within the EC, which curtailed the exports of foodstuffs from Eastern Europe; the failure of CMEA countries to maintain continuity of supply of various exports; the general spread of trade restrictions in the West; and the depressed demand for imports in the industrial countries at various times. As a result, the East European countries changed their attitudes towards trading with the West and their methods of obtaining Western technology. First, they turned to the Western banking system for convertible currency and other loans to finance their import surpluses. By 1980, total net borrowings of the CPEs had risen to $56 billion, with a net debt of $41.2 billion. The major borrowers were Poland, the Soviet Union and Hungary. In that year, it was clear that Poland was faced with a severe debt-servicing problem, for its debt-service ratio (interest commitment plus debt repayments as a percentage of exports) was over 100 per cent. During the early 1980s, attempts to reduce the bloc debt were successful, but after 1985, the debt began to rise again, and at the end of 1988 it exceeded $100 billion. The heaviest debtors were Poland and Hungary, each of which recorded a debt-to-GDP ratio of over 50 per cent.

Second, to conserve scarce foreign currency and to obviate the need for extra loans from the West, many cooperative production agreements were arranged between Eastern and Western firms. These agreements took various forms, but generally they involved the supply of the technology, often including plant and equipment, by the Western to the Eastern firm, with some of the output of the Eastern firm being supplied to the Western company in exchange for the supply of the technology. The supplier of the technology received the benefit of low-cost production, while the recipient received the benefit of Western expertise and the right to sell part of its output in the CPE markets without competition from its Western partner. No foreign currency was required to obtain the technology as it was paid for in commodities.

Foreign Aid and the Centrally Planned Economies

Foreign aid from the CPEs to the poorer countries dates from 1954, when the Soviet Union set up its first aid programme. By 1960, it was followed by other East European countries and China, and total aid commitments of the CPEs reached some $3.6 billion, mostly in the form of loans. Over half of this aid went to South Asia and about one-third to the Middle East, with India and the United Arab Republic (Egypt) being the major recipients and together receiving about 40 per cent of the total commitments.

In the 1960s, total CPE aid commitments averaged around $1 billion per year and this grew in the 1970s and 1980s to an average from East Europe of almost $5 billion per year. The Soviet Union's share declined in the 1960s relative to the shares of Czechoslovakia, China and the German Democratic Republic (GDR).

Over time, the bulk of the aid went increasingly to other CPEs, with Vietnam, Cuba and Mongolia, for example, receiving over 70 per cent of the total by the mid-1980s and other allegedly 'socialist' developing countries around 12 per cent. Non-socialist poor countries accounted for around 7 per cent.

Most of this aid was bilateral, and repayments were often made in the currency of the recipient, in traditional export commodities or in the form of goods produced by the projects aided. A high proportion of the loans went into the creation and modernisation of enterprises in the non-farm sectors and, up to the mid-1970s at least, the ferrous metal industry received special treatment because it was held that this sector was vital to the industrialisation of a developing country. In the 1970s, much attention was also paid to the stimulation of export-oriented activities, with an emphasis on those exports having a ready market in CMEA countries, particularly minerals and fuel. In the 1980s, specific projects of interest to the recipients were financed. There was a general hardening of the terms under which aid was supplied after the early 1970s, and the loans were rendered less attractive to potential recipients. In addition to the financial aid, economic and technical assistance was provided to many of the developing countries over the years. China's foreign aid fluctuated substantially in the 1970s and 1980s but increased in size early in the latter decade, principally to sub-Saharan Africa, where emphasis was placed on agricultural development, transport and health. This aid was appreciated by the poorer recipients in that its technologies were adapted to their needs, especially in small-scale industries such as agriculture and health.

While the bulk of the CPE's aid to developing countries was bilateral, a multilateral aid outlet for CMEA members was created in the mid-1970s, when a Special Fund for development credits was established under the control of the International Investment Bank. A greater degree of coordination of the aid programmes of the CMEA countries also occurred. Nevertheless, by the 1980s, over 85 per cent of foreign aid from CMEA countries came from the Soviet Union.

THE COUNTRIES IN TRANSITION

The poor economic performances of the CPEs in the 1980s led to a movement towards more market coordination. Maddison's figures (1994, p. 62) suggest an average annual decline in the real GDP per capita of Central and Eastern Europe from 1973 to 1992 of 0.8 per cent, with only Hungary holding its own. This contrasted with an annual average increase of 4.0 per cent from 1950 to 1973. The years from 1989 saw massive political, economic and social changes in Central and Eastern Europe and some parts of Asia. There was first the opening of the intra-German border, and soon after the currency union and the integration of the GDR (informally also 'East Germany') into the West German state (the 'Federal Republic') in 1989/90, and thereby its integration into the EU, the break-up of the Soviet Union in 1991 and its replacement by the Commonwealth of Independent States (CIS), comprising Russia, Belarus, Moldova, Ukraine, Estonia, Latvia and Lithuania, and Transcaucasian and Central Asian states of Armenia, Azerbaijan, Georgia, Kazakhstan, Kyrgyz Republic, Tajikistan, Turkmenistan and Uzbekistan, and, further east, Mongolia. The establishment of pro-capitalist governments in Czechoslovakia (later to be divided into the Czech and the Slovak Republics),

Hungary, Poland, Romania, Bulgaria and Albania led to the classification of this group of countries as the Central and East European Countries (CEEC).[4] The countries in transition (CITs) endeavoured to convert from central planning to market economy status.

Out of the former Yugoslavia emerged, in a decade of violence and atrocity, Croatia, Bosnia-Herzegovina, Serbia, Slovenia and the former Yugoslav Republic of Macedonia (Now: North Macedonia). All CEECs sought closer integration with the EU, initially through free trade agreements.

The beginning of this transformation was associated with the dismantling of the former economic and political controls, the establishment of a Western-style banking system, including currency reform and the development of foreign trade and investment, the introduction of free market business legislation and the privatisation of the former state-owned enterprises. It was a formidable set of tasks. At the same time, economic growth faltered, as inefficient firms went into liquidation, trade ties with other CITs were broken and the demand for exportable commodities fell rapidly. Inflation rose to untenable levels and so, too, did unemployment. Advice from the West, especially through the IMF, led to the introduction of stabilisation programmes, including a rapid attack on inflation, the government deficit, the public debt and the introduction of micro-economic reform. The IMF provided financial aid through its drawings and standby procedures, its EFF (Extended Fund Facility), ESAF (Enhanced Structural Adjustment Facility) and the new STF (Systemic Transformation Facility). The rapidity of change required by the West, which initially provided only a minimum of bilateral aid, led to some successes in those countries close to Western Europe — Czechoslovakia, Hungary and Poland — but, for most, the tasks were far too great to guarantee immediate progress, in particular, the further the country was from Western Europe.

The 1990s saw these countries struggle with the problems of economic transition, encouraged by the IMF and other bodies to introduce harsh stabilisation programmes to achieve the short-term goals of balanced budgets, low inflation, monetary stability and micro-economic reform, including the widespread privatisation of industry, and all without any concern for the high levels of unemployment created as a result of these policies. By the mid-decade, inflation rates were being reduced in all except a handful of countries, and economic conditions were beginning to improve in several of them. By 1996, all except five countries (including Russia) recorded positive growth, but all countries still had a long road to follow before they could emulate the Western industrial model. The most advanced of these countries — the Czech Republic, Hungary and Poland — were soon granted associate status within the EU. (In 2004, they would gain full membership in the next EU enlargement round, along with Cyprus, Estonia, Latvia, Lithuania and Malta; see Chapter 22.) Needless to say, little foreign aid issued from these countries during the 1990s. Indeed, financial resources tended to flow in the opposite direction, especially after 1995, from the IMF and mainly private sources in Western Europe.

RECOMMENDATIONS FOR FURTHER READING

For detailed analyses of the world economy in the twentieth century and the roles of the centre as compared to the periphery, essential readings are Bhagwati, (1977, *The New International Economic Order: The North-South Debate*), Landes (1999, *The Wealth and Poverty of*

Nations: Why Some Are so Rich and Some so Poor), Wallerstein (2004, *World-System Analysis*) and Easterly (2006, *The White Man's Burden*).

Reinert (2007, *How Rich Countries Got Rich and Why Poor Countries Stay Poor*) discusses why traditional trade theories may give unhelpful advice to the poorer countries.

Todaro and Smith (2020, *Economic Development*) is a textbook that covers almost every topic of importance for the economic development of the poorer countries.

NOTES

1 In development economics, these considerations are referred as 'Dual Gap Theory'; see, for example, Todaro and Smith (2020).

2 While in terms of total aid received in the 1960s India was one of the most-favoured recipients, in terms of per capita aid it was close to the bottom of the list of recipient countries.

3 This group included the Soviet Union, Czechoslovakia, Hungary, Poland, the GDR, Bulgaria, Romania, Albania (all in Europe), China, Laos, Mongolia, North Korea, Vietnam (in Asia) and Cuba. The European members, except Albania, were members of CMEA, so were Cuba and Mongolia. Although Yugoslavia was centrally planned, it was normally excluded from the group of CPEs because of its more intensive economic relations with the West.

4 The Czech and Slovak Republics formed a customs union in 1992 and also entered into free trade agreements with Hungary and Poland in that year.

CHAPTER **22**

The New Millennium, 2001–24

Michael Graff

INTRODUCTION

The collapse of the German Democratic Republic (GDR; East Germany) in 1989 paved the way for the disintegration of the Soviet Union in 1991. This marked the end of what Eric Hobsbawm called the 'short twentieth century', spanning from the First World War to the end of the Soviet Union. The dismantling of the Berlin Wall and the silent, almost ashamed departure from power of the parties and governments that had claimed to rule over a 'really existing socialism' were greeted warmly by many, if not most, of those directly affected and by observers in the West. Apparently, history had proven that there was no alternative to capitalism, and the 'end of history' seemed to have arrived with the final victory of the liberal market economy along with free elections and parliamentary democracy.[1]

Yet, the twentieth century did not end well, but rather in a 'disintegration of human social relationships … [into] an absolute a-social individualism' (Hobsbawm, 1994, p. 15), along with a series of economic crises. The first years of transition of what had been the centrally planned economies (CPEs) of Eastern and Central Europe into capitalist market economies brought hardship to many, and incredible wealth to the few who succeeded in appropriating for themselves the productive and natural assets through fire-sale privatisations. This 'original accumulation' took only a few years and, along with pronouncedly pro-capitalist leaderships, laid the basis for textbook capitalist economies.

The 'peace dividend' that many expected after the end of the Cold War failed to materialise. The emergence of aggressive nationalism led to the disintegration of multi-ethnic states, basically peacefully in Czechoslovakia, more problematically in parts of the former Soviet Union, and violently to the extreme in a series of civil wars and atrocities from 1991 to 1999, with tens of thousands of deaths, as well as widely practiced 'ethnic cleansing' that haunted what had been Yugoslavia. As this book is finalised, the conflict between Russia and Ukraine that turned into outright fighting between regular forces with the invasion of Russian troops into Ukraine in February 2022 is now in its fourth year. It may already have caused the deaths

DOI: 10.4324/9781003382171-27

of 300,000 combatants and, particularly in the eastern parts of Ukraine, losses of lives of more than 30,000 civilians as well as massive destruction of infrastructure and buildings. At this time, the fighting is continuing as a low- to medium-intensity war of attrition with no end in sight, and it is by no means clear whether this will be the last armed conflict to result from the aggressive nationalism that has gained force since the collapse of the Soviet Union.

Geopolitics as a means to consolidate or gain hegemonic status has definitely re-emerged, and an increasing share of the productive capacity of many economies is now redirected into armaments and troops. It is difficult to witness this without a sense of despair, as at the same time global warming is proceeding virtually unchecked. We are thus facing our perhaps greatest challenge ever, and the efforts to cope with it are clearly insufficient. No decisive steps to bring global warming to a halt have been agreed upon so far, nor are any in sight. Instead, rearmament and military buildup have gained top priority (see Appendices 1 and 2 to Chapter 23).

Looking at standards of living across the globe, high rates of GDP growth have lifted millions of people above the poverty line, particularly in China, but far too many are still left behind. Migrants from the poorer parts of the world are drowning in the seas or perishing on the land routes by the thousands each year in desperate attempts to reach the shores or land borders of wealthier economies and a chance for a better life — the annual number of victims is many times the entire death toll at the infamous Berlin Wall from 1961 to 1989. Those who succeed to arrive alive at their chosen destination must often realise that their dreams do not materialise, as they are forced into clandestine lives with precarious jobs, without medical insurance or social security, but with the permanent threat of denunciation or being accidentally identified as 'illegal' and sent back to where they came from.

As the new millennium approached, the periphery of the world economy recorded serious currency and banking crises. In 1997, the Asian financial crisis hit some of the most promising emerging economies. Foreign capital had flowed in on a large scale, and when the mood changed, contagion spread, capital flows reversed, currencies devalued and the affected economies were faced with short-term debt denominated in foreign currency that corresponded to rapidly increasing amounts in domestic currency. The Russian banking crises of 1998–9 followed, then the Argentinean crisis of 1999–2002. Argentina had installed a currency board in 1991, fixing the peso at 1 to the US dollar, to end its history of hyperinflation. Indeed, inflation was instantly brought down to moderate levels, but it still exceeded US inflation rates so that the peso appreciated in real terms. Exports suffered accordingly, and unemployment rose along with the trade deficit. To maintain the currency board, austerity measures were imposed to improve competitiveness of Argentina's exports. In 1999, GDP dropped by 4 per cent, starting three year, Argentina. In 2001, Argentinians' bank accounts were frozen, and at the end of that year, Argentina defaulted on its external debt. In January 2002, the peg to the dollar was abandoned, which paved the way for recovery.

Meanwhile, in the West the collapse of what some had perceived as a viable 'communist' alternative to capitalism lifted practically all previous restraints on the liberal free market ideology. The roll-back of the welfare state that had started with the extreme pro-business 'laissez-faire' governments under Margaret Thatcher in the UK (1979–90) and Ronald Reagan in the US (1981–9) gained momentum. Reformist left-wing parties and Labour (or Social Democrats, as some of them are also calling themselves) followed suit and, when elected, completed the job. Unemployment benefits, old age and health care provisions were reduced with cynical reference to individual freedom and responsibility. Progressive taxation, which had been the moral backbone of the 'social market economy' and provided the revenue for the welfare state in the 'golden age' up to 1973, was deemed inefficient. Marginal tax rates were cut, and 'simple' — a euphemism for less progressive or completely flat — income tax schedules were embraced. The second long-standing principle of taxation, stating that all income should be taxed independently of the source and at the same marginal rate, was abandoned as a response to increasing international capital mobility. With an increasing number of offshore tax havens offering minimal taxation coupled with 'privacy' (i.e. secrecy), a race to the bottom of capital income taxation set in. While many regarded this as a lamentable but inevitable side-effect of globalisation, more radical market fundamentalists greeted it as a healthy move towards 'slim' government. The absolute minimum of taxes required to ensure the institutional framework for the rule of law and to sustain the police and other armed forces that are perceived as indispensable would ideally be levied on consumption. While these taxes are mostly flat nominally, and in some cases reduced rates are applied for basic goods, they in fact tend to be regressive as the marginal propensity to consume declines with income and wealth. Thus, along with income tax cuts, indirect taxes were increased across the board.

Financial markets grew, and along with them the incomes earned in the financial industry. Liberalisation got rid of precautionary regulation; and innovative 'products' were presented to the admiring public of de facto and would-be investors. At the same time, structural reforms created new financial markets for which there had previously simply been no necessity — student loans as a result of newly introduced or increased tuition fees and the abolition of educational government grants; and pension funds to accumulate mandatory savings on private retirement accounts, where previously tax funded or pay-as-you-go pension schemes had provided reliable and crisis-proof retirement incomes.

Banks widely promoted loans to fund financial investments and willingly accepted these assets as collateral. While this is common practice for mortgage loans for family homes and unproblematic under normal conditions, it turns into systemic risk when it fuels speculation. An important lesson from the Great Depression of the 1930s is that speculative investment based on credit had triggered massive 'margin calls' as the banks watched the collateral prices sliding. The asset price then plunged, as illiquid speculators were forced to sell. It remains a miracle that this could be overlooked in the beginning of the new millennium. In the bubble economies, daily newspapers offered advice to ordinary people to take out loans in order to 'invest' in shares or 'property'. Whatever interest they were charged, they could only gain, as the increase in asset prices was promised to outweigh the costs by far. Tax deductibility for such 'investments' in many countries added to the boom. The usual rule that interest rates for liabilities are higher than for assets, so that it is wise to pay off any loan as quickly as possible was declared invalid. And indeed, as long as the bubble kept inflating, those who stood aside appeared foolish. The housing market boom proved especially significant in macroeconomic terms in countries like the US, where owner-occupied dwellings are the rule rather than the exception, so that the sentiment of increasing net wealth was widely shared. Policies directed at crisis prevention would have undermined the boom and hence have been highly unpopular.

For those who were left behind in terms of real income after taxes and transfers, easily available credit was offered as compensation. In particular, after-tax income distribution inequality had gradually started to increase in the 1970s in the US. As this process accelerated from about 1980, consumers and house buyers, observing their luckier peers engaging in increasingly conspicuous consumption and moving into increasingly spacious dwellings, cut their savings and took on consumer and mortgage debt to keep up with the luckier ones. While not cheap, mortgage loans for real estate could be serviced comfortably as long as the underlying assets experienced reliable price inflation. Thus, the new economic order of mass consumption coupled with increasing inequality relied in fact on a structural asset bubble. Consequently, household indebtedness rose to unsustainable levels.

This neo-liberal 'growth model' could not last, as it was based on a continuous reduction of saving rates by lower-income households, coupled with increasing borrowing, backed by ever-rising asset prices as collateral. The growth of mass consumption within this framework thus inherently depended on asset price inflation. Eventually, saving rates hit zero; for some time, they may become negative, turning the country into a net importer of capital, goods and services, but at some stage the inevitable must happen and the bubble will burst. When this happened for the first time in the new millennium in 2001, the asset price correction wiped out vast amounts of imaginary wealth and slowed down economic growth around the globe, but the financial system as a whole had remained intact, so that this crisis was then largely regarded as the result of overshooting optimism about the profitability of internet-related business projects and stock market price increases as a whole. The correction of 2001 was thus seen as contained within an obviously speculative niche of the otherwise fundamentally healthy economy, and while people had become slightly more sceptical about the promise of huge and practically risk-free profits in the stock market, in particular the 'dot.com' segment, they quickly turned back to normal business.

From then onwards, asset price booms mainly affected the housing market. 'Bricks and mortar' or 'property' sounded more solid than 'dot.com', so confidence in asset price inflation outpacing general inflation was restored, and the neo-liberal growth model could continue for another couple of years. As we now know, the end came in 2007, and the scope of the correction by far exceeded the 2001 crisis. More importantly, this time the stability of the entire financial system had been undermined, as it held huge amounts of assets secured by collateralised household debt. This debt had been skilfully 'packaged' in a variety of multi-layered financial instruments. Their sophistication was admired, and rating agencies awarded them top grades ('triple A'). Seemingly, advances in the theory of finance and their implementation in liberalised, 'flourishing' financial markets had decoupled risk from return. When house prices started to fall, however, these assets turned out to be leveraged and risky beyond any expectation. As valuations plummeted, trade stalled and, consequently, no market prices could be assigned to them. They had turned 'toxic'.

The Asian economies affected by the 1997 crisis, and likewise Russia and Argentina, which were hit by crises in 1998–9 and 1999–2002, respectively, had all by and large followed the recommendations of the 'Washington Consensus', but these crises were nevertheless regarded as events from the periphery, nurtured in an environment of 'crony capitalism', with responsibility attributed to local deficiencies rather than the underlying economic order. But the IT bubble of 1997–2000, and its bursting in 2001, happened right in the centre, as did the 2007 burst of the US subprime mortgage bubble that sent the world economy into the Great Recession of 2008–9.

After recovering from the 2008 to 2009 financial crisis, the global economy faced an unprecedented shock in early 2020 with the outbreak of COVID-19. First detected in Wuhan, China, in December 2019, the virus rapidly spread, resulting in a global pandemic. Swift government action, lockdowns and the rapid development of vaccines kept the death toll at about 7 million according to official reports, though the real number may be much higher due to unreported cases.

However, the economic impact was severe. Unlike traditional recessions caused by internal economic dysfunction, the COVID-19 downturn stemmed from simultaneous supply and demand shocks, leading to a rapid halt in production, surging unemployment and revenue loss. Although recovery was relatively quick once restrictions eased, the pandemic exposed deep vulnerabilities in global supply chains.

The crisis led to a global reassessment of economic globalisation. Supply chain disruptions, symbolised by container pileups in Shanghai, prompted businesses and governments to rethink their reliance on international trade. These concerns intensified with Russia's 2022 invasion of Ukraine, which disrupted grain and energy supplies. Consequently, global trade began shifting from efficiency-driven models to those influenced more by geopolitical considerations.

The experiences of the Great Recession of 2008–9, the sluggish recovery thereafter, and maybe even more so the global economic shocks induced by the COVID-19 pandemic in 2020 and the Ukraine war in 2022 have thus generally led to a more sceptical perception of globalisation, in particular regarding the financial sector and the reliance on global supply chains. Moreover, the large deficits in the trade balance of the US and other economies and — correspondingly — the surpluses of China, Germany and other net exporters persist, and we do not know whether the inevitable reversal will proceed smoothly or not. With the second term of Donald Trump as US president and his imposed and announced drastic import tariffs, which apparently are at the same time aiming at generating government revenue, reducing the US trade deficit, and ensuring geopolitical support or, in some cases, outright political submission, unfortunately, the chances of a soft landing appear less likely than before.

The remainder of this chapter will look at the most important trends and events in the international economy from the end of the last millennium in 2000 to the end of 2024 in more detail. The following and final Chapter 23 will summarise what is known so far about the world economy in 2025, focussing in particular on the likely consequences of the measures imposed by US president Trump. A tentative outlook into the future, outlining and the most likely scenarios for the world economy together with a summary of the most important tasks that lie ahead will conclude.

THE EVOLUTION OF ECONOMIC INTEGRATION IN THE NEW MILLENNIUM

Earlier in this book, we have shown that from 1820 to 1913, the world trade to world output ratio tended to increase. Correspondingly, each unit of output of goods and services went along with more international trade, which directly implies that the international division of labour advanced, so that this ratio can serve as a simple proxy for the complex process of economic

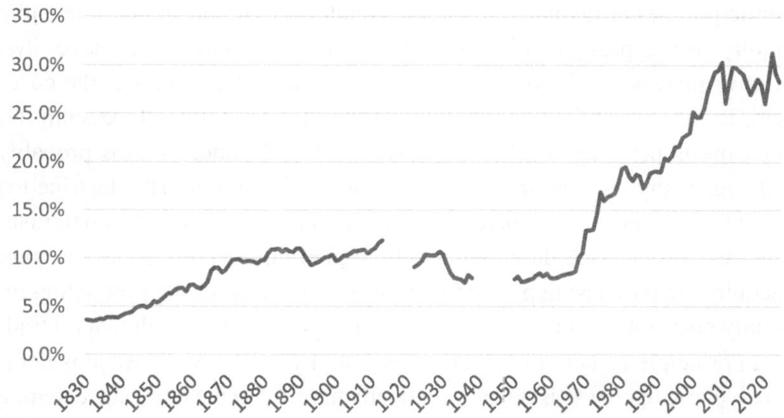

FIGURE 22.1 Global exports/GDP ratio in per cent, 1830–2024

Source: Federico and Tena-Junguito (2019) 1830 sample, constant prices (years 1830–1967); World Development Indicators (years 1968–2024).

globalisation. After the disruptions brought about by the First World War, the interwar period with its trends toward economic nationalism and the epochal violence of the Second World War, the world economy eventually turned back to deepening economic integration; gradually in the 1950s and 1960s, and with unprecedented momentum from the 1970s up to 2008–9.

For the quantitative long-term perspective, historical statistics of annual global exports/GDP ratios have now been estimated, reaching back to the early nineteenth century. The corresponding time series is shown in Figure 22.1.

Economic globalisation, as reflected by the global exports/GDP ratio shown in Figure 22.1, increased rather steadily from 3 per cent in 1830 to the 1880s, when it reached 11 per cent. Then, up to the First World War, the evolution was more volatile, and the trend flattened out. After 12 per cent in 1913, data are missing during the war years until 1922, when the ratio is estimated to have fallen to 9 per cent. It then slowly rose again to 12 per cent in 1929 and then fell back to 8 per cent in 1938 during the Great Depression and the following global trade wars. Data are again missing for 1939 to 1949. For 1950, the estimate is 8 per cent, as in 1938. The ratio then gradually climbed to surpass 12 per cent — the previous historical maximum of 1913 — in 1970. From then on, economic globalisation gained unprecedented momentum, with only short interruptions during the occasional global crises. The world exports to GDP ratio reached a peak of 30 per cent in 2008, before the Great Recession made it plunge as never before to 26 per cent in 2009. In the 15 years since then, the ratio has been more volatile than ever, in 2024 it stood at 24 per cent, and it does not look at all like the evolution could converge back to the pre-2009 growth trend path; quite to the contrary, there is no sign of any upward trend at all.

Apparently, the disruptions in the world economy that triggered the Great Recession have not been resolved, and the shocks to the world economy from COVID-19 in 2020 and the Ukraine war in 2022 have certainly contributed to slowing down or even halting the dynamics of further integration of the world economy. Last but not least, in 2025, the aggressive tariff policies of US president Trump will inevitably distort and reduce global trade, meaning that, for now, economic globalisation seems to have passed its peak.

Economic policies in favour of the home country are of course not a new phenomenon. From antiquity to the present, military, political and economic elites have always seized opportunities to increase their power, influence and economic weight at the cost of the rest of the world. In the economic domain, the doctrine of mercantilism (sixteenth to eighteenth centuries) — the imperative to achieve a positive trade balance — was probably the most pronounced beggar-thy-neighbour trade strategy in modern times. The doctrine lost its influence in the late eighteenth/early nineteenth century when the 'classical' economists, foremost Adam Smith and David Ricardo convincingly argued that exports should be regarded as a means to acquire the purchasing power to import those goods for the production of which the home economy does not exhibit comparative advantage, with the result that *all* trading economies could in principle be better off than under autarky. In this view, trade is not a zero-sum game, and economic openness is not automatically harmful to the domestic economy if it benefits others. Apart from disruptions caused by revolutions and wars, international economic policies were by and large shaped by this new perspective.

Mutual benefits from trade can however not be expected when unequal power prevails and stronger economies are willing to impose their rules on weaker economies. From 'optimum tariffs' that can distort the terms of trade in favour of large economies to outright dictated import and export prices, there is no shortage of instruments that disadvantage weaker economies in international trade. Yet, the lessons learned from the inter-war period — in the end economic nationalism will make *all* countries poorer when trade is reduced and even more when unilateral moves that harm others are met with retaliation — have lately been forgotten or ignored and the potential benefits from trade are being eroded. Since the 1980s, some countries have successfully established positive and persistent trade surpluses, allowing them to be classified as 'neo-mercantilist'; and while the tariffs imposed by President Trump in 2025 are so far the most obvious measures actively chosen to roll back economic integration and globalisation based on mutual benefit, we must not overlook 'Brexit', the UK's exit from the EU in 2020, which, as far as we can assess so far, has been far more damaging to the UK than to the economies of continental Europe.

ECONOMIC TRADE IN THE NEW MILLENNIUM

Chapters 1–21 provided detailed facts and figures and discussed the major trends of world trade up to the end of the 1990s. After the preceding summary of the evolution of economic globalisation and its reflections in theory and policy over the last 200 years, we shall now take a closer look at the data for the new millennium, which mostly cover the years up to 2024.

Table 22.1 shows the shares of the major regions of the world (as categorised by the World Bank) in world exports from 2000 to 2024. Europe (including Central Asia) was the major exporter throughout this period, with close to 48 per cent of world exports at the peak in 2003, but slowly declined thereafter, dropping to 40.6 per cent in 2024.

East Asia (including Oceania) was the next most important region; and its share rose steadily — driven mainly by China — from about 25 per cent in the first years of the period to close to 31 per cent in 2024.

TABLE 22.1 Shares of major regions in world exports (per cent of total)

Year	Europe[a]	East Asia & Pacific	North America	Middle East[b]	Latin America[c]	South Asia	Africa[d]
2000	43.6	24.9	17.9	5.0	6.0	1.0	1.5
2001	45.5	23.8	17.4	4.7	6.1	1.0	1.5
2002	46.3	24.3	16.1	4.6	5.9	1.1	1.4
2003	47.7	24.5	14.6	4.8	5.6	1.1	1.6
2004	47.5	25.1	13.7	5.1	5.5	1.3	1.7
2005	46.1	25.5	13.4	6.0	5.7	1.4	1.9
2006	45.6	25.8	13.0	6.3	5.8	1.5	1.9
2007	46.1	25.9	12.5	6.3	5.6	1.6	2.0
2008	45.7	25.9	12.0	7.1	5.7	1.6	2.1
2009	44.7	26.9	12.4	6.4	5.6	1.9	2.0
2010	41.9	28.8	12.3	6.7	6.1	2.2	2.2
2011	41.7	28.7	11.9	7.3	6.1	2.2	2.2
2012	40.1	29.6	12.2	7.9	6.0	2.2	2.1
2013	40.7	29.6	12.2	7.5	5.8	2.2	2.0
2014	40.9	30.0	12.4	7.0	5.6	2.2	1.9
2015	40.3	31.3	13.0	5.9	5.6	2.2	1.6
2016	40.9	30.7	13.0	5.7	5.6	2.4	1.5
2017	40.8	30.9	12.7	5.9	5.6	2.4	1.6
2018	41.2	30.6	12.3	6.3	5.5	2.4	1.7
2019	41.3	30.4	12.5	6.0	5.6	2.4	1.7
2020	41.5	32.2	11.8	5.1	5.3	2.5	1.5
2021	41.2	32.2	11.3	5.5	5.4	2.6	1.6
2022	40.5	30.7	11.9	6.7	5.7	2.7	1.7
2023	41.2	29.9	12.1	6.5	5.8	2.8	1.6
2024	40.6	30.7	12.1	6.3	5.8	2.8	1.6

Source: World Development Indicators (last updated: 07/01/2025).

Notes: Computed from current US dollar export values. Deviations from 100 per cent for row sums due to rounding. [a] Including Central Asia; [b] including North Africa, Afghanistan and Pakistan; [c] including the Caribbean; [d] excluding North Africa.

North America remains the third most important exporting region, but its share fell sharply compared to Europe and East Asia, declining from close to 18 per cent in 2000 to just above 12 per cent in 2024.

The Middle East (including North Africa, Afghanistan and Pakistan) ranks fourth, contributing roughly between 5 and 8 per cent of world exports (measured in current US dollars). The volatility was high in relative terms, mostly due to fluctuations in oil prices. Latin America (including the Caribbean) ranks next. In 2024, with 5.8 per cent its export share stood only slightly below that of the Middle East (6.3 per cent), but in its share was remarkably stable throughout the period.

Compared to the five major exporting regions mentioned so far, South Asia and Africa (excluding North Africa) are only minor exporters, but whereas the former managed to nearly triple its export share — mainly driven by India — from 1 per cent in 2000 to close to 3 per cent in 2024, the latter remained stagnant at 1.5 per cent in 2000 and 1.6 per cent in 2024.

The overall picture thus reflects of the fading dominance of the economic regions where industrialisation first occurred on a large scale — Europe and North America. At the same time, except for Latin America and Africa, the periphery gained ground in the world market.

Table 22.2 shows the shares of the same regions in world imports. Europe (including Central Asia) was not only the major exporter throughout this period but also the major importer.

TABLE 22.2 Shares of major regions in world imports (per cent of total)

Year	Europe[a]	East Asia & Pacific	North America	Latin America[c]	Middle East[b]	South Asia	Africa[d]
2000	42.1	22.8	22.2	6.2	3.9	1.1	1.4
2001	43.2	22.0	21.7	6.3	4.1	1.1	1.4
2002	43.8	22.2	21.3	5.7	4.0	1.2	1.5
2003	45.5	22.4	19.9	5.2	4.0	1.3	1.5
2004	45.3	23.2	19.1	5.1	4.2	1.5	1.6
2005	44.3	23.4	19.0	5.3	4.4	1.7	1.7
2006	44.5	23.5	18.4	5.4	4.5	1.8	1.7
2007	45.4	23.1	17.0	5.5	5.0	2.0	1.9
2008	44.7	23.9	15.9	5.8	5.5	2.1	2.0
2009	43.3	24.5	15.5	5.8	6.1	2.5	2.2
2010	40.9	26.9	15.7	6.2	5.4	2.7	2.1
2011	40.6	27.9	15.0	6.2	5.3	2.9	2.1
2012	38.4	29.0	15.2	6.4	5.9	2.9	2.2
2013	38.9	29.2	14.8	6.5	5.8	2.7	2.2
2014	38.6	29.2	15.0	6.6	5.9	2.6	2.1
2015	37.8	29.0	16.1	6.1	6.1	2.7	2.1
2016	38.7	28.6	16.0	5.9	5.9	2.8	1.9
2017	38.7	29.1	15.6	5.9	5.7	3.0	1.9
2018	38.8	29.7	15.1	5.9	5.5	3.0	1.8
2019	39.2	29.3	15.3	5.8	5.7	2.9	1.8
2020	39.7	29.8	15.1	5.3	5.4	2.8	1.7
2021	39.0	30.2	14.9	5.8	5.1	3.2	1.7
2022	38.9	28.8	15.3	6.2	5.5	3.4	1.8
2023	39.7	28.3	15.1	6.0	5.8	3.2	1.8
2024	38.7	28.9	15.4	6.0	5.9	3.3	1.8

Source: World Development Indicators (last updated: 07/01/2025).

Notes: Computed from current US dollar export values. Deviations from 100 per cent for row sums due to rounding. [a] Including Central Asia; [b] including North Africa, Afghanistan and Pakistan; [c] including the Caribbean; [d] excluding North Africa.

The peak was likewise in 2003 with 45.5 per cent of world imports, after which its share gradually declined to 39 per cent in 2024.

East Asia (including Oceania) was the second most important importer; it absorbed about 23 per cent of the world's exports at the start of the period and rose to nearly 29 per cent in 2024.

North America was the third most important importing region. Yet, its share continuously declined from just above 22 per cent in 2000 to 15.4 per cent in 2024, reflecting a pronounced change in the distribution of world imports. Latin America (including the Caribbean) ranked next. With 6.0 per cent its 2024 import share stood slightly above that of the Middle East, and mirroring its export performance, it remained remarkably stable throughout the period.

The Middle East (including North Africa, Afghanistan and Pakistan) ranked fifth. Its import share rose by about 50 per cent to just below 6 per cent in 2024 from just below 4 per cent in 2000.

Compared to the five major importing regions, South Asia and Africa (excluding North Africa) are only minor importers. However, South Asia tripled its import share — again mainly driven by India — from just above 1 per cent in 2000 to 3.3 per cent in 2024, while Africa's import share rose by only about 30 per cent, from around 1.4 per cent at the start of the period to 1.8 per cent in 2024.

Thus, the changing distribution of world imports, shifting toward the periphery, also reflects its rising importance in the global economy.

From Tables 22.1 and 22.2, we can directly compute the trade balances of the regions under consideration, where the contributions to the total world trade imbalances in per cent are given by the differences between the regional export and import shares. The results are shown in Table 22.3. By definition, for the world as a whole, the regional balances must sum up to zero in every year. All negative balance shares in Table 22.3 are thus offset by corresponding positive shares.

The most striking observation is the North American contribution to the world's balance of trade. It is negative throughout the whole period, and the numbers are consistently higher in absolute terms than those of any of the other regions. Its absorption of world output has thus significantly outpaced its contribution. Along with this, as an accounting identity, the net debtor position of North America vis-à-vis the rest of the world has increased by the amount of the cumulative trade deficit (net of gains and losses as well as revaluations of the underlying assets due to exchange rate fluctuations). North America has thus to a considerable degree been living on credit, up to 2024 willingly granted by financial and other investors from abroad.

The roles of Europe (including Central Asia) and East Asia & Pacific (including Oceania) in the world economy were largely complementary; their absorption was consistently lower than their production. Notably, except for 2015–16 and 2020, the same holds for the Middle East (including North Africa), a region comprising many oil exporters, though on a somewhat lower scale, reflecting its smaller size in the world economy.

Latin America (including the Caribbean) and Africa (excluding North Africa) recorded positive as well as negative trade balances, but both regions tended more to the negative side, while South Asia consistently recorded relatively small but negative balances.

Especially during the later years of the period under consideration, these three relatively poor regions — in line with theoretical considerations, which predict capital to flow

TABLE 22.3 Shares of major regions in world trade imbalances (per cent of total)

Year	Europe[a]	East Asia & Pacific	Middle East[b]	Latin America[c]	Africa[d]	South Asia	North America
2000	1.5	2.1	1.1	−0.2	0.1	−0.1	−4.3
2001	2.3	1.8	0.6	−0.2	0.1	−0.1	−4.3
2002	2.5	2.1	0.6	0.2	0.0	−0.1	−5.2
2003	2.2	2.1	0.8	0.4	0.0	−0.1	−5.3
2004	2.3	2.0	1.0	0.4	0.0	−0.2	−5.4
2005	1.8	2.1	1.6	0.5	0.2	−0.3	−5.6
2006	1.2	2.4	1.7	0.4	0.2	−0.3	−5.4
2007	0.7	2.8	1.3	0.1	0.1	−0.4	−4.4
2008	1.0	1.9	1.6	−0.1	0.1	−0.4	−3.9
2009	1.4	2.3	0.3	−0.1	−0.2	−0.6	−3.1
2010	0.9	1.9	1.2	0.0	0.0	−0.6	−3.4
2011	1.1	0.9	2.0	−0.1	0.1	−0.7	−3.1
2012	1.7	0.5	2.0	−0.4	−0.1	−0.7	−3.0
2013	1.8	0.4	1.7	−0.7	−0.2	−0.4	−2.6
2014	2.3	0.8	1.1	−0.9	−0.2	−0.4	−2.6
2015	2.4	2.2	−0.3	−0.5	−0.5	−0.4	−3.1
2016	2.1	2.1	−0.3	−0.3	−0.4	−0.4	−3.0
2017	2.1	1.8	0.1	−0.3	−0.3	−0.6	−2.9
2018	2.4	0.9	0.7	−0.4	−0.2	−0.6	−2.8
2019	2.1	1.2	0.3	−0.2	−0.1	−0.5	−2.7
2020	1.8	2.3	−0.4	0.0	−0.2	−0.3	−3.3
2021	2.2	1.9	0.4	−0.4	−0.1	−0.6	−3.6
2022	1.6	1.8	1.2	−0.5	−0.2	−0.6	−3.4
2023	1.6	1.6	0.6	−0.2	−0.3	−0.4	−3.0
2024	1.9	1.9	0.5	−0.2	−0.3	−0.5	−3.3

Notes: Computed from Tables 22.1 and 22.2 as differences of export and import shares. Deviations from 100 per cent for row sums due to rounding. [a] Including Central Asia; [b] including North Africa, Afghanistan and Pakistan; [c] including the Caribbean; [d] excluding North Africa.

from richer too poorer regions — absorbed more than they produced. Europe's trade balance surpluses along with the corresponding capital exports to the rest of the world are likewise in line with conventional economic theory, whereas the trade surpluses of East Asia & Pacific, particularly during the earlier years of the period under consideration, cannot be explained by relative scarcities of capital. North America's huge and persistent trade deficit is even more contrary to conventional economic wisdom. Yet, these two 'anomalies' can at least partly be explained on the one hand by the export-led growth strategy in East Asia, and on the other by the hegemonial position of the US and the role of the US dollar as the world's trade and reserve currency, which so far has allowed the US to accumulate debt vis-à-vis the rest of the world at levels where other economies would almost certainly have defaulted. We will come back to this in the final chapter of this book.

More details on the trade linkages of the international economy can be inferred from international trade-flow matrices. To this end, we refer to the UNCTAD trade matrix, which records annual figures from 1995 to 2024. The regional aggregates are not exactly the same as those of the World Bank displayed in Tables 22.1–22.3, and the UNCTAD data reflect merchandise trade, whereas the World Bank data include trade in services. Having said this, the UNCTAD figures are still highly useful, as many of the present concerns about international trade imbalances are tied to manufacturing and the relocation of production and jobs from the centre to the periphery over the past few decades.

The merchandise trade flow matrix for seven regional aggregates, mostly corresponding to the planet's continents, is shown in Table 22.4. The cells reflect the most recent year, 2024, and the numbers are computed as percentages of total cumulative world trade. The rows display the shares for regions of origin (exports), while the columns show the receiving regions (imports). Since it would overload the presentation to include the corresponding matrices for all previous years since 2000, the following comments will indicate whether any trends are observable in the first quarter of the new millennium.

In 2024, Asia accounted for the largest shares of both world merchandise exports and imports, 43 per cent of exports (up from 32 per cent in 2000) and 39 per cent of imports (up from 28 per cent). At the beginning of the millennium, Europe had still held the first rank, so what we see here is the result of a major shift. In 2024 Europe supplied about 36 per cent of exports (down from 42 per cent in 2000) and received 35 per cent of imports (down from 41 per cent).

North America supplied 11 per cent of exports (down from 17 per cent in 2000) while accounting for 16 per cent of world imports (down from 22 per cent).

The magnitude of the other regions is comparatively small; however, but they consistently gained export as well as import shares. Latin America increased its export share from 5.7 per cent in 2000 to 6.0 per cent in 2024; Africa increased its export share from 2.2 per cent to

TABLE 22.4 Trade flows between major regions, 2024 (per cent of world trade)

Exporting region	Importing region						
	World	Asia	Europe	North America	Latin America[a]	Africa	Oceania
World	100	39.0	34.6	16.0	6.0	2.9	1.5
Asia	43.1	25.3	7.2	6.2	1.8	1.7	0.9
Europe	35.8	6.4	24.0	3.3	0.9	0.9	0.3
North America	10.9	2.8	2.2	3.2	2.3	0.1	0.2
Latin America[a]	6.0	1.5	0.7	2.9	0.8	0.1	0.02
Africa	2.6	1.0	1.0	0.2	0.05	0.4	0.01
Oceania	1.6	1.3	0.1	0.1	0.02	0.02	0.1

Source: UNCTAD Merchandise Trade Matrix (n.d.).

Notes: Percentages scaled to 1 where sum of shares deviate from 100 per cent. Deviations of regional from world shares due to rounding. [a] Including the Caribbean.

2.6 per cent, and Oceania increased its export share from 1.3 per cent in 2000 to 1.6 per cent. Regarding imports, Latin America increased its share from 5.8 per cent in 2000 to 6.0 per cent in 2024; Africa increased its share from 1.9 per cent to 2.9 per cent, and Oceania remained stable at 1.5 per cent.

The diagonal elements of the matrix show the importance of intra-regional trade. To interpret these findings, it is important to recall that intra-regional trade is a positive function of a region's economic size, as well as the intra-regional propensity to trade with each other.[2] Asia and Europe stand out with 25 (down from 31 per cent) per cent and 24 (up from 16 per cent) per cent, respectively. Here too, the reversal over the first quarter of the twenty-first century was profound, as in 2000 Europe's interregional trade still made up 31 per cent of the world's total trade, whereas Asia stood at only16 per cent. In 2024, intra-North American trade accounted for only 3.2 per cent of the total (down from 6.6 per cent in 2000), followed by Latin America (0.8 per cent, down from 1.0 per cent), Africa (0.4 per cent, up from 0.2 per cent) and Oceania (steady at 0.1 per cent). Again, we see a reflection of the dwindling dominance of the historical centre of the capitalist world economy — mostly pronounced for North America.

As the data summarised in Table 22.4 identify the world's net exporter and net importer regions, they also allow to identify the regional pattern of the imbalances. Accordingly, Table 22.5 shows the matrix of inter-regional trade balances as percentages of the total. As the world as a whole and each region taken by itself by definition must have exports equalling imports, the diagonal elements of the matrix are zero. Also, the off-diagonal elements are symmetric, albeit with inverted signs, as one region's surplus must be equal to the trading partner's deficit and vice versa. We shall comment on the findings by looking at net exports, i.e. row by row.

The major contributor to the total cumulative inter-regional trade balances in 2024 was North America (5.1 per cent of the total deficit). The second most important deficit region was Africa, but far behind with 0.3 per cent. All other regions supplied more merchandise than they received, headed by Asia (4.1 per cent), followed by Europe (1.2 per cent) and Oceania (0.1 per cent). Latin America recorded roughly zero net exports. North America's deficit in

TABLE 22.5 Balance of trade between major regions, 2024 (per cent of world trade)

Exporting region	Importing region						
	World	Asia	Europe	North America	Latin America[a]	Africa	Oceania
World	0	−4.1	−1.2	5.1	0.0	0.3	−0.1
Asia	4.1	0	0.8	3.4	0.3	0.7	−0.4
Europe	1.2	−0.8	0	1.1	0.2	−0.1	0.2
North America	−5.1	−3.4	−1.1	0	−0.6	−0.1	0.1
Latin America[a]	0.0	−0.3	−0.2	0.6	0	0.05	0.0
Africa	−0.3	−0.7	0.1	0.1	−0.05	0	−0.1
Oceania	0.1	0.4	−0.2	−0.1	0.0	0.01	0

Notes: Computed from Table 22.3 as differences between bi-directional regional export shares. [a] Including the Caribbean.

2024 was mainly driven by its trade with Asia (–3.4 per cent), followed by Europe (–1.1 per cent) and Latin America (–0.6 per cent). Apart from these, remarkable contributions to the imbalances in world trade were the trade deficits with Asia from Europe (–0.8 per cent), Africa (0.7 per cent) and Latin America (0.3 per cent).

The fact that North America recorded trade deficits with all regions except Oceania, but mainly with Asia, deserves special attention. It is best illustrated by the 'Chimerica' story.[3] Figure 22.2 shows the facts, referring to the UNCTAD merchandise trade matrix. It plots the evolution of the value of US merchandise imports from China, US exports to China and the resulting balance in current US dollars for all available years, from 1995 to 2024. The gap was persistent. It began to widen after 2001 and kept increasing until 2018, when it reached its all-time maximum of 443 billion US dollars.

A couple of observations stand out, however. First, the Great Recession of 2008–9 depressed both US imports from and exports to China, and as the drop of the former was more pronounced than that of the latter, the trade deficit narrowed in 2009. Another reduction occurred in 2016. While US exports to China held steady, imports from China declined by 4.5 per cent. Remarkably, this decline happened *before* the trade war waged by the US against China began, but it coincided with Donald Trump's 2016 pro-tariffs presidential campaign. In 2018, President Trump put his words into action, and in 2019 the resulting decline US–Chinese merchandise trade reduced the US deficit by 18.5 per cent. In 2020, Chinese exports to the US were affected by the strict measures in the People's Republic (lockdowns, quarantines and closed borders) to curb the spread of COVID-19 infections. Under the presidency of Joe Biden (2021–24), Trump's tariffs were not only kept in place, but additional barriers were erected, particularly against Chinese electro-voltaic equipment and electric cars. The recovery of Chinese exports to the US in 2021–2 reflects the post-pandemic rebound, and from then to 2024, the deficit remained steady at close to 150 billion US dollars per annum.

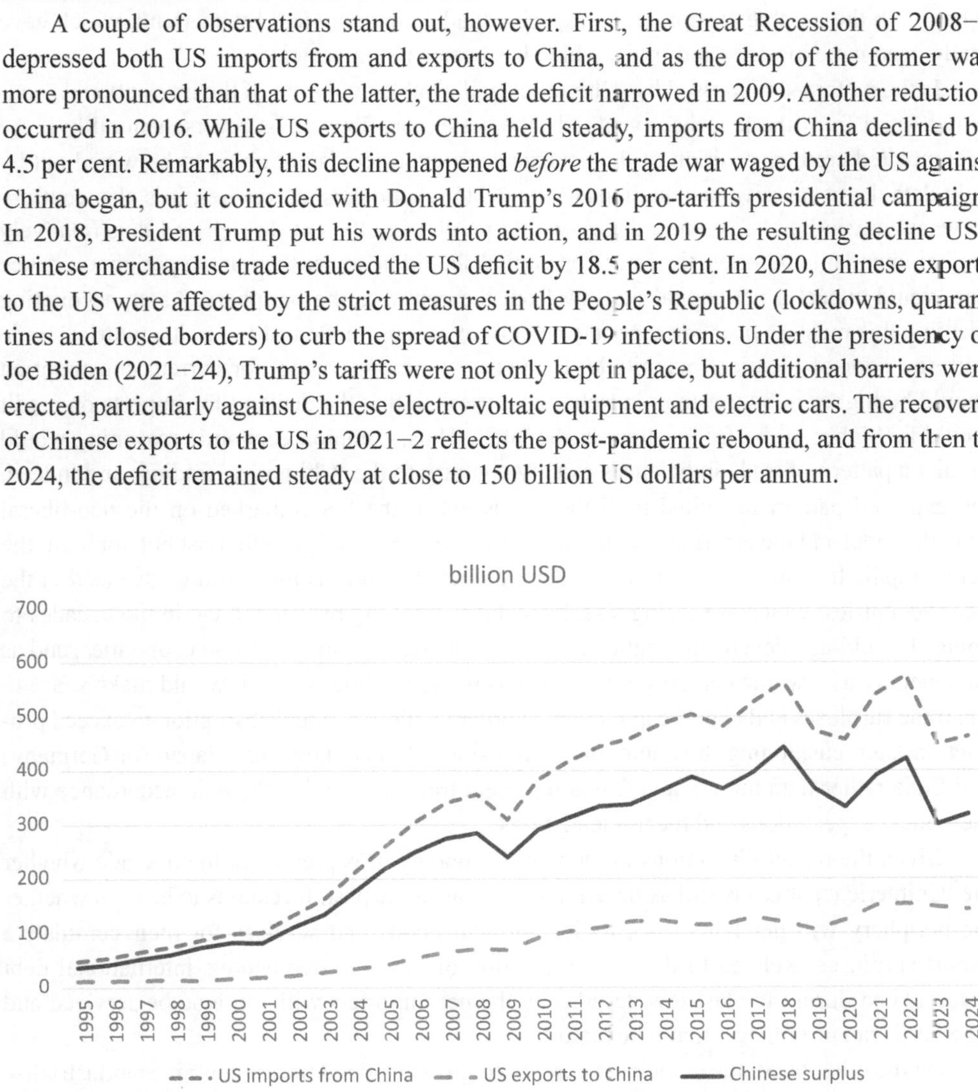

FIGURE 22.2 US–Chinese merchandise trade, billion US dollars, 1995–2024

Source: UNCTAD Merchandise Trade Matrix (n.d.).

The US consumption and investment pattern with absorption exceeding production was to a considerable degree made possible by Chinese exports in excess of imports. Before the Great Recession, this suited all parties involved. On the US side, it supported credit-financed consumption growth, and in China it provided the basis for export-led growth and jobs for the rural poor migrating to the emerging industrial centres of the country. The drawback was the de-industrialisation of the American 'rust belt'; and the disruptions and despair that it created helped Donald Trump to be voted into the Oval Office in 2016 and 2024. During the first months of his second presidency in 2025, it became obvious that he was determined to reduce the US merchandise trade deficits vis-à-vis the rest of the world. (We will return to this in Chapter 23.)

The 'Chimerica' notion is, of course, a stylisation that can readily be expanded to include many successful 'emerging' economies on the one hand and many rich economies on the other, with the notable exceptions of Japan, Canada, Germany and Switzerland, which have lately been net exporters, and India, which has been a net importer.

Is the pattern summarised by 'Chimerica' a desirable evolution of the international economy? Apart from the fact that eventually the net export flows must reverse smoothly if the accumulated creditor position of the persistent net exporters is not going to be wiped out by debt defaults or massive devaluations of the debtor economies' currencies, it is also contrary to what conventional economic theory would predict as efficient. In rich and thus relatively capital-abundant countries, the return on capital should be lower than in the periphery; hence one would expect a net capital outflow from the centre to the periphery. As an accounting identity, this must *ex post* correspond to a current account deficit of the rich countries' trade with the poor of identical magnitude. Likewise, 'time preference' for current consumption should be higher in poorer than in richer countries, so that the demand for imports on credit would be higher in the former than in the latter. Thus, common economic reasoning would predict a pattern of trade imbalances exactly contrary to the 'Chimerica' finding; and indeed, the expected pattern prevailed until the 1980s, when the US embarked on the neo-liberal growth model and the emerging economies turned to export-led growth. Last but not least, the demographic transition that is now affecting the whole world is much more advanced in the richer countries, which are facing sizeable cohorts reaching retirement age in the decades to come. The old-age dependency ratio is thus set to increase sharply in these economies, and as an economy as a whole can only save vis-à-vis the rest of the world, it would make sense to run trade surpluses and export capital now in order to allow national absorption to exceed production later, cushioning the demographic transition. Hence, nowadays Japan (or Germany) and India rather than the US and China represent trade and capital flows in accordance with theoretical expectations and recommendations.

Given the recent disruptions in the world economy, it is premature to conclude whether the 'Chimerica' pattern is still as beneficial as it was in the past. It remains to be seen whether the periphery will get fair compensation through goods and services for their cumulative export surpluses. Related to this is the question of how the tremendous international debt accumulated during the last few decades by the net importers will continue be serviced and whether it can or will eventually be repaid.

On the other hand, the associated export-led growth helped these economies industrialise and advance far on the corresponding learning curves so that once domestic demand picks up, the productivity gains achieved through 'Chimerica' might outweigh its potential drawbacks.

Taken together, it is not unreasonable to assume that the 'catching up' process was accelerated in a number of countries, although there are doubts regarding the wisdom of promoting trade surpluses in some of the poorest countries of the periphery while maintaining continuous deficits in the rich and rapidly ageing economies.

To illustrate the emergence of the current trade imbalances, Figures 22.3 to 22.11 plot the evolution of imports and exports as percentages of GDP from 1980 to 2024 (depending on data availability) for some of the most important economies of the rich parts of the world

FIGURE 22.3 Exports and imports of goods and services (per cent of GDP, US), 1960–2024

Source: World Development Indicators (accessed September 2025).

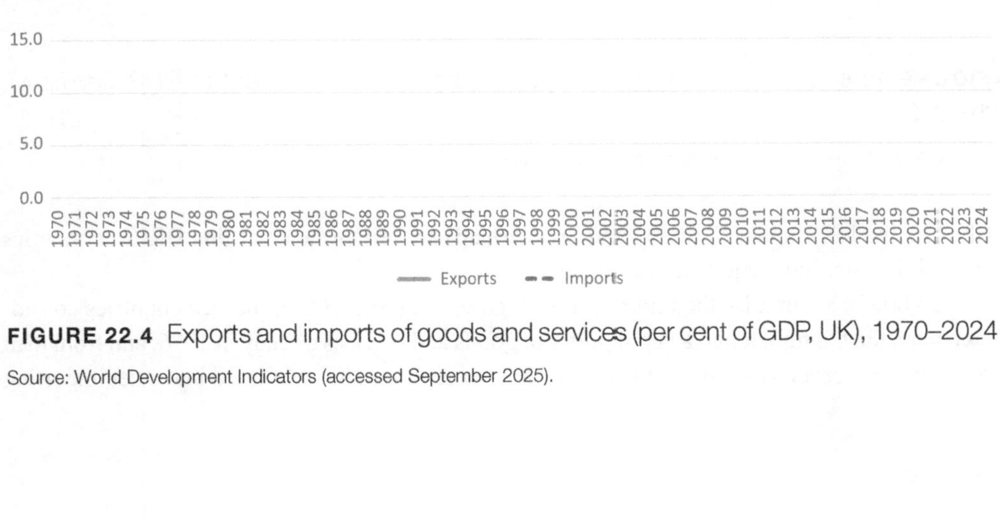

FIGURE 22.4 Exports and imports of goods and services (per cent of GDP, UK), 1970–2024

Source: World Development Indicators (accessed September 2025).

FIGURE 22.5 Exports and imports of goods and services (per cent of GDP, Japan), 1970–2023

Source: World Development Indicators (accessed September 2025).

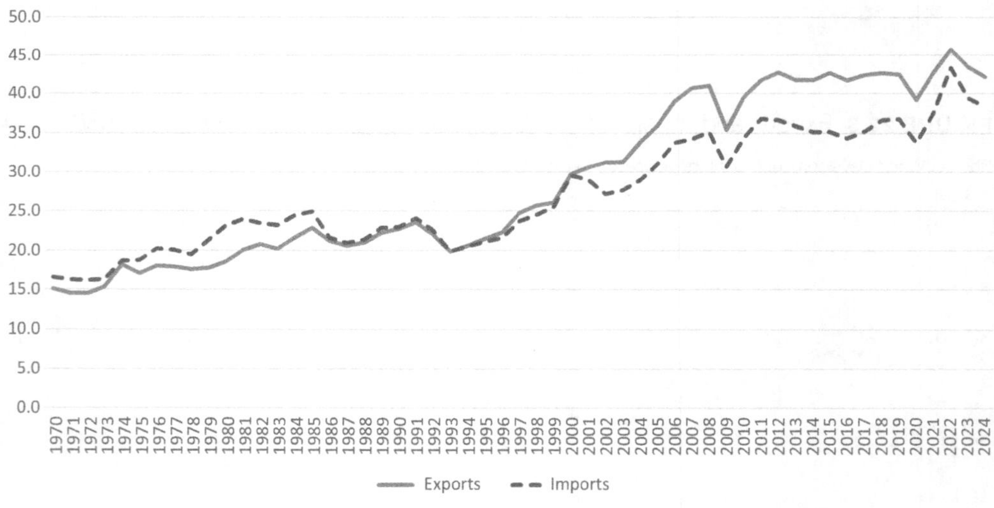

FIGURE 22.6 Exports and imports of goods and services (per cent of GDP, Germany), 1970–2024

Source: World Development Indicators (accessed September 2025).

(the US, the UK, Japan, Germany and Switzerland) as well as the emerging BRIC economies (Brazil, Russia, India and China).

To briefly summarise the findings from Figures 22.3 to 22.11, of the rich countries considered here, the US turned into a net importer of goods and services already in 1976, and from then on, imports exceeded exports in all years without exception. The UK turned into a net importing

FIGURE 22.7 Exports and imports of goods and services (per cent of GDP, Switzerland), 1970–2024

Source: World Development Indicators (accessed September 2025).

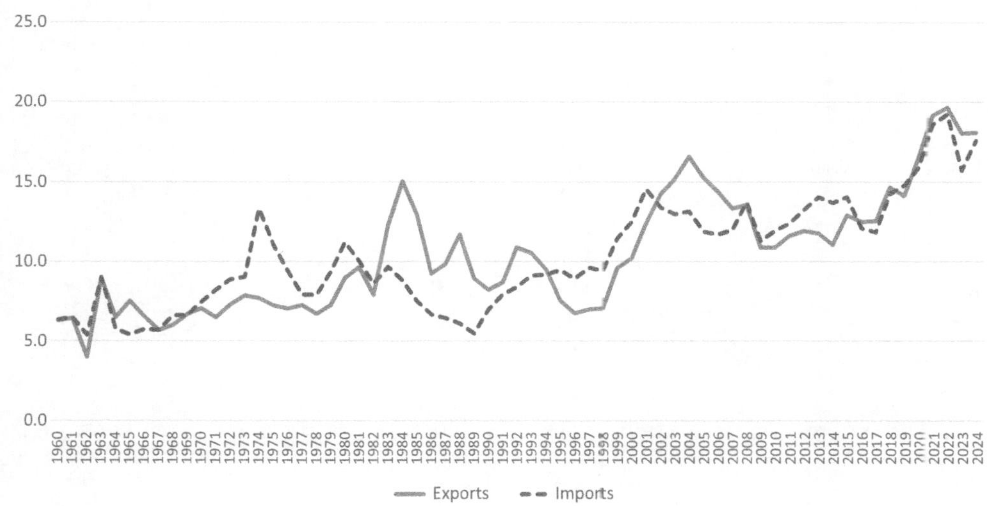

FIGURE 22.8 Exports and imports of goods and services (per cent of GDP, Brazil), 1960–2024

economy considerably later, in 1998, and the trade balance remained negative thereafter, with the exception of 2020, when the onset of the pandemic affected imports more than exports. Japan has been a net exporter for 30 years (1981–2010); after this, the trade balance started to oscillate around zero, which is of course the normal state of affairs. Germany and Switzerland lately stand out amongst the rich countries without a natural-resources exporting sector as persistent net

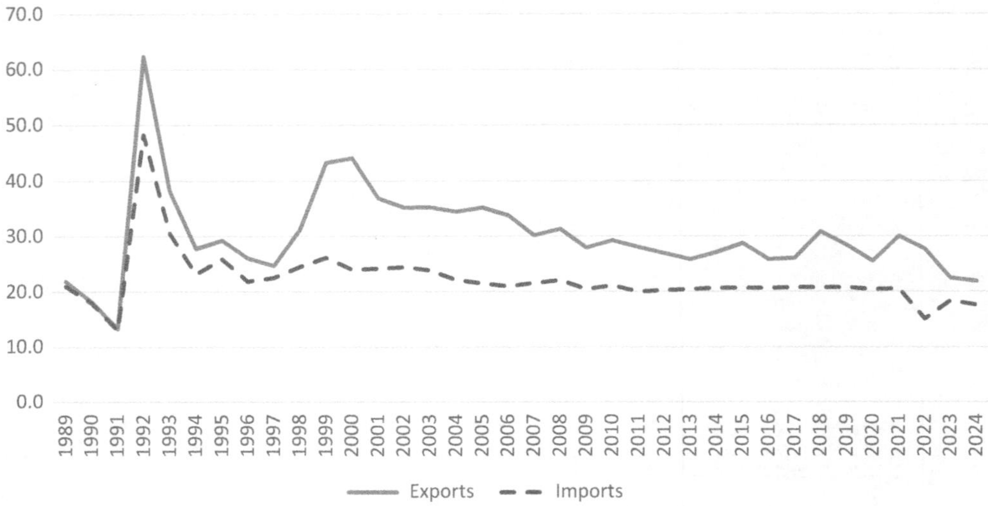

FIGURE 22.9 Exports and imports of goods and services (per cent of GDP, Russia), 1989–2024

Source: World Development Indicators (accessed September 2025).

FIGURE 22.10 Exports and imports of goods and services (per cent of GDP, India), 1960–2024

Source: World Development Indicators (accessed September 2025).

exporters; Germany's balance of trade turned positive in 1993, Switzerland's already in 1984. Of these two 'neo-mercantilist' economies, Switzerland's contribution to the global trade imbalances is smaller in absolute terms, as its economy is much smaller than Germany's. However, while Germany's net exports never exceeded 12.5 per cent of its GDP, Switzerland's have often been in excess of 10 per cent, with the peak in 2022 reaching 14 per cent.

FIGURE 22.11 Exports and imports of goods and services (per cent of GDP, China), 1960–2024

Source: World Development Indicators (accessed September 2025).

Amongst the emerging BRIC economies, Brazil's balance of trade has since 1960 seen surpluses and deficits, at times considerable, but never persistent. Russia, on the other hand, has recorded persistent trade surpluses, in no single year since 1989 have imports exceeded exports, due to the fact that Russia is a major exporter of fossil fuels. India's balance of trade since 1960 confirms what one would expect for a poorer country; with the exception of very few years, imports have exceeded exports, although most of the time not greatly. China balance of trade since 1960 shows that until Chairman Mao Zedong's death in 1976, exports roughly equalled imports, both at low levels. Then, as a result of the economic reforms and the opening-up to the world economy, trade surged, and in 1980, the trade balance turned positive. In line with the export-led growth policy, the value of exports has exceeded that of imports ever since. The export surplus peaked in 2007; it has lately come down to a range of 1 to 3 per cent.

Before we turn to some of the major events in the international economy in the new millennium, it is appropriate to have a look at an increasingly important source of cross-border income flows — remittances of migrants to their home countries. Figure 22.12 plots received personal remittances as percentages of GDP for the World Bank regions South Asia, Sub-Saharan Africa, Latin America & Caribbean as well as for the world as a whole.

It can be seen that for the poorest regions of the world (South Asia, Sub-Saharan Africa and Latin America & Caribbean) remittances add up to 5 per cent of GDP, whereas for the world as a whole, the fraction since 1980 never exceeded 0.8 per cent. Moreover, the income from remittances was pronouncedly volatile, so even if it may be a valuable addition to the income of poor households, it is not a reliable one. Economic shocks in the economies from which the remittances are sent are one factor, attitudes toward immigrants, which make them

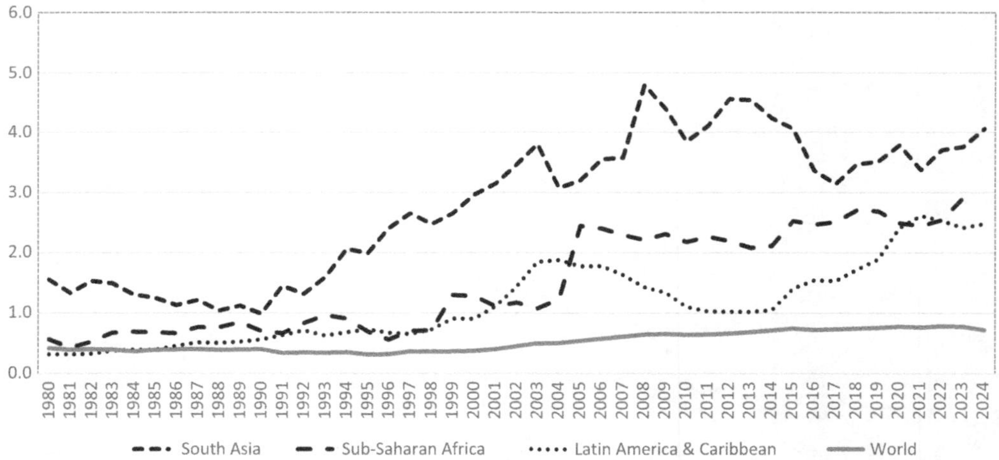

FIGURE 22.12 Personal remittances, received (per cent of GDP), 2000–24

Source: World Development Indicators (assessed September 2025).

more or less welcome are another factor. Yet, for some the poorest countries remittances are essential. Looking at the average over the last 25 years (2000–24), on the world scale, the remittances to gross national income (GNI) ratio amounted to 0.6 per cent, but for 30 countries, it amounted to 10 per cent or more. At the top of the list stands Tajikistan (32 per cent), followed by Tonga and Lesotho (both 30 per cent). The Kyrgyz Republic, Moldova, Lebanon, Nepal, El Salvador and Bermuda received 20 per cent or more of their national income in terms of remittances. Globalisation thus implies that a significant and increasing number of people seek employment abroad, not only to escape from poverty or unemployment, but to support their families at home.

MAJOR FACTS AND EVENTS IN THE INTERNATIONAL ECONOMY, 2001–24

To identify the main events in the international economy during the first quarter of the new millennium to be discussed in the remainder of this Chapter, let us first have a look at the world economy as a whole. To this end, Figure 22.13 shows the world's growth rates of GDP and of the volume of goods and services from 2000 to 2024.

A number of observations stand out. First, in the course of these 25 years, globalisation intensified, as the growth of world trade significantly exceeded that of world GDP. On average, trade grew by 4.1 per cent per year and GDP by 3.0 per cent.

In 2009 and 2020, however, trade *shrank*, and considerably more than GDP, due to the two major economic crises of the new millennium — the Great Recession of 2008–9 and the economic slump caused by the COVID-19 pandemic in 2020. Compared to these shocks, the crises caused by the IT bubble crash in 2001 appears to have been a very moderate

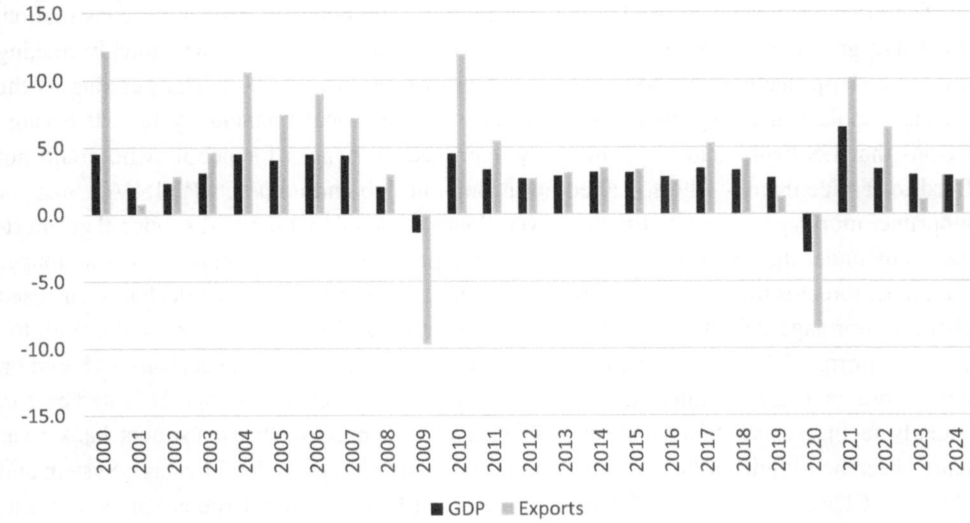

FIGURE 22.13 World GDP and exports of goods and services, growth rates (per cent), 2000–24

Source: World Development Indicators (accessed September 2025).

slow-down — though the growth rate of trade dropped more than that of GDP, they both remained positive.

Lastly, after the Great Recession, globalisation markedly slowed down. While trade growth significantly exceeded that of GDP when the world economy recovered from the Great Recession and the COVID-19 shock in 2010 and 2021–2, after 2010, we not only observe roughly similar growth rates, but in 2016 and 2019, i.e. even before the COVID-19 shock, trade growth fell behind that of GDP. The same is true for the last two years, 2023–4, where the escalation of geopolitical tensions intensified the imposition of embargoes, sanctions and the efforts to achieve autarky in critical sectors. Chapter 23 will discuss whether we are presently witnessing the end or even a reversal of the intensification of globalisation that has characterised the world economy since the Second World War.

The Subprime Mortgage Crisis in the US and the Great Recession

In 2008, the world economy slipped into the most severe recession since the slump of the 1930s. Not only the depth and the global synchronicity of the collapse, beginning in the second half of 2008, were remarkable, but also the fact that this recession became virulent as a liquidity crisis. Because of that, most economies slid into a 'liquidity trap' which made it difficult to stimulate the economy using monetary policy. This induced governments in most developed countries to take refuge in fiscal policy, although the size of the stimulation packages — measured as the share of expenditures in nominal GDP — varied widely across countries.

The crisis originated in the US housing market. The boom in residential construction, which had gained momentum in 2003, slowed down at the end of 2005, quickly making way for a sharp decline. US house prices began to drop in mid-2006. The bursting of the housing bubble had unexpectedly strong effects on the global financial system. It became obvious that US banks had too generously approved mortgages for people who could not afford to service them — the so-called no income, no job and no assets ('NINJA') loans or 'subprime' mortgages. Essentially, these were loans to people who could service their mortgages only under the condition that house prices kept climbing. This condition was no longer valid; thus, foreclosure rates picked up. In an attempt to spread risk, US banks had securitised subprime mortgage debt and sold the resulting asset-backed securities worldwide. With the stream of mortgage interest payments ebbing, these securities — and the derivatives based on them — dramatically devalued. Banks had to write down assets to an unprecedented extent, suddenly facing severe balance sheet problems. In March 2008, the investment bank Bear Stearns became illiquid and was rescued at the last minute by the Federal Reserve System and JPMorgan Chase. In September 2008, the investment bank Lehman Brothers, however, was allowed to go bankrupt, triggering an unforeseen chain of events. Amidst the financial turmoil, the oil price soared from around $90 to over $140 during the first half of 2008. The coincidence of several large adverse shocks — the bursting of the housing bubble in the US and subsequently in a number of European countries, the banking crisis, the oil price hike — made this recession thus hit several key industries simultaneously (construction, banking and insurance, transportation, manufacturing).

The Great Recession began at the turn of the years 2007–8 in the US. By the following quarter it had spread to the rest of the world. Like in the US, in other countries with asset bubbles or excessively large banking sectors, it was triggered by asset price collapses, which in turn led to a banking crisis, as the interbank money market froze and banks became illiquid.[4] Economies that were not vulnerable in these respects nevertheless experienced plunges in demand for their exports, which made them slide into recession or experience depressed growth nonetheless.

As we have mentioned above, the consequences of the Great Recession by far exceeded those of the 2001 crisis. Growth remained positive in the aftermath of the IT bubble, whereas the Great Recession resulted in a massive economic contraction in the high-income economies and a reduction of about 50 per cent of GDP growth in the low- and middle-income countries, although with pronounced variety in the latter group. Within the BRIC economies, Brazil (–0.3 per cent) and particularly Russia (–7.8 per cent) went into recession, but China (9.2 per cent) and India (8.2 per cent) maintained positive, if somewhat depressed, growth rates in 2009, the world economy's worst year for decades. Among the rich countries, the US and Japan slid into recession earlier than the EU. Australia remained largely unaffected thanks to continuing demand for its raw materials from China and swift and bold measures to support domestic demand.

Measures to Curb the Crisis

As the world's leading economies were faced with a recession scenario similar to that analysed by Keynes (1936), 'the liquidity trap' rendered monetary policy ineffective because high 'liquidity preference' increased the demand for money, curtailing the credit supply. At the same time, the 'investment trap' prevented firms from demanding credit despite low interest rates, as genuine uncertainty or pessimistic expectations concerning the business situation in the foreseeable future induced them to postpone most, if not all, investment projects until the situation would noticeably improve.

Central banks across the globe swiftly lowered their interest rates to historical lows in the vicinity of zero, and as this had no perceptible effect on final demand they moved to 'quantitative easing' — unconventional policies with the objective of stimulating demand or at least preventing a slide into deflation by flooding the economy with central bank money. In practice, central banks started to buy commercial paper that they would not consider under normal circumstances and government bonds in massive amounts, at the same time delivering statements that the purchases would continue for extensive periods and without specified limits. The unorthodoxy of quantitative easing thus lies in the fact that it primarily aims at restoring trust in the financial system, subordinating to this purpose all other objectives of the explicit or implicit 'inflation targeting' regime that had emerged since the 1980s and that was believed to have achieved the 'Great Moderation'. Soon sceptics pointed to the fact that quantitative easing in fact amounted to abandoning the new consensus about prudent central banking, which meant that the only objective of monetary policy should be keeping inflation low and stable. Now economies were flooded with liquidity which — once it transformed into demand for goods and services — would inevitably lead to inflation. Furthermore, central banks were bailing out governments, first via purchases of government bonds ('printing money' for the government), and second by a deliberately inflationary policy which would erode the real value of government debt. Up to the present date the critics have continued to raise their concerns, but so far there is no sign that their worries are warranted. Inflation is low across the board, and governments have not been bailed out either.

With monetary policy almost stretched to its limits, expansive fiscal policy became the last resort to avoid a sharp and prolonged contraction. As soon as the world economy found itself in the downturn of 2008–9, economists and policy-makers quickly reconsidered the policy recommendations Keynes had made during the Great Depression. In light of the consensus reached in mainstream economics over the past decades, which saw discretionary fiscal policy at best ineffective and more likely harmful, this reconsideration to some degree came as a surprise. On the other hand, as politicians proved to be pragmatic rather than dogmatic when it became clear that they were facing a situation that had the potential to turn out to be as devastating as the slump in the 1930s, views that had previously been marginalised by the academic mainstream quickly gained acceptance, arguing that in an extraordinary situation, where the means of monetary policy had been exhausted, fiscal policy measures, if carefully administered, might be advised. The debate thus quickly turned from whether discretionary policy should be implemented at all, into how it should proceed, to what extent, and for how long. In technical terms, the magnitude of the 'fiscal multiplier' was discussed. Sceptics saw it as less than the simple arithmetic of expenditure multipliers would have it,[5] due to 'crowding out' or 'Ricardian equivalence'. The first relates to increasing interest rates when the government borrows rather than raising taxes to finance stimulus measures, which could depress private investment, although this is less likely in an 'investment trap', when business is not investing because of excessive uncertainty. Ricardian equivalence, brought forward by the most convinced defenders of the pre-crisis orthodox consensus, is trickier. It states that private agents have perfect foresight and anticipate that credit-financed government expenditure will have to be repaid via increasing tax revenue, so they reduce their consumption accordingly to be able to pay the anticipated additional tax load. In this view, fiscal policy is useless at best, because the multiplier is zero, and likely to be harmful, as it transfers resources from private agents to governments, which is generally seen as detrimental. The rational behaviour and the perfect information assumptions underlying the concept of Ricardian equivalence may be of theoretical interest. In situations where economies are experiencing unprecedented recessions, however, their practical applicability appears more than questionable.

In the end, crowding out as well as Ricardian equivalence were considered irrelevant. Those, whose models — or prior beliefs — predicted higher multipliers, favoured more massive stimulus packages (and vice versa). The more conservative approach favoured tax cuts, whereas the others argued for additional expenditure, unless the tax cuts were directed at lower income earners with a higher propensity to consume out of present income than the rich. In the end, the Anglo-American economies proved to be the most willing to spend massively; and the same holds for relatively large economies as compared with smaller ones.[6]

Table 22.6 summarises the size and structure of discretionary fiscal measures cumulated from 2008 to 2010 for the OECD.[7]

South Korea was reacting more pronouncedly, measured by the fiscal stimulus in relation to GDP, than any other OECD country, followed by the US, Australia, Japan, Turkey and Canada. Switzerland launched the smallest anti-cyclical package. Italy practically remained passive, while fiscal policy that was prematurely directed at curtailing the government's budget deficits in Greece, Iceland, Hungary and Ireland aggravated the downturn.

The IMF, which after the 1997 Asian financial crisis has abandoned its previously orthodox positions in many areas, also surprised in this context. In the October 2012 *IMF Economic Outlook*, two high-ranking IMF economists, Oliver Blanchard (Chief Economist of the IMF from 2008 to 2015) and Daniel Leigh (Senior Economist of IMF Research Division 2009–12) reported that the IMF found its prior estimates of fiscal multipliers in the range of 0.4–1.2 too low in light of evidence and now estimated them at 0.9–1.7. Innocent as this revision may seem, it was made with direct reference to the 'fiscal consolidation' programmes then imposed on the economies affected by the European sovereign debt crisis, which, in the light of the revision, appeared grossly misguided. In fact, the IMF forecasts of the consolidation paths repeatedly proved far too optimistic, as the economies were caught in a downward spiral with GDP, and as a direct consequence, tax revenue, shrinking significantly more than predicted. According to Blanchard and Leigh (2012, p. 41), this is due to the fact that the contractionary effects resulting from the fiscal consolidation have been underestimated, since the fiscal multipliers have been assumed too low. In other words, Keynes' 'paradox of thrift' applies — austerity as a measure to improve the fiscal position of governments does not work in a recession. Accordingly, the IMF became perceivably more sympathetic to fiscal consolidation via debt write-offs than during prior crises.

TABLE 22.6 Size and structure of discretionary fiscal measures, 2008–10 (per cent of 2008 GDP)

	Net effect on fiscal balances			Composition of spending measures		
	Total	Expenditure	Tax Revenue	Consumption	Investment	Transfers
South Korea	−6.1	−3.2	−2.8	0.0	1.2	1.7
US	−5.6	−2.4	−3.2	0.7	0.3	0.5
Australia	−5.4	−4.1	−1.3	0.0	3.0	1.1
Japan	−4.7	−4.2	−0.5	0.2	1.2	2.1
Turkey	−4.4	−2.9	−1.5	0.6	1.2	0.3
Canada	−4.1	−1.7	−2.4	0.1	1.3	0.4
Luxembourg	−3.9	−1.6	−2.3	0.0	0.4	1.2
Spain	−3.9	−2.2	−1.7	0.3	0.7	1.2
New Zealand	−3.7	0.3	−4.1	0.1	0.6	−0.6
Denmark	−3.3	−2.6	−0.7	0.9	0.8	0.1
Sweden	−3.3	−1.7	−1.7	1.1	0.3	0.1
Finland	−3.2	−0.5	−2.7	0.0	0.3	0.1
Germany	−3.2	−1.6	−1.6	0.0	0.8	0.6
Czech Republic	−2.8	−0.3	−2.5	−0.1	0.2	0.2
Netherlands	−2.5	−0.9	−1.6	0.0	0.5	0.1
UK	−1.9	−0.4	−1.5	0.0	0.4	0.2
Mexico	−1.6	−1.2	−0.4	0.1	0.7	0.1
Belgium	−1.4	−1.1	−0.3	0.0	0.1	1.0
Slovak Republic	−1.3	−0.7	−0.7	0.0	0.0	0.7
Austria	−1.2	−0.4	−0.8	0.0	0.1	0.2
Norway	−1.2	−0.9	−0.3	0.0	0.4	0.0
Poland	−1.2	−0.8	−0.4	0.0	1.3	0.3
Portugal	−0.8			0.0	0.4	0.4
France	−0.7	−0.6	−0.2	0.0	0.2	0.3
Switzerland	−0.5	−0.3	−0.2	0.3	0.0	0.0
Italy	0.0	−0.3	0.3	0.3	0.0	0.3
Greece	0.8	0.0	0.8	−0.4	0.1	0.5
Iceland	7.3	1.6	5.7			
Hungary	7.7	7.5	0.2	−3.2	0.0	−3.8
Ireland	8.3	2.2	6.0	−1.8	−0.2	−0.1
G7	−4.1	−2.1	−2.0			
OECD	−3.9	−2.0	−1.9			

Source: OECD (2009).

Notes: Transfers to sub-national governments are omitted; OECD numbers are weighted averages, excluding Greece, Mexico, Norway and Portugal.

Economics and the Great Recession

As the crisis deepened, discontent with academic economics was widely voiced. True, a few economists had been pointing to distress building up in the US housing market. Nouriel Roubini, Robert Shiller and Michael Hudson — to name just a few — correctly predicted the crash and its consequences for the large number of buyers who were lured into taking mortgages to buy 'property' (real estate) at inflated prices on the assumption that house prices would continue to rise at annual rates of 15 per cent or more, and as this proved to be mistaken, they found themselves underwater, with the outstanding mortgage exceeding the property value. But prophets of catastrophe can be found at any time, and these warnings were taken as an attempt to spoil the party. The overwhelming majority of established economists, including economic forecasters, were caught by surprise. As the subprime mortgage market collapsed in 2007, they were quick to reassure politicians and the public that this was a local event that would be safely contained. Yes, growth rates might turn out somewhat lower than previously forecast, but a recession was out of the question. It took until the second half of 2008 for the negative growth rates to be anticipated — that is, well after the fact, as we know now.

It is not without irony that during the first years of the millennium economists discussed the 'Great Moderation'. According to this idea, sound economic policies — most of all a clear focus on inflation targeting by independent central banks, abstinence from fiscal policy as a tool to dampen economic fluctuations, liberalised financial markets that offer sophisticated instruments for credit and for risk management, and low marginal tax rates — in general, a cohesive supply-side policy, had effectively made the business cycle, if not all economic fluctuations, a phenomenon of the past. In this brave new world, only external shocks could temporarily introduce disturbance, but as these are unforeseeable or random, there was no more room for counter-cyclical or related measures.[8] Meanwhile, the credit bubble was steadily inflating, reinforced by opaque credit chains and obscure financial instruments.

How could such a situation have occurred? According to Rajan (2010), the causal factor was the increase in income inequality after the 'golden age' of capitalism had ended in the 1970s. Initially predominantly in the US and Britain, income inequality started to rise, making it increasingly difficult for workers at the lower end of the wage scale to secure their part in the ongoing growth of their economies from labour income. At the same time, the welfare state was dismantled, so that consumption was increasingly financed through credit. The promotion of credit cards (and, of course, credit card debt) among low-income households marked the beginning of this development, and the NINJA loans marked its peak. Politically, this served two goals simultaneously; first, to appease those who otherwise would have been left behind and could have started to doubt the wisdom of the prevailing order and turn rebellious; second, to ensure that aggregate demand would be sustained and thus support continued economic growth. It seemed an almost perfect way of combining wage depression with less redistribution, steadily increasing mass consumption and real estate-related wealth. It was admired as an 'ownership economy' and cheerfully copied in economies like Ireland (the 'Celtic tiger') and Spain (the 'Iberian tiger'), which later found themselves in the centre of the euro crisis that started in 2010.

The new socio-economic model was therefore built on a giant credit bubble which inevitably had to burst. The deleveraging was violent. It triggered the Great Recession and was not fully completed when the next shock struck in 2020. The requirement to save the financial systems from collapsing led to sharp increases in government debt levels. At the same time, financial investors reconsidered their previous assessment of sovereign debt risk, which in addition to increasing interest rates on new debt made all existing debt far more expensive to service as soon as it had to be rolled over. Thus, even governments with sound budgets and otherwise sustainable debt levels came under budgetary pressure. In this context, it is particularly irritating that the direct way to address the problems that caused the current crisis, a reversal of the increasing income inequality, is out of reach of governments, which instead are under pressure to follow strict austerity policies in order to maintain or regain the confidence of the players in the world's financial markets.

Recovery from the Great Recession initially manifested itself quickly and strongly, but second-round effects continued to affect many economies considerably longer, despite the hope that the recovery in 2009 would make this slump 'V-shaped' — sharp but short. Research by Reinhart and Rogoff (2009) on the duration of depressed economic activity following financial crises across centuries found the deleveraging following asset bubbles to be lengthy processes. Real estate prices tend to fall for six years, stock prices for more than three years. Similarly, after the Second World War, government debt rose sharply in the aftermath of banking crises, in part triggered by the rescue measures for the banking system, but mostly due to the drop in tax revenue. Along with this, households and firms struggled to repay outstanding debt and were forced to increase their savings accordingly, which implies prolonged drops in consumption and investment demand, which makes it impossible for governments to cut spending in order to rebalance their budgets, let alone reduce their debt levels without triggering another recession. The 'W-shaped' or 'L-shaped' recessions observed in countries that were forced to adopt austerity measures like Greece and Portugal were thus predictable.

The European Sovereign Debt crisis

The European sovereign debt crisis started in early 2010, after a newly elected government in Greece announced that the government deficit was actually close to 13 per cent of GDP, which was about twice as high as previously communicated, and rating agencies consequently downgraded Greek government debt. Severe austerity measures were soon imposed to improve the budget. In 2010, government final consumption expenditure was cut by more than 7 per cent, and by more than 9 per cent in 2011, triggering strikes and unrest, which further shattered financial investors' confidence, which had already been shaken by the unanticipated defaults elsewhere in the earlier stages of the world's financial crises.

As a result, risk premiums climbed, and the cost of borrowing or refinancing government debt soared. As the Greek economy's share in the euro zone was minor, amounting to about 3 per cent, a quick bail-out could have fixed the problem, but the EU wanted to set an example and not let Greece get away with it, fearing that this would make the euro zone's budgetary discipline guideposts fixed in the 1992 Treaty of Maastricht meaningless once and for all and open the gates widely for irresponsible government finance driven by moral hazard. However, when adherence to principles gained precedence, speculation emerged on whether Greece would sooner or later be forced to resort to depreciation of its currency, which would have meant abandoning the euro.

The exchange rate risk for euro-denominated debt was thus back on the agenda, and default plus exchange rate risk was too much for financial investors in Greek bonds. This, in turn, made Greek debt increasingly unsustainable, with climbing interest rates at every recurrent roll-over. Figure 22.14 shows the long-term interest rates in the euro zone from January 2007 to August 2025 for those countries that had adopted the euro before 2010. Until the end of 2009, the rates moved close to each other, at about 5 per cent. However, in the beginning of 2010, Greek rates started to rise quickly, reaching a staggering peak of more than 29 per cent in February 2012. Contagion soon affected other euro-zone countries. In mid-2020 Portugal and Ireland were 'infected', both their peaks are reached in July 2011 at 12.2 for Portugal and 12.5 for Ireland. Italy (7.1 per cent in November 2011) — the third largest economy of the euro zone (after Germany and France) —, Cyprus (7.0 per cent in September 2011), Spain (6.8 per cent in July 2012) and Slovenia (6.8 per cent in August 2012) were also affected. It took until mid-2015 until the worst was over, but for Greece, interest rates converged to those of the rest of the euro-zone only in mid-2019.

Mid-2019 is another milestone in modern monetary history, as it marks the beginning of negative interest rates on long-term bonds. We shall come back to this further down.

In April 2010 the so-called 'troika' of EU, ECB and IMF launched a first rescue package for Greece in the form of a €110 billion loan at preferential conditions. This proved too little and too late to solve the problem for good, and the euro zone kept 'muddling through', while

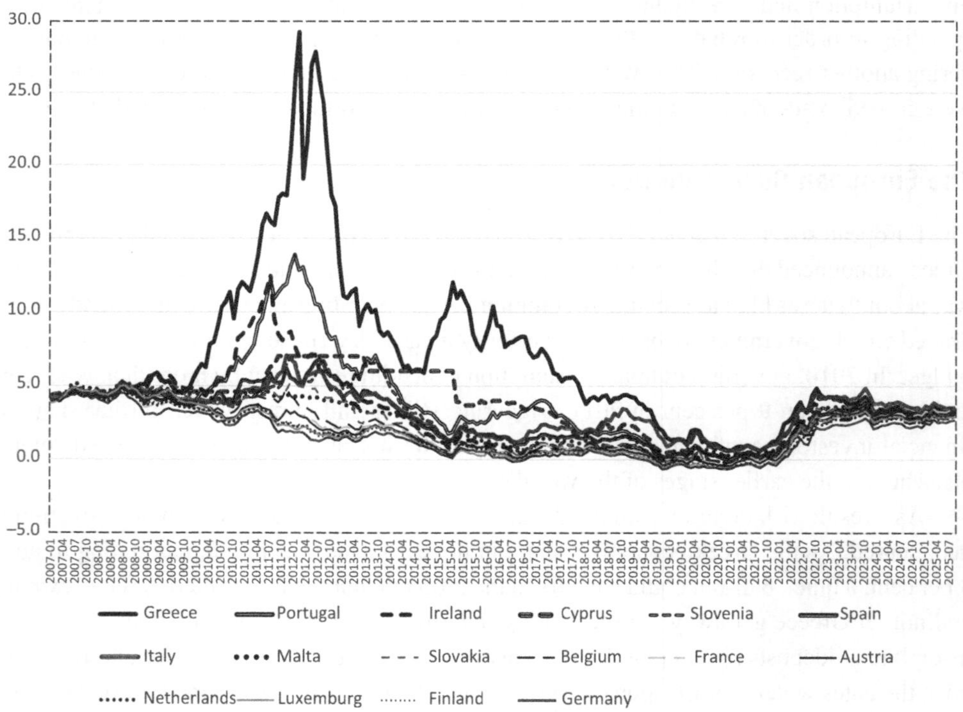

FIGURE 22.14 Long-term interest rates in the euro zone, 2007–25

Source: European Central Bank.

the troika's main concern appeared to be the creditworthiness of the affected economies, as reflected by prices in financial markets. Among the measures taken were the creation of the European Financial Stability Facility (EFSF) and the European Stability Mechanism (ESM), to provide liquidity to euro zone economies under stress in financial markets. Apart from this, the ECB lowered its refinancing rates to historical lows and flooded the European interbank market with liquidity. Most significantly, it committed itself to act as a lender of last resort to governments in the euro zone. Furthermore, a 50 per cent debt 'write-off' — a partial default — was negotiated with holders of Greek government bonds in 2011.

The countries at the periphery of the euro zone, which were plagued by the most severe sovereign debt problems, had mostly experienced persistent current account deficits and, correspondingly, capital inflows during the years preceding the Great Recession and the euro sovereign debt crises, as Figure 22.15 shows. Remarkably, after 2012, with the exception of Greece, Cyprus and Ireland, we see a reversal and capital inflows began reducing the economies' external debts.

It is, however, open to debate what was the cause and what was the effect. The prevailing view refers to a relative increase in labour unit costs that would have eroded competitiveness. On the other hand, it appears that the huge capital inflows were not a reaction to trade deficits but followed their own dynamics. In particular, with the introduction of the euro, financial investors offered cheap credit to countries that had previously faced comparatively high interest rates on international loans due to country risk premiums, as well as interest parity triggered surcharges to take account of these countries' history of devaluations against the ECU. Credit was thus suddenly available from abroad at unprecedentedly low nominal rates, fuelling huge speculative real estate booms. As always in speculative booms, the fantasy of

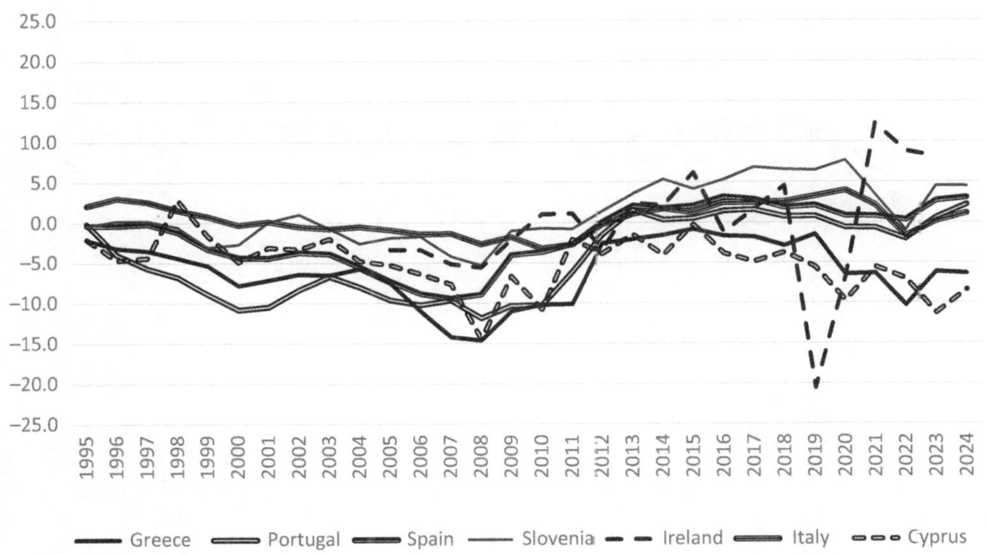

FIGURE 22.15 Current account balances, countries affected by European sovereign debt crisis (per cent of GDP), 1995–2024

Source: World Development Indicators (accessed September 2025).

ever-increasing wealth increased consumption well in excess of income. While some of the additional demand, particularly in construction, would be serviced by the domestic industry, the remainder was imported, hence triggering the trade deficits.

Also, with demand outstripping domestic supply, prices and wages would come under upward pressure, hence the increase in labour unit cost and the price level. Thus, in this view the observed wage increases were a consequence of the speculative bubble rather than its cause.

Finally, there is little evidence for the belief that irresponsible government budgets were the ultimate cause of the 2010 crises. As Cecchetti (2011) pointed out, governments net finance positions in the euro zone had reached historically low deficits, when the subprime mortgage market crashed in and the financial crises led to the Great Recession of 2008–9. Figure 22.16 confirms these findings.

The Irish government had to rescue its banking sector, which until 2007 had expanded beyond reason and became insolvent when the global financial crises hit in 2008. Ireland thus recorded by far the worst deficit in the euro-zone, amounting to 32 per cent in 2010. Yet, from 1997 to 2007 the government recorded budget surpluses in every year except 2002. Cyprus, which was struggling with a banking crisis in 1912–13, had a budget surplus of 3.2 per cent in 2007. Spain's government in 2007 had a budget surplus of 1.9 per cent, and by 2007, the Italian government had managed to reduce its deficit to comply with the first of the two budgetary Maastricht criteria of no more than 3 per cent budget deficit and no more than 60 per cent government debt relative to GDP. Regarding the upper limit of the debt ratio, in 2007 Ireland (23.9 per cent), Cyprus (54.8 per cent) and Spain (35.7 per cent) were well inside the

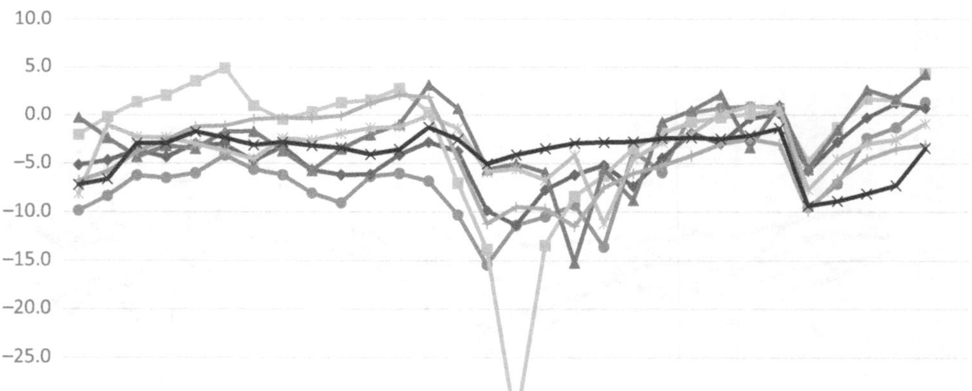

FIGURE 22.16 Central government deficits, countries affected by European sovereign debt crisis (per cent of GDP), 1995–2011

Source: European Central Bank, government statistics.

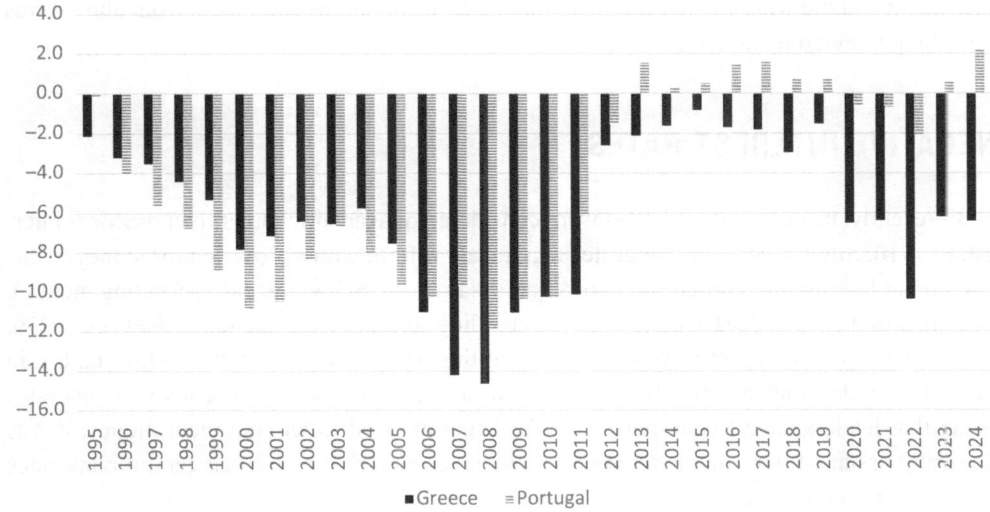

FIGURE 22.17 Current account balances of Greece and Portugal (per cent of GDP), 1995–2024

Source: World Development Indicators (accessed September 2025).

EMU's 'comfort zone'. Italy still recorded a debt ratio of 103.5 per cent, but it was just about to get its budgetary problems under control. Thus, these countries' current budgetary problems were a *result* of the financial crisis, and not vice versa, as the proponents of austerity claim to justify the hardship brought about by the demanded cuts to wages, pensions and health care.

Portugal and, in particular, Greece, however, are a different story. Here, the government deficits exceeded the 3 per cent target consistently in the pre-crisis period, going back years before the introduction of the euro. As a result, their government debt ratios in 2007 exceeded the EMU's upper limit; Portugal recorded 72.7 per cent and Greece 104.6 per cent. In line with this, these two economies stood out in the euro-zone before 2007–8 with long-standing current account balance deficits, as Figure 22.17 shows. Their economies had accumulated increasing debts vis-à-vis the rest of the world.

The cure imposed by the troika first on Greece and then on the other economies that had experienced sharp increases in interest rates for government bonds aimed at improving the competitiveness and in turn the creditworthiness of the highly indebted countries through internal devaluation. As they no longer had currencies that could be devalued against the currencies of their most important trading partners, their internal prices, in particular for tradable goods, were put under pressure, and this was sought to be achieved via wage deflation and cuts of transfer incomes. As can been inferred from Figure 22.17, this worked to some degree; the current account deficits of both countries were significantly reduced, but whereas Portugal's current account balance now appears to be sustainable, the same cannot be said for Greece. Tax fraud and evasion were also targeted to improve the budgetary situation of the government, but increases of corporate taxes were not on the agenda. As a result, these countries experienced drastic declines of purchasing power in the population at large, political discontent and the widespread sentiment that the hardship imposed on them from abroad was punishing the victims rather than the culprits.

NEGATIVE INTEREST RATES

Until recently, negative interest rates were considered of academic rather than practical interest. In 1916, Silvio Gesell had suggested a monetary reform with a provision for money in circulation to lose nominal purchasing power across time — 'Schwundgeld' (shrinking money). The intention of this idea was to prevent hoarding and promote spending. Keynes (1936, p. 175 ff.) paid his respect to Gesell, and up to this date, Gesell has some followers, but in academic circles, they are mostly considered 'as monetary cranks'. As negative interest rates mean that lenders have to pay borrowers for being allowed to lending them money, it was generally assumed that such a situation would never materialise and that central bank rates had a lower bound of zero.

In July 2012, this belief was contradicted by the news that Denmark's Nationalbank had lowered its deposit rate below zero. Other central banks followed — the European Central Bank in June 2014, the Swiss National Bank in December 2014, the Swedish Riksbank in February 2025 and the Bank of Japan in June 2016. The end of negative policy rates in these five economies did not come until January 2020, when the Riksbank's rate was raised to zero. The Bank of Japan eventually finished this remarkable episode in February 2024. Denmark

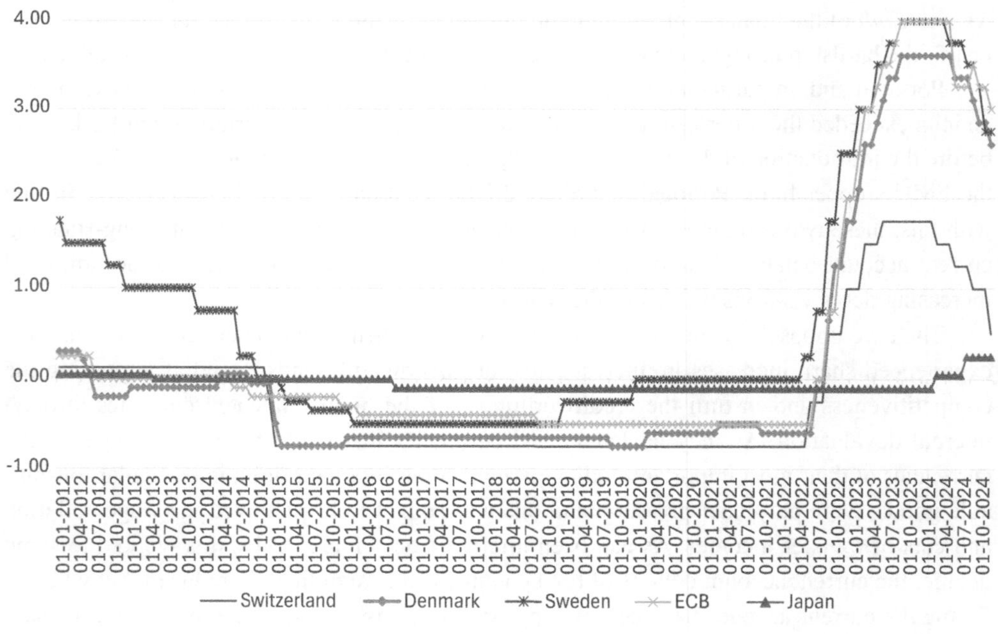

FIGURE 22.18 Central bank rates diving below zero (per cent), 2012–24

Source: Bank of International Settlements, European Central Bank.

and Switzerland had experienced central bank rates as low as –0.75 per cent, Sweden and the euro zone –0.5 per cent and Japan –0.1 per cent, as Figure 22.18 documents.

Central banks pursued different goals with introducing negative interest rates. During the slow recovery from the 2008–9 recession and the following government debt crises, inflation in some economies had come down to uncomfortably low rates. After the Great Recession, Japan and many European economies even went through one or more years of consumer price deflation, and the US recorded a –0.4 per cent CPI decrease in 2009. It was hoped that negative interest rates would prevent inflation expectations from becoming negative. After hyperinflation, negative inflation expectations are perhaps central banker's worst nightmare, as they pave the way for long-lasting deflation. More directly, low central bank rates should diffuse into the economy, stimulate lending and spending and discourage the hoarding of money. Another focus was on exchange rates. The Danish Nationalbank defended its currency's peg to the euro, the Swiss National Bank leaned against appreciation of the Franc.

Given the multitude of factors that have an impact on final demand and prices levels in the affected economies, it is difficult to judge to what extent these extremely 'dovish' monetary policies helped to prevent inflation expectations to become negative; contributed to lowering borrowing costs; or helped exporters. Critics blamed them for hurting savers and pension funds, encouraging excessive risk-taking, asset price inflation and misallocation of investible funds, as with excessively low borrowing rates, investments, which under normal circumstances would never be considered, may become profitable. Last but not least, those who believe that a dollar is always put to better use in the private sector than in the government sector complained that central banks made it easier for governments to service their debts and to run budget deficits.

Then, suddenly, the world economy suffered its next shock, caused by COVID-19 in 2020. After the shutdowns and lockdowns came to an end, in 2021–2, aggregate demand vastly outstripped aggregate supply, so that inflation quickly went up. The price increases caused by the war in Ukraine and the economic disruptions that it triggered, created additional inflationary pressures, so that central banks reversed course and turned 'hawkish'. For the time being, negative central bank rates are off the agenda.

COVID-19

When most economies around the globe had finally recovered from the 2008–9 crisis, an unprecedented shock hit the world economy out of the blue in February 2020. A new coronavirus, triggering the disease COVID-19, had appeared in Wuhan, China, in December 2019, had appeared in Wuhan, China, in December 2019, and within a few months, it spread around the globe and caused the first pandemic of the twenty-first century. According to figures reported to the World Health Organization (WHO), the death toll amounted to about 7 million. Compared to this, the estimated 20 to 50 million lives claimed by the previous pandemic a hundred years ago, the Spanish flu of 1918–20, when the world's population was only one-fifth of today's, make the Spanish flu appear far more deadly, even if the true numbers of COVID-19 victims are likely to be much higher the official 7 million, due to unreported cases.

Having said this, it is only due to the quick and decisive actions of governments and local authorities in most countries of the world to reduce the number of infections and thus curb the spread of the virus — first to avoid a collapse of health services, then to gain time until a COVID-19 vaccine could be developed, produced and distributed — that the death toll did not rise much higher. We do not know the counterfactual, what would have happened if the chains of infection had not been cut as rigorously and if a vaccine had not been made available within just about one year, but the economic slump that resulted from the severe restrictions imposed to mitigate the public health crisis was drastic. The almost instantaneous contraction in the production and distribution of goods and services, the surging unemployment and the abrupt loss of business revenue were unprecedented in modern history. Unlike other recessions, the COVID-19 recession was driven by simultaneous and mutually re-enforcing demand and supply shocks, which made it so abrupt and severe.

The World Bank's *World Development Indicators* presently quantify the reduction of global GDP from 2019 to 2020 at 2.85 per cent, corresponding to a reduction of about $415 per capita. However, to get a more realistic idea of the macroeconomic losses, we need a counterfactual GDP for 2020, as if the virus had never spread across the globe. To this end, let us assume that without the pandemic, world GDP would have grown at the average real rate of the ten years before the pandemic (2010–19), which was 3.20 per cent. The gap between the factual and the counter-factual growth rates thus amounts to more than 6 per cent, and instead of declining by $415, per capita GDP would have risen by about $350. The estimated losses thus amount to about $765 per capita.

Of course, per capita averages hide the enormous economic inequalities, both globally and within countries. For an average income household in one of the richer parts of the world, the impact on disposable income may have gone hardly noticed. For lower income earners, government support for the loss of income during the pandemic would be decisive. In the poorer parts of the world, where governments could not afford the same degree of financial support, the loss of income could be drastic — and outright devastating for the poorest.

The economic impacts of the COVID-19 pandemic varied significantly, not only across countries, but particularly across sectors and occupations. With the imposition of border closures and travel restrictions worldwide, the travel and tourism sector was among the most severely affected. As restaurants, bars, cinemas, theatres, gyms and swimming pools were forced to close, many were threatened by bankruptcy. By contrast, e-commerce experienced rapid expansion, as consumers either opted or were compelled to purchase non-essential goods online during widespread retail closures.

Education frequently went online. The damage to the learning process for pupils and students is difficult to assess; for many children the deprivation of contact with their peers may have the longest lasting negative effects. Also, when childcare, kindergarten and primary schools were closed, many caretakers of young children were faced with difficulties reconciling the demands of their children with those of their employers.

In response, many governments implemented rescue and support packages to save firms that had been running solid businesses before the pandemic survive the shutdowns imposed on them and the occasional lockdowns for the population as a whole. Support for people who had lost their employment income was another priority for governments. Of course, government support required not only the willingness to help but also the financial means or access to affordable credit. According to the IMF (2021), government spending to mitigate the consequences of the pandemic — and of the measures taken to curb the spread of the virus — amounted to about 10 per cent of world GDP. Of this, 1.4 per cent went to the health sector and 8.6 per cent to other support measures. And indeed, the variation was pronounced, from 30.7 per cent in Timor-Leste and 25.5 per cent in the US down to 0.2 per cent in Iraq and 0.1 per cent in Laos. New Zealand, the UK, Singapore, Australia, Greece, Japan, Canada, Germany and Austria were among the most generous (15 to 20 per cent), the BRIC countries spent 9.2 per cent (Brazil), 5.0 per cent (Russia), 4.1 per cent (India) and 4.8 per cent (China). About 50 governments assigned less than 2.5 per cent of GDP to help the victims of the pandemic — not surprisingly the list comprises the poorest countries of the world.

Figure 22.19 illustrates the geographical distribution of government spending and forgone revenue in response to the pandemic in per cent of each country's GDP in 2020. By and large, the map reflects the global distribution of per capita income, with a few exceptions like Sweden and Finland, which managed to keep infection rates low without widespread shutdowns and consequently had relatively few people and businesses who needed income support.

As the origin of this crisis lay outside the economic system, once the virus was under control and the restrictions lifted, recovery on the local scale happened much swifter than during 'normal' recessions that are caused by some dysfunctionality within the economy itself. At the same time, the multiple lockdowns and shutdowns left more lasting impressions, as they had severely affected the global supply chains of the world economy and a hitherto unknown international division of labour. The images of containers piling up in the port of Shanghai are the iconic symbols of the disruptions to world trade, which made business and political leaders around the world reconsider the risks of economic globalisation.

BREXIT

'Brexit' denotes the UK's exit from the EU in 2020, following a referendum in 2016 with 52 per cent of the vote in favour of leaving. Based on false claims about British EU membership costs far exceeding its benefits, and unrealistic promises that after leaving the EU, Britain would conclude free trade agreements with the rest of the world and re-establish its former role as a centre of the world economy, the deceived electorate decided to re-erect economic borders with continental Europe.

The UK formally left the EU in January 2020, and after a transition period of two years, the UK exited the EU single market and the customs union. Although a 'Trade and Cooperation Agreement' was negotiated which continued tariff-free trade for most goods and services, non-tariff barriers such as customs checks, rules-of-origin requirements and regulatory compliance rules led to new costs and barriers and constrained access to EU markets. The images of enormous lorry queues near ports of embarkation are the iconic symbols of these disruptions. The end of free movement of labour has led to shortages, particularly in low-wage sectors like agriculture, hospitality and health care). The UK's attractiveness as a headquarter for multinational corporations was also impaired.

FIGURE 22.19 spending and forgone revenue in response to the COVID-19 pandemic, per cent of 2020 GDP

Source: IMF Database of Fiscal Responses to COVID-19 (n.d.).

It is thus safe to assume that trade volumes went down relative to a counterfactual of continued EU membership and that 'Brexit' has had a negative net effect on output. It reduced integration with its largest trading partner and required massive structural adjustment. In addition, as far as we can assess so far, Brexit has been far more damaging to the UK than to the economies of continental Europe. This is hardly surprising, given the relative economic sizes. In 2020, the UK's GDP amounted to barely 17 per cent of that of the EU. Even if 'Brexit' may be a minor disruption to trade on the global scale, it is still remarkable that a nation that once was the global hegemon should actively choose to disrupt its established trade flows, even if this happened under false promises.[9]

ECONOMIC CONSEQUENCES OF THE RUSSIA–UKRAINE WAR

The Russian invasion of Ukraine in February 2022 has caused economic effects that persist up to this day. We will briefly discuss the most important ones — destruction and disruption of energy and transport infrastructure; commodity price shocks; sanctions and controls of trade with Russia; trade redirection and fragmentation of global supply chains; the impact on low-income countries; and the massive redirection of productive resources towards the military and armaments.

The war has brought massive damage to ports, rail and energy infrastructure. Sabotage and political pressure have disrupted fuel pipelines, leading to higher and more volatile gas and electricity prices in the West. Exports of grain and from the fertile soils of Ukraine were immediately disrupted, resulting in upward pressure on global food prices. Ukraine and Russia are major exporters of wheat, maize, sunflower oil and related inputs. In addition, rising costs of fertilisers — driven by energy prices, trade restrictions and global supply-chain disruptions — have badly affected food security in many poor countries. Low-income food-importing countries have thus borne a disproportionate share of the shock.

The sanctions imposed on Russia and the attempts by the Western camp to reduce reliance on Russian oil and gas imports have led to restructuring of global trade patterns and supply chains, which are now increasingly tilted towards geopolitical considerations rather than comparative advantage. The sanctions directly reduce Russia's trade with the sanctioning countries, force Russia to trade more with non-Western countries — foremost with China and India — and affect neutral countries through complicated compliance rules designed to avoid secondary sanctions.

The Russia-Ukraine war has not only disrupted international trade but also diverted capital and labour from civilian to military purposes. Not surprisingly, this is most pronounced in Ukraine, where military expenditure in 2024 is estimated at about 30 per cent of GDP, and Russia where it has climbed above 6 per cent of GDP. NATO states have also increased military expenditure substantially, the goal of 2 per cent of GDP proclaimed in 2014 was raised in June 2025 to 5 per cent.

According to the Stockholm International Peace Research Institute (SIPRI), global military expenditure increased by 9.4 per cent in real terms from 2023 to 2024, more than ever since the end of the Cold War. Military spending increased across the globe but particularly in Europe and the Middle East. This implies a massive redirection of productive resources into the military and armaments. While military spending can provide short-term economic stimulus, negative externalities tend to prevail in the long-run; foremost inflationary pressure, higher interest rates, reduced private investment and lower productivity growth in non-military sectors. We are already witnessing cuts for social spending, education, infrastructure, and environment and climate in favour of the military. In the long run, this is crowding out investments in a sustainable future by channelling resources into armaments that in the best case will be scrapped in a few decades. Moreover, as governments across the globe are racing to get ready for war, the capacities of the armaments industry are stretched to their limits, which is good news for the shareholders as share prices of the military-industrial complex soar, but bad news for taxpayers and the military, as increasing expenses accompanied by rising prices yield less military capability than desired.

Taken together, the war has raised global inflation, redirected Russian exports toward non-Western economies and increased food and energy insecurity for many poor countries. The policy responses by the Western camp have further exacerbated these disruptions. The long-run productivity and income losses and their global distribution are difficult to quantify, but as the conflict has turned into a war of attrition and is now in its fourth year, with rising geopolitical tensions and, consequently, skyrocketing military and armaments expenses, the negative impacts on welfare can be assumed to be considerable.

INTERNATIONAL ORGANISATIONS, TREATIES AND COOPERATION

WTO Enlargement and the Doha Round

In 2024, WTO membership amounted to 166 countries. Since 2000, 29 countries have joined, the most important among them in terms of economic size being Croatia (2000), China (2001), Saudi Arabia (2005), Ukraine (2008) and Russia (2012). The most recent addition was Timor-Leste, in August 2024. WTO membership is now nearly universal among sovereign states with established trade regimes.

The WTO's mandate and the underlying mechanism (i.e. progressive lowering of trade barriers under most-favoured nation and non-discrimination principle) are as originally designed. Tariff reductions, negotiations and trade-liberalisation remain central in principle, though new issues (digital trade, environment, subsidies, etc.) have gained prominence. Since its establishment in 1995, the WTO has delivered the institutional framework for negotiations, dispute settlements and monitoring of trade policies. However, over the past few years, its importance has eroded, mostly due to new developments in the global political economy. Starting in 2017 with the first presidency of Donald Trump, the US government has followed a confrontational policy toward the WTO, arguing that it disadvantaged US interests and failed to discipline China's trade practices. Since 2017, the US refuses to approve new judges to the WTO's 'Appellate Body'. By December 2019, this left it without the minimum three members required to hear appeals, thus paralysing the WTO's dispute settlement system. The Trump administration gave precedence to bilateral agreements (e.g. with Japan, South Korea) and renegotiated the 'North American Free-Trade' Area (NAFTA) into the 'United States–Mexico–Canada Agreement' (USMCA) in 2020. Managed trade is preferred over multilateral liberalisation.

More generally, the increasing geopolitical tensions have eroded the trust in the benefits of free trade. Trade policy is increasingly subordinated to industrial policy and geopolitical power considerations. The ensuing sanctions, trade barriers and industrial subsidies are often justified under 'national security' exemptions to WTO rules. We are thus witnessing a drift towards a fragmented and multipolar global trade system. This can be quantified by referring to the cumulative number of Regional Trade Agreements (RTAs) in force, collected by the WTO (https://rtais.wto.org/UI/charts.aspx). The database is annual and goes back to 1948. The first two RTAs appeared in 1958, and until 1990 the number gradually rose to 24. By 2000, there were already 91 RTAs in force, rising to 210 by 2010, 312 by 2020, and in 2024, the number stood at 373.

The 'trade rounds', organised every few years as platforms to achieve further trade liberalisation, inherited from the GATT, remain, but their impact has dwindled over time. The first round took place in Doha, in 2001. Beginning in 2003, follow-up rounds were staged in Cancún, Geneva, Hong Kong, Bali, Nairobi and Buenos Aires. Negotiations proved difficult due to widely diverging positions on a range of issues including agriculture, manufacturing, services and intellectual property, mostly between two clearly identifiable camps, the rich economies led by the US, the EU and Japan, and the poorer and emerging countries, including China and India, but also South Korea and South Africa, which in this respect still belong to the periphery of the world economy. The 2008 meeting in Geneva could not resolve a conflict between the US, on the one hand, and China and India, on the other, about special safeguards for poor farmers. The major remaining concerns of the trade rounds relate mostly to agriculture, clothing and textiles and intellectual property. In the Nairobi round in 2015, the agricultural export subsidies in the rich countries came under fierce attack, and as a result, the US and the EU declared the process as 'dead'.

The Doha rounds were an ambitious attempt to reorganise the global trading system in favour of developing countries, and it failed due to the inability of members to reconcile the interests of the rich and the poorer economies. While the latter wanted easier access for their industrial goods, services and better protection of their 'intellectual property'), the former insisted on the interests of their farmers and consumers.

The agricultural products exporting countries keep pushing for free and fair agricultural trade. 20 of them formed a coalition called the 'Cairns Group' in 1986. Its most important achievement was ensuring agriculture was included in global trade rules via the Uruguay Round Agreement on Agriculture (see Chapter 19). It continues to keep their interests — reducing subsidies and barriers that distort agricultural markets — on the WTO's agenda.

EU and Euro Zone Enlargement

In 2000, the EU had the following members: Austria, Belgium, Denmark, Finland, France, Germany, Greece, Ireland, Italy, Luxembourg, the Netherlands, Portugal, Spain, Sweden and the UK. In 2004, this 'EU-15' welcomed the Czech Republic, Cyprus,[10] Estonia, Hungary, Latvia, Lithuania, Malta, Poland, Slovakia and Slovenia as new member states; Bulgaria and Romania followed in 2007. Croatia joined in July 2013. Today, the EU has 27 member states, following the UK's exit in 2020. It includes all countries in the prosperous northwest of the continent, Southwest and Central Europe, except for Iceland, the microstate Liechtenstein. Norway and Switzerland, which would be welcome, but have chosen to stay outside.[11]

Several additional countries are at various stages in the accession process. As of 2025, the EU has granted candidate status to Albania, Montenegro, North Macedonia, Serbia, Turkey, Ukraine, Moldova and Georgia, subject to meeting the Copenhagen political, economic and legal criteria. Bosnia & Herzegovina and Kosovo are potential candidates. Montenegro is among the most advanced candidates — it has opened all negotiation chapters of the EU 'acquis communautaire' (the collection of rights and obligations that constitute the body of EU law) and has provisionally closed several, including critical ones pertaining to rule of law.

Ukraine and Moldova formally began accession negotiations in June 2024, but since the Russia–Ukraine war started in 2022, it is unlikely that they will become EU members any time soon. North Macedonia and Albania, while granted candidate status earlier, continue to progress along the screening and negotiation track. Turkey remains a candidate, but accession is widely understood to be paused or moving very slowly. While some questions remain regarding the prospects for Turkey and Kosovo,[12] EU membership is thus set to cover the entire continent, apart from Belarus, (the European parts of) Russia, which are so far not even treated as candidates for accession in the foreseeable future, Ukraine, and the self-chosen outsiders Iceland, Switzerland, Norway and now also the UK. It is worth noting that with the free movement and settlement of people provisions, EU membership of the states that once constituted Yugoslavia, which was divided along perceived ethnic lines in a series of extremely violent wars with tens of thousands of victims, will to a considerable degree at least practically reverse ex-Yugoslavia's nationalistic separations.

The euro zone has been growing, too. From the original 12 economies in 1999, the following EU member states have joined subsequently: Slovenia (2007), Cyprus and Malta (2008), Slovakia (2009), Estonia (2011), Latvia (2014), Lithuania (2015) and Croatia (2023). Thus, by the end of 2024, the EU had 20 member states that use the euro as their official currency. The remaining EU member states that did not yet use the euro were Bulgaria, the Czech Republic, Denmark, Hungary, Poland, Romania and Sweden. Bulgaria is adopting the euro on 1 January 2026, having recently met the convergence criteria and received formal approval by the European Commission and European Central Bank. Denmark has a legal opt-out under the Maastricht Treaty and is not obligated to adopt the euro. The others (the Czech Republic, Hungary, Poland, Romania and Sweden) are bound by Treaty obligations to adopt once they meet the Maastricht convergence criteria. However, none of them has committed to a firm date, and several have shown no political urgency, citing economic, institutional or public opinion constraints.

Apart from this, a number of economies resorted to 'euroization' without EU membership. The European microstates Andorra, Monaco, San Marino and the Vatican City have sought and received agreement from the ECB to use the euro as legal tender. Two economies from ex-Yugoslavia — Kosovo and Montenegro — unilaterally adopted the euro in 2002, after previously having unilaterally used the German mark. Outside Europe, the euro is legal tender in the following overseas territories linked to EU states: Saint Barthélemy, Saint Pierre and Miquelon, Mayotte, Réunion, Martinique, Guadeloupe, French Guiana and Saint Martin (France), Azores and Madeira (Portugal) and the Canary Islands (Spain).

G7, G20 and BRIC and ASEAN

Apart from supranational institutions such as the United Nations and its specialised agencies, the World Bank, the IMF and the World Trade Organization — which were institutionalised in the wake of the Second World War and the 1944 Bretton Woods Conference — informal arrangements and regular supranational summits also exert influence on global politics and the international economy. These include regional trade or customs areas like the EU and formerly NAFTA, as well as less formal groupings of states and supra-national summits that also exert influence on the international political scene and thereby on the international economy.

The oldest of these informal groups is the 'Group of Seven' (G7), comprising Canada, France, Germany, Italy, Japan, the UK and the US. Since 1976, the G7 has held dozens of summits in which leaders of the West attempted to coordinate policy in areas as varied as defence, energy, taxation and financial stability. Following the collapse of the Soviet Union, Russia participated from 1998 to 2014, during which time the group was known as the G8; when Russia was excluded in 2014, the G8 reverted to G7.

However, without economies such as China, India and Brazil — now among the world's largest — the representativeness and hence the legitimacy of the G7 are increasingly questioned. To address this, the 'Group of Twenty' (G20) was established in 1999. Its stated aim is to serve as 'the premier forum for international cooperation on the most important issues of the global economic and financial agenda' (https://b20brasil.org/about-g20). G20 summits are held annually under a rotating presidency. In 2024, G20 membership included 19 sovereign states plus the EU and, since 2023, the African Union, which now participates as a full member. The G20 members are Argentina, Australia, Brazil, Canada, China, France, Germany, India, Indonesia, Italy, Japan, Mexico, Republic of Korea, Russia, Saudi Arabia, South Africa, Turkey, the UK, the US, the EU and the African Union. Collectively, the G20 members represent around 87 per cent of the global GDP, 62 per cent of the world's population, and over 75 per cent of global trade. Throughout the year, representatives from G20 countries gather to discuss financial and socioeconomic issues. Although the G20 has no formal legislative powers, and its legitimacy rests upon the credentials of its member states and their leaders, it has become one of the most consequential forums for global governance due to its wide coverage and influence. Nonetheless, the G7 continues its meetings, granting more exclusivity to a smaller inner circle.

Partly in reaction to this continuing drive for exclusivity by the Western core group of seven, the BRIC countries (Brazil, Russia, India and China) have in 2009 begun to stage their own exclusive summits. Representing about 40 per cent of the world population, this is a potentially powerful club, but for the time being, the cultural, economic and political diversity of its members is still preventing BRIC from becoming as consequential as the G7, which brings together economically much more similar countries, with a long-standing alliance shaped during the Cold War. Having said this, we may now be witnessing the BRIC gaining importance. With South Africa joining in 2020 and others invited as 'partners', the BRICS+ has expanded to include Indonesia, Iran, Turkey, Egypt, Ethiopia, Nigeria, the United Arab Emirates, Mexico and Argentina. Regional blocs such as ASEAN, the African Union and Mercosur are now also invited to the BRICS+ summits. As a voice of the 'Global South', it can claim some symbolic legitimacy, but more important are its efforts to create its own economic institutions. At the Fortaleza summit in 2014, the 'New Development Bank' (NDB) was created as an alternative to the IMF and the World Bank. With headquarters in Shanghai, it is financing large infrastructure investments. It is issuing bonds and lending in BRIC currencies, thus supporting the BRICS+'s drive towards de-dollarisation. Although the creation of a common reserve currency as an alternative to the dollar is not on the immediate agenda, the BRICS+ countries are increasingly settling trade in their own currencies.

In this context, China's 'The New Silk Route' deserves to be mentioned. Officially called 'Belt and Road Initiative' (BRI), its aim is to connect the 'old world' — Asia, Europe and Africa — through massive investments in transport infrastructure such as rail, pipelines, ports as well as digital communication. Apart from its economic significance, the New Silk Road is clearly an expression of China's rising geopolitical impact; and those who perceive it as a challenge to their entrenched interests fear that it could be a step towards forming a Eurasian bloc in the struggle for hegemony.

In Southeast Asia, ASEAN continues with the ten member states from the region that had joined by 1999, focussing on economic, political and cultural cooperation. It is located along vital global sea shipping routes and represents considerable economic weight, but its weak institutional power has so far prevented it from becoming more than a regional player.

Summits are also staged by the APEC (Asian Pacific Economic Cooperation), bringing together the heads of states of 21 Pacific countries, including the US, China, Japan, Australia and Russia. However, the divergence and hegemonial rivalry within this group make it unlikely that the APEC will in the foreseeable future exert any significant influence in world economic affairs.

CO_2 Emissions and the Kyoto Protocol

There remains no doubt among experts that since the Industrial Revolution in the eighteenth century, human-caused greenhouse gas emissions — predominantly carbon dioxide (CO_2), methane (CO_4), nitrous oxide (N_2O) and fluorinated gases — have significantly contributed to the rise in global average temperature, which is now (2025) estimated to have increased by about 1.2°C relative to the pre-industrial era. Of the estimated total of 1.8 trillion tons of total CO_2 emissions since 1750, about 50 per cent have been released since 1995, i.e. within the last 30 years (https://ourworldindata.org/grapher/cumulative-co-emissions?country=~OWID_WRL). Annual global greenhouse gas emissions (excluding land use and forestry) have more than doubled since 1975, with the balance of responsibility shifting. Figure 22.20 shows the world's greenhouse gas emissions from 1971 to the present, distinguishing between 'low and middle income' and the 'high income' countries, as defined by the World Bank. While high-income countries initially dominated, since 2005, low- and middle-income countries have accounted for the majority of global emissions.

The six largest emitters in 2024 were China, the US, India, the EU, Russia and Brazil (in this order). For much of the post-war period, the US was the single largest polluter, followed by the EU and, at a distance, Japan. China emerged as a major emitter from the mid-1970s onward, but after 2000 its CO_2 output rose at an unprecedented pace. Today, China alone accounts for about 30 per cent of global greenhouse gas emissions. Of the major emitters, only the EU and

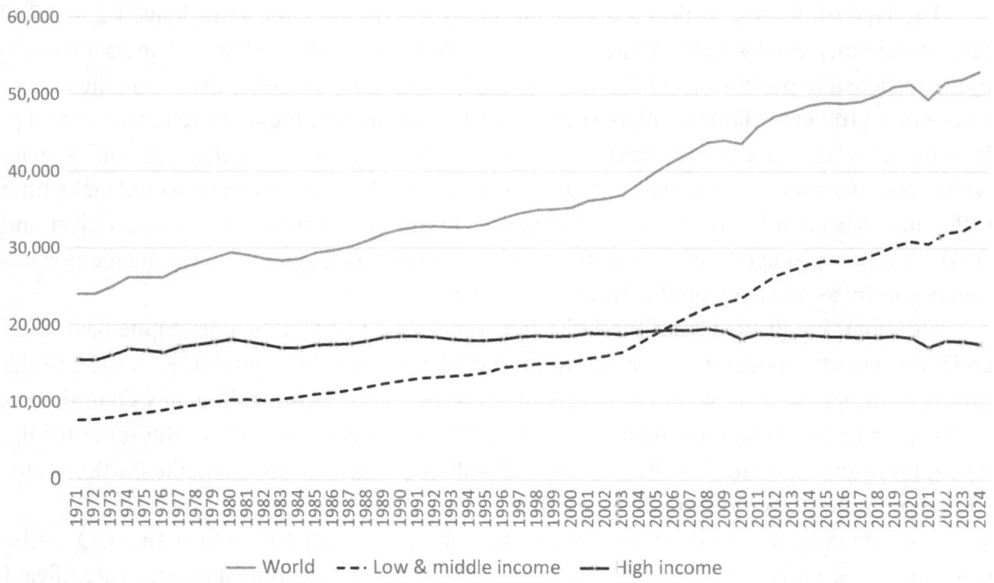

FIGURE 22.20 Total greenhouse gas emissions (excluding land use and forestry), million tons of carbon dioxide equivalent, 1971–2023

Source: World Development Indicators (accessed September 2025).

Japan have managed to stabilise or reduce their emissions in recent decades. It must be kept in mind, however, that the standard attribution of emissions to the locations of economic activity, of which they are harmful side-effects, ignores the fact that it is the use or consumption of goods and services that is the ultimate cause of environmental degradation. Many high-income economies have reduced their domestic emissions partly by outsourcing production to developing countries, thereby inflating the latter's carbon footprint. A truly effective regime of pollution control must therefore consider consumption-based emissions as well as production, to ensure an equitable distribution of responsibility between rich and poor countries of the world.

Because large economies, *ceteris paribus*, pollute more in absolute terms, per capita figures reveal another dimension. In 2024, the highest per capita greenhouse gas emissions were recorded in Gulf states such as Qatar, Bahrain and Kuwait. Among the advanced economies, Australia, the US and Canada rank highest. Russia has recently surpassed the US.

The self-declared aim of the international community, agreed upon in the Paris Agreement (2015), is to limit global warming to 2.0°C compared with pre-industrial levels, which is not overly ambitious. Nevertheless, the measures to achieve this goal and the few commitments to this end have been disappointing so far. Earlier milestones, such as the Kyoto Protocol of 1997, had limited coverage: it set binding reduction targets only for industrialised countries. The Durban (2011) and Doha (2012) conferences extended Kyoto but failed to broaden commitments. Subsequent conferences — including Glasgow (2021), Sharm el-Sheikh (2022) and Dubai (2023) — have stressed coal phase-downs, renewable energy targets and climate finance, but implementation continues to lag behind.

The lack of decisive action has now put the world on track for an estimated 2.5–2.7°C temperature increase by 2100. Apart from the fact that some climate change deniers are occupying responsible positions, and that others simply don't care, the difficulty lies in the collective-action problem. Major emitters such as the US, China and India are reluctant to accept binding constraints that could threaten domestic economic growth. Smaller economies, even with record per capita emissions, can plausibly argue that their actions alone would make little difference. Meanwhile, in advanced economies, fossil-fuel lobbies, climate scepticism and short-term political cycles are preventing decisive action, portraying climate change prevention primarily as an attack on the American/Western way of life.

The emerging giants China and India can point to the fact that on a per capita basis their emissions are still moderate compared to most of the advanced economies, as well as to the historical truth that the now developed countries could industrialise without any commitment whatsoever to the climate or the environment. Whether it is wise to claim the same for the emerging countries while their megacities suffocate in poisonous smog and the Earth's atmosphere continues to warm is another question.

Also, some hypocrisy is involved when the rich economies point to the rising CO_2 emissions in China, India and other industrialising economies. As mentioned above, a significant share of the pollution is due to the new division of labour in the international economy, where increasingly the production of goods that are consumed in the advanced economies is relocated to the periphery. Countries that report reduced domestic emissions in accordance with the Kyoto Protocol are thus at the same time responsible for an increase in global emissions as a response to their demand. Ultimately, then, consumption along with production must be made responsible in order to arrive at a pollution control regime that is acceptable to rich and poor alike. (For a closer look at the policy questions related to global warming, see Appendix 1 to Chapter 23 of this book.)

RECOMMENDATIONS FOR FURTHER READING

For a critique of the intellectual basis of the free-market ideology that started to become increasingly influential in the 1980s, see Skidelsky (2009, *Keynes: The Return of the Master*). Palley (2009, *America's Exhausted Paradigm: Macroeconomic Causes of the Great Recession*) analyses the 'neo-liberal growth model'. Frank et al. (2010, *Expenditure cascades*) elaborate on how 'expenditure cascades' drove household indebtedness that contributed to the severity of the Great Recession of 2008–9.

The economic crises that hit Greece in the aftermath of the Great Recession 2008–9 and the austerity measures imposed by the 'troika' are discussed in detail in Petrakis (2012, *The Greek Economy and the Crisis. Challenges and Responses*).

Graham (2017, *Destined for War. Can America and China Escape Thucydides's Trap?*) is an insightful analysis of the geopolitical rivalry for hegemony between the US and China.

The latest scientific consensus about the global warming as well as about its causes and consequences is given by the IPCC (2023, *Climate Change 2023 Synthesis Report*).

NOTES

1 This view is customarily associated with Francis Fukuyama (1992). It ridicules Marx's vision of the end of history, to be achieved with communism as the voluntary association of the affluent and the free.
2 This is formalised in the so-called 'gravity model' of trade. For an introduction, see Krugman et al. (2011, Chapter 2).
3 The term is attributed to Ferguson and Schularick (2007).
4 In the light of the recent crisis, the success of the theory of finance in becoming a major reference for financial innovation in the last few decades failed to live up to expectations. In line with theoretical predictions, risks were traded more actively and spread across more agents. At the same time, indebtedness and credit chains expanded to unprecedented dimensions, and the financial superstructure of the real economy became increasingly opaque, thus allowing for a menacing but unnoticed accumulation of correlated risk.
5 An analogy to the 'export multiplier' (see Chapter 7 of this book) can be formalised as follows: Aggregate output Y equals private consumption C plus private investment I plus government expenditure G (consumption and investment) plus net exports $X - M$. Assuming that private consumption and imports are constant fractions of income ($C = cY$ and $M = mY$), whereas private investment, government expenditure and exports are autonomous (with respect to Y), implies that $(1 - c + m)Y = X + I + G$. The fiscal multiplier is then given by the partial derivative of Y with respect to G, $\partial Y/\partial G = 1/(1 - c + m)$. This multiplier thus increases in c and decreases in m. As long as $c > m$, it exceeds unity, so that an increase (decrease) in government expenditure increases (decreases) aggregate output by more than the original volume change. Notice that in this context, m can be interpreted as the degree of 'leakage' of domestic government expenditure into imports from other countries.
6 Recall that the propensity to import m in the fiscal multiplier can be interpreted as international 'leakage' of the domestic stimulus measures. Since *ceteris paribus* a country's openness and hence m decreases with the domestic market size, the fiscal multiplier predicts that smaller economies will be more hesitant to resort to fiscal stimulus measures than larger ones.
7 For a discussion of the stimulus packages around the globe, see also Frick et al. (2012).
8 Belief in the 'Great Moderation' shares an important aspect with the belief in the 'end of history' after the collapse of the Soviet Union: an alternative to capitalism is impossible. But with economic crises of the market economy a phenomenon thought to be overcome, there would not even be a point to speculate about alternatives. The crisis-free market economy of the 'Great Moderation' would deliver prosperity to everyone trying hard enough, which is, of course, the best capitalism can possibly promise.
9 With the benefit of hindsight, in June 2025, 56 per cent of people in the UK found it was wrong to leave the EU, while only 31 per cent still thought it was the right decision. (https://www.statista.com/statistics/987347/brexit-opinion-poll/?utm_source=chatgpt.com).
10 In practice, only the Greek-speaking south is integrated into the EU, due to the continuing division of the island into the Greek-speaking south and the Turkish-speaking north as a result of the conflict in 1974.
11 Notice that Norway's and Switzerland's per capita incomes are among the highest in the world. Their reluctance to join the EU can therefore partly be attributed to the fact that they would initially be net contributors to the EU budget, despite the still very limited degree of fiscal transfers from rich to poor within the EU. While this would be an apparently rational (in other words: self-centred) economic motive, it nevertheless disregards the potential benefits from the dynamics triggered by full integration into the world's largest single market. Other aspects are crucial, too: fear of being dominated by Brussels (or Berlin) and the fact that the notoriously protective European Common Agricultural Policy (CAP) is still comparatively *less* protective than Norway's and Switzerland's, which means that once in the EU, their agricultural sectors would come under pressure to shrink.
12 Turkey's membership is so far resisted by Germany and France, partly for fear of unlimited migration from Turkey, partly for 'cultural' reasons, as Turkey, although a secular state for almost a century, would add 75 million predominantly Muslim citizens to the EU. Kosovo is not even recognised as a sovereign state by all present EU members, let alone Serbia.

CHAPTER 23

The International Economy until 2024 and Beyond

Michael Graff

A SUMMARY: 1820–2024

The evolution of the international economy during the period 1820 to 2024 has been largely a response to the changes that have occurred in the political, economic and technological environment within which economic relations between countries are conducted. The record demonstrates a slow but prevailing movement among the regions of the world economy towards greater integration. International trade increased dramatically in the second half of the nineteenth century, outstripping the growth of world output. Particularly significant was the movement towards free trade up to the 1870s, even though it faltered by the 1880s and was kept alive only by the UK and a few Continental countries, as well as the advances in steam transport technology, which rapidly increased the flows of people and commodities across continents and from one continent to another by sea. This expansion of the international economy provided the mechanism for widespread economic growth in Western Europe and its 'offshoots' abroad.

Apart from a vast transfer of population, mainly from Europe to the continents of North and South America, capital funds were made available for economic development in the countries receiving these large inflows of migrants. The evolution of the foreign exchange market throughout the century and the widespread adoption of the gold standard after the 1860s facilitated the international transfers of funds and commodities. Related to this, the growth of world trade was also promoted by the slow spread of a multilateral trade network.

Europe exploited the vast land-intensive resources of the 'new' lands to help feed its growing population and to supply its growing manufacturing industries with many of the required raw materials. Notably, it was the combination of 'war capitalism' in the cotton plantations — slave labour — and 'industrial capitalism' in the 'coke towns' of the emerging industrial centres — formally free wage labour — that helped the cotton industry to grow when local resources became insufficient. As a result, for the industrialising regions, the nineteenth century brought widespread growth of per capita income on a scale never before experienced.

DOI: 10.4324/9781003382171-28

A unique feature of the pre-1914 international economy is that it was dominated by one country, the UK. The first country to industrialise, to adopt the gold standard, and to endorse free trade as its commercial policy, it set the pace for the growth of the world economy by providing the markets, capital and labour needed for the economic development of a large part of the world. After 1870, France, Germany, and, to a lesser extent, the US, Japan and Russia, began to play a more important role in promoting the expansion of the international economy and shaping its character. Even so, Britain's continued pre-eminence in world financial affairs and her adherence to free trade, in a period when there was a general return to protectionism, gave her undisputed leadership in international economic affairs. It is perhaps for this reason that international agreements on financial and other matters were largely unnecessary before 1914. In so far as any guiding influences were exerted on the growth and functioning of the international economy in the nineteenth century, these originated chiefly in Britain, whose importance for world trade and finance was paramount.

Despite the long-run tendency towards international economic integration, the movement also contained the seeds of its destruction in the two decades following the First World War. Such integration depended to a large extent upon a positive British current account, which became much more unfavourable after 1900, ensuring an inevitable collapse of the multilateral trade and payments network, which had already become evident in world trade from the 1870s. In addition to this, the retreat from free trade by several important trading nations, including Germany, the US, France and Russia placed additional strain on world trading patterns and trade by comparative advantage.

The First World War altered the international economy dramatically. First of all, it caused severe disruptions to world trade. In its aftermath, the decline in Britain's international economic position, the emergence of the US as the world's leading industrial and financial power, the economic difficulties experienced by Europe in general and Germany in particular, and the establishment of the Soviet Union on the ruins of the Tsarist Empire made a simple return to the pre-war international economic system impossible. The attempt to restore the gold standard in the 1920s was a complete failure and, in the face of mounting economic difficulties, aggravated later by a worldwide depression and growing political insecurity, countries, or groups of countries, turned in on themselves in order to deal with their economic problems. Moreover, as governments were called upon to deal with these crises by playing a more active role in national economic affairs, international considerations were increasingly subordinated to domestic policies aimed at maintaining employment and output levels. With the collapse of the traditional framework of international economic institutions and the emergence of a more nationalistic approach to economic affairs, there was little hope of intergovernmental cooperation in the search for a multilateral solution to world economic problems and, while the demands of trade finally brought some international agreement on stabilising exchange rates, attempts to deal with trade and financial problems in the 1930s either took the form of bilateral agreements or were made within a framework of discriminatory regional blocs.

The success in obtaining international agreement on a wide variety of economic matters from the mid-1940s onwards contrasted sharply with the more nationalistic outlook prevalent during the interwar years and the much more limited forms of international agreement characteristic of the period before 1914. But this did not come about because countries were less actively concerned in the 1940s with domestic levels of employment and rates of economic growth than they were in previous decades — rather the reverse. It was because governments would not allow domestic economies to be threatened by outside events that it became necessary to create, as an act of deliberate policy, an international economic system within which it was possible for individual countries to exercise economic sovereignty without endangering the welfare of other countries. Moreover, the fact that the attainment of full employment and high growth rates might be helped by the existence of a smoothly functioning world economy also contributed to making countries more willing to cooperate in the setting up of international economic institutions designed to eliminate the financial weaknesses and widespread impediments to world trade and commerce that had brought about the collapse of the international economy in the 1930s. In a sense, then, the emergence of a managed international economy after 1945 was largely the result of the spread of the managed economy at the national level characteristic of the period after 1920.

However, it was not until the 1950s that the trend towards greater globalisation was resumed, largely because of the initiation of a programme of freeing up world trade under the auspices of the GATT and a stable monetary environment created by the establishment of the International Monetary Fund.

Partly as a result of the activities of these supra-national economic institutions set up by collective action or as a by-product of the efforts of the United Nations, and due to internal economic policies based on a broad consensus on progressive taxation, redistribution and social safety networks to avoid poverty for those who, for whatever reasons, happened to be unsuccessful in earning a decent income in the markets, the era from 1950 to 1973 now appears as the 'golden age' for the advanced industrialised countries of the world. Income inequality within these countries, as well as between them, exhibited a tendency to diminish, as countries were 'catching up' with the US, and, internally, the working classes were granted comparatively generous shares in the general increases in GDP, not least to make them less attracted to the alternative — the Soviet system of 'really existing socialism'. Exchange rates were pegged, capital mobility restricted, financial markets closely supervised, and, unlike in the decades to follow, fortunes were made in industrial activity rather than in the financial sector.

Apart from this, the reconstruction efforts following the war played a part initially, while the acceleration in technological knowledge on a broad front was substantially responsible, alone and in combination with other forces, for much of the growth. In fact, one of the major growth-generating features of the post-Second World War era up to the present day has been technological advance on a rapid and intensive scale. Never before have so many important discoveries been made on an annual basis.

During the 1950s and 1960s, the main players were the 'First World' industrialised countries of Western Europe, Canada, the US, Japan, and Australasia. The 'Second World' centrally planned economies (CPEs) were also growing rapidly during these years, so rapidly initially that continuous growth at this rate would have made them surpass the West well before the end of the millennium.

Within the 'Third World', some developing countries also benefited from the growing globalisation, but they all still had a long way to go to achieve comparable standards of living to the leaders. In some cases, foreign aid from the rich countries provided a stimulus to those economies capable of adopting self-sustained growth.[1] Yet, as development assistance was only partly altruistic and to a large degree driven by geopolitical considerations within the Cold War rivalry between the 'First World' and the 'Second World', international aid was not always given to those most in need or most capable of transforming it into pro-poor growth and poverty alleviation. Ruthless dictatorships could count on Western aid as long as they were anti-communist; and reactionary or racist guerrilla formations, as well as the states they could capture, would find support from the Soviet bloc as long as they declared themselves 'freedom fighters' against American, Western or 'Zionist' hegemony.

As in the pre-First World War era, the international economic system of the 1950s and 1960s also contained the seeds of its own downfall. Both the GATT and the IMF operated clearly according to the requirements of the European Economic Community (EEC) and North America. The IMF's exchange rate mechanism was the first to feel the strain in the early 1970s, when the adjustable peg system was abandoned, giving way to currency floating. At the same time, the reductions in tariffs under the guidance of the GATT gave way in the 1970s to systems of quantitative import controls, which were de facto more restrictive than tariffs. At the same time, the establishment and the growth of customs unions and free trade areas also involved some trade discrimination for non-participants, especially in agriculture.

A trans-national economic boom in the early 1970s led to ever-rising inflation rates, which were exacerbated in 1973 and 1974 by unprecedented increases in oil prices. In 1974 the world economy faltered, never again in the twentieth century to return to the halcyon days of the 1950–73 years of low inflation and low unemployment. This marked the end of the international growth phase and the emergence of a difficult period.

After 1974, restrained economic growth occurred in the industrialised countries, generally with high inflation and intractably high unemployment. Moreover, while severe financial crises had formerly usually been confined to the periphery of the world economy, the break-up of the Soviet bloc and the establishment of capitalist market economies in this part of the world not only brought the promise — largely unfulfilled to this day — of increasing prosperity for all, but also the drawbacks of capitalism: financial and banking crises as well as inflation wiping out savings and, worst of all, unemployment due to developments in markets beyond the control of those affected. Unexpectedly for most, the new millennium ridiculed the notions of the 'end of history' and the 'Great Moderation' and brought financial crashes, crises and deep recessions, resulting in intolerable levels of unemployment and severe deterioration in government finances right back to the core of the capitalist world economy.

Meanwhile, the world witnessed the appearance and growth of several newly industrialising countries (NICs) in Asia and elsewhere, including Korea, Hong Kong, Taiwan and Singapore (the 'four tigers'), Brazil, Argentina, Mexico, Israel, Spain, Ireland, Greece and Portugal, to name but a few. Export-oriented growth strategies produced high rates of growth in most of these countries, but especially in the four tigers. By the early 1980s, they had emerged as the coming industrial countries.

In addition, within the already industrialised world, another phase of fundamental change was developing, which Jean Fourastié (1961) aptly called 'La Grande Métamorphose du XXe siècle': During the second half of the twentieth century, employment in, and the output of, manufacturing industry peaked and began a slow relative decline as the tertiary (services) sector rose to prominence. The change in employment began in the late 1960s and, especially, during the 1970s, while the net value-added in manufacturing as a proportion of total output began to peak in the early 1980s, followed by a slow but continuous decline during the 1990s, which continues in the new millennium. The advanced countries are thus gradually de-industrialising.

In the 1980s, the four tigers of East Asia, as well as Israel, were also approaching their zenith as predominantly manufacturing countries and, although manufactured exports still dominated their trading patterns in the 1990s, the services sector became increasingly important in these economies. Thus, in sharp contrast to the experience of the industrially advanced nations of Western Europe, North America and Japan, these newly emerging countries have accomplished in a decade or two a development it took the early developers much longer to achieve. Given these structural changes, it has now become more adequate to classify the leading economies as 'advanced' or 'rich' instead of 'industrialized'. The world economy has thus changed its character significantly during the years since 1975 and is continuing to do so, producing new trade and commercial patterns and new commercially powerful nations.

The pace of globalisation in the world economy — particularly trade, but even more so capital flows — quickened considerably after the mid-1980s, with world trade rising almost twice as fast as world output, following the rapid liberalisation of financial markets in many countries and the acceleration of capital flows to many NICs. This trend resulted in the speedy movement of some Asian countries into a higher income group, while others, such as Malaysia, Thailand and China, began to follow the Asian export-oriented path to their industrialisation. Lately, the traditional North-South pattern of trade has quickly eroded. The newly industrialising economies (NIEs) record persistent trade surpluses with the rich economies, and correspondingly, despite considerable direct investment flowing from richer to poorer economies, there are substantial net capital flows from the poorer to the rich countries. Along with this, South-South trade and capital flows are deepening, and the emergence of large-scale Chinese direct investment in poor but resource-rich Asian and African economies bears witness to the fact that the twentieth-century paradigm of the world economy has come to an end.

We thus have lately been witnessing a profound shift in the locations of economic dynamism and dominance from the traditional industrialised countries of Europe and its former colonies in North America and Oceania as well as Japan to the emerging economies of Latin America and particularly Asia, where China and India are rapidly emerging as economic giants of the twenty-first century. Lately, apart from exports, domestic demand in these countries is increasingly contributing to economic growth. Indeed, the gradual but steady transformation of impoverished landless people and slum dwellers into wage earners and consumers that is taking place in some of the most populous countries in the world — China, India and Brazil — implies that the world's purchasing power and thus demand will increasingly originate from Asia and South America.

MILESTONES, 1989–2024

The collapse of the German Democratic Republic (GDR) in 1989 and the subsequent dissolution of the Soviet Union in 1991 marked the symbolic conclusion of what Eric Hobsbawm described as the 'short twentieth century'. The disintegration of socialist regimes was hailed as a triumph of liberal democracy and capitalism, seemingly validating Francis Fukuyama's thesis of the 'end of history'. Yet, as the following decades revealed, the transition to a capitalist order brought both profound economic dislocation and renewed global instability.

The immediate aftermath of the collapse of centrally planned economies (CPEs) in Eastern and Central Europe was characterised by hardship. Rapid privatisations enriched a narrow elite while much of the population endured unemployment, poverty and the dismantling of social safety nets. The anticipated 'peace dividend' also failed to materialise. Instead, nationalist conflicts tore through the post-socialist landscape. While Czechoslovakia separated peacefully, Yugoslavia's fragmentation produced horrific wars marked by 'ethnic cleansing' and mass casualties. More recently, Russia's 2022 invasion of Ukraine has reignited large-scale interstate warfare in Europe, underscoring the persistence of aggressive nationalism in the post-Soviet era.

Simultaneously, global challenges have intensified. Geopolitical rivalries have fuelled rearmament, diverting resources away from the urgent threat of climate change, which continues unchecked. Despite notable successes in poverty reduction — particularly in China — global inequality persists. Migrants fleeing deprivation face perilous journeys, with annual fatalities far exceeding those of the Berlin Wall era. Even successful migrants often encounter exploitation and precarity in host societies, exposing the limits of globalisation's promises.

The economic dimension of globalisation likewise proved unstable. The late 1990s and early 2000s witnessed a sequence of crises in Asia, Russia and Argentina, each demonstrating the vulnerability of open economies to volatile capital flows. While these were initially dismissed as peripheral failures, subsequent crises struck at the heart of advanced capitalist economies. The dot.com crash of 2001 was followed by the far more devastating 2007–8 global financial crisis, rooted in the collapse of the US housing market. Here, excessive credit expansion, financial deregulation and speculative asset bubbles culminated in systemic collapse, which rapidly spread across the globalised financial markets.

The international economy in the first quarter of the new millennium also experienced consequences of Donald Trump's economic policies during his first term (2017–20), which comprised deregulation, tax cuts and protectionist measures. His first presidency was more restrained and less radical than what would follow in 2025, but it paved the way. The cornerstones of the *domestic* economic agenda was the Tax Cuts and Jobs Act of 2017, which massively reduced corporate and individual income taxes. It increased the federal budget deficit substantially. The tax cuts for individuals were set to expire by 2025 (but since July 2025, we know that this is not going to happen). Trump's *international* economic policy introduced a distinctly protectionist approach, leading to the imposition of tariffs on a range of foreign goods, particularly from China. The US withdrew from the Trans-Pacific Partnership and renegotiated the North American Free Trade Agreement (NAFTA), replacing it with the US-Mexico-Canada Agreement (USMCA).[2] Trump cancelled the US commitment to the Paris Agreement on climate change and rolled back numerous environmental regulations, turning the US into a net exporter of oil and natural gas.

'Brexit', the UK's exit from the EU in 2020, marked the next deliberate political retreat from economic integration in the new millennium. Following the UK's 2016 referendum and formal withdrawal in 2020, the end of participation in the EU single market introduced new non-tariff barriers, disrupted trade flows and reduced labour mobility. Structural adjustments, particularly in agriculture, healthcare and logistics, revealed significant economic costs for the UK, which, given its smaller scale relative to the EU, bore disproportionate losses.

The 2020 outbreak of COVID-19 added another layer of disruption. Unlike traditional recessions, the pandemic-induced simultaneous supply and demand shocks, halting production and exposing vulnerabilities in global supply chains. Although recovery followed the rapid deployment of vaccines and the easing of restrictions, the crisis prompted a reconsideration of globalisation. Reliance on extended, efficiency-driven supply chains appeared increasingly untenable, particularly as the Russia–Ukraine war further disrupted food and energy flows.

The Russia–Ukraine war since 2022 introduced still more sources of global instability. Beyond the human toll, it disrupted food and energy markets, triggered sanctions and trade fragmentation. Another effect was that resources were redirected toward military expenditure, and the armaments industry experienced an immediate surge in share prices. Ukraine's military spending reached an estimated 30 per cent of GDP in 2024, and Russia's over 6 per cent, while NATO in 2025 set a target of 5 per cent of GDP for its members. Since 2022, the armaments industry's share prices have shown massive growth, particularly for leading companies. From the end of 2021 — just before the Russia–Ukraine war — to the end of 2024, in the US, Northrop Grumman saw its stock price rise by 21 per cent. Similarly, over the same period, Lockheed Martin experienced a gain of 41 per cent. In the UK, BAE Systems saw its stock grow by 102 per cent. The German armaments company Rheinmetall even recorded an increase of 645 per cent. From a macroeconomic perspective, however, this is nothing to celebrate. The reallocation of productive capacity toward armaments — which in the best case will be scrapped some day in the future — has stimulated inflationary pressures, and it will crowd out long-term investment in productivity-promoting areas such as education and infrastructure as well as in social and environmental priorities. Taken together, the war has raised global inflation, redirected Russian exports toward non-Western economies and increased food and energy insecurity for many poor countries. The policy responses by the Western camp have further exacerbated these disruptions. The long-run productivity and income losses and their global distribution are difficult to quantify, but as the conflict has turned into a war of attrition and is now in its fourth year, with rising geopolitical tensions and, consequently, skyrocketing military and armaments expenses, the negative impacts on welfare can be assumed to be considerable.

Last but not least, perhaps the most unconventional economic phenomenon of the first quarter of the new millennium — negative interest rates — deserves to be mentioned here. Long considered theoretically implausible, negative policy rates were first implemented by Denmark in 2012, followed by the European Central Bank, the Swiss National Bank, the Swedish Riksbank and the Bank of Japan. At their lowest, rates reached −0.75 per cent in Denmark, Sweden and Switzerland. The objectives varied: preventing deflationary expectations, stimulating lending and spending, and stabilising exchange rates. Yet the efficacy of these measures remains contested. Supporters emphasise their role in countering stagnation after the Great Recession, while critics argue they damaged savers, distorted asset allocation and indirectly subsidised government borrowing. By 2024, amid inflationary pressures triggered by the post-COVID-19 recovery and the war in Ukraine, the era of negative rates ended, giving way to more hawkish monetary policy.

In sum, the promise of a stable, liberal world order following the collapse of the Soviet bloc has proven illusory. The early optimism of the 1990s has given way to an era of geopolitical conflict, recurring financial instability, deepening inequality and mounting ecological peril. Far from the 'end of history', the decades since 1989 have underscored the fragility and contradictions of global capitalism. Since the Great Recession, globalisation has slowed markedly, with trade growth often falling behind GDP growth. Embargoes, sanctions and moves toward autarky have raised the possibility that the long post-Second World War era of deepening globalisation may be reversing. The interplay of unconventional monetary policy, pandemic-induced disruption, political disintegration, geopolitical conflict and climate change has set the stage for a more uncertain and contested international economic order. This evolution unfolded against the backdrop of eroding multilateral cooperation. WTO negotiations stalled after the failed Doha Round, and its dispute settlement system has been paralysed since 2019. Regional and bilateral agreements have proliferated, while geopolitical rivalry increasingly shapes trade. At the same time, groupings such as the G20 and BRICS+ gained prominence, reflecting the redistribution of economic weight toward emerging economies.

2025

The following will summarise what is known so far about the world economy in 2025, focusing in particular on the likely consequences of the measures imposed by US President Trump. On the first day of his second term, he signed a number of executive orders, including his *second* withdrawal from the Paris Agreement on climate change. (The US had first joined in 2016, withdrew in 2020 under Trump and had rejoined again in 2021 under President Biden.)

Regarding his *domestic* economic policy, the 'One Big Beautiful Bill Act' stands out. He ceremoniously signed it on 4 July (!) 2025. It permanently extends the individual tax rate cuts that he had introduced in 2017, and which would have expired at the end of 2025. Fossil fuels are encouraged; renewable energies are discouraged. Spending on social transfers is reduced, while expenditure on military and 'border enforcement' is significantly increased. It will result in massive redistribution from the bottom to the top, and it is estimated that it will increase the annual budget deficit up by around 1 percentage point from currently 6.1 per cent of GDP, which is already huge in international comparison.

Persistent government budget deficits, such as that of the US, can create domestic problems. Specifically, if the interest rate on government debt exceeds the growth rate of the tax base, approximated by GDP, an increasing share of the budget is required to service the debt. In the 2024 financial year, interest costs on outstanding US government debt already exceeded military expenditure. Importantly, a substantial and persistent budget deficit also affects the current account. A balanced current account implies that domestic savings equal domestic investment. A surplus requires national savings to exceed investment, while a deficit indicates the reverse. The latter applies to the US. Domestic absorption of goods and services exceeds domestic production, and the gap is met through net imports.

The resulting large US current account deficit is a looming danger to the world economy. It cannot persist indefinitely, but it remains unclear how long it will continue and whether its reversal will be smooth or painful for both the US and the global economy. The roots of the current situation lie in the late twentieth century. In the 1990s, financial investments in the US were perceived as attractive due to the booming economy and the fact that they were denominated in the world's undisputed reserve currency, which reduced the associated risk premium. As its 'neoliberal growth model' relied on consumption financed by credit, backed by rising prices of largely unproductive assets, and government spending persistently in excess of tax revenue, domestic absorption exceeded output. The growing US current account deficit was financed by corresponding surpluses in Asia — particularly China and Japan — as well as Germany, the oil-exporting states, and several smaller economies. The drawback was the deindustrialisation of the American 'rust belt'. The disruptions and despair that this created helped Donald Trump to be voted into the Oval Office in 2016 and 2024. During the first months of his second presidency in 2025, it became obvious that he was determined to reduce the US merchandise trade deficits vis-à-vis the rest of the world.

To achieve a more balanced trade account — an economic priority of the Trump administration — national savings must align with national investment. Yet, since national savings comprise private and government savings, the record budget deficits of the second Trump presidency are negative government saving, the increasing fiscal deficits will make it difficult to reduce the trade deficit. This notwithstanding, throughout 2025, the US implemented a series of sweeping trade policy measures that substantially increased tariffs on a wide range of imports and restructured the framework governing international trade relations.

On 1 February 2025, the US's 'National Freedom Day', in the White House's Rose Garden, Donald Trump announced a significant shift in US trade policy, focused on imposing tariffs on imports to protect the domestic manufacturing industry, with the ultimate aim of reversing the deindustrialisation of the previous decades and restoring manufacturing employment. At the same time, the new tariffs were declared to be 'reciprocal', with rates determined individually to reduce the US merchandise trade deficits with the respective countries. Trump presented the policy as essential for his 'America First' strategy, despite the risks of international retaliation and higher consumer costs. In particular, on 1 February 2025, executive orders imposed 25 per cent additional tariffs on imports from Canada and Mexico. On the same date, a 10 per cent additional tariff was levied on imports from China, supplementing the extensive duties already in place on many product categories.

Subsequent measures expanded the scope of tariff policy. On 24 March, the US announced tariffs of 25 per cent on goods from countries importing Venezuelan oil, justified by national security. On 2 April, a national emergency was declared on the basis of the US's trade deficits. This measure imposed a baseline 10 per cent tariff on all imports, alongside country-specific 'reciprocal' rates determined case by case, which in some instances reached approximately 50 per cent. The same order also eliminated the exemption for low-value parcels from China.

On 30 May, tariffs on steel and aluminium were doubled to 50 per cent for all trading partners except the UK.

On 30 and 31 July, further executive orders formally removed the $800-parcels exemption for all countries, meaning all imports were henceforth subject to applicable customs duties and full clearance procedures. A detailed country-specific 'reciprocal tariff' list was published, with implementation taking place through August 2025. During this period, India faced additional surcharges — some as high as 25 per cent, while similar tariffs were applied to Brazil, South Korea, Japan, the European Union, Taiwan and Switzerland, among others.

Rates varied significantly by country and product category, with Brazil facing some of the steepest ad valorem duties (up to 40–50 per cent).

A number of observations regarding Donald Trump's latest decisions stand out. First, the process appears somewhat erratic. Tariffs are imposed, then postponed, increased or reduced, which makes it hard to anticipate what will come next. Second, Trump's declared intentions are to reduce or eliminate the trade deficit, to attract foreign direct investment, to increase government revenue, to keep inflation low and to preserve the role of the dollar as the world's trade and reserve currency, but the measures introduced to achieve these goals so far, stand in conflict. Third, some of the tariffs are probably not meant to stay, as Donald Trump's ultimate goal appears to be to make 'deals', where trading partners can negotiate reduced tariffs in exchange for economic or political measures or announcements that he perceives as favourable to US interests. To get a better understanding of the underlying reasoning, it is useful to look at two recent economic policy papers, which appear to constitute the basis of his plans.

According to Michael Pettis (2024), persistent trade imbalances imply that trade is not 'free and equitable'. This terminology clearly deviates from that of conventional economics, where trade is understood as 'free' as long as there are no protectionist obstacles, and 'equitability' is not an issue. However, it is the key to understanding Trump's reference to his tariffs as 'reciprocal'. Conventional economics would label tariffs as such only when they are imposed on a country to retaliate an equivalent tariff, which is obviously not the case for most of Donald Trump's recent tariffs. But according to Pettis, all surplus countries directly or indirectly subsidise their exporting manufacturing industries by policies such as currency undervaluation, wage repression, repressed interest rates, export subsidies and low domestic consumption. The result of such 'beggar-thy-neighbour' policies is that trade patterns are not shaped by comparative advantage, in which economies maximise the value of their exports to obtain the desired imports. Instead, they strive for competitive advantage, which maximises output of the export sector as an end in itself. Deficit countries — in particular the US — have to absorb the effects of global excess savings and face the consequences: loss of manufacturing share, rising debt, constrained consumption and, ultimately, lower growth. Presently, the international economy generates a 'perverse' flow of capital from poorer to richer economies. Powerful deficit countries can and should force surplus countries to alter their distortive policies to restore 'free' trade, which means trade according to comparative advantage, where countries do not operate under persistent trade surpluses or deficits. So far, Trump's tariffs are a precise implementation of Pettis' argumentation.

Another of Donald Trump's obvious intellectual influences is Stephen Miran. Miran (2004) presents a toolbox of policy options for President Trump's second term to reshape the position of the US in the international economy. His message has certainly been received by the addressee, as in mid-2025, Donald Trump nominated him to join the Federal Reserve Board of Governors, filling a vacancy until January 2026. It is thus appropriate to have a closer look at his recommendations, as they have the potential to exert significant effects on the international economy in the years to come. Miran's central proposal is to adopt higher and 'targeted' tariffs on imports, especially from countries with which the US records trade deficits. He argues that — contrary to conventional wisdom — such tariffs would not be borne by US consumers via inflation, which might undermine domestic support for such measures. Instead, due to devaluations of the currencies of the countries facing new or increasing

US tariff rates, a 'currency offset' would shift the burden to foreign exporters. The experience of 2025 suggests that President Trump has so far been acting accordingly, imposing targeted 'reciprocal' tariffs on the rest of the world.

Furthermore, Miran recommends that Trump's trade policy should be subordinated to geopolitical considerations, aiming at maintaining US hegemony. Access to the US market should be 'a privilege that must be earned'. Apart from a country's trade balance with the US, the tariffs on its exports to the US should thus be set based on geopolitical considerations, discriminating between 'friend, foe and neutral trading partner', where the best friends are allies who devote large shares of their resources to the military. The experience of 2025 suggests that President Trump has so far also been acting accordingly, making deals with NATO countries, granting them moderate tariffs in exchange for promises of massive increases in their military spending. The punitive 25 per cent tariff on top of the other ('reciprocal') tariffs on imports from countries buying oil from Venezuela (April 2025), and on India of 25 per cent on top of the earlier tariffs because India is continuing to import Russian oil (August 2025), fall into this category. Somewhat more arbitrary is the punitive tariff imposed on Brazil as a response to the court proceedings against former President Jair Bolsonaro, who shares Trump's political convictions. This is arguably less geopolitics than political intervention in Brazil's internal affairs due to Donald Trump's personal preferences.

Miran also argues that the US dollar is persistently overvalued due to global demand for dollar reserve assets, which harms US exporters, and suggests interventions to correct this. In particular, he recommends a 'Mar-a-Lago Accord' to be implemented during President Trump's second term to devalue the dollar. If successful, this would improve the US' trade balance, but at the same time undermine the US dollar's role as the world reserve currency. As this would weaken US hegemony, Miran recommends resorting to political pressure and to impose punitive tariffs on countries abandoning the dollar in their trade with the rest of the world. However, when details — such as persuading (or forcing) holders of US Treasury Bills to agree to extend the terms or reduce the interest rates on their bonds — became known, financial markets reacted nervously. The imminent danger of sharp rises in interest rates has apparently made the Trump administration for the time being suspend the Mar-a-Lago Accord plan.

Remarkably, on the one hand, the proposals by Pettis and Miran indeed address one of the main problems of the international economy. In the long run, there should be no countries with persistent trade imbalances. The resulting net transfers of goods and services and, along with it, credit, from one part of the world to another jeopardises comparative advantage, leads to debts that will inevitably have to be written off unless the surplus countries start to import more than they export and become deficit countries. On the other hand, there are fundamental contradictions in the proposals and in the measures so far put in place. First, the tariffs are intended to reduce the US trade deficit and at the same time massively to generate revenue for the US government, but achieving one of these goals means failing in the other. To the degree that the main objective — reducing imports to restore balanced trade — is achieved, government revenue is impaired. To generate maximum revenue, the tariffs would have to leave the volume of imports unaffected. Second, tariffs are expected by Miran to strengthen the US dollar, with the result that the dollar prices for US imports will not rise as they would without such 'currency offset'. On the other hand, the US dollar is found to be overvalued, and strong interventionist measures are recommended to depreciate the dollar. Obviously, success with respect to one of the policy recommendations will undermine the outcome of the other. Third, Donald Trump's 'deals' so far not only include promises to import more oil and gas from the US, which indeed would reduce the US trade deficit, but also massive foreign direct investment (FDI) in the US economy. If this amounts to 'green field' investments, jobs will be created locally. Also, foreign firms can evade the new tariffs by relocating headquarters or setting up branch factories in the US, which is another type of FDI that we now start to observe. Crucially, however, all FDI is capital import for the receiving country so that, other things equal, absorption, and along with it imports rise, reducing net exports.

Notwithstanding the former considerations, as mentioned above, the tariffs imposed by US President Trump are hard to understand on a purely economic basis. In line with Miran's recommendation, they are also applied as a means of securing geopolitical support or, in some cases, to impose outright political submission.

The aggressive tariff policies of US President Trump in the first year of his second term have started to change the modus operandi of the world economy, distorting and reducing global trade, meaning that, for now, economic globalisation seems to have passed its peak. Given the latest experiences in 2025, the future of world trade now appears more uncertain than at any time since the Second World War. Remarkably, the only country that has so far resorted to retaliation is China, resulting in the loss of the US's most important export market for soybeans to Brazil. For the time being, the rest of the world is trying to make the best of the situation, consciously avoiding any action that could be perceived as provocative by the White House, and hoping to negotiate 'deals' to safeguard their exporting industries.

The worst outcome would be a global trade war, which will produce only losers, like in the 1930s. The best to hope for is probably a gradual reduction of the global trade imbalances, preserving the benefits of the international division of labour, and allowing enough time for both net-importer and net-exporter countries to manage the required structural adjustments without unnecessary hardship.

PROJECTIONS FOR THE WORLD ECONOMY, 2025 AND BEYOND

Most professional forecasters are reluctant to make forecasts for more than one or two years. The risk that the assumptions are contradicted by the facts increases progressively with the forecast's horizon, and all too frequently forecasters are confronted with their predictions of a few years ago that apparently do not match the facts at all.[3]

Nevertheless, governments, international organisations, trade unions, firms and many others depend on medium-range forecasts to decide on their strategies and policies. For the international economy, forecasts are available from such varied institutions as governments and government-sponsored research institutes, international banks and, last but not least, the two Bretton Woods organisations, the IMF and the World Bank. The IMF's *World Economic Outlook* data (July 2025) go as far as 2026, while the World Bank's *Global Economic Prospects* data (June 2026) include 2027 as well, so we will refer to the latter. The corresponding economic forecasts for the international economy up to 2027 are given in Table 23.1, going back to 2022, when the effects of the Russia–Ukraine war on the international economy began.

TABLE 23.1 The international economy, 2022–27

	2022	2023	2024	2025	2026	2027
World GDP growth rate	**3.3**	**2.8**	**2.8**	**2.3**	**2.4**	**2.6**
World (PPP weights)	**3.5**	**3.4**	**3.3**	**2.9**	**3.0**	**3.1**
High-income countries	2.9	1.7	1.9	1.3	1.5	1.7
Middle-income countries	3.9	4.8	4.4	4.1	4.0	4.0
Low-income countries	4.4	2.8	4.6	5.3	6.1	6.0
United States	2.5	2.9	2.8	1.4	1.6	1.9
Euro area	3.5	0.4	0.9	0.7	0.8	1.0
Japan	0.9	1.4	0.2	0.7	0.8	0.8
China	3.1	5.4	5.0	4.5	4.0	3.9
Russian Federation	−1.4	4.1	4.3	1.4	1.2	1.2
Latin America and the Caribbean	4.0	2.4	2.3	2.3	2.4	2.6
Middle East and North Africa	5.4	1.6	1.9	2.7	3.7	4.1
India	7.6	9.2	6.5	6.3	6.5	6.7
Sub-Saharan Africa	3.9	2.9	3.5	3.7	4.1	4.3
World trade volume	**5.9**	**0.8**	**3.4**	**1.8**	**2.4**	**2.7**
Energy price index	152.6	106.9	101.5	86.2	80.2	84.4
Oil price (US$ per barrel)	99.8	82.6	80.7	66.0	61.0	65.0
Non-energy price index	122.1	110.2	112.5	110.3	106.8	107.1

Source: World Bank (2025), Global Economic Prospects.

The World Bank's projections for key indicators of the international economy from 2022 to 2027 suggest that, following the disruptions caused by the Russia–Ukraine war and the lingering effects of the COVID-19 pandemic, global economic growth is expected to remain subdued throughout the period. World output recovers only gradually, with advanced economies experiencing modest expansion, while developing and emerging market economies show somewhat stronger, though uneven, growth. Inflation, which peaked in 2022, is projected to decline steadily as supply chain pressures ease and monetary policy remains restrictive. Global trade volumes increase at a slower pace than before the pandemic, reflecting weaker demand and heightened geopolitical tensions. Investment growth also remains moderate, constrained by higher interest rates and uncertainty surrounding trade policies. Energy prices, which peaked in 2022, will be steadily declining, but non-energy raw material prices remain elevated. Overall, the forecasts indicate a period of fragile and uneven recovery, characterised by persistent regional disparities.

A number of projections for the long-term outlook of the world economy are also available. The most extended forecast horizon can be found in the *OECD Global Long-Run Economic Scenarios 2025* update. They predict the 'business as usual' GDP growth rate to decline from 2.9 per cent in 2025 to about 2.0 per cent by 2040, and to 1.0 per cent by the end of the twenty-first century. The per capita growth projection shows a gradual decline from

2.0 per cent in 2025 to 1.0 per cent in 2050 and remaining at that level until 2100. In general, economic growth is expected to continue more slowly in the advanced economies compared to the poorer regions of the world, where faster growth is projected owing to higher growth rates of the labour force and industrial catching-up. The locations of high economic growth, and as a result, at some stage, also economic size, will thus continue to shift from the advanced regions of Europe, North America, Oceania and Japan to the emerging economies of Asia, Latin America and Africa. China and India are anticipated to become the economic giants of the twenty-first century.

CHALLENGES FOR THE TWENTY-FIRST CENTURY

The world economy has gone through the first quarter of the new millennium facing severe economic problems and has been far too negligent about concerns regarding the long-term future of the world economy and, ultimately, about the survival of the human species. The depletion of natural resources, pollution of the air, sea and land environments, and global warming due to the greenhouse effect must be addressed far more decisively to prevent the worst from happening. In addition, due to increasing economic and geopolitical rivalry between the military superpowers, the danger of a Third World War and nuclear apocalypse has never, since the end of the Cold War, been as serious as it is today. The situation appears increasingly similar to the years before the First World War, as countries are massively increasing their military spending, and attitudes in some of the states with the most powerful armed forces — many possessing nuclear arms — are becoming increasingly belligerent.

To start with a positive perspective, we can note that, according to the latest United Nations's *World Population Prospects* (2024), the world's population growth rate will continue its decline. From more than 2 per cent annually in the 1960s and 1970s, it has already fallen to currently less than 1 per cent. According to the UN's median variant, growth will come to an end in the 2080s. The world's population will then reach its maximum of 10.2 billion — adding 2 billion people to the present headcount — and then begin to shrink. The most important assumption behind this scenario is a drop in fertility to replacement level and below in all except very few high-fertility countries, and the most important driver is the expansion of women's education. The fact that the ongoing reduction of fertility will reduce the size of the upcoming cohorts of potential parents reduces the uncertainty otherwise characteristic of such long-run projections. The grim Malthusian 'positive checks' — famine, disease and war — which were once feared to prevent the world's population from exceeding the planet's capacity to sustain it, have now fortunately become extremely unlikely. The 'population bomb' has been disarmed.

The next look into the future also appears positive, at least at first sight. As we have shown above, world GDP is predicted to continue growing. With world population growth slowing down significantly and approaching a foreseeable end, average GDP per capita is set to increase. However, there are grounds for concern.

Some of these concerns relate to the negative externalities of economic activity. Humanity must operate within finite resources. While the price mechanism can stimulate innovations that economise on increasingly scarce inputs, either through more efficient use or the development of substitutes, such substitutes are also finite. Also, our planet's capacity to absorb greenhouse gasses without increasing global warming is limited. Despite successive climate conferences, international commitments remain inadequate to limit warming to 2°C. Structural contradictions persist: advanced economies outsource emissions through trade, while emerging economies resist binding constraints, citing historical responsibility and developmental needs. In this context, it is important to distinguish between production- and consumption-based CO_2 emissions measures. With the relocation of an increasing share of the world's 'dirty' manufacturing from the core to the periphery — from where it is exported to rich countries — the latter appear to contribute far less to environmental degradation and global warming than their true ecological footprint, when adjusted for population, consumption and lifestyle, would suggest.

Currently, the outlook for the world economy in relation to climate change is increasingly bleak. With substantial warming and rising sea levels, adaptation to the changing environment will require major transformations of agriculture, tourism and settlement patterns. History will tell whether the current failure to act decisively will prove to be the most spectacular and costly policy failure on a global scale. At some stage — perhaps sooner than anticipated — the world economy may need to evolve towards a sustainable 'steady state', in which conventionally measured GDP no longer grows exponentially (see Appendix 1 to this chapter).

A second concern is a negative externality of nuclear power, namely its inevitable legacy: the requirement to safely store its toxic waste for many thousands of years, for which, to this day, no convincing solution has been found, given that we cannot know how humans in the distant future — if there still are any — will behave towards our toxic legacy.

A third concern is that average GDP is not a reliable indicator of human development and welfare without considering its distribution within and between economies. It remains unclear how unevenly the economic gains of the future will be shared. While it is true that, as countries become richer, most introduce some redistribution to lower-income households to maintain inequality within tolerable limits, this does not hold for inequality between countries. Moreover, redistribution sufficient to ensure an economic basis for a good life for all requires either a broad consensus — including among the better-off — that reducing inequality is necessary to prevent social instability, or desirable as an end in itself, or sufficient political power in the hands of the lower classes to achieve redistribution against the will of the wealthy. Whether such conditions will persist in the future remains uncertain.

The focus on GDP growth and levels as policy goals also neglects the ultimate purpose of economic activity: human happiness and wellbeing. Although the relationship between GDP and wellbeing has historically been positive, it is non-linear. At higher income levels, the marginal damage to wellbeing associated with additional economic growth — through the opportunity cost of foregone non-market activity and the negative externalities discussed above — may eventually exceed the marginal benefit.[4]

The benefits of globalisation, such as increased division of labour and economies of scale, are accompanied by disruptive relocations that create severely affected losers — workers, industries and regions — alongside winners. In theory, the overall balance should be positive, enabling winners to compensate losers and thus achieve a Pareto improvement. In practice, this requires a strong state with the legitimacy to raise adequate tax revenue and redistribute it effectively. Markets and the state are therefore complementary in this process. However, since the rise of the free-market paradigm in the 1980s, which portrayed market intervention as detrimental to efficiency and growth, globalisation has deepened rapidly, while redistributive states have come under attack. Rodrik (2011) aptly termed this the 'paradox of globalisation'. In some economies, the marginal damage may already have exceeded the marginal benefit, suggesting that further expansion should give way to consolidation of its gains.

Remarkably, the lost era of globalisation of the late nineteenth century, which John Maynard Keynes (1920) nostalgically described after the First World War, exhibited characteristics largely absent today. The major trading economies were credibly committed to the gold standard,[5] effectively forming a currency union, albeit one that allowed limited realignments as countries could change their gold parity unilaterally. Moreover, the free movement of people was a reality for almost everyone who could afford it, without even the need for a passport. From an economic standpoint, the world today faces not excessive migration but too little.[6] High barriers to immigration in most OECD countries reflect not economic logic but strong anti-migrant sentiment in potential host nations. Fear of job competition, concerns about welfare burdens and cultural prejudice dominate the often hostile public discourse on migration and asylum, and governments risk electoral defeat if they fail to echo the prevailing mood.

Meanwhile, vast global wage disparities provide powerful incentives for migration. The large sums paid to circumvent legal and physical barriers — and the many lives lost in the process — clearly demonstrate the determination of migrants to reach more prosperous destinations. Yet, for now, the political will to accept migration and to mitigate its adverse effects, such as by compensating affected domestic groups from the broader tax base, appears almost entirely absent. This stands in stark contrast to the willingness to fund ever-tighter border controls and deportations, for which costs appear to be of no concern.

Financial stability remains a major concern. Reinhart and Rogoff (2009) have identified patterns that cast doubt on our ability to prevent or mitigate future financial crises. The 'this time is different' syndrome illustrates how signs of inflating bubbles are repeatedly ignored by successive generations of analysts, speculators and regulators. Historically, a significant proportion of countries have defaulted on debt, and periods of calm are inevitably followed by waves of crises. International crises tend to be contagious, spreading from financial centres worldwide.

The free movement of capital, central to globalisation since the 1980s, is increasingly contested. Economic theory holds that unrestricted capital flows maximise global allocational efficiency. Since the end of Bretton Woods and the integration of former Soviet bloc countries, barriers to capital mobility have largely vanished. Yet experience demonstrates that inflows can become speculative, inflating asset bubbles. With floating currencies, inflows may cause rapid appreciations, damaging export industries. When tides turn, domestic asset markets falter, debt becomes unserviceable, contagion spreads and currencies devalue or pegs collapse. The effectiveness of capital controls in stabilising economies remains an open question

The IMF post-2007 consensus (Ostry et al., 2010) recognises capital controls as a legitimate tool. Restrictions are justified when an economy is near potential and holds ample foreign reserves, the currency is not undervalued and inflows are transitory. This applies to both portfolio and FDI inflows, as some FDI may disguise intragroup debt, making it as risky as debt (Ostry et al., 2010, p. 5). The IMF also notes that controls have helped avoid severe growth disruptions (Ostry et al., 2010, p. 13), marking a departure from decades of orthodox policy.

Offshore banking and currency trading have expanded steadily over five decades. Krugman et al. (2011, p. 622) observe that global trade alone cannot explain this growth. Currently, about 50 per cent of world trade is routed through tax havens — jurisdictions offering political stability, secrecy and minimal taxation to circumvent other countries' regulations (Shaxson, 2011, p. 8). Tax havens effectively prey on other nations' tax bases, an extreme form of beggar-thy-neighbour policy. Their financial sectors are disproportionately large and influential, promoting a discourse of privacy, efficiency and tax avoidance, while silencing critics. The opacity of tax havens undermines supervision and early warning systems, increasing the probability and severity of crises. Some progress has been made with the OECD global minimum tax, agreed by 136 countries and implemented in 2024, setting a 15 per cent minimum on multinational profits. While modest compared to the original 25 per cent proposal and with some tax havens, such as Delaware, noncompliant, it may mark the beginning of the end for aggressive tax competition.

Capitalism also fails to achieve even the efficiency predicted by standard theory. Financial markets repeatedly defy rationality, as evidenced by the 2007 crisis. Crises depress output below potential, and lost cumulative output is irrecoverable. Hysteresis further reduces efficiency: unemployed labour may never return, skills become obsolete and human capital is damaged, contributing to the 'silent reserve'. Official statistics fail to capture the social and economic costs of this displacement. Recessions also slow technical progress and productivity growth, permanently lowering achievable output.

Global deprivation remains stark. Lack of food and safe water causes annual deaths exceeding 10 million. Extreme hunger — daily intake 300 calories below requirement — affects over 300 million people in Africa, the Caribbean and Asia, nearly four per cent of the world population. In a world capable of supporting 1.5 times its current population, preventable starvation is a systemic failure of the global economy, amounting to a crime against humanity (Ziegler, 2002). Ensuring that modern technology and globalisation benefit poorer countries remains one of the century's greatest challenges.

Repeated crises have fostered scepticism towards laissez-faire policies. Many economists advocate a return to Keynesian principles and the 'golden age' of capitalism (1950–73), characterised by high employment, rising real wages, social redistribution and robust welfare systems.[7] Yet global competition and offshore finance have led to tax reductions, undermining national sovereignty and limiting governments' capacity to redistribute, necessitating a revival of social-democratic ideals.

Attempts to correct free-market excesses of the 1990s and 2000s have largely failed. Socialist and communist movements have disappeared, and revolutionary alternatives have been discredited. The final years of the Soviet Union, while better than for much of the global population, fell behind advanced capitalist economies, leaving a difficult legacy for those seeking alternatives to capitalism.[8] Without a vision for an economy guided by rational coordination rather than profit — increasingly synonymous with greed — for the foreseeable future, restraint of capitalism's destructive forces, which have dominated since the 1980s, may be the best achievable outcome.

Financialisation, encompassing speculative housing markets and capital-based pension schemes, exposes ordinary people to systemic risks and amplifies inequality. Powerful financial lobbies resist reform, as failures are often bailed out by taxpayers. In March 2023, Credit

Suisse required over 200 billion francs ($250 billion) in government guarantees to prevent insolvency and avert a global banking crisis.

Global economic integration has not delivered on promises of efficiency and prosperity for all. Instead, inequality within and between countries has widened, and political discontent has shifted to nationalist chauvinism, with migrants and foreigners serving as scapegoats.

Conflicts within and between states have persisted, particularly in the Middle East, Africa, Asia and recently Eastern Europe. Interventions, mostly by the US and Russia, continue, though direct confrontations between great powers have been avoided. Rising geopolitical tensions, the Russia–Ukraine war and fears of a decline in US hegemony amid China's rise increase the risk of direct conflict between nuclear-armed superpowers. Economic rivalry between the US and China, including the ongoing trade war that began in 2018, may escalate to violence — a scenario referred to as the 'Thucydides Trap': When an emerging rival threatens a dominant hegemon — like Sparta challenging Athens in ancient Greece — war may be inevitable if the decision makers in the dominant country are unwilling to accept that the days of hegemony are numbered (see Appendix 2 to this chapter).[9]

If these challenges are addressed, the world economy could take new directions, delivering more sustainable and equitable outcomes. At present, however, the future remains uncertain, and the realisation of a truly globalised world — 'one world, one people' — remains far off.

Appendix 1: Global Warming

Michael Graff

Global warming is no longer a theoretical consideration. The planet is now warmer than at any time since the end of the last Ice Age, when the Neolithic Revolution began to transform our species' way of securing its livelihood. About 250 years ago, the Industrial Revolution marked the beginning of the large-scale use of fossil fuels which — as we now know — created what is today a crucial challenge for humanity. From 1970, the average temperature increase amounted to 0.18°C per decade, and the planet is now at least as warm as during the extremely hot period about 120,000 years ago (Hansen et al., 2025, p. 7). Extreme weather events are becoming more frequent, habitats of plants and animals are shifting and inhabitants of Pacific islands are making plans for evacuation as rising sea levels render them uninhabitable.

The threat emerged unnoticed and initially built up gradually. The impact of CO_2 emissions on the atmosphere, caused by fuel combustion and industry, was negligible until around 1850 and still relatively low until around 1950. Then the increase accelerated, and the data do not yet show an end to the exponential growth in cumulative emissions. The greenhouse effect became widely known in 1980 (Rich, 2018). At that stage, only a third of the cumulative emissions of the industrial era to date had entered the atmosphere. In 1988, when the Intergovernmental Panel on Climate Change (IPCC) was created, still only 42 per cent of the total had been emitted. In the last 30 years, from 1994 to 2024, as much has been emitted as in the entire period before that. Lower-middle-income countries account for only 9.2 per cent of total emissions, and lower-income countries for merely 0.6 per cent (ourworldindata.org/grapher/cumulative-co-emissions). Accordingly, most of the damage was caused knowingly and despite growing concerns, and the rich countries bear the greatest responsibility.

Since 1980, annual CO_2 emissions grew by 2.2 per cent on average and, as a result, doubled. In 2020, emissions shrank considerably for the first time, by 5 per cent, but this was entirely due to the COVID-19 pandemic shutdowns; in 2021, they rebounded by 5.3 per cent. For 2024, the World Meteorological Organization estimates a growth rate of 2.5 per cent.

As a result, 2024 was the warmest year since records began. The average temperature was 1.5°C higher than before industrialisation, reaching the upper limit target set in the

2017 Paris Climate Agreement, which — given the lack of determination — is unlikely to be met. With measures adopted so far, we are heading for 2.7°C by the end of the century (climateactiontracker.org/global/temperatures). Ice melt and sea level rise are accelerating, and the scientific consensus is that, without drastic reductions in greenhouse gas emissions, global warming will threaten the livelihoods of large parts of humanity.

Inaction

With so much at stake, why has so little been done? Denial and appeasement, or the motto that nothing can be done anyway, have successfully justified maintaining the status quo for decades. For one thing, the necessary change is not in the financial interests of the rich and wealthy. The most obvious beneficiaries of the status quo are also the most vehement deniers of anthropogenic climate change and opponents of countermeasures.[10] Their radicalism is also rooted in the fact that the doctrine of the inevitability of free markets clashes with the need for collective action, calling into question the ideological victory of the 1990s. In rich countries, however, many who do not directly benefit from the prevailing economic system as owners of the means of production have also settled into a comfortable existence. Given the repeated assertions in politics and the media that there is no alternative to the status quo (which could at best be given a green veneer) that would not make everyone poorer, the demand for systemic change is seen by many as an attack on their rights and way of life.

Despite climate strikes, green parties and sustainability commitments that extend into the political centre, a radical change in the existing economic system is unimaginable for many. Nevertheless, heterodox economists and imaginative thinkers have long discussed the possibility or desirability of a post-growth society that is less wasteful of natural resources than the current one.

Criticism of Economic Growth

Early concepts of a stationary economy (constant population and constant per capita income) were developed by John Stuart Mill (1848) and John Maynard Keynes (1930). What they have in common is the prospect of prosperity without excess, with sufficient material consumption and short working hours, without questioning capitalism itself. How egalitarian this future would be remained open, but an optimistic attitude is implicitly recognised: a frugal life would also be a good one.

In contrast, the 'Limits to Growth' calculated by the Club of Rome in the early 1970s (Meadows et al., 1972) had a distinctly pessimistic tone. The projected population explosion, together with the depletion of natural resources, would make humanity poorer. However, the analysis did not focus on who would be affected.

The fear of global overpopulation that was widespread in the 1970s is now unfounded: in the Global North, birth rates are already low in many cases, resulting in population decline, and in the Global South they are falling rapidly. As mentioned above, the latest UN projections assume the world population will reach its maximum well before the end of the century and then decline. The so-called 'population bomb' has thus been defused — unlike threats to the material foundations of human life, where there is no all-clear signal.

Just a few years after the Club of Rome's alarm call, André Gorz outlined scenarios in *Écologie et Liberté* (1977) for how (French) prosperity could be maintained in the face of the destructive effects of unregulated economic growth, through a combination of efficiency gains, self-determined production, shorter working hours and frugality. If only those goods were produced that did not privilege anyone, poverty and economic inequality would also disappear.

Since then, numerous proposals for a stationary economy have been made. Recurring elements include ending economic growth and embracing sufficiency, emphasising a communal or needs-based economy instead of a market- or profit-based one, shorter working hours, unconditional basic income, agricultural and commercial self-production, small-scale economic and social organisation and sometimes grassroots democratic decision-making. However, the question whether and how this could be realised within the current economic order is rarely addressed.

Countermeasures

Although the threat posed by resource depletion and global warming is hardly denied by the political and scientific establishment, swift and effective countermeasures are implemented hesitantly, if at all. Required restrictions on economic freedom and changes in personal lifestyles are often considered unacceptable.

Practically, a policy aiming for a stationary economy would have a difficult time, as it would call into question the welfare-state practice of funding social policy and redistribution from growth. A stationary economy would either have to forego social equality or confront questions of ownership and the system itself. The prevailing system therefore necessitates growth. Moreover, with constant working hours and increasing labour productivity, economic growth of the same magnitude is required to avoid rising unemployment. Within the existing order, a socially acceptable stationary economy is therefore difficult to conceive. From the perspective of the propertied class, a stationary economy is not an option: only a steady expansion of profitable investments ensures increasing production and sales, and thus profits.

A hope remains that technical and scientific progress will decouple production and resource consumption, removing the limits to growth.[11] However, observable decoupling is so far *relative*, not *absolute*. While environmental impact per unit produced is decreasing, overall output is still growing faster than environmental production efficiency, so total damage continues to increase. Yet, to prevent the worst-case scenario, emissions must fall significantly and immediately. Moreover, efficiency gains often increase consumption, reducing or eliminating environmental benefits.[12] As long as the economy grows, global decarbonisation will be difficult. Absolute decoupling observed in some rich countries is irrelevant globally, as only domestic emissions are counted. When emissions from imports are included, global emissions continue to rise. The territorial approach is therefore greenwashing for rich countries that outsource dirty production to the periphery, where emissions now appear relatively high simply because they are counted domestically.

Taxes or levies on harmful activities could, in principle, internalise negative externalities, but in the accelerating crisis, they would have to be so high as to function effectively as bans.

This has not been attempted, because resistance from affected companies and their political allies is expected to be as strong as it would be to an explicit ban. Exceptions are made for the highest-emitting industries, as otherwise they would become immediately unprofitable. In other words, exactly what needs to happen is being prevented.

Offsetting emissions through projects elsewhere is popular in rich countries. Proponents argue that the greatest environmental benefit can be achieved by prioritising measures with the best cost-performance ratio, usually in the Global South, but this ignores the need for rapid reductions *everywhere*. Also, most offset projects fail to demonstrate that they achieve the expected emission reductions.

Technical solutions to repair the damage, such as capturing CO_2 from the atmosphere and compressing and storing it in the Earth's interior, are expensive and energy-intensive. They may one day be feasible, but this is not yet foreseeable. Furthermore, CO_2 would need to remain stored permanently, not just until interim reduction targets are met — a condition that cannot be guaranteed.

If market-oriented measures are ineffective and technical solutions remain speculative, what is the alternative? Socially acceptable and ecologically sustainable technological change and efficiency improvements are part of the solution, but given the speed and depth of socio-economic transformation required, change must also break with the profit logic.

A Critical Perspective

The critical perspective to be outlined here sees technical and scientific progress as the decisive potential for a better society, in which sufficient goods and services are available for a good life for all, and tedious, dangerous or even just boring work is increasingly carried out by machines.

For some heterodox economists, capitalism and degrowth are irreconcilable.[13] There will be no voluntary reduction in the quantity of goods and services produced for the market, i.e. in gross domestic product, because this would also lead to a decline in profits; and attempts in recent years to use market-based means to steer the capitalist economy towards sustainability that respects planetary boundaries have failed. The obstacle to ecological and social transformation is structural. In a capitalist market economy, competition forces companies to maximise the difference between the cost of production and the market value of the product. However, market-determined values often differ greatly from utility values, as has become clear during the COVID-19 pandemic. Tax consultancy and investment banking are paid many times more than nursing, education or refuse collection, but in terms of social utility, the opposite is obviously true.

A decisive degrowth policy would, in practice, aim to abolish ecologically harmful and socially superfluous production (SUVs, villas, private jets, weapons, fast fashion, etc.), curb the advertising industry, which increases harmful demand, and promote durable products. A post-capitalist economy would not be hostile to technology, but technical progress would no longer be aimed at maximising profits, but at a better life for all in a society that is ecologically sustainable and at the same time more social and egalitarian than today's. The focus of production would shift away from exchange value and towards the use value of production. Investment decisions would no longer be made by private owners of the means of production, but by the 'associated producers' with a view to the environmentally and socially compatible needs of humankind.

A post-growth economy would have a net investment ratio of zero — if it were higher, the capital stock would grow and so would production. According to economic growth theory, in a dynamic equilibrium, when an economy grows at rate r, this rate is also equal to the profit rate. In a stationary economy ($r = 0$) there would therefore be no profit. However, this does not mean that such an economy would stagnate technologically, because replacement investments for depreciated or obsolete capital goods should lead to the use of the most advanced technologies, with the potential to improve the quality of production and at the same time humanise the world of work.

This would have to begin in the richest countries and would require a radical reorientation of production with the primacy of no longer endangering the foundations of human existence and, given the levels of productivity already attained, guaranteeing a dignified life for all.

With the plundering of non-renewable natural resources and the poisoning of the air, soil and oceans, and, most of all, warming of the planet, the present economic order has become a problem for humanity as a whole. Nature is setting limits that the profit-driven system cannot respect. The main causes of the current environmental crisis lie in past investments in the fossil fuel-based economy, and these will not voluntarily be written off. Justified by geopolitical tension, investment in fossil fuels is experiencing a new boom. The same holds for the production of armaments, which are not only purely destructive, but also massively harming the environment, and should hence not be produced at all if priority were given to dealing with the planetary crisis. According to the *Conflict and Environment Observatory* (2022), before 2022, CO_2 emissions caused by the military already amounted to 5.5 per cent of the global total, and due to the Russia–Ukraine war and the armaments race that it triggered these emissions and their share of the total are very likely to increase in the years to come.

An unfortunate path dependency also results from long-lasting infrastructure, especially in transport, housing and settlement construction. Urban sprawl, long commuting distances and the resulting dependence on cars will not be corrected any time soon. Even if we were to start today, which seems highly unlikely, it would take decades to create compact settlements from the existing ones, with short distances and a prioritisation of community use over private space consumption. Without long-term planning and massive investment in a sustainable future, taking into account the most advanced technologies, it will be difficult to achieve the required transformation soon enough. At the prosperous centre of the global economy, where a more egalitarian distribution than today's already makes a good life possible for all, the focus should be on phasing out environmentally harmful production and ending waste without delay. At the periphery, where poverty prevails and the lack of public services — health, education, transport, etc. — decent housing and other prerequisites for a dignified existence is particularly disgraceful, other priorities would have to be set first, without, however, using the destructive lifestyle in the rich countries as a model for those to be liberated from poverty.

Appendix 2: Hegemony and Current Geopolitics

Michael Graff

This Appendix provides an overview of the historical development of the current geopolitical situation in order to clarify its characteristics. The concept of hegemony is central to this. The ancient Greek word 'hegemon' means 'leader'. In political science, it refers to dominant states whose influence is primarily based on a combination of economic strength and military power and a recognisable willingness to use the latter. 'Geopolitics' refers to strategies for exercising power outside one's own territory, i.e. access to people, resources and markets. Hegemony is thus based on successful geopolitics. As the willingness to use military force is costly, hegemony requires those who are pro forma independent but actually dominated to accept it. In return, participation in so-called 'club goods' is offered.[14] These are primarily military security guarantees, but economic and cultural integration or participation can also play a role. Importantly, hegemony does not last forever, and when an emerging power threatens an established hegemon, danger of war looms. In the US in particular, it is widely believed that there is no escape from the 'Thucydides trap', as the confrontation with China has already begun.[15] How did this come about?

Hegemony from Antiquity to the Present Day

Since ancient times, history has recorded numerous regional and later global hegemonic powers, with the focus initially on the military protection of trade routes.[16] The first truly global hegemony emerged after the Napoleonic Wars with Great Britain at the centre. It was the first industrialised country to supply the world with textiles and other industrial products. In return, it imported food. The Royal Navy secured the transport routes.

The 'Pax Britannica' lasted until the First World War, an imperialist war motivated by claims to land and colonies. The German Empire had challenged British hegemony at sea with a naval arms race, but the other major European powers also pursued imperialist aims. The world war began in the summer of 1914 after the catastrophic failure of international diplomacy. It ended in 1918, when the Central Powers had exhausted their resources. In accordance with the 'right of self-determination of peoples' proclaimed by US President Wilson, the multi-ethnic Austro-Hungarian and Ottoman empires were broken up into 'nation states'. This turned minorities into majorities, and new minorities emerged in many places in the new nation states. It also marked the beginning of the 'ethnic cleansing' of the twentieth century, from the Greek-Turkish 'population exchange' in 1922 to the massacres during the Yugoslav wars of disintegration in the 1990s.

By the end of the First World War, the US outproduced all other countries and became the new global hegemon. US exports had risen dramatically, leading to a massive global debt to the US, which was a decisive factor in the accompanying relocation of the financial centre of the global economy from London to New York. Although the European victorious powers maintained their colonial ambitions, unlike the US they had emerged from the war so weakened that the economic dominance of the US was undisputed. Only the Soviet Union, which had established itself over most of the Russian Empire following the Bolshevik Revolution in 1917, stayed outside the hegemonial reach. As communist revolutions elsewhere had failed to materialise or had been crushed, the internationally ostracised Soviet Union under Stalin pursued a policy of 'socialism in one country' from 1926 onwards and became isolationist and repressive. The young Soviet Union hence made no hegemonic claims.

The rise of the US to global hegemon in the interwar period was preceded by expansion on the North American continent, the annexation of large parts of Mexico (1848), colonial rule over the Philippines (1898–1946) following a war against Spain and the 'Monroe doctrine', which amounted to the declaration of Latin America as the US's exclusive sphere of interest.

The interwar period brought a brief period of recovery, but also hyperinflation, fascism and revanchism, and in the 1930s the worldwide Great Depression. The Second World War began with the German Reich's attack on Poland in 1939. The aim of the aggression was to achieve hegemony on the Eurasian continent. The German successes in the first years of the war encouraged Japan to pursue the conquest of large parts of Asia, which had already begun in 1931 with the invasion of Manchuria. Fascist Italy had conquered Abyssinia (now: Ethiopia) in 1935, intended as the first step towards a modern reincarnation of the Roman Empire. As in 1914, Germany and its allies were dependent on quick successes, as the resources available to the Allies far exceeded those of the Axis powers. In 1941, Germany and its European allies attacked the Soviet Union. When the advance to Moscow was halted in the winter, and with the entry of the US in December 1941, the outcome of the war was sealed. However, the Allies still had to fight for victory until May 1945 in Europe and until August 1945 in the Pacific, when the aggressors were finally defeated.

Over the next four decades, large parts of the world were dominated by the two antagonistic 'superpowers', the US and the Soviet Union. Soviet influence extended as far as the Red Army had advanced in May 1945, with the exception of Yugoslavia and Albania, which sought to find their own paths to socialism. American hegemony extended across Western Europe and Latin America and included numerous fascist and despotic countries.

The Soviet occupation zone in eastern Germany achieved statehood in 1949 as the German Democratic Republic (GDR), and in the same year the Federal Republic of Germany (FRG) was formed from the American, British and French occupation zones. The GDR and FRG were quickly integrated into the Soviet and Atlantic hegemonic zones. Unlike after 1918, the victors did not attempt to keep Germany militarily weak. The GDR and FRG were rearmed as frontline states in the Cold War in the mid-1950s.

In the 1950s, the Soviet Union and China co-operated as informal allies. Later, differences of opinion on Marxism-Leninism led to a rift, and cooperation ended in 1969. In Africa and parts of Asia, the remaining European colonies gained their independence from the 1950s to the 1970s, often after bitter wars. The 'non-aligned' countries outside the two large hegemonic zones were hardly united by anything; hegemony did not emanate from them.

The fact that the US succeeded in producing atomic bombs before the end of the war became decisive for the period after 1945. Two of them were detonated over Hiroshima and Nagasaki in August 1945, and Japan surrendered just a few days later. However, the US's nuclear weapons monopoly lasted only four years; the Soviet Union detonated its first atomic bomb in 1949, followed by Great Britain in 1953, France in 1960 and China in 1964. This did not render war as a political tool obsolete, but at least there has been no major direct confrontation between nuclear powers to this day. The battles of the Cold War (Korea, Vietnam, Afghanistan) took place on the periphery in proxy wars.

US hegemony was accompanied by a combination of supposed divine election and the awareness of having emerged as a democratic state from an anti-colonial war.[17] According to this, US hegemony is a 'mission' and not an ordinary expansion of economic dominance and military reach, but rather the propagation of 'values' of universal validity. This may be seen as a phoney justification of global ambitions, but its impact in the country itself and in many other parts of the world should not be underestimated. US hegemony was formalised through its dominant role in NATO, the IMF, the GATT and WTO and in the World Bank. In addition to the two usual pillars of geopolitical power — economic and military strength — the US was also able to draw on 'soft power' like no hegemon before it: The appeal of the 'American way of life' found its way to every corner of the world through Hollywood and TV soap operas.

The antagonism between the US and Soviet-led blocs continued until the latter began to disintegrate in 1989. The quiet departure of the governments that had claimed to rule over a 'real existing socialism' was greeted with enthusiasm in the West and by many of those directly affected. The US found itself at the centre of a unipolar world and with a political and economic system that would henceforth serve as a model for the rest of the world. Apparently, history had proven that there was no alternative to capitalism, and with the final victory of the liberal market economy over the planned economy, free elections and parliamentary democracy, the 'end of history' (Fukuyama, 1992) seemed to have been reached.

In the US, the euphoria of the 1990s was followed by severe disappointment. The terrorist attacks of September 2001 shattered the conviction of its invulnerability, and the subsequently declared 'war on terror', with its ill-conceived interventions, some of which violated international law, proved to be costly, sacrificial and unsuccessful. In the Middle East and North Africa, no Western-style democracies emerged, but rather a series of failed states. Since the chaotic withdrawal of NATO from Afghanistan in 2021, the Taliban are once again exercising unrestricted violence, with catastrophic consequences, especially for women. Iran is still a theocratic dictatorship, with a nuclear bomb within reach and explicit intentions to destroy Israel. Following the terrorist attack on Israel in 2023 with about 1,200 people killed and 250 taken as hostages, the Israeli army launched an even more devastating attack on Gaza that continues up to this day, and which is not only damaging Israel's reputation in the world, but also that of its closest ally, the US. The economic picture is also sobering. The global recession of 2008–9 was triggered by the bursting of a huge speculative bubble in the US mortgage market. The increasing poverty and the decline of health status in the US are obvious, the infrastructure is in need of maintenance, the budget deficit is chronic, as are the huge trade deficits, which since the 1990s have turned the US from a creditor into the world's largest debtor. The persistent deficits would have already jeopardised the creditworthiness of any other country. It is only thanks to the privilege of being able to borrow in its own currency (still the world's largest reserve currency) that a currency crisis has not yet materialised. Last but not least, 'soft power' has also been damaged. The fact that Donald Trump, a notorious liar and egomaniac, not only held the highest office in the US from 2017 to 2020, but was re-elected in 2024, has been watched by the rest of the world with bewilderment. Police violence, overcrowded prisons and a Supreme Court that restricts women's control over their bodies against the will of the majority of the population do not add to the lustre of America. In addition, the bizarre confrontations between the Democratic and the Republican parties regarding the so-called 'fiscal cliff' that have repeatedly threatened to trigger a fiscal contraction sizeable enough to drag the US economy into recession, and the world economy along with it.

Hegemony and Competition

The hegemonic power of the US has passed its peak, and global hegemony in the future will be shared. The emerging rival is China. The reforms of 1978 marked the beginning of an export-driven growth policy. The one-child policy freed up resources that would otherwise have had to be spent on childcare. The growing industry could then draw on hundreds of millions of potential labourers from rural areas. Record levels of investment massively expanded China's productive capacity. In 2013, the 'New Silk Road' was initiated, a huge investment project in the transport infrastructure of Eurasia and Africa, designed to deepen China's integration with these regions. The geopolitical impact is already undeniable. From 1978 to 2024, China's economic output increased by a factor of 50, that of the US by a factor of 3.3. In 2024, China's GDP amounted to 81.5 per cent of that of the US, but adjusted for purchasing power, China's GDP has already surpassed that of the US in 2016. Economic prosperity, measured by purchasing power-adjusted per capita income, has been above the global average since 2020.

The EU and the countries associated with it in Europe are still an economic heavyweight, but a declining one, and global military hegemony does not emanate from Europe. The military is nationalised and largely integrated into NATO, in which the US plays a leading role. France and the UK have nuclear weapons, but these are probably mainly to maintain a symbolic sense of great-power status. Unlike the US, Europe also lacks a collective sense of mission. France is attached to the 'Francophone world' and endeavours to maintain close relations with its former African colonies. 'Brexit' gave many supporters the illusion that the UK might regain its former global standing. Germany's imperial spirit has disappeared for the time being after two lost wars. Europe's hegemonic aspirations are economic and mostly focused on the European continent. In line with this, after the end of the Soviet Union, they have gradually extended toward the Russian border, a factor that has contributed to the current situation in Ukraine.

Only a few countries on the periphery exercise anything like hegemonic power. Among the BRICS (Brazil, Russia, India, China and South Africa), apart from the rising global hegemon China, regional hegemony is claimed by Russia in Central Asia and the Eastern Slavic states of Belarus and Ukraine, to some extent by India in South Asia, by Brazil in South America and by South Africa in the sub-Saharan region but these countries do not exercise global ambitions. In the South Pacific, Australia is trying to establish regional hegemony as a junior partner to the US.

A look at GDP provides an insight into the extent of the economic underpinning of hegemony. Figure 23.1 shows the shares in global GDP of the ten largest economies (EU combined) in 2024 (constant 2015 US$) from 1990 to 2024.

The US's share fell from 30.8 per cent in 1990 to 23.5 per cent in 2024. The relative loss of importance for the entire Western camp is even more pronounced, as the EU's share fell from 27.8 per cent to 16.2 per cent. Japan, which a few decades ago was still seen as a rising rival for global hegemony, recorded its maximum share of 10.0 per cent in 1991 and has more than halved it since then. Among the emerging economies, India has since 1990 nearly tripled its share of global GDP, but at 3.6 per cent it is still a lightweight from a global perspective. The clear outlier is China. In 1960, then the world's the most populous country, it had a vanishingly small share of 1.5 per cent of global GDP. After the reforms of 1978, it

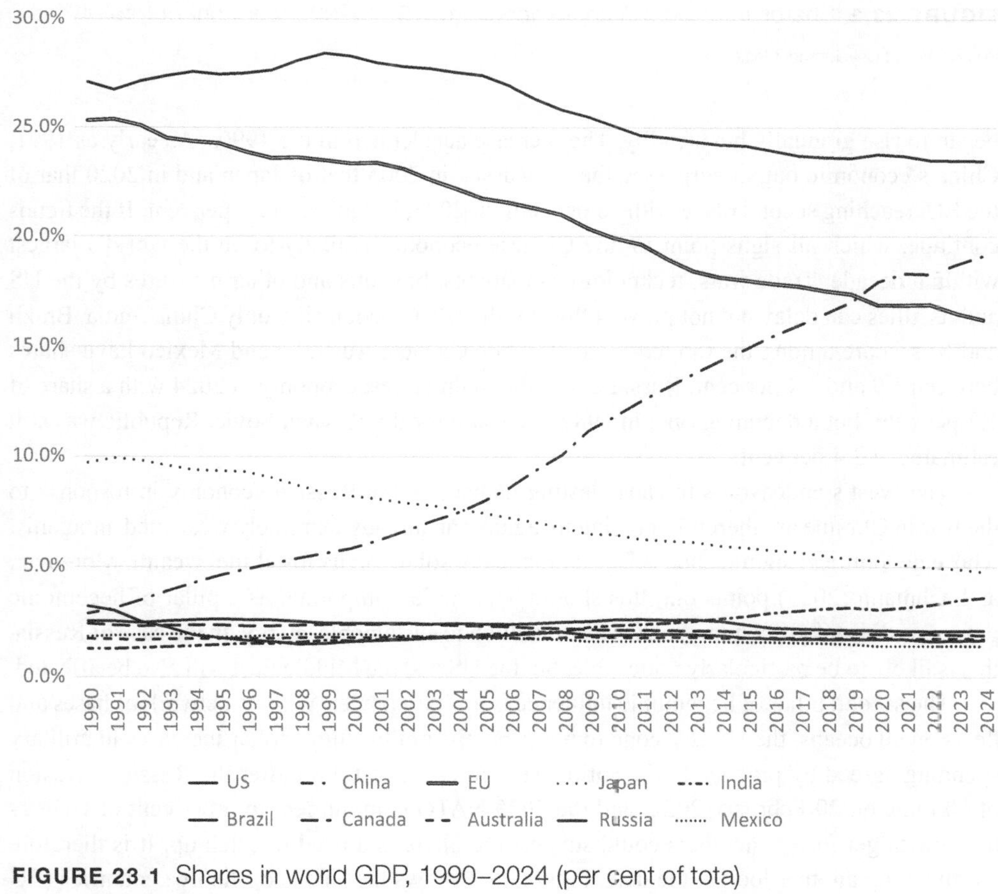

FIGURE 23.1 Shares in world GDP, 1990–2024 (per cent of tota)

Source: World Development Indicators.

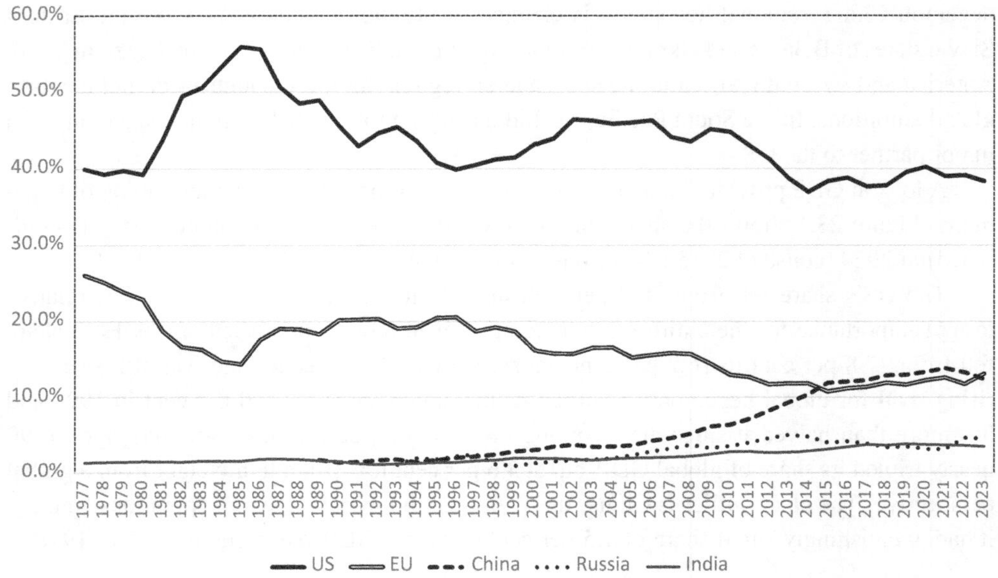

FIGURE 23.2 Shares in world military expenditure, 1977–2023 (per cent of total)

Source: World Development Indicators.

began to rise gradually but steadily. The increase accelerated in the 1990s. As early as 1991, China's economic output surpassed that of Russia, in 2005 that of Japan and in 2020 that of the EU, reaching second place with 18 per cent. In 2024, it stands at 19.1 per cent. If the trends continue, which all signs point to, the Chinese economy is likely to be the world's largest within a decade. Trade wars, technology embargoes, boycotts and other measures by the US and its allies can delay but not prevent this. Of the BRICS countries, only China, India, Brazil and Russia are among the top ten in 2024, while Canada, Australia and Mexico have shares between 1.9 and 1.4 per cent. Russia is still the ninth largest economy in 2024 with a share of 1.7 per cent, but a declining one; in 1989, the share for the Russian Soviet Republic was still estimated at 3.4 per cent.

The West's endeavours to cause lasting damage to the Russian economy in response to the war in Ukraine are therefore coming up against an already extremely weakened antagonist whose geopolitical significance is based practically solely on its fossil fuel wealth. Moreover, as Lachmann (2023) points out, this should become less important as a pillar of hegemonic power, as the global economy makes the transition to sustainable energy. In the case of Russia, this is likely to be particularly noticeable, but the US and the Middle East will also be affected.

The second pillar of hegemonic influence is military power. With its network of bases and fleets on all oceans, the US is second to none, but the multi-billion dollar increases in military spending agreed by practically the entire Western camp just days after the Russian invasion of Ukraine on 20 February 2022, and the 2025 NATO commitment to 5 per cent of GDP as the new target for its members could suggest that there is a need to catch up. It is therefore worth taking another look at the data. Figure 23.2 shows the shares of the five countries (EU combined) with the highest military expenditure in 2023.

US military spending far outstrips that of all other countries. During the last 50 years, the US's share of global spending was never below 37 per cent. In the mid-1980s, when the US forced the Soviet Union into an arms race, it peaked at 56 per cent, after which it fluctuated between 40 and 46 per cent. Together with the EU, Japan, South Korea and Australia, the Western camp had a share peaking at more than 82 per cent during the Cold War; in the last ten years, the joint share has been close to 60 per cent. The US and its closest allies therefore spend far more on the military than the rest of the world combined.

China also stands out here, accounting for 12.4 per cent of global military spending in 2023. Until the mid-1990s, the share was still below 2 per cent. China's ambitions to demonstrate its global military weight are therefore recognisable, but it is also clear that China would not stand a chance in a conventional war of attrition against the West. This applies all the more to Russia. A military dwarf with 1.1 per cent in 1993, it had increased its share to 5.0 per cent by 2013 but has already fallen back to 4.6 per cent by 2023.

The need for rearmament declared in the NATO countries in view of the Russian invasion of Ukraine cannot be justified by these figures. Assuming that relative military spending is a reflection of military power, since the conflict with Ukraine escalated in 2014, Russia was always 12–19 times weaker militarily than the Western camp. In addition, the question arises as to the benefit of the planned increases in military expenditure, as Russia's military aggression in 2022 was not prevented by the West's enormous superiority at that time. As in the Cold War, the geopolitical room for manoeuvre is limited by the deterrent effect of nuclear arsenals. As before, a direct military confrontation between the established major nuclear powers — the US, Russia, China, France or the UK — harbours an incalculable risk, allowing them to engage relatively safely only in local military operations or proxy wars.[18]

The Geopolitical Situation in 2025

The current geopolitical situation is characterised by the relative economic loss of importance of the twentieth-century hegemon and its allies, and the rise of its new rival, China. Unlike before, however, the new rival is not an ideological antagonist but a major economic power that is competing with the West for global influence — access to human labour, resources and markets. China's geopolitical independence and export-driven growth may serve as a model for countries of the periphery. At the same time, 'Chinese-style socialism' is certainly not 'missionary'. It attempts to rationalise the coexistence of an unleashed private sector with a still significant state sector, a one-party system with a party that calls itself 'communist', and 'Chinese traditions'. This is not an ideology that aims for global recognition or reach. China's hegemonic ambitions are geopolitical and, like those of all other major powers without a particular sense of mission, an expression of ordinary economic rivalry.

Of the empires that fell during the twentieth century, two are attempting a renaissance. 'Brexit' was supposed to restore Britain's economic global standing, but this has so far proved to be a complete illusion. Tsarist imperialism had created a multi-ethnic empire which, after 1917, continued to exist practically within the old borders in the Union of Soviet Republics. After the end of the Soviet Union, all 15 declared their independence. Most of the former Soviet republics and Cold War states turned to the West economically and militarily. By 2004, the former GDR, Poland, the Czech Republic, Slovakia, Slovenia, Hungary, Bulgaria, Estonia,

Latvia, Lithuania and Romania had joined NATO. The Russian enclave of Kaliningrad is thus surrounded by NATO countries, and Estonia and Latvia border Russia to the north. However, Belarus and Ukraine lie between the long Russian border to the Black Sea in the south and NATO. The latter are the only Slavic-speaking states of the former Soviet republics apart from Russia, and Russia's last geopolitical 'red line' runs recognisably along their western border.

Since 1992, and increasingly since 2014, there have been ongoing internal Ukrainian disputes over the status of Crimea, the eastern territories, the role of the Russian language and Ukraine's economic and military orientation, with NATO membership becoming an increasingly realistic option, and with the West actively taking sides. Russia's new imperialism, on the other hand, apparently aims at an Eastern Slavic-Orthodox unity based on ethno-linguistic, religious and historical similarities and, not least, at the integration of the Russian, Belarusian and Ukrainian economic areas.

Geopolitics on a nationalistic and religious basis also follow imaginary realities. This makes them potentially irrational and unpredictable, as demonstrated by Russia's attack on Ukraine in February 2022, which was obviously based on a completely unrealistic assessment of the prospects of success. The attempt to take Kiev by surprise with the aim of installing a pro-Russian government failed. The Russian army then established itself in eastern Ukraine. Since then, a war of attrition of medium intensity has been waged. The second miscalculation was the unexpected willingness of the West to provide massive support to Ukraine, logistically and with military material including artillery, tanks and fighter aircraft. In view of the West's massive superiority in conventional armaments, a Russian victory in the war of attrition is impossible as long as Western support continues, and Ukrainian troops are still alive and willing to continue fighting. A Ukrainian victory with Russia's complete withdrawal from eastern Ukraine and Crimea is politically hardly conceivable, as this would force a nuclear power to give up territories that have de facto belonged to Russia since 2014.

It is currently impossible to predict when and on what basis a ceasefire and peace negotiations can take place. On the Western side, the explicit intention is to damage Russia's economic and military potential as much as possible and thus weaken the country permanently. However, as this affects a hegemon that is already well down from the heights, the geopolitical calculation is probably primarily to set an example that expansion and military intervention against the will of the leading Western power will not be tolerated. This is also a signal to China to hold back in the South China Sea and refrain from intervening in Taiwan.

The foreseeable consequences of the war in Ukraine are catastrophic. Loss of life, injuries, excesses of violence against civilians in the shadow of the fighting and massive damage to buildings and infrastructure in Ukraine. The relationship between people who see themselves as Russian and Ukrainian will remain poisoned for a long time to come.

The East Slavic unification envisaged by Russia will not materialise in the foreseeable future, and NATO is experiencing an unexpected increase in importance. Finland and Sweden have joined NATO in 2023 and 2024, and commitment in the Western camp to go to war with Russia has been considerably strengthened.

The current rise in global defence spending is increasing the economic and political importance of the military-industrial complex. Funds that would be urgently needed in the fight against global warming and species extinction are now being invested in unproductive killing machinery, resulting in depletion of resources and massive CO_2 emissions.

Can the US Escape the Thucydides Trap?

War between the US and China is not inevitable. History is not predetermined, but is made by people, which, under the prevailing conditions, means by the ruling elites. But this is precisely why a tragedy could occur. Like the 'sleepwalkers' of 1914, who led the world into the completely senseless catastrophe of the First World War through a combination of militarism, grandstanding and incompetence (Clark, 2012), politicians and opinion-makers in the West are increasingly claiming that a confrontation with China is inevitable (Behrens, 2021). The risk that a direct confrontation between Chinese and US military forces could result from disputes over uninhabited islands, territorial waters or rights of maritime passage in the South China Sea or from China's non-recognition of Taiwan's sovereignty increases with the extent of the bellicose rhetoric and the depth of the conviction that the rivalry with China is not ordinary geopolitical competition, but the expression of a contest of 'values'.

Looking at the relative loss of importance in the US without resentment would mean acknowledging the end of the idea of the chosen country. Finally, it is important to understand that the global economy is not a zero-sum game. A country may defend its *relative* position by keeping others down, but in real terms, it is likely to inflict damage not only on its adversaries, but also on itself.

RECOMMENDATIONS FOR FURTHER READING

For detailed studies of nation building, geopolitics and hegemony, refer to Clark (2012, *The Sleepwalkers. How Europe Went to War in 1914*), Hobsbawm and Terence (2012, *The Invention of Tradition*), Schröder (2022, *The Decline of the American Empire*) and Lachmann (2023, *Trump and the Politics of Imperial Decline*).

Key references for the 'Thucydides Trap' are Gilpin (1988, *The Theory of Hegemonic War*) and Allison (2017, *Destined for War. Can America and China Escape Thucydides's Trap?*).

Rodrick (2011, *The Globalization Paradox*) and Cohen (2009, *Why not Socialism?*) deal with the difficulty of the global economy to address social concerns adequately.

Early economic texts on the stationary economy are by Mill (1848, *Principles of Political Economy with some of their Applications to Social Philosophy*) and Keynes (1930, *Economic Possibilities for our Grandchildren*). Recent contributions by prominent advocates of a more sustainable economic order requiring some kind of 'system change' are Lawn and Clarke (2010, *The End of Economic Growth?*), Foster (2011, *Capitalism and Degrowth: An Impossibility Theorem*), Klein (2014, *This Changes Everything. Capitalism vs the Climate*), Fraser (2022, *Cannibal Capitalism. How Our System Is Devouring Democracy, Care, and the Planet – and What We Can Do about It*), Hickel (2023, *On Technology and Degrowth*) and Huber (2023, *The Problem with Degrowth*).

McAffe (2019, *More from Less – The Surprising Story of How We Learned to Prosper Using Fewer Resources – and What Happens Next*) stands out as an optimist. He portraits the current economic system as innovative and flexible enough to get the planetary crises under control.

NOTES

1 International aid up to this date constitutes a considerable share of gross national income in some of the poorest countries, but its effects usually fall short of the self-proclaimed goals. One of the decisive questions is whether aid distorts incentives. In particular, it can serve as a substitute for domestic saving rather than function as an additional boost to productive investment. Moreover, it can foster an attitude of dependency, which is not helpful in promoting efforts aimed at achieving self-sustaining growth. As long as this is the case, international aid should probably be restricted to humanitarian aid.

2 The USMCA maintained tariff-free trade, but it erected non-tariff barriers, such as rules of origin and wage controls.

3 The reasons for the very limited accuracy of macroeconomic forecasts are manifold. Apart from 'intelligent guessing', which often with the benefit of hindsight proves less intelligent as anticipated, most forecasts are model-based. In principle, these models take account of the last available data and project a return from there to their inbuilt 'equilibrium growth path' within a few years. This approach produces reasonably accurate forecasts as long as the economy is growing smoothly on or close to its equilibrium growth path if the latter exists and is quantified accurately. Obviously, any unforeseeable shock or changes to the concept of 'equilibrium' will cause potentially huge forecast errors even in the short term. Moreover, for poor countries or those that are 'catching up', equilibrium may not be an applicable concept; a better 'model' would presumably be 'creative destruction', coming in irregular waves and with largely unpredictable consequences. Thus, economic forecast for the world economy over decades cannot rely only on a more or less convincing extrapolation of trends, coupled with scenarios of demographic change. Unsurprisingly, such forecasts or projections — when tried at all — are usually performed by research departments in large international banks, where the craving for quantitative data to guide investment decisions is most pronounced.

4 The existence of such a threshold is evident (although not its magnitude). Given full employment, GDP per capita can be increased by longer working hours, later retirement and earlier entry into the labour force. To maximise GDP, this would call for 18-hour shifts, child labour and work until permanent disability or death. Clearly, total wellbeing would be severely impaired despite rising per capita incomes.

5 It must be added that Keynes found the particular version of this de facto currency union — the gold standard — a 'barbaric' relic due to the vast amount of resources it consumed to dig the gold out of the ground, refine it and then bury it again in the vaults of central banks who hoped would never be required to redeem it for their paper money, and also due to the inflexibility it imposed on the money supply, with high volatility of domestic price levels linked to fluctuations of the current account and deflation at the world scale looming as soon as the growth rate of world output exceeded that of the monetary bullion stock. Towards the end of his life, at the Bretton Woods conference in 1944, he proposed a clearing union administered by a supranational central bank and based on the 'bancor' reserve currency, to which all other currencies would be pegged with the provision of re-alignments to prevent persistent imbalances from building up.

6 This argument is elaborated by Hatton and Williamson (2008, Chapters 16 and 17) and Goldin (2010).

7 Representative contributions are — among many others — Jacoby (2008), Palley (2009), Reinhart and Rogoff (2009), Skidelsky (2009), Quiggin (2010), Rajan (2010), Shaxson (2011), Galbraith (2012) and Judt (2012).

8 Has Marxism been refuted by history? Does the collapse of the Soviet Union in 1991 and its satellite states along with it show that there is no alternative to a capitalist market economy? Initially, many, if not all observers approved, but the question 'Why not socialism?' came back on the agenda. This is also the title of a short book by Cohen (2009), in which he argues that the common self-organisation on a camping trip is evidence that, likewise, socialism is achievable as a voluntary association of free individuals.

9 For more details, see Gilpin (1988) and Allison (2017).

10 The Heartland Institute (heartland.org), financed by the fossil fuel industry and private patrons, is notorious for this, and one of the most bizarre deniers of global warming today is US President Donald Trump, arguably the individual with the most political weight in the world.

11 See, for example, McAffe (2019) and Galor (2022).

12 This rebound effect was already described by Jevons (1865).

13 See, for example, Foster (2011), Pirgmaier (2021), Fraser (2022), Hickel (2023) and Huber (2023).

14 See, for example, Nesmashnyi (2023). The economistic jargon is typical of current political science.

15 For an elaboration, see Lachmann (2023).
16 See Bernstein (2008). Sumer (2900–2400 BCE) was the first. Other important regional hegemonic powers were Egypt until the conquest by Rome (30 BCE), the Roman Empire until the year 476, the Eastern Roman Empire until the conquest of Constantinople by the Ottomans (1453), the Muslim 'free trade zone' (seventh to eleventh centuries), the collective hegemony of the Hanseatic League in the twelfth century, the Mongol Empire (thirteenth to fourteenth centuries), Venice and other Italian city states (eleventh to fifteenth centuries). Before 1492, the Maya, the Incas and the Aztecs were important regional hegemonic powers on the American double continent. In the Far East, the Han dynasty ruled from 206 BCE to 220 CE, and the Ming dynasty (1368–1644) even operated as a naval power in the Indian Ocean in the early fifteenth century. From the sixteenth century onwards, Portugal, Spain and the Netherlands took over as hegemonic powers.
17 For an elaboration, see Schröder (2022).
18 For the new nuclear powers India and Pakistan, the need for bilateral deterrence is likely to be dominant, for Israel the fear of annihilation by its neighbours and Iran, and for North Korea nuclear weapons are the life insurance in the conflict with South Korea and its Western allies. Hegemonic ambitions are not expressed by these countries.

Bibliography

Abramovitz, M. (1986), 'Catching up, forging ahead, and falling behind', *The Journal of Economic History*, Vol. *46*, No. *2*, pp. 385–406.

Acemoglu, D. and Robinson, J.A. (2012), *Why Nations Fail: The Origins of Power, Prosperity and Poverty*, Suffolk: Profile Books.

Acemoglu, D., Johnson, S. and Robinson, J.A. (2001), 'The colonial origins of comparative development: an empirical investigation', *The American Economic Review*, Vol. *91*, No. *5*, pp. 1369–1401.

Aldcroft, D.H. (1977), *From Versailles to Wall Street, 1919–1929*, Harmondsworth: Allen Lane

Allen, R.C. (2003), *Farm to Factory: A Reinterpretation of the Soviet Industrial Revolution*, Princeton: Princeton University Press.

Allison, G. (2017), *Destined for War. Can America and China Escape Thucydides's Trap?* Boston: Houghton Mifflin Harcourt.

Ambler, S., Cardia, E. and Zimmermann, C. (2004), 'International business cycles: what are the facts?', *Journal of Monetary Economics*, Vol. *51*, No. *2*, pp. 257–276.

Arndt, H.W. (1944), *Economic Lessons of the Nineteen Thirties*, London: Oxford University Press.

Artis, M. (2003), 'Is there a European Business cycle?', CESifo Working Paper No. 1053.

Bairoch, Paul (1974), 'Geographical structure and trade balance of European foreign trade from 1800 to 1970', *The Journal of European Economic History*, Vol. *3*, No. *3*, pp. 557–608.

Baldwin, R.E. (1958), 'The commodity composition of trade: selected industrial countries, 1900–1954', *The Review of Economics and Statistics*, Vol. *40*, No. *1*, Part 2, pp. 50–68.

Barber, C.L. (1978), 'On the origins of the Great Depression', *Southern Economic Journal*, Vol. *44*, No. *3*, pp. 432–456.

Bastable, C.F. (1923), *The Commerce of Nations*, London: Methuen & Co. Ltd.

Bayly, C.A. (2004), *The Birth of the Modern World, 1780–1914*, New York: Wiley-Blackwell.

Bayoumi, T., Eichengreen, B. and Taylor, M.P. (1996), *Modern Perspectives on the Gold Standard*, Cambridge: Cambridge University Press.

Beckert, S. (2014), *Empire of Cotton. A Global History*, New York: Alfred A. Knopf.

Behrens, U. (2021), *Feindbild China. Was wir alles nicht über die Volksrepublik wissen*, Berlin: Das Neue Berlin.

Bernanke, Ben S. (2000), *Essays on the Great Depression*, Princeton: Princeton University Press.

Bernstein, M.A. (1987), *The Great Depression: Delayed Recovery and Economic Change in America, 1929–1939*, Cambridge: Cambridge University Press.

Bernstein, W. (2008), *A Splendid Exchange: How Trade Shaped the World*, London: Atlantic Books.

Bhagwati, J. (ed.) (1977), *The New International Economic Order: The North–South Debate*, Cambridge: The MIT Press.

Blanchard, O. and Leigh, D. (2012), 'Are we underestimating short-term fiscal multipliers?', in: Blaug, M., O'Brin, D. and Eltis, W. (eds.), *IMF World Economic Outlook*, October, pp. 41–43.

Blaug, M. (1995), 'Why is the quantity theory of money the oldest surviving theory in economics?', in: Blaug, M., O'Brin, D. and Eltis, W. (eds.), *The Quantity Theory of Money*, Aldershot: Edward Elgar Publishing Ltd., pp. 27–49.

Bloomfield, A.I. (1959), *Monetary Policy under the International Gold Standard 1880–1914*, New York: Federal Reserve Bank of New York.

Bloomfield, A.I. (1968), *Patterns of Fluctuation in International Investment Before 1914*, Princeton: Princeton University Press.

Boltho, A. (ed.) (1982), *The European Economy: Growth and Crisis*, London: Oxford University Press.

Born, K.E. (1972), *Die Entwicklung der Banknote vom 'Zettel' zum gesetzlichen Zahlungsmittel*, Mainz: Franz Steiner Verlag.

Born, K.E. (1976), *Geld und Banken im 19. und 20. Jahrhundert*, Stuttgart: Alfred Kröner Verlag.

Broadberry, S. and Harrison, M. (2005), *The Economics of World War I: A Comparative Quantitative Analysis*, Cambridge: Cambridge University Press.

Broadberry, S. and Harrison, M. (2008), 'World wars, economics of', in: Durlauf, S.N. and Blume, L.E. (eds), *The New Palgrave Dictionary of Economics*, London: Palgrave Macmillan. https://doi.org/10.1007/978-1-349-58802-2_1840.

Brunner, K. (ed.) (1981), *The Great Depression Revisited*, Boston: Martinus Nijhoff.

Cairncross, A.K. (1955), 'World trade in manufactures since 1900', *Economia Internazionale*, Vol. *8*, pp. 715–741.

Cairncross, A.K. and Faaland, J. (1952), 'Long-term trends in Europe's trade', *The Economic Journal*, Vol. *62*, No. *245*, pp. 25–34.

Calleo, D.P. (1976), 'The historiography of the interwar period: reconsiderations', in: Rowland, B. (ed.), *Balance of Power or Hegemony?*, New York: New York University Press, pp. 225–260.

Cameron, R. (1961), *France and the Economic Development of Europe 1800–1914*, Princeton: Princeton University Press.

Cameron, R. (1985), 'A new view of European industrialization', *The Economic History Review*, Vol. *38*, No. *1*, pp. 1–23.

Cameron, R. (1993), *A Concise Economic History of the World*, 2nd edn, New York: Oxford University Press.

Carr-Saunders, M. (1936), *World Population*, Oxford: Oxford University Press.

Cecchetti, S. (2011), *Global Imbalances: Current Accounts and Financial Flows*, Chicago: University of Chicago.

Cipolla, C.M. (1972), 'The diffusion of innovations in early modern Europe', *Comparative Studies in Society and History*, Vol. *14*, No. *1*, pp. 46–52.

Cipolla, C.M. (1993), *Before the Industrial Revolution: European Society and Economy, 1000–1700*, 3rd edn, London: Routledge.

Clark, C. (2012), *The Sleepwalkers. How Europe Went to War in 1914*, London: Penguin Books.

Clark, T.E. and van Wincoop, E. (2001), 'Borders and business cycles', *Journal of International Economics*, Vol. *55*, No. *1*, pp. 59–85.

Cohen, G.A. (2009), *Why not Socialism?*, Princeton: Princeton University Press.

Comin, D. and Hobijn, B. (2004), 'Cross-country technology adoption: making the theories face the facts', *Journal of Monetary Economics*, Vol. *51*, No. *1*, pp 39–83.

Conflict and Environment Observatory (2022), *Estimating the Military's Global Greenhouse Gas Emissions*, Mytholmroyd: Scientists for Global Responsibility.

Costigliola, F. (1985), *Awkward Dominion: American Political, Economic and Cultural Relations with Europe, 1919–1933*, New York: Cornell University Press.

Davenport, M. (1986), *Trade Policy, Protection, and the Third World*, London: Routledge.

Davies, G. (1994), *A History of Money: From Ancient Times to the Present Day*, Cardiff: University of Wales Press.

Davis, L.E. and Huttenback, R.A. (1986), *Mammon and the Pursuit of Empire: The Political Economy of British Imperialism*, Cambridge: Cambridge University Press.

De Long, J.B. (2022), *Slouching Towards Utopia. An Economic History of the Twentieth Century*, New York: Basic Books.

De Moor, T. and van Zanden, J.L. (2010), 'Girl power: the European marriage pattern and labour markets in the North Sea region in the late medieval and early modern period', *The Economic History Review*, Vol. *63*, No. *1*, pp. 1–33.

De Vries, J. (2010), 'The limits of globalization in the early modern world', *The Economic History Review*, Vol. *63*, No. *3*, pp. 710–733.

Denison, E.F. (1967), *Why Growth Rates Differ: Postwar Experience of Nine Western Countries*, Washington: The Brookings Institution.

Drummond, I.M. (1987), *The Gold Standard and the International Monetary System, 1900–1939*, London Macmillan Education.

Easterly, W. (2006), *The White Man's Burden*, New York: Penguin Publishing Group.

Edelstein, M. (1982), *Overseas Investment in the Age of High Imperialism: the United Kingdom 1850–1914*, New York: Columbia University Press.

Eichengreen, B. (ed.) (1985), *The Gold Standard in Theory and History*, New York: Routledge.

Eichengreen, B. and Gemery, H.A. (1986), 'The earnings of skilled and unskilled immigrants at the end of the nineteenth century', *The Journal of Economic History*, Vol. *46*, No. *2*, pp. 441–454.

Einzig, P. (1949), *Primitive Money in its Ethnological, Historical and Economic Aspects*, London: Eyre and Spottiswoode.

Eltis, D. and Engermann, S.L. (eds) (2011), *The Cambridge World History of Slavery, Volume 3, AD 1420–AD 1804*, Cambridge: Cambridge University Press.

Eltis, D., Engermann, S.L., Drescher, S. and Richardson, D. (eds) (2011), *The Cambridge World History of Slavery, Volume 4, AD 1804–AD 2016*, Cambridge: Cambridge University Press.

Engerman, S.L. (1986), 'Servants to slaves to servants: contract labour and European expansion', in: Emmer, F.C. (ed), *Colonialism and Migration: Indentured Labour Before and after Slavery*, Dordrecht: Martinus Nijhoff, pp. 263–294.

Fatás, A. (1997), 'EMU: countries or regions? Lessons from the EMS experience', *European Economic Review*, Vol. *41*, No. *3–5*, pp. 743–751.

Federico, G. and Antonio, T.J. (2019), 'World trade, 1800–1938: a new synthesis', *Revista de Historia Económica-Journal of Iberian and Latin America Economic History*, Vol. *37*, No. *1*. online data: 'Federico-Tena World Trade Historical Database', https://doi.org/10.21950/BBZVBN.

Feinstein, C.H. (1960), *Home and Foreign Investment, 1870–1973*, Cambridge: Cambridge University Press.

Ferenczi, I. and Willcox, W.F. (1929, 1931), *International Migration*, New York: National Bureau of Economic Research, Vols. 1–2.

Ferguson, N. and Schularick, M. (2007), 'Chimerica and the global asset market boom', *International Finance*, Vol. *10*, No. *3*, pp. 215–239.

Fischer, F. (1961), *Griff nach der Weltmacht: Die Kriegszielpolitik des kaiserlichen Deutschland 1914/18*, Düsseldorf: Droste.

Fischer, F. (1967), *Germany's Aims in the First World War*, New York: W. W. Norton & Co, Inc.

Fisher, I. (1911), 'Recent changes in price levels and their causes', *The American Economic Review*, Vol. *1*, No. *2*, pp. 37–45.

Fisher, M.M. (2014), *Migration. A World History*, Oxford: Oxford University Press.

Foster, J.B. (2011), 'Capitalism and degrowth: an impossibility theorem', *Monthly Review*, 1 July 2011.

Fourastié, J. (1961), *La grande métamorphose du XXe siècle. Essais sur quelques problèmes de l'humanité d'aujourd'hui*, Paris: Presses Universitaires de France.

Frank, R.H., Levine, A.S. and Dijk, O. (2010), 'Expenditure cascades', Working Paper, European University Institute.

Fraser, N. (2022), *Cannibal Capitalism. How our System is Devouring Democracy, Care, and the Planet – and What We Can Do about It*, New York: Verso Books.

Frick, A., Graff, M., Hartwig, J. and Siliverstovs, B. (2012), 'Are there free rides out of a recession? The case of Switzerland', *International Review of Applied Economics*, Vol. *26*, No. *1*, pp. 27–45.

Friedman, M. (1956), 'The quantity theory of money: a restatement', in: Friedman, M. (ed), *Studies in the Quantity Theory of Money*, Chicago, pp. 3–21.

Friedman, M. (1994), *Money Mischief: Episodes in Monetary History*, San Diego: Harcourt Brace Jovanovich.

Friedman, M. and Schwartz, A.J. (1965), *The Great Contraction, 1929–1933*, Princeton: Princeton University Press.

Fukuyama, F. (1992), *The End of History and the Last Man*, New York: Penguin.

Galbraith, J.K. (2012), *Inequality and Instability: A Study of the World Economy Just Before the Crisis*, Oxford: Oxford University Press.

Galbraith, J.K. (1990), *A Short History of Financial Euphoria*, New York: Penguin Books.

Galbraith, J.K. (1994), *A Journey Through Economic Time*, Boston: Houghton Mifflin.

Galbraith, J.K. (1995), *Money. Whence it Came, Where it Went*, revised edition, Boston: Houghton Mifflin.

Galor, O. (2022), *The Journey of Humanity. The Origins of Wealth and Inequality*, London: Dutton.

Garritsen de Vries, M. (1986), *Balance of Payments Adjustment, 1945–1986: The IMF Experience*, Washington: International Monetary Fund.

Garvy, G. (1943), 'Kondratieff's theory of long cycles', *Review of Economic Statistics*, Vol. *25*, No. *4*, pp. 203–220.

Gerschenkron, A. (1962), *Economic Backwardness in Historical Perspective: A Book of Essays*, New York: The Belknap Press of Harvard University Press.

Gesell, S. (1916), *Die natürliche Wirtschaftsordnung durch Freiland und Freigeld*, Les Hauts Geneveys: Arnstadt i. Thür.

Gilpin, R. (1988), 'The theory of hegemonic war', *The Journal of Interdisciplinary History*, Vol. *18*, No. *4*, pp. 591–613.

Goldin, I., Cameron, G. and Balarajan, M. (2010), *Exceptional People: How Migration Shaped Our World and Will Define Our Future*, Princeton: Princeton University Press.

Golt, S. (1978), *Developing Countries in the GATT System*, London: Trade Policy Research Centre.

Gordon, B. (1987), 'Oresme, Nicholas', in: Eatwell, J., Milgate, M. and Newman, P. (eds), *The New Palgrave Dictionary of Money and Finance*, London: Palgrave Macmillan, Vol. 3, pp. 745–755.

Gordon, M.S. (1941), *Barriers to World Trade*, New York: The Macmillan Co.

Gordon, R.J. and Wilcox, J.A. (1981), 'Monetarist interpretations of the Great Depression: an evaluation and critique', in: Brunner, K. (ed), *The Great Depression Revisited*, Boston: Martinus Nijhoff, pp. 49–107.

Graeber, D. (2011), *Debt: The First 5,000 Years*, Brooklyn: Melville House.

Graeber, D. and Wengrow, D. (2021), *The Dawn of Everything*, New York: Penguin Books.

Gregory, P.R. and Sailors, J. (2003), 'The Soviet Union during the Great Depression: the autarky model', in: Balderston, T. (ed), *The World Economy and National Economies in the Interwar Slump*, London: Palgrave Macmillan, pp. 191–210.

Guerra y Sánchez, R. (1964), *Sugar and Society in the Caribbean: An Economic History of Cuban Agriculture*, London: Yale University Press.

Gupta, S., Schena, M. and Yousefi, S.R. (2020), 'Revisiting IMF expenditure conditionality', *Applied Economics*, Vol. *52*. No. *58*, pp. 6338–6359.

Haffner, S. (1978), *Anmerkungen zu Hitler*, München: Kindler.

Hall, A.R. (1968), *The Export of Capital from Britain, 1870–1914*, London: Methuen.

Hamilton, A. (1791), 'Report on manufactures', https://www.constitution.org/ah/rpt_ manufactures.pdf (accessed December 2012).

Hansen, A.H. (1938), *Full Recovery or Stagnation*, New York W. W. Norton. & Company, Inc.

Hansen, J.E., Kharecha, P., Sato, M., Tselioudis, G., Kelly, J., Bauer, S.E., Ruedy, R., Jeong, E., Jin, Q., Rignot, E., Velicogna, I., Schoeberl, M.R., von Schuckmann, K., Amponsem, J., Cao, J., Keskinen, A., Li, J. and Pokela, A. (2025), 'Global warming has accelerated: are the united nations and the public well-informed?', *Environment: Science and Policy for Sustainable Development*, Vol. *67*, No. *1*, pp. 6–44.

Hanson, J.R. (1980), *Trade in Transition: Exports from the Third World, 1840–1900*, New York: Academic Press.

Hansson, K.E. (1952), 'A general theory of the system of multilateral trade', *The American Economic Review*, Vol. *42*, No. *1*, pp. 59–68.

Harrison, M. (1998), 'The economics of World War II: an overview', in: Harrison, M. (ed), *The Economics of World War II: Six Great Powers in International Comparison,* Cambridge: Cambridge University Press, pp. 1–42.

Harvey, D.I., Kellard, N.M., Madsen, J.B. and Wohar, M.E. (2010), 'The Prebisch–Singer hypothesis: four centuries of evidence', *The Review of Economics and Statistics*, Vol. *92*, No. *2*, pp. 367–377.

Hatton, T.J. and Williamson, J.G. (2008), *Global Migration and the World Economy*, Cambridge: The MIT Press.

Hawtrey, R.G. (1927), *The Gold Standard in Theory and Practice*, London: Longmans, Green and Co. Ltd.

Headrick, D.R. (1988), *The Tentacles of Progress: Technology Transfer in the Age of Imperialism, 1850–1940*, Oxford: Oxford University Press.

Heuman, G. and Burnard, T. (eds) (2011), *The Routledge History of Slavery*, Oxon: Routledge.

Hickel, J. (2023), 'On technology and degrowth', *Monthly Review*, Vol. *75*, No. *3*, pp. 44–50.

Hilgerdt, F. (1942), *The Network of World Trade*, Geneva: League of Nations.

Hilgerdt, F. (1943), 'The case for multilateral trade', *The American Economic Review*, Vol. *33*, No. *1*, Part 2, pp. 393–407.

Hilgerdt, F. (1945), *Industrialisation and Foreign Trade*, Geneva: League of Nations.

Hobbes, T. (1651), *Leviathan or the Matter, Forme, & Power of a Common-Wealth Ecclesiastical and Civill*, London: Printed for Andrew Crooke.

Hobsbawm, E. (1994), *The Age of Extremes: A History of the World, 1914–1991*, New York: Michael Joseph.

Hobsbawm, E. and Ranger, T. (2012), *The Invention of Tradition*, Cambridge: Cambridge University Press.

Hoekman, B.M. and Kostecki, M.M. (2009), *The Political Economy of the World Trading System: WTO and Beyond*, 3rd edn, Oxford: Oxford University Press.

Horie, S. (1964), *The International Monetary Fund*, London: Palgrave Macmillan.

Huber, M. (2023), 'The problem with degrowth', *Jacobin*, 16 July 2023.

Hume, D. (1752), *Political Discourses*, Edinburgh: R. Fleming.

Imbs, J. (2000), 'Sectors and the OECD business cycle', CEPR Discussion Paper No. 2473.

IMF Database of Fiscal Responses to COVID-19 (n.d.). https://www.imf.org/en/Topics/imf-and-covid19/-/media/Images/IMF/Topics/COVID19/fm-database/October-2021/map.ashx (accessed September 2025).

Imlah, A.H. (1952), 'British balance of payments and export of capital 1816–1913', *Economic History Review*, New Series, Vol. *5*, No. *2*, pp. 208–239.

Imlah, A.H. (1958), *Economic Elements in the Pax Britannica*, Cambridge: Harvard University Press.

Inkeles, A. (1983), *Exploring Individual Modernity*, New York: Columbia University Press.

IPCC (2023), Climate Change 2023: Synthesis Report. Contribution of Working Groups I, II and III to the Fifth Assessment Report of the Intergovernmental Panel on Climate Change [Core Writing Team, R.K. Pachauri and L.A. Meyer (eds.)], Geneva.

Issawi, C. (1961), 'Egypt since 1800: a study in lop-sided development', *The Journal of Economic History*, Vol. *21*, No. *1*, pp. 1–25.

Jacoby, S.M. (2008), 'Finance and labor: perspectives on risk, inequality and democracy', UCLA.

Jenks, L.H. (1963), *The Migration of British Capital to 1875*, 3rd edn, London: Thomas Nelson and Sons.

Jevons, W.S. (1865), *The Coal Question. An Inquiry Concerning the Progress of the Nation, and the Probable Exhaustion of Our Coal Mines*, London: Macmillan & Co.

Judt, T. with Snyder, T. (2012), *Thinking the Twentieth Century*, New York: Vintage.

Keynes, J.M. (1920), *The Economic Consequences of the Peace*, New York: Harcourt, Brace, and Howe.

Keynes, J.M. (1930), 'Economic possibilities for our grandchildren', in: Keynes, J.M. (ed), (1963), *Essays in Persuasion*, New York: Norton, pp. 358–337.
Keynes, J.M. (1936), *The General Theory of Employment, Interest and Money*, London: Macmillan.
Kindleberger, Charles P. (1975), 'The rise of free trade in Western Europe, 1820 to 1875', The *Journal of Economic History*, Vol. *35*, No. *1*, pp. 20–55.
Kindleberger, C.P. (1956), *The Terms of Trade: A European Case Study*, New York: John Wiley & Sons, Inc.
Kindleberger, C.P. (1962), *Foreign Trade and the National Economy*, New Haven: Yale University Press.
Kindleberger, C.P. (1978), *Manias, Panics, and Crashes. A History of Financial Crises*, London: Basic Books.
Kindleberger, C.P. (1984), *A Financial History of Western Europe*, London: Allen & Unwin.
Kindleberger, C.P. (1986), *The World in Depression, 1929–1939*, revised and enlarged edition, Berkeley: University of California Press.
Kirk, D. (1996), 'Demographic transition theory', *Population Studies*, Vol. *50*, No. *3*, pp. 361–387.
Klein, N. (2014), *This Changes Everything. Capitalism vs the Climate*, New York: Simon & Schuster.
Kondratieff, N.D. (1935), 'The long waves in economic life', *The Review of Economic Statistics*, Vol. *17*, No. *6*, pp. 105–115.
Körner, N. (2011), *Deutsche Direktinvestitionen 1880–1914: Eine Analyse anhand konkreter Unternehmensbeispiele*, München: GRIN Verlag.
Krugman, P.R. (1979), 'Increasing returns, monopolistic competition, and international trade', *Journal of International Economics*, Vol. *9*. No. *4*, pp. 469–479.
Krugman, P.R., Obstfeld, M. and Melitz, M. (2011), *International Economics: Theory and Policy*, 9th edn, Boston: Addison-Wesley.
Kuznets, S. (1964), *Postwar Economic Growth*. Harvard: Belknap Press of Harvard University Press.
Kuznets, S. (1966), *Modern Economic Growth*, New Haven: Yale University Press.
Kuznets, S. (1967), 'Quantitative aspects of the economic growth of nations: X-levels and structure of foreign trade: long-term trends', *Economic Development and Cultural Change*, Vol. *15*, No. *2*, Part II, pp. 1–140.
Lachmann, R. (2023), 'Trump and the politics of imperial decline', *Political Power and Social Theory*, Vol. *38*, pp. 179–201.
Lamartine Yates, P. (1959), *Forty Years of Foreign Trade*, London: Allen & Unwin.
Lamfalussy, A. (1963), 'International trade and trade cycles, 1950–60', in: Harrod, R. and Hague, D.C. (eds), *International Trade Theory in a Developing World*, London: Macmillan, pp. 241–276.
Landes, D.S. (1999), *The Wealth and Poverty of Nations: Why Some Are so Rich and Some so Poor*, New York: W. W. Norton & Company.
Latham, A.J.H. (1978), *The International Economy and the Underdeveloped World, 1865–1914*, London: Croom Helm.
Latham, A.J.H. (1981), *The Depression and the Developing World, 1914–1939*, London: Croom Helm.
Lawn, P. and Clarke, M. (2010), 'The end of economic growth? A contracting threshold hypothesis', *Ecological Economics*, Vol. *66*, pp. 2213–2223.
League of Nations (1945), *Industrialization and Foreign Trade*, Geneva: League of Nations.
Lenin, V.I. (1917 [1963]), 'Imperialism, the highest stage of capitalism', in: Progress Publishers (ed.), *Lenin's Selected Works*, Moscow: Progress Publishers, Vol. 1, pp. 667–766.
Levin, J.V. (1960), *The Export Economies*, Cambridge: Harvard University Press.
Levine, R. and Zervos, Z.J. (1993), 'What have we learned about policy and growth from cross-country regressions?', *The American Economic Review*, Vol. *83*, No. *2*, pp. 426–430.
Lewis, C. and Schlotterbeck, K.T. (1938), *America's Stake in International Investments*, Washington: The Brookings Institute.
Lewis, W.A. (1949), *Economic Survey, 1919–1939*, London: Allen & Unwin.
Lewis, W.A. (1978), *Growth and Fluctuations 1870–1913*, London: Allen & Unwin.

List, F. (1841), *Das nationale System der politischen Oekonomie*, Stuttgart (The National System of Political Economy, translated by Sampson S. Lloyd, London: Longmans, Green and Co., 1909).

List, F. (1842), *Die Ackerverfassung, die Zwergwirtschaft und die Auswanderung*, Stuttgart: J.G. Cotta.

Luxemburg, R. (1916), *Die Krise der Sozialdemokratie*, Bern: Verlagsdruckerei Union.

MacBean, A.I. and Snowden, P.N. (1981), *International Institutions in Trade and Finance*, London: Allen & Unwin.

MacLaren, D. (1995), 'The Uruguay round agreement on agriculture: a new order?', *Agenda*, Vol. *2*, pp. 281–290.

Maddison, A. (1962), 'Growth and fluctuation in the world economy, 1870–1960', *Banca Nazionale del Lavoro Quarterly Review*, Vol. *61*, pp. 127–159.

Maddison, A. (1964), *Economic Growth in the West*, London: Allen & Unwin.

Maddison, A. (1982), *Phases of Capitalist Development*, London: Oxford University Press.

Maddison, A. (1989), *The World Economy in the 20th Century*, Paris: Development Centre of the Organisation for Economic Co-operation and Development.

Maddison, A. (1991), *Dynamic Forces in Capitalist Development*, Oxford: Oxford University Press.

Maddison, A. (1994), *Monitoring the World Economy, 1820–1992*, Paris: Development Centre of the Organisation for Economic Co-operation and Development.

Maddison, A. (2001), *The World Economy: A Millennial Perspective*, Paris: Development Centre of the Organisation for Economic Co-operation and Development.

Maizels, A. (1963), *Industrial Growth and World Trade*, Cambridge: Cambridge University Press.

Marx, K. and Engels, F. (1848), *Manifesto of the Communist Party*, translated by Samuel Moore in cooperation with Friedrich Engels, London: Progress Publishers, 1888.

McAfee, A. (2019), *More from Less – The Surprising Story of How We Learned to Prosper Using Fewer Resources – and What Happens Next*, New York: Simon & Schuster.

McCallum, B.T. (1990), 'Inflation: theory and evidence', in: Friedman, B.M. and Hahn, F.H. (eds), *Handbook of Monetary Economics*, Amsterdam: North Holland, Vol. 2, pp. 963–1012.

McNally, D. (2020), *Blood and Money. War, Slavery, and Empire,* Chicago: Haymarket Books.

Meadows, D.H., Meadows, D.L., Randers, J. and Behrens III, W.W. (1972), *The Limits to Growth. A Report for the Club of Rome's Project on the Predicament of Mankind*, New York: Universe Books.

Menger, C. (1892), 'On the origin of money', *The Economic Journal*, Vol. *2*, pp. 239–255.

Michie, R. (1988), 'Different in name only? The London Stock Exchange and foreign bourses, c. 1850–1914', *Business History*, Vol. *30*, No. *1*, pp. 46–68.

Mill, J.S. (1848), *Principles of Political Economy*, Vol. II, 3rd edn., London: John W. Parker and Son, 1852.

Milward, A. (1984), *The Reconstruction of Western Europe 1945–51*, London: University of California Press.

Milward, A. and Saul, S.B. (1973), *The Economic Development of Continental Europe, 1780–1870*, London: Allen & Unwin.

Miran, S. (2024), *A User's Guide to Restructuring the Global Trading System*, Stamford: Hudson Bay Capital.

Mitchell, B.R. and Deane, P. (1962), *Abstract of British Historical Statistics*, Cambridge: Cambridge University Press.

Moggridge, D.E. (1969), *The Return to Gold 1925*, Cambridge: Cambridge University Press.

Morgan, T. (1959), 'The long-run terms of trade between agriculture and manufacturing', *Economic Development and Cultural Change*, Vol. *8*, No. *1*, pp 1–23.

Mundell, R. (1998), 'Uses and Abuses of Gresham's Law in the History of Money', *Zagreb Journal of Economics*, Vol. *2*, No. *2*, pp. 3–38.

Neiman, B. (2008), *Multinationals, Intrafirm Trades, and International Macro Dynamics*, Cambridge: The MIT Press.

Nesmashnyi, A.D. (2023), 'European security crisis and U.S. Hegemony. Reversing the decline?', Russia in global affairs, Vol. *21*, No. *1*, pp. 132–152.

Norrbin, S.C. and Schlagenhauf, D.E. (1996), 'The role of international factors in the business cycle: a multi-country study', *Journal of International Economics*, Vol. *40*. No. *1–2*, pp. 85–104.

North, D.C. and Thomas, R.P. (1977), 'The first economic revolution', *The Economic History Review*, Vol. *30*, No. *2*, pp. 229–241.

O'Rourke, K.H. and Williamson, J.G. (1990), *Globalization and History: The Evolution of the Nineteenth-Century Atlantic Economy*, Cambridge: The MIT Press.

OECD (2009), Economic Outlook, Vol. 85.

OECD (2025), *Global Long-Run Economic Scenarios, 2025 update*, Paris: Organisation for Economic Co-operation and Development.

Ostry, J.D., Gosh, A.R., Habermeier, K., Chamon, M., Qureshi, M.S. and Reinhardt, D.B.S. (2010), 'Capital inflows: the role of controls', *IMF Staff Position Note* 10/04.

Overy, R. (1995), *Why the Allies Won*, 2nd edn, London: W.W. Norton.

Palley, T.I. (2009), 'America's exhausted paradigm: Macroeconomic causes of the financial crisis and great recession', *Empirica*, Vol. *38*. pp. 3–17.

Petrakis, P. (2012), *The Greek Economy and the Crisis. Challenges and Responses*, Heidelberg: Springer.

Pettis, M. (2024), *Can Trade Intervention Lead to Freer Trade?* Washington: Carnegie Endowment for International Peace.

Phillips, A.W. (1958), 'The relationship between unemployment and the rate of change of money wages in the United Kingdom, 1861–1957', *Economica*, Vol. *25*, No. *100*, pp. 283–299.

Pirgmaier, E. (2021), 'The value of value theory for ecological economics', *Ecological Economics*, Vol. *179*, January 2021, p. 106790.

Polanyi, K. (1944), *The Great Transformation: The Political and Economic Origins of our Time*, Boston: Farrar & Rinehart.

Pollard, S. (1981), *Peaceful Conquest: the Industrialization of Europe 1760–1970*, Oxford: Oxford University Press.

Pomeranz, K. (2000), *The Great Divergence: China, Europe, and the Making of the Modern World Economy*, Princeton: Princeton University Press.

Pomfrey, R. (1988), *Unequal Partners: The Economics of Discriminatory International Trade Policies*, Oxford: Blackwell.

Prebisch, R. (1950), *The Economic Development of Latin America and its Principal Problems*, New York: United Nations Department of Economic Affairs.

Quiggin, J. (2010), *Zombie Economics: How Dead Ideas Still Walk Among Us*, Princeton: Princeton University Press.

Radford, R.A. (1945), 'The economic organisation of a P.O.W. Camp', *Economica*, New Series, Vol. *12*, No. *48*, pp. 189–201.

Rajan, R.G. (2010), *Fault Lines: How Hidden Fractures Still Threaten the World Economy*, Princeton: Princeton University Press.

Rediker, M. (2007), *The Slave Ship. A Human History*, New York: Viking Press.

Reinert, E.S. (2007), *How the Rich Countries Grew Rich and why Poor Countries Stay Poor*, London: Constable.

Reinhart, C.M. and Rogoff, K.S. (2009), *This Time is Different: Eight Centuries of Financial Folly*, Princeton: Princeton University Press.

Ricardo, D. (1809), *The High Price of Bullion: A Proof of the Depreciation of Bank Notes*, London: Printed by Harding & Wright, St. John's-square, for John Murray.

Ricardo, D. (1817), *On the Principles of Economy and Taxation*, London: John Murray, Albemarle-Street.

Rich, N. (2018), 'Losing earth. The decade we almost stopped climate change', *New York Time Magazine*.

Rittmann, H. (1975), *Deutsche Geldgeschichte 1484–1914*, München: Battenberg.

Roberts, G.W. and Byrne, J. (1966), 'Summary statistics on indenture and associated migration affecting the West Indies 1834–1918', *Population Studies*, Vol. *20*, No. *1*, pp. 125–134.

Rodrik, D. (2011), *The Globalization Paradox*, New York: W. W. Norton & Co.
Rostow, W.W. (1978), *The World Economy: History and Prospect*, London: University of Texas Press.
Saul, S.B. (1960), *Studies in British Overseas Trade, 1870–1914*, Liverpool: Liverpool University Press.
Scammell, W.M. (1964), *International Monetary Policy*, London: Macmillan.
Scammell, W.M. (1965), 'The working of the gold standard', *Yorkshire Bulletin of Economic and Social Research*, Vol. *17*, No. *1*, pp. 32–35.
Schröder, H.J. (2022), 'The decline of the American empire', in: Schröder, M., Rollinger, R. and Strolbl, P. (eds.), *The End of Empires*, Wiesbaden, pp. 697–744.
Schumpeter, J.A. (1912), *Theorie der wirtschaftlichen Entwicklung*, Berlin (The Theory of Economic Development, Cambridge, 1934).
Schumpeter, J.A. (1939), *Business Cycles: A Theoretical, Historical, and Statistical Analysis of the Capitalist Process*, Vols. 1 and 2, New York: McGraw-Hill Book Company.
Scott, F.D. (ed.) (1968), *World Migration in Modern Times*, Englewood Cliffs: Prentice-Hall.
Scott, J.C. (2016), *Against the Grain. A Deep History of the Early States*, New Haven and London: Yale University Press.
Scott-Smith, G. and Rofe, J.S. (eds) (2017), *Global Perspectives on the Bretton Woods Conference and the Post-War World Order*, Cham: Palgrave Macmillan.
Shaxson, N. (2011), *Treasure Islands: Tax Havens and the Men Who Stole the World*, London: Vintage.
Singer, H. (1950), 'The distribution of gains between investing and borrowing countries', *The American Economic Review, Papers and Proceedings*, Vol. *40*, No. *2*, pp. 473–485.
Skidelsky, R. (2009), *Keynes: The Return of the Master*, New York: PublicAffairs.
Smith, A. (1776), *An Inquiry into the Nature and Causes of the Wealth of Nations*, London: Printed for W. Strahan; and T. Cadell, in the Strand.
Solomou, S. (1988), *Phases of Economic Growth, 1850–1913: Kondratieff Waves and Kuznets Swings*, Cambridge: Cambridge University Press.
Sombart, W. (1916), *Der moderne Kapitalismus, Vol. I: Die Vorkapitalistische Wirtschaft, Vol. II: Das europäische Wirtschaftsleben im Zeitalter des Frühkapitalismus, Vol. III: Das Wirtschaftsleben im Zeitalter des Hochkapitalismus*, 2nd edn, München: Duncker & Humblot.
Spencer, D.L. and Woroniak, A. (eds) (1967), *The Transfer of Technology to Developing Countries*, New York: Praeger.
Spufford, P. (1988), *Money and Its Use in Medieval Europe*, Cambridge: Cambridge University Press.
Stiglitz, J.E. (2002), *Globalization and Its Discontents*, New York: W. W. Norton.
Temin, P. (1976), *Did Monetary Forces Cause the Great Depression?*, New York: W. W. Norton & Co.
Tew, B. (1960), *International Monetary Co-operation*, London: Hutchinson University Library.
Thorp, W.L. (1926), *Business Annals*, New York: National Bureau of Economic Research, Inc.
Todaro, M.P. and Smith, S.C. (2020), *Economic Development*, 13th edn, Boston: Pearson Education.
Tooze, A. (2006), *The Wages of Destruction: The Making and Breaking of the Nazi Economy*, London: Allen Lane.
Toussaint, É. (2023), *The World Bank. A Critical History*, London: Pluto Press.
Triffin, R. (1960) *Gold and the Dollar Crisis*, New Haven: Yale University Press.
Triffin, R. (1968), *Our International Monetary System: Yesterday, Today and Tomorrow*, New York: Random House.
Tyszynski, H. (1951), 'World trade in manufactured commodities, 1899–1950', *The Manchester School*, Vol. *19*, No. *3*, pp. 272–304.
Ulmer, M.J. (1960), *Capital in Transportation, Communications and Public Utilities: Its Formation and Financing*, Princeton: Princeton University Press.
UNCTAD Merchandise Trade Matrix (n.d.). https://unctadstat.unctad.org/datacentre/dataviewer/US.TradeMatrix (accessed September 2025)
UNCTAD (1997), *World Investment Report 1997: Transnational Corporations, Market Structure and Competition Policy*, New York: UNCTAD Division on Investment, Technology and Enterprise Development.

United Nations (1949), *International Capital Movements During the Inter-War Period*, New York: United Nations.
United Nations (2024), *World Population Prospects*, New York: United Nations.
Urquhart, M.C. and Buckley, K.A.H. (1965), *Historical Statistics of Canada*, Cambridge: Cambridge University Press.
US Bureau of Census and Statistics (1960), *Historical Statistics of the U.S., Colonial Times to 1957*, Washington: U.S. Census Bureau.
Van der Wee, H. (ed.) (1972), *The Great Depression Revisited: Essays on the Economics of the Thirties*, The Hague: Martinus Nijhoff.
Van Duijn, J.J. (1983), *The Long Wave in Economic Life*, London: Allen & Unwin.
Van Schaik, C. and Michel, K. (2016), *The Good Book of Human Nature: An Evolutionary Reading of the Bible*, New York: Basic Books.
Wallerstein, I. (2004), *World-System Analysis: An Introduction*, Durham: Duke University Press.
Weber, M. (1924), *Wirtschaftsgeschichte. Aus den nachgelassenen Vorlesungen von S. Hellmann and Dr. M. Palyi*, 2nd edn, München: Duncker & Humblot.
Wilkins, M. (1970), *The Emergence of Multinational Enterprise: American Business Abroad from the Colonial Era to 1914*, Cambridge: Harvard University Press.
Williamson, J.G. (1964), *American Growth and the Balance of Payments 1820–1913*, Chapel Hill: University of North Carolina Press.
Williamson, J.G. (1982), *The Lending Policies of the International Monetary Fund*, Washington: Institute for International Economics.
Woodruff, W. (1966), *Impact of Western Man*, New York: St. Martin's Press.
World Bank (2025), *Global Economic Prospects*, Washington: World Bank.
Woytinsky, W.S. and Woytinsky, E.S. (1953), *World Production and Population*, New York: The Twentieth Century Fund.
Woytinsky, W.S. and Woytinsky, E.S. (1955), *World Commerce and Governments*, New York: The Twentieth Century Fund.
Wright, C.M. (1955), 'Convertibility and triangular trade as safeguards against economic depression', *The Economic Journal*, Vol. *65*, No. *259*, pp. 422–435.
Ziegler, J. (2002), *Les nouveaux Maîtres du Monde et ceux qui leur résistent*, Paris: Seuil.

Index

Note: Page numbers followed by "n" refer to end notes.

For Product Safety Concerns and Information please contact our
EU representative GPSR@taylorandfrancis.com Taylor & Francis
Verlag GmbH, Kaufingerstraße 24, 80331 München, Germany